ASIAN DISCOURSES
OF RULE OF LAW

Rule of law is one of the pillars of the modern world, and widely considered necessary for sustained economic development, the implementation of democracy and the protection of human rights. It has, however, emerged in Western liberal democracies, and some people question how far it is likely to take root fully in the different cultural, economic and political context of Asia. This book considers how rule of law is viewed and implemented in Asia. Chapters on France and the USA provide a benchmark on how the concept has evolved, is applied and is implemented in a civil law and a common law jurisdiction. These are then followed by 12 chapters on the major countries of East Asia, and India, which consider all the key aspects of this important issue.

Randall Peerenboom is a Professor of Law at UCLA Law School. He obtained a B.A. in Philosophy, M.A. in Chinese Religion and Ph.D. in Philosophy before obtaining a J.D. from Columbia Law School. He has written extensively on Chinese law and philosophy, including *China's Long March toward Rule of Law* (2002). From 1994 to 1998, he practiced law with a major international law firm in Beijing. In addition to advising on various aspects of foreign investment in China, he often serves as an expert witness on PRC legal issues and is Of Counsel at Yiwen Law Firm.

ROUTLEDGECURZON LAW IN ASIA
Series editor: Randall Peerenboom

ASIAN DISCOURSES OF RULE OF LAW
Theories and Implementation of Rule of Law in
Twelve Asian Countries, France and the U.S.
Edited by Randall Peerenboom

ASIAN DISCOURSES OF RULE OF LAW

Theories and implementation of rule of
law in twelve Asian countries,
France and the U.S.

Edited by Randall Peerenboom

Routledge
Taylor & Francis Group
LONDON AND NEW YORK

First published 2004 by RoutledgeCurzon
This edition published 2012
by Routledge
2 Park Square, Milton Park, Abingdon, Oxon OX14 4RN

Simultaneously published in the USA and Canada
by Routledge
711 Third Avenue, New York, NY 10017

Routledge is an imprint of the Taylor & Francis Group, an informa business

Typeset in Times by Taylor & Francis Books Ltd

British Library Cataloguing in Publication Data
A catalogue record for this book is available from the British Library

Library of Congress Cataloging in Publication Data
A catalog record has been requested

ISBN 0-415-32613-3 (hbk)
ISBN 0-415-32612-5 (pbk)

CONTENTS

CONTENTS

NOTES ON CONTRIBUTORS

Upendra Baxi is an expert on human rights and the Indian legal system, author of many books and articles, and a well-known social activist.

Hahm Chaihark is Assistant Professor at the Graduate school of International Studies, Yonsei University, where he also serves as the Chair of the Korean Studies Program. He specializes in constitutional law and Confucian political theory. His recent publications include *Politics of Relationality: Family and the Public Good in East Asia* (co-edited with Daniel A. Bell, forthcoming) and *"Law, Culture and the Politics of Confucianism"* (in Columbia Journal of Asian Law, 2003).

Albert Chen is the former Dean of Hong Kong University Law School, Member of the Committee for the Basic Law of the Hong Kong Special Administrative Region under the Standing Committee of the National People's Congress of the People's Republic of China, an honorary professor at the People's University of China, Tsinghua University, Jilin University, Zhongshan University, Shantou University and the Southwestern University of Politics and Law, and an honorary research fellow of the Dongwu Institute for Comparative Law at Suzhou University. He is also a member of the Academic Advisory Committee of the Sun Yat-sen Institute for Social Sciences and Philosophy of the Academia Sinica, Taipei, a member of the international editorial board of *Social and Legal Studies*, and an associate member of the International Academy of Comparative Law. In addition to over 70 articles published in various English-language and Chinese-language journals, he has authored or co-authored six books and co-edited three others. His books include *Hong Kong's Legal System and the Basic Law* (1986), *Human Rights and the Rule of Law: The Challenges of Hong Kong's Transition* (1987), *Law and Politics in Hong Kong* (1990), *The Rule of Law, Enlightenment and the Spirit of Modern Law* (1998).

Anne S. Y. Cheung is in the Department of Law, University of Hong Kong.

Sean Cooney is a Senior Lecturer in the Faculty of Law at the University of Melbourne. His research has focused on East Asian labour and constitutional law. He has published in a range of international journals in English and Chinese. He most recently co-edited (with Tim Lindsey, Richard Mitchell, and Ying Zhu) the Routledge publication *Law and Labour Market Regulation in East Asia* (2002).

John Gillespie is an associate professor at the Law School, Deakin University, Melbourne, specializing in Asian comparative law. He teaches courses on comparative Asian commercial law and Indonesian commercial law and has published widely, especially on the Vietnamese legal reform. His publications include the book *'Commercial Legal Development in Vietnam: Vietnamese and Foreign Commentaries'* in 1997. In addition, he has worked as a consultant on legal reform projects for the World Bank, UNDP, IFC and AusAid in Vietnam, Laos and Indonesia.

Professor John O. Haley is Wiley B. Rutledge Professor of Law at the Washington University in St. Louis and the author of numerous books and articles on Japanese law.

Professor H. P. Lee holds the Sir John Latham Chair of Law at Monash University. He is currently the Deputy Dean, Faculty of Law. He is a member of the Australian Press Council and the Deputy Chair of the Freedom of the Press Committee. Professor Lee is the co-author of *The Australian Judiciary* (2001) and the author of *Constitutional Conflicts in Contemporary Malaysia* (1995).

Tim Lindsey is Associate Professor of Law and Director of the Asian Law Center at the University of Melbourne.

Vitit Muntarbhorn is Law Professor at Chulalongkorn University and Former United Nations, Special Rapporteur on Sale of Children, Child Prostitution and the General Rapporteur for the Second World Congress against Commercial Sexual Exploitation of Children.

Raul C. Pangalangan is Professor and Dean of Law at the University of the Philippines, where he teaches Constitutional Law, Jurisprudence and International Law. He has served as Visiting Professor at the Harvard Law School (1998); Director of Studies at The Hague Academy of International Law (2000), and Philippine delegate and Drafting Committee member at the Rome Conference to establish the International Criminal Court.

Dr. Laurent Pech of the University of Aix–Marseille is an expert on French, German, and E.U. law.

Randall Peerenboom is a Professor of Law at UCLA Law School. He has written extensively on Chinese law and philosophy. From 1994 to 1998 he practiced law with a major international law firm in Beijing. In addition to advising on various aspects of foreign investment in China, he often serves as an expert witness on PRC legal issues and is Of Counsel at Yiwen Law Firm. His most recent book is *China's Long March toward Rule of Law* (2002). He is now working on a study of the relation between culture and human rights; an empirical survey of supervision of the judiciary in the PRC; and a philosophical exploration of a form of Confucian collectivism as an alternative to Western liberal democracy.

Brian Z. Tamanaha is Professor of Law at St. John's University Law School and author of the widely acclaimed *A General Jurisprudence of Law and Society* (2001) and *Realistic Socio-Legal Theory: Pragmatism and a Social Theory of Law* (1997).

Veronica Taylor is Professor of Law and Director of the Asian Law Center at the University of Washington.

Dr. Li-ann Thio is a leading constitutional scholar in Singapore and co-author of the standard casebook *Constitutional Law in Malaysia and Singapore* (1997). She is the corresponding editor on Singapore for the series *Constitutions of the Countries of the World*, and Chief Editor of *Singapore Journal of International & Comparative Law*.

PREFACE:

Overview of project goals, methodology, and structure

This volume on rule of law in Asia, France, and the U.S. is the first install-
ment of a multi-year, multi-volume project that seeks to provide a better
understanding of legal systems in Asia and their relationship to economic
development, democracy, the protection of human rights, and geo-political
stability in the region and the world. It also seeks to provide a much-needed
empirical foundation to what has hitherto been an excessively abstract and
overly politicized debate about "Asian values," or its more recent, politically
correct reformulation "values in Asia."

Values in Asia

Debates over "Asian values" have often produced more heat than light.[1]
Supporters of universal human rights frequently dismiss the claims of some
Asian governments as the self-serving rhetoric of dictators and (mis)repre-
sent their position as a morally reprehensible and philosophically absurd
anything-goes cultural relativism. Defenders of Asian values often respond
by attacking Western governments for past and present violations of human
rights, and accuse them of cultural imperialism and ethnocentricity.

Clearly, authoritarian regimes have at times used the rhetoric of Asian
values for self-serving ends, playing the cultural card to deny citizens their
rights and then fend off foreign criticism. Just as clearly, there are many
different voices within Asia, and anyone professing to speak for all Asians or
of Asian values runs the danger of discounting these voices. Yet we need to
be careful not to dismiss Asian values as merely a cynical strategy seized on
by authoritarian regimes to deny Asian citizens their rights. More philosophical and nuanced accounts point out that, whatever Asian governments'
political motivations, there are legitimate differences in values at stake.

While a number of sophisticated theoretical works have been written,
what has been lacking to date in the discussion about values in Asia are
systematic empirical studies to back up the strong theoretical (and in some

cases polemical) claims being made on both sides about the differences or lack thereof in fundamental values. Accordingly, this project will provide an empirical basis for the debate by examining the range of values in Asia through concrete legal cases and social-political events, and – to the extent that there are differences within Asia or between some or all Asian countries and Western countries such as France and the U.S. – explore the reasons for such differences.

The project involves a series of conferences to which specialists in twelve different Asian countries or jurisdictions (Japan, the Philippines, South Korea, China, Taiwan, Hong Kong, Singapore, Thailand, Malaysia, Indonesia, Vietnam, and India), along with specialists from the U.S. and France or Germany, have been or will be invited. The first volume sets the stage for subsequent volumes by providing a general overview of the dominant conceptions of law, organized around the theme of rule of law; and the institutional framework. Subsequent volumes examine specific areas of law or topics in law to determine:

- whether there are differences/similarities between the countries with respect to the rules;
- outcomes in particular cases (or the way events are handled if they are not subject to formal legal resolution);
- the justifications/explanations for such outcomes (legal reasons, cultural/philosophical explanations, or economic, political, institutional explanations).

Universalist advocates of human rights argue that there is an expansive overlapping consensus regarding human rights as set forth in the so-called International Bill of Human Rights – the Universal Declaration of Human Rights, the International Covenant on Economic, Social and Cultural Rights, and the International Covenant on Civil and Political Rights. In response, some Asian governments argue that the hard core of universal rights is extremely limited. There is little disagreement that some acts are bad, such as torture, disappearances, genocide and slavery, though even in these areas little disagreement does not mean no disagreement. For example, is cruel and unusual punishment, as allowed in Singapore and previously in Europe but now prohibited by the European Court of Human Rights bad? What about capital punishment? Is it cruel and unusual to keep people waiting on death row for more than five years, two years, one year?

Although there are many rights that people agree are desirable when stated at very high level of abstraction, agreement at this level of abstraction is not helpful in resolving most pressing social issues. What may seem like a pragmatic or overlapping consensus quickly breaks down once one moves beyond discussions about the desirability of the broad wish-list of rights contained in human rights documents to the difficult issues of the justifications for such rights and how they are interpreted and implemented in practice. Undeniably, there is greater acceptance of the general idea of human rights than in the past, and even more agreement among more countries and people about particular human rights and how they are to be interpreted and implemented. There is also good reason to believe that the scope of agreement will increase over time. Nevertheless, there is still ample room for reasonable people to disagree over the content, justification, interpretation, and implementation of rights.

Systematic empirical studies will clarify the range of diversity with respect to other rights issues such as free speech, freedom of association, and freedom of the press. For instance, Thailand, one of the more tolerant countries in Asia in terms of freedom of speech and the press, prohibits the advocacy of communism, criticism of the government, and incitement of ethnic, racial or religious tensions. Yet without an examination of actual cases and the specific context it is not clear where exactly the lines are drawn, how onerous such restrictions are, what the penalties are, and whether the laws are applied fairly or used to attack opposition party figures and so on.

Empirical studies will also shed light on sexuality/gender issues (same-sex marriage, homosexuality, pornography, prostitution, transsexuality); obscenity laws; the public–private distinction and privacy issues (urine tests, mandatory treatment for drug addicts, identity cards, the right of companies to read employees' emails); the value of life (abortion, female infanticide, euthanasia, the right to die, eugenics, sale of body parts); paternalism and the limits of autonomy and consent (can experienced business persons consent to unconscionable contract provisions? Can dwarfs consent to dwarf-tossing contests where the participants compete in bars to see who can throw the dwarf the farthest? Can people consent to sadomasochistic acts that amount to criminal offenses in the case of non-consenting parties? Can criminal defendants consent to trial without counsel?); family law issues (domestic violence, spousal rape, children's duty to support their parents, parents' duty to take care of children, the right to divorce, child custody, the division of property upon divorce, inheritance laws, surrogate motherhood); labor issues (the right to form a union and to strike, minimum wage, child labor, the promotion of the family through the adoption of workplace rules and government-supported childcare programs); economic rights (the right to housing, medical care); cultural rights (the rights to the use of language, culturally important lands and waterways); freedom of religion; and collective rights such as the right to self-determination and the right to a clean environment as reflected in environmental laws.

Focusing on concrete legal issues across a wide variety of areas of law will clarify just how extensive the overlapping consensus actually is. It will also identify common ground and rationales that could be useful in expanding the overlapping consensus. And in some cases it will no doubt demonstrate that overlapping consensus is not likely, or at least not likely given the current circumstances.

Legal cases show most clearly where societies draw lines on controversial issues that involve the rights and interests of individuals versus the rights and interests of the group or state. Although this issue has often been construed as a battle between Asian communitarians and Western liberals, it is a truly universal issue that everyone of whatever persuasion must face. It is certainly possible that the majority of Asians may prefer a different balance than the majority of Westerners, though again we need more detailed empirical studies to examine differences in practice across a wide range of specific issues. Of course, simply noting a majority preference one way or the other will not end the debates – those in the minority can continue to claim that they are right. But before we can turn to such normative arguments we must have a better sense of the differences and the reasons for them.

Nowadays, rights are increasingly the medium through which different factions struggle for power. Highlighting legal cases reveals much about who has power within a society. At the same time, legal cases generally result in legal opinions, scholarly articles, and coverage in the media that can be used to understand the rationales and justifications for reaching the particular decisions. Because there will generally be critiques and counterarguments, one can also get some sense of the diversity of views within a country. In some cases, poll results and other relevant survey data may be available to provide a better sense of the intensity of particular viewpoints within a given society. As not all issues will necessarily be resolved through the formal legal system, our study will also include important social and political events that do not make it to court and other issues dealt with through informal mechanisms.

Reference to "Asian values" should not be taken as an a priori endorsement of the concept as meaningful or useful, or of Asian values over other values. Asia is a big place, with tremendous diversity – too much, critics suggest, to speak about a singular set of Asian values. On the other hand, a pluralism of Asian values is still Asian values. There is nothing wrong with noting a diversity of values and still claiming that they are Asian. Nor need each country within Asia share every single feature. There may still be dominant patterns within Asia. It is true that "Asian values" is a construct. But then so are "the West" and "liberalism," both of which encompass a tremendous diversity of views. Nevertheless, there are still dominant trends in Western thought. Liberalism clearly has a stronger hold than communitarianism in the West, for example, whereas the opposite seems to be true in much of Asia (though perhaps collectivism is a more apt description than communitarianism). Any comparative project must begin by constructing categories that highlight certain features and thus simplify to some extent quotidian reality – what William James referred to as the boomin', buzzin' confusion. The problem has not been that the East and West, Asian values and Western values are constructs, but that they have been overly simple constructs that lacked a firm empirical foundation.

In the final analysis, the key question is whether Asian countries share enough common ground for the term "Asian values" to be useful. To some extent, that will depend on what one's project is. There may be more common ground in certain areas of laws or with respect to certain issues than in others. It may very well be the case that "Asian" is too broad a qualifier to capture the significant differences for most comparative purposes, for example with respect to legal systems and conceptions of rule of law. However, at this stage, we need more detailed empirical studies across a range of issues in a number of Asian and Western countries before we can conclude that there is not enough in common among Asian countries and different from Western countries to render the term "Asian values" otiose.

Because "Asian values" has been tainted by misuse by politically oppressive regimes, one common suggestion is to replace it with "values in Asia." This change has the salutary effect of signaling a desire to move away from the overtly political use of the term by some Asian governments toward a more sophisticated approach sensitive to the pluralism within Asia. But eliminating references to "Asian values" and replacing it with "values in Asia" will not put an end to substantive debates about the universality of rights or shed any light whatsoever on how rights are to be interpreted or implemented in particular contexts in Asia. At best, it simply shifts the focus to a less grand level, whether that be country by country, area of law by area of law, or issue by issue.

Comparative law

Asian legal systems have historically been given short shrift in studies of comparative law. Attempts to classify the world's legal systems often begin with the concept of a modern legal system found in some economically advanced Western countries as the paradigmatic or core example. Max Weber, for instance, attributed the success of some Western countries in part to their legal systems, which he described as logical, formal, and rational. In contrast, Weber considered the legal system of many Asian countries to be nothing more than a kind of arbitrary or irrational *kadi* justice where wise men allegedly determined what was best in a given situation based on their own judgment and interpretation of customary norms rather than by appeal to fixed standards or principles of general applicability.

The legal systems of Asia have fared no better in other more recent schemes,[2] often being dumped into the category of religious or Oriental systems or unceremoniously swept into the dustbin category of "other" (or in some cases not even considered to be legal systems at all).[3] Rene David's influential taxonomy, for instance, consists of three families – civil, common, socialist – and the dreaded, descriptively empty, alien "other," into which he places China and Japan, along with African countries and states with Islamic, Hindu, or Jewish legal systems.[4]

Objecting to the Euro-American centrism of existing taxonomies, the renowned comparative legal scholar Ugo Mattei has proposed a new grouping. He describes three types of legal systems based on whether the primary source of social norms and order is law, politics, or philosophical and religious traditions.[5] In a *rule of professional law* or *rule of law* system, law is the main mechanism for resolving disputes and the state and state actors are subject to law. In addition, law is largely secularized and independent from religion, morality, and other social norms. In contrast, in a *rule of political law* system, the separation between law and politics is absent or minimal. Legal institutions are weak, and the law often does not bind government officials. This form of law is characteristic of former socialist states in transition and developing states.

The third category is *traditional law*, or what Mattei calls "the Oriental view of the law." These systems lack a separation between law and religion and/or are based on a "traditional transcendental philosophy in which the individual's internal dimension and the societal dimension are not separated." They are characterized by a reduced role for lawyers in dispute resolution and an increased role for mediators and "wise men," a high rate of survival of diversified local customs, an emphasis on duties rather than rights, a high value placed on harmony, the importance of a homogeneous population as a means of preserving social structure, family groups rather than individuals as the building blocks of society, a strongly hierarchical view of society, a high level of discretion left to decision-makers, a greater emphasis on the role of gender in society, a hurried and largely unsuccessful attempt to transplant Western legal codes and relationships, and a rhetoric of supernatural legitimization rather than an appeal to democracy and rule of law for legitimacy.

This family allegedly consists of Islamic law countries, Indian law and Hindu law countries, and countries with "other Asian and Confucian conceptions of law." It supposedly includes such widely disparate Asian countries as Japan, China, Thailand, Laos, Cambodia, Burma, Indonesia, India, Malaysia, the Philippines, Vietnam, North and South Korea, and Mongolia, as well as Islamic countries not in the Asian region such as Morocco, Tunisia, and Algeria.

Not surprisingly, such classification schemes have given rise to charges of Orientalism. A particular kind of law is considered not only necessary for economic development but an indicator of cultural achievement and civilization. Whereas the West has law, order, rule, reason, rational bureaucracies, predictability, and certainty, others have violence, chaos, arbitrary tradition, and coercive despotism imposed by rulers with too much discretion. In some cases, Asian countries are seen as incapable of implementing "the rule of law" or a modern legal system because of cultural factors. In other cases, the superiority of Western legal systems is seen as justifying a missionary-like effort to transplant Western laws, institutions, norms, and values to Asia.

This project seeks to update our understanding of legal systems in Asia. The rapid change in many legal systems in Asia and the likelihood of further rapid development require new conceptual frameworks for understanding the purposes of law, the various roles of the legal systems, the ways in which they operate, and the development paths of legal institutions in Asian countries. The first volume examines these issues through the prism of rule of law. Subsequent volumes enrich this panoramic overview of the many ways rule of law is conceptualized and theorized in Asia and the institutional infrastructures through which legal systems in Asia operate, by examining in detail the operation of the legal systems across a wide range of issues and areas of law.

Given the tremendous diversity within Asia, one must wonder about the value of any category so broad as to include all of the very different countries in Asia, just as one must wonder about the utility of a concept as broad as Asian values. Accordingly, this project seeks to avoid distorting, strong-arm attempts to force all Asian systems into a single preconceived mold, model, or family by having country experts develop theories or models for understanding legal developments in their respective countries based on their extensive, in-depth local knowledge of indigenous discourses, debates, and issues.

While not expressly developed for comparative purposes, such categories and theories may prove useful for comparative law. Some countries appear to be confronting similar issues, and as a result some of the conceptual frameworks or theories may be useful in understanding legal developments across borders. Although developing an adequate taxonomy is at best the first step in explaining or predicting how, when, and why legal systems change, articulating different conceptions of law and the interest groups backing such conceptions may assist in predicting the likely path of development of a legal system. Taxonomies may also be useful in ensuring that legal reforms are appropriate for the particular type of system and existing conditions. To the extent that there are competing conceptions of law, taxonomies also enhance the process of normative evaluation by clarifying the differences and what is at stake. In short, while comparative law has suffered from attempts to oversimplify Asian legal systems and squeeze them into a single category, developing conceptual frameworks that capture the diversity of legal systems within Asia and different views within particular Asian countries may prove valuable in providing heuristic devices for understanding domestic legal development and for broader comparative purposes.

Transplantability of law: conditions for success and reasons for failure

A key issue in comparative law, and a pressing concern of countries in Asia, as well as of multilateral and bilateral programs aimed at promoting rule of law and legal reforms in Asia, is the transplantability of law. What accounts for the ability of some countries to develop functional legal systems, often by borrowing and adapting foreign laws and institutions, while other states continue to suffer from dysfunctional legal systems despite efforts to reform?

The diversity within Asia provides fertile ground for exploring the possibilities for, and limitations on, legal transplants. There is a wide range of countries at different stages of legal system development. Some countries studied here – France, the U.S., Japan, South Korea, Hong Kong, Taiwan – have mature legal systems. Others, such as China and Vietnam, are still in the early stages of institutional development. Legal systems vary from civil law to common law to mixed (civil-common and civil-common-socialist). Some of the states have mature market economies; others, such as China and Vietnam, have only recently endorsed market reforms. While globalization and the reach of the international legal and economic regimes have affected all, some countries are more integrated into the global economic order and international legal regime than others.

Political systems run the gamut: well-established democracies, states struggling to consolidate democracy, soft-authoritarian regimes, and reformist Marxist–Leninist, effectively single-party, socialist states. Some have good human rights records across the board. Others have pockets of problems, often with respect to certain civil and political rights. Still others offer little protection when it comes to many civil and political rights but do better with respect to other rights – or at least they are not significantly worse than other countries when it comes to economic, social, and cultural rights.

Some countries have built their legal systems largely on the basis of transplanted laws and institutions, often as a result of colonialism. Indeed, only Thailand did not experience colonialism, at least directly. Singapore, Malaysia, Hong Kong, the Philippines, and India are all now grappling with postcolonial attempts to reconcile the colonial legal system with local conditions, leading in some cases to movements to give greater expression to indigenous traditions and values. To that end, a variety of cultural and religious traditions, including Buddhism, Islam, Confucianism, and Daoism, may provide valuable resources. These countries also vary widely with respect to homogeneity and ethnic diversity, and with respect to wealth distribution and the existence of poverty. They also range in size from small city-states to the most populous country in the world, and from heavily urbanized to predominantly rural.

Relationship between rule of law and economic development

The role of law in economic development in Asian countries has been the subject of great debate. Some scholars argue that law has not played a significant role. Rather, growth has been attributed to Asian varieties of capitalism, which for some means a strong developmental state in which a technocratic bureaucracy determines industrial policy, picking and choosing winners and in some cases deliberately "getting the prices wrong." In a similar vein, some attribute economic success to a close relationship between government and business, described by some as clientelism or corporatism – or more disparagingly by critics as cronyism. Still other explanations highlight cultural factors that diminish the importance of clear property rights or emphasize diligence, hard work, education, and saving; the large number of family businesses; informal networks; and relation-based contracting and business practices.

The contrasting view holds that law has played a more important role in the growth of those Asian countries that have experienced high growth rates over long periods of time than is usually assumed, and that law is likely to play an even greater role in the future as some of the economies develop and countries become entrenched in the global economy. All parties realize, of course, that a functional legal system is not sufficient for economic growth. Other factors may be more important, including sound macroeconomic fundamentals and management; a stable business environment with low inflation; prudent fiscal policies; exchange rates to support exports; high savings and investment rates; high-quality human capital (good education and high literacy rates); merit-based bureaucracies; low income inequality; export promotion; success in attracting foreign direct investment and political stability.

Whatever the outcome of this debate, it is clear that the desire for economic growth and reforms in the economy have propelled legal system development in Asia. All of the Asian countries in this study have, or have committed to the development of, a formal legal system. Accordingly, the issue is not a mutually exclusive choice between formal and informal law or between public and private ordering. Formal and informal law, public and private ordering-each offer advantages and disadvantages, and are complementary in many ways. Since they are not perfect substitutes, each can support and help overcome the weaknesses of the other. The more difficult task is to determine *when* each type of ordering is best.

Legal systems that comply with the requirements of a thin or formal conception of rule of law are compatible with a variety of economic systems.[6] Conversely, substantive or thick theories of rule of law may be distinguished by differences in economic systems or varieties of capitalism. A conference on corporate law will explore how the various countries handle a common set of issues, thus shedding light on the relation between rule of law and varieties of capitalism within Asia.

This project will also explore an issue that has yet to receive adequate attention in the political economy or economics literature regarding law and development: the possibility of countries pursuing a form of "economic rule of law" where the legal system operates (for the most part) independently of political influence with respect to commercial issues but where other areas of law are subject to greater, if varying, degrees of politicization. Such systems raise a number of theoretical and practical issues. Is a system that complies with the usual requirements of a thin rule of law at all times except for cases involving political opposition figures a defective rule of law or another kind of system altogether? Is it possible in practice to develop a professional and autonomous judiciary and legal system capable of handling commercial laws fairly and independently and yet maintain control in politically sensitive cases? Or will there be spillover effects as institutions exercise their muscles and newfound authority, and demonstrate their growing sense of professionalism, by claiming the right to decide all cases in accordance with legal norms? These questions raise crucial issues about the relationship between law and politics, and the possibility for the full implementation of rule of law in non-democratic societies.

Law and politics

Two issues stand out regarding the relationship between law and politics. The first involves the evolutionary theses of modernization theorists, the early law and development movement of the 1960s and 1970s, and many though not all multilateral and bilateral programs today, that legal and economic reforms will lead to political reforms, and in particular the establishment of liberal democracies. The second concerns the political foundations of rule of law. Is it true, as is often asserted, that rule of law must go hand in hand with democracy and human rights, and that full implementation of even a thin rule of law is not possible in non-democratic and/or non-liberal regimes?

Although democracy is notoriously difficult to define, the following may serve as a provisional working definition. A genuine democracy requires at minimum open, competitive elections, under universal franchise, of those in posts where actual policy decisions are made (*the electoral dimension*). It also requires sufficient freedom of association, assembly, speech, and press to ensure that candidates are able to make their views known and compete effectively in the elections, and so that citizens are able to participate with reasonable effectiveness in the electoral process (*the participatory process dimension*). In addition, it requires the legal institutions to ensure that these freedoms are in fact realized and the election is carried out fairly (*the rule of law dimension*). In this view, elections are a necessary but not sufficient condition for democracy. Democratization is a process, which can occur even within a single-party state, even though full realization of genuine democracy is not possible in such a state. Moreover, while democracy implies rule of law, the opposite is not necessarily the case, at least as a conceptual matter.

Several countries in Asia are not democratic in the above sense, most clearly Vietnam, China, and Hong Kong, but arguably also Singapore and

Malaysia given the ways in which election outcomes are influenced by political factors, including the use of the legal system to harass opposition figures. These countries therefore provide important test cases for determining the extent to which legal reforms can proceed and rule of law can be implemented in non-democratic or democratic but non-liberal states. Close examination also sheds light on the interplay between legal, economic, and political reforms, and how legal and economic reforms may contribute to the process of democratization even in the absence of more expansive genuine elections.

Other states in the region are relatively new democracies still in the process of working out the kinks, including Taiwan, South Korea, Thailand, and the Philippines. As they attempt to consolidate democracy, they face a number of issues not faced by more mature democracies, including transitional justice concerns and basic constitutional law issues involving fundamental rights, checks and balances, and separation of powers. Having made the transition from authoritarianism to democracy, they too offer insights for other countries regarding the nature of that transition. Examining a wide range of rights issues will also demonstrate to what extent, if at all, the democratic states in Asia differ from *liberal* democracies in France and the U.S.

Rule of law, supranational and international legal regimes, and geo-political stability

Globalization is influencing legal systems in Asia, as elsewhere in the world. This is most noticeable in the growing importance of international law and its effects on domestic law systems. Much of the attention has been on human rights. However, other areas of law are also impacted. Commercial law is affected by international organizations such as the World Trade Organization and International Labor Organization and by regional trade systems, while environmental law is the subject of a number of international treaties. In addition, domestic systems may be affected when their courts draw on international norms or case law or the case law and jurisprudence of other states. Such changes raise interesting theoretical and practical issues about the limits of sovereignty and the possibilities for the development of an international or supranational rule of law. These last issues are addressed in the contribution on France to the first seminar on rule of law, which is currently struggling to reconcile traditional state sovereignty with the legal order of the European Union premised on a supranational rule of law.

A volume on international law and geo-political stability will explore a number of related issues, including dominant conceptions of international law and international relations in Asian countries; compliance with international treaties (economic, military, environmental, human rights); regional alliances; and disputes both within and outside the region, and the mechanisms for resolving such disputes, whether legal or otherwise.

List of future conferences/volumes

A number of areas of law or issues merit study and would advance our understanding of values in Asia and the role of law more generally in the region. The following is a tentative list of conferences:

- **Public Law: Constitutional and Administrative Law**: the focus will be on constitutional designs and structures; the role of the military; mechanisms for constitutional review and separation of powers issues; administrative law institutions and mechanisms for controlling discretion (including administrative litigation, administrative review, ombudsmen); and specific issues such as jurisdiction, standing and the basis for challenging state acts.
- **Constitutional Rights**: (1)**Civil and Political Rights**: free speech, freedom of religion, free press, freedom of assembly/limitations on civil society, the priority of civil and political versus economic, social and culture rights; (2) **Economic-Social and Cultural Rights**: right to education, housing, employment; right to use of language and support of particular cultural practices or minority groups.
- **Criminal and Criminal Procedure Law**: arrest and other compulsory enforcement rules (standards; approval requirements for warrants; rules on arbitrary detention); search and seizure; interrogation (access to a lawyer; line-ups; right to silence; admissibility of tainted evidence).
- **Law and Morality**: **Law and Morality**: (1) perfectionism versus a neutral state: paternalism, moralism; (2) sexuality/gender issues, including same-sex marriage, homosexuality, pornography, prostitution, transexuality; (3) public–private distinction and privacy issues (urine tests, mandatory treatment for drug addicts, identity cards, the right of companies to read employees' emails); (4) value of life issues such as abortion, euthanasia, female infanticide, eugenics, genetic experimentation and cloning.
- **Corporate Law**: corporations as short-term profit maximizers versus corporations' right or obligation to consider the impact of businesses on local communities; employee rights; minority shareholder rights; mechanisms for holding management accountable; regulatory framework; government's role in supporting research and development and disseminating results.
- **Family Law**(as outlined above).
- **International Law**(as outlined above).

Concluding volume

Once we have finished the series of conferences on specific areas of law, we will hold a final conference to analyze the results and place them within a broader framework. To that end, we will invite not only legal scholars but economists, political scientists, sociologists, and philosophers to participate. We hope thereby to overcome some of the potential limitations of focusing on legal cases or adopting a narrow legalist approach to the issues. The final conference will also try to draw some lessons with respect to comparative law; the extent to which legal systems differ in the U.S., France, and Asian countries, the degree of variation within Asia and the reasons for the differences; variations in theory and practice of human rights; the effect of colonialism on the subsequent development of rule of law; the importance of culture and religion (including Islam, Buddhism, and Confucianism) on the development of contemporary legal systems; the relation between law and economic development; the relation of legal reforms, economic growth and political reform (and in particular democratization); the effect of globalization and trends toward convergence and/or divergence in legal systems and particular areas of law.

Notes

1   Debates over Asian values involve a number of issues and have evolved over time. Round one, which took place in the early and mid-1990s, had two main focal points. The first area of contention was human rights, especially the issue of universalism versus relativism, but also including other issues such as the priority of rights and the compatibility of Confucianism, Buddhism, and Islam with democracy and human rights. The other main area of contention was economics, and in particular whether authoritarian or democratic regimes are better able to achieve sustained economic growth and whether Asian versions of capitalism are superior to the varieties of capitalism found in Western liberal democracies. The second round of debates arose in response to the Asian financial crisis. For an overview of the debates, see R. P. Peerenboom, 'Beyond Universalism and Relativism: The Evolving Debates about "Values in Asia",' Indiana International and Comparative Law Review (forthcoming, 2003).
2   Roberto Unger, *Law in Modern Society: Toward a Criticism of Social Theory* (1976), New York: Free Press; published simultaneously in London: Collier Macmillan Publishers (categorizing legal systems in terms of customary law, bureaucratic or regulatory law and rule of law). Customary law is neither codified nor public but inheres in the norms and practices of a society. Bureaucratic law arises when state and society become distinct. The problem with bureaucratic law, which is similar to an instrumental rule by law, is that there is a tension if not contradiction between instrumentalism and legitimacy. In contrast, in a rule of law legal order, law is general and autonomous, and thus allegedly more legitimate. Unger argues that China's premodern legal system was unable to develop beyond bureaucratic law due largely to the absence of separation between state and society and the lack of a transcendent deity. For a critique of Unger's views of the Chinese legal system, see William Alford, "The Inscrutable Occidental? Implications of Roberto Unger's Uses and Abuses of the Chinese Past," 64 *Texas Law Review* (1986), pp. 915–72.
3   For a discussion and critique of the views that China lacks either a *legal* system or a legal *system*, see R. Peerenboom, *China's Long March Toward Rule of Law* (Cambridge: Cambridge University Press, 2002).

4 Rene David and John E. C. Brierley, *Major Legal Systems in the World Today: An Introduction to the Comparative Study of the Law*, pp. 28–30, 518–33 (1985).
5 See U. Mattei, "Three Patterns of Law: Taxonomy and Change in the World's Legal Systems," 45 *American Journal of Comparative Law* (1997), pp. 5–44.
6 For the distinction between thin/formal and thick/substantive theories of rule of law, see Chapter 1.

VARIETIES OF RULE OF LAW
An introduction and provisional conclusion

Randall Peerenboom

In search of a conceptual framework for rule of law: the many meanings, uses and abuses of rule of law

Rule of law is an essentially contested concept. It means different things to different people, and has served a wide variety of political agendas, from Hayekian libertarianism to Rawlsian social welfare liberalism to Lee Kuan Yew's soft authoritarianism to Jiang Zemin's statist socialism. That is both its strength and its weakness. That people of vastly different political persuasions all want to take advantage of the rhetorical power of rule of law keeps it alive in public discourse, but it also leads to the worry that it has become a meaningless slogan devoid of any determinative content.

Given such wide usages, it is far from clear how to approach a comparative discussion of rule of law. Analytically minded philosophers tend to want to clarify the minimal content of rule of law by specifying the necessary conditions that any legal system must possess to merit that honorific label. Social activists and critics prefer a more normative approach. Rule of law becomes an expeditious means toward a greater end – achieving their favored political agenda. Positively, rule of law serves as an aspirational ideal, pointing the way toward a more just world. Elided with justice, rule of law becomes an empty vessel into which each person pours his or her hopes for a better tomorrow. Negatively, rule of law is seen as an ideological mask of oppression, the legal system a bastion of conservatism that serves the rich and powerful and thwarts attempts at realizing a more just world by reifing the status quo. Wondering about the evolution of rule of law and rule of law discourse, the more historically and linguistically minded take yet another tack. They reflect on the connotations of the various terms used to translate "rule of law," the discourses that were replaced or superseded by rule of law, and how the discourse has changed over time. Others broaden the historical study to look at the factors that led to the development of rule of law in the West or explain the success or failure in transplanting rule of law from modern Western liberal democracies with mature economies to foreign lands that may not be liberal, may not be democratic, and may not have developed economies. Spurred by such worries, political theorists and legal scholars debate endlessly the relationship between rule of law, democracy, human rights and constitutionalism. Focusing their lens a little more narrowly, neo-institutionalists inquire into the institutions needed to implement rule of law, whether that be an independent judiciary and legal profession, a systems of checks and balances or a particular form of separation of powers.

No single approach will satisfy everyone. Each produces its own insights, and has its own drawbacks. However, if we are to have meaningful discussions with others with different backgrounds, it may help to begin with some definitions and a provisional conceptual framework to clarify whether we are all talking about the same thing, and, if not, how and why we differ. Fortunately, despite the many debates over rule of law and its contested nature, there is a fairly well-accepted conceptual or analytical framework that at least clarifies some of the terms and disputes, though without resolving many important related but oftentimes somewhat broader issues.

Thin and thick conceptions of rule of law

The fact that there is room for debate about the proper interpretation of rule of law should not blind us to the broad consensus as to its core meaning and basic elements. At its most basic, rule of law refers to a system in which law is able to impose meaningful restraints on the state and individual members of the ruling elite, as captured in the rhetorically powerful if overly simplistic notions of a government of laws, the supremacy of the law and equality of all before the law. In contrast, states that rely on law to govern but do not accept the basic requirement that law bind the state and state actors are best described as a rule *by* law or *Rechtsstaat*.[1]

Conceptions of rule of law can be divided into two general types, thin and thick. A thin conception stresses the formal or instrumental aspects of rule of law – those features that any legal system allegedly must possess to function effectively as a system of laws, regardless of whether the legal system is part of a democratic or non-democratic society, capitalist, liberal or theocratic.[2] For present purposes, the constitutive elements of a thin conception include, in addition to meaningful restraints on state actors, the following. There must be rules or norms for determining which entities (including courts) may make law, and laws must be made by an entity in accordance with such rules and norms to be valid. Laws must be made public and readily accessible. Law must be generally applicable: that is, laws must not be aimed at a particular person and must treat similarly situated people equally for the most part. Laws must be relatively clear, consistent on the whole, relatively stable, and generally prospective rather than retroactive. Laws must be enforced – the gap between the law on books and law in practice should be relatively narrow – and fairly applied. Moreover, laws must be reasonably acceptable to a majority of the populace or people affected (or at least the key groups affected) by the laws.[3]

There is general agreement not only about these criteria, but that these criteria cannot be perfectly realized, and may even in some cases be in tension with each other. While marginal deviations are acceptable, legal systems that fall far short are likely to be dysfunctional. Of course, a thin theory requires more than just these elements. A fully articulated thin theory would also specify the goals and purposes of the system as well as its institutions, rules, practices and outcomes.

Typical candidates for the more limited normative purposes served by thin theories of rule of law include:[4]

- ensuring stability, and preventing anarchy and Hobbesian war of all against all;
- securing government in accordance with law by limiting arbitrariness on the part of the government;
- enhancing predictability, which allows people to plan their affairs and hence promotes both individual freedom and economic development;
- providing a fair mechanism for the resolution of disputes;
- bolstering the legitimacy of the government.

States may agree on these broad goals and yet interpret or weigh them differently, leading to significant variations in their legal regimes. For instance, a greater emphasis on stability rather than individual freedom may result in some states limiting civil society, freedom of association and speech (see Chapters 4, 6 and 7). Moreover, in periods of rapid economic or social transformation, some of these goals, such as predictability, may be sacrificed for other important social values.

A variety of institutions and processes are also required. The promulgation of law assumes a legislature and the government machinery necessary to make the laws publicly available. Congruence of laws on the books and actual practice assumes institutions for implementing and enforcing laws. While informal means of enforcing laws may be possible in some contexts, modern societies must also rely on formal means such as courts and administrative bodies. Furthermore, if the law is to guide behavior and provide certainty and predictability, laws must be applied and enforced in a reasonable way that does not defeat people's expectations. This implies normative and practical limits on the decision-makers who interpret and apply the laws and principles of due process or natural justice such as access to impartial tribunals, a chance to present evidence and rules of evidence. One must also look beyond the traditional branches of government to the legal profession, civil society, private actors who increasingly take on government functions, and the military, which in many countries continues to be a force capable of undermining the legal system and rule of law.

3

In contrast to thin versions of rule of law, thick or substantive conceptions begin with the basic elements of a thin conception but then incorporate elements of political morality such as particular economic arrangements (free-market capitalism, central planning, "Asian developmental state" or other varieties of capitalism), forms of government (democratic, socialist, soft authoritarian) or conceptions of human rights (libertarian, classical liberal, social welfare liberal, communitarian, "Asian values," etc.).

Thus, a liberal democratic version of rule of law incorporates free-market capitalism (subject to qualifications that would allow various degrees of "legitimate" government regulation of the market), multiparty democracy in which citizens may choose their representatives at all levels of government, and a liberal interpretation of human rights that generally gives priority to civil and political rights over economic, social, cultural, and collective or group rights. Liberal democratic rule of law may be further subdivided along the main political fault-lines in Europe and America: a libertarian version that emphasizes liberty and property rights, a classical liberal position, a social welfare liberal version, and so on.

Although rule of law has ancient roots and may be traced back to Aristotle, the modern conception of rule of law is integrally related to the rise of liberal democracy in the West. Indeed, for many, "*the* rule of law" means some form of a liberal democratic version of rule of law. The tendency to equate rule of law with liberal democratic rule of law has led some Asian commentators to portray the attempts of Western governments and international organizations such as the World Bank and the International Monetary Fund (IMF) to promote rule of law in Asian countries as a form of economic, cultural, political and legal hegemony.[5] Critics claim that liberal democratic rule of law is excessively individualist in its orientation and privileges individual autonomy and rights over duties and obligations to others, the interests of society, and social solidarity and harmony.[6] This line of criticism taps into recent, often heavily politicized, debates about "Asian values," and whether democratic or authoritarian regimes are more likely to ensure social stability and economic growth.[7] It also taps into post-colonial discourses and conflicts between developed and developing states, and within developing states between the haves and have-nots over issues of distributive justice. In several countries, arguably in *all* countries, it has resulted in an attempt to inject local values into a legal system established by foreign powers during colonial occupation or largely based on foreign transplants (see, especially, Chapters 6, 7, 8 and 10).

It bears noting that many of the critiques of liberal democracy in Asia are shared by Western critics as well. Such odd bedfellows as the critical left, conservative right and communitarians all find common ground in maintaining that liberals overstate the importance of autonomy and individual freedom at the expense of a more holistic approach that fosters community

4

and social solidarity. Such diversity suggests that "the West" has been just as much a simplified construct as "Asia"/"the East" in recent debates about Asian values and the universalism of human rights.

Whatever the normative merits or limitations of liberalism, the liberal democratic model is of limited use in understanding several of the legal systems in Asia. China and Vietnam are effectively single-party socialist states. While there are democratic elections in Singapore and Malaysia, both countries are frequently characterized as non-liberal, soft-authoritarian regimes. Several other countries are in the process of consolidating democracy. But even many of the democratic regimes show signs of being less liberal than their Western counterparts. Some countries remain politically unstable and torn by ethnic strife, resulting in various restrictions on individual liberties. Many are confronting widespread poverty and the social ills that follow from it. Worried about meeting the basic needs of sustenance, expansive social welfare programs seem a distant pipedream.

In striking contrast to the many volumes on rule of law in the Western literature, relatively little work has been done on clarifying alternative conceptions of rule of law in other parts of the world, including Asia.[8] What emerges from the following country studies is a rich portrait of diverse conceptions of rule of law both across the region and within individual countries, from liberal views to authoritarian views, from top-down statist views to the bottom-up perspectives of oppressed individuals seeking to harness the power of rule of law to redress individual instances of injustice and the broad-ranging systemic problems that empower a few at the expense of the many.

A point of clarification: the relationship between thin and thick theories

While thin and thick versions of rule of law are analytically distinct, in the real world there are no freestanding thin rule of law legal systems that exist independently of a particular political, economic, social and cultural context. Put differently, any legal system that meets the standards of a thin rule of law is inevitably embedded in a particular institutional, cultural and values complex, whether that be liberal democratic, statist socialist, soft authoritarian, communitarian, some combination of them, or some other alternative. In Singapore, for instance, the government sometimes seems to advocate a thin rule law against the thicker normative conception of liberals. However, the government's conception of a thin rule of law is itself embedded in a particular non-liberal thick conception as evidenced in its views on democracy, the importance of stability and economic growth, and various rights issues.

Theoretically, one way of conceptualizing the relationship between a thin rule of law, particular thick conceptions of rule of law, and the broader context is in terms of concentric circles. The smallest circle consists of the core elements of a thin rule of law, which is embedded within a thick rule of law conception or framework. The thick conception is in turn part of a broader social and political philosophy that addresses a range of issues beyond those relating to the legal system and rule of law. This broader social and political philosophy would be one aspect of a more comprehensive general philosophy or worldview that might include metaphysics, religious beliefs, aesthetics, and so on.

The advantages and disadvantages of thin and thick theories

Thin and thick conceptions are analytical tools. It is not a question of one being the right way to conceive rule of law and the other wrong. They have different advantages and disadvantages, and serve different purposes. Thin conceptions highlight certain features and purposes of a legal system. Even a more limited thin rule of law has many important virtues. At minimum, it promises some degree of predictability and some limitation on arbitrariness, and hence some protection of individual rights and freedoms. While the notion of legality may seem like all too thin a normative reed in cases where the laws themselves are morally objectionable, even the harshest critics of rule of law acknowledge that getting government actors to act in accordance with, and to abide by, the laws is no small achievement. Certainly dissidents rotting away in jail after being denied the right to a fair trial and other procedural protections appreciate the importance of even a thin rule of law. Similarly, business people and the average citizen alike appreciate a legal system in which laws do not change daily and are regularly applied in a fair manner by competent administrators and judges free from corruption. By narrowing the focus, a thin theory highlights the importance of these virtues of rule of law.

Conversely, because thick theories are based on more comprehensive social and political philosophies, rule of law loses its distinctiveness and gets swallowed up in the larger normative merits or demerits of the particular social and political philosophy. As Joseph Raz observes,

> If rule of law is the rule of the good law then to explain its nature is to propound a complete social philosophy. But if so the term lacks any useful function. We have no need to be converted to the rule of law just in order to believe that good should triumph. A non-democratic legal system, based on the denial of human rights, of extensive poverty, on racial segregation, sexual inequalities, and religious persecution may, in principle, conform to the requirements of the rule of law better than any of the legal systems of the more enlightened Western democracies.[9]

As a practical matter, much of the moral force behind rule of law and its enduring importance as a political ideal today is predicated on the ability to use rule of law as a benchmark to condemn or praise particular rules, decisions, practices and legal systems. But all too often, rule of law is simply invoked to criticize whatever law, practice or outcome does not coincide with one's own political beliefs. For example, in Singapore liberal critics of the government's conservative policies have invoked rule of law to object to the lack of "adequate" workers' rights legislation, limitations on the right of peaceful demonstration, and a regulatory framework that restricts the freedom of the local press. Contrast such complaints with the following. A law provides that contractors must have five years of experience and meet various other requirements to obtain a license; nevertheless, a government official denies a license to a contractor who meets all of the requirements, and a court refuses to overturn the decision because local courts are funded by the local government. Two government agencies issue conflicting regulations, and there is no effective legal mechanism to sort out the conflict. A suspect is entitled to legal counsel according to law, but in practice the authorities refuse to allow him to contact his lawyer. Your dispute with your insurance company regarding payment for hospital bills incurred as a result of a car accident remains pending in court after seven years due to judicial inefficiency. The rich and powerful are regularly exempted from prosecution of certain laws whereas others are prosecuted in similar circumstances.

Distinguishing between thin and thick theories makes it possible to use rule of law more effectively as a benchmark for evaluating legal systems by clarifying the nature of the problem. Several of the countries in Asia are still in the process of establishing functional legal systems. Their legal systems are plagued by thin rule of law issues such as weak legal institutions, incompetent and corrupt administrative officials and judges, excessive delays, and limitations on access to justice including high court costs and the lack of legal aid.[10] These kinds of problems are qualitatively different than more political issues such as how broad free speech or freedom of association should be, or whether labor should have the right to form unions and strike. Obviously, these latter issues are tremendously important and deserve to be discussed. But whether the most effective way to do so is by riding into battle hoisting the banner of rule of law is debatable. When invoked by parties on both sides of an issue to support diametrically opposed results, rule of law quickly becomes conceptually overburdened and unstable.

A thin theory therefore facilitates focused and productive discussion of certain legal issues among persons of different political persuasions. Being able to narrow the scope of the discussion and avoid getting bogged down in larger issues of political morality is particularly important in cross-cultural dialogue between, for example, American liberals and Chinese socialists or Muslim fundamentalists. Criticisms of a legal system in a country such as China and Vietnam that point out the many ways in which the system falls short of a liberal interpretation of rule of law are likely to fall on deaf ears

7

and may indeed produce a backlash that undermines support for rule of law, and thus, ironically, impede reforms favored by liberals. Conversely, criticisms are more likely to be taken seriously and result in actual change given a shared understanding of rule of law. To the extent that there is common ground and agreement on at least some features of a thin theory of rule of law, parties can set aside their political differences and focus on concrete reforms. For instance, the U.S. and the People's Republic of China (PRC), notwithstanding the U.S.'s liberal democratic conception of rule of law and the Chinese government's statist socialist conception, have been able to agree on a wide range of reforms to improve the PRC legal system, including judicial exchange and training programs aimed at improving the quality of PRC judges; programs to assist in the development of a legal aid system; exchanges to strengthen the securities regulatory system and the administrative law system; seminars on electronic commerce, corporate law, and the enforcement of arbitral awards and court judgments; and even a symposium to discuss the legal aspects of protecting human rights, including issues such as China's legal responsibilities under international rights agreements, the rights of criminal defendants and the legal protection of religious freedom.

As discussions of contentious criminal law issues show, relying on a thin rule of law as a benchmark to assess a legal system does not allow one to completely avoid all substantive issues of the type that must be addressed by advocates of a thick theory of rule of law. It merely reduces the range of issues where such substantive values will be relevant and hence the scope of possible conflict. Although the features of a thin rule of law are common to all rule of law systems, they will vary to some extent in the way they are interpreted and implemented depending on substantive political views and values. For instance, socialists and liberals may agree that one of the purposes of a thin rule of law is to protect individual rights and interests but disagree about what those rights and interests are. Or they may agree that rule of law requires that laws be made by an entity with the authority to make laws but disagree as to whether members of that entity must be democratically elected. Accordingly, legal systems that meet the standards of a thin rule of law will still diverge to some extent with respect to purposes, institutions, rules and outcomes due to the different contexts in which they are embedded.

One of the dangers of eliding rule of law with an open-ended concept like justice is that it tends to produce confusion, and eventually disillusionment. As Vitit Muntarbhorn (Chapter 11) explains:

> The Thai term for the rule of law is "*Luck Nititham,*" implying a precept of law based upon a sense of justice and virtue – not an easy notion to grasp in a concrete sense. There is thus a kind of mythification of the term as a linchpin of our society, when in reality it is steeped in popular incomprehension rather than

comprehension. This mythification dilutes the impact of the notion of the rule of law, precisely because the distance between people and the notion itself is often extreme – and that gap results in what can be described as the *rule of lore*.

Simply put, there is little agreement over what justice is. As Upendra Baxi (Chapter 10) reminds us:

> the "good" that triumphs, as a "complete social philosophy," may be, and indeed has often been, defined in ways that perpetuate states of Radical Evil. Complete social philosophies have justified, and remain capable of justifying, varieties of violent social exclusion.

Given the fact of pluralism,[11] thick conceptions of rule of law must confront the issue of whose good, whose justice? Liberals, Socialists, Communitarians, Neo-authoritarians, Soft Authoritarians, New Conservatives, Old Conservatives, Buddhists, Daoists, Neo-Confucians and New Confucians all differ in their visions of the good life and on what is considered just, and hence what rule of law requires. By incorporating particular conceptions of the economy, political order or human rights into rule of law, thick conceptions decrease the likelihood that an overlapping consensus will emerge as to its meaning. Conversely, limiting the concept of rule of law to the requirements of a thin theory makes it possible to avoid getting mired in never-ending debates about the superiority of the various political theories all contending for the throne of justice.

The more concrete, practical downside of conflating rule of law with justice is that it gives rise to unrealistic expectations of rule of law. No legal system to date has produced a perfectly just society, and none ever will. People should not expect a legal system or rule of law to address all social ills. You may win a lawsuit, but if the other party is insolvent, no legal system will be able to enforce the judgment for you. Regardless of whether abortion is allowed or prohibited, some people will find the outcome unbearable. When the legal system falls short of one's particular conception of what is just, it is then criticized, leading to a backlash against rule of law as an empty concept or, worse yet, a mask of oppression.

On the other hand, thick theories have their advantages as well. Articulating different thick conceptions makes it possible to relate political and economic problems to law, legal institutions and particular conceptions of legal systems. By highlighting differences in viewpoints across a range of issues, thick theories bring out more clearly what is really at stake in many disputes. Moreover, activists and legal reformers in repressive regimes generally prefer thick theories because they allow them to discuss certain controversial political issues. For instance, in China, legal reformers have

9

used a broad conception of rule of law as a means of discussing democracy, separation of powers and human rights issues.

As a matter of legal sociology, it seems most people object to the normative deficiencies of a thin rule of law, and are unwilling to describe states such as Nazi Germany or apartheid South Africa as rule of law states.[12] Whatever the merits of this view, conceiving rule of law in thin terms will mean that rule of law will give way to other important values in some instances, and many of the most important public issues will be debated in terms other than rule of law. Where laws are deeply unjust, citizens will engage in civil disobedience or seek to overthrow the ruling regime. Similarly, if rule of law is narrowly conceived to curtail all discretion, then rule of law and its virtues of predictability and certainty will sometimes give way to considerations of equity and the desire for a context-specific and just outcome.

In sum, the choice of thin or thick theories depends on one's purpose. Investors seeking a basis for assessing legal system risk may be better served by a rule of law index that closely approximates the standards of a thin theory. Similarly, governments wishing to promote legal reform in a country such as China or Vietnam may find their offers to assist in implementing rule of law more readily accepted if they are couched in terms of a thin rule of law rather than as part of a larger package of political reforms that includes democracy and an expansive liberal interpretation of civil and political rights. Conversely, human rights non-governmental organizations (NGOs) might find that a broader conception of rule of law suits their purposes better. Social activists and political dissidents will no doubt want an expansive conception of rule of law that furthers their political agenda.

The limits of this conceptual framework and rule of law

Law has its limits, and so does rule of law, conceptually, normatively and practically. Rule of law assumes some degree of separation between law and politics, even though the line is not always a bright one and varies according to one's thick conception. Revolutions and coups present a particularly difficult challenge for rule of law. How are courts to respond to situations such as in the Philippines, where Marcos' amendment of the constitution was ratified by a show of people's assemblies, a procedure not in conformity with the constitution at the time (Chapter 12)? Should they stand up for the rule of law principles of legality, predictability and certainty in the face of political reality? What, then, when Cory Aquino becomes president and replaces the Marcos-era constitution with her Freedom Constitution, again without complying with the rules in place at the time? By sticking up for rule of law, the court runs the risk of forcing a constitutional crisis. In the first case, Marcos may very well have replaced the judges, as happened in Malaysia in 1986 when the court dared to oppose Mahathir. In the Aquino case, the court would have incurred the wrath of the people, compromising its legitimacy and authority and undermining its efforts to emerge as a political force in the new regime. In both cases, what the court did do was simply bow to political reality. In South Korea, the court has also struggled with the issue of how to handle leaders who come to power as a result of a coup. The court recognized that as a practical matter generally it will not be possible to prosecute those who took power after a successful coup while they remain in office, yet insisted nonetheless on the legal possibility of prosecution. To be sure, that these acts, especially by Marcos, could be challenged in court suggests that rule of law is a powerful motivating ideal, one which even dictators cannot dismiss without tarnishing their legitimacy.

For all of its rhetorical appeal, however, rule of law, whether thick or thin, cannot provide much guidance with respect to certain issues. As will become quickly apparent from the following chapters, the minimal requirements of rule of law are compatible with considerable diversity in institutions, rules and practices. For example, the way powers are distributed and balanced between the executive, legislature and judiciary varies widely. Constitutional review is conducted by a variety of entities that enjoy different powers. The nature and degree of judicial independence, as well as the manner in which it is achieved, also vary. In some cases judges are appointed (through a variety of mechanisms) and in some cases they are elected. Nor will appeals to rule of law alone put an end to debates about what type of theory of adjudication is best – strict interpretation, purposive, the social activist approach of Indian courts or Dworkin's (liberal, equality-based) make-law-the-best-it-can-be approach.[13] Indeed, appeals to rule of law alone will not even resolve many specific, thin rule of law issues such as how clear rules must be or when retroactive rules are acceptable.

Institutional choices are often highly path-dependent: the initial choice of institutions and the way they operate and evolve over time is influenced to a large extent by a host of contingent, context-specific factors. Seemingly similar institutions, sometimes transplanted from one system to another, are likely to function differently from place to place. Assessing the appropriateness and effectiveness of institutions requires an evaluation of their results in the particular context. For example, while China is not the only country in which the local governments fund the local courts and judges are appointed by local authorities, the combination has led to a severe problem with local protectionism.

To take a more pervasive issue, most if not all states preclude some political and administrative acts from judicial review. Such decisions include certain decisions by police as to whom to arrest and by prosecutors regarding whom to prosecute; decisions regarding national defense, war and covert operations; and some highly technical issues left to administrative agencies. Rule of law therefore cannot require that every decision be subject to judicial review or else no country would merit the label of rule law.

Nevertheless, rule of law does require some limits on discretion and arguably the ability to challenge most government decisions in some way, whether that be through internal administrative mechanisms or the electoral process, whereby citizens can vote governments that misuse their power out of office. But exactly what is required is far from clear. Singapore, for instance, has a number of laws that allow for the restriction of individual liberties without judicial review. The Maintenance of Religious Harmony Act, observes Li-ann Thio (Chapter 6), "allows the minister to issue pre-emptive 'restraining orders' to 'gag' politicians or religionists thought to be mixing an incendiary cocktail of religion and extremist politics." The government argues that, given the sensitive nature of religion in multiethnic Singapore, issues involving religious harmony are crucial for the survival of the nation, and better left to the executive than to the judiciary or the legislature. The executive's decision is subject to review by the elected president, and advisory councils composed of bureaucrats or religious and civic leaders are sometimes consulted to further diminish the dangers of a concentration of unchecked powers in the executive's hands. Nevertheless, critics contend that such justifications and mechanisms are inadequate, and call for a more robust judicial review.

Cases involving the declaration of national emergency and derogation of rights raise equally difficult issues. Although Asian governments have frequently been criticized for invoking national security as an excuse to limit rights, Western governments have also reacted to real or perceived threats in a heavy-handed way, most recently in the wake of September 11.[14] While the dangers of abuse of powers are apparent, advocates of different thick conceptions are likely to disagree about when national emergencies should be declared, who has the right to declare them and what type of review, if any, there should be. In Malaysia, the king, the titular head of the executive, acts on the advice of the cabinet in deciding whether a state of emergency exists. Parliament, not the judiciary, has the power to review the decision and overturn it. Appealing to rule of law will not suffice to sort out these issues. Both sides can appeal to their own particular thick conceptions, and a thin conception does not require all important decisions to be left ultimately to the courts. In any event, concluding that a practice or decision is consistent or inconsistent with a thin rule of law or a particular thick conception of rule of law is not the end of normative debate. In the end, we need to look at how a system or particular rule or practice works and then evaluate it.

Given that rule of law cannot resolve many of these issues, wouldn't it be better simply to discuss particular issues without reference to rule of law? While there is considerable merit in the suggestion that what matters most is not the label but the substance of particular issues, abandoning reference to rule of law is neither possible nor desirable. As a practical matter, people will continue to invoke rule of law. Faced with that fact, it is better to try to bring some clarity to the different uses of the term, by distinguishing between rule by law and rule of law and between thin and thick conceptions of rule of law and different types of thick conceptions, than to insist futilely that the term be avoided altogether.

In addition, rule of law provides a useful heuristic guide for legal reforms in that the elements of a thin (or even thick) theory may be used to clarify and prioritize areas in need of reform and to see the relationships between the various elements. It provides some structure to what otherwise could be a chaotic, piecemeal reform process. It also helps avoid misunderstandings and wasted efforts in ensuring that reforms that might work in one system are not attempted in legal systems whose purpose and political and legal infrastructure differ.

Moreover, even though relying on the concept of rule of law will not put an end to debates in many cases, it does highlight important issues and may be determinative in some cases. For instance, the Korean Bar Association, a number of prominent law professors, and other "conservative" intellectuals have accused President Kim Dae-jung of violating rule of law by using a general tax audit of all the major news media companies as a cover for persecution of his political opponents (Chapter 13). A thin rule of law is ideologically neutral in requiring governments, whether democratically elected or authoritarian, to act according to law and to treat similarly situated persons equally. Assuming it turns out that Kim was using the law only or primarily against political opponents, critics will be able to argue that his acts violate rule of law, a powerful objection in any setting, but particularly in the case of a president in a newly democratic state who made his name by opposing the abuse of law for political purposes by the prior authoritarian regime.

The construction, de(con)struction and reconstruction of rule of law and rule of law discourse

One of the striking conclusions of this comparative survey is that, while rule of law is invoked everywhere nowadays, rule of law discourse is much more vibrant and hotly contested in some countries than in others. Rule of law plays a major role in political debates in China, Hong Kong, Singapore, Malaysia and even Vietnam. In contrast, as Hahm Chaihark remarks (Chapter 13), "It is fair to say...that, until very recently, the term rule of law remained largely irrelevant to most Koreans. It was either a cover for legitimizing oppressive authoritarian regimes, or the subject of naïve and sentimental musing on the part of law professors. The utterance of the term generally evoked fear or suspicion." Rule of law only became a central part of pubic discourse after democratization. Meanwhile, Thailand, after decades of semi-democracy followed by repeated coups, passed a new constitution in 1997 that entrenches rule of law. Yet democracy and human rights attract more attention than rule of law. Conflated with justice, rule of law is poorly understood, and in the wake of the Asian financial crisis, there is some hostility to rule of law as a hegemonic tool of the IMF.

While the diversity in legal systems and rule of law discourses belies easily generalizations, several conclusions may be drawn. As one would expect, the nature and subject matter of the debates vary widely. In Vietnam (and some would say China), the main issue is whether the ruling regime is willing to accept the basic requirement of rule of law that the state and state actors are bound by law. The value of even a thin rule of law is seen most clearly in such countries, where the fundamental principle of legality is still contested. Thin conceptions of rule of law are most useful as a benchmark for states that are still in the process of establishing a modern, functional legal system. In such countries, much of the discussion is about which reforms are required to bring the system into compliance with the requirements of a thin theory.

In more mature legal systems, the discussion is more likely to focus on thick conceptions of rule of law or, in the absence of deep conflicts about thick conceptions of rule of law, on particular issues often involving consti-tutional law, judicial interpretation, human rights and the separation and balance of powers. In countries where social, economic and political cleav-ages give rise to sharply contested political positions and in turn competing thick conceptions of rule of law, much of the attention is on articulating and comparing the different conceptions, and arguing for the superiority of one over the other(s). Untethered by the more limited conception of a thin rule of law, parties invoke rule of law in the name of widely disparate political causes.

The relationship between law and politics is a recurring theme, particu-larly but not only in non-democratic societies, as the *Bush v. Gore* case in the U.S. shows. In Singapore and Malaysia, the heavily politicized use of law at least in a narrow range of cases raises difficult theoretical and practical issues regarding rule of law. The line between law and politics also becomes blurry in newly democratized states confronting constitutional moments and transitional justice issues. While in the process of consolidating democracy, the Philippines, South Korea, Taiwan, Thailand and Indonesia are all strug-gling with central constitutional issues involving the delineation and balancing of the powers of the various branches, as well as fundamental rights. At the same time, in most of these countries the legal system remains weak, falling short of basic thin rule of law requirements.

The U.S., France and Japan are mature democracies with well-developed legal systems. In Japan, there are many calls to radically reform the legal system, overhaul legal education, reconfigure the administrative law regime and so on. But rule of law is not often invoked. In France, rule of law discourse has centered on issues of constitutional review, and more recently the idea of a constitution for the E.U. In the U.S., parties of every political

14

persuasion continue to invoke rule of law, notwithstanding an extensive critical literature that calls into question its meaning and value. Such extensive criticism has led to fears that the public's faith in the legal system will be undermined. As a result, a retrenchment is taking place where rule of law is defended by making it less ambitious.

Vietnam: toward rule of law?

Vietnam is at a stage of economic, political and legal development where rule of law is still more of a distant aspiration than a reality. Even the most basic issue of whether the Party will accept limits on its authority and be bound by law remains up in the air. On the one hand, according to the *nha nuoc phap quyen* doctrine, the Party is supposed to confine itself to policy formulation, leaving the state apparatus to enact and implement law. Moreover, the 1992 Constitution provides that Party organizations are subject to law. Nevertheless, as John Gillespie (Chapter 5) observes, in practice Party leaders still do not accept that Party policy needs state legislation to acquire coercive force.

Socialist ideology remains significant, much more so, it seems, than in China. The Party continues to limit political discourse, though not as strictly as in the past. The economy is mainly relational in nature, and foreign direct investment is limited. The population is largely rural. As a result, the demand for rule of law from the commercial sector is limited. The supply side is equally problematic. Legal institutions are weak and undeveloped. The courts are corrupt, incompetent, and lack independence and authority. The legislature is beginning to show signs of professionalization, but many wonder how far it can go within the existing framework (as is also true in China). The administrative law system is very much a work in progress.

While the prospects for significant change may seem bleak, there are clearly forces pushing for legal reforms and rule of law. The government's desire for legitimacy both domestically and internationally is one factor. Because today being a good member of the international community includes supporting rule of law, Vietnam's desire for foreign aid has opened a window of opportunity for the IMF and other donor agencies and bilateral programs promoting rule of law. To the extent that legitimacy is performance based, the need to ensure economic growth has led the government to endorse *doi moi* reforms, which involve normalizing social and economic transactions through legal means rather than on the basis of ideology and morality. They also involve an open-door policy that fosters cooperation and trading relationships between Vietnam and other countries. Foreign investors will no doubt continue to demand reforms. As the domestic economy grows and expands beyond relational contracts and companies accumulate valuable tangible and intellectual property interests, they too are likely to push for reforms that protect them from an over-reaching state.

Although it may be too early to expect a rich discussion about alternative conceptions of rule of law, there are various thick conceptions of rule of law emerging, some of them fairly well articulated while others are only beginning to take shape and develop a constituency. Not surprisingly given the nature of the ruling regime, the government's statist socialist conception of rule of law is dominant. Multilateral agencies are divided between those that wish to de-emphasize political factors and focus on institution-building and thin rule of law concerns, and those that favor a thick liberal democratic rule of law with all of the usual political institutions and practices. There also appears to be some support within Vietnam for a soft-authoritarian form of rule of law. In addition, there is a diversity of views on a wide range of issues that do not add up to particular coherent conceptions.

Rule of law is only one form of discourse competing for space in Vietnam today. While foreign agencies and elite intellectuals are likely to invoke rule of law, local discourses often treat similar issues in other terms. As we have seen, however, rule of law is rhetorically powerful. The equivocation between thick and thin conceptions allows it to be used by different factions to push their own agenda. As the Party's role in establishing the dominant discourse diminishes, or at least its capacity to control public discourse wanes, rule of law may come to serve those seeking further reforms. But the emergence of rule of law discourse is only the first step in a long road toward establishing a rule of law legal system. At present, the main issues would seem to be to get the Party to accept that it must act according to law, to separate the Party from the state and business, and to strengthen legal institutions.

Rule of law in (soft-)authoritarian, non-democratic or limited democratic states: competing conceptions of rule of law in China, Malaysia, Singapore and Hong Kong

China, Malaysia, Singapore and Hong Kong are non-liberal states in which there are clearly different thick conceptions of rule of law competing for ascendance. In addition, each is confronting in its own way issues relating to the relationship between law and politics. While China and Hong Kong do not allow elections of top leaders, in Malaysia and Singapore critics complain that the ruling party uses the legal system to harass political opponents and undermine democracy. Thus all are important test cases with respect to the relationship between rule of law and democracy.

In China, rule of law re-entered public discourse in the late 1970s as China entered the modern reform era. Throughout the 1980s, much of the emphasis was on legislation and institution-building. In the early to mid-

1990s, attention turned to the quality as well as the quantity of laws, issues of implementation, the powers of government institutions, and the purposes of law and legal reforms. The view that the Party and government must act according to law gained ground, reinforced by the passage of numerous administrative laws and institutional reforms aimed at establishing and then strengthening the administrative law system. During the mid-1990s, rule of law became a central topic, leading in 1996 to the regime's endorsement of a new official policy of "rule the country according to law, establish a socialist rule of law state," which was subsequently incorporated into the Constitution in 1999.

As in Vietnam, China is still at an early stage in implementing rule of law. Unlike in Vietnam, however, regime norms and policies clearly endorse basic rule of law principles, including that the Party and state must act within the limits of law. However, practice lags behind. Considerable efforts are still needed to change attitudes and to establish institutions to give effect to rule of law. While problems in implementing rule of law are often attributed to the Party, many of the most serious problems are institutional in nature. The legislative system, judiciary, legal profession and administrative law system are all weak.[15] Thus much of the attention is on the more technical aspects of legal reform and institution-building.

There is, however, also a wide range of sharply divergent political views in China, which leads to radically different thick conceptions of rule of law. As elaborated in Chapter 4, statist socialists, neo-authoritarians, communitarians and liberals differ over forms of government, the enduring value or poverty of socialism, the advantages and disadvantages of government by elites versus populist democracy, whether an authoritarian regime or democratic one is more likely to ensure economic growth and social stability, a number of issues that fall under the rubric of varieties of capitalism, the proper balance between laws serving the state's interests and protecting the rights and interests of individuals, and a whole range of issues regarding individual rights.

In contrast to China, Malaysia enjoys a relatively well-developed legal system, a product of British colonialism. As H. P. Lee (Chapter 7) points out, after Independence, Malaysia's first three prime ministers, having been trained abroad, continued to support judicial independence and rule of law. However, as in other countries, independence from colonial rule has led to attempts to infuse the legal system with local values. In 1969, the government promoted *Rukunegara* as a five-point national philosophy to facilitate national unity in the wake of racial disturbances. The five principles – belief in God, loyalty to king and country, upholding the constitution, rule of law, good behavior and morality – provide a radically different normative basis and ideological framework for rule of law than the social-contractarian, Enlightenment liberalism of some contemporary Western states, with their emphasis on separation of state and church and a neutral state that refuses to favor any particular substantive moral conception of the good (described by Brian Tamanaha in Chapter 2).

Since the 1990s, Mahathir has sought to distance Malaysia even further from the liberal model by infusing Asian values into the legal system. As a result, many disputes in the name of rule of law involve competing thick conceptions, and in particular the government's Asian-values-based, soft-authoritarian brand versus more liberal interpretations, though there is also evidence of communitarian strands and a "traditionalist" or fundamentalist strand that reflects the resurgence of Islam.[16] Broad security laws and powers of preventive detention highlight differences between the government and liberals with respect to fundamental rights, the proper balance between individual freedoms and the interests of society, and the relative importance of stability and economic growth versus freedom. Notwithstanding attempts to dismiss invocations of Asian values as cynical ploys by authoritarian rulers to deny people their rights, public opinion polls show that the majority of Malaysian citizens rank economic growth and social stability higher than individual liberties and freedoms, and Mahathir has been repeatedly re-elected by wide margins.[17]

At the same time, the government's use of the legal system to influence the electoral process and attack opposition figures raises questions about the limits of rule of law and the legitimacy of elections. The highly politicized prosecution of Anwar Ibrahim calls into question the separation between law and politics and the independence and authority of the courts, at least with respect to certain politically sensitive cases.

In Singapore, rule of law is a hotly debated topic. As in Malaysia, the legal system is well developed, and thus most of the issues involve competing thick conceptions rather than thin rule of law concerns. Indeed, as Li-ann Thio (Chapter 6) reminds us, the Singaporean legal system is regularly ranked among the world's best, if not the best, for efficiency, fairness and lack of corruption. Yet critics question whether Singapore enjoys rule of law. They decry the politicization of the legal system and the use of law to undermine political opposition, limit civil society and advance the conservative, statist substantive agenda of the People's Action Party (PAP). In commenting on the widespread perception of judicial bias, the U.N. special rapporteur on the independence of the judiciary and legal profession wryly noted

> the very high number of cases won by the Government or members of the ruling party in either contempt of court proceedings or defamation suits brought against critics of the Government, be they individuals or the media, particularly from a liberal perspective.[18]

While on the whole less authoritarian than China, the softer form of authoritarianism in Singapore involves limited democracy where elections are dominated by the PAP and opposition is tamed through the use of

defamation suits against political opponents, manipulation of voting procedures, gerrymandering, and short campaign times.[19] Given the dominance
of the PAP, accountability in Singapore is achieved not so much through
elections as through other means such as allocating limited participation
rights to the opposition, inviting members of the public to comment on
legislation, and the use of shadow cabinets where PAP members are asked to
play an opposition role. Law is meant to strengthen the state, ensure stability
and facilitate economic growth. Many decisions are left to the state and
political actors, primarily the cabinet headed by the prime minister. Civil
society is limited, and characterized by corporatist relationships between the
state, businesses, labor unions and society. Administrative law tends to
emphasize government efficiency rather than protection of individual rights.

While individual rights are constitutionally guaranteed, they are not
interpreted along liberal lines. The government's soft-authoritarian perspective of rule of law emphasizes a positivist account of law and a utilitarian
conception of rights, with rights seen as a grant from the state, as opposed
to a deontological conception of rights or the view that rights are grounded
in a social contract and thus possessed by individuals in a state of nature
prior to the formation of the state. Lee Kuan Yew and other government
officials have invoked Asian values to emphasize group interests over individual interests, and to justify limitations on civil and political rights,
including limits on free speech such that citizens are not allowed to attack
the integrity of key institutions like the judiciary or the character of elected
officials without attracting sanction in the form of contempt of court or
libel proceedings. Labor rights are also limited in the name of social stability
and economic growth.

Rejecting liberal neutrality, the government favors a more paternalistic
approach where the state promotes a substantive normative agenda and
actively regulates private morality and conduct. The government has
appealed to Confucianism not only to support its paternalist approach, but
to promote social harmony and consensus rather than adversarial litigation. On the whole, the judiciary tends to follow the government's lead.
Although the reason for that seems to be a genuine congruence of views on
the part of most judges rather than overt political pressure on the courts, in
some cases judges who have challenged the PAP have been reassigned and
the government does retain leverage over some judges appointed on a
temporary basis.[20]

The most vocal challenge to the government's view comes from liberals.
But there is also a communitarian or collectivist perspective that seeks a
middle ground between the more statist orientation of the government's soft
authoritarianism and the excessive individualism of liberals. According to
constitutional scholar Kevin Tan, Singaporean-style communitarianism is
an axiom of faith in governing nowadays, resulting in a premium being
placed on national security, economic growth and nation-building. While

"legal rights are not trampled upon at will, in balancing the rights of the individual and community, the state-articulated concerns of public interests have gained precedence." Although Tan suggests that most of the support for communitarianism comes from political elites, he also allows that the community-based approach toward rights has acquired popular resonance in mainstream Singaporean society.[21]

Like Singapore and Malaysia, Hong Kong has a well-developed legal system that is largely the product of British colonialism. Until the handover in 1997, the system was widely considered to be an exemplar of rule of law, notwithstanding the lack of democracy and a restricted scope and interpretation of individual rights during the colonial period. Prior to the handover, alarmists predicted the imminent demise of rule of law. As one would expect, the novel one-country, two-systems arrangement in which a special autonomous regime with a common law heritage and one of the most laissez-faire economies in the world co-exists under the larger umbrella of a socialist state with a civil law heritage has led to some bumps along the way. Nevertheless, the legal system's reputation for rule of law remains largely intact.[22]

With the change of government, however, has come a different value orientation. Tung Chee-hwa has on occasion invoked Asian values, suggesting to some that Hong Kong might be evolving toward a more Singaporean model. Signs of a possible shift toward a more soft-authoritarian or collectivist model include pressure on the media to toe the government's line; limitations on free speech and assembly, and in particular the requirement that demonstrators obtain prior approval from the authorities; consideration of a bill on religious sects, urged by Beijing, to control Falungong, along with the recent conviction of Falungong demonstrators; and the recent brouhaha over regulations required under Article 23 of the Basic Law dealing with a variety of potential threats to national security, from sedition to disclosure of state secrets.

Although Hong Kong under British rule was hardly a fortress of liberalism, liberals nowadays invoke "rule of law" to oppose government acts and further their own liberal agenda. The battle between the liberals and the more conservative or soft-authoritarian forces tracks to a considerable extent the conflicts between the "fundamentalists" and the "pragmatists" described by Albert Chen and Anne Cheung in Chapter 8, though there are some liberal pragmatists and non-liberal fundamentalists. The fundamentalists insist that certain rule of law principles are sacred and inviolable, and cannot be sacrificed even if there are weighty policy considerations that suggest otherwise. In contrast, the pragmatists recognize the importance of rule of law principles but are open to other considerations that also deserve to be taken seriously. For the most part, the government takes a more pragmatic approach, whereas liberals generally are more fundamentalist. Whether the fundamentalist/pragmatist distinction is merely a strategic cover for substantive political views would require test cases involving a conflict between them.[23] For instance, it would be interesting to see if the fundamentalists still rigidly insisted on upholding rule of law when the outcome would be at odds with their political agenda and substantive conception of justice. As noted previously, rule of law is only one of many important social values, and thus one suspects that, while fundamentalists may be somewhat more committed to thin rule of law values than pragmatists, all would be willing to sacrifice rule of law on the alter of their preferred form of justice in some cases.

Rule of law, democracy, constitutionalism, and transitional justice: the Philippines, South Korea, Taiwan, Thailand, Indonesia and India

The Philippines, South Korea, Taiwan, Thailand and Indonesia are in the process of consolidating democracy and strengthening legal institutions and the legal system. They are all confronting fundamental constitutional issues such as the relation of democracy to rule of law; balance of powers issues involving the power of the executive, legislature and increasingly activist judiciaries; and a wide range of human rights issues from freedom of the press to gender issues to the rights of criminal suspects. While India differs from the others in a number of ways, most notably in the fact that it is a longer-standing democracy, it too is grappling with many of the same types of constitutional, balance of power and human rights issues.

While struggling to consolidate democracies and establish a constitutional order, new democracies must also often wrestle with controversial issues of transitional justice. Newly formed governments must decide whether prosecuting former leaders and their siblings and cronies will help or hinder reform and national healing. The time-consuming and frustrating attempts to retrieve some of the riches stashed away overseas by Marcos and his family led to complaints that the legal system was too formalistic and protected bandits. The public wanted a faster, rougher form of popular justice. In South Korea, the trials of ex-presidents involve a complicated story in which money and murders combined to create the political force to prosecute. Yet the path to justice was hardly straightforward, and in the end President-elect Kim Dae-jung pardoned both Chun Doo-hwan and Roh Tae-woo as a goodwill gesture toward political conservatives.

In some cases pardons or amnesties may smooth the transition. In Cambodia, however, the government must now decide whether to honor past amnesties, and whether to try those accused of past atrocities in international tribunals or in its own courts, with or without an international presence. Some fear that trial in domestic courts will lead to a mockery of justice. Yet the government sees intervention by the U.N. as a violation of its sovereignty and as undermining the integrity and authority of the judiciary. In other cases, truth commissions might offer a better alternative.

Indonesia and East Timor are also grappling with how to do justice to

21

the past while looking to the future. Reflecting political and practical realities as well as the desire to achieve both retribution and reconciliation, a complex system has been established involving the U.N.-authorized Commission for Reception, Truth and Reconciliation, special panels for serious crimes in Dili consisting of international and East Timorese judges, and an ad hoc human rights court in Jakarta. Building on experiences elsewhere, the Truth and Reconciliation Commission provides immunity to individuals but not groups, provided individuals make a full disclosure of their acts for which reconciliation is sought and such acts do not constitute "serious crimes."[24]

In contrast to the largely favorable assessment of the Truth and Reconciliation Commission, the serious crimes unit and the ad hoc human rights court in Jakarta have been subject to intense criticism.[25] The head of the serious crimes unit resigned in protest over the lack of funding. As the unit's term approaches its end, there have been only a dozen or so convictions. Many of the 100-plus persons indicted reside in Indonesia and are unlikely to face trial given the government's refusal to turn them over to Dili. Meanwhile, Amnesty International and the Judicial System Monitoring Programme (JSMP) have complained that the trials in the Jakarta human rights court have been seriously flawed, resulting in neither truth nor justice. Jurisdiction has been limited so that only a small number of those who engaged in serious crimes in 1999 are potentially liable; the indictments in early cases failed to capture the widespread and systematic nature of the crimes and glossed over the role of the Indonesian security forces; and key witnesses summoned to testify refused to appear because of the lack of adequate measures to ensure their safety.

Indonesia and especially East Timor are confronting not only difficult issues of transitional *justice*, but equally if not more difficult problems in transitional *governance*. As in Kosovo, the U.N. was ill prepared to assume responsibilities for running East Timor after the East Timorese opted to no longer be part of Indonesia and Indonesians in key political, administrative and judicial positions fled.[26] To gain some feel for the enormity of the challenge, there were no East Timorese lawyers with experience as judges or prosecutors because none had been appointed to such positions under Indonesian rule. Similarly, the exodus of prison guards and the burning of prisons forced the U.N.'s International Force for East Timor to rely on U.N. civil police officers to run overcrowded makeshift detention centers, and to release individuals accused of serious crimes to make room for those charged with grave violations of humanitarian law.[27]

Judiciaries emerging from an authoritarian past are frequently eager to demonstrate their newfound independence, bolster their legitimacy and expand their authority by becoming "activist" across a range of issues. The courts in all of the countries in this group (with the exception of Indonesia, where most of the attention so far has been on constitutional amendments by the legislature) are now regularly deciding a large number of constitutional cases, frequently striking down laws as unconstitutional.[28] In some cases this is to be expected, given that many laws are the product of the previous authoritarian regime. But it also shows the tendency for courts to demonstrate their independence and expand their authority. In South Korea, the justices of the Constitutional Court went out of their way to overcome distrust and ignorance, writing long opinions that signaled their desire to hear more cases. In Taiwan and India, the courts have even struck down constitutional amendments as unconstitutional.[29]

Taking an activist approach on a wide range of issues, including many social and economic issues for which the judges do not necessarily possess the necessary expertise, may lead to overreaching, ideologically driven decisions that have negative social, economic and political consequences. In Eastern Europe, courts decided cases based on neo-liberal economic dogma that did not always fit the times and conditions.[30] In the Philippines, a recurring complaint is that the courts interfere too much in "economic decision-making" by second-guessing government policy-makers and issuing injunctions against business decisions. In South Korea, the Constitutional Court stretched to decide in favor of a *chaebol* forced into bankruptcy under the previous regime, even though technically the bankruptcy was caused by a bank, a private entity. Eager to reinforce the separation of state and business, shore up private property and support an economy based on neo-liberal principles rather than the developmental state model of the previous regime, the court – for better or worse – seized the opportunity to limit the power of the government and the president to regulate and interfere with the business activities of private corporations.

Lacking the legitimacy that comes from elections, courts in newly democratized states will frequently cater to the public to shore up their political base. In several of the South Korean cases, the judiciary has cultivated a populist and progressive image. In part, this may be a reflection of Korean concerns over national identity and the ongoing preoccupation with modernity. For instance, in striking down a law providing for an apology as one remedy in defamation cases, the Constitutional Court expressly noted that no modern country other than Japan provides for apology. Its decision in the *chaebol* case was arguably populist in nature and served to portray the courts as in line with the practices of modern countries elsewhere. Similarly, the court again sided with modernity, upsetting cultural conservatives, when it ruled against a prohibition on marriage between people with the same surnames, although the court did not decide what degree of relations would be allowed to intermarry, kicking that politically sensitive issue back to the democratically elected legislature. In India, the activist court has gained popular moral support by transcending received liberal notions of the judicial function and engaging in a broad social action program.[31]

In the Philippines, the court has sought the support of the people to the

23

point where rule of law is in danger. As Raul Pangalangan observes (Chapter 12), the post-Marcos constitutional order aimed at two competing goals: on the one hand, to restore the primacy of the rule of law – "a government of laws and not of men," while, on the other, institutionalizing the gains of "People Power" – the direct but peaceful exercise of democracy that ousted the Marcos regime and adopted a social reform agenda. Popular democracy was written into the constitution, which gave the people the power to directly amend the constitution, recall local government officials, and revise or reject statutes and ordinances. Given the weakness of the courts in the Marcos era and the role of the people in rising up against authoritarianism, the people have enjoyed an elevated moral status and legitimacy. Thus, while the courts have been eager to expand their authority and to "juridify" policy debates by expanding access to the courts through liberalized rules of standing, they have been wary of challenging popular opinion. The result has been an overreaching judicial review that has led to a non-normative, outcome-oriented jurisprudence,

> as if the courts were in a perpetual popularity contest refereed by polling groups and single-interest lobbies, all of them oblivious to the intricacies of legal reasoning and attuned solely to the question of "who won" and "are we on the same side."

The wavering, unprincipled jurisprudence has "abetted an unabashed derision for law as 'legal gobbledygook'" and undermined the legitimacy of the legal system and rule of law. While all courts take into consideration public opinion in some cases, the predictability and certainty promised by a thin rule of law are lost when court decisions regularly turn on the capricious whims of the public.

The issue came to a head in the case of former president Estrada. The court was faced with what seemed to be a choice between catering to the desires of the masses to expedite Estrada's removal or upholding time-consuming procedures for impeachment set out in the constitution. When the impeachment procedures became bogged down because of legal niceties such as rules of evidence, the people took to the street to oust Estrada. After Vice-President Arroyo was sworn in, a challenge was brought to the court. In finding that the transfer of power was squarely within the constitution, the court refused to endorse People Power as a basis for changing presidents. The court went out of its way to emphasize the dangers of People Power to rule of law. In the words of one justice, "Where does one draw the line between the rule of law and the rule of the mob, or between People Power and Anarchy?" To be sure, the decision may appear to some to be yet another capitulation to public opinion, notwithstanding the court's rhetoric to the contrary, as the final result was to uphold the legally dubious replacement of Estrada with Arroyo. But the court arguably showed similar backbone in standing up to the public when it rejected a private initiative to amend the constitution to allow Ramos to run for another term.

The counter-majoritarian difficulty is, of course, not unique to the Asian countries. The *Bush v. Gore* debacle, in which the Supreme Court to all intents and purposes decided the election and truncated the political process (with most justices abandoning their previous positions), also highlighted the issue of allowing unelected justices wide powers of judicial review. But the issue may take slightly different forms in newly democratized states. In Taiwan, for instance, rather than pandering to the public, the government's need to shore up its political base with Western allies and differentiate itself from the PRC has led the political elite to endorse liberal democracy. Yet polls show the populace as a whole is lukewarm at best in its support for liberal values.[32] The courts, then, are torn between different constituencies, which may lead to inconsistencies in jurisprudence and exacerbate the kinds of systems-failure or slippage problems that occur when legal norms are transplanted from one society to another, as discussed by Sean Cooney in Chapter 14.

In some newly democratized states, the legislature may not enjoy much authority or legitimacy either as a result of tightly controlled or otherwise flawed elections or processes. In Thailand, the legislature itself has been criticized for being politicized, and critics have objected to the lack of transparency of various selection processes under the Constitution. In other situations, the newly elected president may have been a popular figure in the movement for democracy, and thus enjoy a heightened moral status. Courts may therefore be reluctant to challenge the president. In South Korea, however, when President Kim, a former activist, encouraged, in the name of popular sovereignty, civic groups to violate laws preventing unregistered political groups from engaging in political campaigns, he was criticized for showing disrespect for rule of law. The laws were subsequently amended to allow civic groups to campaign subject to a number of time, place and manner restrictions. But when civic groups continued to violate the laws, they were convicted, and the Supreme Court upheld their convictions.

Because the activist approach often puts the judiciary in conflict with other branches of government, courts in newly democratized states must balance their desire to expand their authority with the risk that their actions might provoke a reaction from the other branches of government and lead to a constitutional crisis and challenges to judicial authority. Thus, they must carefully pick and choose their issues and calibrate their power relative to other state actors. In Taiwan, for instance, the increasingly aggressive Council of Grand Justices issued an ambiguous interpretation enabling the president, the premier and the legislature to save face when the legislature sought to impeach the president. In Thailand, although the Constitutional Court held against a number of government officials who failed to declare their assets as required by law, thus leading to their disqualification from public office, the Court reached the opposite conclusion in a case involving Thailand's billionaire prime minister. In Korea, the Constitutional Court has dealt with a number of balance of powers issues, including judicial review of the legislative process in determining whether the legislature abused procedural rules to ram through a bill, the executive's authority to invoke emergency powers, and the jurisdiction of the Constitutional Court *vis-à-vis* the Supreme Court. The Constitutional Court has been careful to decide these cases in ways that do not unduly challenge other organs of state power while still maintaining legality and the court's status in the political pecking order. For instance, while upholding the government's decision in the emergency powers case, the court laid the foundation for expanding its own power in future cases. Likewise, in reviewing the legality of legislative procedures, the court allowed the laws to stand to avoid problems with retroactivity even though it found the procedures defective, thus avoiding a direct conflict with the legislative and executive branches, while requiring changes in the future.

On the other hand, courts are quick to impose their will on less powerful sectors. While wary of upsetting the general public, the Filipino Supreme Court has not hesitated to flex its muscles in a turf battle with the newly established Human Rights Commission, consistently barring the Commission from exercising judicial power. Meanwhile, in Thailand the judiciary has taken aim at the police, no longer allowing them to arrest people without a proper writ from the courts.

While most scholarly attention focuses on these large legal issues such as judicial activism, the counter-majoritarian difficulty, the proper balance of powers, along with important normative issues involving fundamental human rights, it bears noting that India, Thailand, the Philippines, Indonesia, and to a lesser extent Taiwan and South Korea are still dealing with many thin rule of law problems such as access to justice, inefficient courts that lead to interminable delays in deciding cases, and corruption. Indeed, corruption remains a major issue throughout much of Asia, with the notable exception of Singapore and Hong Kong and, to a lesser extent, Taiwan and South Korea. As Muntarbhorn puts it, the Thai legal system is plagued by the five Cs: corruption, collusion, cronyism, clientelism and crime. The average citizen may be as concerned, if not more concerned, about these types of thin rule of law problems as with broader concerns about balance of power or even many rights issues.

In contrast to China, Vietnam, Malaysia, Singapore and Hong Kong, where a sharp divergence in fundamental views has fueled heated debates about competing thick conceptions of rule of law, there is less explicit discussion of competing thick conceptions in these newly democratized countries. This may in some cases be a function of the nature of legal scholarship. In South Korea and Taiwan, for instance, constitutional scholars tend to follow the civil law tradition in focusing on doctrinal issues rather than engaging in more theoretical jurisprudence, as is the case in the U.S. and some other common law countries. In the case of Taiwan, South Korea, Indonesia and perhaps Thailand as well, it may also be that the focus until recently has been on democratization and fundamental rights. The fundamental divide was between authoritarianism and democracy. With the battle for democracy only recently won, political philosophers and legal theorists may not yet have had the time to turn their attention to articulating new social-political philosophies. Assuming that philosophers and theorists tend to systematize and reflect existing social phenomena rather than create new systems out of whole cloth, it may be that new, clearly differentiated political factions and positions have not yet formed. If so, then we could expect competing thick conceptions to emerge over time as political factions form, just as in the U.S. and other mature democracies a wide range of political views has led to competing thick conceptions.

Another possibility, however, is that the dominance of liberalism has suppressed reflective thought and stifled imaginative, creative theorizing that more accurately reflects local beliefs and the way legal systems actually operate in these countries. Many of the scholars in these countries have been trained abroad or, even if not, are more familiar with the Western political and legal philosophy literature than the literatures in their own countries. Indeed, facility with the latest debates and terminology in Western academia is frequently the surest means to publication, funding from international agencies, invitations to visit abroad, positions in multilateral organizations and promotion.[33]

All of these countries are *rights-based democracies* as opposed to majoritarian democracies: that is, democracies in which individual rights sometimes trump the majoritarian decision-making process. But whether they are *liberal* rights-based *democracies* is another issue. A *liberal rights-based democracy* is a particular type of democracy that emphasizes individual rights and autonomy to a greater extent than communitarianism, for example. The ongoing debates over Asian values (or the more politically correct, pluralist variant "values in Asia") and the attempts to articulate a Confucian alternative to liberalism suggest that competing thick conceptions of rule of law may emerge over time in Taiwan and South Korea.

Whereas in Malaysia, Singapore, Indonesia, China and Hong Kong senior government leaders (as well as academics and citizens) have invoked Asian values, in Taiwan, South Korea and Japan senior government leaders have been critical of the notion.[34] As we have seen, the political elite in these countries frequently seeks to position itself as democratic, progressive, modern and even "liberal," though often its policies are more conservative than liberal by the standards of Western countries. In any event, we must avoid the overly hasty and mistaken conclusion that the rejection of Asian values by some government leaders means that Asian values discourse does not exist or that there is no support within these countries for alternatives to liberalism (just as we must resist the equally mistaken opposite conclusion that a government's invoking of Asian values means there is no domestic opposition to the concept).[35] Although we currently lack an adequate empirical basis regarding outcomes in specific cases across a wide range of legal issues to draw firm conclusions about the degree of difference between Asian countries and Western countries and within Asia, and about the reasons for any such difference, an abundance of polling evidence suggests that there are significant differences in values.[36] Given the heated debates about how to resolve rights issues and balance the interests of the individual with the interests of the group and society within Western countries, and the different outcomes in Western countries, it should not be surprising that there would also be significant differences in Asian countries. Having democratized, these countries must now decide *what kind of democracy* they want to be. Vague appeals to liberal democracy and liberalism are not likely to capture the highly textured debates and conflicts that will inevitably arise, just as they have arisen in the U.S. and other well-established Western democracies.

As Tim Lindsey points out in Chapter 9, talk of Asian values appeared to die out rapidly in Indonesia after the fall of Suharto, as the new regime sought to distance itself from the previous regime by adopting liberal democratic institutions and incorporating an expansive array of individual rights. Yet it is far too early to write off Asian values. Although many endorse the democratic ideal, "there is little understanding and little consensus on the detail of what that democratic ideal might look like in Indonesia. The debate is fragmented and confused." One possibility is the emergence of a hardline Islamic regime. A second possibility is the rise of a military regime that might use the specter of Islamic fundamentalism, the failure of the new regime to achieve economic growth, or the breakdown of law and order to grab power. But a military coup may not be necessary. A third possibility is that Indonesian citizens, like their fellow citizens in various former Soviet republics, will vote for an authoritarian ruler if the economy continues to drag or there is a significant rise in crime or breakdown of law and order. While these possibilities contemplate the coming to power of a regime that would fall on the more authoritarian end of the Asian-values spectrum, a fourth possibility is the emergence of a more communitarian or collectivist-oriented regime of the type arguably found in Japan, South Korea or Taiwan. As noted below, many of the newly enacted constitutional rights are more consistent with traditional conceptions of the role of the state in Asia than they are with the limited state of classical liberalism or even the most expansive social welfare state of Northern Europe. Indeed, Habibie's unilateral actions, whatever their final result, were more characteristic of traditional authoritarian leaders than the heads of state in liberal democracies.

To be sure, other variants that do not fall along the liberal/communitarian axis or directly implicate the Asian values debates are surely possible and indeed probable. As Hahm points out (in Chapter 13), political orientations in South Korea are ambiguous and unstable. In the contemporary political ideological terrain, "conservative" generally refers to a position characterized by a strong anti-communism, nostalgia for the state-led, export-driven economic policy of the 1970s and 1980s, a pro-business stance, and a strong state *vis-à-vis* society. "Progressive," on the other hand, means a more open attitude toward North Korea, a pro-labor stance, support for a more robust civil society, and a neo-liberal economic policy marked by deregulation and marketization.

There is also support in the chapters on India, Thailand, the Philippines and Indonesia for what might be called a *developmental, redistributive justice* model of rule of law. This form, with different variants in each of the four countries, emerges out of a fundamental difference between these countries and economically advanced countries: the brutal reality of crushing poverty combined with severe disparities in income.[37] Observing that nearly 60 per cent of the nation's material resources are in the hands of some 20 per cent of the population in Thailand, Muntarbhorn (Chapter 11) warns that this lack of equity "has dire consequences for the rule of law and human rights, precisely because the inequity may breed violence, if not disrespect for the law." He asks, "How can the rule of law help to foster equity and social justice?" Baxi (Chapter 10) raises a similar query, challenging academics to broaden their views to incorporate the concerns of the disenfranchised into a bottom-up, social activist conception of rule of law.

While social welfare liberals in the West are also concerned about the plight of the least well off, their ability to articulate a compelling story is hampered by a strong current in liberal thought from Locke to Hayek that emphasizes property rights and the right to enjoy the fruits of one's labor, thereby fostering possessive individualism and a materialistic, acquisitive capitalism. In contrast, activists in some Asian countries seeking a more egalitarian distribution of wealth may be able to draw on indigenous traditions such as the Islamic principle of *zakat*, which requires one to contribute part of one's wealth to help the poor. Or they may appeal to Buddhist principles of kindness and consideration for one's neighbors to support a humane response to those in need. "These values-in-Asia", claims Muntarbhorn, "add much value to the rule of law and human rights, not only in material terms but also in spiritual terms." It remains to be seen whether the existence of such traditions in Asia will be sufficient to overcome selfishness (which exists in Asia as much as elsewhere), counter the inherent tendency of governments to serve entrenched interests, or offset other traditions such as casteism in India or the Confucian privileging of the family that leads to attenuated moral obligations towards others.

Substantively, the developmental redistributive model of rule of law has two main planks. The first is an international dimension that highlights the radical disparity between North and South and emphasizes the right of development, debt forgiveness and the obligation of the North/developed countries to aid the South/developing countries. The second plank is a domestic one and reflects the particular circumstances of each state.

In the Philippines, one catches glimpses of an alternative redistributive conception in the way rule of law is frequently linked to social and political philosophies that promise justice, social welfare and People Power democracy. Whereas Western countries on the whole have been reluctant to assume obligations to allocate sufficient resources to satisfy economic, social and cultural rights, the 1987 Filipino Constitution contained a long list of open-ended "directive principles" that, as Pangalangan points out (in Chapter 12), reflect the tendency of the activist drafters of the Constitution to codify 'new' rights, e.g. to education, food, environment and health. In Thailand, concerns for redistributive social justice are found in the government's policies to achieve sustainable development, including rural development. Thus the government has adopted a series of populist policies, including a universal healthcare scheme, a development fund for each village, and debt moratorium for farmers.

Similarly, a series of constitutional amendments has provided Indonesian citizens, at least in theory, with an impressive array of rights extending well beyond those guaranteed in most developed states, including a right to work and live in human dignity, a right to receive just and appropriate rewards for work, a right to protection from violence, a right to the certainty of just laws and equal treatment before the law, a right to obtain the same opportunities in government and to assistance and special treatment in order to gain the same opportunities and benefits in the attainment of equality and justice, and a right to physical and spiritual welfare. Such rights greatly exceed not only classical liberalism's emphasis on primarily negative civil and political rights but also the rights provided by even the most generous of European social welfare states. The provision of such robust positive rights arguably reflects traditional views where the legitimacy of the state turns on its ability to provide for the material and moral well-being of its citizens. At the same time, these rights are constrained by concerns for the community and state and the need for public order and stability. Thus, each person has a duty to respect the basic human rights of others *in orderly life as a community, as a people, and as a nation.* Moreover, these broad rights may be limited by law in order to take into consideration morality, religious values, security and public order.

Like the Philippines, the Indian constitution codifies both first-generation civil and political rights and second-generation rights. However, whereas the former are considered fundamental and justiciable, the latter are considered progressive, although there is some legally binding language that suggests that second-generation rights may play a greater role than they have in the constitutional jurisprudence of the U.S. and other Western countries. The Indian constitution also seeks to redress historical imbalances that have led to the subjugation of some groups, reaching beyond the state to private groups and practices. It thus outlaws in the name of equality caste-based practices of "untouchability." Likewise, the constitutional right against "exploitation" prohibits bonded labor, serfdom, traffic in human beings, and certain forms of child labor. And a system of reservations or quotas ensures some representation for disadvantaged groups, including the poor. In addition, the constitution enshrines a policy of affirmative action that creates a two-track system obligating the state "to specifically reform the 'dominant'/'majoritarian' 'Hindu' religious traditions in a fast forward mode, while leaving the reform of 'minority' communitarian/religious traditions to slow motion, minuscule change." Institutionally, the constitution creates a number of federal agencies to protect and promote the rights of "discrete and insular" minorities. Significantly, the judiciary has taken an activist approach to public-interest litigation or social action in an effort to breathe life into these broad constitutional provisions and to move beyond formal equality toward a more equitable allocation of social and legal resources.[38]

Given that the state in these countries may be weak, lack adequate resources to address many social problems or simply tend to side with vested interests, social activists cannot rely only on the state and activist courts. They must look to civil society as well. Thus, in Thailand little progress has been made in addressing distortions in land holdings despite constitutional provisions regarding an appropriate system. Nor have provisions protecting labor produced much in the way of results. Accordingly, NGOs such as Work of the Assembly of the Poor have had to step in to deal with grievances ranging from displacements to slow compensation from government agencies. Portraying the rule of law as a "terrain of struggle of the multitudes against the rule of the minuscule," Baxi as well calls attention to the importance of grassroots movements to ensure social justice for the disenfranchised.

Mature democracies and legal systems: rule of law in Japan, France and the U.S.

Japan, the U.S. and France are mature democracies with mature legal systems. Many of the basic constitutional issues have already been decided, though new issues continue to arise from time to time and old issues continue to be debated ad infinitum. Much of the focus is on particular constitutional or rights issues that reflect different substantive political philosophies.

In Chapter 2, Brian Tamanaha shows how rule of law in the U.S. is integrally linked to liberalism broadly understood to include four types of liberty: legal liberty (freedom to do whatever is not prohibited by law), private liberty (protected spheres free from government intrusion), institutionalized liberty (separation of powers), and political liberty (democracy). While all four are found together in the U.S., they need not all go together.

31

Non-democratic states could enjoy the other three types of liberty. Moreover, there is considerable variation within each of these areas, and disagreements about how the four categories should fit together. As we have seen, conflicts between private liberty (individual rights) and democracy give rise to counter-majoritarian issues. Meanwhile, libertarians, classical liberals, social welfare liberals, conservatives, and communitarians disagree about the scope of private liberty, among other issues.

In Japan, past discussions relevant to rule of law have often focused on administrative guidance, criminal law issues, the seemingly small number of lawyers and the large role of informal versus formal law. Today, as John Haley and Veronica Taylor point out in Chapter 15, Japan's legal system is the subject of major reforms and controversies. The poor economic performance of Japan recently and the Asian financial crisis have led to the restructuring of the bureaucracy and the curtailment of administrative guidance, which is now subject to tighter legal restrictions and judicial review, the passage of the Administrative Procedure Law and Information Disclosure Law, and a cabinet resolution requiring public notice of administrative rule-making. Globalization and domestic pressures have also led to proposals to overhaul the legal profession and legal education (a hot issue in South Korea as well). Constitutional debates range from Japan's commitment to pacifism and the legality of sending military forces to join in U.N. peacekeeping activities to electoral law reform, whether to impose controls on political funding, and the role of the prime minister. Although Japan has the lowest crime rate of any industrialized democracy, critics of the criminal justice system question whether the pre-trial procedures afford adequate protections to suspects and charge that the system lacks transparency, police and prosecutors are unaccountable, and defense lawyers are impotent. There is an ongoing active debate as to whether Japan is and should be moving away from its traditional criminal law system based on "paternalistic benevolence," prosecutorial discretion, particularized justice, and rehabilitation, toward a more "American" model that ironically combines greater protection for individual rights with a punitive emphasis on incarceration.[39]

The far-reaching recommendations of the Justice System Reform Council issued in June 2001 involve major institutional changes to the judiciary, legal profession and prosecutors, as well as specific recommendations regarding civil, criminal, administrative, labor and intellectual property law. In so doing, they raise fundamental questions about the purpose of law in Japan and the nature of the legal system. Not surprisingly, the Council expressly invokes rule of law as the guiding principle for the reforms, though the term is not defined. Even less surprisingly, Council members have understood it in different ways. Reflecting the German influence on Japan's legal system, some scholars interpret rule of law in the more minimal sense of the traditional civil law notion of *Rechtsstaat*, where the emphasis is on a law-based order in which the people's daily life is ruled by law. On the other hand, others take the approach we have taken here, and characterize such a system as rule by law rather than rule of law, reserving the latter for a legal system in which law serves to hold accountable and restrain the state and state actors.

Some of the Council's recommendations are aimed at redressing thin rule of law concerns regarding access to justice, legal aid and the efficiency of the judicial system. Others center on thick of rule of law concerns such as the nature of the political system and the Japanese state, the role of the government in the economic order, state–society relations and the need for expanded participation by civil society in governance, and the balance between the rights of individual criminal suspects and the interests of society as a whole in maintaining order in the face of increasing, albeit still relatively low, crime rates. The nature and range of issues being debated, and the depth of disagreement among different political interest groups, including political parties, business, and social activists, would seem to provide fertile ground for legal theorists seeking to articulate competing thick conceptions of rule of law. However, as in South Korea and Taiwan, legal scholars in Japan have yet to step back, synthesize the various discrete debates and develop comprehensive theories of rule of law, including non-derivative local variants to liberalism that capture the main fault-lines of domestic political debates.

Lest one incorrectly assume, based on the dominance of liberal democratic conceptions of rule of law, that rule of law discourse has evolved in a uniform way in Western countries, Laurent Pech begins Chapter 3 by noting two peculiarities about rule of law in France. First, there was no French equivalent for "rule of law" until the beginning of the 20th century, when *Etat de droit* became popular among scholars. Second, in contrast to other Western democracies, France has experienced considerable constitutional instability. Between 1789 and 1959, in addition to 16 constitutions, France had 21 "semi-constitutional governments" and "*de facto* regimes." The failure of constitutionalism to take root in France owes much to the principle of legislative supremacy and a deep distrust of judicial power that precluded judicial review of statutory law. This distrust grew out the negative experience with the royal courts of pre-revolutionary France, where the courts impeded the work of the royal administration and thwarted legislative reforms by refusing to apply relatively progressive and enlightened royal edicts. Since then, French citizens, fueled by Rousseauian visions of parliamentary law as an expression of the general will, have been wary of a rule by judges.

The aversion to judicial review led to the creation in 1799 of a separate administrative court, the *Conseil d'Etat*. Over time, the Council of State expanded its powers, emerging as a guardian of human rights that has prevented abuses of executive power in the absence of any effective mechanism to restrain the legislator. The rise of the modern regulatory state and the shift of powers to the executive under the Fifth Republic, however, eroded the traditional rationale for legislative supremacy. Accordingly, the 1958 Constitution established the *Conseil Constitutionnel* to ensure that the parliament did not overstep its bounds and encroach upon the executive. In time, it began to review the constitutionality of legislative acts of parliament.

Nevertheless, the Constitutional Council's ability to protect rights remains hampered by the limitation to ex ante review of legislation and the lack of standing for individuals or ordinary courts to bring cases before the Council. Barred from raising constitutional claims in domestic courts, French citizens have been forced to appeal to international human rights law, a trend strengthened by the entry into force of the European Convention on Human Rights in the French legal order in 1974, and by the possibility of referring the decisions of ordinary French tribunals to the European Court of Human Rights as of 1981.

Today, some of the most interesting and complex rule of law issues involve the relationship between French domestic law and the supranational law of the European Union. The threshold issue of how to translate the concept of a "Community based on rule of law" suggests some of the difficulty, as existing glosses of "rule of law" such as *Etat de droit* or *Rechtsstaat* entail a state. As Pech notes,

> the terms "rule of law," "*Etat de droit*," and "*Rechtsstaat*" are nowhere defined in the treaties, and national understanding of these terms shows that there is still some disagreement about the precise meaning of a Union founded on rule of law...or a Community based on rule of law.

Nor do traditional notions of separation of powers or federalism apply to the novel institutional arrangements of the E.U.

Critiques and defenses of rule of law: saving rule of law by clipping its wings

Despite the popularity of rule of law nowadays, its critics are legion, especially in the U.S. and states with well-developed legal systems. Unable to afford the luxury of belittling rule of law, citizens, social activists and scholars in countries where governments regularly and capriciously ignore the law and trample on individual rights tend to be more appreciative of its virtues and more enthusiastic in advocating it. To be sure, many of the criticisms of rule of law are worthy of attention. Collectively, they point to a variety of conceptual, normative and practical deficiencies in the way rule of law is understood and how it is implemented. Most importantly, they demonstrate unequivocally that rule of law is no panacea. With these reservations, few advocates of rule of law would have any quarrel. Yet at times the criticisms are overstated or simply based on unrealistic expectations of rule of law. Rule of law may not be an answer for all of the social ills of modern societies, but it is a minimal requirement for any decent society. Perhaps because of an awareness that the legitimacy of the legal system and the image of rule of law are rather more fragile than we might think even in countries such as the U.S.,[40] there has recently been something of a retrenchment, with a number of scholarly works coming to the defense of rule of law.[41] In order to defend rule of law, however, it has been necessary to clip its wings, to be more modest in the conceptual claims about rule of law and more circumspect in the normative claims about what rule of law can achieve.

As many of the criticisms and responses have been discussed above or are developed at length elsewhere, including in the chapters that follow, I will merely highlight some of the more prominent issues. One common complaint is that rule of law is inadequately theorized.[42] Even acknowledging considerable agreement about the basic elements of a thin theory, there is still considerable room for disagreement about the details. Some of the elements are vague, a matter of degree and subject to exceptions. What precisely is meant by "consistent"? Some laws may not be directly contradictory, but may have inconsistent purposes. Sometimes laws are changed and even made effective retroactively. The notion of equality before the law raises the question of equal in what respect: what are the morally and legally relevant factors in deciding whether two people are similarly situated? More generally, in some instances it is difficult to say whether a legal system merits the label rule of law, as in the case of the developed legal systems in Singapore and Malaysia and in the much improved but still maturing system in China.[43]

Briefly put, the response to such criticisms is to accept that rule of law is vague at the margins, agree that there may be disputes in some cases about whether a country merits the label rule of law, and allow that appealing to rule of law does not resolve many issues; and yet still maintain that there is sufficient agreement to make the concept useful and that in most cases there will be rough agreement of the "I know it when I see it" type about whether a legal system should be described in terms of rule of law. After all, most, if not all, important political concepts are contested, vague at the edges and subject to various interpretations. But we don't abandon concepts such as justice, democracy or human rights simply because they are contested. Indeed, in comparison to a widely disputed concept such as justice, there is considerably greater consensus about the basic elements of a thin rule of law.

Another common worry is that law is much more indeterminate than rule of law advocates presume, and that such indeterminacy undermines rule of law's promise of predictability and blurs the line between law and politics. Critical legal scholars, critical race theorists and feminists have demonstrated that the seeming neutrality of (rule of) law may reinforce existing power structures at the expense of certain vulnerable members of the society. The legislative system may reinforce the tyranny of the majority and fail to provide adequate representation to disadvantaged minorities. Conservative judiciaries may exacerbate the inequities by siding with powerful entrenched interests. Historically, legal systems that met the standards of a thin rule of law have undeniably accommodated colonial repression, apartheid, discrimination against women or gays and other forms of social exclusion. As Baxi reminds us, at times people's movements from Mahatma Gandhi to Nelson Mandela involving civil disobedience and mass illegalities have been necessary to remedy injustices.

The response to such criticisms is again to accept that law is neither always determinate nor always just but to deny that these observations somehow undermine the importance or value of rule of law. As Tamanaha points out (in Chapter 2), the weight of empirical studies supports the contentions of the vast majority of judges and lawyers that most cases are easy cases and that the indeterminacy thesis is overstated. Nor is there any need to deny that rule of law is compatible with great injustice. Indeed, proponents of thin theories readily admit that point. Even those who favor particular thick conceptions of rule of law readily allow that all legal systems fall short of the ideal of rule of law and cannot always ensure a just outcome in all cases. As discussed previously, the fact of pluralism inevitably results in the violation of someone's conception of justice: no law or legal decision will please everyone. In the case of unjust or unworkable laws, the rule of law virtues of predictability and certainty may at times need to give way to higher moral principles and considerations of equity, justified civil disobedience, or even "mass illegalities" and populist movements that seek to overthrow the political system. Yet the desire to do what is perceived as right in the particular circumstances must be balanced against the benefits of predictability and certainty and tempered by the realization that what is right is often contested.

A related line of criticism attributes indeterminacy to the rise of the regulatory state. Today, administrative officials are given considerable discretion, and asked to pass regulations and make decisions based on broad standards. The response to such concerns is twofold. The first line of defense notes that rule of law is consistent with administrative discretion provided that such discretion is subject to legal, political, institutional and cultural restraints. Critics then point out that these mechanisms for review are often ineffective, leaving administrative officials with wide-ranging discretion, or that they simply shift the discretion to another entity such as the courts, which are then called on to make policy decisions based on the same broad standards. The second line of response is that a certain amount of discretion is inevitable and indeed desirable, and thus should be incorporated into the concept of rule of law or else no legal system will meet the standards of rule of law. Moreover, as noted previously, failure to build in any room for discretion or equity will result in rule of law being set aside to secure more equitable results in particular cases. Indeed, some scholars argue that laws may be *too determinate*, and that rule of law amounts to a perverse kind of fetish for clear rules and bright lines when life is far too complex and filled with nuances and fine shades of gray to be reduced to any simple set of black and white rules. Apart from allowing that a legal system should incorporate a certain amount of discretion in the form of doctrine of equity or laws stated as broad standards rather than more narrow rules, defenders of rule of law once again acknowledge that in some cases the virtues of predictability and certainty may need to give way to civil disobedience or broader claims of justice.

Drawing on the perceived failures of the law and development movement of the 1960s and 1970s, some critics worry that efforts to export rule of law and improve the legal system may strengthen authoritarian regimes and undermine efforts to promote political reforms and democratization. There is no gainsaying the fact that the instrumental aspects of legal reforms may enhance the efficiency of authoritarian governments, and that in the absence of democracy and pluralist institutions for public participation in the lawmaking, interpretation and implementation processes law may come to serve the interests of the state and the ruling elite (as it may do even when these elements are present in democratic states, though the likelihood is greater in authoritarian regimes). Of course, those who unapologetically reject democracy and believe that an authoritarian government is necessary to oversee economic reforms and maintain stability will see the state-strengthening aspect as desirable. At any rate, given the choice between an authoritarian regime committed to some form of rule of law and one that rejects the basic obligation to govern in accordance with law, there is little doubt as to which is preferable. At minimum, even a thin rule of law entails limits on the state and the ruling elite, who are also bound by the law, provides a basis for challenges by citizens of government arbitrariness, and serves to protect the rights and interests of the non-elite.[44] Where legal rules are applied with principled consistency to both the state and its citizens, as required by rule of law, they generally restrain rather than expand the arbitrary exercise of state power. In the long run, implementing rule of law usually will alter the balance of power between the state, society and individuals, while alterations in the balance of power resulting from economic reforms and factors beyond the legal system will simultaneously create further pressure to implement rule of law. While a robust civil society is not inevitable, it is more likely in a state that implements rule of law than one that does not. A robust civil society is arguably more likely to seek and more likely to obtain political reforms aimed at further limiting the power of authoritarian states and increasing the power of society, though again this is not inevitable if the civil groups are themselves closely bound by clientist or corporatist ties to the ruling regime. Thus, even if the goal is democracy and protection of human rights, it makes sense to ensure, at minimum, that a thin rule of law is realized. A more likely result than a stronger authoritarian regime is that rule of law will be a force for liberalization and come to impose restraints on the rulers, as in Taiwan, South Korea and even Indonesia.

In countries such as China where democratization is not a viable option at present, legal reform aimed at implementing rule of law is one of the main channels for political reform. On the other hand, softer, wealthier authoritarian states like Hong Kong and Singapore may use legal reforms and redistributive social welfare policies to buy off the citizenry and delay or forego more fundamental political reforms.[45]

In sum, there are undeniably certain conceptual or theoretical problems with rule of law. There are various competing conceptions, including different conceptions within countries and between countries, none of which will satisfy everyone. Moreover, rule of law is a not fully realizable ideal in practice, and even where implemented to a reasonable extent hardly promises that justice is around the corner. The question is: then what? Choices include: abandoning talk of rule of law, which, as discussed previously, is not possible in practice and has various adverse consequences for those who want to take advantage of rule of law rhetoric for its considerable potential to improve their lives over the status quo; attempting to clarify its meanings, conceptions, uses and limits, as we have done in this volume; and simply critiquing it without offering a constructive alternative, which may be necessary but is never sufficient. In the end, it is hard to avoid the conclusion that, despite its many shortcomings, rule of law has played a positive role on balance, and so let's keep using it.

The success and failure of rule of law: transplants, homegrown varieties and hybrids

Assuming rule of law is desired, what does this comparative study tell us about the factors that are likely to lead to the successful implementation of rule of law or, alternatively, impede its implementation? Some skeptics claim that current efforts to promote rule of law in Asian countries such as China and Vietnam are likely to fail because of the radically different conditions in the target countries. More fundamentally, others object to the efforts of Western countries and multilateral agencies such as the IMF and World Bank to promote (liberal democratic) rule of law as a form of imperialism, as alluded to earlier. Both of these issues can be addressed in part by avoiding ethnocentric attempts to impose an overly narrow form of rule of law and by taking seriously differences in local circumstances, including levels of economic development, existing institutions, and local traditions and values. As we have seen, rule of law is consistent with considerable variation. There is therefore ample room to adopt a form of rule of law that meets the requirements of a thin conception and fits the circumstances of countries in Asia.

Moreover, the problems with transplantability should not be overstated. Clearly efforts to transplant legal institutions, rules and practices have been successful to a considerable degree in many cases in Asia and elsewhere.[46] To be sure, some comparative legal scholars continue to insist on lumping all Asian countries into a single category and denying even well-developed legal systems in such countries as Japan the label rule of law. But this untenable position seems to be the result of a lingering orientalism, lack of up-to-date information about Asian legal systems, and a tendency to interpret rule of law over-narrowly as necessarily liberal democratic rule of law.[47] Despite their differences, Asian countries are facing many of the same problems as other countries. They are all market economies or moving in that direction; they all seek to attract foreign technology and investment; they are all increasingly part of a global economic and legal order. Not surprisingly, there is then little dispute about the desirability of a thin rule of law, notwithstanding different thick conceptions. Differences in thick conceptions, along with different initial starting conditions and the path-dependent nature of reforms, ensure, however, a certain amount of divergence in the way legal systems operate and evolve even as they tend to converge as a result of the forces of globalization and the increasing reach of the international legal order. Thus, what we find is a rich diversity of transplants, homegrown varieties and hybrids.

The most important factor behind the move toward rule of law in Asia has been the transition toward a market economy. In China, the slogan "a market economy is a rule of law economy" has been repeated in mantra-like fashion and invoked to support China's accession to the World Trade Organization (WTO). Even in Vietnam, where the regime continues to hold out hopes for a socialist economy, all the while moving in the direction of a more market-based economy, the government has realized the importance of rule of law to foreign investors and economic development. Although some scholars claim that economic growth in Asia has occurred in the absence of clear property rights and rule of law, formal law has played a much greater role than they claim.[48] Indeed, the issue in many Asian countries has not been whether rule of law is necessary for economic growth, but whether rule of law can be limited to commercial law without spilling over into other areas.

Legal systems may be rule of law compliant in some areas and not in others. However, over time, there is likely to be spillover from the commercial area into other areas such as family law, environmental law, criminal law and administrative law. A legal system that is able to deliver competent, efficient, fair decisions in economic cases requires certain institutions and norms among the judiciary and state actors, as well as an investment in their professionalization and legal training. Such reforms, however, tend to take on a life of their own as institutions evolve and seek to expand their authority, as judges and other state actors begin to internalize professional norms, and as citizens come to expect judges and administrative officials to ensure that the government lives up to its commitment to rule of law. This type of runaway institutional development is true in the West, as evidenced by the U.S. Supreme Court's grab for power in *Marbury v. Madison* or the way the French Constitutional Council and Council of State overcame their humble origins to steadily expand their jurisdictions and claim a more robust role in the constitutional order. And it is equally true in Asia, as evidenced by the increasingly aggressive judiciaries in South Korea, Taiwan and even Indonesia. Indonesia is a particularly interesting example in that significant developments occurred prior to the recent democratization. Initially, the Soeharto government's desire to obtain legitimacy abroad and to deal with corruption and patrimonial practices that were adversely affecting business confidence led to the establishment of administrative courts. But then the courts turned on Soeharto, pursuing key allies on corruption charges and defiantly striking down the government's decision to ban a popular weekly news magazine. In response to a groundswell of public support, the judiciary became increasingly aggressive in challenging the government, to the point where after the change in the regime Soeharto himself has been brought up on charges of corruption.[49] Considerable institution-building was possible therefore under authoritarian rule, just as it has been in China and Vietnam. Taking advantage of the space for reform may have accelerated the transition to democracy in the case of South Korea, Taiwan and Indonesia. At minimum, it laid some of the foundations for a post-authoritarian order. Rather than having to start from scratch, these countries were able to build on existing institutions, which were poised for further development and ready to take on new responsibilities after the regime changed.

Among the most controversial issues is the relation between democracy and rule of law, and the extent to which rule of law may be realized in non-democratic states. Despite considerable institutional reforms, the limited ability of the legal system to check political power in South Korea, Taiwan and Indonesia suggests that ultimately the lack of democracy imposed limits on the implementation of rule of law. On the other hand, Malaysia, Singapore and, even more so, Hong Kong seem to offer legal systems that comply with the requirements of a thin rule of law within the context of a non-democratic or limited democratic polity to a large extent. Even critics allow that the legal system in these places operates fairly and effectively with respect to most issues, including most commercial, family, environmental and criminal law matters, and even in most administrative law cases and many constitutional cases. To be sure, many of the cases do not result in decisions favored by liberals, but that is to be expected given the differences in political views and thick rule of law conceptions.

Nevertheless, the legal system is highly politicized, particularly in Malaysia and Singapore, though again the nature and degree of acceptable politicization varies depending on one's thick conception. As noted previously, in Singapore, for example, courts have protected PAP officials against defamation while on the whole tolerating attacks on the character of opposition figures, and at least one judge who challenged the PAP was removed, though the government claimed that his transfer had been scheduled for a long time. In the past, the constitution could be amended by a simple majority, which strengthened the hand of the PAP, although even a two-thirds requirement would have been no obstacle given the PAP's dominance at the polls. The PAP's electoral dominance has been supported, however, by anti-hopping laws that prevent politicians from switching parties before the next election and gerrymandering of electoral districts. Perhaps more significantly for rule of law, the highest court has acquiesced in these laws, and indeed has never held any legislation unconstitutional.[50]

In contrast, Hong Kong's legal system, at least until recently, has not suffered from the same degree of politicization. Recent cases involving selective prosecution and preferable treatment of the rich and powerful and their offspring raise the central thin rule of law issue of equality before the law. The reality, however, is that all systems fall short of the ideal to some degree. Democratic countries do not necessarily treat the rich and powerful just like everybody else. One need only consider Gerald Ford's pardoning of Richard Nixon or Bill Clinton's pardoning of the former housing secretary Henry Cisneros and congressman Daniel Rostenkowski. Indeed, the light slap on the wrist Clinton received for lying under oath – suspension of his license to practice law for two years and a fine of $25,000 – smacks of special privilege. Hilary Josephs concluded in her comparison of legal accountability for corruption in China and the U.S. that they

> are quite alike in their general reluctance to prosecute high officials. Despite fundamental differences in political systems, and a common commitment to equality before the law, those in power are rarely called to task in either country for criminal misconduct associated with discharge of their official duties.[51]

She also points out that in both countries prosecutors' decisions are influenced by political factors, including party affiliations, with a greater readiness to target someone from the opposing political party or faction. In the end, it seems that rule of law is more difficult to implement fully in the absence of democracy, although democracy is not necessary for the implementation of rule of law in all cases. Moreover, democracy provides no guarantee that rule of law will be implemented adequately.

Other factors contributing to the establishment and likely implementation of rule of law include integration in the global economy and international law regime, and an economy dominated by industry, foreign trade, and large-scale foreign direct investment by multinational companies. The more isolated a regime, the less subject it is to international pressure to implement rule of law. Although Vietnamese leaders may oppose liberal democracy, their desire for aid has opened a window for the IMF and other agencies to promote "technical" legal reforms. In China, while the main impetus for legal reforms comes from domestic forces, the demands of foreign investors have led to changes in the commercial law regime, and pressure from the international human rights community was influential in the process of amending the Criminal Procedure Law. In addition, China's joining the WTO has clearly resulted in further changes to the legal system and strengthened the hand of legal reformers. Similarly, as the economy has grown and diversified, the limits of social networks and informal mechanisms for resolving disputes have become more apparent in China. In contrast, the largely rural economy in Vietnam has generated less demand for rule of law.[52]

A legacy of colonialism may also affect the development of the legal system and the likelihood of implementing rule of law, though the direction of influence may be positive, negative or both. As Hahm observes (in Chapter 13), the modern legal system was tainted by Japanese imperialism and ideologically suspect. Many Koreans distrusted judges and lawyers, who were held in low esteem, although their distrust did not prevent them from using the legal system entirely. In Hong Kong the legal system was also perceived as an alien imposition and an instrument of colonial rule, with little concern for the individual rights of Hong Kong citizens. The language of the courts was English, and most judges were expatriates. On the other hand, the legal systems in Hong Kong, Singapore and Malaysia were widely perceived to be central to economic growth and stability. Although multi-country empirical studies are somewhat ambiguous, they tend to support the view that a history of British colonialism is associated with a stronger legal system and better protection of human rights in the post-colonial order.[53]

Ethnic tensions also shape the development of rule of law because law is one of the primary means of mediating political conflicts between different interest groups, redressing past injustices, and maintaining social harmony. Ethnic divisions may impede the development of democracy, strengthening the argument of authoritarian governments that a strong state with limits on civil society and freedom of religion, speech and assembly is necessary to ensure stability. At minimum, ethnic diversity may give rise to particularly sharp counter-majoritarian issues and lead to complicated systems of rights. The constitutions in Singapore, Malaysia and India clearly reflect the importance of ethnic diversity in providing (or *not* providing) for representational voting, affirmative action, the establishment of novel institutions and mechanisms to ensure the protection of minority rights, and strong emergency powers that can be readily invoked should ethnic conflicts erupt. In Singapore, for example, the Malay Muslims enjoy some degree of cultural autonomy through the Administration of Muslim Law Act, which regulates marriage, testamentary disposition and the like. Singapore has made reservations to protect these religious and cultural particularities when acceding to U.N. human rights treaties like the Convention for the Elimination of All Forms of Discrimination against Women in 1975. While the Singaporean constitution reflects a concern for minorities, it adopts an individual rather than a group rights approach as found in Malaysia. And whereas Singapore refused to endorse any particular religion, Islam is the official religion in Malaysia, although the Malay constitution provides for the freedom to practice other religions. As we have seen, India has a complicated two-track system that emphasizes reform to certain Hindu practices while leaving other ethnic and religious issues to be sorted out over time.

Governments no doubt adopt rule of law in part because it bolsters their legitimacy. That said, legitimacy narratives vary from country to country; states differ in their need to appeal to rule of law to shore up their legitimacy; and rule of law – particularly a thin rule of law – may not provide much of a legitimacy boost if the laws themselves are perceived as unjust. Consent has provided the main basis for legitimacy in Western political theory since Hobbes, Locke and the Enlightenment fable of rights-bearing individuals in the state of nature who agree to concede some (for Hobbes, virtually all) of their rights to the sovereign in exchange for security and the protection of the state. Not surprisingly, this myth (or at least parts of it) strikes many Asians and for that matter many Westerners as bizarre, as do more recent attempts to ground the legitimacy of the political system, legal system or particular laws in some form of actual or hypothetical consent (whether from behind a veil of ignorance or not), or in some form of idealized account of deliberative democracy or Habermasian theory of communicative action.[54] In China, legitimacy traditionally was based on the moral character of the rulers, their special insights into the Way (*dao*), and the Mandate of Heaven, which was ostensibly conferred on the son of heaven who possessed the requisite moral character and normative insights. Rulers had an obligation to ensure the material and spiritual well-being of the populace, with the people retaining the right to revolt, according to Mencius, if this fiduciary-like obligation was breached. In practice, however, dynastic rule was based on heredity, with dynasties continuing until they collapsed or were overthrown, often by outside forces such as the Mongols or Manchus. The narrative of the morally enlightened ruler leading the way continues to surface in Vietnam, linked now with the scientific infallibility of Marxist-Leninism, and in Singapore, where Lee Kuan Yew combines assurances that elite government officials know what is best for the people with rigorous, and largely successful, attempts to wipe out corruption and establish an efficient, highly respected corps of civil servants. In both China and Vietnam, however, the appeal of socialism and the charisma of revolutionary leaders appear to be on their last legs, as revolutionary leaders die off, retire or become obsolete in the face of market reforms that are rendering socialist ideology increasingly incoherent and irrelevant.

Nowadays, legitimacy is primarily performance based, and tied to the government's ability to maintain stability and ensure economic growth. As Lee Kuan Yew puts it, "as long as the leaders take care of their people, they will obey their leaders."[55] What matters is practical success, not abstract theories dreamed up by political philosophers. "Our citizens live with freedom and dignity in an environment that is safe, healthy, clean and incorrupt. They have easy access to culture, recreational and social amenities, good standards of education for our children and prospect of a better life for future generations." Skeptics warn that authoritarian regimes that rely on performance-based legitimacy are likely to suffer when economic growth slows, as it inevitably must given the cyclical nature of modern economies. Yet empirical studies show that wealthy (soft-)authoritarian regimes are relatively stable.[56] Moreover, economic downturns are no less destabilizing for democracies at low levels of economic development than for poor authoritarian regimes, although once democratic states reach a certain level of wealth, economic downturns rarely if ever produce a reversion to authoritarianism.[57] Focusing on the recent Asian financial crisis, the results do not support the skeptics' view. Whereas democracy arguably exacerbated Thailand's economic problems,[58] China continued to prosper, while Singapore and Hong Kong suffered less than other economies in the region.[59]

Nationalism has provided a further basis for legitimacy in Asia. Lee Kuan Yew and other government leaders appeal to Asian values in part because the notion resonates with segments of the population that were never comfortable with "Western values" and always saw their own civilization as superior. The economic rise of some Asian countries gave them the confidence to stand up for their own traditions and to argue that they succeeded by combining Western institutions and indigenous values. The negative side of this resurgent pride in homegrown traditions is the sharp rise in identity politics and a tendency to slip into a jingoistic nationalism easily manipulated by state leaders to detract attention from domestic problems and the lack of significant political reforms.

While cultural traditions undoubtedly influence the development and implementation of rule of law in a variety of ways, in no case has culture been an absolute bar to its establishment. In China, for example, legal reforms have been slow to take hold in part because historically law has been held in low regard. The importance of social networks (*guanxi*), a history of privileging substantive justice over procedural justice, and arguably a preference for avoiding formal law in favor of informal means of resolving disputes have made it somewhat more difficult to implement a law-based order. Nevertheless, such factors also existed in Hong Kong, South Korea and Singapore, all of which have managed to establish highly law-based orders.

Conclusion and roadmap

The concept of rule of law has evolved, and will continue to evolve. The rise of the modern regulatory state challenged a strict rule-bound interpretation of rule of law. As a result, the conception of rule of law was relaxed to allow for a certain degree of discretion, generally subject to legal and other limits. Whereas in the past rule of law was state-centered, the rise of supranational law has caused further modifications in the way it is conceived. The E.U. example discussed above points to a more general issue in this era of increasing globalization and internalization of law: to what extent can we speak of an international rule of law? How does such a conception differ from more traditional state-bound conceptions of rule of law? Does the lack of effective enforcement mechanisms that plagues much of international law, especially human rights law, deprive the legal order of the certainty and predictability required by a thin rule of law?

Rule of law is a protean concept, and rule of law discourses in Asia and elsewhere encompass multiple strands, some of them at odds with or at least in tension with each other. Nevertheless, the requirements of a thin rule of law are widely shared and provide a certain degree of universalism. This universalism breaks down, however, when it comes to competing thick conceptions and the myriad of institutional arrangements.

The most striking point about Asian conceptions of rule of law is that there is a variety of different conceptions within Asia and within particular countries, especially once one takes into consideration non-governmental voices offering alternatives to the conception favored by the state. In all states, there is a tension between a liberal democratic rule of law and alternatives that reflect local values, traditions, and in many cases differences in levels of economic development and institutional arrangements. As is seen time and again, local diversity is ensured by the path-dependency and context-specificity of rule of law and legal reforms. France's experience with a conservative judiciary hindered the development of judicial review and constitutionalism for centuries. In the U.S., courts emerged as a powerful political force, but now many worry about the democracy deficit and fear that the judiciary has become too strong. Whereas in the U.S. judicial activism is a threat to democracy, in the Philippines People Power is a threat to rule of law. Sometimes a conservative but activist judiciary impedes political reforms, thwarts efforts to strengthen democracy and restricts human rights, whereas in Singapore and Malaysia a conservative and decidedly non-activist court accomplishes the same. In China many of the obstacles to rule of law reflect historical conditions. It will take time to build a competent corps of judges and lawyers, to change the attitudes and working style of bureaucrats, and to realign power between the branches of the government. It also takes time to change the attitudes of the populace, to inculcate a respect for law, and to overcome traditional reluctance to challenge authority and make use of the administrative litigation law to sue government officials. Meanwhile, in Thailand a history of coups combined with Buddhist traditions has led to a constitutional right of non-violent protest: "A person shall have the right to resist peacefully any act committed for the acquisition of the power to rule the country by a means which is not in accordance with the modes provided in this Constitution".

Although the competing conceptions of rule of law in Asia and the many institutional and doctrinal developments and innovations all merit attention and study, they unfortunately have been largely neglected due to the dominance of the liberal democratic rule of law paradigm and the presumption among Western exporters of rule of law that, while the rest of the world has much to learn from Euro-America, Euro-America stands to gain little from comparative study of other traditions and legal systems. Rather than the rest learning from the West, it would seem that the communitarian strands of rule of law and the developmental, redistributive model of rule of law may offer useful resources to address shortcomings in the liberal democratic forms of rule of law that prevail in Western countries today. However, to benefit from the experiences of Asian countries we in the West must be able to move beyond our smug complacency and be willing to listen to different voices and suspend our own views long enough to consider the views of others. We can only hope that this volume and subsequent volumes will contribute to that process.

Perhaps a few additional comments will help make transparent the underlying logic to the organization of the following chapters. We begin, in Chapter 2, with Tamanaha's account of rule of law in the U.S., in part because of the importance of the U.S. as a benchmark (whether positive or negative) for other countries and its role in exporting rule of law abroad, and in part because the chapter provides an excellent overview of the philosophical issues relating to rule of law as the concept has developed in the West. This is followed by Pech's chapter on rule of law in France, which helps remind us that as an analytical category "the West" is an oversimplified expedient, and that rule of law has evolved differently in Western countries. France's civil law legal system also contrasts with the common law system of the U.S., and provides a basis for comparison to some of the legal systems in Asia that grew out of the civil law tradition.

Chapter 4 takes up competing conceptions of rule of law in China. The existence in China of strongly divergent views about fundamental political issues such as socialism, soft authoritarianism, communitarianism and (liberal) democracy makes it possible to clearly articulate parallel competing thick conceptions of rule of law. The chapter which follows it, on Vietnam, highlights the importance of even a thin rule of law to countries that have yet to accept the basic principle that government actors must abide by the law. The chapters on China and Vietnam highlight the need to distinguish between socialist conceptions of rule of law and liberal democratic conceptions, and call attention to the problems of implementing rule of law in a socialist political system, albeit with Vietnam appearing to lag a decade or more behind in the process.

Chapters 6, 7, and 8 explore rule of law in soft-authoritarian or limited democratic states, respectively Singapore, Malaysia and Hong Kong. As the legal systems in these countries are fairly well developed and generally comply with the requirements of a thin rule of law at least with respect to commercial matters, debates tend to focus on competing thick conceptions of rule of law. Although the main fault-lines are between liberal democratic and soft-authoritarian conceptions, there is also some support for communitarian versions. Chapters 9, 10, 11, 12, 13 and 14 take up, in order, Indonesia, India, Thailand, the Philippines, South Korea and Taiwan. These are newly democratized states, with the possible exception of India, although even in India the consolidation of democracy and the struggle for basic human rights continue in a context very different from that of some economically advanced liberal democracies in the West. The first four are also less developed economically, and perhaps for that reason have given rise to the developmental, redistributive justice model(s) of rule of law discussed previously.[60] They also continue to confront challenges in achieving reasonable compliance with thin rule of law requirements, in particular in improving the efficiency of the legal system and eliminating corruption. In contrast, South Korea and Taiwan are much wealthier. Like Japan (which is covered in the last chapter), they are counted among the East Asian Tigers (along with China and Singapore). Wealthy and democratic, South Korea, Taiwan and Japan have legal systems that are generally compliant with the requirements of a thin rule of law with respect to commercial as well as political issues. Perhaps for that reason as well as other reasons discussed previously, much of the current legal and political debate has occurred without explicitly raising the banner of rule of law, though competing thick conceptions of rule of law lie just beneath the surface, awaiting more systematic articulation.[61]

Notes

1   As with rule of law, *Rechtsstaat* has been interpreted in various ways. While some interpret it in more instrumental terms similar to rule by law, others would argue that the concept entails at minimum the principle of legality and a commitment on the part of the state to promote liberty and protect property rights, and thus some limits on the state. In any event, the concept *Rechtsstaat* has evolved over

time in Europe to incorporate democracy and fundamental rights. Accordingly, it is often now used synonymously with (liberal democratic) rule of law.

2 See, for example, Joseph Raz, "The Rule of Law and Its Virtue," in Joseph Raz, ed., *The Authority of Law* (Oxford: Clarendon Press, 1979); Robert Summers, "The Ideal Socio-Legal Order: Its "Rule of Law" Dimension," *Ratio Juris,* vol. 1, no. 2 (1988), pp. 154–61; Robert Summers, "A Formal Theory of Rule of Law," *Ratio Juris,* vol. 6, no. 2 (1993), pp. 127–42.

3 For Hart, citizens need not like the laws or find them normatively justified. As long as people obey the laws (and officials accept the rule of recognition), the legal system could exist and function. However, as a practical matter, relying on compulsory enforcement for every law or most laws is costly and impractical. Such a legal system might still qualify as rule of law, but it would not last long. H. L. A. Hart, *The Concept of Law* (Oxford: Clarendon Press, 1961).

4 Perhaps the most formal and substantively minimal basis for rule of law is that suggested by Raz (1979), who takes as his departure point the "basic intuition" that law must be capable of guiding behavior.

5 See Carol Rose, "The New Law and Development Movement in the Post-Cold War Era: A Viet Nam Case Study," *Law & Society Review,* vol.32 (1998), p. 93; Barry Hager, "The Rule of Law," in Mansfield Center for Pacific Affairs, ed., *The Rule of Law: Perspectives from the Pacific Rim* http://www.mcpa.org/rol/perspectives.htm (summarizing complaints of critics).

6 See Takashi Oshimura, "In Defense of Asian Colors," in Mansfield Center, *Rule of Law*, at p. 141 (claiming that the individualist orientation of [liberal democratic] rule of law is at odds with Confucianism and "the communitarian philosophy in Asia"). See also Joon-Hyung Hong, "The Rule of Law and Its Acceptance in Asia," in id. at p. 149 (noting the need to define rule of law in a way that is acceptable to those who believe in "Asian values").

7 On the various debates that go under the label "Asian values" and their evolution, see Randall Peerenboom, "Beyond Universalism and Relativism: The Evolving Debates about 'Values in Asia'" *Indiana International & Comparative Law Review*, (2003).

8 For a welcome exception, see the essays in Kanishka Jayasuriya, "Introduction: Framework for the Analysis of Legal Institutions in East Asia," in Kanishka Jayasuriya, ed., *Law, Capitalism and Power in Asia* (London: Routledge, 1999). Jayasuriya's commendable effort to develop an alternative to a liberal conception of rule of law is marred somewhat by his strong-arm attempt to force all Asian countries into his statist model. As several of the other contributors to that volume point out, his model fails to capture the diversity within Asia. The model is even less applicable to three countries conspicuously missing from the volume – Japan, South Korea and the Philippines. Nor does it fit well with Thailand, which is also only dealt with in passing. Moreover, it tends to privilege ideology and the view of the state while overlooking or discounting the perspectives of different segments of society.

9 Raz, supra note 2, at p. 211.

10 To be sure, even these thin rule of law issues may also be politicized.

11 The fact of pluralism, as Rawls uses that phrase, is both a factual claim about the existence of irreconcilable comprehensive moral views and a normative claim that such views are reasonable. See John Rawls, *Political Liberalism* (New York: Columbia University Press, 1993).

12 Criticizing thin conceptions for their normative shortcomings seems to me to be a category mistake in that thin conceptions do not purport to be an adequate moral theory by themselves. A dictator who commits racial or ethnic genocide or a corrupt authoritarian leader who misuses the legal system to advance the

economic interests of his family and cronies while turning a blind eye to widespread abject poverty and human suffering surely deserve to be subject to moral censure. But to claim that they are violating rule of law somehow misses the point. Surely there are more direct and telling normative criticisms. To focus on rule of law violations in the case of Hitler, Pol Pot or South Africa highlights the wrong normative issues. Expanding the concept of rule of law makes such criticisms possible but at the price of obscuring the primary virtues of rule of law.

Taking the opposite approach, David Dyzenhaus criticizes Paul Craig, who distinguishes between procedural (thin) and substantive (thick) conceptions of rule of law and suggests that one should not stretch the concept of rule of law to include criticisms that a government is not acting justly. Dyzenhaus argues that "the very claim that the rule of law is best understood formally – detached from a substantive theory of justice – is deployed in [Craig's] hands in order to make a substantive claim about the best way to conduct political and legal debate." As I have taken pains to show, however, the very notion of there being a "best" way to conduct political and legal debate is misguided. How one conducts political debate will depend on one's purposes and goals (not to mention that there are purposes other than political debate for which the distinction may be useful). Similarly, Robert Alexy revisits the Hart–Fuller debates, which, as Dyzenhaus concedes, most commentators take Hart to have won, examining seven different arguments for and against positivism. Following Gustav Radbruch, who famously argued that the dominance of legal positivism was one of the contributing factors in undermining resistance of lawyers to Nazism, Alexy suggests that judges are less likely to resist applying evil laws if they cannot hide behind a circumscribed positivist conception of law to justify their decisions. Unfortunately, the empirical evidence to back up the claim that natural law stiffens the resolve of judges asked to apply evil laws is lacking: indeed, as Alexy notes, Hart accused Radbruch of "extraordinary naivete." But even if it were the case that natural law (and thick theories of rule of law) is normatively superior to positivist law (and thin conceptions of rule of law), that would hardly destroy the analytical utility in clearly distinguishing the two. Nor would it undermine the usefulness of thin theories for certain purposes such as assessing risk investment or persuading recalcitrant non-democratic governments worried about "peaceful evolution" to cooperate in legal reforms. See David Dyzenhaus, "Recrafting the Rule of Law," in David Dyzenhaus, ed., *Recrafting the Rule of Law: The Limits of Legal Order* (Oxford: Hart Publishing, 2000), p. 6; Robert Alexy, "A Defence of Radbruch's Formula," in *Recrafting the Rule of Law*.

13 Ronald Dworkin, *Law's Empire* (Cambridge: Belknap Press, 1986).
14 See, generally, Joshua Zelman, "Recent Developments in International Law: Anti-Terrorism Legislation – Part One: An Overview," *Journal of Transnational Law and Policy*, vol. 11 (2001), p. 183. See also Pech, Chapter 3; Peerenboom, supra note 7.
15 See Randall Peerenboom, *China's Long March Toward Rule of Law* (Cambridge: Cambridge University Press, 2002).
16 See, for example, Vidhu Verma, *Malaysia: State and Civil Society in Transition* (Boulder: Lynne Reiner, 2002) (distinguishing between Mahathir's nationalist [or statist, Asian-values] perspective, a less state-oriented communitarianism that shares some of the nationalist disenchantment with Western liberalism, and a "traditionalism" that also rejects liberalism but is based on Islam).
17 See Bridget Welsh, "Attitudes Toward Democracy in Malaysia," *Asian Survey*, vol. 36, no. 9 (September 1996), p. 882 (reporting that a survey of Malaysians in 1994 found that the majority was willing to limit democracy, particularly when social order was threatened, and that fears of instability and Asian values led to

limited support for democracy; also noting that respondents were willing to sacrifice freedom of speech in the face of threats to social order).

18 Paragraph 218, Report of the Special Rapporteur on the independence of judges and lawyers, Dato Param Cumaraswamy, U.N. Doc. E/CN.4/1996/37 (Commission on Human Rights, 52nd Session).

19 Tan points out that Singapore has been described as a semi-democracy, pseudo-democracy, illiberal democracy, limited democracy, mandatory democracy, a "decent, non-democratic regime," and a despotic state controlled by Lee Kuan Yew. Eugene K. B. Tan, "'WE' v. 'I': Communitarian Legalism in Singapore," *Australia Journal of Asian Law*, vol. 4 (2002), p. 1.

20 See Thio, Chapter 6.

21 See, for example, Tan, supra note 18, at pp. 1, 4. Tan himself calls for a more robust judicial review that places greater weight on the rights of individuals. See also Li-ann Thio, "An i for an I: Singapore's Communitarian Model of Constitutional Adjudication," *Hong Kong Law Journal*, vol. 27, no. 2 (1997), p. 152, 185 (1997) (also objecting to the deferential, positivist/textualist approach of the judiciary for failing to produce a "robust constitutional jurisprudence respectful of individual rights and human dignity").

22 Albert Chen, "Hong Kong's Legal System in the New Constitutional Order," in Jianfu Chen, Yuwen Li, and Jan Michiel Otto, eds., *Implementation of Law in the People's Republic of China* (The Hague: Kluwer Law International, 2002); Report of the Joseph R. Crowley Program, "One Country, Two Legal Systems?," *Fordham International Law Journal*, vol. 23 (1999), p. 1; U.S. Department of State, *United States Report on Hong Kong*, http://www.usconsulate.org.hk/ushk/pi/20010731.htm.

23 This concern does not apply to pragmatic liberals.

24 Carsten Stahn, "Accommodating Individual Criminal Responsibility and National Reconciliation: The UN Truth Commission for East Timor," 95 *American Journal of International Law* 952 (2001).

25 See, generally, the joint press release of JSMP and Amnesty International on August 15, 2002, "Indonesia: East Timor Trials Deliver neither Truth nor Justice," www.jsmp.minihub.org/News/15-8-2-02.htm.

26 Ian Martin, *Self-Determination in East Timor* (Boulder: Lynne Reiner, 2001).

27 Hansjorg Strohmeyer, "Making Multilateral Interventions Work: The U.N. and the Creation of Transitional Justice Systems in Kosovo and East Timor," 25 *Fletcher Forum of World Affairs* 107 (2001). In Rwanda, the inability of the decimated formal court system to try the 60,000 people being detained in jail has resulted in informal dispute mechanisms, the *gacaca* tribunals, normally used to resolve civil claims and minor crimes, being pressed into service to handle serious crimes. Human rights activists have questioned whether allowing untrained members of the local community to sentence defendants who may not be represented by legal counsel to terms up to life imprisonment complies with international human rights law and rule of law more generally.

28 As Hahm notes (Chapter 13), activist does not necessarily mean liberal. In Thailand, the courts have shown a conservative inclination to side with entrenched interest groups. See Muntarbhorn, Chapter 11. Baxi (Chapter 10) also observes that, although the courts have come to the aid of the disenfranchised in a variety of ways,

> Indian activists recoursing judicial power and process know rather well the "one-step-forward, two-steps-backward" nature of judicial activism. Even as they engage activist judiciary in the tasks of Indian democratic renewal, their politics of hope remains moderated by the acknowledgement of the

brute institutional fact that Courts and Justices remain, at the end of the day, State-bound and permeated.

29 See Tay-sheng Wang, "The Legal Development of Taiwan in the 20th Century: Toward a Liberal and Democratic Country," *Pacific Rim Law and Policy Journal*, vol. 11 (2002), p. 931, note 1 (observing that just a few years ago no one could imagine that the Council of Grand Justices would find newly amended constitutional provisions unconstitutional). For a discussion, see Cooney, Chapter 14.

30 Bojan Bugaric, "Courts as Policy-Makers: Lessons from Transition," *Harvard International Law Journal*, vol. 42 (2001), p. 247.

31 See Baxi, Chapter 10; Jamie Cassels, "Judicial Activism and Public Interest Litigation in India: Attempting the Impossible?," *American Journal of Comparative Law*, vol. 37 (1989), pp. 495, 515 (drawing on earlier works by Baxi).

32 In recent years, the Constitutional Court has exercised its newfound authority by greatly expanding the rights of criminal suspects, notwithstanding a Taiwanese public that overwhelmingly favors tough treatment for criminals. In 1991, 58 percent of Taiwanese approved of executing criminals in public, 68 percent endorsed passing special laws to attack crime, and 59 percent believed that punishment was more important than compensation for the injured. In 1999, over two-thirds thought punishments were too lenient, while only 1 percent thought they were too harsh. And over 42 percent believed that suspects could be detained even if there was not sufficient evidence to prove them guilty of serious crime as long as there were grounds for reasonable suspicion. See Tsung-fu Chen, "The Rule of Law in Taiwan: Culture, Ideology, and Social Change," in *Understanding China's Legal System* 374, 400 (ed. Stephen Hsu, New York: New York University Press, 2003) (arguing that without support for the protection of human rights it is doubtful that rule of law can be realized in Taiwan [or at least the liberal democratic version of rule of law entailed by such rights]).

33 Granted, many scholars may simply be liberals. Whether the views of liberal academics are representative of the larger society is another issue. Even in the U.S., liberals dominate the academy. As foreign scholars tend to be liberals for the most part, they are more likely to oppose than support local variants that challenge liberal tenets. And surely one cannot expect much sympathy for Asian values or other indigenous alternatives to liberalism from Western governments or the Western-dominated international agencies and human rights organizations that are the main exporters of liberal democratic rule of law. Of course, individual scholars, governments, agencies, rights groups and individuals within these governments, agencies and groups may be more or less accommodating of diversity.

34 Any such reservations did not prevent Japan and South Korea from voting in favor of the Bangkok Declaration, the manifesto for Asian values (Taiwan did not have a vote).

35 There are many reasons for rejecting "Asian values" that do not bear on the issue of whether there are different values in Asia, including that the concept has been overly politicized and misused by authoritarian governments to trample on individual rights, or that the concept is analytically untenable given the pluralism of Asia.

36 For instance, one survey found that, while 86 percent of Malaysian respondents supported a free press, only 40 percent thought the press should be free to discuss sensitive issues and only 52 percent thought it should be free to criticize the government, with many of those favoring constructive criticism. See Bridget Welsh, supra note 17. When asked to choose between democracy and economic

prosperity and political stability, 71 percent of Hong Kong residents chose the latter, and only 20 percent chose democracy. Similarly, almost 90 percent preferred a stable and peaceful handover to insisting on increasing the pace of democracy. Kuan Hsin-chi and Lau Siu-kai, "The Partial Vision of Democracy in Hong Kong: A Survey of Popular Opinion," *China Journal*, vol. 34 (1995), pp. 239, 261–2. For similar findings in Taiwan, see Cooney, Chapter 14. For the PRC, see, for example, Yali Peng, "Democracy and Chinese Political Discourses," *Modern China*, vol. 24 (1998), pp. 408–40. See also Minxin Pei, "Racing Against Time: Institutional Decay and Renewal in China," in William A. Joseph, ed., *China Briefing: The Contradictions of Change* (Armonk: M. E. Sharpe, 1997), p. 11. Pei cites polls showing that two-thirds of the people thought that the economic situation was improving while half thought their own living standards were improving, and that the majority of respondents (54 percent) placed a higher priority on economic development than democracy. Over two-thirds of those polled supported the government's policy of promoting economic growth and social stability, and 63 percent agreed that "it would be a disaster for China to experience a similar change as that in the former Soviet Union" (id. at p. 18). Even 40 percent of non-CCP (Chinese Communist Party) member respondents said they voluntarily supported the same political position as the CCP (id.). See alsoXia Li Lollar, *China's Transition Toward a Market Economy, Civil Society and Democracy* (Bristol: Wyndham Hall Press, 1997), p. 74, citing results of poll in which 60 percent of respondents assigned highest priority to maintaining order, while another 30 percent chose controlling inflation, whereas only 8 percent chose giving people more say in political decisions and free elections, and only 2 percent chose protecting free speech. Wan Ming cites survey data showing growing support for the Party, and concludes that a development consensus that emphasizes stability has emerged. See Wan Ming, "Chinese Opinion on Human Rights," *Orbis,* vol. 42 (1998), p. 361. Another study showed Chinese to be the least tolerant of diverse viewpoints among all of the countries surveyed. It also found little support for a free press and the publishing of alternative views. See Andrew Nathan and Shi Tianjian, "Cultural Requisites for Democracy in China: Findings from a Survey," *Daedalus*, vol. 122 (1993), p. 95. For further polling evidence, see Suzanne Ogden, *Inklings of Democracy in China* (Cambridge: Harvard University Asian Center, 2002).

37 To be sure, the U.S. also suffers from an inegalitarian distribution of income. While gross national product (GNP) reached a historic high in the U.S. in 1990, having grown over 25 percent in a decade, child poverty increased by 21 percent so that one in five American children lived in poverty. The U.S. ranked 14th in the world in terms of life expectancy and 20th in terms of infant mortality. Almost 30 percent of the poor had no medical insurance in 1991. Somewhere between 5 million and 10 million Americans experienced homelessness in the late 1980s. See John Gledhill, "Liberalism, Socio-Economic Rights and the Politics of Identity: From Moral Economy to Indigenous Rights," in Richard Wilson, ed., *Human Rights, Culture and Context* (Chicago: Pluto Press, 1997), pp. 70, 72–3. Globally, in 1980 the top 20 percent of the world's population captured 84.4 percent of the world's gross domestic product (GDP). In 2000, the top 20 percent took 85.6 percent. See Gary Clyde Hufbauer, "Polarization in the World Economy," 5:1 *Milken Institute Review* 26, 28 (2003).

38 See Baxi, Chapter 10; see also Cassels, supra note 31, at p. 498 (describing distinctive features of social action litigation as liberalization of standing requirements, procedural flexibility, a creative and activist interpretation of rights, remedial flexibility and ongoing judicial participation and revision). Sharing Baxi's caution about the limits of public-interest litigation, Cassels

warns that India's activist judges have been criticized for violating rule of law, and that not all judicial decisions have favored the oppressed and less fortunate.

39 Critics sometimes frame the issue as whether the system is consistent with rule of law. Susan Maslen, "Japan and the Rule of Law," *UCLA Pacific Basin Law Journal*, vol. 16 (1998), p. 281.

40 See Randy Barnett, "Constitutional Legitimacy," 103 *Columbia Law Review*, 111–148 (2003) (arguing that neither "consent of the governed" nor "benefits received" justifies obedience to even "constitutionally valid" laws). If citizens begin to believe the view popular among some academics that law is all politics and that judges simply decide cases based on their political preferences, respect for the legal system will wane. Courts have won this respect over a long time, sometimes overcoming deep distrust, as in France. In many Asian countries, the courts are still fighting to gain respect and legitimacy. Respect for the courts and the legal system is a valuable resource. It allows the courts to resolve in a peaceful manner problems that the majoritarian democratic process may not be able to resolve. It also facilitates a peaceful transition of power, which is no small feat in many countries. Whatever one thinks of *Bush v. Gore*, that Gore and his supporters did accept the decision was telling. While many of my Chinese colleagues saw in the court's decision a kind of politicization of the legal system with which they were all too familiar, they did express admiration for the peaceful transition that followed.

41 See, for example, Ronald Cass, *The Rule of Law in America* (Baltimore: John Hopkins University Press, 2001); see also Tamanaha's balanced assessment in Chapter 2. Even Unger has moderated his views. Whereas he complained in 1976 that "the very assumptions of the rule of law appear to be falsified by the reality of life in liberal society," 20 years later he acknowledged that rule of law may play a positive role, and that when rule of law prevails, "people enjoy security in a regime of rights." Roberto Unger, *Law in Modern Society: Toward a Criticism of Social Theory* (New York: Free Press, 1976), p. 181; *What Should Legal Analysis Become?* (London: Verso, 1996), p. 64.

42 For the argument that this might be an advantage given the wide diversity of legal systems, see Peerenboom, supra note 15, at p. 175.

43 For a discussion of approaches to assessing whether a country meets the minimal conditions for rule of law, see id.

44 Even the critics of the law and development movement found value in rule of law as a weapon against authoritarianism. Gardner, for instance, objected to the original law and development movement on the ground that its "legal instrumentalism proved vulnerable because it lacked, indeed rejected, any carefully developed philosophical or ethical perspective and because it offered a vision of law inadequately differentiated from state and power, and thus was unable to discriminate between 'ends' externally defined." Yet he also noted that the ideology of rule of law was useful in limiting the arbitrary acts of the government. James A. Gardner, *Legal Imperialism* (Madison: University of Wisconsin Press, 1980). Similarly, Yash Ghai has remarked based on the experiences of African countries that although the neutral façade of liberal constitutions that portray law as autonomous and impartial often masks social and economic inequities, the ideology of rule of law nevertheless acts to restrain rulers and protect individuals' rights and freedoms. Ghai, "Constitutions and Governance in Africa: A Prolegomenon," in Sammy Adelman and Abdul Paliwala, eds., *Law and Crisis in the Third World* (London: Hans Zell Publishers, 1993).

45 Carol Jones, "Politics Postponed: Law as a Substitute for Politics in Hong Kong and China," in *Law, Capitalism and Power in Asia*, supra note 8.

46 The spillover can be in either direction. As Chen and Cheung point out (in Chapter 8), Hong Kong has been downgraded as an investment site due in part to the erosion of Hong Kong's political autonomy from the mainland as well as concerns about transparency, corruption and allegations of favoritism by the government toward certain firms. Other non-legal factors included the continuously deteriorating economic condition and the lack of relevant skills among workers.

47 See Ugo Mattei, "Three Patterns of Law: Taxonomy and Change in the World's Legal Systems," *American Journal of Comparative Law*, vol. 45(1997), p. 5, discussed in the Preface to this volume.

48 Those who attribute the success of Asian countries to relation-based capitalism often underestimate the role law has played in economic development in the region, in part because they tend to elide rule of law with democracy and a liberal version of rights that emphasizes civil and political rights. I discuss this issue at length and review a number of multi-country empirical studies that also support the contention that a thin rule of law is necessary if not sufficient for sustained economic growth in Peerenboom, supra note 15, ch. 10. See also Katharina Pistor and Philip A. Wellons, *The Role of Law and Legal Institutions in Asian Economic Development 1960–1995* (New York: Oxford University Press, 1999); Samantha Ravich, *Marketization and Democracy: East Asian Experiences* (Cambridge: Cambridge University Press, 2000); Henry Rowen, "The Political and Social Foundations of the Rise of East Asia,"in Henry S. Rowen, ed., *Behind East Asian Growth* (New York: Routledge, 1998).

49 See David Bourchier, "Between Law and Politics: The Malaysian Judiciary Since Independence," in *Law, Capitalism and Power in Asia*, supra note 8.

50 Although a lower court held an Act unconstitutional, the decision was overturned on appeal.

51 Hilary Josephs, "The Upright and the Low-down: An Examination of Official Corruption in the United States and the People's Republic of China," *Syracuse Journal of International Law and Commerce*, vol. 27 (2000), pp. 269, 271.

52 To be sure, there is generally some demand for rule of law even among rural citizens, small businesses or companies locked into tight social networks. See Peerenboom, supra note 15, ch. 10.

53 Compare Steven Poe and C. Neal Tate, "Repression of Human Rights to Personal Integrity in the 1980s: A Global Analysis," *American Political Science Review*, vol. 88 (1994), p. 853 (finding no evidence that British colonialism has a positive impact on human rights), with Neil Mitchell and James M. McCormick, "Economic and Political Explanations of Human Rights Violations," *World Politics*, vol. 40 (1988), pp. 476, 497 (finding only slight evidence to support the claim that British colonial influence has a positive impact on human rights); Steven Poe, C. Neal Tate, and Linda Camp Keith, "Repression of the Human Right to Personal Integrity Revisited: A Global Cross-National Study Covering the Years 1976–1993," *International Studies Quarterly*, vol. 43 (1999), pp. 291, 310 (finding British colonialism did have positive impact on human rights).

54 Habermas locates the legitimacy of moral principles, political decisions, his elaborately conceptualized legal system and particular legal rules in the possibility of rational consensus: "Just those action norms are valid to which all possibly affected persons could agree as participants in rational discourses." While moral norms require universal assent, certain legal norms may be justified by ethical and pragmatic reasons. Thus, Habermas defines the notion of "rational discourse" broadly to include, with respect to certain legal norms that involve non-generalizable interests, fairly negotiated compromises that result in a rational balancing of competing value orientations and interests. But the condi-

tions for a fairly negotiated compromise, including sufficient parity of material resources to participate meaningfully in political debates, are not now, or ever likely to be, present in the real world. Jürgen Habermas, *Between Facts and Norms*, trans. William Rheg (Cambridge: MIT Press, 1996).

55 See Thio, Chapter 6.

56 Adam Przeworski and Fernando Limongi, "Modernization: Theories and Facts," *World Politics*, vol. 49 (1997), p. 155.

57 Id.

58 Pasuk Phongpaichit and Chris Baker, *Thailand's Crisis* (Thailand: Silkworm Books, 2000).

59 China has reported growth rates over 7 percent for the last several years, with predictions for future growth in the near term in the same range. See also, G. Pascal Zachary, "From Iceland to Botswana, Small Nations Prosper," , 25 February 1999, p. B1 ("Singapore, the smallest country in Southeast Asia, has been the least hurt by the region's economic crisis."). Hong Kong's growth rate of GDP fell in 1998, rebounded to 3.1 percent in 1999 and 10 percent in 2000, and then fell sharply in 2001 to 0.1 percent due to the general economic slowdown in industrial countries. Growth picked up in 2002 but then dropped in 2003 as a result of the SARS (severe acute respiratory syndrome) crisis. See the Asia Development Bank's outlook for Hong Kong, available at http://www.adb.org/documents/books/ado/2002/hkg.asp.

60 According to the CIA's World Factbook, in 2001 the GDP per capita of the U.S. was $36,300, Japan $27,200, Singapore $24,700, South Korea $18,000, Taiwan, $17,200, Thailand $6,600, the Philippines $4,000, Indonesia $3,000, and India $2,500.

61 I have received many helpful comments on this chapter from the participants of the conference, as well as from Michael Dowdle, Jonathan Ocko and an anonymous reviewer.

2

RULE OF LAW IN THE UNITED STATES

Brian Z. Tamanaha

This chapter will articulate the theoretical understanding of the rule of law in the United States. Three underlying themes will be pressed in the course of this articulation. One theme is that there is a debate among theorists within the U.S. regarding the nature and consequences of the rule of law, which is glossed over in the promotion of the rule of law to the rest of the world. Interestingly, this promotion has occurred at the same time that theorists from both the right and left of the political spectrum have identified a decline in the rule of law in the U.S. A second theme is that the rule of law as understood in the U.S. is connected to a liberal culture and a liberal political system. A third theme is that, while the rule of law undeniably furthers freedom, in the dominant theoretical understanding it is also consistent with inequality and oppression, and it exists in tension with democracy. The overarching point of these themes is that rule of law is not a panacea. Its strengths must be understood along with its limitations.

Liberal theory

The rule of law in the United States must be understood within the political theory of liberalism. The core of liberalism is its emphasis on individual liberty.[1] Liberalism holds that: "The only freedom which deserves the name, is that of pursuing our own good in our own way, so long as we do not attempt to deprive others of theirs, or impede their efforts to obtain it."[2]

In the liberal social contract tradition, initiated by Hobbes and Locke, the starting point of law is the coming together of autonomous, rights-bearing individuals who enter a covenant to form a government authorized to promulgate and enforce a body of laws in the interest of preserving order. Life without law is prone to strife and insecure. Hence individuals give up their natural freedom in exchange for the protection and order afforded by law. What renders the arrangement legitimate is the individual consent that gives rise to the government and legal system. Consent respects the autonomy of individuals even as they become subject to the dictates of the law. Equality is added to liberty as a prime liberal value by virtue of the moral equivalence accorded to all individuals as autonomous, rights-bearing beings. Ronald Dworkin explained how, under liberalism, liberty and equality require that the government must remain neutral on the "question of the good life":

> Since the citizens of a society differ in their conceptions, the government does not treat them as equals if it prefers one conception to another, either because the officials believe that one is intrinsically superior, or because one is held by the more numerous or more powerful group.[3]

Four themes of liberty

The classic dilemma raised by the decision to submit oneself to law is the apparent trade-off between order and liberty. Giving up liberty in the interest of self-preservation is a poor exchange if the result is to subject oneself to a legally enforced oppression. The modern liberal answer to this dilemma is fourfold. First, the individual is free to the extent that the governing laws are democratically enacted. By virtue of democratic mechanisms, citizens have authored the rules they are obliged to follow; the individual is at once ruler and ruled – citizens thus rule themselves. This is consistent with liberty because one is not subject to the will of another but rather to one's own will. "[O]bedience to a law one prescribes to oneself is freedom,"[4] Rousseau declared. "A people, since it is subject to laws, ought to be the author of them."[5] Moreover, presumably under a democracy citizens would not enact laws to oppress themselves – their power to make law is their own best protection. Self-rule is *"political liberty."* To be effective, the full realization of political liberty implies the right to vote, and the protection of freedom of speech, assembly and association.

Second, the individual is free to the extent that government officials are required to act in accordance with law. This requirement promotes liberty by allowing individuals to predict when they will be subject to interference from the government, enabling them to avoid the law by not running afoul of it. This entails that the rules be stated in general terms in advance, and that the application and interpretation of laws be certain. The seminal example of this version of liberty is the notion that criminal punishment may not be imposed in the absence of a pre-existing law. *"Legal liberty"* is the freedom to do what one wishes outside of what the law proscribes. The rule of law, as will be made clear, is most closely identified with legal liberty.

Third, the individual is free insofar as the government is prohibited from taking certain kinds of actions against individuals. Such restrictions are often contained in Bills of Rights. These restrictions may be substantive (strictly prohibiting government incursion in protected spheres) or only procedural (the government must satisfy a high burden, like demonstrating necessity, before interference in these protected spheres is allowed). This is *"private liberty."* Although it is now often phrased in terms of "individual rights" or "human rights," the heritage of private liberty lies in natural law.[6] Private liberty, to the extent that it is recognized, is controversial and variable in content, but must at least include the freedom of religion and conscience, as well as the more general idea that a person may not be punished by the state for beliefs alone. The essential idea is that people are entitled to a minimum core of integrity of body and mind, which in its fullest form amounts to a sphere of personal privacy.

Finally, freedom is enhanced when the powers of the government are divided into compartments – typically legislative, executive, and judicial (horizontal division), and sometimes municipal, state, and national (vertical division) – with the application of law entrusted to an independent judiciary. This division promotes liberty by preventing the accumulation of power in any one institution, setting up a form of competitive interdependence within the government. Separating legislative from judicial powers is essential if there are to be standing laws in advance of the moment of application. Allocating the application of law to an independent judiciary insures that a legal institution is the final tribunal before which all governmental actions can be held accountable for consistency with the law. *"Institutionalized liberty"* exists where institutional structures and processes have been devised to enhance prospects for the realization of the liberty of citizens through the division of government power, and especially through the availability of recourse to an autonomous judiciary. This is qualitatively different from the previous three themes of liberty, in the sense that it is a system for bringing about liberty rather than a kind of liberty itself.

The characteristic form of liberal democracy formulates a tight correspondence between political liberty and legal liberty that can be succinctly stated in the following two-step terms: freedom requires that citizens create the laws under which they live; and it requires, furthermore, that when government officials enforce and apply these laws, they do so according to the laws as written, not subject to the will or discretion of the person who happens to be the government official. At the first step citizens rule themselves; at the second step citizens are ruled by law, which they established for themselves. In neither instance are citizens subject to the rule of another. Liberal democracies also often add protection for private liberty through Bills of Rights; they often have a separation of powers, especially with an independent judiciary; and they often establish all of this in a written constitution.

Although these four themes of liberty are regularly found together, that is not necessarily required. Legal liberty (freedom to do whatever is not prohibited by law), private liberty (protected spheres free from government intrusion), and institutionalized liberty (separation of powers) may all (separately or together) exist without political liberty (without democracy). All

58

three forms of liberty could be present, for example, in a system in which the laws are established by a non-democratic (philosophical or scientific) elite, as many political theorists from Plato onward have proposed. Furthermore, legal liberty may exist without private liberty – whether there is a restricted sphere free from government interference is an entirely separate issue from whether the government must act according to standing law.

Political liberty (democracy) and private liberty (individual rights) conflict

These answers by no means resolve the tension between order and freedom. Perhaps the most formidable difficulty is that private liberty and political liberty conflict. As Isaiah Berlin observed, "there is no necessary connexion between individual liberty and democratic rule. The answer to the question 'Who governs me?' is logically distinct from the question 'How far does government interfere with me?' "[7] The goal of private liberty is to curb the intrusion of governmental authority against individuals, whereas the goal of political liberty is to control the exercise of that authority.[8] The concern of the former is tyranny against the individual, and democracies can be tyrannical. The concern of the latter is to determine who gets to shape the social and political community through legislation, an objective which is inhibited by the limitations of private liberty. "These are not two different interpretations of a single concept, but two profoundly divergent and irreconcilable attitudes to the ends of life.... These claims cannot both be fully satisfied."[9]

Liberalism has always promoted liberty of the individual as the preeminent value. Many early liberals were against popular democracy – not widely instituted until the twentieth century – which they viewed with trepidation as leading to rule by the ignorant masses, susceptible to demagogues, a recipe for anarchy, a threat to the property of the elite, and an invitation to disorder. Even apparently strong pro-democratic sentiments expressed by liberals, like Kant's assertion that a citizen has a "lawful freedom to obey no law other than the one to which he has given his consent," are often less than they might appear; for Kant disqualified from voting all "passive" citizens, which included apprentices, servants, all women, sharecroppers, and more generally all "persons under the orders or protections of other individuals."[10] The right to vote advocated by classic liberals was usually restricted to the propertied class.

The fear of democracy was a central theme of James Madison and Alexander Hamilton in *The Federalist Papers*, a classic work of applied liberalism. Madison reiterated the core dilemma of liberal democracies: To secure the public good and private rights against the danger of such a [majority] faction, and at the same time to preserve the spirit and form of popular government, is then the great object to which our inquiries are directed.[11]

Both Madison and Hamilton, in various writings, voiced repeated concern about democracy as a threat to contract and property rights, fears which had been magnified by recent events in state legislatures.[12] Despite these concerns, they were committed to democracy as the best form of governance, and paid careful attention to lessening its attendant risks.

They identified three ways to limit the dangers of democracy. Representative (not direct) democracy, first of all, was supposed to produce rule by a reasoned elite who would be less swayed by popular passion. Vertical and horizontal separation of powers, second, would also operate to restrain the masses. The underlying idea was to make it difficult for the government apparatus to be captured by an oppressive majority. "[T]he society itself will be broken into so many parts, interests and classes of citizens, that the rights of individuals, or of the minority, will be in little danger from interested combinations of the majority."[13]

The third mechanism was judicial review, articulated by Hamilton:

> By a limited Constitution, I understand one which contains certain specified exceptions to the legislative authority;...Limitations of this kind can be preserved in practice no other way than through the medium of courts of justice, whose duty it must be to declare all acts contrary to the manifest tenor of the Constitution void. Without this, all the reservations of particular rights or privileges would amount to nothing.[14]

Hamilton's argument is that the supremacy of the Constitution would be vitiated if contrary legislation could not be invalidated. This reasoning does not determine who should have the power to declare invalidity. For that Hamilton offered the prudential argument that the judiciary is the weakest branch, which poses no threat to the others, and added that "the interpretation of the laws is the proper and peculiar province of the courts."[15]

Chief Justice John Marshall followed this reasoning to find that judicial review was constitutionally required (notwithstanding that it was not explicitly mentioned in the Constitution), observing that constitutions secure "a government of laws, and not of men."[16] A written constitution, including a bill of rights,[17] provides legal controls on the law-maker in explicit terms. Judicial review is the mechanism through which this legal limitation is effectuated, which – taking the judiciary as the oracle of the law – is presented as the law itself speaking, or as close to this as is humanly possible.

Because judicial review (which extends beyond protection of individual rights) involves the power to invalidate legislation, it has serious anti-democratic implications. Judicial review can be justified in democratic terms, as necessary to the effectuation of the Constitution, which was itself democratically created. But that does not lessen the fact that it results in judges overriding laws enacted by democratically elected legislators who believed the laws they produced were consistent with Constitutional requirements.

Liberalism and moral pluralism

The liberty central to liberalism is a liberty to pursue one's own vision of the good. Whether this is understood as a default position owing to the failure to identify universal moral principle or as the right position to take given the conclusion that there is no single good but many legitimate alternative forms of the good attached to different cultures or forms of life,[18] the result is the same: liberalism, especially in its protection of spheres of individual liberty, is constructed in a manner that accommodates moral pluralism. Moral pluralism can function within liberalism comfortably in either of two forms – when more than one community or culture with its own version of the good coexists within the ambit of a single system, or when there is a pluralism of moral views among the individuals who exist within the system.

Liberalism purports to be neutral with regard to these alternative visions of the good; that is, it cannot adopt and promote as the state-sanctioned good (or religion) one such vision over another, with the caveat that it may prohibit or sanction visions of the good that threaten others or the state. This abstention from endorsing any particular substantive conception of the good does not mean that liberal systems are completely neutral – in an important respect they are not. Liberalism takes the position that neutrality is the *right* principle upon which to construct a government and system of laws,[19] at least in situations of pluralism, and the values of individual autonomy and tolerance are actively promoted in liberal systems. Were this not the case, liberalism would fail to reproduce itself, would indeed lead to its own destruction, which would occur if anti-tolerant views came to prevail within society, then seized control over the governmental apparatus and instituted a non-liberal regime.

Liberalism and capitalism

The final piece of liberalism to be related is its economic component. Liberalism has been called a "bourgeois" political theory for reasons of both its origins and its content. Its articulation by Locke coincided with the emergence and newly established prominence of the merchant class in the towns and cities of England.[20] During this period the bourgeoisie was engaged in a struggle against the privileges of the aristocracy and the church, and the onerous taxation of the monarchy, while wrapped in a straitjacket of feudal laws that inhibited their activities and accorded them no respect. An individualist political theory that touts liberty and the protection of rights, especially the rights of contract and property, as Locke's theory did, obviously mirrored the interests of the bourgeois.[21] The right of property protected (and promoted) their accumulation of capital; freedom of contract inhibited government interference in their contractual arrangements with other merchants and with workers; enforcement of contract provided security for their transactions, and allowed them to invoke the state apparatus to insure compliance with agreements.[22] Above all else, merchants required predictability in the enforcement of contractual and property rights in order to calculate in advance the potential costs and benefits of anticipated transactions. Max Weber famously established the ways in which liberalism's formal rational legal system – the rule of law – facilitates capitalism through increasing predictability and security.[23]

Arguments over the decline of the rule of law in the U.S.

Hayek's account of the rule of law and its decline

Friedrich Hayek is the leading conservative theorist on the rule of law. Hayek argued that the rule of law was the cornerstone of liberty, and he decried the grave threat posed to this ideal by the vast expansion of administrative action that accompanied the rise of the social welfare state. Hayek offered a concise and influential definition of the rule of law:

> Stripped of all technicalities, this means that government in all its actions is bound by rules fixed and announced before-hand – rules which make it possible to foresee with fair certainty how the authority will use its coercive powers in given circumstances and to plan one's individual affairs on the basis of this knowledge.[24]

In the previous section this idea was given the label "legal liberty." The rule of law in this sense promotes liberty by allowing individuals to know the range of activities – those not prohibited by the law – in which they are completely free to do as they please without being exposed to government coercion.

According to Hayek, "true law" has three attributes that all rule of law systems must possess: "the laws must be general, equal and certain."[25] The attribute of *generality* requires that the law be set out in advance in abstract terms not aimed at any particular individual. The law then applies, without exception, to everyone whose conduct falls within the prescribed conditions of application. Hayek, when elaborating this attribute, quoted Rousseau's description of the generality requirement: "When I say that the province of the law is always general, I mean that the law considers all subjects collectively and all actions in the abstract; it does not consider any individual man or any specific action."[26] Hayek added that the separation of powers between legislature and judiciary is virtually required by the attribute of generality, for only in this manner can the law be set out in abstract terms apart from its possible application to any particular individual; legislative and judicial separation thus is by implication also an "integral part" of the rule of law.[27] *Equality* requires that the laws apply to everyone without making arbitrary distinctions among people. When distinctions do exist (as in government imposed male but not female conscription), Hayek insisted that to be legitimate they must be approved by a majority of people inside as well as outside the group targeted for differential treatment.[28] *Certainty* requires that those who are subject to the law be able to predict reliably what legal rules will be found to govern their conduct and how those rules will be interpreted and applied. Predictability is what allows one the freedom of action beyond what the law proscribes.

Hayek acknowledged that it was impossible for any legal system to attain perfectly these three attributes, but he believed that they could nonetheless be approximated. He summarized how these aspects of the rule of law preserve liberty:

> when we obey laws, in the sense of general abstract rules laid down irrespective of their application to us, we are not subject to another man's will and are therefore free. It is because the lawgiver does not know the particular cases to which his rules will apply, and it is because the judge who applies them has no choice in drawing the conclusions that follow from the existing body of rules and the particular facts of the case, that it can be said that laws and not men rule.[29]

Hayek postulated a fundamental antithesis between law and discretion, and he equated discretion with arbitrary will.

The exercise of discretion by administrative officials does not necessarily fall foul of the rule of law, according to Hayek, as long as the discretion exercised by officials is pursuant to legal rules that possess the qualities of generality, equality, and certainty, and as long as their decisions are subject to judicial examination.[30] The problem was that too often these legal restraints were absent. Any administrative authority that tries to achieve particular policy results in concrete situations involving the application of coercion, which many did, inherently violates the rule of law, Hayek insisted, because the generality requirement cannot be satisfied.[31] "This pursuit of 'social justice' made it necessary for governments to treat the citizen and his property as an object of administration with the aim of securing particular results for particular groups."[32] He believed that the growth of administrative actions had "already led very far away from the ideal of the Rule of Law."[33]

While pressing his attack on administrative actions, Hayek argued that the related goals of substantive equality and substantive – better known as "distributive" – justice are inherently inconsistent with the rule of law.[34]

Substantive equality is the notion that equality requires treating differently situated people differently in order to equalize their situations. Distributive justice is the notion that there must be a fair distribution or allocation of goods in a society, with fairness determined in accordance with some standard of merit or desert. The connection between these ideas is that unfair distributions often lead to unequal opportunities, and vice versa. In more concrete terms, people born rich or born poor cannot be said in moral terms to have deserved, respectively, their relative advantages and disadvantages (distributive injustice); for them to be treated equally the disadvantage suffered by the poor person must somehow be offset (substantive equality). Hayek's first objection to distributive justice was that there is no certain system of values according to which a society can determine what is a fair distribution, so the views of some will have to prevail over those of others.[35] Even in a society with a consensus on a system of values, conflicts will nonetheless still arise between incommensurable values; there will still be dissenters from the majority; and in any case it would seem impossible to obtain agreement about the relative and appropriate values of each of the innumerable activities of individuals, and their just rewards. Any such system would by necessity be particularistic in nature, Hayek asserted, and therefore inconsistent with the rule of law, because the infinite variety of the situations that arise cannot be governed by general rules set in advance. Substantive equality violates the rule of law for the same reason, and additionally because the differential treatment it entails violates the equality requirement.

Hayek unapologetically embraced the implications of this position:

> A necessary, and only apparently paradoxical, result of this is that formal equality before the law is in conflict, and in fact incompatible, with any activity of the government deliberately aiming at material or substantive equality of different people, and that any policy aiming directly at a substantive ideal of distributive justice must lead to the destruction of the Rule of Law. To produce the same result for different people, it is necessary to treat them differently.... It cannot be denied that the Rule of Law produces economic inequality – all that can be claimed for it is that this inequality is not designed to affect particular people in a particular way.[36]

Lamentable as the resulting disparity might be, Hayek asserted, the poor in liberal societies still had more absolute wealth than the supposedly equal masses in socialist societies, and they enjoyed greater freedom, including the freedom to take initiatives which would improve their own economic position. And he allowed that the government could provide a minimum level of support, and insurance against catastrophe, for the unfortunate in society, especially since this can be established in non-coercive ways.[37]

Critical left opposition to liberalism

According to the critical left, liberalism promised liberty and equality, but instead resulted in different forms of domination and inequality. Freedom from government domination was indeed advanced by liberalism, but with no commensurate gain in freedom from some individuals being dominated by others. Private domination takes many forms, the most obvious of which are control over conditions of employment, and acting upon racial, gender, religious, or ethnic prejudices. Similarly, inequality based upon social hierarchies tied to status at birth was abolished by liberalism, but new inequalities based on the unequal distributions of wealth and talent were established.[38] Private domination and unequal distribution of wealth and talent often interact to reinforce one another, because those with greater wealth and talent are often the ones who have the ability and opportunity to dominate others. More specifically, it is especially the poor, less able, or social outcasts who get short shrift under liberalism. Rather than liberty for all, from the standpoint of those at the bottom it appears that liberalism creates liberty for some to dominate others. Moreover, it appears that the public power of law is inordinately at the call of those at the top of the new hierarchies, enforcing their already ample ability to exercise their private power. Public resources thereby reinforce the advantage already granted by private resources, in much the same way as occurred prior to liberalism, just along new lines.

To the extent that these new forms of domination and inequality are acknowledged by liberalism, they are most often excused as unfortunate but necessary side-effects that come with the benefits of formal equality and freedom from government domination. The trade-off is still preferable, liberal apologists (like Hayek) assert, in that government domination can be absolute, including the infliction of physical pain and death, which is not allowed to private domination, and under liberalism individuals at least have the *opportunity* to move from one economic class to another, which status hierarchies or totalitarian governments foreclosed. This response is cold comfort to the losers in the new system. Private oppression can pervasively affect one's life, and inequality hurts no matter how it is constructed.

Unger on the breakdown of the rule of law

Roberto Unger is the leading philosopher of the critical left. Unger's account of the rule of law is much like Hayek's: law must be set out in advance in general terms, and cases should be heard in autonomous courts of law.[39] Unger asserted, with Hayek, that "the rule of law has been truly said to be the soul of the modern [liberal] state."[40] Moreover, he cited,[41] and echoed, Hayek's core argument that the social welfare state was bringing about "the dissolution of the rule of law."[42]

Unger elaborated how the problems Hayek identified went beyond the administrative context to pervasively infect the law itself. Two crucial changes in law were generated by the social welfare state, according to Unger. First, judges were asked increasingly to apply open-ended standards like fairness, good faith, reasonableness, and unconscionability. Second, courts – not just administrative officials – were required increasingly to engage in purposive reasoning; that is, they were asked to render decisions about how best to achieve legislatively set policy goals, a process which immersed judges in making choices from among a range of alternative means with different value implications. According to Unger, these two changes were inconsistent with the traditional judicial role of formal rule application, and departed from the ideal of a regime of rules with the qualities of generality, equality, and certainty:

> Open-ended clauses and general standards force courts and administrative agencies to engage in ad hoc balancing of interests that resist reduction to general rules.[43]...
>
> Purposive legal reasoning and nonformal justice also cause trouble for the ideal of generality. The policy-oriented lawyer insists that part of interpreting a rule is to choose the most efficient means to the attainment of the ends one assigns to it. But as the circumstances to which decisions are addressed change and as the decisionmaker's understanding of the means available to him varies, so must the way he interprets the rules. This instability of result will also increase with the fluctuations of accepted policy and with the variability of the particular problems to be resolved. Hence, the very notion of stable areas of individual entitlement and obligation, a notion inseparable from the rule of law ideal, will be eroded.
>
> The quest for substantive justice corrupts legal generality to an even greater degree. When the rage of impermissible inequalities among social situations expands, the need for individualized treatment grows correspondingly. No matter how substantive justice is defined, it can be achieved only be treating different situations differently.[44]

These new demands placed on judges had the further effect of eroding the autonomy of law. "As purposive legal reasoning and concerns with substantive justice began to prevail, the style of legal discourse approaches that of commonplace political or economic argument."[45] Judicial decision-making increasingly resembled administrative and political decision-making, raising serious questions about its legitimacy, which had previously rested upon a claimed distinction between law and politics. It offended the notion of political liberty to have unelected judges make political decisions no different in nature from legislatures. As a consequence of these changes, the legal system consisted of an unstable oscillation between rule application, instrumental reasoning, the application of open-ended standards, and ad hoc balancing. On top of these changes wrought by the social welfare state on the rule of law, Unger observed in liberal societies what he called a growing "corporatism": the increase in the power and reach of corporate institutions in society and their domination over the lives of individuals.[46] Corporations also exerted a greater role in shaping government actions, especially through influence on administrative officials and politicians. This blurring of the lines between public and private enhanced the bitterness experienced under liberalism from social and economic inequalities, and the de facto lack of freedom of many.

Led by Unger, and informed by a revolt against liberalism taking place within political theory,[47] critical left scholars argued that liberalism is a deeply flawed theory owing to its starting presupposition of autonomous individuals and overarching focus on individual liberty. In a myriad of ways the liberal approach to society and law failed to appreciate the role of community. People are born to, nurtured by, and always exist within communities; they take their language, morals, roles, and very patterns of thoughts from communities; their identity is a function of how others in the community view them; they love others and need love from others; solidarity with others, expressed in friendship and altruism, gives meaning to life; individuals are social beings through and through. All of this was forgotten by liberalism, according to critical scholars, or at least was not adequately acknowledged. The rule of law was constructed on the individualist presuppositions of liberalism, and thus suffers from the same failure to account for community.

Many critical theorists took the view that the solution lies in enhanced community, which would solve the contradictions within liberalism by aligning the interests of the individual with the interests of society. Unger explained why:

> Community is held together by an allegiance to common purposes. The more these shared ends express the nature of humanity rather than simply the preferences of particular individuals and groups, the more would one's acceptance of them become an affirmation of one's own nature; the less would it have to represent the abandonment of individuality in favor of assent and recognition. Thus, it would be possible to view others as complementary rather than opposing wills; furtherance of their ends would mean the advancement of one's own. The conflict between the demands of individuality and of sociability would disappear.[48]

Not only is there no conflict between the individual good and the social good, the rule of law is no longer preeminent in a community of shared values. The dominant orientation in situations of conflict, instead of strict rule application, will be to come to an outcome that furthers the shared community purpose. The government is an extension of the community that shares in and facilitates this achievement of the common good, and hence need not be feared or restrained. The will of all, connected with the will of one; so discretion by judges and government officials was no longer a problem but a useful flexibility that enhanced their ability to promote the common good.

To his credit, Unger recognized the totalitarian potential inherent in the promotion of greater community, and he acknowledged that all too often the supposedly shared community values are really values that promote the interests of some over others. He warned that the communitarian goal may be chimerical and dangerous.[49]

The debate over indeterminacy

The critical left did more than just identify the decline of the rule of law; it attempted to further this decline by pressing the indeterminacy thesis to argue that the rule of law is a fraud. The debate in the U.S. over the indeterminacy of law was especially lively in the 1980s and 1990s, spawning a sizable body of literature that covered a range of subjects from the indeterminacy of language, to the indeterminacy of standards, to the indeterminacy of particular areas of the law.[50] Fortunately much of the debate can be bypassed without loss. As the debate progressed, leftist critics of the rule of law narrowed their claims about the indeterminacy thesis. When the initial heat subsided, substantial agreement emerged among disputants over the presence (though not the precise extent) of indeterminacy, with remaining disagreement focused mostly on how the indeterminacy was to be characterized and whether it threatened the ideal of the rule of law.

The indeterminacy thesis – which focuses on judicial decisions – asserts that, in a significant subset of cases, the law does not produce a single right answer, and sometimes the available body of legal rules even allows contradictory outcomes.[51] Owing to said indeterminacy, the decision made by the judge in such cases must be the product of factors other than the legal rules. Indications of this indeterminacy are the presence of rules that can lead to different outcomes, gaps in the rules, the ready availability of exceptions to rules, the openness of legal standards, all reflected in the seeming ease with which skilled lawyers are able to formulate arguments on both sides of a case, and in the fact of regular disagreement over the law manifested in dissenting opinions and disagreements among courts.

The main response put forth by opponents of the indeterminacy thesis is to point out the relatively high degree of predictability in law.[52] There are many "easy cases." These are cases in which lawyers can reliably predict the outcome, cases in which there will be little or no disagreement among judges. These cases are routinely resolved prior to court proceedings because each side can evaluate the likely outcome. The bulk of cases are like this.

Critical legal scholars agree that most cases are predictable. But they make three further points. First, most of the plentiful supply of easy cases are not necessarily determined by the legal rules (given that they often allow conflicting outcomes), as opposed to other factors (i.e. the shared indoctrination into the patterns of thought of the legal tradition, the shared socio-economic background of judges). Second, a fair number of cases, especially cases with important issues at stake, are not easy cases, in which judges must chose from among alternative possible outcomes, none compelled by the legal rules. In this subset of cases accurate prediction is difficult. Third, in many instances what was initially thought to be an easy case can be transformed into a problematic one, with sufficient motivation and skill exercised by lawyers or judges who wish to obtain an outcome different from that evidently required by prevailing interpretations.

Opponents of the indeterminacy thesis have ready answers for the second and third arguments by critical theorists. All legal systems have a certain unavoidable degree of indeterminacy, owing to the openness of language to different interpretations, to the generality of rules, which irrepressibly allows alternatives at the stage of application, and to the fact that every situation cannot be anticipated or provided for in advance by legislators. Furthermore, nothing can prevent a judge from manipulating the rules to achieve an outcome if so determined. All systems depend upon judges acting in good faith not to exploit the latent indeterminacy in law. Most critical scholars do not strongly contest either of these points.

So the debate over the indeterminacy thesis comes down to the issue of the source of the acknowledged high degree of predictability in law. Critical scholars attribute the source of this predictability to factors other than the law, including the shared social economic background of judges (upper-middle-class white males). Many critical scholars also refer to the indoctrination into the legal culture as a source of predictability:

> The legal culture shared by judges and theorists encompasses shared understandings of proper institutional roles and the extent to which the status quo should be maintained or altered. This culture includes "common sense" understandings of what rules mean as well as conventions (the identification of rules and exceptions) and politics (the differentiation between liberal and conservative judges).[53]

This is a conventionalist explanation for the predictability in law.

Opponents of the indeterminacy thesis agree with the latter explanation for the predictability in law, and assert that the error of critical theorists is their failure to recognize that all meaning is conventional in this sense, and therefore it is not only proper, but inevitable.[54] Legal professionals constitute an interpretive community with a shared language, culture, and sets of beliefs, which provide stability and determinacy in the interpretation and application of rules. What seem to be indeterminate rules when viewed in the abstract, will, in the context of application, be determinate, because shared conventions within the legal tradition (as well as institutional factors, like appellate review) will rule out certain interpretations as unacceptable. This explanation expands what it means to be a part of the "law" beyond the rules to now include the entirety of the legal tradition.

This explanation for the prevalence of easy cases must compete with the alternative explanation that judges' decisions are predictable owing to the fact that they are all from the elite class (a doubtful assertion in the U.S. today), which leads them to interpret and apply law in the same ways. And this explanation says nothing about the evident disagreements in law. However, when combined with the acknowledgement that a substantial majority of cases are easy, and that the legal tradition is a major reason for this uniformity, the indeterminacy thesis has lost much of its punch. Perhaps that explains why there is not much discussion of it in legal theory circles today.

Widespread agreement about the predictability of law, moreover, suggests that the indeterminacy thesis does not necessarily threaten at least one core aspect of the rule of law. Recall that predictability was, for Hayek, *the* key way in which the rule of law preserves liberty: it allows people to plan and take action with notice of what will subject them to legal coercion. An indeterminate and unpredictable legal system would fail in this respect. An indeterminate legal system that is nevertheless predictable will continue to preserve this kind of liberty.

Two theoretical versions of the rule of law

It is widely understood among theorists in the U.S. that there are two basic theoretical versions of the rule of law: formal and substantive. Presenting this contrast in the simplest terms, formal versions consist exclusively of procedural characteristics, whereas substantive versions include content requirements.

Formal versions of the rule of law

A majority of U.S. theorists advocate the formal version, which has been prominently articulated by Joseph Raz, Lon Fuller, and Robert Summers. Raz's account is the most influential. Raz followed Hayek to identify "the basic intuition" underlying the doctrine of the rule of law to be that "the law must be capable of guiding the behavior of its subjects."[55] He derived the elements of the rule of law from this single idea. According to Raz, these elements include that the law must be prospective, general, clear, public, and relatively stable. To this list Raz added several mechanisms he considered necessary to effectuate rules of this kind: an independent judiciary, open and fair hearings without bias, limited review of legislative and administrative officials, and limited discretion of the police. With minor variations, the first set of requirements is representative of all formal versions of the rule of law; the second set, with minor variations, is also often recognized, usually with the understanding that it stands in a supportive or supplemental relation to the first set.[56]

Raz agreed with Hayek that the rule of law furthers human autonomy and dignity by allowing people to plan. "But it has no bearing on the existence of spheres of activity free from governmental interference and is compatible with gross violations of human rights."[57] "It says nothing about how the law is to be made: by tyrants, democratic majorities, or any other way. It says nothing about fundamental rights, about equality, or justice."[58] For those who refuse to accept this account of the rule of law, it should be remembered that the U.S. adhered to the tenets of the rule of law even when slavery was legally enforced and racial segregation legally imposed, and that apartheid South Africa abided by the rule of law even when the majority of its citizens had no right to vote.[59] To restate its defining negative characteristic: the formal version of the rule of law does not incorporate any separate criteria of the good or just.

Although there are differences among the various formal accounts of the rule of law, they show a remarkable degree of agreement on fundamental issues. They all emphasize that the primary value of the rule of law – the essence of what it does – is to provide predictability, thereby allowing people to plan, and that this is highly valued because it enhances *individual autonomy*.[60] Above all, the rule of law is about legal liberty. Another point of unanimity is that the rule of law is *neutral* with regard to a wide range of substantive content. Fuller asserted that his notion of legality was "indifferent toward the substantive aims of the law and is ready to serve a variety of such aims with equal efficiency."[61] Summers asserted that this neutrality is a strong reason to prefer the formal over the substantive version:

> a relatively formal theory is itself more or less politically neutral, and because it is so confined, is more likely to command support on its own terms from right, left, and center in politics than is a substantive theory which not only incorporates the rule of law formally conceived but also incorporates much more controversial substantive content.[62]

Yet another area of agreement can be found in the almost complete overlap in core elements identified as definitive of the rule of law: generality, certainty, clarity, publicity, prospectivity. All of these theorists derived their elements following the same basic strategy: by deduction from the primary value served by the rule of law *qua* law. All of these theorists emphasized that these elements required that the law as enacted be faithfully and routinely adhered to by all government officials, especially judges. These theorists (at least those who addressed the point) acknowledged that judges could not regularly depart from the rules to achieve substantive justice (or equity), that this should occur only in exceptional circumstances if at all, for otherwise the certainty of the rule of law would be destroyed.[63] All of these theorists recognized the necessity for institutional mechanisms to effectuate these basic elements, specifically an independent judiciary (and legal profession) achieved through some form of separation of powers (institutionalized liberty). All of these theorists recognized that no system could perfectly realize these criteria, that approximation was good enough, and that Western legal systems had achieved the necessary levels. And all of these theorists concurred that the formal rule of law is necessary but not sufficient to constitute a completely just legal system, that the substantive content of the law must also be just.

On one key point there is not complete agreement among advocates of the formal rule of law. A number of formal theorists, including Raz and Summers, reject Hayek's assertion that the rule of law is inconsistent with the social welfare state and trying to achieve a greater degree of substantive equality. Raz's basic point is that the rule of law is one virtue among others, and that it can give way when necessary to achieve other compelling social values like distributive justice. A different response to Hayek is that, as long as the dominant orientation of the government remains rule oriented (certainly at least in the area of criminal prosecution), the rule of law can comfortably coexist with substantial areas of discretionary activity on the part of the government officials, especially when involving non-coercive activities, without leading to the collapse of the rule of law. The past century of experience in Western social welfare states has conclusively established this proposition.

Substantive version of the rule of law

All substantive versions of the rule of law incorporate the elements of the formal rule of law, then go further, adding on other elements in various combinations, including some requirement with respect to the content of law. Among U.S. legal theorists the most renowned substantive account of the rule of law is Ronald Dworkin's, which he set out by way of contrast to the formal ("rule-book") version:

> I shall call the second conception of the rule of law the "rights" conception. It is in several ways more ambitious than the rule-book conception. It assumes that citizens have moral rights and duties with respect to one another, and political rights against the state as

a whole. It insists that these moral and political rights be recognized in positive law, so that they may be enforced *upon the demand of individual citizens* through courts or other judicial institutions of the familiar type, so far as this is practicable. The rule of law on this conception is the ideal of rule by an accurate public conception of individual rights. It does not distinguish, as the rule-book conception does, between the rule of law and substantive justice; on the contrary it requires, as a part of the ideal of law, that the rules in the rule book capture and enforce moral rights.[64]

Dworkin insisted that these rights are not themselves granted by the positive law, but are instead in some sense prior to and an integral aspect of the positive law. He avoids resort to metaphysics by identifying the source of those rights in the community. The rule-book "represents the community's effort to capture moral rights."[65] But the rule-book is not the exclusive source of these rights, and the rule-book can be silent or can produce conflicting interpretations. In such instances it is the role of the judge to make the decision which "best fits the background moral rights of the parties" by framing and applying an overarching political principle that is consistent with the body of existing rules and principles.[66] These principles may not be in direct contradiction with existing democratically created rules, but they can go beyond the rules, and they can resolve apparent conflicts between the rules. When engaging in this task judges do not ask what the legislators did do or would have done had they anticipated the problem at hand, but what they *should* have done had they been acting consistent with the political principles underlying the system and infusing the community.

Dworkin acknowledged the obvious objection to his rights conception: it is "often the case" that "it is controversial within the community what moral rights they have."[67] If that is so, how, then, is the judge supposed to formulate the supposedly prevailing political principles? Dworkin does not satisfactorily address this question, resting largely upon the faith that in most cases the application of a controlling principle will be evident, and upon the faith that within liberal societies the basic principles cohere. Scant support for this sanguine attitude can be found in philosophical or public discourse. As the moral philosopher Alastair MacIntyre recently observed, "no fact seems to be plainer in the modern world than the extent and depth of moral disagreement, often enough disagreement on basic issues."[68]

To suggest that society's views on these subjects cohere at the highest level of political and moral principle, such that an answer to each disagreement exists if only the judge considered the issue with enough acuity, fails to appreciate the ultimately contestable nature of the disputes – for example over abortion, affirmative action, homosexual rights, the death penalty – and the heartfelt depth of the opposition involved. Perhaps the most problematic implication of this approach is that it removes important issues from the political arena. These are decisions that must be made by individuals and societies following discussion and persuasion, not matters of calculus to be discovered by the proper hierarchic alignment of pre-existing political and moral principles.

Dworkin's incorporation of individual rights and political principles into the rule of law has substantial anti-democratic implications, the same implications identified in the earlier discussion of judicial review. In Dworkin's approach, final say over the content of rights is accorded to judges, who are told to consult unwritten political principles. When judges are not elected, as is the case with many U.S. judges, this grants to a group of individuals not accountable to democracy the power to impose restraints on democracy. No concern would be merited by this allocation of authority if the content and implications of rights were readily apparent, but often they are not. If the judges consult their own subjective views to fill in the content of the rights, the system will no longer be the rule of law, but the rule of the man or woman who happens to be the judge. Substitute one judge for another with different views, or get a different mix of judges, and the result might well be different. This is patently inconsistent with the idea of the rule of law.

Dworkin denied that judges consult their *own* subjective views of the governing principles but instead (should) seek to find the community's latent or emergent principles. He construed this as democratic in nature, as a furtherance of democracy rather than inconsistent with it.[69] Judicial opinions are a part of public political discourse. The Court, like the legislature, is a political institution participating in and reflecting the political process.[70] Skeptics of this argument point out that it is still the judge's view of the community's principles, which is difficult to separate from the judge's own set of principles. The latter invariably shapes the former. The suspicion that the personal views of the judges have a determinative role in shaping the content of the rights is difficult to repress, especially since judges often disagree sharply among themselves. It is not obvious that there is any other way to understand a right like privacy other than by consulting one's own view of the matter, for there is no acknowledged authority to consult on the societal view.

Finally, it is questionable to construe judges as democratic actors when the thrust of the institutional design establishing the rule of law – specifically the separation of powers and an independent judiciary – is to insulate judges from political forces in order that they may render decisions based exclusively upon the law. Rights are widely understood to be "anti-majoritarian," which is one of the reasons their protection is thought best laid in the hands of the (non-democratic) judiciary. Indeed judges are universally condemned if seen to be acting politically. Dworkin's argument is that this condemnation is merited only when judges base decisions on political "policy" as opposed to political "principle," and the latter is what he advocates as consistent with democracy. But the line between policy and principle, if it can be drawn at all, is permeable and contestable, never mind the difficult question of how to decide from among competing principles and questions of scope.

Conclusion

For the most part this essay has focused on elaborating the liberal political and cultural ideas surrounding the rule of law, and the various doubts about and debates over the rule of law within U.S. legal theory. In addition to providing this information for the edification of the reader, my intention was to encourage that the rule of law be approached with a degree of critical engagement. Its liberal underpinnings might not fit comfortably in all non-liberal societies or circumstances. It has been used – inappropriately – to push an agenda that would promote substantive inequality. It has significant anti-democratic implications, even though it is often identified with democracy. It is not the highest value in the relations among citizens and between citizens and their governments. It must not be forgotten that the rule of law is a *political* ideal. What the rule of law means and how it actually works in a given society are decisions that must be made by and within that society.

Having said all that, I would be remiss if I did not conclude by reaffirming my conviction that, when properly established and adapted to fit local conditions, the rule of law is an essential good of benefit to all societies. The state is an institutionalized apparatus of power. It is not the only such institution in the modern world, but it is a dominant one, and it is an institution that claims to wield power on behalf of, or at least in the interest of, its citizens. Unfortunately there is always a risk that the state, or persons who control the state apparatus, will visit harm on its citizens. The rule of law ideal cannot by itself prevent this from happening, but it does provide a resource with which to resist it. The ultimate inspiration underlying the rule of law is that the state should operate within legal restraints. To the extent that this is achieved, there is little doubt that individuals as well as communities within a society will be better off.

Notes

1 See Jeremy Waldron, "Theoretical Foundations of Liberalism," 37 *Philosophical Quarterly* 127, no. 147 (1987).
2 John Stuart Mill, *On Liberty and Other Writings* (Cambridge: Cambridge University Press, 1989), p. 16.
3 Ronald Dworkin, *A Matter of Principle* (Harvard: Harvard University Press, 1985), p. 191.
4 Jean-Jacques Rousseau, *The Social Contract* (Middlesex: Penguin, 1968), p. 65.
5 Id., at p. 83; Rousseau meant direct, not representative, democracy.
6 See Joseph M. Snee, "Leviathan at the Bar of Justice," in *Government Under Law*, ed. Arthur Sutherland (Cambridge: Harvard University Press, 1956).
7 Berlin, *Four Essays on Liberty* (Oxford: Oxford University Press, 1969), p. 130. Berlin made his famous distinction between negative liberty (private liberty) and positive liberty (political liberty) along the lines of my contrast between, respec-

tively, private liberty and political liberty. To avoid a confusion of terminology, I have not referred to his distinction, informative as it is.

8 Id., at pp. 118–72.
9 Id., at p. 166.
10 Immanuel Kant, *Metaphysical Elements of Justice*, 2nd edn., trans. John Ladd (Indianapolis: Hackett Publishing, 1999), pp. 120–1.
11 James Madison, Alexander Hamilton, and John Jay, *The Federalist Papers* (New York: Arlington House, 1966), no. 10, p. 82.
12 Gottfried Dietze, *The Federalist: A Classic on Federalism and Free Government* (Baltimore: John Hopkins University Press, 1965), pp. 41–102.
13 *Federalist Papers*, no. 51, p. 324.
14 Id., no. 78, p. 466.
15 Id., no. 78, p. 467.
16 *Marbury v. Madison*, 1 Cranch 137, 177 (1803).
17 Hamilton actually opposed the inclusion of a bill of rights on the grounds that it was unnecessary because the government had only limited powers, and out of the fear that listing rights would limit protection to those stated. *Federalist Papers*, no. 84, pp. 512–15.
18 See John Gray, *The Two Faces of Liberalism* (Cambridge: Polity Press, 2000).
19 See Stephen Mulhall and Adam Swift, *Liberals and Communitarians* (Oxford: Blackwell. 1992), pp. 9–33. Ronald Dworkin, "Liberalism," in *A Matter of Principle* (Cambridge: Harvard University Press, 1985).
20 The two most elaborate accounts of this connection are Harold J. Lasky, *The Rise of European Liberalism* (New Brunswick: Transaction, 1997), and C.B. Macpherson, *The Political Theory of Possessive Individualism* (Oxford: Oxford University Press, 1962).
21 Lasky, *The Rise of European Liberalism*, pp. 161–96.
22 See Fianfranco Poggi, *The Development of the Modern State* (Stanford: Stanford University Press, 1978), p. 119.
23 See Max Weber, *On Law in Economy and Society*, ed. Max Rheinstein (Cambridge: Harvard University Press, 1954), pp. 39–40; David Trubek, "Max Weber on Law and the Rise of Capitalism," *Wisconsin Law Review*, 720 (1972).
24 F. A. Hayek, *The Road to Serfdom* (Chicago: University of Chicago Press, 1994), p. 80.
25 F. A. Hayek, *The Political Ideal of the Rule of Law* (Cairo: National Bank of Egypt, 1955), p. 34.
26 Rousseau, *The Social Contract*, supra, note 4, p. 82.
27 Hayek, *The Constitution of Liberty* (Chicago: University of Chicago Press), pp. 210–12.
28 Id., at pp. 207–8.
29 Id., at p. 153.
30 Id., at pp. 212–17.
31 Id., at pp. 214–15.
32 Hayek, *Law, Legislation and Liberty: The Mirage of Social Justice*, vol. 1 (Chicago: University of Chicago Press, 1976), p. 142.
33 Hayek, *The Political Ideal of the Rule of Law*, p. 56.
34 Hayek, *The Road to Serfdom*, pp. 80–111. Although he presses this argument elsewhere, its most concise articulation is still in this initial text. See also Hayek, *Law, Legislation and Liberty*, vol. 2, pp. 62–100.
35 See Gray, *Hayek on Liberty* (New York: Routledge, 1998), pp. 72–5.
36 Hayek, *The Road to Serfdom*, pp. 87–8.
37 Hayek, *Law, Legislation and Liberty*, vol. 3, pp. 41–64.

38 See Robert Unger, *Knowledge and Politics* (New York: Free Press, 1975), pp. 145–90. This account is informed by Unger's analysis.

39 Unger, *Law in Modern Society* (New York: Free Press, 1976), p. 273, n. 11.

40 Id., at p. 192.

41 Id., at p. 291, n. 40.

42 Id., at p. 200.

43 Id., at p. 197.

44 Id., at p. 198.

45 Id., at p. 199.

46 Id., at pp. 200–3.

47 See Michael J. Sandel, *Liberalism and the Limits of Justice* (Cambridge: Cambridge University Press, 1982); Alastair MacIntyre, *After Virtue* (Notre Dame: University of Notre Dame Press).

48 Unger, *Knowledge and Politics*, supra, note 38, p. 220.

49 Id., at ch. 6.

50 An overview of this debate can be found in Brian Z. Tamanaha, *Realistic Socio-Legal Theory: Pragmatism and a Social Theory of Law* (Oxford: Oxford University Press, 1997).

51 The critical literature on this subject is substantial. The articles that helped informed this account are cited below. See Joseph William Singer, "The Player and the Cards: Nihilism and Legal Theory," 94 *Yale Law Journal* 1 (1984); Allan C. Hutchinson and Patrick J. Monahan, "Politics and the Critical Legal Scholars: The Unfolding Drama of American Legal Thought," 36 *Stanford Law Review* 199 (1984); James Boyle, "The Politics of Reason: Critical Legal Theory and Local Social Thought," 133 *University of Pennsylvania Law Review* 685 (1985); Mark Tushnet, "Defending the Indeterminacy Thesis" 16 *Quinnipiac Law Review* 339 (1996); John Hasnas, "Back to the Future: From Critical Legal Studies Forward to Legal Realism, or How Not to Miss the Point of the Indeterminacy Argument," 45 *Duke Law Journal* 84 (1995).

52 There is a sizable body of literature contesting the indeterminacy thesis. The following were the most helpful sources of the points made in the text. Lawrence B. Solum, "On the Indeterminacy Crisis: Critiquing Critical Dogma," 54 *University of Chicago Law Review* 462 (1987); Ken Kress, "Legal Indeterminacy," 77 *California Law Review* 283 (1989); Jules L. Coleman and Brian Leiter, "Determinacy, Objectivity, and Authority," 142 *University of Pennsylvania Law Review* 549 (1995); Steven J. Burton, "Reaffirming Legal Reasoning: The Challenge From the Left," 36 *Journal of Legal Education* 358 (1986); Christopher L. Kutz, "Just Disagreement: Indeterminacy and Rationality in the Rule of Law," 103 *Yale Law Journal* 997 (1994).

53 Singer, "The Player and the Cards," supra, note 51, p. 22.

54 See Owen Fiss, Objectivity and Interpretation," 34 *Stanford Law Review* 739 (1982); Owen Fiss, "Conventionalism," 58 *Southern California Law Review* 177 (1985); Burton, "Reaffirming Legal Reasoning," supra, note 52.

55 Joseph Raz, "The Rule of Law and its Virtue," in *The Authority of Law* (Oxford: Clarendon Press, 1979), p. 214.

56 See Summers, "A Formal Theory of the Rule of Law," 6 *Ratio Juris* 127 (1993); Robert B. Summers, "Propter Honoris Respectum: The Principles of the Rule of Law," 74 *Notre Dame Law Review* 1,691 (1999).

57 Raz, "The Rule of Law and its Virtue," supra, note 55, pp. 220–1.

58 Id., at p. 214.

59 A. van de S. Centlivres, "The Constitution of the Union of South Africa and the Rule of Law," in *Government Under Law*, ed. Arthur Sutherland (Cambridge: Harvard University Press, 1956).

60 See Waldron, "The Rule of Law in Contemporary Liberal Theory," 2 *Ratio Juris* 70 (1989), pp. 84–5.
61 Lon Fuller, *The Morality of Law* (New Haven: Yale University Press, 1964) p. 153.
62 Summers, "A Formal Theory of the Rule of Law," supra, note 56, p. 136.
63 Id., at p. 137.
64 Ronald Dworkin, "Political Judges and the Rule of Law," 64 *Proceedings of the British Academy* 259, 262 (1978).
65 Id., at p. 269.
66 Id., at p. 268.
67 Id., at pp. 263–4.
68 Alastair MacIntyre, "Theories of Natural Law in the Culture of Advanced Modernity," in *Common Truths: New Perspectives on Natural Law*, ed. E. B. McLean (Wilmington, Delaware: ISI Books, 2000).
69 See Dworkin, "Political Judges and the Rule of Law," supra, note 64.
70 See Allan C. Hutchinson, "The Rule of Law Revisited: Democracy and Courts," in *Recrafting the Rule of Law*, ed. David Dyzenhaus (Oxford: Hart Publishing, 1999).

3

RULE OF LAW IN FRANCE

Laurent Pech[1]

Introduction

If the idea of a "rule of law" – as a means to restrain the exercise of political power by subjecting it to certain abstract principles – has ancient roots in Western political thought, the term itself has a more specific origin. It is peculiar to England and, more specifically, to Albert Van Dicey, who defined rule of law in his *Introduction to the Study of the Law of the Constitution* (1885) as "the absolute supremacy or predominance of regular law as opposed to the influence of arbitrary power, and exclud[ing] the existence of arbitrariness of prerogative, or even of wide discretionary authority on the part of the government."[2] Later, this abstract notion was generally understood as a broader concept:

> First, the rule of law expresses a preference for law and order within a community rather than anarchy, warfare and strife. In this sense, the rule of law is a philosophical view of society that is linked with basic democratic notions. Secondly, the rule of law expresses a legal doctrine of fundamental importance, namely that government must be conducted according to law, and that in disputed cases what the law requires is declared by judicial decision. Thirdly, the rule of law should provide in matters both of substance (for example, whether the government should have power to detain citizens without trial) and of procedure (for example, the presumption of innocence in criminal trials, and the independence of the judiciary).[3]

This broad understanding of the concept of rule of law will not create much debate today in France. There are, however, two French peculiarities that must be considered in order to fully understand the modern conception of rule of law and its institutional and legal manifestations in France. First, the term "rule of law," for a long time, was without any equivalent in French legal vocabulary. Second, in contrast to most Western democracies, constitutionalism did not take deep roots in France as no effective constitutional review mechanisms were sought.

The first French peculiarity is the lack of any French expression, until the beginning of the twentieth century, with a meaning similar to the concept of rule of law. It was only then that the term *Etat de droit* – usually used today to loosely translate the term rule of law – became familiar among scholars.[4] However, originally, the French term was only conceived as the literal translation of the German term *Rechtsstaat*, first introduced into French legal doctrine by Professor Léon Duguit in 1907.[5] The main French theorist of *Rechtsstaat* remains, however, Professor Raymond Carré de Malberg, who extensively tried to adapt the German principle to French needs.[6] The close relation of the French term *Etat de droit* to the concept of *Rechtsstaat* requires a brief account of what German legal doctrine understands under this concept.[7]

Although it is customary to consider Immanuel Kant as the spiritual father of the concept of *Rechtsstaat*,[8] the term itself was apparently first used in 1798 by Johan Wilhelm Placidus in his *Litteratur der Staatslehre. Ein Versuch*.[9] This neologism was then popularized by Robert von Mohl, who defined the main objective of a *Rechtsstaat* as "organiz[ing] the living together of the people in such a manner that each member of it will be supported and fostered, to the highest degree possible, in the free and comprehensive exercise and use of his strengths."[10] If this very wide concept of *Rechtsstaat* was much used in the first half of the nineteenth century, its history is quite turbulent. It almost disappears from constitutional doctrine at the end of the nineteenth century, retaining a meaning only in administrative law, where the concept was transformed into a mere principle of legality.[11] However, since the entry into force in 1949 of the Basic Law (*Grundgesetz*), the German constitution, the concept of *Rechtsstaat* has come to be considered as a principle to which all state activity must conform.[12] It has also found a much broader meaning which implies some fundamental organizational principles of the State: separation of powers, judicial review, principle of legality, fair procedure, legal certainty, principle of proportionality, etc. Since 1949, the term *Rechtsstaat* has been widely used both by the legal academy and the Federal Constitutional Court. This success has caused some skepticism and criticism. One major criticism points out the relative and elusive nature of the concept of *Rechtsstaat*. As the Belgian historian R. C. van Caenegem puts it: "the problems...start with the very word."[13] The same is actually true of the concept of rule of law. According to Jeffrey Jowell, "[t]he rule of law has meant many things to many people."[14] Regarding the concept of *Rechtsstaat*, we can indeed question the dogmatic value of such a concept, as it is supposed to imply so many different principles and rules which are guaranteed, on the other hand, by the Basic Law.[15] Hans Kelsen himself questioned the usefulness of the concept of *Rechtsstaat*, as it is redundant with the concept of *Staat* – the term *Rechtsstaat* being, therefore, little more than a pleonasm.[16] With the complex history of the concept of *Rechtsstaat* in mind, it is no wonder that, in France, the concept of *Etat de droit* has had a similarly turbulent history.[17]

Indeed, given the late appearance of the concept of *Etat de droit* at the beginning of the twentieth century – and then only as a literal translation of *Rechtsstaat* – one might wonder whether France was actually a State governed by law. However, one cannot conclude from the absence of such a concept in French legal doctrine that principles of rule of law were not present in France, even if no synthetic term was formulated.[18] It may be sufficient to cite Article XVI of the Declaration of the Rights of Man and of the Citizen of 1789 ("Any society in which the guaranty of rights is not assured or the separation of powers established, has no Constitution") to see that the concept of rule of law was implicitly present, as this Article did in fact equate constitutional government with two decisive components of "a State governed by law": separation of powers, and the protection of human rights. The lack of any term similar to the English "rule of law" or the German "*Rechtsstaat*" may be explained by the centrality and the liberal definition of two other terms in French legal vocabulary: *Etat* and *République*. Indeed, the word *République* has multiple meanings. It can imply not only a government of the people, by the people, and for the people, but also the principles of 1789: freedom, equality, etc. Moreover, for Jean-Jacques Rousseau, "every State governed by law" can be described as a *République*.[19] The word *Etat* is usually analyzed as describing the phenomenon of the submission of political power to law. According to Montesquieu, the State could be described, in its essence, as a "society where you have laws."[20] Given this background vocabulary, the term *Etat de droit* is in a way meaningless, as it is difficult to see what could be meant by a "State" which is not a "State governed by law." In theory, a society where arbitrariness is the only rule cannot have a "State," as the concept of State is identified with a State subjected to law. It can also be added that for Rousseau the words *Etat* and *République* (in its meaning of *res publica*) were absolutely synonymous. The long-time lack of a concept similar to that of *Rechtsstaat* could then be explained by the specific French ideal of the State or of the Republic, whose basic principles are essentially those associated, in theory, with the concept of rule of law or *Rechtsstaat*.

Another distinctive French feature, which also explains the turbulent history of the concept of *Etat de droit*, is that, in contrast to most Western democracies, where the Constitution is the fundamental legal document, constitutionalism did not take deep roots in France.[21] Revolutionary France, for example, went through five constitutions in fifteen years.[22] Since that time, constitutions have had greatly diminished practical and symbolic importance. During the Revolution and the volatile years which followed, the French people experienced a constitutional monarchy, a radical republic, moderate reaction, dictatorship, and, finally, the restoration of the monarchy. Subsequently, from 1814 to 1875, each major political upheaval resulted in a new constitution.[23] Successive constitutions differed signifi-cantly with respect to their treatment of governmental structure and fundamental values. However, a certain constitutional stability has prevailed since the adoption in 1875 of the Constitution of the Third Republic. This political regime endured for 65 years, until the French military defeat of 1940 in the Second World War. After the short-lived Fourth Republic (1946–58), France has lived under the Constitution of the Fifth Republic since 1958.

One explanation for this constitutional instability may be that, unlike the American Revolution, which was one against alleged abuses of public power, the French Revolution was directed primarily against private oppression: the remnants of the feudal system and the power and privileges of the Church and aristocracy, which were protected by the judicial class.[24] Thus, the docu-ments embodying the revolutionary programs and expressing the aspirations of each society necessarily took different forms:

> a Constitution in the United States, with its emphasis on the separa-tion and limitation of (public) power; and a code of private law in France (*Code civil*), based on the principles of legislative supremacy, equality, the personal and economic autonomy of the individual, and absolute ownership and freedom from alienation of property.[25]

From a legal point of view, however, the failure of constitutionalism in France can be explained more fundamentally by the long-time triumph of a dominant conception associating the idea of human rights with the principle of legislative supremacy and, at the same time, a deep distrust of judicial power.[26] This conception precluded any effective judicial review of statutory law. When the concept of *Etat de droit* emerged at the beginning of the twentieth century, it was actually promoted by professors in favor of judicial review of statutory law. Their failure to end the supremacy of Parliament finally resulted in the disappearance of the concept in French legal doctrine until the 1970s.[27] The symbolic starting point of a new influence of the concept of *Etat de droit* was the speech given on November, 8, 1977, by the President of the Republic, Valéry Giscard d'Estaing, in the salons of the *Conseil constitutionnel*, the French constitutional court and one of the major innovations of the Constitution of the Fifth Republic:

> When each authority, from the modest to the highest, acts under the control of a judge who insures that this authority respects the entirety of formal and substantive rules to which it is subjected, the *Etat de droit* emerges.[28]

The newfound success of the concept of *Etat de droit* lies essentially in the fact that with the entry into force of the Fifth Republic the ideas of (1) judicial review of statutory law and (2) the limitation of executive power by courts pursuant to substantive constitutional standards had begun to make much actual headway in France. Since 1958, significant developments, especially the rise of a true judicial review of statutory law by the Constitutional Council, have taken place, elevating the status and importance of the Constitution and constitutionally based decision-making in the political life of the nation.[29] Today, France can be fully described as an *Etat de droit*, if we believe the standard conception of French constitutional doctrine, which essentially equates the *Etat de droit* with judicial review of statutory law in accordance with formal and substantive rules stated in the Constitution, located at the top of the hierarchy of norms.[30]

If the process of establishing the *Etat de droit* was a long evolutionary one (see pp. 000–00), since the entry into force of the Constitution of the Fifth Republic in 1958, the *Etat de droit* became a reality (see pp. 000–00). Today, on the verge of a European Constitution, it also seems necessary to examine briefly how the European Union is subjected to the rule of law (see pp. 000–00).

The long evolutionary process toward rule of law

Although French constitutional thought was quite prolific, Revolutionary France did not succeed in achieving constitutional stability, and, ever since, constitutions have had greatly diminished practical and symbolic importance. The idea of rule of law became synonymous with the concept of parliamentary sovereignty. The *Etat de droit* was thus prevented from emerging by the triumph of the *Etat légal*.

The unsuccessful quest for constitutional stability

Before the French Revolution of 1789, political authority was vested in the person of the king.[31] To sustain the unity of the Kingdom and prevent disorder, scholars provided rationales for strong central authority, at first emphasizing the idea of sovereignty[32] and later, as the monarchy grew in power, particularly during the reigns of Henry IV, Louis XIII, and Louis XIV, the theory of the divine right of kings.[33] According to Jean Bodin, sovereignty is "the distinguishing mark of a commonwealth," and "the principal mark of sovereign majesty and absolute power is the right to impose laws generally on all subjects regardless of their consent." Whereas Bodin accepts the possibility that sovereignty can reside in different persons or bodies, the theory of the divine right of kings, building on the concept of sovereignty elaborated by Bodin, locates sovereign power in the hereditary monarch. Royal power flows directly from God. The royal prerogative is thus absolute and is subject to no limitations except for the obligation to respect the laws of God and nature, the "fundamental laws" of the kingdom, and treaties.[34]

With the clear triumph of the monarchy over particularist internal forces that threatened the existence of the nation as such, as doctrines of *jus divinum* and natural law began to lose their binding character, the problem arose of how to limit royal absolutism. Looking to the English system as a model, Montesquieu, in *De l'Esprit des Lois* (1748), developed a political analysis that focused on the idea of "constitution" as "the indispensable term to describe the fundamental order of a state, the models of political existence of a nation or people, the essential disposition of the elements or powers composing a form of government."[35] More specifically, Montesquieu advocates a constitution based on the principle of separation of powers: "To assure liberty, legislative, executive, and judicial powers must be kept separate." In his view, however, the judicial power is subordinate to the legislative power, as the sole function of the judge is to apply the law, for "the judges of the nation are...nothing but the mouth which pronounces the words of the law; some inanimate beings who cannot moderate either the force or rigor of the law."[36]

While Montesquieu's introduction of the idea of a written constitution into the intellectual mix of the times would prove important during the early years of the Revolution, revolutionary political thought was opposed to giving expression to an existing "constitution," but in favor of a constitution created by an act of sovereign national will and instituted in accordance with abstract principles of political right. Indeed, Enlightenment philosophy promoted an active use of political power aimed at the abolition of the old feudal power and its customary law underpinnings, and their replacement by a new coherent legal order based on the requirements of reason. The fundamental political change brought about by the French Revolution started a gradual process of transfer of sovereignty from the monarch to a new abstract entity. The problem in 1789 was to determine which new abstract entity could substitute the people in place of the king. This new abstract entity was to be known as the Nation. According to Article III of the Declaration of the Rights of Man and of the Citizen of 1789: "The principle of all sovereignty resides essentially in the Nation. No body and no individual may exercise authority which does not derive expressly therefrom." The word "Nation" was used to convey that the sovereignty which used to belong exclusively to the king had now passed to the citizens, i.e. the Nation. Emmanuel Sieyès provided the political rationale for the adoption of such a principle in the first French constitution, the Constitution of 1791.[37] He argued that the people are in fact the Nation and that, in consequence, the people, acting through its representatives, can adopt a constitution and rule the country on behalf of the nation.[38] In this conception, the State is only an artifice, a machine animated by law that is the expression of the general will.

Contrary to what one might think, the idea of the supremacy of the Constitution was admitted in France after 1789. Indeed, Article XVI of the

Declaration of the Rights of Man made respect for human rights and the separation of powers an officially recognized condition of the legitimate exercise of public authority. And, in theory, if the new sovereign, the Nation, retained the right to change the Constitution, it could do so only by following the forms that it had prescribed in the Constitution itself. In practice, however, the French conception of rule of law would not be identified with the idea of supremacy of the Constitution but with the supremacy of the Parliament.

One major explanation lies in the transposition made by the revolutionaries of the providential qualities which Rousseau, in *Du Contrat social* (1762), attributed to laws voted by the people, to laws which were passed by representatives.[39] Rule of law was thus identified with rule by legislation, and the supremacy of law is understood as the supremacy of Parliament. In Rousseau's view, indeed, the law is "sacrosanct." As an expression of the general will, law is enacted by the entire populace for the entire populace and is thus "infallible." Article VI of the Declaration of the Rights of Man actually states: "The law [*loi*] is the expression of the general will." It follows, then, that the law must be applied as written by judges and by administrative and government officials; it may not be displaced by anyone but the sovereign body politic itself. Another factor lies in the "inalienable" sovereignty of the people proclaimed by Rousseau. In his view, the fundamental law can be malleable, since it must express the current will of the people. Consistent with this view, the Constitution of 1793, which was never applied, states explicitly: "A people always has the right to review, reform, and change its Constitution. One generation cannot subject future generations to its laws" (Article 28).

It is no wonder in these conditions that the "representatives" of the Sovereign did not pay much attention to the supremacy of the Constitution. Emmanuel Sieyès' proposal of a *Jurie constitutionnaire*, which would have entrusted the mission of examining complaints brought by citizens for alleged violations of the Constitution to a body of representatives especially selected for this purpose, did not find favor with the revolutionaries. Afterward, no effective mechanisms to defend the supremacy of the Constitution were developed. On the contrary, the French experience has led to caricatures of constitutional review which depreciated the institution. Under the Napoleonic Constitution, the power given to the Senate to void any unconstitutional act, including legislation, served purely political purposes, since the Senate was merely a tool in the hands of the emperor to assert his control over the other institutions of government. The Senate of the Second Empire (Constitution of 1852), though less servile, was not more efficient in its role as judge of constitutional conformity. The last attempt, made under the Fourth Republic (Constitution of 1946), had given rise to a Constitutional Committee which bore a certain resemblance to a court judging the constitutionality of laws, but access to it was very difficult and the Constitution itself formally forbade the invalidation of a text which would violate the rights and liberties laid out in its Preamble.

Finally, it must be said that until the entry into force in 1958 of the Constitution of the Fifth Republic France lived under constitutional systems in which, despite appearances from the texts, there was near absence of a Constitution. Without any effective mechanism to defend the supremacy of the Constitution, France went through numerous political regimes and 16 Constitutions (and even more if one takes into account partial revisions and aborted constitutional projects) in less than two centuries. The rapid succession of different political regimes could only lead to the undermining of the supremacy of the constitution. Political opinion about constitutions became skeptical and disrespectful because, in the end, constitutions changed even more frequently than other merely legislative dispositions.[40] This long-time failure of constitutionalism led to the triumph of parliamentary sovereignty until 1958.

The triumph of parliamentary sovereignty

After the Republican form of government had been firmly established in the Third Republic (1870–1946), rule of law was increasingly conceived as rule of the law made by Parliament. This view could find some measure of support in the Declaration of the Rights of Man and of the Citizen of 1789, which had left the implementation of the various individual rights to the law, and had expressly confirmed its special status as the expression of the general will. As we have seen, this veneration of the law was the result of the tradition of "supremacy of law" derived from the works of Rousseau. According to this tradition, it was inconceivable that the law as expression of the general will could in any way infringe upon the liberties of citizens. Indeed, Article VI of the Declaration of the Rights of Man affirms that the law cannot be harmful to those citizens who have the right "to participate, personally or through their representatives, in its formation." The mere generality of its will also excluded any arbitrary act since the vice of arbitrariness was exclusively associated with the pursuit of individual and group interests. The rule of law was thus achieved if the will of the legislator prevailed and the administration could only act on the basis of its instructions, which implied the strict subordination of executive decrees to legislation. It was therefore no surprise that under the Third Republic and the Fourth Republic, which rested on explicit commitment to the tradition of the French Revolution, the idea of rule of law became synonymous with the concept of parliamentary sovereignty and its corollary, the principle of legality – i.e. the principle that administrative action will be submitted to law.

The supremacy of the law was nevertheless questioned during the first part of the twentieth century in the influential writings of Raymond Carré de Malberg.[41] Although Carré de Malberg's conceptions of the Nation and the State reinforced the notion of the malleability of the constitution, he did not recognize the premise that the law is the expression of the general will. For Carré de Malberg, this premise is merely a legal fiction. And because a law enacted by Parliament is not the expression of the general will but of a political majority, whereas the constitution is brought into force by approval in a popular referendum, legislative acts, just like the acts and decisions of the executive branch or the judiciary, should be subject to the constitution, which is the common source of parliamentary, executive, and judicial powers. Thus, for Carré de Malberg there was, in theory, no obstacle to the establishment of judicial review of statutory law in France.[42]

Let us emphasize, no obstacle *in theory*. Indeed, another essential political feature in France since the Revolution has been the suspicion of judicial power among politicians as well as among legal theorists. This was a result of the negative experience with the royal courts or *"Parlements"* of pre-Revolutionary France, which had not only interfered in the work of the royal administration but also impeded the limited legislative reforms the monarchy sought to introduce by refusing to apply relatively progressive and enlightened royal edicts. Since that time, French political tradition has rested on a rejection of a *"gouvernement des juges."*[43] The idea of a judicial body modifying the will of the elected legislature, and therefore the sovereign will of the people whom the legislature represents, has traditionally been rejected as a distortion of the democratic process and the rule of law. In practice, the revolutionaries prohibited judges from meddling in the exercise of legislative power, either by means of orders denying jurisdiction, or by preventing or suspending the execution of laws. Moreover, in order to exclude encroachments upon the administration similar to those of which the old parliaments were guilty, ordinary courts were forbidden to cite the members of the administration before them for acts done in their offices.[44] The resolution of administrative controversies was instead entrusted to the administrative bodies themselves. The creation by Napoleon in 1799 of the *Conseil d'Etat* (Council of State) and its progressive emergence as a respected administrative court and a guardian of human rights would at least prevent abuses of executive power, in the absence of any effective mechanism to sanction the legislator in such circumstances.

Although the Council of State was finally given the task of resolving difficulties which might occur in the course of the administration,[45] its judicial activity continued to be hampered for most of the nineteenth century.[46] By the end of the twentieth century, however, the Council of State had begun to extend its control beyond formal and procedural requirements to the content of administrative measures. On the basis of its general jurisdiction in litigation involving the administration, the Council of State has succeeded in developing the modern *droit administratif* as a coherent body of rules whose purpose was no longer to shield the use of administrative prerogative from judicial scrutiny, but to regulate and limit its exercise in the interest of the society whose needs and interests the administration was deemed to serve.[47]

The *Conseil d'Etat* saw its role increased even more after the end of the First World War and the resulting ascendancy of the executive branch of government. Faced with a situation where the parliamentary statute had largely lost its function as a precise guideline for the administration in its dealings with the citizen, the Council of State understood that strict adherence to the principle of legality could no longer serve as a meaningful substitute for the rule of law. The Council of State responded to this new situation by recognizing some "general principles of law" (*principes généraux du droit*), which were not explicitly laid down in statutes but could be derived from the republican tradition and the general principles of legislation, as being part of the concept of legality.[48] Their function was to fill the considerable gaps left by the legislature and to protect citizens against arbitrary or illegal acts of the government. Among the diverse sources from which the Council of State derives these general principles of law are "constitutional" documents such as the 1789 Declaration of the Rights of Man and the Preamble to the 1946 Constitution of the Fourth Republic. It is important to recognize, however, that these principles do not owe their binding force to any particular text, such as the Constitution, but are, rather, the application by the Council of State of principles that it deems inherent in the liberal tradition of 1789, in the natural law ideas of justice and equity, and in the necessities of social life. Over time, these principles have come to be associated with the body of jurisprudence of the Council of State rather than the documents of the 1789 Declaration of the Rights of Man and the Preamble to the 1946 Constitution of the Fourth Republic, which were deemed to be without normative value.

The scope of the "general principles of law" is not limited to procedural rules. They also serve to protect a number of substantive fundamental rights, like, for example, the principle of equality before the law,[49] freedom of thought and opinion,[50] or the principle of non-retroactivity of administrative acts.[51] These "general principles" cannot bind Parliament itself, as they were not considered to be supra-legislative principles. Although these principles have retained their function as a safeguard for individual liberties in the Fifth Republic, as we shall see their practical significance has been somewhat diminished by the decisions of the *Conseil constitutionel* on the direct effect on fundamental rights provisions in the Preamble of the Constitution of 1946 and the Declaration of 1789. Though it is at times an unorthodox jurisprudence, the Council of State's activism is generally praised as serving as a control organ that protects citizens against executive regulations by applying principles contained in the Declaration of 1789 and in the Preamble of 1946.

The lack of constitutional review of statutory provisions was not specific to France. It is interesting to note that in Germany the concept of

Rechtsstaat was increasingly defined in a formal way and transformed into a mere principle of legality in the second half of the nineteenth century. One of the major reasons for such a development was the failure of the liberal revolution of 1848–9, and the subsequent renouncement of a Constitution which provided for an elaborate catalogue of fundamental rights and an extensive constitutional jurisdiction of the Imperial Supreme Court. The new doctrine focused on the development of general principles of administrative law which would provide the individual with a sufficient measure of protection against an abuse of powers by administrative authorities. Its main element was the principle that the administration could interfere with personal liberty or private property only on the basis of a specific statutory authorization which entitled it to do so. Decisions taken by the administration in individual cases were subject to judicial control with respect to their legality. The idea of judicial review of statutory law, on the other hand, was rejected by national authorities.[52] In this way, the situation in Germany was quite similar to that in France, where only the Council of State, through the judicial review of the legality of administrative acts, protected fundamental rights from being violated by the executive power.

This lack of constitutional review of statutory provisions was identified by Carré de Malberg as the distinctive feature of the *Etat légal* practiced in France as opposed to the concept of *Etat de droit*.[53] The *Etat légal*, according to Carré de Malberg, is conceived as a means of securing the legislative supremacy of the elected assembly, whereas the *Etat de droit* is designed to protect the rights and liberties of the citizen from the tyranny of the majority. The two principles embody, in other words, two different concepts of law: the democratic ideal of law, and the liberal theory of fundamental rights as an inherent limit to the democratically legitimized exercise of legislative power. Carré de Malberg's conclusion, however, that the *Etat de droit* would not be complete before a constitutional review of statutory laws had been established, remained unheeded for several decades. But, as we shall see, when a real control of the constitutionality of statutory laws was finally established in the Fifth Republic, this was not seen, at first, as a triumph of the *Etat de droit*. Rather, it was perceived as a necessary corollary to the new concept of separation of powers, which strengthened the role of the executive and curtailed the powers of Parliament, namely in the legislative field.

The emergence of the *Etat de droit* under the constitution of the Fifth Republic

By the mid-1950s France was once again in the midst of political crisis. The dominant role accorded to Parliament by the Constitution of 1946 continued to produce short-lived coalition governments that proved incapable of dealing with the pressing problems of the period, particularly those occasioned by post-war decolonization. By the spring of 1958, extreme dissatisfaction with the government, particularly on the right and among the military, made a coup d'état or even civil conflict a distinct possibility. In May, after the resignation of Prime Minister Pierre Pfimlin, President René Coty invited Général de Gaulle to form a government. Général de Gaulle accepted the invitation. On June 1, the National Assembly accorded a vote of confidence to the de Gaulle government, and on June 3 the Assembly enacted a law authorizing the revision of the Constitution. The new Constitution was submitted to referendum on September 28 and was overwhelmingly approved by the people. The Constitution of the Fifth Republic was promulgated on October 4, 1958. There are certain innovative aspects of the 1958 Constitution that should be noted.

First, the Constitution of the Fifth Republic defines the president as the supreme arbiter of national institutions.[54] Although the Constitution, as promulgated in 1958, provided for the indirect election of the president, a 1962 amendment provided for the direct election of the president for seven years[55] by direct universal suffrage. It is significant, however, that the Constitution does not establish a Bonapartist-type government. In fact, the Constitution of 1958 represents something of a novelty in France: it establishes a "mixed" form of government, one which combines aspects of a "rationalized" parliamentary system with a strong executive power. Regarding the executive power, in its practical operation since 1958 this system has resulted in the concentration of governing power in the hands of the president and not of those of the prime minister.[56] Presidential supremacy is usually explained by the stronger legitimacy gained by the president through an election by direct universal suffrage since 1965. Except for three brief periods (1986–8, 1993–5, and June 1997–June 2002), called "*cohabitations*,"[57] the president and the prime minister have been members of the same political party or coalition. At the same time, that political party or coalition would control the National Assembly, which has the last word on legislation. This conjunction of executive and legislative power by a stable political majority has led, since 1958, to an extraordinary concentration of power in the hands of successive presidents. Indeed, in such a scheme the prime minister is the candidate selected by the president before being the chief of the majority at the National Assembly, and the rule of governmental accountability to Parliament loses any useful purpose when the same political majority controls both the executive and the legislative power.

The second innovation of the 1958 Constitution is that it clearly limits the domain of the law and accords significant rule-making power to the executive branch. Article 37 of the Constitution, in particular, states that the matters in which Parliament is competent should be strictly enumerated and limited by the Constitution. For all matters not reserved to the Legislative branch by the Constitution, the executive would be in charge. An omnipotent Parliament and an unstable executive power (a new government every six months, on average) under the Fourth Republic caused the people to call into question the supremacy of the legislative power. Legislation became more and more technical and specific, and thus clearly not the general and timeless expression of natural reason of the "Rousseauian" tradition. Consequently, the law as enacted by Parliament increasingly lost its claim to superior status, and the Constitution of the Fifth Republic illustrated the growing dissatisfaction of the French people with the traditional conception of parliamentary sovereignty.

The Constitution of 1958 would eventually give legal expression to these developments by establishing a mechanism for assuring that Parliament does not overstep its assigned domain at the expense of the executive: the *Conseil constitutionnel*.[58] Created primarily as a watchdog of the legislative branch of government, its principal role was originally to enforce the allocation of competence between the executive and legislative branches. However, within a few years after 1958, the Constitutional Council had magnified its importance by undertaking strict constitutional review of legislation.

Taken together, these innovations in the Constitution of the Fifth Republic represent a manifest departure from the "Rousseauian" tradition of parliamentary domination of both the political and legal systems. But the institution created by the Constitution of 1958 which ultimately had the most significant impact on contemporary French law and ways of thinking about rule of law was the *Conseil constitutionnel*.

Constitutional review of legislation as a decisive step toward the Etat de droit

The invalidation of an Act of Parliament on the grounds that it infringes upon constitutionally protected rights of the citizen is alien to French constitutional tradition. The doctrine of separation of powers, the notion that parliamentary legislation constitutes the authentic expression of the general will, and an aversion to "government by judges" formed a seemingly insurmountable barrier to the introduction of constitutional review in France.[59] The Constitution of the Fifth Republic indirectly undermined these traditional views by creating a *Conseil constitutionnel* with power to determine whether legislation adopted by Parliament, when submitted to the Council for review, is in "conformity with the Constitution."[60] However, as previously demonstrated, according to the drafters of the 1958 Constitution the principle purpose of constitutional review was to insure that Parliament did not encroach upon the law-making domain accorded to the executive branch of government by the Constitution. After 1971, however, this view was no longer relevant.[61]

Indeed, in a landmark decision in 1971, *Liberté d'Association*,[62] which can be called France's *Marbury v. Madison* because of its tremendous impact on constitutional law,[63] the *Conseil constitutionnel* refused to allow the promulgation of a law enacted by Parliament on the grounds that it was substantively unconstitutional. Even though the law in question was within the enumerated parliamentary domain and thus raised no separation of powers problems, in the Council's view it violated a substantive prohibition of constitutional status. The Constitutional Council voided the statute on the basis of the fundamental rights provisions contained in the Declaration of the Rights of Man of 1789 and in the Preamble of the Constitution of 1946. With this decision, the Constitutional Council qualified these two texts as legally binding. Its reasoning was based on the fact that the Constitution's Preamble – which provides that "[t]he French people hereby solemnly proclaim their attachment to the Rights of Man and the principles of national sovereignty as defined by the Declaration of 1789, reaffirmed and complemented by the Preamble of the Constitution of 1946" – is itself legally binding. The Constitutional Council would push its creative reasoning even further. It argued that the reference to the Preamble of the Constitution of 1946 – which provides that "the French people solemnly reaffirm...the fundamental principles recognized by the laws of the Republic" – allows considering liberty of association as one of such fundamental principles.

Prior to the Constitutional Council's decision of 1971, it was never thought that, simply because the Preamble of the Constitution of 1958 referred to the Declaration of 1789 and the Preamble of the Constitution of 1946, those documents were legally binding. In one short sentence ("Considering the Constitution and its Preamble..."), the Constitutional Council not only created a vast body of substantive constitutional law, with all the human rights and principles contained in the 1789 Declaration and the Preamble to the Constitution of 1946, but also laid the foundation for an active definition of "the fundamental principles recognized by the laws of the Republic."[64] Taken together, the sources of law that have "constitutional status" – the Constitution of 1958, the Declaration of 1789, the Preamble to the Constitution of 1946, and the fundamental principles recognized by the laws of the Republic – have become known as *le bloc de constitutionnalité*, i.e. the entire body of rules and principles which have supra-legislative value, any violation of which would cause a statute to be invalidated.[65]

While the *Liberté d'Association* decision established the right of the Constitutional Council to review statutory laws pursuant to a broad set of constitutional standards and principles, it did not extend the Council's scope of review. The significance of the Constitutional Council's review powers was, however, much enhanced by the constitutional reform of 1974. This reform granted the power to petition for judicial review of statutory law – a power that had previously been limited to the President of the Republic, the prime minister and the presidents of the parliamentary chambers – to any group of at least 60 deputies or 60 senators.[66] Article 61, as currently written, thus assures that virtually all legislation can be brought before the *Conseil*, as it is extremely unlikely that the opposition will fail to win 60 seats in one of the two chambers (577 seats for the National Assembly and 321 seats for the Senate) in a nation where political life is essentially bi-polarized.

Since 1971, and essentially because of the 1974 constitutional reform, the *Conseil constitutionnel* has increased and consolidated its role as a protector of fundamental freedoms, and an entire series of statutes have been struck down on the grounds that they violated rights and freedoms.[67] Over the years, practically every freedom, and some principles deemed to be essential in a State governed by rule of law, have been expressly protected by the *Conseil constitutionnel*: the principle of equality before law,[68] legality of crimes and punishments,[69] non-retroactivity of criminal laws,[70] freedom of opinion,[71] freedom of expression,[72] freedom of the press,[73] human dignity,[74] etc. Thus, even beyond the decisive protection of fundamental rights, one of the major achievements of the Constitutional Council's jurisprudence may have been the clear formulation of the principle that the respect of principles and rules of constitutional value is binding on all organs of government, including the legislature. In a 1985 decision, under the influence of Dean Vedel, the Constitutional Council offered a synthesis of what has become the new cornerstone of French public law:

> The law expresses the general will only when it respects the Constitution.[75]

The Constitutional Council's jurisprudence finally put an end to the traditional conception of parliamentary sovereignty. By providing an effective mechanism to control the Parliament but also the executive, the Constitution of the Fifth Republic has insured France a long period of constitutional stability. By protecting the rights and liberties of the people from the legislature, the Constitutional Council gained its legitimacy and France has indeed transformed itself from an *Etat legal* into an *Etat de droit*, where a majority of elected representatives cannot pass statutory laws which are not in conformity with the Constitution. However, constitutional review of legislation still suffers in France from its limited scope.

The limited scope of constitutional review of legislation

France represents one variation of the "European model" of constitutional justice, that of a separate jurisdictional apparatus created for the purpose of adjudicating constitutional questions upon request by political or judicial authorities.[76] According to this model, only the Constitutional Council is empowered to decide constitutional questions. Of course, it is perfectly legitimate not to adopt the American model of constitutional justice, i.e. a unitary judicial apparatus that hears both constitutional and non-constitutional questions. Nevertheless, the French system of constitutional review remains quite limited in scope, even in comparison with Germany, Italy or Spain.

Constitutional review operates only on an *a priori* basis and this is one of the main sources of dissatisfaction. Contrary to the situation of the United States Supreme Court or that of other constitutional courts in Europe, French constitutional review is essentially an *ex ante* review (*contrôle a priori*). It must occur before a voted statute comes into force and, consequently, it is an abstract review: it is not exercised on the basis of an actual case, but consists in an abstract examination of the text of the contested law. The problem is that, in the present system, once a law is in fact promulgated it is no longer subject to constitutional challenge, even though serious constitutional questions may arise in its application. This problem also extends to treaties, which cannot be subjected to constitutional challenge once they have entered into force.

Of course, *ex ante* constitutional review also has advantages. In particular, one major advantage is the certainty it provides as to the validity of a statute.[77] When a statute is passed and appeal made to the *Conseil constitutionnel*, one month later (maximum period of time to render a decision) the French people know if the statute is valid or not. And in a country that has traditionally given great deference to the will of the legislator, *ex ante* review has the advantage of allowing the legislator to revise a law based on the Council's decision, thereby correcting constitutional defects and permitting promulgation of the law.

But one major disadvantage of an *ex ante* constitutional review is that laws not submitted to the Constitutional Council for review may be promulgated even if they contain unconstitutional provisions. Article 61 of the Constitution indeed permits referral of any proposed statute to the Constitutional Council only upon request of national political authorities (the president, the prime minister, the president of either legislative body, or, since 1974, any group of 60 senators or deputies). If these authorities are unwilling, for political or other reasons, to refer a voted statute, it is not possible to challenge the constitutionality of the statute. This is not pure hypothesis. Following the 9/11 attacks in the United States, the Parliament voted a law on public order which was not referred to the Constitutional Council,[78] although it contains at least one provision expressly not in conformity with the Council's past jurisprudence.[79]

Such prejudicial consequences could be avoided if the French system of constitutional review allowed for individual access to constitutional justice or, at least, allowed for the referral of court decisions to the Constitutional Council on the grounds that statutory provisions violate fundamental rights protected by the Constitution.[80] In Germany, for example, the respect of fundamental rights can be enforced by a special individual complaints procedure before the Federal Constitutional Court. In addition, ordinary courts – if they believe the statute which governs the case to be unconstitutional – can refer the question to the Constitutional Court.[81] Consequently, as a last resort, all state activity which has a negative impact on fundamental rights will be subject to constitutional review in Germany. The judicial activism displayed by the Federal Constitutional Court in interpreting the Basic Law and the frequent use of individual constitutional challenges has led to an increasing "constitutionalization" of the legal order. As a result, any kind of human behavior is protected by at least one of the fundamental rights guaranteed by the Constitution against state interference.[82]

In the absence of such individual constitutional challenges, the "constitutionalization" of the French legal order has been less extensive. Certainly, the Constitutional Council has defined, over the years, a comprehensive body of constitutional principles, and its jurisprudence has considerably enriched the protection of fundamental rights in France. Further, according to Article 62 of the Constitution the decisions of the Constitutional Council are binding on all administrative and judicial authorities. Although the *Conseil d'Etat* and the *Cour de cassation* have expressly relied on principles enunciated by the *Conseil constitutionnel* and accepted its interpretative authority,[83] the use of constitutional norms in judicial and administrative adjudication, though of great significance, still suffers from the lack of a possibility for ordinary courts or citizens to bring cases before the Constitutional Council. As an alternative, plaintiffs tend to cite international norms instead of constitutional norms in front of ordinary French courts. This attitude severely undermines the existence of constitutional jurisprudence.[84]

The Constitutional Council itself ruled that it is up to ordinary courts to resolve conflicts between treaties and statutory provisions,[85] while the Council retains the sole competence to resolve, on an *a priori* basis, conflicts between treaties and the Constitution. This jurisprudence leads to a paradoxical result. Based on the traditional prohibition of constitutional review of statutory laws, French laws, once promulgated, are not subject to constitutional control, regardless of whether they violate the constitutional text. However, this basic prohibition can no longer bind ordinary courts wherever French legislation is in conflict with international norms. And, as Article 55 of the Constitution states that international norms prevail over legislation, the result is that ordinary judges must give precedence to international norms over conflicting statutory laws. This is of significant importance in areas regulated by European Community law, where national courts are obliged to give precedence to Community law over conflicting statutory laws, even when more recently enacted.[86]

Given the anomalous fact that neither citizens nor courts can refer cases to the Constitutional Council, whereas any ordinary tribunal can rule, at any time, on the conformity of laws in relation to treaties, it is no surprise that plaintiffs tend to forget about constitutional claims, preferring to press claims that specific legislation violates an international obligation. This trend of appealing to a transnational Bill of Rights in fundamental rights cases has only been encouraged by the entry into force of the European Convention on Human Rights in the French legal order in 1974, and the possibility of referring the decisions of ordinary French tribunals to the European Court of Human Rights since 1981.[87] The authority of the Constitutional Council has also been undermined by the fact that its rulings can now be indirectly overturned by decisions taken by supranational juris-dictions. Indeed, since France is a member of both the European Community and the Council of Europe, its domestic norms, even approved by the Constitutional Council, are subject to challenge by European tribunals such as the European Court of Justice in Luxembourg or the Human Rights Court in Strasbourg.[88]

This trend tends to limit the authority of the Constitutional Council and the usefulness of its jurisprudence. To be more precise, it must be said that ordinary courts can, however, rule on problems of constitutionality pertaining to administrative acts, judicial acts, or acts of private law. Ordinary French judges, after initial reluctance, do also apply today the Constitution where appropriate, and have recognized not only the authority of the Constitutional Council under Article 62 of the Constitution but also its jurisprudential interpretative authority. Still, since plaintiffs tend to focus mostly on international norms, ordinary courts will not apply, subsequently, constitutional norms in individual cases, especially where violations of fundamental rights are at issue.

Nevertheless, one cannot deny that the *Conseil constitutionnel* has today emerged as a major force among French institutions. It should be remembered that, initially, most authorities were in full agreement that the role of the Constitutional Council would be minor, and many were suspicious of an instrument which was denounced as more political than judicial, seeming to serve the sole purpose of protecting the executive from the Parliament. In spite of this skepticism, the Constitutional Council has not been the "docile crea-ture" that some imagined it would be. Since 1971, the importance of its jurisprudence should not be underestimated. By engaging in substantive review of legislative enactments, it has overthrown the revolutionary legacy of the *de facto* supremacy of statutory law over constitutional law. In several decisions of the early 1980s the Constitutional Council solemnly affirmed that all organs of the state, including the legislature, are bound by the principles and rules of constitutional rank, a step which has been hailed by French scholars as the completion of the *Etat de droit* as described by Carré de Malberg.

And, in a constitutional system where members of the same political majority may hold the positions of president and prime minister and the majority in the National Assembly, the Constitutional Council's existence is essential. On one hand, it contributes to the pacification of political life by assuring the opposition that it has the means to make the majority respect constitutional limits. On the other hand, it has the potential to prevent abuse and preserve the rights of individuals. Multiple changeovers since 1981 between right-wing and left-wing political parties have actually reinforced the legitimacy of the Constitutional Council. The Council is attacked for its partiality by different political majorities each time it invalidates an important statute,[89] and public opinion thus retains the fact that the *Conseil* is an essential actor on the political stage and, more importantly, that it is an independent institution and a useful instrument for appeasing political passions.

Having become the guardian of rights and freedoms with which no public authority can interfere, the Constitutional Council is today hailed as an institution which allowed France to move from a mere democracy to a full-fledged *Etat de droit*, and contributed to the noteworthy *"judicialisation"* of politics.[90] The same conclusion can also be drawn for Germany, where the Constitutional Court, due to its wide range of review powers,[91] has in past decades reviewed a considerable number of political conflicts, conflicts that have been conceived in legal terms.[92] In France, as in Germany, the *Etat de droit* or the *Rechtsstaat* are, in sum, shorthand for the concept of constitutional supremacy and of the protection of fundamental rights over any public authority, especially over the legislature. In both countries, the emphasis on the effective protection of fundamental rights as a core element of the *Etat de droit* or the *Rechtsstaat* also has far-reaching implications for the balance of powers between the different branches of government. First of all, it stresses the subordination of the executive to the legislative power by extending the requirement of a statutory basis for administrative action to areas where fundamental rights are at stake. Moreover, it strengthens the hand of the judiciary in the exercise of its review powers concerning administrative action or judicial decisions, by requiring that any measure taken by any public authority interfering with the fundamental rights of individuals – guaranteed by the constitution or international texts – be subject to judicial review.[93]

This is a considerable change, especially for France, where, it should be remembered, since the Revolution the judicial function has been regarded as subservient to the legislative power. In fact, one of the principal goals of the French Revolution was to remove power from judges, or, as Professor Merryman has remarked, "to make the law judge-proof."[94] This post-Revolutionary attitude toward the judicial function has had a long-time demeaning effect on the French judiciary. The entry into force of the Constitution of the Fifth Republic fundamentally altered this conception.[95] In the words of Dean Vedel:

> In reality, there has been a revolution since 1958. But even if it assumes the appearance of the *Conseil constitutionnel*, it is situated outside it and above it. It consists in making constitutional superiority, until then ineffective and purely theoretical, a rule of law meaningfully applied.[96]

This idea of rule of law, or, more precisely, of the *Etat de droit*, is mostly identified in France by the legal academy with judicial review of statutory law by a constitutional court and the *"judicialisation"* of politics. Of course, it can also have a larger meaning. The concept of *Etat de droit* could thus be identified with a whole set of political and legal principles which govern the exercise of public authority in a liberal democracy. This larger meaning seems to be the one influencing the European Union's expansion.

Rule of law on the verge of a European constitution

Speaking about the president of the "European Convention," who is today in charge of preparing a fundamental institutional reform of the European Union (EU),[97] Peter Norman said: "Mr. Giscard d'Estaing will be piloting an untested vessel with an untried crew to a destination that is far from obvious."[98] Indeed, the European Council on 14–15 December 2001 was quite ambitious when it adopted a Declaration on the Future of the EU[99] and established a "Convention" which will bring together representatives of national governments and parliaments, European institutions, non-governmental organizations (NGOs), and the general public. The task of this Convention, which held its inaugural meeting on February 28, 2002, is unique and historical, as for the first time governments and parliaments from both Eastern and Western Europe met together with NGOs and civil society to chart the future course of the EU and perhaps to define a unique Constitution for the EU.[100] Some commentators are actually comparing it with the Philadelphia Convention of 1787, which defined the U.S. Constitution. Not surprisingly, studying the conception and institutional manifestations of rule of law within the EU system will need, in the near future, to be reassessed.

Although the EU has its own legal order, it has neither a formal Constitution nor a formal Bill of Rights, as the final status of the Charter of Fundamental Rights adopted in December 2000 has yet to be decided. Moreover, the EU is neither a new State replacing existing ones, nor is it comparable to other international organizations. Its Member States delegate sovereignty to common institutions representing the interests of the Union as a whole on questions of joint interest. All decisions and procedures are derived from the basic treaties ratified by the Member States. The French Constitution, for example, was amended to integrate the transfer of power to European institutions laid down in the Maastricht Treaty and the Amsterdam Treaty. According to Article 88–1: "The Republic shall participate in the European Communities and in the European Union constituted by States that have freely chosen, by virtue of the treaties that established them, to exercise some of their powers in common."

Although not a "State" in the classical meaning of constitutional law, the EU is said to be based on rule of law and democracy. The European Court of Justice was the first to formulate such an idea by defining the EU, in a

1986 decision, not as a "State governed by law" – it is not yet a State – or simply based on rule of law, but as a "Community based on the rule of law":

> It must be first emphasized in this regard that the European Economic Community is a Community based on the rule of law, inasmuch as neither its member states nor its institutions can avoid a review of the question whether the measures adopted by them are in conformity with the basic constitutional charter, the treaty. In particular..., the treaty established a complete system of legal remedies and procedures designed to permit the Court of Justice to review the legality of measures adopted by the institutions.[101]

In a 1991 opinion, the European Court of Justice reaffirmed its analysis of the political and legal nature of the EU, qualifying the European Economic Treaty of "the constitutional charter of a Community based on the rule of law," which established a new legal order:

> Indeed, the EEC [European Economic Community] Treaty aims to achieve economic integration leading to the establishment of an internal market and economic and monetary union and the objective of all the Community treaties is to contribute together to making concrete progress towards European unity....In contrast, the EEC Treaty, albeit concluded in the form of an international agreement, nonetheless constitutes the constitutional charter of a Community based on the rule of law. The Community treaties established a new legal order for the benefit of which the States have limited their sovereign rights and the subjects of which comprise not only Member States but also their nationals. The essential characteristics of the Community legal order which has thus been established are in particular its primacy over the law of the Member States and the direct effect of a whole series of provisions.[102]

The formula "Community based on the rule of law" is actually the translation of the German term *Rechtsgemeinschaft*, formulated for the first time by Walter Hallstein, president of the European Commission from 1958 to 1967.[103] The term is translated in French by *Communauté de droit*.[104] The European Court of Justice avoided using the classical terms *Etat de droit* or *Rechtsstaat* in order to escape the difficulty of qualifying the EU as a "State" governed by law. The term "Community" indeed leaves open the question of the legal nature of the EU. However, since the Maastricht Treaty of 1992 and the Amsterdam Treaty of 1997, new developments have occurred. Even though the EU is nowhere defined as a "Community based on the rule of law," the treaties expressly state that the EU is based on the principle of rule of law.

For the first time in 1992, the term "rule of law" appeared twice in the Maastricht Treaty. The third paragraph of the Preamble stipulates that, with the Treaty, States confirm "their attachment to the principles of liberty, democracy and respect for human rights and fundamental freedoms and of the rule of law." In Article 11 (former Article J.1), the treaty defines as one of the objectives of a common foreign and security policy: "to develop and consolidate democracy and the rule of law, and respect for human rights and fundamental freedoms." With the Amsterdam Treaty, a third essential provision reaffirms the commitment of the EU regarding rule of law. According to Article 6 § 1: "The Union is founded on the principles of liberty, democracy, respect for human rights and fundamental freedoms, and the rule of law, principles which are common to the Member States." Paragraph 2 of the Preamble of the European Charter of Fundamental Rights, not yet legally binding, also states that the Union is based on the principle of rule of law: "Conscious of its spiritual and moral heritage, the Union is founded on the indivisible, universal values of human dignity, freedom, equality and solidarity; it is based on the principles of democracy and the rule of law."

When looking at the French or the German version of the treaties, it is interesting to note that the term "rule of law" is directly translated by "*Etat de droit*" or "*Rechtsstaat*." However, it is questionable to speak of *Etat de droit* or *Rechtsstaat*, i.e. a State governed by law, since the EU is not yet a State. This theoretical difficulty can only be resolved if Article 6 is construed to mean that the term *Etat de droit* or *Rechtsstaat* does not apply to the EU but to the Member States.[105]

A more fundamental difficulty lies in the use of three national concepts, all of which are deemed to be equivalent. Nevertheless, the terms "rule of law," "*Etat de droit*," and "*Rechtsstaat*" are nowhere defined in the treaties, and national understanding of these terms shows that there is still some disagreement about the precise meaning of a Union founded on rule of law according to Article 6 quoted above, or a Community based on rule of law according to the Court of Justice.[106] The German legal academy seems to understand the concept of *Rechtsstaat* within the EU as a concept which encompasses a large number of principles: separation of powers, judicial review, principle of legality, fair procedure, legal certainty, principle of proportionality, etc.[107] These legal requirements expected from the EU system will not then be that different from what is expected of the German legal system. In France, few scholars insist on the concept of *Etat de droit* at the European level.[108] While not excluding, like in Germany, the recognition of a certain number of principles (principle of legality, legal certainty, etc.) as "constitutional" principles, the concept of *Etat de droit* is essentially identified in France with judicial review of statutory law by a constitutional court. Such a review is quite problematic within the EU system, as the principle of separation of powers finds no application in its original institutional arrangement.

To be brief, it must be said first of all that the EU is built on a complex institutional system that is the result of a difficult bargaining process between the defenders of a supranational scheme of integration for Europe and the defenders of an institutional scheme as the most respectful of national sovereignty. Consequently, the principle of separation of powers is not, to say the least, classically applied. Decisions are taken by an "institutional triangle." In this triangle, the Commission represents the interests of the Union as a whole and it has the sole right of initiative. The main decision-making institution is the Council of Ministers, where each national government is represented. It is up to this Council to enact Union "legislation" (regulations, directives, and decisions). The treaties require adoption by a simple majority, a qualified majority, or by unanimity according to the area regulated. It is actually the Union's true "legislature." Although citizens directly elect the European Parliament, the Parliament does not formally have the power to vote laws, but provides a democratic forum for debate. And although the Parliament can put forward amendments to the "legislation," at most, it can block the decision-making process when in disagreement with the Council,[109] but retains the power to dismiss the Commission by a motion of distrust whereas the Commission is not, in reality, the main decision-making institution within the EU.

To speak of *Etat de droit* in describing the EU is thus difficult in light of its institutional arrangement, as the principle of separation of powers makes no sense in a system where, for example, the "Parliament" has no power to enact legislation. Actually, the European Court of Justice, when referring to the EU as a "Community based on the rule of law," essentially emphasizes the idea that all acts of the Community's institutions are subject to judicial review within a new legal order and that the EU enforces respect for fundamental rights.

Regarding judicial review, the Court of Justice's main task is to ensure that Community law is interpreted and implemented uniformly within Europe and in line with the treaties. The first set of competencies of the Court of Justice is to ensure the supremacy of the treaties over the supranational institutions. For example, the Court may rule that a Member State has failed to act on an obligation under the treaties; review the instruments enacted by the Community institutions for compatibility with the treaties when an action for annulment is brought; and censure any institution for failure to act. The second essential area of judicial review is when the Court of Justice gives a preliminary ruling, i.e. an opinion on the correct interpretation of the treaties or the validity and interpretation of instruments enacted by the Community institutions when requested to do so by a national court. Finally, since the Amsterdam Treaty, the Court can check Community instruments regarding the respect of fundamental rights.

As far as fundamental rights are concerned, Article 6 § 2 of the European Union Treaty specifies that the Union shall respect fundamental rights, as guaranteed by the European Convention on Human Rights, and as they result from the constitutional traditions common to the Member States. Since 1969, however, it is "the general principles of European Community law" which have provided the foundation for the protection of fundamental rights.[110] Indeed, the Court decided in the *Stauder* decision that fundamental rights form part of "the general principles of Community law" that it is required to uphold.[111] Where the European Community intervenes in the protected sphere of a fundamental right, it may neither violate the principle of proportionality nor affect the essential content of that right.

The Amsterdam Treaty has formally empowered the European Court of Justice to ensure the respect of fundamental rights and freedoms by the European Community institutions, thereby extending its powers.[112] In theory, it is solely the European Community which is obliged to respect fundamental rights when adopting acts of secondary Community law, but Member States are also required to respect fundamental rights when implementing Community law.[113] The most widely utilized remedy for the protection of fundamental rights against European Community Acts is found in the preliminary rulings procedure of Article 234 of the European Community Treaty. Also providing protection against human rights violations is Article 230, which gives individuals the right to initiate annulment proceedings against Acts of the Community institutions when they are directly affected by such Acts. If the action is well founded, the Court of Justice declares the challenged Act to be void, with retroactive and universal effects.

Nevertheless, protection of fundamental rights within the European Union is still based on a hybrid system lacking the federative potential of its American counterpart, under which the United States Supreme Court ultimately enforces respect for the same constitutional rules by the authorities of the Union and those of the States, each acting within its respective sphere of competence. Such a degree of coherence could be achieved only if the Member States entrusted to the Court of Justice the task performed by the United States Supreme Court, that of protecting any individual citizen, on the basis of a "federal" standard of respect for fundamental rights, against any public authority of any kind and in any area of substantive law. The lack of such a "federal" standard is, however, not that problematic in a "Community based on the rule of law," in which each Member State is committed to rule of law and the protection of fundamental rights, and in which all the Community's institutions act under the control of the Court of Justice, which insures that the institutions respect the entirety of formal and substantive rules to which they are subjected.

If the term "rule of law" was without any equivalent in French legal vocabulary for a long time, this is not because France was not a State governed by law, but because this idea was more often translated by the terms *République* or *Etat*. In fact, it was not until the beginning of the twentieth century that a specific term would emerge: *Etat de droit*, which was actually the literal translation of the German term *Rechtsstaat*. Within French legal doctrine, until the entry into force of the Constitution of the Fifth Republic the lack of constitutional review of statutory provisions was identified as the distinctive feature of the *Etat légal* practiced in France, as opposed to the concept of *Etat de droit*. The latter is designed to protect the rights and liberties of citizens by subjecting the legislative power to the respect of the Constitution. Since the creation of the Constitutional Council in 1958, France can be fully described as an *Etat de droit*, where each authority, including the legislature, acts under the control of a judge who ensures that this authority respects the entirety of the formal and substantive principles of constitutional value. In France and Germany, the concepts of *Etat de droit* and of *Rechtsstaat* are, in sum, shorthand for the principle of constitutional supremacy and of the protection of fundamental rights from any public authority, and especially from the legislature.

It is evident that today the terms "rule of law," "*Etat de droit*," and "*Rechtsstaat*" form the new creed of political discourse in Western Europe since the collapse of communism in Central and Eastern Europe. For the first time in the history of European treaties, the term "rule of law" appeared in the Treaty of the European Union in 1992, in which the Member States confirmed their commitment to this principle and their attachment to some other indissociable principles: liberty, democracy, and respect for human rights and fundamental freedoms. However, one may wonder if widespread dissemination of the term "rule of law" could possibly result in an even greater lack of precision.[114] The consequential risk associated with such widespread usage is detrimental to the concept itself, especially if used in the form of rhetorical alibi and as a substitute for democracy.

Notes

1 Doctor of Law, Institut d'Etudes Politiques, Aix-en-Provence, Université de Droit, d'Economie et de Sciences Aix–Marseille III. Laurencpech@aol.com

2 Albert Van Dicey, *Introduction to the Study of the Law of the Constitution*, 8th edn. 1915 (Indianapolis: Liberty Fund, 1982), p. 120, quoted by K. P. Sommermann, 'The Rule of Law and Public Administration in a Global Setting', *Introductive Report, Twenty-fifth International Congress of Administrative Sciences*, p. 3.

3 Anthony W. Bradley and Keith D. Ewing, *Constitutional and Administrative Law*, 12th edn. (London: Longman, 1997), p. 105.

4 For a classic study, see Jacques Chevallier, *L'Etat de droit*, 3rd edn. (Paris: Montchrestien, 1999), and for a brilliant comparative study and a comprehensive conceptual analysis, see Luc Heuschling, *Etat de droit, Rechtsstaat, Rule of Law* (Paris: Dalloz, 2002). For a similar study in English of a more concise content but not less interesting, see Rainer Grote, "Rule of Law, Etat de droit and

Rechtsstaat – The Origins of the Different National Traditions and the Prospects for Their Convergence in the Light of Recent Constitutional Developments," in Christian Starck, ed., *Constitutionalism, Universalism and Democracy – A Comparative Analysis* (Baden-Baden: Nomos, 1999).

5 Léon Duguit, *Manuel de droit constitutionnel. Théorie générale de l'Etat – Organisation politique* (Paris: Fontemoing, 1907). See also Maurice Hauriou, *Principes de droit public* (Paris: Sirey, 1910).

6 Raymond Carré de Malberg, *Contribution à la théorie générale de l'Etat*,2 vols. (Paris: 1920–2; reprinted CNRS, 1962).

7 For a general and historical overview, see Ernst-Wolfgang Böckenförde, "The Origin and Development of the Concept of the Rechtsstaat," in Ernst-Wolfgang Böckenförde, *State, Society and Liberty* (New York: Berg Publishers, 1991). In French, see also Olivier Jouanjan, ed., *Figures de l'Etat de droit. Le Rechtsstaat dans l'histoire intellectuelle et constitutionnelle de l'Allemagne* (Strasbourg: Presses Universitaires de Strasbourg, 2001).

8 In his theory of the State, Kant defined the State as the union of a multitude of men under laws of justice. Any lawful State has to be a State governed by the law of reason, i.e. one that is based on the principles of freedom of every member of society, the principle of equality and of individual autonomy. The laws of the State had to preserve and promote these principles. Kant's definition of the lawful state exerted a considerable influence on the liberal constitutional law theories which developed in Germany in the first half of the nineteenth century. For a brief introduction to the concept of Rechtsstaat, see Donald P. Kommers, *The Constitutional Jurisprudence of the Federal Republic of Germany*, 2nd edn. (Duke University Press, 1997), pp. 36–7.

9 Luc Heuschling, *Etat de droit, Rechtsstaat, Rule of Law* (Paris: Dalloz, 2002), no. 32.

10 Robert von Mohl, *Die Polizeiwissenschaft nach den Grundsätzen des Rechtsstaates*, vol. 1 (Tübingen: Laupp, 1844), p. 8.

11 See Otto Mayer, *Deutsches Verwaltungsrecht* (1895–6), translated in French, *Le Droit administratif* (Paris: Giard & Brière, vol. 4, 1903–4).

12 Article 28 § 1 of the *Grundgesetz* states: "The constitutional order in the States must conform to the principles of the republican, democratic, and social state under the rule of law, within the meaning of this Constitution." See Michel Fromont, "République Fédérale d'Allemagne: l'Etat de droit," *Revue de droit public* (1984), p. 1,203.

13 Raoul C. van Caenegem, "The 'Rechtsstaat' in Historical Perspective," in Raoul C. van Caenegem, *Legal History: A European Perspective* (London: Hambledon Press, 1991), p. 185.

14 Jeffrey Jowell, "The Rule of Law Today," in Jeffrey Jowell and Dawn Oliver, eds., *The Changing Constitution*, 3rd edn. (London: Clarendon Press, 1994), p. 57.

15 For a critical study of the traditional understanding of the concept of Rechtsstaat, see Philip Kunig, *Das Rechtsstaatsprinzip. Überlegungen zu seiner Bedeutung für das Verfassungsrecht der Bundesrepublik Deutschland* (Tübingen: Mohr, 1986).

16 Hans Kelsen, *Reine Rechtslehre*, 2nd edn., 1960 (Wien: Österreichische Staatsdruckerei, 1992), p. 314. Through a normativist approach, Hans Kelsen concluded, by identifying the State with law, that "the State of law" does not exist as a particular State-model because every State is a "State of law." See also, in French, Michel Troper, "Le Concept d'Etat de droit," *Droits*, no. 15, 1993, p. 51. If this particular criticism would be difficult to make with regard to the concept of "rule of law," it seems to be more in reason of particular historical circumstances, as John Locke used the term "Lawful Government" in his *Two*

Treatises of Government before the term rule of law became more influential with the work of Albert van Dicey.

17 For an account of the difficulties of the legal thinking in France of grasping the notion of *Etat de droit*, see recently Alexandre Viala, 'La notion d'Etat de droit: L'histoire d'un défi à la science juridique', *Revue européenne de droit public* (2001), p. 673. The author shows that, despite the will to capture the concept on the basis of an approach devoid of any value judgments, in order to explain how the State is governed by law, Professor Raymond Carré de Malberg and Professor Léon Duguit ultimately let themselves guided by their axiological preferences, R. Carré de Malberg by his attachment to the individualistic philosophy of the French Revolution, L. Duguit by an underlying legitimisation of what was later called Welfare State.

18 For a comprehensive study of the French concept of *Etat de droit*, see, recently, Marc Loiselle, *Le Concept d'Etat de droit dans la doctrine juridique française*, doctoral thesis (Paris: University of Paris II, 2000).

19 *"Tout Etat régi par des lois," Contrat social* (1762), Livre II, ch. VI.

20 *"Société où il y a des lois," L'Esprit des lois* (1748), Livre XI, ch. 3.

21 Between 1789 and 1959, in addition to 16 constitutions, France had 21 "semi-constitutional governments" and "*de facto* regimes."

22 Constitution of 3 September 1791; Constitution of 24 June 1793; Constitution of 26 August 1795; Constitution of 13 December 1799; Constitution of 18 May 1804.

23 Charter of 4 June 1814; Charter of 14 August 1830; Constitution of 4 November 1848; Constitution of 14 January 1852, Constitutional Laws of 24–25 February and 16 July 1875.

24 See the classic work of Alexis de Tocqueville, *L'Ancien régime et la révolution* (1856). For a brilliant synthesis about the Revolution of 1789, see the studies offered by François Furet and Mona Ozouf, eds., *A Critical Dictionary of the French Revolution* (Cambridge: Belknap Press of Harvard University, 1989).

25 Martin A. Rogoff, "A Comparison of Constitutionalism in France and the United States," *Maine Law Review*, Vol. 49 (1997), p. 23.

26 See Maurio Cappelletti, *The Judicial Process in Comparative Perspective* (Oxford: Clarendon Press, 1989), pp. 190–8.

27 See Luc Heuschling, *Etat de droit, Rechtsstaat, Rule of Law* (Paris: Dalloz, 2002), no. 392.

28 Quoted by Jacques Chevallier, *L'Etat de droit*, 2nd edn. (Paris: Montchrestien, 1994), p. 128.

29 See the comprehensive and challenging study of Alec Stone, *The Birth of Judicial Politics in France. The Constitutional Council in Comparative Perspective* (London: Oxford University Press, 1992). See also F. L. Morton, "Judicial Review in France: A Comparative Analysis," *American Journal of Comparative Law*, Vol. 36 (1988), p. 89.

30 See, e.g., L. Favoreu, P. Gaïa, R. Ghevontian, J.-L. Mestre, O. Pfersmann, A. Roux, and G. Scoffoni, *Droit constitutionnel*,4th edn. (Paris: Dalloz, 2001), no. 116–18.

31 For an inspired synthesis, see Martin A. Rogoff, "A Comparison of Constitutionalism in France and the United States," *Maine Law Review*, Vol. 49 (1997), pp. 46–64.

32 The classic work on sovereignty is by Jean Bodin, *Les Six Livres de la république* (1576).

33 See James B. Collins, *The State in Early Modern France* (New York: Cambridge University Press, 1995).

34 See the classic work of Jacques Bénigne Bossuet, *Politique tirée des propres paroles de l'Escriture sainte* (1709).
35 Keith M. Baker, "Constitution," in François Furet and Mona Ozouf, eds., *A Critical Dictionary of the French Revolution* (Cambridge: Belknap Press of Harvard University, 1989), p. 481.
36 *De l'Esprit des lois*, Livre XI, ch. 6.
37 Emmanuel Sieyès, *Qu'est-ce que le Tiers Etat?* (1789).
38 Keith M. Baker, "Sieyès," in François Furet and Mona Ozouf, eds, *A Critical Dictionary of the French Revolution* (Cambridge: Belknap Press of Harvard University, 1989), p. 313.
39 See Jean Carbonnier, "La Passion des lois au siècle des Lumières," in *Essais sur les lois* (Paris: Defrénois, 1979). The author mentions, as one of many examples of the new revolutionary "passion" for law, the opening in Paris in 1790 of a *"club des nomophiles."*
40 As Professor Rivero has observed, the rapid succession of constitutions inevitably diminished their value in the eyes of the people, and it was difficult to subordinate the law, which endures, to respect for the Constitution, which passes away so often. See Jean Rivero, *Le Conseil constitutionnel et les libertés*, 2nd edn. (Paris/Aix-en-Provence: Economica–PUAM, 1987), p. 131.
41 See, essentially, La Loi, expression de la volonté générale, 1931 (Paris: Economica, 1984). For a presentation in English, see Alec Stone, The Birth of Judicial Politics in France. The Constitutional Council in Comparative Perspective (London: Oxford University Press, 1992), pp. 23–45.
42 See Eric Maulin, "Le Principe du contrôle de la constitutionnalité des lois dans la pensée de R. Carré de Malberg," *Revue Française de Droit Constitutionnel*, no. 21 (1995), p. 79.
43 For a comparison with the attitude toward the judicial power in the United States, see the classic work of John H. Merryman, *The Civil Law Tradition – An Introduction to the Legal Systems of Western Europe*, 2nd edn. (Stanford: Stanford University Press, 1985), ch. 3.
44 See Article 13 of the Law of 16–24 August 1790.
45 During the course of the nineteenth century, a section of the Council of State, which eventually came to be called the *Section du Contentieux*, emerged as a court of general jurisdiction. See, generally, Lionel Neville Brown and John S. Bell (with the assistance of Jean-Michel Galabert), *French Administrative Law*, 5th edn. (Oxford: Clarendon Press, 1998).
46 According to the doctrines of *"ministre juge"* and *"justice déléguée,"* the minister remained the competent authority to decide upon complaints brought by individual citizens against the administration, and the Council of State, acting on appeal against the decision of the minister, could only present a proposal to the head of state but not pronounce judgment itself. It was not until the end of the Empire and the firm establishment of a Republican form of government that these doctrines were officially renounced.
47 For the text of major decisions and an evaluation, see the classic work of M. Long, P. Weil, G. Braibant, P. Delvolvé, and B. Genevois, *Les Grandes Décisions du Conseil d'Etat*, 13th edn. (Paris: Dalloz, 2002).
48 See, e.g., Y. Gaudement, *Traité de droit administratif*, 16th edn. (Paris: LGDJ, 2001), no. 1,199–1,212.
49 See, e.g., C.E. Sect., March 9, 1951, *Société des concerts du conservatoire*, Rec. 151.
50 See, e.g., C.E. Ass., April 1, 1949, *Chaveneau*, Rec. 161.
51 See C.E. Ass., June 25, 1948, *Société du Journal l'Aurore*, Rec. 289.

52 Only with the Weimar Republic (1919–33), did the idea of constitutional review of statutory provisions re-emerge, and only with the entry into force of the Basic Law (1949) were effective mechanisms actually created. See David P. Currie, *The Constitution of the Federal Republic of Germany* (Chicago: University of Chicago Press, 1994), pp. 6–8.

53 See, generally, Marie-Joëlle Redor, *De l'Etat légal à l'Etat de droit. L'Evolution des conceptions de la doctrine publiciste française 1879–1914* (Paris/Aix-en-Provence: Economica–PUAM, 1992).

54 According to Article 5:

> The President of the Republic shall secure respect for the Constitution. He shall ensure, by his arbitration, the regular functioning of the governing authorities as well as the continuity of the State. He is the guarantor of national independence, territorial integrity, and respect for Community agreements and treaties.

55 A 1999 amendment to the Constitution reduced the president's term of office from seven to five years.

56 The president appoints the prime minister (Article 8), he presides at meetings of the Council of Ministers (Article 9), he can dissolve the National Assembly (Article 12), he conducts foreign affairs (Article 52), he is commander-in-chief of the armed forces (Article 15), and he can exercise emergency powers in certain grave situations (Article 16). From a literal reading of the Constitution, it can be concluded, however, that the prime minister should be institutionally pre-eminent. Indeed, it is up to the prime minister to direct the activities of the government (Article 21), which is charged with determining and directing the policy of the nation (Article 20). The prime minister also exercises the executive rule-making power (Article 21), he may seek delegation of parliamentary law-making power for a designated period (Article 38), and he has the power to initiate legislation (Article 39).

57 From a strict reading of the Constitution, it can be concluded that the Constitution allows *cohabitation*. The constitutional text is indeed quite ambiguous. In a situation of cohabitation, i.e. when the president faces a hostile political majority at the National Assembly, the president has no other choice than to appoint the leader of the new parliamentary majority as prime minister. In these circumstances, Article 20 – which entrusts the prime minister with determining and directing the policy of the nation – finds its literal meaning. See J. V. Poulard, "The French Double Executive and the Experience of Cohabitation," *Political Science Quarterly*, Vol. 105 (1990), p. 243.

58 The Council is made up of nine members, whose terms are renewable by thirds. As a guarantee of their legitimacy, members are appointed by the President of the Republic and those of the two chambers of the Parliament in equal numbers. As a guarantee of their independence, members cannot be reappointed. For a comparative analysis of the functions of the Constitutional council, see Michael H. Davis, "The Law/Politics Distinction. The French *Conseil Constitutionnel*, and the U.S. Supreme Court," *American Journal of Comparative Law*, Vol. 34 (1986), p. 45; Burt Neuborne, "Judicial Review and Separation of Powers in France and the United States," *New York University Law Review*, Vol. 57 (1983), p. 363.

59 See, generally, Georges Vedel, "The Conseil Constitutionnel: Problems of Legitimization and Interpretation," in Eivind Smith, ed., *Constitutional Justice under Old Constitutions* (The Hague: Kluwer Law International, 1995).

60 According to Article 61 of the 1958 Constitution:

Organic laws before promulgation, and regulations of the parliamentary assemblies, before they take effect, must be submitted to the Constitutional Council for a ruling on their conformity to the Constitution. For the same purpose, before promulgation, legislation may be referred to the Constitutional Council by the President of the Republic, the Prime Minister, the President of the National Assembly, the President of the Senate, or sixty deputies or sixty senators.

Article 62 provides that "[a] provision held to be unconstitutional may be neither promulgated nor put into effect. Decisions of the *Conseil constitutionnel* are not appealable. They bind the public powers and all administrative and judicial authorities."

61 This view became irrelevant not only because the Constitutional Council fundamentally increased its role as a guardian of fundamental freedoms, but also because the Council contributed to the reinforcement of the legislative powers of Parliament through a "reading down" of Articles 34 and 37 of the Constitution. See Louis Favoreu, "The Constitutional Council and Parliament in France," in Christine Landfried, ed., *Constitutional Review and Legislation* (Baden-Baden: Nomos Verlag, 1990).

62 C.C., July 16, 1971, no. 71–44 DC, Rec. 29. For the text of major decisions and an evaluation, see the classic work of Louis Favoreu and Loïc Philip, *Les Grandes Décisions du Conseil constitutionnel*,11th edn. (Paris: Dalloz, 2001).

63 George D. Haimbaugh, Jr., "Was It France's Marbury v. Madison?," *Ohio State Law Journal*, Vol. 35 (1974), p. 910.

64 In this matter, the *Conseil constitutionnel* has shown some self-restraint. It was careful only to declare, through this notion, a certain number of rights and freedoms which did not appear *expressis verbis* in either the Declaration of 1789 or the Preamble of 1946, and which were considered as being fundamentally linked to the notion of democracy by the legislator of the Third Republic between 1870 and 1940. In practice, very few nullifications were based on these "fundamental principles," and by the end of the 1980s this reference had disappeared, since Dean Vedel argued that the Constitutional Councilshould rely only on textual sources of constitutional principles in order to demonstrate interpretative restraint and thus solidify its legitimacy. See Georges Vedel, "Le Précédent judiciaire en droit public français," *Journées de la Société de législation comparée*, Vol. IV (1984), p. 265.

65 Louis Favoreu, "Le Principe de constitutionnalité: Essai de définition d'après la jurisprudence du Conseil constitutionnel," in *Mélanges Eisenmann* (Paris: Ed. Cujas, 1975), p. 33.

66 Constitutional Act no. 74–904, October 29, 1974, modifying Article 61 of the Constitution.

67 For an instructive case study in English, see C. Vroom, "Constitutional protection of individual liberties in France: The *Conseil Constitutionnel* since 1971," *Tulane Law Review*, Vol. 63 (1988), p. 265.

68 C.C., December 27, 1973, no. 73–51 DC, Rec. 25.

69 C.C., January 19–20, 1981, no. 80–127 DC, Rec. 15.

70 C.C., January 9, 1980, no. 79–109 DC, Rec. 29.

71 C.C., November 23, 1977, no. 77–87 DC, Rec. 42.

72 C.C., October 30–31, 1981, no. 81–129 DC, Rec. 35.

73 C.C., October 10–11, 1984, no. 84–181 DC, Rec. 73.

74 C.C., July 27, 1994, no. 94–343–344 DC, Rec. 100.

75 C.C., August 23, 1985, no. 85–197 DC, Rec. 70.

76 See Louis Favoreu, "American and European Models of Constitutional Justice," in *Comparative and Private International Law – Essays in Honor of J.H. Merryman* (Berlin: Duncker and Humblot, 1990).
77 For a discussion of the advantages and disadvantages of an *ex ante* review system, see Maurio Cappelletti, "Repudiating Montesquieu? The Expansion and Legitimacy of Constitutional Justice," *Catholic University Law Review*, Vol. 35 (1985), p. 1.
78 *Loi relative à la sécurité quotidienne*, Act no. 2001–1,062, November 15, 2001, J.O. no. 266, November 16, 2001.
79 The new legislation gives the police broad powers to search vehicles in order to fight crime. An identical provision was nullified by the Constitutional Council in a decision of January 12, 1977 (no.76–72 DC, Rec. 31). The Council rejected the law on the grounds that, by giving police virtually unlimited authority to search vehicles, the law failed to provide adequate controls on police activity and violated individual freedom.
80 An amendment to the Constitution was actually proposed in 1990 to allow the two supreme jurisdictions, the *Conseil d'Etat* and the *Cour de cassation*, to refer a "question of constitutionality" to the *Conseil constitutionnel*. The proposal failed due to a political conflict between the president and the Senate. On this project and the proposal to allow individuals to lodge a constitutional complaint before the *Conseil constitutionnel*, see, recently, Louis Favoreu, "Sur l'Introduction hypothétique du recours individuel devant le Conseil constitutionnel," *Les Cahiers du Conseil constitutionnel*, no. 10 (2001), p. 99.
81 According to Article 93(1)4a of the Basic Law, the Federal Constitutional Court decides "on complaints of unconstitutionality, being filed by any person claiming that one of his basic rights or one of his rights under Article 20 (4) or under Article 33, 38, 101, 103 or 104 has been violated by public authority." According to Article 100(1):

> Where a court considers that a statute on whose validity the court's decision depends is unconstitutional, the proceedings must be stayed, and a decision must be obtained from the State court with jurisdiction over constitutional disputes where the constitution of a State is held to be violated, or from the Federal Constitutional Court where this Constitution is held to be violated. This also applies where this Constitution is held to be violated by State law or where a State statute is held to be incompatible with a federal statute.

82 See David P. Currie, *The Constitution of the Federal Republic of Germany* (Chicago: University of Chicago Press, 1994), pp. 8–30.
83 Ordinary courts have no obligation to follow non-dispositive holdings of the *Conseil constitutionnel*, but do so in practice. See Symposium, *Le Conseil constitutionnel et le Conseil d'Etat* (Paris: Montchrestien, 1988); Symposium, *La Cour de cassation et la Constitution de la République* (Aix-en-Provence: PUAM, 1994).
84 See Guy Carcassonne, "Faut-il maintenir la jurisprudence issue de la décision no. 74–54 DC du 15 janvier 1975?," *Les Cahiers du Conseil constitutionnel*, no. 7 (1999).
85 C.C., January 15, 1975, no. 74–54 DC, Rec. 19.
86 See Cass. ch. mixte, May 24, 1975, *Administration des Douanes v. Société Cafés Jacques Vabre, Recueil Dalloz* (1975), p. 497, concl. Touffait. Traditionally, the *Cour de Cassation* had no power whatsoever to refuse to apply a law enacted by Parliament. See also, regarding the principle of supremacy of European Community law, C.E. Ass., October 20, 1989, *Nicolo*, Rec. 190.

87 See Guy Scoffoni, "The influence of the European Convention on Human Rights on the National Law of a Member State," *Journal of Chinese and Comparative Law*, Vol. 2 (1996), p. 21.
88 See the decision of the European Court of Human Rights, *Zielinski & Pradal v. France*, October 29, 1999, Rec. 1999–VII.
89 For decisions invalidating statutes which were deemed essential for the left-wing majority and severe criticism: C.C., January 16, 1982, no. 81–132 DC, Rec. 18 (nationalization of private firms); C.C., October 10–11, 1984, no. 84–181 DC, Rec. 73 (regulation of the press). For decisions invalidating statutes which were deemed essential for the new right-wing majority: C.C., September 19, 1986, no. 86–217 DC, Rec. 141 (regulation of audiovisual sector); C.C., August 13–14, 1993, no. 93–325 DC, Rec. 224 (immigration law).
90 Louis Favoreu, "De la Démocratie à l'Etat de droit," *Le Débat*, no. 64 (1991), pp. 158–62.
91 The constitutional rules are enforced by the Federal Constitutional Court, which not only acts as a court of last instance in fundamental rights cases, but is also competent for the adjudication of all sorts of disputes between the different organs of government (Article 93(1)1a) and the review of the constitutionality of parliamentary statutes (see Article 93(1)2).
92 See Rainer Grote, "Rule of Law, Etat de Droit and Rechtsstaat – The Origins of the Different National traditions and the Prospects for their Convergence in the Light of Recent Constitutional Developments," in Christian Starck, ed., *Constitutionalism, Universalism and Democracy – A Comparative Analysis* (Baden-Baden: Nomos, 1999).
93 Article 19(4) of the German Basic Law provides that, "[s]hould any person's rights be violated by public authority, recourse to the court is open to him. Insofar as no other jurisdiction has been established, recourse is available to the courts of ordinary jurisdiction." The French Constitution does not expressly formulate such a principle. The Constitutional Council, however, has recognized it as a "fundamental principle recognized by the laws of the Republic." See C.C., January 23, 1987, no. 86–224 DC, Rec. 8.
94 John H. Merryman, "The French Deviation," *American Journal of Comparative Law*, Vol. 44 (1996), p. 109.
95 Constitutional review is still sometimes identified with an illegitimate "government of judges." For a discussion of such an identification: See Séverine Brondel, Norbert Foulquier, and Luc Heuschling, eds., *Gouvernement des juges et démocratie* (Paris: Publications de la Sorbonne, 2001).
96 Georges Vedel, "Le Précédent judiciaire en droit public français," *Journées de la Société de législation comparée*, Vol. IV (1984), p. 288, translated and quoted by C. Vroom, "Constitutional Protection of Individual Liberties in France: The *Conseil Constitutionnel* since 1971," *Tulane Law Review*, Vol. 63 (1988), p. 334.
97 The Maastricht Treaty, which was signed in 1992, created the European Union, a concept comprising the European Communities (which was amended to the term "European Community" on the same occasion), as well as other forms of cooperation.
98 *Financial Times*, February 25, 2002. See Research Paper, *The Laeken Declaration and the Convention on the Future of Europe*, no. 02/14, House of Commons, 8 March 2002, http://www.parliament.uk/.
99 According to this declaration, four areas of reform have to be considered in order to prepare the next reform of the EU in 2004. The four areas are: a more precise delimitation of competencies between the EU and the Member States in accordance with the subsidiarity principle; the status of the Charter of Fundamental Rights; simplification of the Treaties to make them clearer and

more accessible; and the role of national parliaments in the European architecture. The declaration also allowed for a wider agenda by establishing a "Convention" whose purpose is "to consider the key issues arising for the Union's future development and try to identify the various possible responses."

100 A "Future of Europe Web-Site" has been opened: see http://www.europa.eu.int/futurum/. It includes a Citizens Discussion Forum, to which written contributions are welcome.

101 E.C.J., April 23, 1986, *Les Verts v. Parliament*, 294/83, Rec. 1339, § 23. With this decision, the European Court of Justice extended its competencies under Article 173 of the Treaty of Rome to review decisions of the Parliament, whereas Article 173 was only providing expressly for such a review regarding decisions of the Council and of the Commission.

102 E.C.J., December 14, 1991, *Opinion 1/91*, C–1/91, Rec. I–6079, § 1.

103 M. Zuleeg, "Die Europäische Gemeinschaft als Rechtsgemeinschaft," *Neue juristische Wochenschrift* (1994), p. 546, quoting Walter Hallstein, *Die Europäische Gemeinschaft*,5th edn. (Dusseldorf: Econ-Verlag, 1979), p. 51.

104 See, recently, Joël Rideau, ed., *De la Communauté de droit à l'Union de droit* (Paris: LGDJ, 2000).

105 This interpretation seems to be in conformity with the treaty in Article 7 and Article 49, which only provide for some actions against States which do not respect the principles mentioned in article 6 § 1. Article 7 of the European Union Treaty enables the Council to take measures against Member States (suspension of certain rights of the Member State concerned) when there is a serious and persistent breach by a Member State of principles mentioned in Article 6 § 1. Article 49 also provides that any European State wishing to become a Member of the Union must respect the principles on which the Union is founded.

106 For an analysis insisting on the genealogical link between the concepts of *Etat de droit*, *Rechtsstaat*, rule of law, and the European concept of "Community based on the rule of law," see D. Simon, *Le Système juridique communautaire*, 2nd edn. (Paris: PUF, 1998), pp. 50–5.

107 For a synthesis, see Delf Buchwald, "Zur Rechtsstaatlichkeit der Europäischen Union," *Der Staat* (1998), p. 189; Helmut Schmitt von Sydow, "Liberté, démocratie, droits fondamentaux et Etat de droit: Analyse de l'Article 7 du traité UE," *Revue du droit de l'Union européenne* (2001), p. 292.

108 For a synthesis, see Luc Heuschling, *Etat de droit, Rechtsstaat, Rule of Law* (Paris: Dalloz, 2002), no. 312.

109 See Article 251 of the European Community Treaty. The so-called "co-decision procedure" was introduced by the Maastricht Treaty and provides for two successive readings, by Parliament and the Council, of a Commission proposal; and the summons, if the two "co-legislators" cannot agree, of a "conciliation committee" in order to reach an agreement. This agreement is then submitted to Parliament and the Council for a third reading with a view to its final adoption. If the Parliament rejects the agreement, no text can be adopted.

110 The Court's creation of a Community human rights doctrine is often explained as motivated by a wish to protect the well-established, but sometimes challenged, ambition of Community law to reign supreme over any norm of national law, including constitutional human rights norms. The idea is that the Court could not expect full respect for the supremacy principle from national courts unless acts of the Community institutions were subject to human rights review by the Court.

111 E.C.J., November 12, 1969, *Stauder v. Ulm*, 29/69, Rec. 419.

111

112 Article 46 (formerly Article L) of the EU Treaty has been amended to extend the powers of the Court of Justice to cover Article 6 § 2 (formerly Article F.2) of the Treaty, as far as action by the European institutions is concerned.

113 E.C.J., May 29, 1997, *Kremzow v. Austrian Republic*, C–299/95, Rec. I–2629.

114 See Jacques Chevallier, "La Mondialisation de l'Etat de droit," in *Mélanges Phillipe Ardant* (Paris: LGDJ, 1999), p. 325.

4

COMPETING CONCEPTIONS
OF RULE OF LAW IN CHINA

Randy Peerenboom

In 1996 Jiang Zemin adopted the new *tifa,* or official policy formulation, of ruling the country in accordance with law and establishing a socialist rule of law state (*yifa zhiguo, jianshe shuhui zhuyi fazhiguo*), which was subsequently incorporated into the Constitution in 1999. However, while China's leaders have officially endorsed rule of law, they have not sanctioned the liberal democratic version. Significantly, there is relatively little support for liberal democracy, and hence a liberal democratic rule of law, among state leaders, legal scholars, intellectuals, or the general public. On the contrary, study after study shows most people are more concerned about stability and economic growth than democracy and civil and political liberties.[1]

Accordingly, if we are to understand the likely path of development of China's legal system, and the reasons for differences in its institutions, rules, practices, and outcomes in particular cases, we need to rethink rule of law.[2] We need to theorize rule of law in ways that do not assume a liberal democratic framework, and explore alternative conceptions of rule of law that are consistent with China's own circumstances.

To that end, I describe four competing thick conceptions of rule of law: Statist Socialism, Neo-Authoritarian, Communitarian and Liberal Democratic. In contrast to Liberal Democratic rule of law, Jiang Zemin and other Statist Socialists endorse a state-centered socialist rule of law defined by, *inter alia*, a socialist form of economy (which in today's China means an increasingly market-based economy but one in which public ownership still plays a somewhat larger role than in other market economies); a non-democratic system in which the Party plays a leading role; and an interpretation of rights that emphasizes stability, collective rights over individual rights, and subsistence as the basic right rather than civil and political rights.

There is also support for various forms of rule of law that fall between the Statist Socialism type championed by Jiang Zemin and other central leaders and the Liberal Democratic version. For example, there is some support for a democratic but non-liberal (New Confucian) Communitarian variant built on market capitalism, perhaps with a somewhat greater degree of government intervention than in the liberal version; some genuine form of multiparty democracy in which citizens choose their representatives at all levels of government; plus an "Asian values" or communitarian interpretation of rights that attaches relatively greater weight to the interests of the majority and collective rights as opposed to the civil and political rights of individuals.[3]

Another variant is a Neo-authoritarian or Soft Authoritarian form of rule of law that like the Communitarian version rejects a liberal interpretation of rights but unlike its Communitarian cousin also rejects democracy. Whereas Communitarians adopt a genuine multiparty democracy in which citizens choose their representatives at all levels of government, Neo-authoritarians permit democracy only at lower levels of government or not at all.[4]

Historical and institutional overview

A brief and necessarily simplified overview of China's legal history and the current political, economic, and legal systems will help situate the ensuing discussion of the four dominant thick conceptions of rule of law in China today, and highlight the extent to which it would be a major achievement for China to implement any thick version of rule of law that complies with the requirements of a thin rule of law.[5]

Classical theories of law were dominated by Confucianism and Legalism. Confucians believed that law should play a complementary role to morality and virtuous rulers as a means of governing. Legal punishments might alter people's behavior, but they could not change people's character and produce the kind of person required to realize a harmonious society in which each person flourished in community with others. Moreover, generally applicable laws were incapable of providing the fine-toothed, context-specific resolutions required to ensure substantive justice and to maintain harmony.

In contrast, Legalists believed the Confucian system was nothing more than "rule of man" (*ren zhi*).The Confucian sage determined what was best in a given situation based on his own judgment rather than by appeal to fixed standards or laws of general applicability. In response, the Legalists advocated clearly codified, publicly promulgated laws applicable to commoner and noble man alike. While advocating the impartial application of publicly codified laws, Legalism was hardly rule of law in the contemporary sense, which, at minimum, refers to legal limits on the ruling elite. Rather, the Legalist *fa zhi* is better understood as rule *by* law. Law was simply a pragmatic tool for obtaining and maintaining political control and social order. While constrained to some extent by moral norms and social expectations, the ruler remained the ultimate authority, both in theory and in practice. In the final analysis, law was what pleased the ruler. Accordingly, the ruler retained the authority to promulgate and change laws, and remained above and beyond the law.

The Imperial legal system combined Confucian and Legalist elements. As such, it reflected their inherent weaknesses. It failed to provide effective restraints, particularly institutionalized legal restraints, on the power of the ruler. Moreover, law was seen as a tool to serve the interests of the state, and thus the system failed to adequately address the need to protect individuals against the state. The shortcomings of the system led to a reform movement at the end of the Qing. A number of reformers advocated learning from the West, and showed particular interest in Western legal systems and the notions of rule of law, constitutionalism and human rights. Several concrete steps were taken to improve the legal system. China drafted its first constitution in the early 1900s. It adopted legal codes modeled on statutes primarily from Germany and Japan, and sought to modernize the judiciary by restructuring the courts (including the establishment of administrative courts) and increasing the professionalism of judges and the newly established private bar. Unfortunately, such reforms could not take root during the turbulent Republic period, and thus the first wave of legal globalization had little lasting impact.

During the Mao period, the legal system served primarily as a handmaiden to politics. As in earlier periods, law was conceived of as an instrument to strengthen a paternalistic state. The purpose of law was to serve the state, not to protect individual rights. There was little if any separation between law and politics. There was neither an independent judiciary nor an autonomous legal profession. Most important, there were no effective legal limits on state power, particularly the power of the ruler and the ruling elite. Although a number of laws were administrative in nature, the purpose of such laws was to enhance government efficiency and to ensure that lower-level government officials obeyed the ruler's orders or central Party dictates, whether in the form of law or of policies. There were few legal channels for citizens to challenge government decisions, and there was little opportunity for public participation in the lawmaking, interpretation, or implementation processes.

Since Mao's death in 1976, China has undertaken unprecedented economic, political, and legal reforms. The drive to implement rule of law has received wide support from various groups. For China's rulers, many of whom suffered under the arbitrary rule of Mao, the dangers of unlimited government were readily apparent. The leaders' desire for legitimacy both at home and abroad mandates that the government be held accountable for its actions. In particular, the problem of corruption within the government has eroded support for the Chinese Communist Party (CCP). Perhaps most importantly, economic reforms require a more predictable and accountable administration. Clearly, the ruling regime sees administrative law as a way to rationalize governance, enhance administrative efficiency, and rein in local governments. At the other end of the spectrum, rule of law responded to people's demands for greater protection of their rights and interests. As economic reforms progressed, people began to have more property and business interests to protect.

115

One of the main theoretical and practical issues in establishing rule of law has been how to reconcile the leading role of the Party with the basic rule of law principle of the supremacy of law. Theoretically, the issue has been resolved by allowing the CCP to set the general direction for society while requiring that the Party's policies must be translated into law to be legally binding. Moreover, both the state and CCP constitutions provide that the Party and individual Party members are bound by law. In practice, however, many of the Party's powers and actions lack a clear legal basis and in some cases they are at odds with the law. Given the differences between single-party socialism and democracy, the role of the Party as the leading party will clearly be different than in liberal democratic rule of law states. One of the challenges for rule of law in China is to define more clearly what an acceptable role for the Party would be consistent with general requirements of a thin rule of law. Of course, an arguably more difficult task is to ensure that the Party then complies with that role and acts within the acceptable limits of law.

In any event, many of the most pressing obstacles for the implementation of rule of law have nothing to do with the Party. Rather, they are institutional in nature. In the current constitutional structure, the National People's Congress (NPC) is the highest state organ. It is responsible for supervising the executive branch, judiciary, procuracy, and military (which has not been an independent source of authority or instability). As in other parliamentary supreme states, there is no separation of powers in the American sense of three constitutionally equal and independent branches, though the judiciary and executive do have functional independence within their respective spheres. Unlike in democratic parliamentary supreme states, people's congress delegates are not directly elected, and are subject to a *nomenklatura* system of Party approval. Nevertheless, the Party's diminished role in the lawmaking process and even more minimal role in the process of creating lower-level regulations has shifted the responsibility for the making of laws and regulations to the NPC, local people's congresses, governments, and administrative agencies. Thus, people's congresses have become increasingly independent, professional, and powerful. However, the lawmaking and rulemaking processes still lack transparency, and opportunities for public participation are limited, notwithstanding some improvements since 1978. The quality of much legislation remains low, in part due to the lack of practical experience and competence of drafters. Laws and regulations are subject to frequent change. Even more worrisome, there is a shockingly high incidence of inconsistency between lower and superior legislation.

In general, the courts are plagued by problems of limited competence of judges, the lack of independence, and limited authority and powers. Many judges are poorly trained, and judicial corruption is widespread and threatens to undermine the legitimacy of the system. Judges are subject to approval by the Party, and Party organs continue to play a role in setting general policies for the courts. However, Party organs are rarely involved directly in deciding the outcomes of specific cases. Rather, interference by government officials motivated by local protectionism is much more common.[6] The courts inability to fend off local officials is structural in nature: local people's congresses select judges and local governments fund the courts, including not only judicial salaries but more discretionary items such as housing and other welfare benefits. The problems with judicial incompetence and corruption have given rise to calls for more external supervision by people's congresses and the procuracy. While such supervision is justified on grounds of judicial accountability, it undermines the already fragile independence and authority of the courts. As in civil law countries, courts have limited power to make or interpret law. The courts' limited authority to conduct judicial review and in particular the inability to overturn abstract acts (generally applicable laws and regulations) that are inconsistent with higher legislation exacerbate the aforementioned legislative inconsistency problems. Moreover, there is still no effective mechanism for constitutional review, although various proposals for some form of constitutional review court or body have been debated for years.

The legal profession has made remarkable strides in terms of both numbers and quality. However, on the whole the profession is still plagued by both quantitative (particularly in rural areas) and qualitative shortcomings. Many lawyers have received little if any formal legal training, though recent changes have raised the standards and now require a four-year degree in law and passage of a unified national exam for lawyers, procuratorates, and judges. The legal profession also suffers from problems with corruption and professional responsibility, despite the passage of a code of ethics and ongoing efforts by the Ministry of Justice to emphasize professional responsibility.

As for the administrative law system, whereas in the past the purpose of administrative law was considered to be to facilitate efficient government and ensure that government officials and citizens alike obey central policies, administrative law is now understood to entail a balancing of government efficiency with the need to protect individual rights and interests. Moreover, China has established institutions and mechanisms for reining in the bureaucracy similar to those in countries known for rule of law, including legislative oversight committees, supervision committees that are the functional equivalent of ombudsmen, internal administration reconsideration procedures, and judicial review. At the level of legal doctrine, China has passed a number of laws that not only resemble but are modeled on laws from other countries. Even in the area of outcomes there are signs of convergence with the legal systems of Western countries, albeit rather limited convergence.[7]

Despite convergence with respect to goals, institutions, mechanisms for checking administrative discretion, and legal doctrines, China's administrative law regime produces comparatively suboptimal results because of a variety of context-specific factors. Although some of the troubles are specific to the administrative law system – such as loopholes or shortcomings in particular laws – most of the problems have little to do with the administrative law system as such. Rather, the system is undermined by deficiencies in the legislative system, a weak judiciary, poorly trained judges and lawyers, and general problems such as a relatively low level of legal consciousness among the citizenry, many of whom are afraid to challenge government officials.

Without doubt, China has made considerable progress in establishing a legal system that meets the requirements of a thin rule of law. Nevertheless, a number of obstacles remain. Many of the legal reforms have involved passing legislation based on foreign models or attempting to establish similar institutions and mechanisms for making, interpreting, and implementing law. Such attempts at legal transplants always give rise to issues of compatibility with indigenous traditions and conditions. The problems are perhaps more severe in China's case given the fundamental differences between its philosophical traditions and contemporary liberalism and the differences between a single-party state and a democratic one. Thus, many scholars in the People's Republic of China (PRC) have questioned whether rule of law, and especially a liberal democratic version of rule of law, will take root in China's very different soil.[8] What is needed, they suggest, is an indigenous theory of rule of law – rule of law with Chinese characteristics – one that takes into consideration China's native resources and China's particular circumstances, its culture, traditions and history, as well as other such contingent factors as ideology, the current stage of development of its legal and political institutions, and the fact that China is still in the midst of a dramatic transition from a centrally planned economy to a more market-oriented one. Others argue that what is needed is an explicitly socialist theory of rule of law.[9] In short, while there is little disagreement over the elements of a thin theory of rule of law or its desirability, there is considerably more debate over thick conceptions of rule of law.

Four ideal types: Statist Socialist, Neo-authoritarian, Socialist, Neo-authoritarian, Communitarian, Liberal Democratic

Given the wide variety of political beliefs and conceptions of a just socio-political order, it is in theory possible to categorize thick rule of law theories in a number of ways. In order to facilitate discussion, however, I have divided PRC views into four schools: Statist Socialist; Neo-authoritarian, Communitarian and Liberal Democratic. A few preliminary observations about these conceptions may help avoid misunderstandings.

First, a full elaboration of any of these types requires a more detailed account of the purposes or goals the regime is intended to serve and its institutions, practices, rules, and outcomes, as provided in the rest of the chapter and more fully elsewhere.[10] Second, these four ideal types were constructed with the present realities of China in mind. For instance, I attribute to Statist Socialism a belief in a market economy. This is not to rule out the possibility of a Statist Socialist rule of law that adopts a centrally planned economy. However, China can no longer be described in such terms. My purpose is not to create an exhaustive set of categories that can be applied to all countries and legal systems, or even all Asian countries. The categories may not be applicable at all to other countries, or, even if applicable in a general sense, they may need to be redefined in light of the particular circumstances and issues.

Nor are these categories exhaustive with respect to China. For instance, given the wide regional differences and the importance of religion and non-Han values in some areas such as Tibet and Xinjiang, a form of semi-religious rule of law might be more appropriate. Moreover, the ideal types could be further subdivided. Thus, Communitarian rule of law could come in a more statist "Asian values" version, a pragmatic New Confucian version or a Deweyan civic republicanism version that assumes much of the value structure and institutional framework of a liberal democratic order.[11] Indeed, one could create an ever-expanding taxonomy by making finer specifications of any of the variables or introducing new ones. However, at some point, one begins to lose the forest for the trees.[12] For present purposes, these four types are sufficient to capture the main differences in the dominant prevailing political and legal views.

The four variants are ideal types in the sense that they are representative models. As such, they are intended to reflect real positions. It is therefore possible to identify schools of thought and individuals that fall into each of the categories.[13] At the same time, they are a distillation of the views of many different individuals, drawn from not only written sources but thousands of conversations with scholars, legal academics, judges, lawyers, and citizens over the years.[14] Consequently, no one type may fit exactly the position of any one person or group. For instance, while most New Conservatives would support Neo-Authoritarianism, some might favor Statist Socialism or Communitarianism.[15] Others might not fit easily into any category, but rather endorse elements from different schools. Moreover, although certain individuals may have expressed general support for some of the central tenets of the various ideal types, they will not have addressed all of the specific issues that I address. At times, therefore, the positions attributed to their variant of rule of law are a logical extension of their ideas based on inferences from their general principles.

Each of the various types is compatible with a variety of institutions, practices, rules and, to some extent, outcomes. Within Western Liberal Democratic legal orders, for example, there is considerable variation along each of these dimensions. Take such a basic issue as separation of powers. In the U.S., separation of powers refers to a system in which the legislature, executive, and judiciary are constitutionally independent and equal branches. In contrast, the U.K. and Belgium, among others, are parliamentary supreme states. On the other hand, despite these structural differences, no country – not even the U.S. – adheres to the simplistic separation of powers where the legislature passes laws, the executive implements them and the courts interpret and enforce them by adjudicating disputes. For better or worse, administrative agencies everywhere make, implement, and adjudicate laws.

Similarly, some liberal states have written constitutions; others, such as the U.K., do not. Some are common law systems; others are civil. Civil law countries tend to prefer broadly drafted laws; common law countries more narrowly drafted laws. In some liberal states, judges are elected; in others, judges are appointed; in still others, some judges are elected and some are appointed. In some, the legal profession is self-regulating; in others, the legal profession is subject to supervision by a government body such as the Ministry of Justice.

Conversely, different regimes may share similar purposes, institutions, practices, and rules. Given a general consensus on the purposes and elements of a thin theory, one would expect, of course, a certain amount of convergence in institutions, practices, and rules. For instance, in order to enhance predictability and limit government arbitrariness, China has established many of the same mechanisms for controlling administrative discretion as have other regimes. It has also enacted a number of administrative laws modeled on comparable laws in the U.S. and Europe.

Notwithstanding the wide variation within particular regime types on the one hand and the overlap among different regime types on the other, the ideological differences that underlie different thick conceptions of rule of law tend to be reflected in variations in institutional arrangements, practices, rules and, most importantly, in outcomes. Indeed, even were China to import wholesale the institutions and legal doctrines of the U.S., the outcomes in particular cases would still differ as a result of fundamental differences in values, political beliefs, and philosophies. The four ideal types, therefore, serve an heuristic purpose in capturing some of the basic differences between alternative thick conceptions of rule of law in the PRC.

For the purposes of comparison, I refer to a rule by law regime where relevant. Of course, rule by law systems come in different varieties as well. There are more moderate and more extreme versions. The legal system during the Mao era, particularly during the Cultural Revolution, was a good example of an extreme version, to the point where at times it hardly could be described as even a rule by law legal system, which after all implies some form of law-based order. Notwithstanding variation within the category of rule by law, rule by law is distinguishable from rule of law in that the former rejects the central premise of rule of law that law is to impose meaningful limits on even the highest government officials.

Nevertheless, a rule by law system, especially a more moderate form than that of the Mao era, may share some features with some versions of rule of law, particularly the Statist Socialist and Neo-Authoritarian ones: for example, the rejection of elections in favor of single-party rule. This is hardly surprising given that institutions, rules, or practices may serve more than one purpose or end. On the other hand, in some cases certain features appear to be the same but differ in degree or the role they play in rule of law and rule by law regimes. For instance, while Communitarians accept some limits on civil society, the limits are much more restrictive in a rule by law system, even a moderate rule by law regime. Similarly, a rule by law system aims at a much higher degree of thought control than the others.[16]

The economic regime

Although all four rule of law variants favor a market economy, they differ with respect to the degree, nature, and manner of government intervention. Notwithstanding the significant differences in the economies of Western liberal democracies that have led neo-institutionalists and political economists to posit varieties of capitalism even within Europe,[17] economies in liberal democratic states tend to be characterized by minimal government regulation intended primarily to correct market failures, a clear distinction between the public sphere and private commercial sphere, and limited administration discretion to interfere in private business. In contrast, economic growth in many Asian countries, including China, has been attributed to a form of managed capitalism in which the state actively intervenes in the market, government officials blur the line between public and private spheres by establishing clientelist or corporatist relationships with private businesses, and universal laws are complemented, and sometimes supplanted, by administrative guidance, vertical and horizontal relationships, and informal mechanisms for resolving disputes.[18] In these Asian development states, the government relies on its licensing power and control over access to loans, technology, and other information and inputs to steer companies in the direction determined by the state. In some cases, the government will champion particular companies or sectors of the economy. The government may also have a direct or indirect economic interest in certain companies. Of course there is considerable variation in the amount, nature, and form of government intervention in Asian countries. Surely Hong Kong's economy has been as laissez-faire as any in the West. On the whole, however, Asian governments have taken a more interventionist approach to managing the economy.

China's economy is currently heavily regulated and characterized by clientelism and corporatism[19] Moreover, governments at all levels have both direct and indirect economic interests in companies. To be sure, there is considerable debate about the merits of such heavy government intervention and close government–business relations. While a more laissez-faire economy has its supporters, there is ample support for the view that China's transition from a centrally planned economy to a market economy requires a strong (Neo-authoritarian) government able to make tough decisions without fear of having to appease the electorate.[20] Although Statist Socialists and Neo-authoritarians (and rule by law proponents) are most likely to adopt such views, many if not most Communitarians also support them. The difference between them is that Statist Socialists arguably favor a higher degree of government regulation than Neo-authoritarians and Communitarians.

Statist Socialists and Neo-authoritarians are also somewhat more likely to favor corporatist or clientelist relationships between government and businesses than Communitarians on the grounds that they increase the state's control over economic activities. However, all are concerned about the negative effects of corporatism and clientelism, in terms of both economic efficiency and increased corruption. Thus some shift away from such relationships as they currently exist toward a more open, transparent process based on generally applicable laws is likely, even if in the end there remains a higher degree of interaction between government and business than in the West.

Public ownership is one pillar, albeit a shaky one, of Jiang Zemin's socialist rule of law state. To be sure, all states allow for some public ownership. Nonetheless, in comparison to the others, Statist Socialists can be expected to favor somewhat higher levels of public ownership, more limitations on the kinds of shares that can be held by private and foreign investors, and more restrictions on the industries in which private and foreign companies may hold majority shares.

The political order

Liberal democracies are characterized by genuine democratic elections for even the highest level of government office, a neutral state in which the normative agenda for society is determined by the people through elections and a limited state with an expansive private sphere and robust civil society independent of the state.[21] In contrast, Statist Socialism is defined by single-party rule, elections at only the lowest level of government and, at present, a *nomenklatura* system of appointments whereby the highest-level personnel in all government organs, including the courts, are chosen or approved by the Party. Rather than a neutral state, the Party in its role as vanguard sets the normative agenda for society, which currently consists of the four cardinal principles: the leading role of the Party, adherence to socialism, the dictatorship of the proletariat, and adherence to Marxism–Leninism–Mao Zedong thought. In addition, there is a smaller private sphere and a correspondingly larger role for the state in supervising and guiding social activities. If Statist Socialists had their way, there would be at most a limited "civil society" characterized by a high level of corporatist and clientelist relationships with government.[22] In these respects, there is little to distinguish Statist Socialists from rule by law advocates, although the latter might favor an even more totalitarian form of government.

Neo-authoritarians prefer single-party rule to genuine democracy. They would either do away with elections or, if that was not politically feasible, limit elections to lower levels of government. If forced to hold national-level elections, they would attempt to control the outcome of the elections by imposing limits on the opposition party or through their monopoly on major media channels. Like the Statist Socialists, they reject the neutral state and favor a large role for the government in controlling social activities. Nevertheless, they would tolerate a somewhat smaller role for the government and a correspondingly larger civil society, albeit one still subject to restrictions and characterized by clientelism and corporatism.

In contrast, Communitarians favor genuine multiparty democratic elections at all levels of government, though not necessarily right at the moment. Given their fear of chaos, distrust of the allegedly ignorant masses, and lack of requisite institutions, they are willing to postpone elections for the moment and to accept a gradual step-by-step process where elections are permitted at successively higher levels of government. Like the Statist Socialists and Neo-authoritarians, they believe state leaders should determine the normative agenda for society, and hence allow a larger role for the state in managing social activities than in a liberal democratic state. However, they prefer a somewhat more expansive civil society. Although some groups, particularly commercial associations, might find close relationships with the government helpful, other more social or spiritual groups might not. The latter would be permitted to go their own way, subject to concerns about social order, public morality, and specific harms to members of the group or society at large. Rather than hard or statist corporatism, Communitarians favor a soft or societal version.[23]

Perspective on rights

Liberal Democrats favor a liberal understanding of rights that gives priority to civil and political rights over economic, social, cultural, and collective or group rights. Rights are conceived of in deontological terms as distinct from and normatively superior to interests.[24] Rights are considered to be prior to the good (and interests) both in the sense that rights "trump" the good/interests and in that rights are based not on utility, interests, or consequences but on moral principles whose justification is derived independently of the good.[25] To protect individuals and minorities against the tyranny of the majority, rights impose limits on the interests of others, the good of society, and the will of the majority. Substantively, freedom is privileged over order, individual autonomy takes precedence over social solidarity and harmony, and freedom of thought and the right to think win out over the need for common ground and right thinking on important social issues.[26] In addition, rights are emphasized rather than duties or virtues.

In contrast, Communitarians endorse a communitarian or "Asian values" interpretation of human rights that emphasizes the indivisibility of rights. Greater emphasis in placed on collective rights and the need for economic growth, even if at the expense of individual civil and political rights. Rather than a deontological conception of rights as anti-majoritarian trumps on the social good, rights are conceived of in utilitarian or pragmatic terms as another type of interest to be weighed against other interests, including the interests of groups and society as a whole.[27] Accordingly, stability is privileged over freedom; social solidarity and harmony are as important, if not more so, than autonomy and freedom of thought; and the right to think is limited by the need for common ground and consensus on important social issues. Communitarians, Neo-authoritarians, Statist Socialists and rule by law advocates also pay more attention than liberal democrats to the development of moral character and virtues and the need to be aware of one's duties to other individuals, one's family, members of the community, and the nation.

Like Communitarians, Neo-authoritarians and Statist Socialists conceive of rights in utilitarian or pragmatic terms. However, they have a more state-centered view than Communitarians. Statist Socialists in particular are likely to conceive of rights as positivist grants of the state and useful tools for strengthening the nation and the ruling regime. They are also more likely than Neo-authoritarians to invoke state sovereignty, "Asian values" and the threat of cultural imperialism to prevent other countries from interfering in their internal affairs while overseeing the destruction of the communities and traditional cultures and value systems that they were allegedly defending. Nevertheless, Communitarians and Neo-authoritarians in China are also likely to object to strong-arm politics and the use of rights to impose culture-specific values on China or to extract trade concessions in the form of greater access to Chinese markets.[28] Moreover, like Communitarians, Neo-authoritarians and Statist Socialists privilege order over freedom. They go even farther than Communitarians, however, in tilting the scales toward social solidarity and harmony rather than autonomy, and are willing to impose more limits on freedom of thought and the right to think. While Neo-authoritarians would restrict the right of citizens to criticize the government, Statist Socialists would impose such broad restrictions that criticism of the government would be for all practical purposes prohibited. Indeed, Statist Socialists much prefer unity of thought to freedom of thought, and right thinking to the right to think.[29] Were it possible (without undermining their other goals, such as economic growth), they would return to the strict thought control rule by law regime of the Mao era. At minimum, they draw the line at public attacks on the ruling party or challenges to single-party socialism. Despite the changes in society over the last twenty years that have greatly reduced the effectiveness of "thought work," they continue to emphasize its importance to ensure common ground and consensus on important social issues defined by the Party line.[30]

The rule by law regime of the Mao era differed from any of these rule of law regimes in considering the concept of rights as a bourgeois liberal device to induce false consciousness in the proletariat. Although the Mao regime did include some rights in its various constitutions, such rights were considered programmatic goals to be realized at some future date. In addition, duties were privileged over rights, especially duties to the state; civil society was extremely limited; and efforts at thought control were pervasive.

Purposes of rule of law

Proponents of the various conceptions see rule of law serving certain similar purposes: enhancing predictability and certainty, which promotes economic growth and allows individuals to plan their affairs; preventing government arbitrariness; increasing government efficiency and rationality; providing a mechanism for dispute resolution; protecting individual rights; and bolstering regime legitimacy. They differ, however, with respect to the priorities of the various purposes, their degree of support or enthusiasm for any given purpose, and the details of how the goals are interpreted. Broadly stated, Liberal Democrats emphasize the role of rule of law in limiting the state and protecting the individual against government arbitrariness, whereas Communitarians favor a more balanced role for rule of law as a means of both limiting and strengthening the state. In contrast, Neo-authoritarians place somewhat greater emphasis on the state-strengthening aspect, which is assigned an even higher priority by Statist Socialists.

Indeed, although Statist Socialists accept – at least in theory – the primary requirement of rule of law that government officials and citizens alike are subject to law and must act in accordance with it, they accept such limits grudgingly. Not surprisingly, to date the reach of the law has been limited, with high-level government officials typically subject to a separate system of Party discipline rather than to the formal legal process. Moreover, while Statist Socialists appreciate the benefits of limiting government arbitrariness, they also prefer a system that allows them sufficient flexibility to pursue their legitimate (and sometimes illegitimate) ends. And while they regularly declare that rule of law is necessary to protect individual rights, it is not a high priority. In any case, the ability of the legal system to protect individual rights is severely hampered by their statist conception of rights and the extreme emphasis on stability and order over freedom.

Differences in the purposes of rule of law are evident in the weights attached to stability. All – even Liberal Democrats – agree that stability is important. Clearly one purpose of law in Western traditions has been to prevent anarchy and a Hobbesian war of all against all. China, for its part, has suffered tremendous upheaval in the last 150 years, from the uprisings against and eventual collapse of the Qing, through the chaos and internal struggles of the Republican period, to the turbulence of the anti-rightist movement, Great Leap Forward, and Cultural Revolution of the Mao era. With a quarter of the world's population, many of them below or near the poverty level, China (and the rest of the world) can hardly afford political chaos or anarchy. The current economic reforms have already resulted in massive unemployment and rising unrest. As the reforms continue and the number of unemployed shoots up, the potential for traumatic disruptions of the social order increases accordingly.[31]

Rule of law could serve the goal of stability in a variety of ways. First, it could limit the arbitrary acts of government. One of the biggest sources of instability in the last fifty years has been the Party itself and the arbitrariness of senior leaders. One of the main reasons for promoting rule of law after the death of Mao was to avoid the chaos of the Cultural Revolution, where the whims of Party leaders substituted for laws. Rule of law is meant to make governance more regular and predictable. It is also needed to address the perennial problem confronting socialist regimes of political succession.[32] Whereas the death of Mao set off a struggle for power, rule of law is supposed to ensure a more seemly and seamless transition of power.[33]

In addition, rule of law serves stability by regularizing central–local relations. Conflicts between the central and local governments have increased dramatically as a result of economic reforms that have given local governments both more authority and more responsibility. In their desire to promote local economic development, local governments regularly ignore central laws and policies, issue regulations that are inconsistent with national-level laws, or engage in local protectionism. While there seems little chance of the central government losing control over local governments to the point where local governments emerge as Republican-era-type warlords, as some alarmists have suggested, authority has become fragmented to such an extent that China arguably now has a de facto federalist form of government. Predictably, Jiang Zemin and other Statist Socialists emphasize the value of rule of law as a means of disciplining local governments and recentralizing power.

On the other hand, some scholars have noted that stability is often a code word in Chinese politics for greater centralization of power, an emphasis on collective over individual rights, and the continued dominance of the Party.[34] In this view, the government's emphasis on stability is overstated and is really just an attempt to limit challenges to Party rule. Former vice-director of China Academy of Social Sciences Li Shenzhi, for instance, argues that subsistence is no longer such a major problem. Accordingly, more emphasis should be paid to political reform and citizens' civil and political rights.[35] Similarly, Yu Keping has argued that political reform need not lead to instability.[36] To some extent, the differences turn on empirical issues. How unstable is China? How likely is it that the activities of any one dissident or even a group of dissidents could endanger national security? But they also reflect fundamental differences in values. Although all appreciate the need for stability, liberals would place greater importance on freedom whereas Statist Socialists, Neo-authoritarians, and Communitarians would privilege, to varying degrees, order over freedom.

Broad agreement over other purposes also gives way to subtle differences upon further probing. All agree, for instance, that predictability and certainty are crucial for economic growth. But predictability and certainty may serve other purposes as well. Liberal Democrats value predictability because it enhances freedom by allowing people to plan their affairs and realize their ends in life, and thus promotes human dignity.[37] Underlying this view is a liberal view of the self as moral agent that emphasizes autonomy and the importance of making moral choices. But not all ethical traditions share this view of the self or place such importance on choice-making. The dominant Chinese view of the self as social and the Confucian emphasis on doing what is right rather than the right to choose call into question justifications of rule of law that appeal to this interpretation of human dignity.[38] Of course, the ability to plan one's affairs is valuable to some degree in China. However, the weight attached to the ability to plan one's affairs and the reasons given in support are likely to differ between Liberal Democrats and the others, with Statist Socialists assigning it the least weight.[39]

Similarly, all hope that rule of law will enhance the legitimacy of the ruling regime. However, by allowing elections and ample opportunities for public participation in lawmaking, administrative rulemaking, interpretation and implementation processes, legitimacy for Liberal Democrats and Communitarians is based on consent. In contrast, in the absence of elections and with only limited opportunities for public participation, legitimacy for Statist Socialists and Neo-authoritarians is primarily performance based: that is, legitimacy depends on whether the laws, the legal system, and the regime as a whole produce good results.[40]

In contrast, in a rule by law regime law is merely a tool to serve the interests of the state, and there are no meaningful legal limits on the rulers. Law serves the state by enhancing government efficiency, although that goal is often compromised by the heavily politicized nature of law and the dominance of policy. Law is not meant to protect the rights of individuals. Whereas rule of law regimes rely on the courts to resolve disputes, in the Mao era, for instance, the formal legal system was used primarily to suppress enemies. Disputes among the people were settled through mediation, and economic conflicts between state-owned entities were resolved administratively or by Party organs.

Institutions and practices

According to Max Weber, the defining feature of a modern legal system that merits the label rule of law is autonomy. Law is distinct from politics, and independent judges decide cases impartially in accordance with generally applicable laws using a distinct type of legal reasoning. To be sure, the line between politics and law is not always a clear one, as critical legal scholars repeatedly remind us.[41] Nevertheless, as Alice Tay observes:

> The difference between law and decree, between government procla-mation and administrative power on the one hand and the genuine rule of law on the other, is perfectly well understood in all those countries where rule of law is seriously threatened or has been abol-ished.[42]

While the outer extremes between a system dominated by politics – such as the legal system in the Mao era, particularly during the Cultural Revolution – and a rule of law system in which legal institutions and actors enjoy a high degree of autonomy are reasonably clear, there is considerable room for variation in the middle. Advocates of alternative conceptions of rule of law are likely to disagree over where to draw the line between law and politics due in part to their divergent views about the economy, the political order, the nature and limits of rights, and the purposes that law is meant to serve.

Liberal Democrats favor a high degree of independence and autonomy. The legislature that makes laws is freely elected rather than appointed by the ruling party. The judiciary as a whole and individual judges are independent. Judges generally enjoy lifetime tenure and can be removed only for limited reasons and in accordance with strict procedures. The appointment process is relatively non-politicized.[43] There are a variety of mechanisms for reining in administrative discretion, and the legal system is capable of holding even top-level government officials accountable. The legal profession is indepen-dent and often self-governing.

At the other end of the spectrum, Statist Socialists favor only a moderate to low level of separation between law and politics. In keeping with the minimal requirements of rule of law, CCP policy is now to be transformed into laws and regulations by entities authorized to make law in accordance with the stipulated procedures for lawmaking, whereas in the Mao era CCP policies substituted for or trumped laws. Although the legislature is not freely elected, Party influence on the lawmaking processes has diminished radically since the beginning of reforms.[44] To be sure, like ruling parties in parliamentary systems in other countries, the Party is able to ensure that major policy initiatives become law when it is united and willing to expend the political capital to do so.[45]

Statist Socialists also favor a more limited judicial independence. Courts have a functional independence in the sense that other branches of government are not to interfere in the way courts handle specific cases. Unlike the Mao era, courts may decide cases without Party approval of the judgment. However, the courts may still be subject to macro-supervision by the NPC, the procuracy and other state organs, and even Party organs. While the courts as a whole enjoy limited functional independence, the autonomy and independence of individual judges are even more restricted. Accordingly, most cases are decided by a panel of judges, and a special adjudicative supervision committee within the court has the right to review particular decisions in case of manifest error.

The legal profession is granted a similar partial independence. Although not the "workers of the state" of the Mao era, lawyers still must meet political correctness standards to practice law and pass the annual inspection test (though in practice there appear to be no reported cases in which a political litmus test has been invoked to deny a license). While the Ministry of Justice (MOJ) shares responsibility for supervising the legal profession with lawyers associations, the MOJ retains most of the authority, including the power to punish lawyers. In part because of such political reasons, but mainly due simply to corruption and rent-seeking by the MOJ and its local affiliates, lawyers try to forge close clientelist relations with the MOJ.

In the administrative law area, government officials are granted considerable discretion, in part so that they may be more responsive to shifts in Party policy, but mainly for other reasons, including the need to respond quickly and flexibly to a rapidly changing economic environment.[46] Limits on civil society, freedom of the press, and public participation in the lawmaking, interpretation, and implementation processes make it difficult for the public to monitor government officials. The lack of elections eliminates whatever leverage the public has over officials resulting from the possibility of voting the current government out of office.

Neo-authoritarians prefer a moderate separation between law and politics. As with Statist Socialism, the legislature is not elected. However, Neo-authoritarians favor greater judicial independence than Statist Socialists, although many would still limit the independence of the courts and individual judges in various ways. For instance, they may prefer China's unitary system, in which the NPC is supreme and exercises supervision over the courts to a U.S.-style separation of powers system. On the other hand, they support the development of a more professional and honest civil service, and an administrative law system capable of reining in wayward government officials and combating corruption.[47] They also advocate greater public participation and more expansive, though still limited, freedom of association, speech, and the press so that the public can play a greater role in the monitoring of government officials. The primary purpose of administrative law, however, remains rational and efficient governance rather the protection of individual rights. The elite corps of civil servants is to be given considerable flexibility in formulating and implementing administrative rules, which are the main form of legislation in daily governance. The legal profession would be granted limited independence and be subject to supervision by the MOJ, albeit a cleaner and more professional one. Nevertheless, lawyers would still seek to establish clientelist ties to the MOJ due its control over licensing for special forms of business and other commercial reasons.[48]

Communitarians prefer a moderate to high degree of separation between law and politics. The legislature would be freely elected. There would be ample opportunities for public participation in rulemaking, interpretation, and implementation. The public would also be able to throw out a government that is corrupt or performs poorly; as a whole, the administrative law system would be sufficiently strong to hold even top-level government officials accountable. Although Communitarians are sympathetic to the argument that a strong economy, particularly in times of transition, requires a strong executive, they balance the need for efficient government against the need to protect individual rights. Moreover, like the Liberal Democrats, they support an autonomous judiciary, with life tenure for judges and relatively apolitical processes for appointing and removing judges. At the same time, they reject the liberal notion of a neutral state. Accordingly, they favor the practice whereby courts decide cases in light of a substantive moral agenda for society determined by the ruling elite. In that sense, they do not differ from Statist Socialists or Neo-authoritarians.[49] Rather, what distinguishes them is the particular normative agenda. The Communitarians believe that judges should emphasize harmony, stability, and the interests of the community over the interests of individuals as well as economic development. Neo-authoritarians and State Socialists agree in general but place more emphasis on economic development and upholding the authority of the state. In particular, State Socialists insist that the courts uphold the four cardinal principles – a position not supported by either Neo-authoritarians or Communitarians.

Rules

Although there is room for disagreement among liberal democrats on specific issues, on the whole Liberal Democrats prefer liberal laws. For instance, liberal laws provide strong protections for broadly defined civil and political rights. For some, free speech may be subject to only narrow time, place, and manner restrictions. Social groups are free to organize without having to register with government authorities. Persons accused of crimes have the right to a lawyer, who may be present at all stages of formal interrogation; the accused may only be held for a very limited time without being charged; and the state may not rely on illegally obtained evidence in making its case. Euthanasia laws may allow individuals to choose to end their life or to ask others to assist them in doing so. Parents may keep their children out of school and educate them at home if they choose.

Communitarians, Neo-authoritarians, and Statist Socialists all endorse laws that limit individual freedom to one extent or another. For instance, all allow registration requirements for social groups to ensure public order. All accept substantive limits on speech as well as time, place, and manner restrictions. No one is free to walk into a courtroom with a jacket that says "Fuck the Draft" on it.[50] Flag burning is outlawed. The accused have a right to a lawyer, but only after the police have had an initial opportunity to question them. The accused may be held for longer periods without being charged, and the period may be extended upon approval of the authorities. Illegally obtained evidence may be used in certain instances, though forced confessions and police torture are not allowed. Children are required to attend state-authorized schools and to study a curriculum approved by the Ministry of Education. More controversially, Statist Socialists and Neo-authoritarians, and perhaps even Communitarians, endorse broadly drafted laws to protect the state and social order, such as state secrets laws and prohibitions against endangering the state.

Outcomes in specific cases

Institutions in a broad sense include ideology, purposes, organizational structures and cultures, norms, practices, rules, and outcomes in specific cases. Although I have separated them for the sake of a clearer exposition, in reality they overlap and blend together, as is evident from the following examples concerning constitutional, administrative, and criminal law.[51]

In general, constitutions in socialist countries have played a very different role than constitutions in liberal democratic rule of law states, in part because socialist states have made little pretense of abiding by the basic requirements of rule of law and accepting any constitutional limits on the ruling regime's power. Reflecting their origins in Enlightenment theories of social contract, liberal constitutions emphasize a limited state and a separation between state and society. Rule of law plays a central role in imposing limits on the state and protecting the individual against an over-reaching government by ensuring that the state does not encroach on the fundamental rights of individuals set out in the constitution. Liberal constitutions set out fundamental principles that are supposed to stand the test of time, including the basic rights of citizens.

In contrast, socialist constitutions are characterized by frequent change. The frequent change in socialist constitutions is consistent with socialist legal theory, which conceives of law as a superstructure that reflects the economic basis of society and in particular the ownership of the material modes of production. When the economic base changes, law – and the constitution – must change accordingly. Moreover, since Marxism posits an evolution toward an ideal state, when the economy passes through various stages amendment of the constitution is to be expected. In the PRC, the 1978 Constitution was replaced in 1982 by a more market-oriented constitution that reflected Deng Xiaoping's economic open-door and reform policies. The 1982 Constitution has subsequently been amended three times as economic reforms have deepened and the economy has steadily moved away from a centrally planned economy toward a more market-oriented economy. Each time the amendments incorporated the more market-oriented policies.

Although changes in PRC constitutions reflect transformations in the economic base of society, they also reflect fundamental shifts in political power. Again, this is entirely consistent with socialist legal theory, which conceives of law as a tool of the ruling class. Whereas in a capitalist society law serves the bourgeoisie, in a socialist state law allegedly serves the people. However, in a Leninist socialist state the Party acts as the vanguard of the people. Thus law becomes a tool of the Party. The constitution changes when there are major changes in Party leadership or Party policy. The 1954 Constitution therefore reflected the victory of the CCP and the Party's consolidation of power. The 1975 Cultural Revolution Constitution codified Mao's victory over his opponents and embodied his radical vision for a society that must engage in permanent revolution and ceaseless class struggle to defend socialism against the enemy within and abroad. The short-lived 1978 Constitution signaled Deng's victory over Mao loyalists, the turn toward a more law-based order and the need to concentrate on economic development rather than class struggle. However, Deng had yet to consolidate his power. By 1982 he was firmly in control. Thus the 1982 Constitution confirmed the new emphasis on economic development. It also continued the trend, begun in the 1978 Constitution, to downplay the dominance of the CCP, separate the Party from government, and turn over the functions of day-to-day governance to state organs. Although the 1982 Constitution incorporated Deng's four cardinal principles, they were placed in the preamble. In contrast, the principles of the supremacy of the law and that no individual or party is beyond the law were incorporated into the body of the constitution. Nevertheless, the constitution did not explicitly endorse rule of law, even a socialist rule of law, until the amendment in 1999.

What role the constitution will play in the future depends in part on which version of rule of law prevails. Should Statist Socialism win out, given the relatively low level of separation between law and politics, the constitution is likely to continue to change frequently to reflect major changes in policies as determined by state leaders. Because Statist Socialists see rule of law as a means to strengthen the state, the role of the constitution in protecting rights will remain limited. The constitution might not be directly justiciable; individuals would generally be able to avail themselves of the rights provided in the constitution only if such rights are implemented by specific legislation. On the other hand, even if Statist Socialism prevails, the constitution is likely to play a more important role as a baseline for measuring the legitimacy of state actions. To maintain credibility, the ruling regime will have to take the constitution more seriously. As a result, the ruling regime will appeal to the constitution more often to justify its acts. Indicative of the transition toward rule of law, Beijing has already begun to appeal to the constitution at critical times, including when the government imposed martial law in 1989 and banned Falungong in 1999.

The constitution will play an even more important role if a Neo-authoritarian or Communitarian form of rule of law is adopted. Although the tension between strengthening and limiting the state would still be manifest in constitutional law, at minimum there would be greater emphasis on individual rights. As a result, the constitution would probably become directly justiciable.[52] It might also be subject to less change. The process for amending the constitution would differ, at least for Communitarians. Whereas non-elected state leaders would make the decision to amend the constitution for Statist Socialists and Neo-authoritarians, democratically elected representatives would make the decision in a Communitarian state.

Like constitutional law, the administrative law regime will vary depending on which version of rule of law wins out. Until recently, in China the main purpose of administrative law was considered to be to facilitate efficient administration. This view has now largely given way to the belief that administrative law must strike a balance between protecting the rights of individuals and promoting government efficiency.[53] Although the tension between the two goals is evident in every system, how China balances the two will depend on which of the various alternatives of rule of law is adopted. To date, there is very limited public participation in the administrative law process. An Administrative Procedure Law is being drafted, however, that will increase opportunities for public participation. Should the Communitarian or even the Neo-authoritarian conception prevail, one should expect the law to allow for greater public participation than if the Statist Socialist conception prevailed.

Differences in conceptions of rule of law are also evident in the outcomes of administrative litigation cases. PRC courts have been reluctant to review aggressively administrative decisions. On the whole, they have shown considerable deference to administrative agencies, for example by interpreting very narrowly the abuse of authority standard for quashing administrative decisions. In particular, they have been reluctant to interpret abuse of authority to include a concept of fundamental rights, as have courts in some Western liberal democracies.[54] There are many reasons for the courts' deference other than ideology, including institutional limits on the power of the courts.[55]

But even setting aside the various institutional obstacles, given the weak support for liberalism in China, PRC courts are less likely than their counterparts in liberal democratic states to take full advantage of the abuse of authority standard as a means to protect individual rights and rein in government officials at the expense of government efficiency.

Criminal law is another area where outcomes are especially sensitive to differences in ideology and in the conceptions of rule of law. In light of the importance of stability to most Chinese, civil and political rights are likely to be subject to more limits than in liberal democratic states. Statist Socialists in particular will object to criticisms of the government that challenge single-party socialism. Accordingly, the continued persecution of dissidents is likely to continue if Statist Socialists (and perhaps if Neo-authoritarians) prevail. At present, the authorities often rely on re-education through labor (*lao jiao*), an administrative sanction whereby dissidents may be detained for one to three years, with a possible extension for another year, without many of the procedural rights afforded criminal suspects under the Criminal Procedure Law. Although Liberal Democrats object to re-education through labor, others are likely to support it as necessary for social stability. Hence the complete elimination of re-education through labor does not appear to be politically feasible at this point. Arguably, the best that Liberal Democrats can hope for is that the process is changed to incorporate more procedural protections of the kind incorporated in the Criminal Procedure Law.

On the other hand, rule of law is not infinitely elastic. Any supporter of rule of law will question the manner in which the government has suppressed dissidents. Even in criminal cases, dissidents are often denied their rights under the Criminal Procedure Law, including a right to an open trial, to communicate with their lawyers and families and so on.[56]

In short, the outcomes of many particular issues will turn on the specific substantive moral, political, and economic beliefs that define a particular thick conception of rule of law. How much criticism of government should be allowed and under what circumstances? Should one be able to use offensive language in public? Should beggars be allowed on the street? Under what circumstances can someone be stopped and searched? Do the police need a warrant to enter your house and, if so, how and when can they obtain one? Must individuals carry an identification card? Is the "anger of the people" a legitimate basis for meting out capital punishment? Should adultery be a crime? Are gay marriages consistent with family values, a way of strengthening a newly envisioned family, or a threat to the very notion of family? Liberal Democrats, Communitarians, Neo-authoritarians, and Statist Socialists will disagree over these issues, and indeed there will be many disagreements within any given school, just as there are many disagreements over such issues in countries known for liberal democratic rule of law. Nevertheless, despite such disagreements there is also considerable common ground about the basic requirements of rule of law as captured in thin theories, and general acceptance that rule of law differs from rule by law in that the former entails meaningful legal limits on government actors.

Conclusion

Given that "rule of law" has become associated with Liberal Democratic rule of law, one might argue that the term should not be stretched to include other variants. When talking about China, one should simply forgo use of "rule of law" in favor of other terms. Obviously, one is free to reserve the label "rule of law" for a particular version if one so chooses. However, one problem with this approach is that forcing PRC ideas about rule of law into our prevailing yet contingent categories smacks of cultural imperialism.

Second, the debate about legal reform in China has been couched in terms of rule of law, both in China and abroad. Of course, one could protest every time the term "rule of law" is used, or at least point out that the term is being misused. But given that "rule of law" is a contested concept even in the West, any attempt to appropriate the term for a particular usage will be futile: the debate will continue to be posed in terms of rule of law, by those both inside and outside of China. Rather than restricting the use of the term with respect to China, it might be more useful to try to figure out what those who use the term mean by it and why they want to invoke it. How one defines rule of law will depend on what one's purpose is. Investors, governments and multilateral agencies, non-governmental organizations (NGOs), moral philosophers, and political scientists all have different purposes for invoking rule of law, and may therefore find some ways of defining or measuring it more suitable to their particular purpose than others. That does not mean that they are free to define rule of law as they like. Enough people in the relevant discourse community must accept the usage for the speech act to be meaningful and for the definition to serve a useful purpose. There is, however, enough common ground to the various conceptions of rule of law provided by the basic requirements of a thin rule of law to render the invocation of rule of law in the Chinese context intelligible and useful.

Third, many reformers in China want the debate couched in terms of rule of law for strategic reasons: rule of law entails at minimum some restraints on government leaders and opens up other possibilities for political reform.

Fourth, simply relying on either Liberal Democratic rule of law versus rule by law is no longer sufficient to capture what is happening in China. It is descriptively incorrect – the legal system is no longer a pure rule by law. Nor can we capture all of the nuances in the PRC debates about rule of law if we only have the overly simplistic categories of rule of law (i.e. our Liberal Democratic version) or else rule by law.[57] Without more refined categories, we simply will not be able to understand what is happening, either in terms of the evolution of PRC discourse or in practice with respect to the development of the legal system.

Fifth, the practical import of forcing PRC discourse and practice into our preconceived boxes of Liberal Democratic rule of law or authoritarian rule by law is that we are likely to come to the wrong conclusions about reforms. We are likely to be either too pessimistic or too optimistic – either there is no fundamental change or China is becoming "like us." But neither seems to be the case. Misreading what is happening is likely to lead to bad policy choices. Foreign governments and aid agencies could miss opportunities to support reforms that would improve the PRC system, for example by failing to provide adequate resources for certain reforms because they do not believe such changes could possibly work in a rule by law system meant to serve the interests of the Party and nothing more. Alternatively, time and resources could be wasted on projects that are not consistent with the form of rule of law likely to emerge in China. Some rules or practices that work in the context of a Liberal Democratic rule of law might require liberal institutions and perhaps liberal values to succeed. They may fail to take hold in a different legal order, exacerbating the gap between law and practice.

Sixth, objecting to the application of rule of law to China and other states that are not liberal democracies overstates the differences and fails to capture the considerable agreement with respect to the basic elements of a thin rule of law. Despite considerable variation, all four variants of rule of law accept the basic benchmark that law must impose meaningful limits on the ruler, and all are compatible with a thin conception of rule of law. Predictably, as legal reforms have progressed in China the legal system has converged in many respects with the legal systems of well-developed countries; and it is likely to continue to converge in the future.

At the same time, however, there will inevitably be some variations in rule of law regimes even with respect to the basic requirements of a thin conception due to the context in which they are embedded. Hence signs of both divergence and convergence are to be expected. Indeed, whether one finds convergence or divergence depends to a large extent on the particular indicators that one chooses, the timeframe and the degree of abstraction or focus. The closer one looks, the more likely one is to find divergence. That is, however, a natural result of narrowing the focus.

Turning from theory to practice, implementation of rule of law, however conceived, leaves much to be desired in China at present. Ultimately, the key to the future realization of rule of law in China is power. How is power to be controlled and allocated in a single-party socialist state? To the extent that law is to limit the Party, how does the legal system obtain sufficient authority to control a party that has been above the law? In a democracy, the final check on government power is the ability of the people to throw the government out and elect a new one. In the absence of multiparty democracy, an authoritarian government must either voluntarily relinquish some of its power or else have it taken away by force. Naturally, Party leaders will resist giving up power so readily. They may therefore be disinclined to support reforms that would strengthen rule of law but also allow institutions to become so powerful that they could then provide the basis for challenging Party rule. The result may be that, at least on those issues that threaten the survivability of the Party, the needs of the Party will continue to trump rule of law for some time (though it bears noting that most issues do not threaten the Party).

I have argued elsewhere that there are reasons to believe that the issue of power can be resolved in favor of rule of law and that law will come to impose ever more meaningful restraints on Party and government leaders.[58] It is possible that the ruling regime will be forced to accept limitations on its power as a condition for staying in power. At the same time, while China is not likely to embrace democracy in the near future, in the long run it may need to allow genuine democratic elections to enhance accountability and to provide a peaceful mechanism for alleviating growing social cleavages. Yet even if China becomes democratic, that does not mean that it will necessarily become a liberal democracy or adopt a Liberal Democratic form of rule of law.

Notes

1   See, for example, Yali Peng, "Democracy and Chinese Political Discourses," *Modern China*, vol. 24, no. 4 (1998), pp. 408–44; see also Minxin Pei, "Racing Against Time: Institutional Decay and Renewal in China," in William A. Joseph, ed., *China Briefing: The Contradictions of Change* (Armonk, N.Y.: M. E. Sharpe, 1997), pp. 11–49. Pei cites polls showing that two-thirds of the people thought that the economic situation was improving while half thought their own living standards were improving, and that that the majority of respondents (54 percent) placed a higher priority on economic development than democracy. Over two-thirds of those polled supported the government's policy of promoting economic growth and social stability, and 63 percent agreed that "it would be a disaster for China to experience a similar change as that in the former Soviet Union." Id., p. 18. Even 40 percent of non-CCP member respondents said they voluntarily supported the same political position as the CCP. Id. See also Xia Li Lollar, *China's Transition Toward a Market Economy, Civil Society and Democracy* (Bristol, Indiana: Wyndham Hall Press, 1997), p. 74, citing results of a poll in which 60 percent of respondents assigned highest priority to maintaining order, while another 30 percent chose controlling inflation, whereas only 8 percent chose giving people more say in political decisions and free elections, and only 2 percent chose protecting free speech. Wan Ming cites survey data showing growing support for the Party, and concludes that a development consensus that emphasizes stability has emerged. See "Chinese Opinion on Human Rights," *Orbis*, vol. 42, no. 3 (1998), pp. 361–74. Another study showed Chinese to be the least tolerant of diverse viewpoints among all of the countries surveyed. It also found little support for a free press and the publishing of alternative views. See Andrew Nathan and Shi Tianjian, "Cultural Requisites for Democracy in China: Findings from a Survey," *Daedalus*, vol. 122, no. 2 (1993), pp. 95–123. Granted, polling results must be used with caution. Often, the design of the question influ-

ences the outcome, as may be the case when people are simply asked to choose between economic growth and democracy. Moreover, respondents may feel inhibited and provide what they feel are safe answers or the answers desired by the pollers. On the other hand, nationals of the PRC living abroad often make similar arguments about democracy and economic growth and exhibit similar values. Nor are such views limited to mainland PRC citizens. When asked to choose between democracy and economic prosperity and political stability, 71 percent of Hong Kong residents chose the latter and only 20 percent chose democracy. Similarly, almost 90 percent preferred a stable and peaceful handover to insisting on increasing the pace of democracy. Cited in Daniel Bell, *East Meets West: Human Rights and Democracy in East Asia* (Princeton: Princeton University Press, 2000), p. 119.

2   Given the many possible conceptions of rule of law, I avoid reference to "the rule of law," which suggests that there is a single type of rule of law. Alternatively, one could refer to the concept of "the rule of law," for which there are different possible conceptions. The thin theory of rule of law would define the core concept of rule of law, with the various thick theories constituting different conceptions. Yet from the perspective of philosophical pragmatism, how one defines a term depends on one's purposes and the consequences that attach to defining a term in a particular way. As thick and thin theories serve different purposes, I do not want to privilege thin theories over thick theories by declaring the thin version to be "the rule of law."

3   For an overview and analysis of the Asian values debates, see Randall Peerenboom, "Beyond Universalism and Relativism: The Evolving Debates about Values in Asia," *Indiana International and Comparative Law Review* (2003).

4   Alternatively, the Neo-authoritarian state might give the appearance of allowing genuine multiparty elections at all levels but in fact control the outcome by limiting the ability of opposition parties to campaign (as in Singapore).

5   For a more extensive discussion of the evolution of rule of law in China, see Randall Peerenboom, *China's Long March Toward Rule of Law* (Cambridge: Cambridge University Press, 2002).

6   See Gong Xiangrui, ed., *Fazhi de lixiang yu xianshi* [The Ideal and Reality of the Rule of Law] (Beijing: China University of Law and Politics Press, 1993), p. 33.

7   See, for example, Minxin Pei, "Citizens v. Mandarins: Administrative Litigation in China," *China Quarterly* no. 152 (1997), for a discussion of the outcomes of administrative law cases.

8   Su Li, "Bianfa, Fazhi Jianshe Ji Qi Bentu Ziyuan" [Change of Law, Establishment of the Rule of Law and its Native Resources], 41 *Zhongwai Faxue* 1(1995) (emphasizing China's native resources – *bentu ziyuan*); Sun Guohua, "Cong Zhongguo de Shiji Chufa, Zou Ziji de Daolu" [Start from China's Actual Circumstances, Take Our Own Road], in Liu Zuoxiang, ed., "Zhongguo Fazhi Shixian Fanglue (Bitanhui)" [Strategy for the Realization of the Rule of Law (Written Exchange of Ideas)], 71 *Falü Kexue* 3 (1996) (emphasizing the need to consider China's "national character" – *guoqing*). Ma Xiaohong suggests that rule of law in China must take into account the traditional emphasis on morality and substantive justice. Ma Xiaohong "Yifa Zhiguo Jianshe Shehuizhuyi Fazhi Guojia Xueshu Yantaohui Jiyao" [Excerpts from the Academic Conference on Ruling the Country According to Law, Establish a Socialist Rule of Law State], 3 *Faxue Yanjiu* 17 (1996). Su Li, "Ershi Shiji Zhongguo de Xiandaihua He Fazhi" [Twentieth Century China's Modernization and Rule of Law], 20 *Faxue Yanjiu* 3 (1998) (noting that China is still predominantly an agrarian society). In the villages, custom and traditional informal means of resolving disputes remain strong. However, as he acknowledges, society is changing and reliance on custom

and traditional informal means of resolving disputes is no longer sufficient. But see Zhang Wenxian, "Lun Lifazhong de Falu Yizhi" [On the Legal Transplant of Legislation], 1 *Faxue* 6 (1996), arguing that China has little choice but to import laws given the needs and rapid pace of economic reforms.

9 Shao Cheng, "Jiaqiang Lianzheng Fazhi de Jianshe" [Strengthen the Establishment of Good Governance, Rule of Law], in "Zhongguo Fazhi Shixian Fanglue (Bitanhui)" [Strategy for the Realization of Rule of Law (Written Exchange of Ideas)], 3 *Falu Kexue* 3 (1996).

10 See Peerenboom, *China's Long March*.

11 As Michael Davis notes, communitarianism in Asia is different than in the West in that Western communitarians assume a liberal democratic framework. Michael C. Davis, "Constitutionalism and Political Culture: The Debate Over Human Rights and Asian Values," *Harvard Human Rights Journal*, vol. 11 (1998), pp. 109–47. In contrast, Asian communitarians tend to be more conservative and authoritarian. Asian neo-conservative communitarians emphasize hierarchy and order rather than pluralism and a vibrant social discourse. Western communitarians put more stress on equality and liberation of the members of the community. For an attempt to develop a Deweyan–Confucian alternative to liberalism, see David Hall and Roger Ames, *Democracy of the Dead: Dewey, Confucius and the Hope for Democracy in China* (Chicago: Open Court, 1999). Wm. Theodore de Bary, *Asian Values and Human Rights: A Confucian Communitarian Perspective* (Cambridge: Harvard University Press, 1998) argues for a more liberal form of Confucian communitarianism. While they are admirable preliminary attempts to sketch a philosophical theory of Confucian communitarianism, neither account addresses in any detail the issue of rule of law or provides details regarding political or legal institutions, legal rules or outcomes with respect to particular controversial issues. In *East Meets West*, Daniel Bell assesses the arguments for and against a communitarian system based on non-liberal democratic traditions and values, suggesting that such a system may suit certain states. Critics of Asian communitarian have pointed out that often citizens in Asian countries exhibit precious little concern for the community. Indeed, in China today the principal units of normative concern and allegiance appear to be the family and the state, with little regard shown for what falls between the family and state. Accordingly, "collectivism" might be a better descriptive term than communitarianism.

12 If China's legal system does at some point reach a stable equilibrium state, for example coming to rest in some form of communitarian rule of law, it would become necessary to draw increasingly fine distinctions between the various forms of communitarian rule of law. By way of comparison, the category of Liberal Democratic rule of law, while useful for comparative purposes with respect to competing conceptions of rule of law in China, is of little use without further specification for capturing competing conceptions of rule of law in Western developed liberal democracies. With respect to the U.S., for instance, one would need to distinguish between libertarians, conservatives, communitarians, and liberals, and then between various schools of liberals, including traditional liberals, welfare liberals, postmodern liberals, and so on. Moreover, particular issues might be more important in one context than another. For example, in the U.S., the fault-lines for competing conceptions of rule of law tend to run along the lines of different theories of constitutional interpretation. See Richard Fallon, "'The Rule of Law' as a Concept in Constitutional Discourse," *Columbia Law Review*, vol. 97, no. 1 (1997), pp. 1–56.

13 Jiang Zemin's report at the 15th Party Congress is an excellent example of Statist Socialism. See "Jiang Zemin's Congress Report," *FBIS–CHI–97–266* (September

23, 1997). Neo-authoritarianism is generally associated with Zhao Ziyang and members of his think tank. See, for example, Barry Sautman, "Sirens of the Strongman: Neo-Authoritarianism in Recent Chinese Political Theory," *China Quarterly*, no. 129 (1992), pp. 72–102. However, I use the term in a more inclusive way. For instance, Neo-authoritarianism has resurfaced in the form of New Conservatism, the New Left and elitist democracy. See Edward X. Gu, "Elitist Democracy and China's Democratization," *Democratization*, vol. 4, no. 2 (1997), pp. 84–112, who notes that despite some differences New Conservatives and elitist democrats share the same basic views with respect to democracy and the role of the elite in bringing about social order and harmony. Pan Wei, a political scientist at Beijing University, has put forth a "consultative rule of law" that incorporates and builds on the basic principles of Neo-authoritarianism, including the rejection of democracy in favor of a strong state, albeit with a much reduced role for the Party. See Pan Wei, "Democracy or Rule of Law – China's Political Future" (unpublished manuscript presented at the Conference on China's Political Options, May 19–20, 2000, Vail, Colorado). Liberal Democratic rule of law is well represented by Liu Junning (albeit with libertarian leanings) and many living abroad in exile, such as Baogang He. See Liu Junning, "Cong fazhiguo dao fazhi" [From *Rechtsstaat* to Rule of Law], in Dong Yuyu and Shi Binhai eds., *Zhengzhi Zhongguo* [Political China] (Beijing: Jinri Zhongguo Chubanshe, 1998), pp. 254–6, at p. 233; Baogang He, *The Democratization of China* (New York: Routledge, 1996). Within China, He Weifang, a professor at Beijing University Law School, is a leading example among legal scholars. No PRC scholar has articulated a comprehensive theory of a communitarian rule of law. However, PRC scholars have criticized aspects of the current system, taken exception to various features of a Liberal Democratic order, and developed pieces of a communitarian alternative. For instance, Xia Yong has attempted to construct a virtue-based theory of rights. Similarly, scholars in China and abroad have defended communitarian positions against liberal democratic critics, but generally on highly abstract philosophical grounds and primarily with respect to alternatives to democracy and liberal human rights, as noted in note 12. The Communitarian position captures the views of the majority of Chinese citizens, who may wish for democracy, but not right now, as reflected in the polling data cited previously. They value individual rights but fear even more disorder and chaos. Accordingly, they draw a different balance than liberals between individual rights and group interests. This position is evident in the legal and philosophical literature in the long-running debates over collectivism and the relation between rights and duties. See, for example, Chih-yu Shih, *Collective Democracy: Political and Legal Reform in China* (Hong Kong: Chinese University Press, 1999), discussing such debates. The four positions also track the result of Peng's survey of political discourse in China. Peng's four categories overlap to a large extent with the four positions I have identified, with radical democracy representing the Liberal Democratic view; established conservativism representing Statist Socialism; concerned traditionalism representing Neo-authoritarianism; and alienated populism aligning to some degree with Communitarianism, albeit a jaded and somewhat cynical communitarian view. One of the striking features is that despite radically divergent views on democracy all four groups strongly support rule of law. See Yali Peng, "Democracy and Chinese Political Discourses," *Modern China*, vol. 24, no. 4 (1998), pp. 408–44.

14 In some cases, I have drawn on current institutions, rules, practices, and outcomes to demonstrate features of the various positions, particularly Statist Socialism and Neo-authoritarianism but also to some extent Communitarianism and rule by law. Similarly, while the current system does not exhibit many

features of a Liberal Democratic order, it is possible to appeal to Western countries for concrete "real-life" examples. The Communitarian variant is the most hypothetical (in the sense of not being grounded in existing institutions and practices) of the positions, as the current system remains more state-dominated than the Communitarian view would allow. One advantage of defining a Communitarian rule of law in a rigorous way is that it becomes possible to design a survey instrument to gauge the degree of support for it among the populace.

15 Xiao Gongqin, one of the leading New Conservatives theorists, considers himself a Neo-authoritarian. However, his support for the Party also aligns him with Statist Socialists. On New Conservatives, see Merle Goldman, "The Potential for Instability Among Alienated Intellectuals and Students in Post-Mao China," in David Shambaugh, ed., *Is China Unstable?* (Armonk, N.Y.: M. E. Sharpe, 2000); Barret McCormick and David Kelly, "The Limits of Anti-Liberalism," *Journal of Asian Studies*, vol. 53, no. 3 (1994), pp. 804–31.

16 Many skeptics question whether China's ruling regime accepts the principle that law binds the state and state actors. Some argue that many of the reforms are actually consistent with a more efficient rule by law, especially a softer authoritarian version than that of the Mao era. Chen Jianfu, for instance, suggests that legal reforms are not meant to change the nature of law as a tool but just to make law a better tool. Chen Jianfu, "Market Economy and the Internationalisation of Civil and Commercial Law in the People's Republic of China," in Kanishka Jayasuriya, ed., *Law, Capitalism and Power in Asia* (London: Routledge, 1999), pp. 69–94. Yet there are good reasons to be skeptical about the skeptics' view. Undeniably, some of the recent reforms and developments, such as a certain amount of institution-building, greater reliance on law rather than policy, and even some devolution of power, are consistent with the view that the purpose of legal reforms is a more efficient rule by law. However, they are also consistent with a transition to rule of law. As is often the case, much turns on which side bears the burden of proof. Those who see reforms as supporting rule by law insist that those who perceive a transition toward rule of law provide conclusive proof of the transition. Turning the tables, however, why assume the skeptics' view is correct? Taken to the extreme, diehard skeptics will be satisfied with nothing less than the full realization of the rule of law ideal. Yet the establishment of rule of law is a long-term process. No legal system can transform itself from rule by law into a fully implemented rule of law over night. All countries now known for rule of law initially went through a period in which legal institutions were weak and rule of law only imperfectly implemented at best. Although it may be impossible to pinpoint the exact moment the tide turned toward rule of law, at some point preceding the actual implementation of some reasonable approximation of the ideal of rule of law, there was inevitably a credible commitment to it. Moreover, while skeptics can explain away some reforms as consistent with a more efficient rule by law, other reforms cannot be dismissed so readily. The express commitment to rule of law and the efforts to establish a viable administrative law system that aims both to protect individual rights and to enhance government efficiency, for instance, are at odds with the establishment of a more efficient rule by law. For a fuller discussion, see Peerenboom, *China's Long March.*

17 For an assessment of the variety of capitalism literature, see Peter Hall, "The Political Economy of Europe in an Era of Independence," in Herbert Kitschelt, Peter Lange, Gary Marks, and John D. Stephens, eds., *Continuity and Change in Contemporary Capitalism* (New York: Cambridge University Press, 1999), pp. 135–63.

18 See, for example, John Gillespie, "Law and Development in 'the Market Place': An East Asian Perspective," in Jayasuriya, ed., *Law, Capitalism and Power in Asia*, pp. 118–50; Carol A. G. Jones, "Capitalism, Globalization and Rule of Law: An Alternative Trajectory of Legal Change in China," *Social & Legal Studies*, vol. 3, no. 2 (1994), pp. 195–221. Whether Asian countries grew because of or in spite of such practices is, of course, much contested.

19 See, for example, David Wank, *Commodifying Communism: Business, Trust, and Politics in a Chinese City* (New York: Cambridge University Press, 1999), describing the importance of clientelism for private businesses in Xiamen.

20 See Sautman, "Sirens of the Strongman." For a critique of the alleged advantage of authoritarianism, see Jose Maria Maravall, "The Myth of the Authoritarian Advantage," *Journal of Democracy*, vol. 5 (1994), pp. 17–31.

21 That democracy should be neutral is, of course, contested by communitarians, conservatives, and philosophical perfectionists. See Michael Sandel, *Democracy's Discontent: America in Search of A Public Philosophy* (Cambridge, Massachusetts: Belknap Press of Harvard University Press, 1996). Similarly, welfare liberals allow for a greater role of the state than classical liberals, whereas libertarians favor an even more restricted role. It bears noting that these models are not ideal types in the sense that they necessarily represent the most normatively attractive or defensible interpretation of these positions. For example, some form of deliberative democracy that rejects the state neutrality principle might be a more attractive conception of democracy. Rather, the models were developed for their explanatory value. They represent common interpretations of the various positions, with features selected in part to bring out the differences between the various positions. Choosing a common interpretation rather than the most normatively defensible version has the advantage that the model will then have greater explanatory power as a descriptive tool and also as a predictor of how the legal system might develop and actual cases be decided. Conversely, a normatively superior but very narrowly supported version of some view (say a version supported only be elite intellectuals and philosophers with no political power) might be interesting as philosophy but relatively useless in predicting *Realpolitik* issues such as how the legal system is likely to develop and how controversial cases will be decided in practice. Once the basic differences between the various positions are clear, philosophers and others can debate the relative merits of each position and try to persuade others as to their own normative favorites.

22 Gordon White, Jude Howell, and Shang Ziaoyuan, *In Search of Civil Society: Market Reform and Social Change in Contemporary China* (Oxford: Clarendon Press, 1996), describing the close relations of many civil organizations with the state; Tony Saich, "Negotiating the State: The Development of Social Organizations in China," *China Quarterly*, vol. 161 (2000), p. 124–41, pointing out that the Leninist tendency to thwart organizational plurality is compounded by the fear of the potential for social unrest resulting from economic reforms, but also observing that the state's capacity to exert formal control is increasingly limited.

23 For a discussion of hard or statist corporatism versus soft or societal corporatism, see Howard J. Wiarda, *Corporatism and Comparative Politics: The Other Great "Ism"* (Armonk, N.Y.: M. E. Sharpe, 1997).

24 Randall Peerenboom, "Rights, Interests, and the Interest in Rights in China," *Stanford Journal of International Law*, vol. 31, no. 2 (1995), pp. 359–86.

25 John Rawls, *A Theory of Justice* (Cambridge: Harvard University Press, 1971); Ronald Dworkin, *Taking Rights Seriously* (Cambridge: Harvard University

Press, 1977). Of course, not all liberals accept that the right should be privileged over the good or endorse a deontological theory or rights.

26 Randall Peerenboom, "Confucian Harmony and Freedom of Thought," in Wm. Theordore de Bary and Tu Weiming, eds., *Confucianism and Human Rights* (New York: Columbia University Press, 1998), pp. 234–60.

27 Peerenboom, "Rights, Interests and the Interest in Rights in China."

28 In a survey of 547 students from thirteen universities in China, 82 percent claimed that for other countries to initiate anti-China motions before the U.N. Commission on Human Rights constituted interference in China's internal affairs; 71 percent believed that the true aim of the United States and other countries in censuring China was to use the human rights issue to attack China and impose sanctions on it, with 69 percent maintaining that this constituted a form of power politics. See "Students' Attitudes Toward Human Rights Surveyed," *BBC Summary of World Broadcasts*, May 4, 1999.

29 Peerenboom, "Confucian Harmony and Freedom of Thought."

30 Daniel Lynch, *After the Propaganda State: Media, Politics, and "Thought Work" in Reformed China* (Stanford: Stanford University Press, 1999).

31 For an analysis of the likelihood of China becoming unstable and the factors that might contribute to it, see David Shambaugh, ed., *Is China Unstable?* (Armonk, N.Y.: M. E. Sharpe, 2000). The contributors discuss conflicts among the ruling elite and government–military relations, the declining role of the Party at the grassroots level, economic reforms, urban and rural unrest, and minority regions.

32 Wang Jiafu, "Lun Yifa Zhiguo" [On Governing the Country in Accordance with Law], *Faxue Yanjiu*, vol. 18, no. 2 (1996), pp. 3–9.

33 In fact, the transition from Deng to Jiang was relatively smooth, as was the shuffling of top leaders, including Li Peng's move from the State Council to the NPC when his term expired. To be sure, one could question what, if anything, rule of law had to do with it. Nevertheless, the fact that there are term limits does provide the backdrop against which political maneuvering occurs. In any event, the hope is that in the future succession will proceed in accordance with legal rules and that when senior officials reach the end of their terms they will step down or move to another post as required by law.

34 Shi Qinfeng asserts that, whereas the purpose of rule of law is to limit the state, in China the purpose of rule of law is stability to ensure that the current regime remains in power. This view is typical of the Statist Socialist variety but not of the others. "Yifa zhiguo jianshe shehuizhuyi fazhi guojia xueshu yantaohui jiyao" [Excerpts from the Academic Conference on Ruling the Country According to Law, Establish a Socialist Rule of Law State], *Faxue Yanjiu*, vol. 18, no. 3 (1996), pp. 13–23.

35 Li Shenzhi, "Yei yao tuidong zhengzhi gaige" [Push Ahead with Political Reforms Too], in Dong Yuyu and Shi Binhai, eds., *Zhengzhi Zhongguo* (Beijing: Jinri Zhongguo Chubanshe, 1998), p. 21.

36 Yu Keping, "Zouchu 'Zhengzhi gaige – shehuiwending' de liangnan jingdi" [A Way Out of the Two Trouble Areas: "Political Reform – Social Stability"], in Dong Yuyu and Shi Binhai, eds., *Political China* (Beijing: Jinri Zhongguo Chubanshe, 1998), pp. 49–53.

37 Joseph Raz, "The Rule of Law and Its Virtue," *Law Quarterly Review* 93 (April 1977) pp. 195–221; John Finnis, *Natural Law and Natural Rights* (Oxford: Clarendon Press, 1980), p. 272.

38 Peerenboom, "Confucian Harmony and Freedom of Thought." Joseph Chan, for example, develops a Confucian alternative to a liberal or Kantian conception of moral autonomy. The former is a more minimal conception of autonomy than

the latter, and supports civil liberties to a lesser degree. Joseph Chan, "Moral Autonomy, Civil Liberties, and Confucianism," *Philosophy East & West*, vol. 52, no. 3 (July 2002), pp. 281–310.

39 A survey of academics, think tank experts, officials, businesspeople, journalists, and religious and cultural leaders found significant differences between Asians and Americans. The former chose an orderly society, harmony, and accountability of public values, in descending order, as the three most important societal values. In contrast, the Americans chose freedom of expression, personal freedom, and the rights of the individual. See Susan Sim, "Human Rights: Bridging the Gulf," *Straits Times* (Singapore), October 21, 1995, p. 32.

40 Jiang Zemin seems to believe that rule of law can help shore up the regime's legitimacy in a more direct way by providing a normative basis for a market economy. For a discussion of why the CCP's legitimacy is unlikely to be significantly enhanced by rule of law reforms, see Peerenboom, *China's Long March*.

41 See, generally, David Kairys, ed., *The Politics of Law*, 3rd edn. (New York: Basic Books, 1998).

42 Alice Ehr-Soon Tay, "Communist Visions, Communist Realities, and the Role of Law," *Journal of Law and Society*, vol. 17, no. 2 (1990), pp. 155–69.

43 In practice, the degree of politicization varies widely from country to country. See Shimon Shetreet and Jules Deschenes, *Judicial Independence: The Contemporary Debate* (Boston: Martinus Nijhoff Publishers, 1985).

44 Michael Dowdle, "The Constitutional Development and Operations of the National People's Congress," *Columbia Journal of Asian Law*, vol. 11, no. 1 (1997); Murray Scott Tanner, *The Politics of Lawmaking in China* (Oxford: Clarendon Press, 1999).

45 See P. P. Craig, *Administrative Law*, 3rd edn. (London: Sweet & Maxwell, 1994), p. 74, for the idea that "the government can always ensure that its policies become law in much the way that it desires." G. Craenen, "Legislators," in G. Craenen, ed., *The Institutions of Federal Belgium* (Leuven: Acco, 1996), pp. 71, 77, describes a change in the center of gravity away from the parliament to the executive such that the latter is able to "push its initiatives to the foreground and to obtain from Parliament what it considers necessary," and argues that parliament's main function is now less legislative and more to keep the government in check. This is not to claim of course that the Party is similar in all respects to ruling parties in parliamentary liberal democracies.

46 This paragraph depicts the current situation. See Randall Peerenboom, "Globalization, Path Dependency and the Limits of Law: Administrative Law Reform and the Rule of Law in the People's Republic of China," *Berkeley Journal of International Law*, vol. 19, no. 2 (2001), pp. 161–264.

47 See, for example, Pan Wei, "Democracy or Rule of Law." Statist Socialists might also favor an honest and professional civil service, though they may put greater emphasis on ideology and political factors in appointing civil servants and prefer that Party discipline committees be responsible for dealing with corruption among senior officials.

48 Communitarians share a similar view of the legal profession as the Neo-authoritarians, though they view the legal profession's obligations as being more toward society than the state and differ over specific issues such as when lawyers' obligations to the state and society will trump their obligations to their clients.

49 Kanishka Jayasuriya, "Introduction: Framework for the Analysis of Legal Institutions in East Asia," *Law, Capitalism and Power in Asia: The Rule of Law and Legal Institutions* (London: Routledge, 1999), p. 19, argues that judicial independence in East Asia is influenced by a statist ideology that rejects the liberal notion of a neutral state in favor of a paternalist state which grounds its legiti-

macy in its superior ability to fathom what constitutes "the good" for society. Thus, he claims, courts are more likely to serve as an instrument for the implementation of the policy objectives of the state and ruling elite.

50 In *Cohen v. California*, 403 U.S. 15 (1971), the U.S. Supreme Court held that an individual's right to free speech extends to wearing a jacket with "Fuck the Draft" on it in court, even though others may find such language offensive.

51 Indeed, focusing on each dimension separately is somewhat misleading. While different regime types tend to be correlated with different institutions and rules, in some cases advocates of alternative conceptions of rule of law might espouse seemingly similar purposes or adopt similar institutions or rules. Yet in practice the outcomes will still differ widely. This is to be expected in that there is generally some degree of indeterminacy to legal rules. Thus, even in the U.S., for example, conservative judges are likely to come to different conclusions in some cases than liberal judges, notwithstanding the fact that they share the same institutional context.

52 Many PRC scholars maintain that the constitution should be justiciable. Interestingly, the Supreme People's Court recently issued a potentially landmark interpretation in its reply to an inquiry from Shandong High People's Court. The Supreme Court stated that the plaintiff's basic right to an education as provided in the constitution should be protected even though there was no implementing law regarding the right to education. While a number of questions remain as to the Court's interpretation, it would appear that the decision opens the door to parties to directly invoke the constitution when at least their basic (*jiben*) constitutional rights have been violated, even in the absence of implementing legislation, thus making the constitution directly justiciable. See the Supreme Court's Reply, no. 25, issued on August 13, 2001.

53 See, for example, Luo Haocai, ed., *Xiandai xingzhengfa de pingheng lun* [The Balance Theory of Modern Administrative Law] (Beijing: Beijing University Press, 1997).

54 Compare P. P. Craig, *Administrative Law*, 3rd edn. (London: Sweet & Maxwell, 1994), pp. 17–18, claiming that the standard of *ultra vires* is being reinterpreted along lines consistent with respect for fundamental rights in the U.K., with Pei, "Citizens v. Mandarins," p. 856, tbl. 12, reporting that abuse of authority was invoked in only 16 of 219 cases where PRC courts quashed the illegal acts of agencies, in comparison with 60 times for exceeding legal authority, 48 for insufficient principal evidence, 40 for incorrect application of law, and even 32 for violation of legal procedures.

55 Peerenboom, "Globalization, Path Dependency and the Limits of Law."

56 Id. See also, *Human Rights Watch World Report 1998: China* (December 8, 1998) www.hrw.org/hrw/campaigns/china-98/chn-wr98.htm.

57 Nor is it possible simply to rely on Jayasuriya's statist rule of law as an alternative. The statist version fails to capture the differences between the Statist Socialist and Neo-authoritarian versions, and is at odds in significant respects with the Communitarian variant.

58 See Peerenboom, *China's Long March*.

5

CONCEPTS OF LAW IN VIETNAM

Transforming statist socialism

John Gillespie[1]

Introduction

In 1986 the Communist Party of Vietnam (CPV) committed Vietnam to *doi moi* (renovation) economic and political reforms.[2] Fearing political isolation and economic decline, the party wanted investment and technology from the outside world, but the door closed on many democratic liberal ideas. *Doi moi* reforms aimed to liberalize private production and to attract foreign investment (FDI) and overseas development assistance (ODA). But the party is attempting this transformation to a market-oriented legal system by preserving many Soviet-inspired legal institutions and CPV leadership (*su lanh dao cua dang*) over the state.

Legal reform is shaped by tensions between economic development and a political desire to preserve party power. Lawmakers must reconcile the needs of a rights-based commercial legal framework and a ruling party that has not decided to unconditionally accept legal limits to its power. As a compromise, borrowed laws are superimposed over Soviet-inspired legal institutions, with little theoretical consideration given to compatibility. The factors constraining legal discourse are numerous and varied, but they include Marxist–Leninist ideology, low demand and respect for legal rules, and poor institutional enforcement of laws. This chapter traces the legal discourse concerning the role of law in post *doi moi* society and canvasses changes required to enhance social demand for the "rule of law."

Constructed from different systems of knowledge, the new overlaying the old, legal discourse in Vietnam traverses distinct ways of conceiving social regulation.[3] Randy Peerenboom (Chapter 4) outlined four rule of law taxonomic models comprising the main sets of legal practices and norms shaping legal discourse in China: statist socialism, neo-authoritarianism, communitarianism, and democratic liberal rule of law. Broad cultural, ideological, and economic similarities make the statist socialist model roughly applicable to Vietnam.

Law reform everywhere comprises a set of conscious strategies to improve state–society relationships; as such, any account must discuss the agents for change in addition to conceptualizing legal discourse. Law is a central process used by competing social agents to structure state power.[4] Efforts to reform law inevitably touch the foundation of power, legitimacy, and domination embedded in basic state and social structures. In order to understand legal discourse in Vietnam, it is necessary to contrast competing visions for law and their social impact.

Vietnamese agents for change come from within party–state circles and externally from farmers, entrepreneurs, and other social groups. Though pursuing different interests, their demands are largely articulated within the parameters of the statist socialist version of the rule of law. Contests within statist socialist discourse revolve around orthodox Marxist–Leninist "socialist legality" and *nha nuoc phap quyen* [law-based state] (see pp. 000–00). Socialist legality promotes party paramountcy and state bureaucratic management, whereas *nha nuoc phap quyen* advocates limiting party and state power with law.

Foreign agents for change, such as donors, investors, and international treaty partners, aim to transplant a thin rule of law and a thicker democratic liberal rule of law (see Chapter 1).[5] Some foreign donors (especially multilateral donors such as the World Bank, the United Nations Development Program [UNDP] and the Asian Development Bank [ADB]), foreign investors, and treaty partners advocate a thin version of democratic liberal rule of law.[6] Their principle concern is generating a stable and transparent environment where businesses can plan their affairs according to law. Their reform program also promotes substantive neo-liberal economic goals, such as limiting state powers over private property and contractual rights.

Some bilateral donors (e.g. Sweden), non-governmental human rights organizations (NGOs) (e.g. Human Rights Watch), and various overseas Vietnamese dissident groups advocate both a thin rule of law and a thick democratic liberal rule of law. They accuse Vietnamese authorities of constraining free speech, religious worship, ethnic culture, and due process in criminal trials.[7] In contrast to neo-liberal economic ideals promoted by multilateral donors, this group funds legal assistance programs promoting representative democracy, procedural justice, and civil rights.

Regrettably, the idealized representation of democratic liberalism projected into Vietnam rarely mentions the intense political struggles in Western countries required to generate social consensus on personal liberties.[8] Post September 11 debates in which civil rights are traded for national security are not conveyed to Vietnamese audiences. Perhaps, in time, more textured representations of democratic liberalism will penetrate Vietnamese censorship barriers, but, for the present, democratic pluralism and civil rights are presented as ahistorical immutable principles.

We have seen that "rule of law" discourse in Vietnam is contested. The sections which follow outline the debates within statist socialism and then explore the four main sites of contention with other "rule of law" discourse: separating party and state, democratic processes, transplanting market law, and institutional regulation. In the interests of clarity, it is useful first briefly to outline the main institutional structures in Vietnam.

Institutional overview

Vietnam has a unitary state system comprising five arms: National Assembly (NA), president, government (executive), People's Courts, and People's Procuracy. Any discussion concerning the state makes little sense without first discussing the role of the CPV (*Dang Cong San Vietnam*). Vietnam is a one-party state governed by the CPV, which is the "force leading the state and society."[9] The party is led by a politburo and central committee that meet two or three times a year to formulate policy on every aspect of Vietnamese society. There is an extensive, organizational network mirroring the four state levels: central, provincial/city, district, and ward/village.

Resisting periodic campaigns designed to formalize party–state linkages, party and state remain symbiotically enmeshed. The Ordinance on Public Employees 1998, for example, requires all state employees to follow party resolutions and the party line as if they were law. Central party commissions (*Ban Trung Uong*) regulate state bodies with internal, secret operational guidelines, and "party affairs sections" (*ban can su dang*) operating in every state organ "lead and motivate members in the organization…to implement the party line and policies."[10] The *nomenklatura* further secures "party leadership" by ensuring that party members occupy key state positions.[11] Finally, political qualities determined by party seniority and ideological loyalty are still more important than professional proficiency in determining promotion.

The National Assembly (*Quoc Hoi*), Vietnam's supreme legislature, historically performed a largely ceremonial function, approving and passing laws drafted by the party and state executive. Before *doi moi* reforms it sat infrequently, leaving the Government Council (*Hoi Dong Chinh Phu*) and ministers to rule though administrative edicts.[12] State power in principle is unified (*thong nhat*) and centralized (*tap trung*) in the National Assembly.[13] Its importance as a legislative body has undoubtedly increased since the early 1990s, though real power resides with the government. The ideological and institutional limits to legislative reform are considered below in the context of changing democratic processes (pp. 000–00).

The Government (*Chinh Phu*) is constitutionally divided among central (ministries) and local executive bodies (provincial/city, district, and village people's committees). Central authority is devolved (*phan bo*) through branch (*nganh*) and vertical (*doc*) central–local power-sharing.[14] Police and taxation powers are implemented by provincial agencies directly under central control. Other executive powers are devolved to functionally specialized departments attached to people's committees (*uy ban nhan dan*).

Court hierarchy in Vietnam reflects the three main levels of the unitary state. The Supreme People's Court (*Toa An Nhan Dan Toi Cao*) is responsible for judicial work (*cong tac xet xu*), hearing appeals and supervising and reviewing decisions made by provincial courts. It is headed by a president and several vice-presidents, and consists of the Council of Judges (the highest adjudication body) and three Appeals Courts (*Toa Thuc Tham*). Judges are organized into chambers of courts that specialize in criminal, civil, economic, military, and administrative law. At the second hierarchical level, provincial/city courts hear first-instance and appellate cases. Over 600 district-level courts comprise the lowest level in the court system, hearing first-instance cases in rural *huyen* districts or urban districts (*quan*).

The people's procuracy was established in Vietnam in 1960 as the fifth arm of the state. The Supreme Procuracy vertically controls provincial/city- and district/village-level branches.[15] Blurring policing and juridical functions, procurators investigate and prosecute criminal violations in the courts, while supervising the legality and enforcement of court decisions. Finally, the president is the ceremonial head of state, and exercises limited legislative and political powers.

The next section traces "rule of law" discourses in Vietnam and identifies four main areas of contest: separating party and state, democratic processes, transplanting market law and institutional regulation. These issues are discussed in subsequent sections.

Mapping statist socialist "rule of law" discourse in Vietnam

Pre-doi moi *period*

Vietnamese perceptions of law were profoundly influenced by imported neo-Confucian ideology. With increasing dedication, emperors from the Lê Dynasty (1428–1788) onwards borrowed Chinese laws and governmental structures. As in China, the Confucian elite in Vietnam saw no inconsistency in championing rule through ritual principles (*li*) while controlling social behavior with draconian penal laws. Just as Confucius analogized from moral principles, Vietnamese authorities treated legal rules expressing Confucian morality as optional instruments rather than immutable divine principles. Laws were primarily used to preserve Confucian hierarchies and social order.[16] For most Vietnamese, unwritten moral codes based on Confucian, Buddhist, Taoist, and animistic precepts governed village life.

From its inception, the party conflated neo-Confucian moral principles with Marxist–Leninism to legitimize its rule. Taken together, neo-Confucian morality rule (*duc tri*), assertions of moral righteousness (*chinh nghia*), and

Marxist scientific infallibility invested the party with a moral and historic mission to lead the nation.[17] Ho Chi Minh put the moral leadership of the party beyond doubt where he declared that "the party is morality."[18] Moral virtue legitimized both political power and rule through moral leadership and administrative edict.

Moral leadership deeply influenced state–societal legal relationships. Socialist law and legal institutions imported from the Soviet Union during the 1960s and 1970s were filtered through neo-Confucian moral precepts.[19] While socialist legal ideology was imported largely intact, the modus operandi of imported Soviet institutions was peculiarly Vietnamese. Socialist legality (*phap che xa hoi chu nghia*), the core statist socialist rule of law doctrine, is defined in Vietnamese writings as a tool of proletarian dictatorship (*chuyen chinh vo san*) to defeat enemies, and protect the revolution and the collective democratic rights of people to organize, manage, and develop a command economy. It has two main elements:

- class-based legality;
- "legal enforceability" (*tinh chat cuong che*).

The class element is reasoned from Marxist theory that worker-controlled societies require legal systems that reflect proletarian aspirations. The connection between law and class is explained by the familiar metaphor that law is part of the "superstructure," which reflects the "will of the ruling class" (*y chi cua giai cap thong tri*) and their domination over the means of production.[20]

Legal ideology obscured the precise relationship between party "policy" (*chinh sach*) and law with opaque class rhetoric. Three syllogistic principles are, nevertheless, discernable in party writings.[21] First, as the leader and defender of working-class interests, the party is the executive committee of the ruling class and directs its "dominant will" (*y chi toi thuong*). Second, class leadership gives the party a monopoly to formulate policy that binds everyone. Third, since law reflects the "dominant will," party policy is considered the "soul and spirit" (*linh hon*) of the law.[22] The conflation of party policy and law enabled the party and state to use law as a "management tool" (*cong cu quan ly*) to adjust or balance (*dieu chinh*) social relationships – a practice allowing the substitution of policy for law.

Vietnamese writings also stressed that law has coercive force. Linking socialist legality to "state discipline" (*ky luat nha nuoc*), legal violations were considered revolutionary betrayals. Quoting Lenin, Vietnamese commentators wrote: "only the slightest violation of the law, the slightest loss of social order provides a loophole to be immediately taken advantage of by the enemies of the working people."[23] State officials and citizens were exhorted to "respect and act within the law" (*phai ton trong va thuc hien phap luat*).[24]

To summarize, socialist legality in Vietnam evinced three main principles.

First, law is not above the state, but rather emanates from the state. As an extreme manifestation of legal positivism, there is no space in socialist legality for customary rules or natural rights.[25] Second, socialist legality invested the party and state with prerogative powers to substitute policy for law. Law facilitates, but never constrains, state power. Third, the party leads and the state manages society using moral "exemplary behavior" (*guong mau*). Echoing Imperial claims to a heavenly mandate, party paramountcy – the supremacy of party policy/morality over law – evolved into a transcending moral principle.

Importing nha nuoc phap quyen *(law-based state)*

After decades of socialist orthodoxy, questions were raised during the Fifth National Congress of the CPV in 1982 on whether revolutionary ideology should continue dominating legal thinking.[26] Reformers argued for a separation of the party from the day-to-day running of the government, and regulation through law, rather than moral rule and edict. Little was done until the Sixth National Congress of the CPV in 1986. By this time, rampant inflation, falling production, a vibrant informal economy, and the booming economies of Vietnam's capitalist neighbors could no longer be ignored. Admitting past economic errors, party leaders introduced *doi moi* (renovation) reforms promoting law rather than morality to regulate the economy. Striving to catch up with regional neighbors, the party-state gradually accepted that socialist legality could no longer regulate a mixed-market economy.[27]

In searching for a new legal ideology, Vietnamese lawmakers turned once again to the Soviet Union for inspiration.[28] During the mid-1980s Mikhail Gorbachev introduced a series of constitutional changes designed to formalize economic and social liberalizations (*perestroika*) without fundamentally disrupting Communist Party power.[29] Soviet lawmakers developed a constitutional doctrine – *pravovoe gosudarstvo* (law-based state) – that proclaimed the supremacy of law and the constitution.

Pravovoe gosudarstvo was based on German *Rechtsstaat* (state-law) principles.[30] Developed in autocratic nineteenth-century Prussia, *Rechtsstaat* promoted the implementation of state policy through legislation. It de-emphasized social customs and precedents derived from sources outside the state that were capable of checking political and bureaucratic power. Contrasting with Diceyan common law notions of the "rule of law," there were no unwritten legal conventions that the state was powerless to change. *Pravovoe gosudarstvo*, nevertheless, radically departed from Leninist socialist legality with its emphasis on party paramountcy and legal exceptualism.

In a speech delivered to the Seventh Congress of the CPV in 1991, General Secretary Do Muoi introduced *nha nuoc phap quyen* (state-legal rights), a Vietnamese adaptation of *pravovoe gosudarstvo*.[31] Like *pravovoe gosudarstvo*, *nha nuoc phap quyen* required stable, authoritative, and compul-

sory law; equality before the law; and the use of law to constrain and supervise enforcement and administration. It also proposed a binary separation of
party and state functions. The party was supposed to formulate socioeco-
nomic objectives, leaving state apparatus to enact and implement the party
line.

Unlike their Soviet mentors, Vietnamese legal theorists refused to
abandon socialist legality and are endeavoring to create a "socialist law-
based state" (*nha nuoc phap quyen xa hoi chu nghia*). By juxtaposing socialist
legality and *nha nuoc phap quyen* principles, policymakers set in motion
ideological contests within statist socialist discourse.

Current directions in statist socialist rule of law

Recent legal writings highlight areas of tension between socialist legality
and *nha nuoc phap quyen*.[32] As it is more a conceptual label for new legal
thinking than a coherent ideology, writers use *nha nuoc phap quyen* as a
convenient rubric to smuggle socialist legality and democratic liberal ideas
into the "rule of law" discourse. Five main themes are discernable in *nha
nuoc phap quyen* writings:

1 Law rather than morality must adjust basic social relationships. Calls
   for legal formalism periodically appeared in socialist legality writings,
   but the principle of party paramountcy legitimized the substitution of
   policy for law. Whether party paramountcy and legal exceptualism are
   countenanced in *nha nuoc phap quyen* thinking is explored below in the
   sections dealing with the separation of party and state (pp. 000–00) and
   transplanting market law (pp. 000–00).
2 State power belongs to the people and is used to elect state bodies. Also
   found in socialist legality, this rhetorical proposition rests on Lenin's
   assertion that democracy is only possible where the working class
   "centralize power in their hands." The section below concerning democratic processes (pp. 000–00) examines whether the shift towards legal
   formalism advocated by *nha nuoc phap quyen* discourse contemplates
   more democratic accountability.
3 State organs and citizens "must respect and act within the law." This
   proposition superficially resembles "legal enforceability" in socialist
   legality. The sections below dealing with separating party and state
   (pp. 000–00) and transplanting market law (pp. 000–00) explore
   whether there has been a conceptual shift from treating law as a
   management tool to a "rule of law" that binds party and state institutions.
4 Legislative, executive, and judicial powers are distributed among state
   bodies (*hoc thuyet tam quyen phan lap* – division of powers doctrine).
   The 1992 Constitution rejected Montesquieu's separation of powers

doctrine and retained the socialist organizational principle that unifies (*thong nhat*) and centralizes (*tap trung*) state power in the National Assembly. Efforts under *nha nuoc phap quyen* to clarify bureaucratic and judicial powers are examined below in the sections dealing with transplanting market law (pp. 000–00) and implementing law (pp. 000–00).

5   Courts should operate independently from local government organs (people's committees) and resolve disputes with *phap che* (legality). Contemporary writers unambiguously call for courts to take center-stage in resolving social grievances, but are less clear whether justice is done by realizing party objectives or pursuing due process.[33] The interplay between socialist legality and *nha nuoc phap quyen* notions of justice is examined below in the implementing law section (pp. 000–00).

Separating party and state

The central ideological struggle in Vietnam is between a thin "rule of law" (requiring the party and state to follow economic law), promoted in *nha nuoc phap quyen* discourse, and party paramountcy in socialist legality doctrine. At stake are the norms, rules, and processes that establish the appropriate ways of legitimizing and exercising state power.

Class-based theory

Party paramountcy arose from the Marxist–Leninist axiom that by leading and defending "ruling-class" interests the party acquired prerogative rights to substitute political power for state law. The class theory underpinning party paramountcy is, however, unraveling in the mixed-market economy. As private enterprises and foreign investors become more economically important, party theorists have been forced to expand the ranks of the "working-class peasant" alliance. The 1992 Constitution added intellectuals to the ruling class. More recently, the ruling class enlarged further to include the "interests of the entire people" (*loi ich cua toan the nhan dan*), including entrepreneurs.[34] The final class barrier collapsed when in 2002 the Party Central Committee officially permitted party members to engage in private business.

The recruitment of former class enemies into the "ruling class" forced a radical rethinking of the Marxist–Leninist foundations of party paramountcy. Class struggle, for example, was transmogrified into class cooperation. Contemporary theorists deduce from an obscure injunction issued by Ho Chi Minh in the 1940s encouraging cadres to filter Soviet class struggle doctrines through "East Asian ethnology" that class-cooperation reflects East Asian yearnings for social harmony.[35] Theorizing of this kind draws on precepts outside Marxist–Leninism, and the party has been unable to mount a convincing class-based argument for maintaining party paramountcy in a mixed-market economy.

Searching for moral legitimacy

Party paramountcy has always rested on more solid foundations than Marxist theory. Stephen Young argued that "Vietnamese invest true authority with those who possess the quality of *uy tin* (moral legitimacy)."[36] Party theorists have long used the moral legitimacy conferred by the "working class" cause to justify party paramountcy. Since the leadership was not accountable to an electorate, legitimacy rested on the politically connected public believing assertions of party moral superiority.

Once again, however, class cooperation excited by the market economy is unsettling longstanding conventions. If the party protects – even creates markets – for entrepreneurs it loses the revolutionary moral high ground. For this reason, party theorists find imaginative, but unconvincing, reasons to justify why private enterprise in Vietnam is non-exploitative. Some argue that Vietnamese small businesses are not capitalists, because profits are equivalent to wages, while others contend that intellectual labor in the service sector does not exploit the "surplus value" of other workers. Still others maintain that capitalism is a necessary stage on the way to socialism and that, by implication, the party has not abandoned the working class.[37] As market mechanisms replace socialist redistribution, revolutionary morality is losing its power to legitimize party paramountcy.

There are mixed signals that the party-state is seeking moral legitimacy from domestic and, especially, foreign audiences by stressing thin "rule of law" elements in *nha nuoc phap quyen* discourse. Market forces increasingly require the party-state to regulate private commercial relations with greater regularity, due process, and transparency. But because the market affects people differently not everyone responds positively to "rule of law" imagery. Fairer tax collection, regulation of market failures, and credible dispute resolution generate legitimacy for those (primarily large private companies and foreign investors) engaged in the state-regulated economy. For the vast majority working in the relational economy, promises of a thin rule of law are much less important than other representations of *uy tin*.

High-profile criminal trials designed to generate legitimacy by showing due process have also been ineffectual, even counterproductive. In the Minh Phung corruption trial, for example, 200 witnesses were called during a 67-day trial.[38] Orchestrated images showing exhaustive investigations and rigorously tested evidence were subverted when party-prerogative powers favored high-ranking party and state officials. As an ideal, a thin "rule of law" is permitted until it conflicts with the central tenet of socialist legality – law must not constrain the party line. There are indications, discussed below (pp. 000–00), that the party is contemplating a thin "rule of law" in commercial, but not criminal and labor, cases.

The party has been more successful in generating moral legitimacy by appealing to developmentalist and nationalist sentiments. Invoking nostalgic visions of wholesome village traditions, party writers portray the party as defender and definer of core social customs and values.[39] Manufactured cultural values are reproduced in popular films like "*Thuong Nho Dong Que*" (Our Beloved Countryside), depicting serene village morals providing refuge from the "whirlwind of the market economy."[40] Party resolutions select from a wide range of "traditional" values to reinvent *the* "national identity" (*ban sac dan toc*) in a mixed-market economy. "Traditional" values include "well-established" historical values, especially patriotism, national independence, collective values that tie individuals, families, communities and the homeland, kindness, tolerance, appreciation of *nghia tinh dao ly* (Confucian values), diligence, creativeness, elegance, and modesty. They differ from revolutionary morality in downplaying Marxist–Leninism. The party avoided the anti-Western "Asian values" discourse elsewhere in Southeast Asia, perhaps from concern that it might inadvertently discredit the European roots of Marxist–Leninism.

Party leaders use invented values to tap into a visceral nationalism obsessed with "protecting the fine cultural traditions and values of the country" from foreign enemies.[41] The party legitimizes paramountcy by connecting moral values and Marxist–Leninist ideology. This is a dynamic process. At the beginning of the twentieth century, revolutionary morality vilified neo-Confucianism as rigid and hierarchical – an impediment to socialist modernization. At the beginning of the 21st century the party is increasingly appealing to neo-Confucian essentialism and shared economic prosperity to legitimize authoritarian government. The moral images promoted by the party have changed, but not legitimacy through morality.

Party control over state organs

Nha nuoc phap quyen doctrine requires the party to confine itself to policy formulation, leaving the state apparatus to enact and implement law. The 1992 Constitution formalized this principle by placing party organizations under the law, an ideological shift that appeared to signal the demise of party paramountcy.[42] In practice, constitutionalism never penetrated party thinking. CPV leaders did not accept that party policy needed state legislation to acquire coercive force.[43]

The relationship between party and state is complicated by the party's dual roles. In some circumstances the party functions as a type of political bureaucracy that formulates policy for the state. Resembling Western political parties, in this manifestation the party is functionally separate from, and frequently competes with, state institutions. But the party also functions like a mass organization, infiltrating, managing, and controlling state institutions through resolutions, "party affairs sections," and the *nomenklatura* system.[44] In this manifestation the party functions like an elitist secret society, linking family members, classmates, and military comrades in relational networks.

Public administration reforms aim to rationalize and modernize state structures by engineering a legal-rational Weberian bureaucracy, as distinct from a "class" state.[45] Attempts to control party "leadership" over the state are opposed by those believing this will "weaken both the Party's leading role and the State's managerial role and the people's right to mastery."[46] They argue that "[l]ife is richer and more complicated than stipulations…it is not always possible to establish clear demarcation lines between the areas within the competence of the Party and those within the competence of the administration."[47] Party leaders have refused to contemplate state institutions, such as constitutional courts, that could check party prerogative powers with law.[48]

External challenges to party paramountcy

Thin rule of law ideals promoted by foreign donors directly contest party paramountcy. As we have seen, the party is unwilling to accept legal constraints on its management of sensitive criminal and political matters. There are indications (discussed below, pp. 000–00) that the party is voluntarily moderating prerogative powers over market transactions.

Substantive democratic liberal values also threaten party leadership. Western human rights interventions treat separate party and state functions as a universal good or political "truth." Naturally, the separation between political and state power in Western countries is never absolute or unchanging; nor should it be in representative democracies.[49] Conceptual divisions between political morals and state law nevertheless enable a functional separation of party and state. In plural societies the separation of party and state is necessary to ensure that states appear neutral between different values and ways of life. For Western critics, moral legitimacy (whether grounded in fact or myth) does not justify the party interfering in legislation passed by the National Assembly and criminal trials.[50] Their condemnation reflects conflicting understandings of political legitimation.

Party paramountcy in Vietnam primarily (though not entirely) arises from a shared belief in the party's moral mission to lead the state and society. Functional separation of party and state diminishes moral legitimacy by damaging party prestige. When discussing regime legitimization in communist countries, Muthiah Alagappa stated that "[w]hile acceptance by the citizens would enhance the moral basis and self-esteem of such regimes, their legitimacy depends on acceptance by state institutions or 'political forces to be found within the circle of power.' "[51] For over 70 years political legitimacy in Vietnam has rested on perceptions of moral legitimacy more than legal conformity and popular consent. Party paramountcy (and statist socialism) depends on the 2.1 million party members forming the "circle of power" controlling state and ideological apparatus believing the moral images projected by party leaders. Their support reduces the need for the party to seek alternative sources of legitimacy through representative democracy.

All the same, party power-sharing is not immune from internal and external forces. Some Western commentators have shown that Vietnamese party leaders are forced voluntarily to concede power in order to gain coop- eration from revival groups.[52] A quiet, sometimes covert, process of negotiation and compromise adjusts power-sharing arrangements among power-brokers, and even with those outside the party-state orbit. Ben Kerkvliet characterizes these exchanges as "dialogue in the broadest sense of the word, which incorporates communication of contentious ideas and pref- erences in ways that, in Vietnam, are often indirect and non-verbal."[53] "Dialogical" exchanges renegotiate party–state power-sharing using rules developed over decades of political discourse.

Contests generally come down to how much decision-making power the party should transfer to state organs (especially the National Assembly and government) and non-state agents. From a "rule of law" perspective, this becomes a question of whether constitutional rules can effectively resolve competition for political power. As we shall see, movement in this direction is most evident in the economic arena, where the party economic commis- sion is beginning to transfer constitutional power to state bodies to formulate and implement economic policy. It is equally possible that eventu- ally "rule of law" discourse will resolve political issues directly threatening party security more effectively than party-based dialogical exchanges.

Democratic processes

Democratic representation

Views regarding representative processes in statist socialism are traceable to Lenin's assertion that democracy is only possible where the working class "centralize power in their hands."[54] Socialist democracy (*dan chu xa chu nghia*) was conceived in two ways. Drawing on democratic liberalism, theo- rists argued that popularly elected legislatures (National Assembly and provincial legislative councils) should supervise state power on behalf of the people. Socialist "democracy" also borrowed from Lenin's revolutionary conception that bourgeois democracy abandoned the people's democratic rights wholly into the hands of elected representatives. Democratic rights were better safeguarded, he thought, by "proletarian dictatorship" (*chuyen chinh vo san*) where the "ruling class" directly supervised state organs through their proxy – the communist party.

157

Revolutionary terminology such as "proletariat dictatorship" has meta-morphosed into internationally respectable slogans – "a socialist law-based state of the people from the people for the people" – but core illiberal, authoritarian proclivities remain in democratic discourse. The question remains whether increasingly complex state–society relationships in the post-*doi moi* environment will force the party to transfer more decision-making power to elected legislative bodies.

NA influence has undoubtedly grown in line with the demand for legislation in the mixed-market economy. While it is not yet a policy-making body – and is unlikely to develop this way under existing constitutional settings – delegates behave more like legislators. NA sitting times have become more frequent and debates more robust. Issue-oriented coalitions combine to block or amend draft laws that might potentially harm political patrons. The Press Law, for example, was amended 27 times before adoption.[55] More recently, delegates representing provincial people's committees unsuccessfully opposed the Enterprise Law 1999, which threatened provincial discretionary powers.

Reform-minded lawyers within the NA believe that more assertive NA delegates and occasional voter resistance to party-sanctioned candidates do not necessarily foreshadow representative democracy.[56] For this to happen, they think the party must relax strict nomination rules that ensure that over 90 percent of NA delegates are party members.[57] They also believe recent changes increasing the number of full-time delegates and supervisory powers were intended to improve legislative efficiency, satisfy candidate quotas, and meet conditions imposed by foreign donors.[58] Reforms have not tipped the balance of power away from party-dominated standing committees that currently conduct NA work between the two brief annual sittings.

Informants speculate that increased media scrutiny of NA debates aims to show provincial constituents that they have a voice in central policy-making.[59] For example, provincial delegates in recent televised discussions on sensitive land corruption cases were given prominent seats to emphasize their involvement in resolving these problems. Democratic discourse is orchestrated to convince voters that representative bodies resolve sensitive issues. The transfer of actual decision-making power from the party to the NA is difficult to predict in an environment where delegates are punished for expressing views beyond the narrow parameters permitted by the party.

What is currently lacking is a political morality supporting effective choice between different outlooks. Only the party defined revolutionary ethics (*dao duc cach mang*) last century, and only the party is permitted to modernize political morality for the 21st century. Those outside the virtuous circle (party–state) play only a limited role in shaping moral discourse. Worse still, those challenging party views are perceived as violating public morals and are charged with crimes against public order.[60] Without a political morality supporting views from beyond the party–state orbit, discourse concerning democratic reforms takes place underground or within narrow political boundaries designed to preserve party paramountcy.[61]

Civil rights

From Imperial times, state–society relations were based on asymmetric (*co che xin cho* – asking–giving) processes. Members of the public petitioned authorities to redress administrative abuses, while mandarins, as morally "superior men," instructed those slower to understand.[62] In contrast with democratic liberal notions that citizens have inherent civil rights, in neo-Confucian Vietnam mandarins bestowed rights.

On gaining power, Ho Chi Minh exhorted cadres not to dictate from above like "new mandarins" (*quan moi*).[63] But party leaders soon discovered that imported egalitarian socialist ethics could not easily displace neo-Confucian values and hierarchical practices. It is nonsense to look for total continuities; nevertheless, contemporary officials share a similarity in moral outlook and administrative style with pre-modern mandarins. State corporatism and collective approaches to civil rights nurture these attitudes.

Recent official responses to rural "hotspots," where villagers directly and occasionally violently protested land and public finance abuses, exemplify contemporary attitudes to civil rights.[64] The state reacted with a mixture of repression and consultation. Reforms introduced by the Decree No. 29 on Grassroots Democracy (*dan chu tan goc*) in 1998 endeavored to make village officials more publicly accountable through greater procedural transparency and public forums. Disclosure and complaint procedures seemed to invest individuals, more than party collectives, with rights to take action against malfeasants. The Decree sent mixed signals that the state was moving from socialist management and *co che xin cho* processes towards civil rights.

Some commentators skeptically dismiss these reforms as *su chung luat* (legal vaccinations) designed to forestall far-reaching change, while others believe grassroots democracy is cautiously making *co che xin cho* relationships more accountable to civil rights.[65] Evidence that the state responds to social pressure does not necessarily intimate movement towards civil rights. Progress in this direction requires a profound change in state toleration of political "lobbying" (*chay lo thu tuc*), demonstrations, and ultimately political pluralism. "Grassroots" democracy sanctions spontaneous demonstrations as a safety-valve for public frustration, without recognizing a state–society compact where public dissent is recognized as a legitimate means of influencing government policy. The right to protest is bestowed by benevolent regulators and is not an inherent or achieved right. The party and state do not recognize civil rights generated by autonomous social relations such as religions, workplaces, and professional organizations. As a result, there are few non-state pathways (or civil space) where the public can sway political decision-making.[66]

Far from achieving civil rights through political discourse, the state granted rights to appease public hostility towards wayward provincial officials. An inability to control strong provincial governments and corrupt officials implies a weak central state more than movement towards civil rights.[67] For example, the party encourages public accountability at the provincial and district/village level while doing nothing to give citizens civil rights enforceable against central government and party officials.

Despite a decade of Public Administrative Reform (PAR) designed to induce bureaucratic accountability through administrative appeals and court actions, most complainants prefer to petition junior officials.[68] The continuation of the *co che xin cho* (asking–giving) relationships is only partially attributable to low rights consciousness in Vietnamese society. Administrative courts were ostensibly introduced to check *co che xin cho* relationships with legal rights, but have failed so far to influence official behavior and attract public confidence.[69]

Party theory, moreover, does not recognize legal space beyond the party and state.[70] *Xa hoi cong dan* (citizen society) theory locates legal obligations and civil rights in citizenship, but explicitly rejects the possibility that personal legal rights (civil rights) are inherent attributes.[71] Naturally, the party-state is not monolithic and does not aspire to control all public voices, though in rejecting a legal role for *xa hoi dan su* (civil society) it reserves the ultimate right to establish the quality and extent of civil rights.

The impact of democratic liberalism

Liberal representative democracy seriously challenges party power.[72] Western donors advocating Lockean notions that governments derive legitimacy from popular mandates urge the party to accept multiple political voices and open political-moral discourse to competing social interests. The question of how much space governments should allow citizens to pursue personal interests varies among and within liberal democratic countries. Nevertheless, there is general agreement among donors that states should refrain from interfering with basic freedoms (natural and positive rights) such as religious and political organization.

Fearing political competition, party theorists consider multiparty democracy "peaceful evolution" (*dien bien hoa binh*) – an attempt by Vietnam's enemies to achieve through peaceful means what they could not do through force: remove the party from power. The party has not developed effective theoretical responses to multiparty democracy and instead recycles socialist democracy rhetoric that "mastership" (*quyen lam chu*) of the people through "grassroots" democracy safeguards the people's interests.

Research finds meager public support for representative democracy and civil rights. The Lockean mythology that state legitimacy requires popular consent appears alien and contrived to those conditioned to view civil rights as concessionary privileges granted by the state. In a society where political authority primarily rests on moral legitimacy (*uy tin*), state–society relations are generally conceived in moral rather than legal (civil rights) terms.

Language also constrains the passage of thick democratic liberal ideals. The Vietnamese word for rights, "*quyen loi*," is derived from the Chinese "*quanli*," which was in turn borrowed from the Japanese "*kenri*," coined in the late 19th century.[73] As with its Chinese and Japanese derivations, "*quyen loi*" invokes notions of might, power and interest that impede civil rights discourse in Vietnamese.[74] With the exception of a few disaffected members of the urban elite, it does not occur to the vast majority that constitutional rights could or should convey more than mere rhetorical aspirations. Indeed, the very idea of a society governed by civil rights is anathema to many.[75] Private rights are widely perceived as promoting individualism (*chu nghia ca nhan*) and undermining collective values by substituting the self for group membership. Evincing communitarian thinking, media commentators worry that constitutional rights will promote a culture of runaway self-seeking individualism and consumerism.

To recap, there are few signs that human rights discourse is changing party attitudes towards political pluralism and civil rights. It is possible that the increasing complexity of state–society relations in the mixed-market economy may eventually force the party to transfer power to elected representatives to resolve social disputes that are intractable to "dialogical" exchanges. Once some discretionary authority is devolved, representative bodies may arrogate more power for themselves. Social demand for democratic reforms and civil rights is limited, however, in a society conditioned to accept that benevolent rulers confer rights. Agitation for democratic reforms is almost entirely confined to small, but vocal, offshore Vietnamese political organizations and human rights agencies.[76]

Transplanting market laws

More than any other factor, economic discourse has changed the meaning of law in Vietnam. Contrasting with Western *lex mercatoria*, which primarily evolved from domestic commercial exchanges, commercial law in Vietnam relies on legal imports.[77] Starting with the Law on Foreign Investment 1987, lawmakers borrowed a commercial legal framework from Western legal sources. But the meanings ascribed to legal imports are shaped by domestic economic and legal discourse.

Bilateral and multilateral (e.g. World Bank and UNDP) donors technically assisted commercial law reforms. Japanese and multilateral donors offered divergent but by no means mutually exclusive visions for legal change.[78] Both agreed that a thin rule of law encourages market stability and predictability, but Japanese advisors were more sympathetic towards state-directed economic reform and bureaucratic regulatory powers. Multilateral and

Western bilateral donors, on the contrary, championed a neo-liberal economic agenda in which private commercial rights were promoted as a means of keeping the government from interfering with the market.[79]

More than 10 years after western legal borrowing began, a Legal Needs Assessment (LNA) project coordinated by the Ministry of Justice, though largely sponsored and conceived by the UNDP, recommended in 2001 sweeping commercial law reforms.[80] Three proposals reveal the thin rule of law template underpinning donor-assisted reforms:[81]

- citizens may do everything not expressly prohibited by law;
- the "State must not do anything, except that which is expressly permitted by law;"
- citizens should have increased powers to "know, discuss, and check" state power.

The first principle is a core democratic liberal rule of law value that invests individuals with "natural" personal liberties. The other principles reflect the thin rule of law concern that legal rules should circumscribe state power. Local responses to thin and thick versions of the "rule of law" are divided along geographical (North–South, highland–lowland and urban–rural) and hierarchical fault-lines. The sections which follow map the main discourses shaping imported commercial laws. Research suggests that communication between the discourses is imperfect, forming socially layered responses to the rule of law.

Receiving market laws

The party elite

Even the thin democratic liberal "rule of law" principles underlying donor-assisted commercial law reforms contest the core socialist legality principles: party paramountcy, morality rule, and legal exceptualism. That a rule of law was ever contemplated by party leaders suggests two possibilities: that laws constraining party paramountcy are politically acceptable when applied to commercial relationships; and/or that the state intends to tame private commercial rights with prerogative powers.

Internal debates within the politburo remain opaque; however, high-level officials responsible for law reforms provide some glimpses into elite-level thinking.[82] Three reasons for reform are advanced. Imported facilitative law is attractive, because it recentralizes economic power by closing provincial licensing gateways. More importantly, political leaders believe that rapid economic development requires a market-oriented legal system to attract and regulate foreign and domestic investors. Following from this point, legal harmonization required by international treaties is a necessary precondition for gaining entry into foreign markets.[83]

Swimming against the tide of international legal integration, many within the elite are concerned that imported neo-liberal economic norms will exacerbate existing social inequalities.[84] For them, contractual and property rights are needed to attract foreign investment and satisfy ODA conditionalities, but discretionary powers must preserve the "state benefit" (*loi ich cua nha nuoc*). They also believe that a thin "rule of law" will constrain the state's ability to *quan ly* (manage) the economy and reduce the negative social impact of capitalist property and contract rights. Their thinking reflects underlying command economic doctrine that states are obligated to "*quan ly*" the economy to protect working-class interests. Exposing deep divisions within party discourse, this group recently prevented reformers from removing references in the Constitution to state and cooperative ownership forming the "foundation of the national economy."

Some foreign observers speculate that the party elite use orthodox Marxist–Leninism and international economic integration as ideological weapons in "palace wars." In addition to gaining political advantage, there is evidence that ideology advances personal economic opportunities. Some party leaders oppose market law reforms that may increase competition and damage family businesses, while others see commercial opportunities in international integration.[85]

Elite-level technocrats

Elite-level legal and economic technocrats working in central ministries are responsible for importing borrowed law and adapting it to Vietnamese conditions. Many within this group fit Alan Watson's description of elite "globalized" lawmakers attuned to the epistemology of neo-liberal economic regulation.[86] Working closely with foreign legal advisers, they treat legal ideas as technical fragments unconstrained by cultural borders, and evince an unwavering conviction in the instrumental power of law to engineer social change.[87]

They are also influenced by domestic dialogues. Contacts between entrepreneurs and lawmakers developed during the initial periods of regulatory change.[88] Many state and party officials had family and friends in businesses and through these connections were personally acquainted with the difficulties faced by entrepreneurs in a legal systems run by socialist-trained bureaucrats.

Middle-level bureaucrats

If legal imports are abstract technical rules to elite technocrats, for lower-level bureaucrats implementing the law, rule of law reforms have personal consequences. Imported neo-liberal economic reforms directly contest prerogative powers invested in middle-level bureaucrats to manage (*quan ly*) society. In the command economy, officials used party morality and economic planning to manage commercial behavior. Devised in the Soviet Union to link state planning and economic production, "state economic management" (*quan ly nha nuoc kinh te*) in Vietnam unified political and economic leadership in the party-state. Since statutory rules were insufficiently developed to control complex economic transactions, officials routinely applied political and moral pronouncements (derived from the *tinh dang cong san* – party element) to plan and regulate the economy.[89]

Command planing has now been largely replaced by market mechanisms, but "dialogical" and behavioral patterns engrained over decades of "state management" are not easily changed. In many cases the economic vocabulary used in bureaucratic discourse resists neo-liberal economic principles. Enduring neo-Confucian "asking–giving" (*co che xin cho*) attitudes, a Soviet-style education that emphasized public over private interests, and an antipathy to the private sector have produced a "manage in order to manage" (*quan ly de quan ly*) mentality that treats state management as an objective in its own right. Thin "rule of law" reforms that streamline procedures and close licensing gateways have encountered bureaucratic resistance, even sabotage.[90] Officials have shown great ingenuity in blocking regulatory transparency by introducing new controls by stealth and shifting prerogative powers from one area to another. Socialized by the "manage in order to manage" culture, officials perceive imported market-based laws that facilitate private-sector development – and, worse still, reduce rent-seeking opportunities – as culturally alien and inappropriate.

Entrepreneurial responses to commercial laws

Research indicates that domestic entrepreneurs, the group supposedly benefiting from legal imports, are indifferent, even hostile, towards some legal reforms.[91] They see more value in a thin rule of law that checks bureaucratic action than in substantive neo-liberal economic rules governing contractual, property, and corporate rights. Take, for example, the Enterprise Law 1999. Entrepreneurs supported changes that liberalized market entry procedures, but were less enthusiastic about reforming substantive provisions governing internal management rules, rights of minority shareholders, and legal relations with third parties.[92]They worried that elaborate, corporate governance imports were remote from everyday practices, would impose onerous reporting obligations and further isolate entrepreneurs from the law.

Evidence suggests that substantive provisions in the Enterprise Law have failed to attract support, because existing informal business structures were reasonably reliable and cost effective. Relational business structures have endured socialism, and more recently market forces, and continue to order most private business organizations and transactions.[93] Proverbs like *gia dinh la trien het* (family first, others second) invoke a social ordering where close family connections form the bonds generating dependable and trustworthy management structures. When external skills are required, family members turn first to friends from the same village or those with longstanding personal ties. Recruitment is often based on common linkages through villages, university classes, or military units. In each case, attempts are made to find sentimental attachments that replicate *trung thanh* (loyalty), *tinh cam* (sentiment towards others), and *tin* (trust) to bind family members.[94] Transacting parties rely on sentimental (*tin cam*) relationships to enforce and adjust non-performing commitments. Penalties for non-performance are linked to reputation, opportunities to engage in future trade, and the criminalization (*hinh su hao*) of commercial relations through police debt collection.[95] Relational networks and institutions played a key role in the rapid expansion of household and private business from the early *doi moi* period.[96]

Local demand for the rule of law is largely attributable to the economic benefits conferred. Surveys show that in Vietnam's "state-managed economy" (*nha nuoc quan ly kinh te*) entrepreneurs enthusiastically support a thin rule of law promoting legal transparency and rules checking bureaucratic discretion. Vietnamese entrepreneurs, like their Western counterparts, want law reforms to wind back state inspections and simplify taxation and land procedures. They complain that bureaucrats use unclear rules to interfere with decision-making and generate rents. For politically well-connected state-owned enterprises, however, a thin rule of law threatens valuable relational networks binding party-state officials and private business.

Entrepreneurs are less enthusiastic about imported contract, property, and company norms. Development patterns elsewhere in East Asia suggest that as firms grow and become internationally integrated relational institutions are unable to deal with "outsiders" such as regional and international customers, bankers, and other formal market institutions. Vietnamese lawyers confirm that local firms are becoming increasingly aware that their interests are preserved by formal contracts in transactions with some foreigners. Contracts are used in transactions with Western and Japanese firms, but dealings with other "strangers" (Koreans, Taiwanese, Singaporeans, Chinese, and Malaysians) generally rely on relational structures.

It is difficult accurately to evaluate demand for contract and property norms, since the courts and debt enforcement agencies in Vietnam are dysfunctional. Research indicates that relational connections reduce transaction risk and provide satisfactory enforcement mechanisms. Rather than ordering business relationships, imported commercial laws are primarily used to gain market entry, finance, land, and import/export quotas. Businesses transact within the shadow of bureaucratic power more than normative law.

Empirical research shows that entrepreneurs and the general public have a low *y thuc phap che* [legal consciousness].[97] Not only are laws poorly disseminated and understood, but, perhaps more importantly, business standards are negotiated through moral more than legal discourse. The gap between legal and moral discourse is greatest where imported neo-liberal rules designed for integrated capitalist markets are superimposed on relational transactions designed to avoid state regulation.

It is perhaps too early in the reform cycle to assess whether relational structures can compete with, or even complement, a thick "rule of law" system. As the economy grows and domestic firms transact more frequently with foreigners (especially those requiring formal contracts), imported contract and property norms may increasingly supplement personal sentimental bonds in commercial exchanges. Demand for substantive legal rights is likely to stimulate more interest in independent, efficient courts (the thin rule of law).

The impact of democratic liberalism on market regulation

Imported market laws have significantly reoriented statist socialist thinking. Some high-level lawmakers believe that a very thin rule of law and neo-liberal commercial laws should govern commercial transactions. Their enthusiasm for laws binding economic regulators contrasts with their reluctance to bring party power more generally within constitutional structures. Kanishka Jayasuriya labels democratic liberalism applied to markets, but not other social transactions, "economic constitutionalism."[98] He notes that regimes elsewhere in East Asia (such as China, Singapore, and Malaysia) have confined a thin rule of law (coupled with neo-liberal commercial rights) to market transactions, while applying statist socialist or illiberal rule to other state–society relationships.

Even a very thin rule of law faces considerable hurdles to entering Vietnamese legal discourse. Rule of law ideals have transferred rapidly to elites benefiting from recentralized economic power and private investments, but are resisted by orthodox socialists wanting state intervention to preserve equality of outcomes. Middle-level bureaucrats are ideological and organizationally opposed to rules that diminish their social prestige and rent-seeking opportunities. As domestic markets become more integrated into world trading networks, it is possible that large Vietnamese companies and foreign investors will increasingly benefit from rules constraining bureaucratic interference and setting normative commercial standards. Small traders, on the contrary, are likely to remain embedded for decades in the "peasant legal culture" (*nen phap ly nong dan*) ordering relational networks.[99]

Rather than posing a reception–rejection dichotomy, socially layered responses to imported market rules intimate that different rule of law discourses coexist within the same the legal system. The rule of law means different things to different social groups according to their ideological, cultural, and economic capacity to benefit from the market. Reception patterns also raise important questions about the proper relationship between formal and relational systems. As the organizational limits of personal relationships are reached, entrepreneurs look for familiar normative rules to order dealings with strangers. Finding complementarities between neo-liberal legal transfers and underlying relational structures will greatly enhance the prospects for the rule of law in the commercial arena.[100] For this to happen lawmakers need to expand dialogical exchange with entrepreneurs.

Implementing law

From its inception, socialist legality promoted "independent" (*doc lap*) courts. Democratic liberal versions of the rule of law go further by requiring independent courts that check bureaucratic power and adjudicate commercial disputes according to predetermined law.[101] This section examines complementarities between judicial "independence" in statist socialist and rule of law discourse. Only courts are discussed, because decisions made by other dispute resolution bodies (i.e. foreign and domestic arbitration centers) are reviewable by judges.[102]

Contrasting with extensive changes in economic law, judicial discourse remains embedded in orthodox socialist thinking. Both the socialist 1980 Constitution and post-*doi moi* 1992 Constitution required courts to protect "the socialist legal system, the socialist regime, the people's right to mastery, the state and collective rights, and the lives, property, freedom, honor and dignity of citizens."[103] In an ideological environment where courts are expected to protect party and state interests, the meaning of judicial independence is ambiguous – independent from what or whom.

One issue is clear: judges are not "independent" (*doc lap*) from "party leadership" (*su lanh dao cua dang*).[104] Like other public employees, judges are required to "strictly abide by the Party's lines and policies."[105] Compliance with party leadership is supervised by party groups (*dang bo* or *chi bo*) operating inside each court and the *nomenklatura*. This mechanism ensures that only party members are appointed to senior judicial posts and that sitting judges unquestioningly follow the party line.[106] For example, judges in Ho Chi Minh City hearing bankruptcy cases follow internal party rulings not to evict debtors until creditors provide alternative accommodation.[107]

Independence is understood by judges to mean freedom from party "interference" (*su can thiep*).[108] Informants admit that the distinction between leadership and intervention has never been clarified. Evidently rulings based on party consensus constitute leadership, and non-consensual directions are unacceptable interference. For example, in politically sensitive corruption and human rights trials, formal party decisions directing judicial outcomes are treated as party leadership. Informants intimate that improper interference occurs where party organs or officials circumvent party decision-making processes and directly pressure judicial officials. This is most likely to occur where pecuniary interests are put at risk in commercial cases.

Supreme Court controls over inferior court decision-making constitute another form of interference. Historically, judicial committees composed of superior and inferior judges reviewed all inferior court decisions.[109] Though in principle majority decisions prevailed, in practice chief judges dictated most outcomes. Judicial committees compromised independent decision-making by encouraging a culture of "first decide then try" (*quyet dinh truoc khi xet xu*) or, as popularly expressed, "the decision is in the judge's pocket" (*an bo tui*).

Gradually replacing "collegiate" decision-making, judges hearing commercial cases are now encouraged to use biannual similar-fact case summaries (*tong ket chuyen de*) and professional instructions issued by the Supreme Court. These internal documents guide judges in applying law to facts and are incrementally forming commercial law doctrines. Strict prohibitions against judicial activism inhibit the development of legal techniques beyond civil and commercial cases. Superior court judges worry that broad jurisprudential principles may dignify legal processes with the authority to challenge party paramountcy. This concern recalls the historical suspicion in socialist legal thinking towards jurisprudence.[110]

In the command economy, courts functioned like executive arms of the state. Provincial and district judges were (and still are) appointed with the approval of local governments and passively relied on local agencies to gather evidence and assess liability.[111] Ministry of Justice officials to a lesser extent sought influence over the judiciary. While lawyers believe that horizontal influence from people's committees continues, they also report tentative signs that judges hearing commercial and civil cases are increasingly using legal principles to assess liability. The struggle towards legality is hindered by the constitutional doctrine that privileges socialist (party-state) interests in court hearings. For example, criminal prosecutions for judicial corruption overwhelmingly target litigants bribing judges; party and state interference is ignored.[112]

Domestic entrepreneurs have greeted growing legalism in commercial courts with indifference. Commercial litigation levels are extremely low in Vietnam. Economic courts, which hear debt, bankruptcy, and commercial disputes, considered 500 cases in 1995 but fewer than 400 cases in 2001.[113] Litigation rates declined over a period in which private economic activity almost doubled.

Lawyers report that domestic entrepreneurs only reluctantly approach courts for adjudication. Litigation aversion is not unique to Vietnam. Entrepreneurs everywhere are unwilling to jeopardize trading relationships and incur legal expenses.[114] The difference lies in the social importance of court rulings. In the West, they set commercial standards that influence pre-court negotiations. In Vietnam, indifference towards substantive commercial norms induces a low social demand for law-based dispute resolution. Law-based adjudication generates justifiable anxiety that courts will use alien statuary norms to regulate highly contextualized family and patronage-based trading networks. At the same time, relational structures provide comparatively effective dispute resolution and enforcement processes.

Public skepticism about the competency and impartiality of judges further discourages litigation.[115] Judges are considered unsympathetic towards the private sector, basing decisions on party-state status and bribes, and treating legal rules as convenient but optional ways of getting things done. Under questioning by delegates of the National Assembly in 2002, the Chief Judge of the Supreme Court admitted that "judges in civil cases can make any party win" (*xu dan su, xu the nao cung duoc*). The perception of systemic bias, incompetence, and corruption influenced more than 90 percent of private-sector respondents recently surveyed to conclude that courts would not satisfactorily resolve commercial disputes.[116]

Democratic liberal rule of law and judicial change

Party leaders support reforms transferring power to the courts over commercial and civil disputes.[117] Having committed to a thin rule of law in the commercial arena, a question arises whether judicial power will extend over administrative and politicized criminal cases? Evidence that judicial review over administrative action is deliberately constrained by the party comes from the Supreme Court Annual Report 2000, which directs administrative court judges to decide such cases cautiously, in consultation with state bodies.[118]

Party influence is most blatant in criminal court interventions designed to punish party enemies and exculpate loyal cadres.[119]

Personal networks linking judges and senior party-state officials collapse the personal distance and anonymity necessary for genuine autonomy. Interpersonal linkages do not affect private commercial and civil cases provided party-state interests are unaffected. Depoliticizing courts is much more difficult where decisions directly impinge on political and executive power.[120] Experience in democratic liberal countries implies that courts are the last state institutions to gain power over political decision-making.[121]

The missing ingredient for judicial reform is popular support for formal adjudication. Relational mechanisms provide relatively efficient dispute resolution mechanisms and most demand for court-based dispute resolution comes from foreign litigants excluded from local relational networks. It is difficult to gauge whether attitudes would change if courts provided an efficient and impartial alternative or supplemented relational transactions.

Conceptualizing legal thought in Vietnam

Two rule of law models – statist socialism and a very thin version of democratic liberalism – dominate Vietnamese legal discourse. Statist socialism is defined by a commitment to party paramountcy and legal exceptualism.

Beyond these core principles there is considerable conceptual variation. The replacement of class conflict with class cooperation marked a shift in party mythologizing towards developmentalism, nationalism, and legal formalism. This expansion of legitimizing symbols opened space in the *nha nuoc phap quyen* (law-based state) discourse for new legal thinking.

The legitimizing symbols are sufficiently vague to enable the central elite to promote their own normative and political agendas in "palace wars." Party factions alternatively invoke orthodox socialist legality to protect members from criminal litigation, and "rule of law" rhetoric to prosecute competitors in the courts. Those down the hierarchy understandably resent legal inequality, without necessarily objecting to party paramountcy as a general principle. Most agree with a political outlook that favors political stability and economic growth over democratic representation and rights-based civil liberties. Movement towards representative democracy is unlikely until rules governing NA discourse more effectively resolve political contests than informal party "dialogical" exchanges. This transformation will also require party support for a political morality that values democratic pluralism. What is more probable in the short term is greater responsiveness to the needs and aspirations of the Vietnamese people through consessionary "grassroots" democracy.

Economic discourse has profoundly influenced legal discourse. Some within the party-state elite promote a neo-liberal economic agenda privileging private commercial rights over "state economic management." Under their guidance a thin rule of law is making inroads into socialist legality thinking. Rival factions query whether regulatory regimes constrained by a thin rule of law are flexible enough to deliver equitable outcomes. They also contest thicker, neo-liberal regulatory norms that reduce state powers to ameliorate inequalities generated by market forces.

Most middle- and low-level bureaucrats strenuously resist thin rule of law reforms designed to increase discretionary accountability. Although private entrepreneurs in general favor tight legal controls over bureaucrats, malfeasance and unfair business practices are perceived as moral rather than legal lapses. There is a conceptual disconnection between ethical and legal standards. Ultimately, many believe that rule through moral leadership is ethically superior to law-based arrangements.

Support for a thin "rule of law" is growing within Vietnam, but this does not necessarily foreshadow the demise of statist socialism. A thin rule of law promotes transactional certainty and constrains bureaucratic discretion, but by definition lacks a transcending political morality capable of rivaling substantive norms in statist socialist discourse. The notion that capitalist contractual relationships generate human dignity does not resonate in Vietnamese relational society. Kanishka Jayasuriya's "economic constitutionalism" suggests an alternate trajectory where illiberal socialist legality and a thin rule of law are ideologically reconcilable – even symbiotically beneficial. The thin rule of law regularizes commerce and centralizes power in state bodies, while party-prerogative powers depoliticize the commercial arena by limiting special-interest groups hostile to economic producers (e.g. consumer associations taking product liability actions).

Beyond these broad generalizations there is insufficient common ground to make other rule of law concepts appear intelligible in Vietnam. Clearly, certain individuals believe that neo-authoritarian or communitarian rule of law should replace party domination. Some private entrepreneurs quietly express a vision for change loosely based on "soft"-authoritarian rule in Singapore and pre-democratic South Korea and Taiwan. They envisage representative democracies distributing political power and autonomous legal rights ordering relational transactions. Even within the business community this is a marginal view, especially now that the party gives entrepreneurs a role to play in the economy.

A small, but vocal group of dissident party members and overseas Vietnamese (*viet kieu*) advocate multiparty democracy qualified by strong state discretionary powers.[122] It is their determination to remove the CPV from power, more than a desire to introduce civil rights and representative government, that distinguishes this discourse. So far vigorous state repression has kept these views very much as minority positions.

Postulating a future for rule of law discourse

The preceding discussion suggests that longstanding state–society "dialogical" pathways are increasingly unable to resolve social issues generated by market and global forces. Recognizing these shortcomings, party leaders are experimentally applying thin "rule of law" principles to more effectively resolve commercial, and perhaps eventually political, contests. Thicker substantive rule of law precepts are less attractive, because they clash with existing norms. Despite its intuitive appeal, this analysis oversimplifies the way "rule of law" ideas engage with Vietnamese legal discourse.

The meanings contained in imported versions of the rule of law are profoundly shaped by the epistemological assumptions ordering Vietnamese discourse. Vietnamese legal and cultural borrowings from China during Imperial times established enduring patterns of legal borrowing. In contrast to Imperial China, where the Confucian canon was treated as an all-encompassing source of political, social, and moral authority, Vietnamese emperors used imported Confucian texts as persuasive precedents guiding state policy. The moral and historical precepts that gave coherence and context to the canon were often ignored.[123] This approach engendered a comparative lack of coherence or unity in Vietnamese moral and legal traditions.

Little attempt was made during the socialist command period, as in Maoist China, to manufacture a coherent moral philosophy. Instead, using a

171

technique called *thao dang* (situational validity), fragments of Soviet legal ideology were syncretized with neo-Confucian morals, forming a conceptual pot-pourri. Skillfully applying local and imported legal values to resolve social problems to the satisfaction of interested parties is much more highly valued than consistently following established procedures and immutable legal ideals.[124] Vietnamese legal thinkers rarely attempt to construct overarching theoretical explanations for state and society relationships.[125] As a result, the grafting of new "rule of law" principles on to a syncretized legal discourse has unsurprisingly generated opaque thinking about state–society relationships.

Syncretic thinking allows new and contradictory substantive ideas to enter and enlarge the range of values applied to new situations. Imported precepts are understood in a dialogical context that constructs social truths in different ways from democratic liberal discourse. Behind the statist socialist façade, the legal discourse may eventually include communitarian and even democratic liberal civil rights in forms that are not easily recognizable to foreign observers. Syncretism enables Vietnamese lawmakers to construct a modern governance system from a mishmash of borrowed and local precepts.

Notes

1   The author gratefully acknowledges Australian Research Council funding, assistance from many Vietnamese officials, business leaders and lawyers, and the numerous insightful comments on an earlier draft by Randy Peerenboom.
2   *Doi moi* reforms promote a multi-sectored economy, regulated by "socialist-oriented market mechanisms" (*co che thi thruong theo dinh xa hoi chu nghia*); normalizing social and economic transactions through legal, rather than ideological and moral apparatus; and pursuing an "open-oor" (*mo cua*) policy and international economic integration. See Vo Dai Luoc, *Vietnam's Industrialization, Modernization and Resources* (Hanoi: Social Sciences Published House, 1996), pp. 15–47; Ngo Quang Xuan, "Vietnam: Potential Market and New Opportunities," *Fordham International Law Journal*, vol. 19 (1995), pp. 32–3.
3   Niklas Luhmann and Gunther Teubner offer the valuable insight that social discourse has fragmented into "discrete discursive systems." Transplanted institutional structures such as democracy and the "rule of law" are susceptible to multiple and perhaps competing conceptualizations in host countries. The rule of law, for instance, has a highly contextual meaning in Western legal discourse that may change when conceptualized in other discourses. It is, accordingly, important to know how particular discourses in Vietnam conceive institutional change. See Gunther Teubner, *Law as an Autopoietic System* (Oxford: Blackwell, 1993), p. 69; Niklas Luhmann, *A Sociological Theory of Law*, trans. Elizabeth King and Martin Albrow (London and Boston, Massachusetts: Routledge & Kegan Paul, 1987). This study uses the discourse theory without accepting the exaggerated "Autopoietic systems" argument that legal discourse is a closed self-reproducing system. See Anthony Beck, "Is Law an Autopoietic System," *Oxford Journal of Legal Studies*, vol. 14, no. 3 (1994), pp. 401, 404–15; Hugh Baxter, "Autopoiesis and the 'Relative Autonomy' of Law," *Cardozo Law Review*, vol. 49 (1988).

4 See Yves Dezalay and Bryant G. Garth, *The Internationalization of Palace Wars* (Chicago: University of Chicago Press, 2002), pp. 246–50.
5 Debates concerning legal transplantation have polarized around Lawrence Friedman's contention that law mirrors society and does not easily transplant, and Alan Watson's belief that legal transfers are primarily governed by legal elites, who borrow laws according to "chance and prestige." It is suggested that both views are correct, but that each examines different facets of transplantation. Watson looks at why laws are borrowed, while Friedman and others examine the deeper issues concerning legal implementation and social reception. See, generally, Otto Kahn-Freund, "On Uses and Misuses of Comparative Law," *Modern Law Review*, vol. 37 (1974), pp. 6, 7–11, 27; Gunther Teubner, "Legal Irritants: Good Faith in British Law or How Unifying Law Ends Up in New Divergences," *Modern Law Review*, vol. 61, no. 1 (1998), pp. 11, 25–7; William Ewald, "Comparative Jurisprudence (II): The Logic of Legal Transplants," *American Journal of Comparative Law*,vol.43 (1995), pp. 498–502.
6 See UNDP, *Completion of Viet Nam's Legal Framework for Economic Development* (Hanoi: UNDP Discussion Paper 2, 1999), pp. 52–4; also see Carol V. Rose, "The 'New' Law and Development Movement in the Post-Cold War Era: A Vietnam Case Study," *Law and Society Review*, vol. 32 (1998), p. 106.
7 For example, the New York-based Human Right Watch group alleges harassment and imprisonment of Buddhist and Catholic clergy organizing outside party-sanctioned religious organizations. See Human Rights Watch, *World Report 2002, Vietnam*, www.hrw.org/wr2k2/asia11.html.
8 Finding a balance between rights, equality, and social order has preoccupied Western political thought since the 17th century. See Michael Freeman, "Human Rights, Democracy and "Asian Values," *Pacific Review*, vol. 9, no. 3 (1996), pp. 355–405.
9 Constitution 1992, article 4.
10 See Mark Sidel, "Generational and Institutional Transition in the Vietnamese Communist Party," *Asian Survey*, vol. 37, no. 5 (1997), pp. 483–4. Party Statute articles 42(3), 43(1). See also David Marr, "The Vietnam Communist Party and Civil Society" (unpublished paper), presented at "Vietnam Update 1994 Conference: *Doi Moi*, The State and Civil Society," Australian National University, November 10, 1994, pp. 8–9.
11 Party Statute, article 41(2). See Mark Sidel, "Vietnam:The Ambiguities of State-Directed Legal Reform," in Poh-Ling Tan, ed., *Asian Legal Systems* (Sydney: Butterworths, 1997), p. 364.
12 See Nguyen Cuu Viet, "Nhan Thuc Ve Nguyen Tac Tap Quyen va Vai Khia Canh Trong Van De Ve Quan He Giua Lap Phap va Hanh Phap O Nuoc Ta Hien Nay" [Some Perceptions of the Principles of Centralism and a Few Aspects of the Relationship Between the Legislative and Executive Bodies of Vietnam Today], *Nha Nuoc va Phap Luat*, no. 2 (1997), pp. 47–9.
13 See Dao Tri Uc, "Xay Dung Nha Nuoc Phap Quyen Xa Hoi Chu Nghia Su Lanh Dao Cua Dang" [Building Up the Law-Based State Under the Leadership of the Communist Party], *Nha Nuoc va Phap Quyen* [State and Law], no. 7 (2001), pp. 3–4.
14 Vietnamese Constitution 1992, articles 112, 118, 124.
15 See Vietnamese Constitution 1992, articles 137–140; Law on the Organization of the People's Procuracy 2002.
16 See, generally, William Alford, "The Inscrutable Occidental," *Texas Law Review*, vol. 64 (1986), pp. 943–8.
17 See Truong Chinh, "Forward Along the Path Charted by Karl Marx," in *Truong Chinh: Selected Writings* (Hanoi: Gioi Publishers, 1994), p. 547; Le Duc Tho,

"Report Summarizing Party Building Work and the Amended Party Statues," *Nhan Dan*, December 20, 1976, pp. 2, 3; *FIBIS Asia and Pacific Daily Report*, January 1977, p. 14.

18 See Ha Xuan Truong, "Ho Chi Minh – A Cultural Look Through the Century," *Vietnam Social Sciences*, no. 2 (2001), pp. 15, 16.

19 See Nguyen Khac Vien, *Tradition and Revolution in Vietnam* (Berkeley: Indochina Resource Centre, 1974), p. 50; see also Truong Chinh, *supra* note 17, pp. 563–8.

20 Both Ho Chi Minh and Truong Chinh placed the Marxist "base (mode of production) determines the superstructure (ideals, culture and law) metaphor" at the center of state ideology. See Song Thanh, "President Ho Chi Minh Laid the Foundation for a Law-Governed State in Vietnam," *Vietnam Law and Legal Forum*, vol. 1, no. 9 (1995), pp. 4–6; see also Truong Chinh, *supra* note 17, pp. 540–6.

21 See Vu Duc Chieu, *Phap Che La Gi?* [What is Legality?], Nha Xuat Ban Pho Thong (Hanoi, Popular Publishing, 1974), pp. 40–1.

22 Id., p. 40.

23 See V. I. Lenin, *Selected Works*, vol. II (Hanoi: Su That Publishing House, 1959), p. 246; cited in Nguyen Nien, "Several Legal Problems in the Leadership and Management of Industry Under the Conditions of the Present Improvement of Economic Management in Our Country," *Luat Hoc* [Legal Science], no. 14 (1976), pp. 33–43, trans. JPRS 67995, 30 September 1976, p. 37.

24 See Le Minh Tam, *Giao Trinh Ly Luan Nha Nuoc va Phap Luat* [Themes on State and Law] (Hanoi: People's Police Publishing, 1998), pp. 497–503.

25 "Socialist legality, likewise, is always the *modus operandi* of the socialist state and cannot become an impediment to the realization of its historical tasks." This passage is quoted from an English-language version of a Soviet text entitled "The Theory of the State and Law," which was translated into Vietnamese and widely circulated in legal training institutions. Interviews, Nguyen Nhu Phat, Director, Center for Comparative Law, Institute of State and Law, January, October 1997; June, July 1998. Also see S. A. Golunskii and M. S. Strongovich, *The Theory of State and Law* (Moscow: Institute of Law of the USSR, Academy of Sciences, 1940), trans. *Soviet Legal Philosophy* (Cambridge, Massachusetts: Harvard University Press, 1951), p. 393.

26 See Circular no. 3831/TP Concerning Some Immediate Work to be Done by the Judiciary Sector to Implement the 5th Party Congress Resolution, June 11, 1982, Minister of Justice, first reproduced in *Phap Che Xa Hoi Chu Nghia* [Socialist Legality], no. 2, April 1982, pp. 8–10, 15, trans. JPRS–1978, January 25, 1983, p. 90.

27 See Central Committee CPV, "Resolution on Industrialization from the Central Committee (Communist Party Seventh Session Seventh Party Congress)," *Voice of Vietnam*, August 11, 1994, trans. *BBC Monitoring Service* Asia–Pacific, August 19, 1994. For a detailed account, see Adam Fforde, "From Plan to Market," in Anita Chan, Ben Kerkvliet, and Jonathon Ungar, *Transforming Asian Socialism: China and Vietnam Compared* (Sydney: Allen & Unwin, 1999), pp. 44–63; Tu Tuan Anh, *Vietnam's Economic Reform: Results and Problems* (Hanoi: Social Science Publishing House, 1994), pp. 15–26.

28 Although numerous party and state bodies were involved in this project, Professor Doan Trong Truyen, Chairman of the National Administrative School (now National Administration Institute) coordinated research. See Hoc Vien Hanh Chinh Quoc Gia [The National Administrative School], *Ve Cai Cach Bo May Nha Nuoc, [On the Reform of the State Apparatus]* (Hanoi: Truth Publishing House, 1991).

29 The literature is vast, but see Robert Sharlet, *Soviet Constitutional Crisis from De-Stalinistion to Disintegration* (New York: M. E. Sharpe, 1992), pp. 85–98; John N. Hazard, "The Evolution of the Soviet Constitution," in Donald Barry, ed., *Towards the Rule of Law in Russia?* (New York: M. E. Sharpe, 1992), pp. 103–11; M. Gorbachev, *Perestroika* (London: Collins, 1987), p. 110.

30 The concept of *pravovoe gosudarstvo*, or *Rechtsstaat*, upon which it is based, asserts that the state is the highest, if not the only, source of law. The basic form and source of law is legislation, rather than custom and precedent. See H. J. Berman, "Some Jurisprudential Implications of the Codification of Soviet Law," in Richard M. Buxbaum and Kathryn Hendley, eds., *The Soviet Sobranie of Laws: Problems of Codification and Non-Publication* (Berkeley: University of California Press, 1991), p. 173.

31 SeeDo Muoi, *Sua Doi Hien Phap Xay Dung Nha Nuoc Phap Quyen Viet Nam, Day Minh Su Nghiep Doi Moi* [Amending the Constitution, Establishing a Law-Based State and Promoting *Doi Moi* Achievements], Nha Xuat Ban Su That (Hanoi: Truth Publishing House 1992), pp. 30–8.

32 The literature concerning *nha nuoc phap quyen* is as confusing as it is large. Since writers rarely acknowledge sources, ideological precepts are frequently thrown together with little explanation, much less logical organization. See, generally, Le Hong Hanh, *Giao Trinh Ly Luan Nha Nuoc va Phap Luat* [Themes on State and Law] (Hanoi: People's Police Publishing, 1998), pp. 322–5; Nguyen Duy Quy, "On the Problem of Building a Juridical State in Our Country," *Vietnam Social Sciences*, vol. 3 (1993), pp. 10–11; Anonymous, *Nhung Van De Ly Luan Co Ban Ve Nha Nuoc va Phap Luat* [Basic Theoretical Issues about State and Law] (Hanoi: National Political Publishing House, 1996), pp. 112–16.

33 See, e.g., Le Cam, "To Chuc Bo May Quyen Luc Nha Nuoc Trong Giai Doan Xay Dung Nha Huoc Phap Quyen Viet Nam: Mot So Van De Ly Luan va Thuc Tien" [State Apparatus in Building Up a Law-Based State in Vietnam: Some Theoretical and Practical Issues], *Nha Nuoc va Phap Luat* [State and Law], no. 8 (2002), pp. 10–11.

34 Article 1 of the 1992 Constitution added intellectuals to the "peasant and worker alliance." Only "socialist intelligentsia" were considered part of the "ruling class" in the 1980 Constitution (article 3). See also Le Hong Hanh, *supra* note 32, pp. 324–5.

35 See Quang Can, "Some Reflections on Marxist Philosophy in the Perspective of Eastern Culture," *Vietnam Social Sciences*, no. 1 (2001), pp. 9–10.

36 Stephen Young, "Unpopular Socialism in United Vietnam," *Orbis*, vol. 22, no. 2 (1977), pp. 227, 228. Interview, Hoang Ngoc Hien, Sociologist, Nguyen Du School of Creative Writing, Hanoi, June 2002.

37 See Luu Ha Vi, "Vietnam: Industrialization Viewed from the Interplay between Productive Forces and Relations of Production," *Economic Development Review.* (January 1997), pp. 1–4; Nguyen Phu Trong, "Market Economy and the Leadership of Role of the Party," *Tap Chi Cong San* [Communist Review] (January 1994), pp. 29–33.

38 See John Gillespie, "Self-Interest and Ideology: Bureaucratic Corruption in Vietnam," *Australian Journal of Asian Law*, vol. 3, no. 1 (2001), pp. 13–23.

39 There is extensive literature in this area, but see Le Thi, *The Role of the Family in the Formation of the Vietnamese Personality* (Hanoi: Gioi, 1999), pp. 140–6.

40 See Ngo Phoung Lan, "The Changing Face of Vietnamese Cinema During Ten Years of Renovation," in David Marr, ed., *The Mass Media in Vietnam,* Political and Social Change Monograph 25 (Canberra: Australian National University, 1998), pp. 95–6.

41 See Le Kha Phieu, "Party Leader Addresses Cultural Officials," *Nhan Dan*, October 9, 1998, pp. 1, 5.
42 Previous constitutions in 1959 and 1980 placed the party under the constitution, but not law.
43 In 1996 party paramountcy was reaffirmed in the Party Statute – "the Party rules and uses the State as a tool to manage society." See Party Statute 1996, articles 41–3.
44 Nguyen Nham, "Why is the Management of the State by Law Still Weak?," *Quan Doi Nhan Dan*, June 13, 1997, p. 3.
45 Thaveeporn Vasavakul, "Rethinking the Philosophy of Center–Local Relationships in Post-Central-Planned Vietnam," in Mark Turner, ed., *Central–Local Relations in Asia–Pacific* (Basingstoke: Macmillan, 1999), p. 176.
46 Do Muoi, *Vietnam: New Challengers and New Opportunities* (Hanoi: Gioi Publishers, 1995), p. 162.
47 *Ibid.*
48 Proposals to give courts powers to interpret the validity of laws according to the Constitution were rejected during the last amendment of the Constitution in 2001. See, e.g., Le Cam, *supra* note 33, pp. 10–11.
49 See generally David Kairys ed. *The Politics of Law*, 3rd ed. (New York: Basic Books, 1998).*Cf.* H. Berman, *Law and Revolution: The Formation of the Western Legal Tradition* (Cambridge, Mass: Harvard University Press, 1983).
50 This power is not publicly acknowledged, however. The final draft approved by the National Assembly occasionally differs from the code or law published in *Nhan Dan*, the official party newspaper. Clauses increasing state management powers appeared in the published version of the Enterprise Law 1999.
51 Muthiah Alagappa, "The Anatomy of Legitimacy," in M. Alagappa, ed., *Political Legitimacy in South East Asia* (Stanford: Stanford University Press, 1995), p. 28.
52 See Adam Fforde, "Law and Socialist Agricultural Development in Vietnam: The Statute for Agricultural Producer Cooperatives," *Review of Socialist Law*, vol. 10 (1984), pp. 315, 317–19; Melanie Beresford, *Vietnam: Politics, Economics and Society* (London: Pinter, 1988), pp. 116–18.
53 Benedict J. Tria Kerkvliet, "An Approach for Analyzing State–Society Relations in Vietnam," *Sojourn*, vol. 16, no. 2 (2001), pp. 1, 2–3; Benedict J. Tria Kerkvliet, "Dialogical Law Making and Implementation in Vietnam," in Alice Tay, ed., *East Asia – Human Rights, Nation-Building, Trade* (Baden-Baden: Nomos, 1999), p. 372.
54 Vietnamese writers cited V. I. Lenin in *Nha Nuoc va Cach Mang* [State and Revolution], chs. 2 and 3. Lenin proposed that the working class should centralize power in their hands and power should be distributed on the basis of democracy. This ideology gave political and social meaning to democratic centralism. See Dinh Gia Trinh, *Nghien Cuu Nha Nuoc va Phap Quyen* [Studies about State and Legality] (Hanoi: Historical Studies Publishing House, 1964), pp. 90–2.
55 See Russell Heng Hiang Khng, "Leadership in Vietnam: Pressure for Reform and Their Limits," *Contemporary Southeast Asia*, vol. 15, no. 1 (1993), p. 102.
56 The term "reform-minded" is used here to denote those favoring a law-based society in either a statist socialist or neo-authoritarian mold. Interviews with Office of National Assembly officials, Hanoi, October 1997, March 2000; January 2002. Also see Le Quang Thuong, "Mot So Van De Ve Cong Tac Dang Vien Trong Tinh Hinh Hien Nay" [Several Problems Concerning Cadres Work Under the Current Situation], *Tap Chi Cong San*, no. 14 (July 1996), pp. 18–19.

57 In the 1997 elections 663 candidates stood for 450 NA seats; CPV members stood for every seat. Among the 450 winners, 384 were CPV members; only 3 "self-nominated" candidates won seats. See James Riedel and William Turley, "The Politics and Economics of Transition to an Open Market Economy in Vietnam" (Paris: Technical Paper no. 152, OECD, 1999), pp. 44–5.

58 The assembly is now comprised of 500 delegates; only 125 are full time, the rest are part time and must work to generate a living income. The accumulation of professional skills is also impeded by high turnover rates: only 25 percent of delegates are re-elected after each five-year term. This is attributed to party policy that requires balanced representation from the "class alliance." Peasant delegates must be replaced by intellectuals, for example. Interview, Nguyen Si Dung, Director, Center for Information, Library, and Research, Office of the National Assembly, Hanoi, February 17, 2000.

59 Informants working in the Office of the National Assembly for the Law Committee are not privy to high-level party deliberations, but as party members they are given internal party instructions concerning the purpose and function of NA reforms.

60 For example, the dissident intellectual Ha Si Phu (Nguyen Xuan Tu) was placed under house arrest and threatened with charges of treason for drafting an open letter appealing for more democracy. See Human Rights Watch, *World Report, Vietnam 2001*, www.hrw.org/wr2k1/asia/vietnam.html.

61 See Shaun Kingsley Malarney, "Culture, Virtue and Political Transformation In Contemporary Northern Viet Nam," *Journal of Asian Studies*, vol. 56, no. 4 (1997), pp. 906–10.

62 Mandarins monopolized the right to interpret the neo-Confucian cannon, while the principle of *chinh giao* (government merged with teaching) encouraged them to rule through moral persuasion. See Alexander Woodside, "The Triumphs and Failures of Mass Education in Vietnam," *Pacific Affairs*, vol. 56, no. 3 (1983), p. 414; Alexander Woodside, "Exalting the Latecomer State," in Anita Chan, Ben Kerkvliet, and Jonathon Ungar, eds., *Transforming Asian Socialism: China and Vietnam Compared* (Sydney: Allen & Unwin, 1999), pp. 23–4.

63 Cadres were warned to avoid laziness (*benh luoi bieng*), boasting (*benh ba hoa*), "narrow-mindedness"*(benh hep hoi)*, "commandisim" (*loi menh lenh*), "bureau-cratism" (*loi quan lieu*), the excessive use of Sino-Vietnamese words (*benh dung chu Han*), and arrogance (*benh kieu ngao*). See, generally, Nguyen Khac Vien, *supra* note 19, pp. 45–52.

64 "Hotspots" usually arise from disputes concerning the allocation of land-use rights and excessive taxation. See Associated Press, "State Media Break Silence on Vietnamese Unrest, Blame Bureaucracy," *Associated Press* (unpublished report), September 9, 1997, pp. 1–2.

65 Interviews with Hanoi-based Vietnamese lawyers in October 2000 and March 2001.

66 See Michael Gray, "Creating Civil Society? The Emergence of NGOs in Vietnam," *Development and Change*, vol. 30 (1999), pp. 693–713; Joerg Wischerman and Nguyen Quang Vinh, "The Relationship between 'Civil Organizations' and 'Government Organizations' in Viet Nam – Selected Findings of an Empirical Survey" (unpublished paper), "Vietnam 2001 Update Conference," Singapore, November, 19–21, 2001.

67 Although Kerkvliet challenges monolithic representations of a "dominating state," it does not necessarily follow that social space leads to civil rights. See Kerkvliet, "An Approach for Analyzing State–Society Relations in Vietnam," p. 238.

68 A general right to denounce malfeasance has been available to Vietnamese citizens since the Constitution of 1960. The Office of State Inspection revealed that state officials at the district and inferior levels attracted approximately 40 percent of all petition complaints between 1992 and 1994. Most complaints concerned false charges, illegal arrests, and unfair treatment. See "Tinh Hinh va Ket Qua Giai Quyet Khieu Nai, To Cao Trong Thoi Gian Qua, Nhung Giai Phap Trong Thoi Gian Toi"[Situation and the Results of the Handling of Petitions and Letters of Criticism in the Past and Measures for the Future], *Thong Tin Cong Tac Tu Tuong* (1995), pp. 10–15; Nguyen The Nghia, "Cai Cach Thu Tuc Hanh Chinh: Mot Van De Buc Thiet Hien Nay Cua Cai Cach Mot Buoc Nen Hanh Chinh Nha Nuoc" [The Reform of Administrative Procedures: An Important Aspect of the Reform of State Administration], *To Chuc Nha Nuoc*, vol. 2, nos.11–12 (1995), pp. 12–14.

69 Foreign investors initiate most cases. Narrow jurisdictional powers have limited interest in judicial redress to fewer than 30 actions since the courts were formed in 1996. Few cases are successful. Pham Tuan Khai, "Some Suggestions on the Administrative Courts in Vietnam," *Vietnam Law and Legal Forum*, vol. 2, no. 15 (1995), p. 9.

70 Le Minh Tong, "Mot So De Ve Nha Nuoc Pha Quyen Trong Boi Canh Viet Nam" [Some Issues about the Law-Based State in the Context of Vietnam] (unpublished paper), "Rule of Law and its Acceptance in Vietnam," Institute of State and Law, Hanoi, September 11, 2000, pp. 1–2.

71 See Le Hong Hanh, *supra* note 32, p. 437. Other writers acknowledge a correspondence between social ethics and law. See Hoang Thi Kim Que, "Mot So Suy Nghi ve Moi Quan Giua Phap Luat va Dao Duc Trong He Thong Dieu Chinh Xa Hoi" [Some Thoughts on the Relationship between the Law and Ethics in the Social Regulatory System], *Nha Nuoc va Phap Luat* [State and Law], no. 7 (1999), pp. 16–19.

72 At the insistence of the Swedish International Development Agency, the final Legal Needs Assessment Report prepared by the Ministry of Justice contained a broad statement that "The law must develop legal protection for freedom and people's democratic rights." See "Comprehensive Needs Assessment for the Development of Vietnam's Legal System for the Period 2001–2010" (Hanoi: Ministry of Justice, 2001). More specific attempts to introduce clearer procedures for public complaints or rules governing NA debates have been comprehensively rejected by Vietnamese authorities.

73 The term "*kenri*" was composed from a translation of the English "human" (*jinken*) "rights" (*ken*). See Marina Svensson, "The Chinese Conception of Human Rights: The Debate on Human Rights in China 1894–1949" (unpublished paper), Department of East Asian Languages, Lund University (1996), p. 84.

74 See Ta Van Thai, *The Vietnamese Tradition of Human Rights* (Berkeley: University of California, 1988), p. 2; Randy Peerenboom, "Rights, Interests and the Interest in Rights in China," *Stanford Journal of International Law*, vol. 31 (1995), p. 365.

75 See Nguyen Chi My, "Chu Nghia Ca Nhan va Cuoc Dau Tranh De Khac Phuc No" [Individualism and the Struggle Against It], *Tap Chi Cong San*, June 1983, pp. 37–8; Pham Huy Ky, "Chu Nghia Ca Nhan: Dac Diem Bieu Hien va Bien Phap Khac Phuc" [The Ways of Avoiding Individualism in Society], *Nghien Cuu Ly Luan* [Theoretical Studies], no. 2 (1999), pp. 46–8; also see David Marr, "Concepts of 'Individual' and 'Self' in 20th Century Vietnam," *Modern Asian Studies*, vol. 34, no. 4 (2000), pp. 788–96.

76 See, e.g., oversees Vietnamese political organizations; Vietnam Democracy Association, www.thongluan.org; www.vinsight.org/insight.html; www.Imvntd/.org/dossier/thaothuc.

77 Even Alan Watson, who believes that Western law is primarily constructed from Roman law transplants, agrees that the *lex mercatoria* evolved slowly over centuries from indigenous European commercial practices. See Alan Watson, *The Evolution of Law* (Baltimore: Johns Hopkins University Press, 1985); Alan Watson,"Evolution of Law: Continued," *Legal History Review*, vol. 5 (1987), pp. 337–560.

78 Interviews, Japan International Cooperation Agency (JICA) long-term legal representatives Kawazu Shinsuke, Legal Coordinator, and Takeuchi Tsutomu, Judicial Expert, Hanoi (January 2002). See, generally, Lawrence Tshuma, "The Political Economy of the World Bank's Legal Framework for Economic Development," *Social and Legal Studies*, vol. 8, no. 2 (1999), pp. 75–96.

79 See, generally, Ann Seidman and Robert Seidman, *State and Law in the Development Process* (London: Macmillan, 1994).

80 Resolution no. 8 2002 of the Central Committee of the CPV established an inter-agency steering committee to coordinate legal reform in the judicial sector. Its powers will extend to overseeing reform to courts, procurators, and lawyers.

81 The three propositions are contained in section 3 of the "Comprehensive Needs Assessment for the Development of Vietnam's Legal System for the Period 2001–2010" (Hanoi: Ministry of Justice, 2001).

82 These views are based on interviews with Le Dang Doanh, Director of the Central Institute of Economic Management, Hanoi (January 2000, January 2002). Also see Pham Duc Thanh, "The Economic, Social and Cultural Impacts of Globalization on Vietnam," *Vietnam's Socio-Economic Development*, no.28 (2001), pp. 36–41.

83 Broad party views about commercial reforms are contained in the Resolutions of the 4th Plenum of the 8th Party Congress, 1997; the 9th Congress, 2001; and the 5th Plenum of the 9th Party Congress, 2002.

84 See, generally, Dao Duy Tung, *Qua Trinh Thanh con duong di len Chu Nghia Xa Hoi o Viet Nam* [The Process of Developing the Path Ascending to Socialism in Vietnam] (Hanoi: Chinh Tri Quoc Gia, 1994).

85 See Quan Xuan Dinh, "The Political Economy of Vietnam's Transformation Process," *Contemporary Southeast Asia*, vol. 22, no. 2 (2000), pp. 360–88.

86 See Allan Watson, "Comparative Law and Legal Change," *Cambridge Law Journal*, vol. 37 (1978), pp. 313, 314–15.

87 See Pham Duy Nghia, "Phap Luat Thuong Mai Viet Nam Truoc Thach Thuc Cua Qua Trinh Hoi Nhap Kinh Te Quoc Te" [Commercial Law Faces the Challenges of International Economic Integration], *Nha Nuoc va Phap Luat*, no. 6 (2000), pp. 11–15; Pham Duy Nghia, "Mot So Anh Huong Truc Tiep Cua Qua Trinh Hoi Nhap Kinh Te Khu Vuc va The Gioi Doi Voi Phap Luat Viet Nam" [Some Direct Influences of the World and Regional Economic Integration into Vietnamese Law], *Tap Chi Nghien cuu Lap Phap* [Legislative Studies], no. 2 (2001), pp. 3–7.

88 See Ray Mallon, "Approaches to Support the Development of an Enabling Environment for Small Enterprises" (unpublished report), GTZ Country Report, Hanoi (2002), p. 16.

89 Interviews, Nguyen Nhu Phat, *supra* note 25; Le Kim Que, President, Bar Association, Hanoi, July 1998, October 1999.

90 See Nguyen Phuong Quynh Trang, "Doing Business Under the New Enterprise Law: A Survey of Newly Registered Companies" (Hanoi: Private Sector Discussion Paper 12, MPDF, 2001), pp. 14–17, 20–1, 24.

91 See John Gillespie, "Transplanted Company Law: An Ideological and Cultural Analysis of Market-Entry in Vietnam," *International and Comparative Law Quarterly*, vol. 51, pp. 641–72.

92 These impressions are based on interviews with Nguyen Dinh Cung Director, Enterprise Department Central Institute of Economic Management, Hanoi, September 2000, March 2001; and Hanoi-based Vietnamese private legal practitioners from Investconsult, Leadco and VILAF law firms. Also see Report, "Ban Dong Gop Y Kien vao Du An Luat Cong Ty va Luat Doanh Nghiep Tu Nhan" [Report Contributions and Opinions to the Draft Company Law and Private Investment Law] (unpublished report) (Hanoi: Hanoi Union of Associations of Industry and Commerce, 1999).

93 See David Marr, "Politics of the Family" (unpublished paper) (2001), pp. 20–6; Hoang Kim Giao and Nguyen Dac Thang, "A Profile of Vietnamese Owners of Private Enterprise," *Vietnam Economic Review*, no. 4 (1995), pp. 29–30.

94 These views are based on interviews with private entrepreneur associations in Hanoi and Ho Chi Minh City. Vu Duy Thai, Vice-Chairman and Secretary, the Hanoi Associations of Industry and Commerce (member of the Central Committee of the Fatherland Front), Hanoi (April 1999, February 2000); Nguyen Trung Truc, Chairman, Vietnam German Entrepreneurs' Club, Hanoi (1999, 2000); Pham Thi Thu Hang, Deputy General Director, VCCI (Small and Medium-sized Enterprise Promotion Center), Hanoi (1998, 1999); Nguyen Hoang Luu, General Secretary, *Hiep Hoi Cac Doanh Nghiep Vua Va Nho Ha Noi* (Hanoi Small and Medium-sized Enterprises Council), Hanoi (1999, 2000); Cao Thi Kim Dung, Information Service Manager, Union of Associations of Industry and Commerce (*Hiep Hoi Cong Thuong Thanh Pho Ho Chi Minh*), Ho Chi Minh City (1998, 1999).

95 See Pham Duy Nghia, "Hinh Su Hoa Cac Giao Dich Dan Su Kinh Te: Quan Niem Bieu Hien va Mot So Giai Phap Khac Phuc" [The Process of Criminalization of Civil and Economic Transitions: Ideas, Manifestations and Some Solutions], *Tap Chi Nghien Cuu Lap Phap* [Legislative Research Review], no. 6 (2000), pp. 30–42.

96 This experience is not unique to Vietnam. See Raymond Mallon, "Experiences in the Region and Private Sector Incentives in Vietnam," in S. Leung, ed., *Vietnam and the East Asian Crisis* (London, Edward Elgar, 1999); Per Ronnas and Bhargavi Ramamurthy, eds., *Entrepreneurship in Vietnam: Transformation and Dynamics* (Singapore: ISEAS, 2001).

97 The term "y thuc phap che" [legal consciousness] was imported from the Soviet Union in the 1960s, but in Vietnam means that it is immoral to disobey the law. See Tran Dinh Hao, "Nha Nuoc Phap Quyen va Kinh Te Thi Truong O Viet Nam" [Law-Based State and Market Economy in Vietnam] (unpublished paper), The Mansfield Dialogues, "Rule of Law and its Acceptance in Vietnam" Conference, Hanoi, September 11, 2000.

98 See Kanishka Jayasuriya, "The Rule of Law and Governance in the East Asian State," *Australian Journal of Asian Law*, vol. 1, no. 2 (1999), pp. 119–21.

99 See Pham Duy Nghia, *supra* note 87, pp. 15–18.

100 One difficulty with this approach is that relational practices developed to avoid state regulation and promote secrecy and taxation avoidance. Selecting practices that complement open markets and competition is difficult. Because foreign donors have shown little interest in this area, research funding has been scarce and little is known about the actual modus operandi of small and medium-sized enterprises.

101 See, P. O"Malley, *Law, Capitalism and Democracy* (Sydney: Allen & Unwin, 1983), pp. 122–3; see also Ronald Dworkin, *Taking Rights Seriously* (London: Duckworth, 1977).

102 A draft Law on Arbitration in 2002 proposed domestic arbitration without judicial review. Arbitration awards were still subject to court ratification. See Statute on the Vietnam International Arbitration Center 1993; Decree on the Organization and Operation of Economic Arbitration 1994. Thuy Le Tran, "Vietnam: Can an Effective Arbitration System Exist?," *Loyola Los Angeles International and Comparative Law Journal*, vol. 20 (1998), pp. 361–86.

103 Vietnamese 1980 Constitution, article 127; Law on the Organization of People's Courts 1992, article 1; see also Vietnamese Constitution 1992, article 126. See, generally, Trinh Hong Duong and Dang Quang Phuong, "Hien Phap Nam 1992 Ve Vi Tri Chuc Nang va Nhiem Vu Cua Toa An Nhan Dan" [The Constitution of 1992: Role, Functions and Responsibilities of the People's Courts] (unpublished paper) (1998), pp. 1–12.

104 The LNA projects actively promoted judicial independence by streamlining appeal mechanisms, increasing judicial salaries, promoting open trials, and forbidding "improper" intervention into court cases. Significantly, no restrictions on party prerogative powers were contemplated. See "Comprehensive Needs Assessment," *supra* note 72, p. 27.

105 Ordinance on Public Employees 1998, articles 1(4), 6(2).

106 See Nguyen Van Canh, *Vietnam Under Communism, 1975–1982* (Stanford: Hoover Institution Press 1983), p. 79.

107 Interviews, Chief Judge of the Civil Court, Ho Chi Minh City Provincial Court, June 2001.

108 Interviews, Nguyen Khac Cong, Judge, Supreme Court, Hanoi (October 1997); Nguyen Thi Loi, Deputy Chief Judge, Civil Division, Hanoi People's Court, Hanoi (July 1998, March 1999); Nguyen Van Dung, Judge, Economic Division, Supreme Court (July 1998).

109 The court system was reorganized following the 1959 Constitution to implement the principles of democratic centralism. See Dinh Gia Trinh, *Nghien Cuu Nha Nuoc va Phap Quyen*, [Studies about State and Legality], Nha Xuat Ban Su Hoc (Hanoi: Historical Studies Publishing House, 1964), p. 104.

110 See Richard Kinsey, "Karl Renner on Socialist Legality," in David Sugarman, ed., *Legality, Ideology and the State* (London: Academic Press, 1983), pp. 36–9.

111 Law on the Organization of People's Courts 2002, article 40.

112 See Pip Nicholson, "The Vietnamese Courts and Corruption," in Tim Lindsey and Howard Dick, eds., *Corruption in Asia* (Sydney: Federation Press, 2002), pp. 215–17.

113 Petitions from enterprises in economic courts fell by 28 percent in 2000. See Pham Xuan Tho, "Economic Courts Failed to Win Enterprise Confidence," *Vietnam Law and Legal Forum*, vol. 7, no. 77 (2001), p. 20.

114 Although relational theorists find aversion to judicial dispute resolution in the West, they also find that few trading relationships of any significance are consummated without legal advice. While judicial hearings are infrequent, courts decisions strongly influence settlement and negotiations between litigants, which proceed within the "shadow of the law." See, generally, John O. Haley, "The Myth of the Reluctant Litigant," *Journal of Japanese Studies*, vol. 4, no. 2 (1978), pp. 366–89.

115 These views are based on numerous interviews with private lawyers from Investconsult and Leadco, Hanoi, and IMAC, Ho Chi Minh City, between 1997 and 2001, and interviews with Supreme Court, Hanoi Economic Court, and Ho Chi Minh City Economic Court judges between 1994 and 2000. High on the list

of concerns is a chronic shortage of experienced commercial judges. Statistics informally provided by Ministry of Justice officials in 2000 suggest an overall shortage of 1,714 judges. Litigants also complain that judges base their decisions on internal guidelines that are unavailable to creditors and debtors.

116 John McMillan and Christopher Woodruff, "Interfirm Relationships and Informal Credit in Vietnam," *Quarterly Journal of Economics*, vol. 114, no. 4 (1999), pp. 1,285–86.

117 Resolution no. 20 of Party Politburo, 2001, established an inter-agency steering committee to oversee judicial reforms.

118 See Toa An Nhan Dan Toi Cao [Supreme People's Court], *Giai Dap Mot So Van De Ve Hinh Su, Dan Su, Kinh Te, Lao Dong, Hanh Chinh va To Tung* [Annual Report on Criminal, Civil, Economic, Labor, Administrative and Military] (1 February 2000), pp. 60–1.

119 See John Gillespie, "The Political-Legal Culture of Anti-Corruption Reforms in Vietnam," in Tim Lindsey and Howard Dick, eds., *Corruption in Asia* (Sydney: Federation Press, 2002), pp. 186–93.

120 See Oskar Weggel, "The Vietnamese Communist Party and Its Status Under Law," in D. Loeber, ed., *Ruling Communist Parties and their Status Under Law* (The Hague: Martinus Nijhoff Publisher, 1986), pp. 418.

121 France, for example, did not establish a constitutional court until 1958. See Chapter 3.

122 Overseas dissident groups publish their views on several websites. See, e.g., Alliance for Democracy in Vietnam, Mission Statement, www.lmdcvn.org/documents; International Committee for a Free Vietnam, Mission Statement, www.icfv.org/home.

123 As O. W. Wolters opined, "they localized the Confucian corpus by fragmenting it and detaching passages, drained of their original contextual meaning, in order to appropriate fragments at their discretion and fit them into the context of their own statements." See O. W. Wolters, "Assertions of Cultural Well-being in Fourteenth-Century Vietnam: Part I," *Journal of Southeast Asian Studies*, vol. 10 (1979), p. 437. Also see David Marr, *Vietnamese Anticolonialism, 1885–1925* (Berkeley: University of California Press, 1971), pp. 19–20.

124 Brian Tamanaha queries the centrality of law in Western societies and, by implication, the integrative role of law in society. See Brian Tamanha, "The View of Habermas from Below: Doubts About the Centrality of Law and the Legitimation Enterprise," *Denver University Law Review*, vol.76 (1999), pp. 996–8.

125 These comments are based on interviews with a Vietnamese sociologist specializing in state–village relations. Interviews, Hoang Ngoc Hien, Sociologist, Nguyen Du School of Creative Writing, Hanoi (June 21, 1998; April, September 1999; August 2000, June 2002). Nguyen Van Huyen vividly described syncretism in villages:

> In this jumble of spiritual things, the cult of ancestors and the cult of the village patron can be distinguished. The great majority of the people in the country have a very flexible and very soft popular religion characterized by a certain number of practices, some related to Confucianism, others to Taoism or to Buddhism, that are automatically obeyed on different occasions in life.

Nguyen Van Huyen, *The Ancient Civilization of Vietnam* (Hanoi: Gioi Publishers, 1995), pp. 277–88. Marr *supra* note 123, p. 20.

6

RULE OF LAW WITHIN A NON-LIBERAL 'COMMUNITARIAN' DEMOCRACY

The Singapore experience

Li-ann Thio

Introduction: statist and liberal models of the rule of law

Two primary competing conceptions of 'rule of law' are evident within Singapore constitutional practice and discourse. The dominant state-sponsored version rests on a statist or 'soft authoritarian' model which emphasises strong executive control over public order, pursuant to community interests in preserving security and harmony within a multicultural, multi-religious state. Duties of politicians to 'rule by virtue' and citizens to make responsible decisions are stressed over legal modes of regulating governance through rights and institutional restraints.

Although formal political pluralism exists insofar as political parties compete in regularly held elections (although the electoral system advantages the incumbent party[1]), politics and law operate within a dominant-party state based on the Westminster parliamentary system. Singapore has not experienced political turnover since Independence in 1965. The ruling People's Action Party (PAP), fronted by Prime Minister (PM) Lee Kuan Yew (Lee) until 1990, exercises strict paternalistic control, micro-managing citizens' lives through educational streaming and campaigns promoting Mandarin-speaking, courtesy and public-toilet flushing, for example. State neutrality is rejected in favour of an espoused Neo-Confucian state ideology, encapsulated in a 1991 white paper on shared values.[2] These 'communitarian-oriented' values minimise individual autonomy while prioritising government-defined collective goals. The PAP 'manages' democracy, aided by its overwhelming parliamentary majority, unimpeded by an emasculated political opposition.[3] Demands for more public consultation are accommodated, without ceding any genuine political power, through informal feedback channels rather than consultation rights, and by amending the constitution to create an ersatz parliamentary opposition by guaranteeing a minimal opposition presence and nominated parliamentarians, both with truncated voting powers. This marginalises adversarial oppositional politics. Close checks on civil society are maintained, and the PAP influence stretches to 'grassroots' bodies, particularly through government-run Community Development Councils, which promote community governance and bonding by administering government-funded welfare-related programmes. Tight social control is preserved by maintaining symbiotic ties between the government and umbrella body for labour unions.[4]

The government scrupulously adheres to legal formalities and procedures and has even erected institutional restraints on political power, through innovative institutions like the elected president, though the effectiveness of such institutional cuffs is questionable. Narrow legalism informs both constitutional ordering and interpretation. The judicial interpretation of constitutional liberties manifests a 'corporatist' or pro-communitarian slant, prioritising statist over humane values by expansively construing derogation clauses to curtail individual rights to serve public 'goods' relating to order, health and morality. Positivistic understandings of 'law' reduce such rights to state grants rather than inalienable entitlements. Administrative law decisions indicate that efficiency routinely trumps fairness concerns, even when constitutional rights are implicated.[5]

Thus, rule of law is appreciated in instrumental terms, to preserve the socio-political stability necessary to attracting foreign investment, fuelling economic growth.

The secondary version, espoused by opposition politicians and other critics, is liberal and rights oriented, emphasising civil-political rights, political liberalism, the intrinsic importance of limited government and holding state power accountable through formalised constraints.

This chapter examines how the protean, contested concept of rule of law has been understood and utilised within Singapore. It has been the subject of parliamentary debates, ministerial statements, media discussions and judicial pronouncements, informing the nature of a state's economic system, political ideology and human rights practice. It sparks controversy in engaging substantive justice theories, blurring the law/politics dichotomy evident in debates over 'formal' and 'substantive' visions of rule of law.[6]

The essential contest in Singapore may be located, first, in assertions that rule of law is 'no cliché',[7] as evidenced by existing political stability and social cohesion. This 'soft authoritarian' model associates rule of law with 'content-independent' evaluative criteria often associated with 'thin' rule of law conceptions. The key tenets are the Law's supremacy, equality before the law and 'notions of the transparency, openness and prospective application of our laws, observations of the principles of natural justice, independence of the Judiciary and judicial review of administrative action'.[8] However, a substantive layer is discernible in advocating strong centralised government, consonant with 'Asian values', to maintain order and propel national development goals.

Contrariwise, rule of law allegedly amounts to 'empty legalism'.[9] Liberal versions of rule of law have been propounded. Veteran opposition politician

J. B. Jeyaretnam grounded a plethora of claims on this, including alleged breaches of fundamental liberties, discriminatory application of licensing laws and undemocratic practices prejudicing opposition politicians. Jeyaretnam envisaged a substantive conception of rule of law in criticising its inadequacy regarding deficient workers rights legislation and disregarding rights to peaceful demonstration.[10]

Both views appreciate the rule of law's legitimating function. The government regularly cites laudatory reports about Singapore's legal framework in facilitating commercial transactions; for example, the *World Competitiveness Yearbook* consistently ranks Singapore first for legal framework.[11] Rule of law through sustaining a sound business environment becomes synonymous with law and order, buttressing the view that economic productivity and political stability are closely correlated. Critics equally insist that the rule of law in Singapore is 'in decline',[12] being systematically 'dismantle[d]'[13] by a 'compliant judiciary'.[14] This 'misRule of Law',[15] reflects 'legal terrorism',[16] as 'the rule of Lee has displaced the Rule of Law' as Singapore judges 'know which side of the judicial bread is buttered'.[17] Evidently, 'soft authoritarian' apologists focus on the role and rule of law in the commercial field, while detractors highlight public law and social justice issues.[18]

The critique against mere legalism channels the enquiry beyond the normative contest to the essential question: while a diversity of constitutional arrangements may embody the rule of law in the abstract, does the existing institutional infrastructure provide meaningful legal restraints to exercises of government powers?

The first section (pp. 000–00) provides a brief Singapore legal history, describing the constitutional framework. The second (pp. 000–00) considers the economic system and the politico-legal culture shaping governance, evident in government policy and institutional values. The subsequent two sections (pp. 000–00 and 000–00) discuss specific instances where rule of law has been contested, examining institutional development, processes and rights jurisprudence, thus elucidating dominant and marginal conceptions of rule of law, its functional utility and underlying values. The final section (pp. 000–00) offers concluding observations.

Singapore legal history and institutional framework

The directors of the British East India Company might be considered Singapore's founding fathers, given its trading centre origins. Sir Stamford Raffles arrived at the island of some 120 fisher folk in 1819; thereafter, Singapore became a thriving port. British control over Singapore as part of the Straits Settlement and a Crown Colony lasted until 1959, when it became self-governing. It joined the Federation of Malaysia in 1963, seceding and gaining Independence on 9 August 1965.

Legal history: reception of the common law and subsequent (in)fusion of influences

The common law was imported into Singapore through the 1823 Charter of Justice. At Independence, the English legal framework and institutions were pragmatically retained to preserve the confidence they inspired in regulating commercial transactions, remaining the basis of the legal system.[19]

However, there is a distinct move towards 'indigenising' (or 'sinifying') the legal system to meet local exigencies. This aspiration towards autochthony is most apparent in the public law field (criminal,[20] constitutional and administrative law). As Singapore is the 'most occidental of the oriental societies', the legal system supposedly reflects a 'creative synthesis' of 'the best of Western Law and Eastern tradition'.[21]

The catalyst is the government's championing of a cultural approach towards government and governance consonant with 'Asian values' and consistent with the PAP's brand of pragmatism.[22] This espouses a communitarian or 'illiberal' democracy. Given the close historical associations between rule of law, Western liberal democracy and free market capitalism, the question is whether 'rule of law' can evolve or be sustained within an illiberal democracy.

The British common law colonial legacy familiarised its recipients with 'the basic principles' underlying Western rule of law conceptions. As a 'force for freedom', it attributed the 'highest value' to individual rights to life, liberty and security.[23] The question is whether 'Singapore values' are consistent with or repudiate the common law's protective philosophy towards individual dignity, given the 'communitarian' model of constitutional adjudication dominating the past decade.[24] Has the common law 'shell' been retained with the 'vicarious respectability'[25] it affords, while denying its pro-individual dignitarian values? The Singapore case study presents insights on how 'rule of law' is understood in an avowedly 'Asian' society and shaped by its local culture (insofar as is clearly identifiable).

Constitutional history

Initial plans to draft a new constitution were jettisoned; the preferred expedient was to retain the existing 1963 state constitution Singapore had as part of the Malayan Federation, making later amendments as necessary.[26]

Lee initiated the establishment of the 1966 Wee Chong Jin Constitutional Commission to make proposals concerning safeguards against discriminatory laws and protecting minority concerns.[27] It recommended accommodating racial minority concerns within a democratic setting to stabilise the immigrant nation. State survivability issues were foremost, given pressing socio-economic problems like poverty, unemployment and housing shortages, exacerbated by communalist and communist threats.

To facilitate economic growth, colonial preventive detention laws were retained to combat triads and communist insurgents threatening public order.[28] The Wee recommendations were departed from as the constitutional amendment process was expediently modified to require only a simple parliamentary majority (not two-thirds), making the supreme law as flexible as ordinary legislation. To facilitate land acquisition pursuant to economic restructuring, a more limited constitutional bill of rights (compared with the Malaysian one) was adopted, conspicuously excluding the article 13 right to property and 'adequate compensation' for compulsory land acquisition by the state. Legislation[29] serving the community's interests authorised land acquisition for public housing and industrial development.

Attempts to forge a distinct Singapore identity were apparent. First, secularism was affirmed, contrasting with the constitutional enshrinement of Islam as the Malaysian Federation's official religion.[30] Second, an egalitarian ethos was preferred over according special Malay rights flowing from a claimed *bumiputras* (sons of the soil) status. Individual rather than group rights would safeguard minority concerns.[31] However, article 152 declares the government responsible for caring for the interests of 'racial and religious minorities', recognising 'the special position of the Malays' as Singapore's indigenous people. Limited legal pluralism is mandated through article 153, authorising legislation to regulate Muslim religious affairs, thus preserving some cultural autonomy in relation to personal laws regulating marriage and testamentary disposition.[32] Singapore has appended reservations to protect these religious, cultural particularities in acceding to UN human rights treaties like the Convention for the Elimination of All Forms of Discrimination against Women.[33]

Constitutional framework

Singapore retained the essential structure, with incipient modifications,[34] of the Westminster parliamentary system,[35] which rests on parliamentary supremacy, the rule of law and common law principles, the pillars of British constitutionalism. Aside from the political check of elections, the chief brakes on abuses of power include judicial review over administrative action, incorporating heightened scrutiny in fundamental liberties cases.[36]

Government is organised around the familiar trichotomy of powers: the legislature, the executive and the judiciary are established under separate constitutional chapters, underscoring the judicially affirmed separation of powers principle.[37] Functional, not institutional, separation of powers is evident as certain offices straddle government branches; for example, the president's consent is necessary to enact legislation. Singapore's Parliament is not supreme, as legislative power is constitutionally delineated.[38]

187

Legislature and executive

Singapore adopted a unicameral legislature based on the 'first past the post' electoral system. A quasi second chamber called the Presidential Council on Minority Rights (PCMR)[39] was established to review legislation to insure against laws with 'differentiating measures' that were practically 'disadvantageous' to racial–religious community members.[40] However, the PCMR's institutional weakness is widely acknowledged, as it lacks coercive powers. It may make adverse reports, but has issued none.[41] Its composition raises problems, as members include senior cabinet members, the attorney-general (AG) and the chief justice. Were a law with a 'differentiating measure' to be judicially challenged, the chief justice could be placed in a difficult position in hearing this case. In addition, since the cabinet authors most laws, it is basically a case of the same people checking themselves. Such 'self-regulation' surfaced in subsequent constitutional experiments.

The executive composes a cabinet executive headed by the PM and a ceremonial head of state, the president. The cabinet is formally collectively responsible to Parliament, although the PM actually controls Parliament through the 'Whip', buttressed by the PAP's overwhelming parliamentary majority, a chief fixture in Singapore politics, effectively fusing legislative–executive power. Political power is further centralised through anti-hopping laws.[42]

A season of constitutional experimentation created two classes of non-elected parliamentarians in 1984 (Non-Constituency MP) and 1990 (Nominated MP). In 1988 the electoral system was transformed to include, while retaining a nominal number of single member constituencies, group representation constituencies where voters choose a team of four to six MPs, with at least one stipulated minority member.[43] In 1991 the presidency became an elective office vested with minimal supervisory powers over stipulated fields of government activities. These include custodial powers over financial reserves, the appointment of key civil servants and limited supervision over specified civil liberties.[44]

The judiciary

As the partisan administration of law erodes rule of law, a central institutional requirement is an independent, accessible judiciary.

Part VIII of the Constitution establishes the judiciary and provides safeguards for judicial independence by insulating it from political pressure, fixing tenure at 65 and guaranteeing against adverse remunerative changes.[45] Singapore judges enjoy generous annual salaries: chief justice ($347,000), judges of appeal ($253,200) and Supreme Court judges ($234,600).[46] Article 93 vests judicial power in the judiciary, and practice confirms the power of judicial review.[47] The Supreme Court consists of a permanent three-member

Court of Appeal and a High Court. Subordinate courts are regulated under the Subordinate Courts Act (Cap 321). The abolition of jury trials broke with British practice.[48] Until 8 August 1994, the Privy Council was the final court of appeal for civil and criminal trials.[49] The reason for retaining the Privy Council to head the judicial hierarchy offered by Lee in March 1967 apparently no longer applied. This had allowed 'some other tribunal where obviously undue influence cannot be brought to bear'[50] to review Singapore courts. Dissenting judgements are generally absent in public law cases.

Singapore judges enjoy broader judicial powers than English judges and 'an even greater responsibility',[51] particularly in public law, as judicial control extends beyond applying administrative law principles to striking down unconstitutional laws, after *Marbury v. Madison*.[52] No Act has ever been successfully invalidated.[53]

The judiciary is guardian of Part IV fundamental liberties. Although no constitutional right of access to a judicial remedy exists, this is accepted in practice.

Under article 100, introduced in 1994, the president, with cabinet approval, may refer a question to an ad hoc constitutional tribunal regarding a constitutional provision's actual or prospective effect. The impetus for this stemmed from the 1994 dispute over the scope of presidential powers under the newly minted elected presidency (EP) scheme, specifically, whether presidential discretion to withhold assent to certain bills purporting to curtail EP powers existed.[54] This remains the sole constitutional reference, although opposition politician Jeyaretnam wanted the tribunal to consider the constitutionality of the Public Entertainments Act[55] and whether parliamentary and presidential approval were necessary before making substantial loans to Indonesia.[56]

The Singapore judiciary is efficient in terms of speedy case management and disposition. Nevertheless, it has been criticised for lacking impartiality. The UN Special Rapporteur on judicial independence said that 'the perceived judicial bias favouring the government "could have stemmed from the very high number of cases won by the Government or members of the ruling party in either contempt of court proceedings or defamation suits" against government critics, whether media or individuals'.[57] Government ministers allegedly utilise the judicial machinery to deluge their political opponents with litigation, subsequently causing financial bankruptcy and removal from the political scene.[58] In *AG v. Lingle*, the AG adduced evidence that between 1971 and 1993 'there had been 11 cases of opposition politicians who had been made bankrupt after being sued'.[59] While the courts are lauded for protecting property rights, critics perceive a judicial pro-government bias in politically sensitive cases.

These allegations have been denied in parliamentary debates.[60] Lee noted that '[o]ur judiciary and the rule of law are rated by WEF [World Economic Forum], IMD [International Institute for Management Development] and

189

PERC [Political and Economic Risk Consultancy] as the best in Asia'.[61] Further, judiciary efficiency in 'clearing court cases continues to command wide admiration...their fair and efficient administration of justice...has enhanced the rule of law'.[62]

Undoubtedly, innovative judicial reforms have successfully reduced case backlogs through proactive case management, holding night courts and through information technology, improving accessibility.[63] This is complemented by an initiative making Singapore legislation freely available online.[64] A recent judgement affirming an expansive reading of standing where constitutional rights are infringed also vindicates the rule of law by allowing concerned parties to mount legal challenges against unlawful action.[65] However, there are concerns about financial accessibility with rising court costs,[66] but the prospect of delayed justice has been curtailed.[67]

Other concerns about judicial independence exist. One relates to tenure, where judges over 65 are hired as contract judges, explicitly authorised by article 98; for example, the 77-year-old chief justice has a three-year contract until 2004.[68] Extensions of judicial terms by contract are not automatic,[69] raising the unsavoury possibility of judges being 'beholden' to the executive.[70] This same concern applies to the Judicial Commissioners (JC) scheme. Inaugurated in 1986, this sought to attract private practitioners to the bench by instituting a probationary 'trial period' of perhaps one to two years. JCs desiring a career judgeship may not act 'without fear or favour'. The scheme also provides short-term judges for six-month periods or more, or to hear specific cases.[71]

Further, the lower judiciary is susceptible to extraneous political pressures, as subordinate court judges lack tenure and form part of the executive branch. The president appoints subordinate court judges on the recommendation of the chief justice (also the chairman of the Legal Services Commission, which determines appointment terms). Thus, district court judges are routinely shuffled between the executive and judicial branches, sustaining concerns that they might imbibe the executive's corporatist ideology,[72] carrying that into adjudication, as a 'judiciary of amateurs'.[73]

There have been complaints of executive interference with the judiciary, such as over transferring District Judge Michael Khoo to the AG's Chambers after he heard a criminal case against opposition politician Jeyaretnam, where he imposed a fine not entailing the loss of Jeyaretnam's parliamentary seat. The case was tried in January 1981; in August 1981 Khoo was removed from the bench it what was perceived as a politically motivated punitive transfer, although the AG characterised it as coincidental and long overdue.[74] A commission led by Judge T. S. Sinnathuray, whose judgments are largely pro-government, investigated and declared these allegations unfounded.

Economics and politico-legal culture

In November 1995 the AG publicly rebuked the Law Society for failing to defend Singapore's legal system and judiciary against foreign criticism about unfair trials.[75] He insisted that to collaborate in Singapore's development the Law Society had to accept 'a concept of the rule of law which should not be substantially different from that understood and accepted by the government of the day', heeding the 'necessary conditions' allowing it to 'exist and thrive'.[76]

The AG identified the 'rule of law' as embedded in the local politico-cultural context, not a universal legal principle. The Law Society president replied that the ongoing English debate about balancing the principles of parliamentary supremacy[77] and the 'rule of law' warranted reconsideration in Singapore, perhaps motivated by the fear that a government-stipulated version would make rule of law subject to political expediency, not principle.[78] This section examines how 'rule of law' is appreciated within Singapore's legal-politico context.

The rule of law as instrumental to economic growth and development

Within a heavily internationalised national economy where foreign trade is triple the national product, the government is a significant economic actor, retaining the primary economic policy-making role.[79] Statutory boards like the Economic Development Board help shape economic policies. The government maintains direct or indirect interests in certain companies, and restricts the types and quantity of shares foreign investors can hold, for example in the publishing industry.[80] Temasek Holdings, a government investment company (GIC) controls one-third of the Singapore stock market, with substantial shareholdings in Singapore government-linked companies (GLCs) like Singapore International Airlines, SingTel and DBS Bank Limited, which generate 60 per cent of the gross domestic product (GDP). Singapore's planned capitalist economy is growth oriented and heavily interventionist, with a strong free trade commitment.

The 'economics first' argument and economic legitimacy

Singapore's economic success, led by an authoritarian government ready to subsume individual liberties to community interests in public order, has been presented as an Asian law and development alternative,[81] rejecting the European welfare model that promotes a dependency ethos.[82] The high level of enjoyment of socio-economic rights serves to ground the government's economic legitimacy. 'Basic needs' are satisfied, home ownership is promoted through public housing schemes,[83] there are excellent transportation facilities, reasonable healthcare services, a much admired – albeit criticised – public education system, and mandatory retirement schemes like the Central Provident Fund (CPF).[84] Delivering economic goods sustains 'political stability', ensuring the PAP's successive re-election 'with solid majorities',[85] since, 'as long as the leaders take care of their people, they will obey their leaders'.[86] Singapore validates its policies by 'the more rigorous test of practical success', ignoring its critics and abstract theories,[87] attracting admirers among developing nations.

The phenomenon of the 'politically inert and economically dynamic'[88] state apparently contradicts Western constitutionalism's theoretical assumptions about economic growth and constitutional government.[89] Indeed, this empirical success fuelled the articulation of the 'Singapore school', which hinges the interpretation and application of human rights upon cultural values[90] and the stage of economic development, justifying an 'economics first' policy. This prescribes economic modernisation, aided by social discipline and political liberalisation, to precipitate economic growth.[91] Thus, the rule of law is primarily conceived as an instrument to facilitate economic transactions, through clear investment laws and credible dispute resolution mechanisms securing property rights, rather than in terms of intrinsic justice values. The rule of law guarantees a certain environment, giving 'our people...MNCs [multinational corporations] and other foreign investors...the confidence to invest in our physical, industrial as well as social infrastructure...the fundamental bases of our economic growth and our social development'.[92]

This stability is maintained through a strong criminal law system and preventive detention laws where order trumps criminal process rights. References to Singapore's vulnerability justify these strict measures, a recurrent theme in political discourse. Threats to public order may stem from economic vagaries or security issues arising from communist insurgents, fundamentalist Islamic terrorism or internal racial tensions. Further, cultural ('Confucian') values are lauded as underlying Singapore's progress[93] because they prioritise community interests, reverence for scholarship and respect for government leaders. This allowed the establishment of a meritocratic civil service, compulsory military service and a limit on trade union powers, neutering a source of political opposition or strike-induced economic setbacks.[94]

Guarding against corruption

The antidote to corruption, cronyism and nepotism lies in the government's meritocracy policy.[95] Allegations of preferential treatment have been publicly addressed, as when Senior Minister (SM) Lee called for parliamentary debates to air the issue of alleged special discounts conferred on him and his son, Deputy PM Lee Hsien Loong, in relation to discounted luxury property purchases.[96] Upon investigation by the Corrupt Practices Investigation

Bureau (CPIB) called for by PM Goh, the matter was declared above board, a finding which attracted parliamentary consensus.[97] SM Lee praised the 'impersonal and effective' system he had established, which could scrutinise his conduct, demonstrating that 'no one is above the law',[98] as 'the Government upholds the rule of law'.[99] This illustrates the importance the PAP places on moral legitimacy.

Further anti-corruption initiatives include the criticised policy of high ministerial salaries, which brushes aside 'naïve' calls to public service in favour of hard-headed economic rationality. Since 1994, ministerial pay has been pegged to top private-sector salaries, despite disquiet and calls for a referendum, which were rejected as 'childish talk' entertained by weak governments.[100] PM Goh noted in 2000 that paying good people to assume government posts was an ancient Confucian precept, necessary to establish a 'self-sustaining system' generating good governors and economic growth.[101]

Politico-legal culture, moral and political legitimacy and the rule of law

In addition to performance-based economic legitimacy, the PAP government seeks to buttress its position through moral and political legitimacy. This shapes the contours of legal culture, providing insight into the components of the Singapore government's soft authoritarian 'thick' conception of the rule of law. Notably, this legal culture conditions judicial values.

Singapore's legal culture is constructed within a hegemonic dominant-party state; the PAP has monopolised political power since Independence,[102] garnering a resounding 75.3 per cent of the vote in the August 2001 general elections.[103] Notably, only 33 per cent of the eligible voters could vote, since most electoral wards went uncontested, returning the incumbent government to power on Nomination Day.[104]

The PAP's pervasive influence over Singapore's broad political middle ground is effectuated by managing dissent through co-opting critics,[105] creating institutional channels for alternative viewpoints, harnessing the domestic media as a national partner in creating consensus[106] and saturating the grassroots with pro-establishment committees.[107] This conflates the state, government and society, as is evident in election campaigning strategies urging voters in marginal wards to vote PAP and enjoy prioritised ward upgrading. This exercise in asset enhancement underwritten by public funds indicates the politicisation of the public-housing programme, extending even to promising voters this priority in precincts within opposition wards which demonstrate a minimum of 50 per cent PAP support.[108] This means that numbered voting slips can be traced to specific precincts, undermining secret voting. Opposition politicians have criticised the PM for behaving as 'the Secretary-General of the ruling party' in safeguarding party interests over national interests.[109]

Political legitimacy

Electoral validation, which confers political legitimacy, is equated with a blanket endorsement for the PAP style of governance and policies. The law minister has rhetorically stated that a 'sophisticated electorate' would be intolerant of government power abuses, particularly the Internal Security Act.[110]

Since elections theoretically provide a peaceful way to oust a repressive or unresponsive regime, repeated electoral success is taken to validate government practices and policies, proving the health of rule of law. However, this reasoning turns on the actual ability of political checks to gauge popular opinion and facilitate peaceful government changes. Since political turnover remains unlikely for the foreseeable future,[111] elections present a feeble political check.

Moral legitimacy: the junzi and the scallywag

Moral legitimacy is asserted in speaking of a government of virtuous Confucian *junzi*, superior gentlemen morally obliged to lead, enjoying popular 'trust and respect'. This notion was deemed more apt than 'the Western idea' of limiting government power and treating governors 'with suspicion unless proven otherwise'.[112]

In 'good governance' discourse, demonstrated virtue may be equal to or weightier than rule of law. When PAP leaders' reputations are impugned, judicial vindication against alleged libel is sought.[113] A corollary tactic is demonising certain opposition politicians as dishonourable,[114] while affirming others![115]

Constructing a national ideology and the valorisation of pragmatic Confucianism

The government champions cultural relativist arguments in engaging international human rights discourse. 'Asian values' were concretely identified in the *Shared Values White Paper*, which sought to craft a unifying national identity. Five values meant to shape individual–society relations were declared:

- nation before community and society above self;
- family as the basic unit of society;
- regard and community support for the individual;
- consensus instead of contention;
- racial and religious harmony.[116]

Proposals to include 'belief in God' were rejected.

This reactionary project sought to stem the growing tide of 'Western' values and individualism infecting Singaporeans.[117] The values' neo-Confucian tenor stirred disquiet among non-Chinese ethnic groups and more liberal Chinese citizens. The need to buttress neo-Confucian prescriptions like filial piety through legal processes was recognised in the Maintenance of Parents Act (Cap 167B).[118]

Though it is now commonplace for PAP ministers to insist that Singapore is a 'Confucian' society, scholars had to be imported to draft a Confucian syllabus in the 1980s, indicating a lack of local scholarly resources and interest. Kuo notes that the Confucian movement was a 'top-down' nation-building exercise, given Confucianism's compatibility with the dominant political culture characterised by 'paternalism, communitarianism, pragmatism and secularism'.[119]

Constructing a version of Singapore culture from selective cultural traits to forge a neo-Confucian variant was criticised as artificial.[120] While drawing heavily on Confucian tradition, with a cursory nod to Malay and Indian traditions, aspects of Confucianism such as recognising the validity of criticism against an unjust government went ignored.[121] The self-serving focus was on traits emphasising obedience to authority.[122] A degree of ambivalence is evident too as not all Western values were considered since some, like 'parliamentary democracy and the Rule of Law', were 'rightly adopted'.[123] In warning the middle class of dangerous foreign influence, the white paper addresses citizens as beneficiaries of the state's care. Rather than an 'individual rights protection mechanism', the rule of law serves only to prepare citizens 'for the requirements of a national plan formulated by a wise and virtuous bureaucratic elite'.[124] This reflects the belief that morality is closely aligned with economic progress,[125] with the shared values representing a culture-based justification for socio-political control.

'Shared values' and styles of governance: hierarchy, paternalism and deference

Singapore's paternalistic, interventionist government, with its feudalistic personality-oriented mode of governance, endorses hierarchical ruler–ruled relationships, a modified version of Confucian relational hierarchies (*wulun*). The Father is replaced by the State as the *paterfamilias*, with the Child as citizenry. PM Goh stated that, while his predecessor ruled like 'a stern father', he sought to govern 'like an elder brother'.[126] This hierarchical sense has filtered into expectations that, in engaging political debate, deference ought to be accorded the government as senior partner, given its sensitivity to criticism.[127] This offends liberal egalitarian sensibilities. While the government is more open to promoting civic participation, the desire remains to contain debate without capitulating to the robust debate which is characteristic of liberal democracies.[128] In past practice, the government has lambasted groups, including professional societies like the Law Society, for venturing into what it considers to be political criticism,[129] stipulating that only members of political organisations could participate in politics.[130] This chills debate and stultifies the development of a democratic ethos, sustaining the belief that opposition politics is a risky business.

'Shared values', government policy and the primacy of community interests

Community interests in stability are paramount, being integral to maintaining primary economic growth objectives.

Given the alien quality of the loyal opposition concept, competitive politics and the adversarialism it breeds have been damned as destabilising, with the PAP advocating a 'one-party [system with] many small parties to keep us on our toes'.[131] This gels with the Confucian valuing of harmonious social relations.[132]

Localising judicial review: 'communitarian values' and the rule of law

A presumptive bias in community interests against individual rights is also evident in the dominant public law values Singapore judges apply.

First, in construing constitutional liberties qualified by 'public good' derogation clauses, the quality of individual protection rests on whether individual dignity is intrinsically respected, as embodied in contemporary Euro-American common law philosophy. Lord Diplock considered that the common law embodies fair dealing principles. Thus, the judicial function extends beyond interpreting written law to declaring unwritten common law and equity.[133] Alternatively, have individual interests been instrumentally subsumed to collective interests?

The Privy Council in *Ong Ah Chuan v. PP* (public prosecutor)[134] advocated a pro-individual bias in interpreting bills of rights in commonwealth constitutions, giving citizens the 'full measure' of fundamental liberties, avoiding 'the austerity of tabulated legalism'.[135] This contrasts with the less liberal approaches towards residual common law liberties extant in English jurisprudence for many centuries.

Of late, this approach has been discounted, with statist concerns accorded determinative weight. A 1994 judicial statement on precedents, issued after ending Privy Council appeals, stated that the development of Singapore law should reflect local socio-political and economic changes and 'the fundamental values of Singapore society'[136] in shaping an autochthonous public law.

Subsequent cases evidenced a broad reading of public order as exceptional qualifications to individual rights, whereupon the exception may be argued to have become the rule. In *Colin Chan v. PP*,[137] publicorder included non-violent threats. The court agreed with the government's view that the national interest was prejudiced by the existence of the Jehovah's Witnesses (JWs), a religious sect whose pacific tenets compelled members not to perform compulsory national military service. This justified their de-registration under the Societies Act (Cap 311) and the 'content-blind' ban of all Watchtower (JW publishing arm) publications under the Undesirable Publications Act (Cap 358). Prima facie, these actions violated articles 14 and 15 rights to free speech, association and religion. Yong CJ (chief justice) rejected the need to show a clear or reasonably foreseeable danger in relation to religious expression and public order. He considered that an administration which perceived the possibility of trouble over religious beliefs but preferred to wait before taking action was 'pathetically naïve' and 'grossly incompetent'.[138] He thus endorsed a jurisprudence of pre-emptive strikes. He further cemented the primacy of public order in stating that, while religious beliefs merited 'proper protection', religious acts had to conform to 'the general law relating to public order and social protection'. Anything running contrary to 'the sovereignty, integrity and unity of Singapore' warranted leashing.[139]

Applying this logic, the statutory duty of national service was anointed a 'fundamental tenet', brooking no derogation.[140] This exalts duty to the country over a right to religious liberty.[141] Notably, this concern for public order stems not from a cultural but from a statist imperative.

Second, a shift from a teleological to a literalist or positivist approach to constitutional adjudication is evident, which shies away from requiring laws to accord with substantive constitutional values. In *Ong*, it was stated that an Act purporting to deprive one of life and liberty, protected under article 9,[142] had to comport with 'fundamental principles of natural justice', as 'law' bore a non-literal meaning.[143]

However, in *Jabar v. PP*[144] the court flatly refused to read a substantive element into the word 'law', curtailing the scope of the review. At issue was whether the 'death row phenomenon' was constitutional or constituted cruel and inhumane treatment such that it fell below standards of fairness embodied in the law, breaching article 9. The court opted to read 'law' as merely legislative will enacted in accordance with correct procedure, maintaining judicial indifference over whether that law was 'fair, just and reasonable'.[145] This approach implicitly defers to parliamentary sovereignty, reflecting a thin positivist conception of rule of law shorn of ethical content. Only government sensibility or a conscious popular political morality barred the enactment of morally reprehensible laws.

In 1998, a strange if undeveloped attempt to articulate a natural rights theory surfaced in *Taw Cheng Kong v. PP*,[146] concerning the unequal application of an anti-corruption law. Karthigesus JA (judge of appeal) affirmed the Privy Council's view of 'law' in *Ong* as something consistent with fundamental principles of natural justice,[147] subjecting all laws to the principle of constitutionality – the highest law.[148] He argued, drawing from social contractarian theories, that constitutional rights were inalienable rather than reciprocal exchanges between state and citizen, or 'carrot and stick privileges'.[149] This affirms the intrinsic worth of individuals as holding rights the state could not alienate[150] and was a rare successful challenge to an Act's constitutionality, though it must be considered an aberration in the larger scheme of utilitarian cases.

While adopting a parochial 'four walls'[151] approach, the courts have dismissed international and comparative civil liberties standards as unsuited to local 'social conditions'.[152] However, these social conditions were not elaborated,[153] which is unfortunate as it behoves a judiciary intent on developing a local public law jurisprudence to expound clearly what these social conditions are, which values are prioritised or discounted. This would elucidate how individual rights would take shape within a duty-oriented 'communitarian' culture. Indeed, concerns for control rather than culture are evident in the importation into peacetime Singapore of 'Western' cases from a more conservative,[154] wartime era reticent towards strong legal curbs on executive power, to buttress decisions. This demonstrates the 'siege' mentality that makes law the servant of a broadly construed, illiberal notion of public order.[155] This augurs ill for efforts to develop a strong rights culture, as only a minimalist conception of government accountability and a 'thin', procedural rule of law are envisaged.

The speech cases implicating the reputations of politicians or public institutions disclose the judicial endorsement of 'communitarian' or feudal values like deference to authority and respect for hierarchy; that is, political libel and contempt of court suits. These cases have minimised the importance of free speech as an individual right and as a community interest in free, informed debate within a democratic society, promoting transparent, accountable government.[156] Paramount consideration is accorded politicians' reputations, as manifested by the huge damage awards[157] (inducing self-censorship), rejecting a US 'public figure' doctrine[158] or the recognised broader limits of acceptable criticism for politicians in European jurisprudence.[159] The Court of Appeal in *J. B. Jeyaretnam v. Lee Kuan Yew*[160] argued that this would 'do the public more harm than good' as 'sensitive and honourable men' would be deterred from seeking public offices of trust and responsibility, where they might be vulnerable to 'others who have no respect for their reputation'.[161] Singapore public officials are not expected to demonstrate forbearance to political criticism. Unlike the US, the PM was entitled to have his reputation protected no less than a private individual: *Goh Chok Tong v. J. B. Jeyaretnam*.[162] While acknowledging the 'undeniable public interest' in protecting free speech, which can expose public wrongdoing, allowing public officials 'to execute their duties unfettered by false aspersions' was 'an equal public interest'.[163] Intangible qualities of good character were stressed and could result in increased damages flowing from the plaintiff's high standing,[164] an approach consistent with a non-liberal system. The community interest in maintaining politicians' public characters trumped the community interest in holding public officials accountable.

The privileging of judicial reputation is also evident in contempt cases.[165] In *AG v. Wain*, speech critical of the judiciary which had the 'inherent tendency'[166] (a tenuous link) to interfere with the administration of justice, a public concern, satisfied the 'scandalising the court' offence. This test, which is biased in favour of institutional interests, discounts the importance of free speech, even regarding the operation of a primary constitutional organ. The suggested test struck by Canadian courts in *R v. Kopyto*,[167] requiring 'real, substantial and immediate' danger to the justice system, was rejected. The Canadian approach is instructive in recognising the significance of elevating a common law free speech liberty to a constitutional right, requiring an evaluation of the gravity of harm involved, its reasonable forseeability and the speaker's motive. This identifies and considers both competing public interests in free speech – which helps expose public deceptions – and protecting the judicial process from unfounded attacks.

Consciousness of rights and law?

Attitudes towards law and authority apparently manifest reticence towards formal adversarial litigation, in contrast with Western liberalism's strong rights orientation. Singapore's predominantly Chinese population shares with other East Asian cultures a preference for a 'strong, decisive and authoritarian form of government',[168] prioritising social harmony, relational obligations and informal dispute resolution modes.[169] However, leading politicians display a zealous litigiousness in seeking the judicial vindication of their political reputations. Indeed, government recommendations that critics seek judicial solutions for charges of unfair electoral processes and allegations of official malfeasance[170] display a legalistic mentality.

An underdeveloped sense of rights or 'law' consciousness manifests at various levels. First, constitutional supremacy and what this entails are only apprehended formalistically. Although the supreme law,[171] the Constitution, may be amended as easily as ordinary legislation, the theoretically more onerous amendment procedure (two-thirds parliamentary majority)[172] designed to enhance mature deliberation is a formality in a dominant-party state, a consequence of unchecked political power. Although it attracted controversy, many innovative constitutional institutions were enacted in the 1980s, ignoring calls for referenda.[173] As the fact of election apparently gave a government carte blanche during its tenure, it may alter the Constitution's basic structure without further ado. Indeed, the government considers easy amendability desirable, as this has allowed its expeditious introduction in 1991 and subsequent fine-tuning of institutions like the elected presidency in 1994, 1996, 1997 and 1998 to enhance institutional workability.[174]

Second, the Constitution has been judicially discounted in some cases. In deciding the status of the Military Court of Appeals and whether it was immune from judicial review in *Abdul Wahab bin Sulaiman v. Commandant, Tanglin Detention Barracks*,[175] Judge Sinnathuray did not reference relevant constitutional provisions. He ignored article 93 (the judicial power clause) and article 9 (process rights), preferring to consider English cases and *Halsbury's Laws of England*, in an unfortunate display of inapt Anglo-centric reasoning. Judge Sinnathuray's stressing of the paramountcy of 'local conditions' in discounting foreign contempt of court cases is ironic, since he ignored the most local of local conditions in *Abdul Wahab* – the Constitution.

Third, constitutional litigation constitutes a minor percentage of the Supreme Court's docket, where commercial cases predominate. This flows partly from unfamiliarity with asserting claims against the state. Confucian tradition holds no notion of individual rights as a protective shield against state abuses. Order is prioritised, and insofar as this sustains the commercial objectives of Singapore Inc. this hard-line stance attracts public acquiescence.

The individual in an Asian community is not an atomistic rights recipient but is contemplated in terms of needing community support. Furthermore, state obligations towards citizens are couched as programmatic goals, not justiciable entitlements. Policies potentially infringing article 12 (equality clause)[176] or Singapore's international women's rights obligations[177] go unchallenged, for example the one-thirds quota for female medical students. Potential reform is expressed in terms of optional policy choice rather than a legal obligation to vindicate gender equality, manifesting an antipathy for invoking 'rights', which limits state power, in framing state–individual relations.[178]

The perception of rights as undesirable focal points of contention is evident in the negative government reaction towards an opposition party's 1997 initiative to establish a Malay rights group. This was criticised as harmful to racial harmony, and might spark more rights claims from other ethnic groups. Rather than 'rights talks', running constructive social programmes to tackle drug abuse problems and rising divorce rates were advocated.[179] Similarly, the government downplayed the prospect of constitutional litigation for religious liberty infringements when four Muslim schoolgirls were banned from attending public school in January 2002 for wearing *tudung* (headscarves), which was contrary to educational policy.[180] Urging that *tudung* was not religiously mandated, the PM urged the parents to prioritise their daughters' education and send them back to school sans *tudung*. Dialogue was preferred over legal action,[181] particularly given strained ethnic relations.

Individuals have exceptionally won public law cases; for example, acquittal concerning Official Secrets Act[182] charges and a Manpower

Ministry dismissal decision were found unjust for breaching natural justice.[183] Successful administrative lawsuits rest on procedural unfairness or technicalities rather than substantive grounds.[184] In balancing administrative efficiency against individual interests in fair treatment, the former is prioritised. The 'content-blind' ban on all Watchtower publications in *Colin Chan v. Public Prosecutor*[185] was upheld because it was administratively inefficient, if not impossible, to evaluate each publication, expressive rights notwithstanding.

The role of the rule of law and institutional developments

Singapore's constitutional experiments bear the imprimatur of their chief architect (Lee Kuan Yew)[186] in moulding parliamentary democracy and review mechanisms to suit local exigencies.

Managing parliamentary democracy in Singapore

The Westminster model's predicate of a functioning adversarial bipartisan system never materialised in Singapore. Damned as destabilising, dissent is managed through reordering parliamentary democracy along more 'harmonious', 'consensual' lines.

After its parliamentary monopoly was breached in 1981, the government introduced novel institutions for articulating alternative (non-government) voices through the NCMP and NMP schemes in 1984 and 1991. These balanced the PAP's desire to maintain control over the parliamentary process with being responsive to demands for increased political accountability.

Creating a quasi-opposition

Breaking with the 1970s strategy of deploying PAP backbenchers to act as parliamentary opposition, the PAP created a quasi-opposition to 'check' the parliamentary executive and promote citizen participation in an otherwise 'monolithic' government process.

To expose younger PAP MPs to robust parliamentary debate, the NCMP scheme offers parliamentary seats to the top three losers from opposition parties capturing a minimum of 15 per cent of their constituency's vote.[187] This constitutes a placatory distraction from electing opposition MPs.

The NMP scheme allowed the incorporation of a slew of non-elected 'independent' voices into Parliament, reminiscent of the practice of appointing natives to colonial legislative assemblies. 'Talented', non-partisan individuals unwilling to contest elections[188] would supply the government-perceived deficiency that opposition MPs expressed insufficient alternative views. This institutionalises an exception to the PAP stricture that only

201

politicians (party political members) should engage in politics,[189] although NCMPs and NMPs lack full voting rights.[190]

These constitutional innovations assume the continued inability of parliamentary opposition to discharge debating and oversight functions, let alone form a substitute government. A decade after introducing three differentiated tiers of parliamentarians, the NCMP scheme still operates, given the PAP's continued dominance.[191] The press and PAP have feted the NMP scheme, democratic illegitimacy notwithstanding, as enhancing parliamentary debate, muting the prospect of alternative government while emphasising the accommodation of alternative, albeit politically impotent, voices. This evolving 'Asian' democracy consolidates the dominant-party state surrounded by a token opposition and government-vetted critics offering 'constructive' dissent. Recent proposals to select NMPs from functional groups like academia and business contradicts its non-partisan rationale; it could introduce interest-group politics, albeit under PAP managerial oversight, consonant with soft authoritarianism.

Buttressing political dominance through electoral regimes: the group representation constituency (GRC) and gerrymandering

The GRC, introduced in 1988, now dominates the electoral system and buttresses political stability.[192] It ostensibly seeks to prevent minority under-representation by institutionalising multi-racialism in Parliament. Three former single-member constituencies (SMCs) were merged into one GRC, contested by three candidates teams, including a designated minority.[193] Team sizes have increased to between four and six members.[194] Opposition parties, who encounter difficulties in fielding suitable teams, have never won a GRC; 75 of 84 contested parliamentary seats come from mostly uncontested GRCs,[195] the remainder from SMCs.[196]

Though theoretically neutral, GRCs practically entrench the incumbent party and facilitate its self-renewal by fielding political neophytes in teams anchored by strong ministerial candidates.[197] Minority representation could be just as effectively guaranteed by the original 1982 'twinning proposal', joining two constituencies to be jointly contested by two MPs, one a minority representative. Reasons for enlarging GRC sizes were superfluous to this original rationale.[198] Thus, the scheme dilutes democratic precepts of government chosen by competitive elections rather than electoral default.

Prioritising expediency over democratic legitimacy manifests itself on two counts. First, GRC by-elections are not required where a member is lost through death or resignation. The need to focus on economic recovery excused not holding by-elections in Jalan Besar GRC in 1999 when an MP convicted for fraud resigned.[199] Second, electoral boundaries are regularly changed shortly before general elections, subsuming opposition or marginal wards within larger GRCs. The political element cannot be discounted, as

PM-appointed civil servants compose the Electoral Boundaries Review Committee. Rule of law demands certainty to enable planning, absent where opposition politicians find, with little pre-election notice, that wards they were cultivating no longer existed.[200] It is desirable to create an independent elections agency which delineates boundaries based on logical, demographical criteria, rather than expediency, without unduly stifling democratic principles.[201]

Me and my shadow: the lifting of the Whip

After winning 82 of 84 parliamentary seats in 2001, the government proposed creating a 'shadow cabinet,'[202] composed of about 20 PAP parliamentarians free from the Whip, to enliven debates.

This latest incarnation of the PAP's preference for internal self-regulation in framing politics and decision-making[203] is inherently limited, promoting consensus over confrontation in casting Parliament as a place where in-house critics fine-tune government policy, rather than a competitive politics site.[204]

The elected presidency as a mechanism of control

In 1991, the ceremonial presidency was transformed into the EP, charged with checking possible specific abuses of untrammelled government powers. However, the EP's role in the constitutional scheme of institutional checks is marginal.

The EP was to be the 'second key' over national financial reserves, guarding against fiscal mismanagement and preventing nepotistic or ill-conceived key public appointments made by an irresponsible government 'freakishly' elected.[205] The EP has only negative 'veto' discretionary powers.

The government apparently was 'clipping its own wings' in institutionalising checks through the EP against a 'weak or bad government ruining Singapore'.[206] To ensure autonomy, party political membership was prohibited. A legal system cannot perpetually guarantee good men, although EP is the institutional embodiment of the PAP's morally and fiscally conservative Confucian *junzi*. This is evident in the Presidential Elections Committee (PEC) administered filtering process requiring candidates to show they are of 'integrity, good character and reputation'. A subjective contrary finding might be defamatory, but the PEC, composed of three bureaucrats, enjoys immunity.[207] In addition, candidates must satisfy criteria more exacting than those required of the PM or even the US president! Candidates are mostly 'pro-establishment', as they must be high political or public office-holders (minister, chief justice, AG) or have managed a company with a minimum of $100 million paid-up capital.[208]

However, this institutional check is weak. Veto powers relating to Internal Security Act (ISA) (Cap 143) detention orders and restraining orders issued under the ISA (Cap 143) and Maintenance of Religious Harmony Act (MRHA) (Cap 167A) restraining orders were later added to the EP's bundle of powers.[209] However, the EP's powers are not initiatory, may be overridden, and are exercised by committee in tandem with a Council of Presidential Advisors (CPA) or other civil servants. Under article 22, the EP may refuse assent to certain public appointments after consulting the relevant authority. If the CPA's recommendation differs, the EP's decision may be overridden by a two-thirds majority parliamentary resolution. If the PM refuses consent, the director of the Corrupt Practices Investigation Bureau may proceed with an investigation with the EP's concurrence.[210]

The scope of EP powers has been disputed, culminating in the seminal 1995 constitutional reference.[211] The EP's powers have been consistently restrictively construed and truncated by amendments.[212] The 'two keys' principle (Cabinet and EP) has been diluted since the government 'changed the locks'.[213] It was admitted that the EP's role is 'mostly 99% ceremonial as before' in the absence of a rogue government.[214] As such, the strict pre-qualifying criteria seem somewhat excessive.[215]

Ousting judicial review: the move towards non-legal or bureaucratic control

The Court of Appeal in *Chng Suan Tze v. Minister of Home Affairs* considered absolute ministerial discretion as contrary to rule of law, affirming an objective test as 'all power has legal limits' which are judicially reviewable.[216]

However, an array of laws authorise the curtailment of individual liberties without judicial redress, to serve public order imperatives. These ouster clauses concentrate unchecked power in executive hands, tempered by a felt need to provide substitute checks. Consequently, non-legal control over executive powers was conferred on political bodies like the EP or the bureaucrat-staffed advisory council, but are these checks effective?

MRHA and restraining orders

The MRHA allows the minister to issue pre-emptive 'restraining orders' to 'gag' politicians or religionists thought to be mixing an incendiary cocktail of religion and politics. While this implicates both speech and religious liberty rights, judicial review is precluded, as 'religious harmony' issues affecting national 'survival'[217] are best left to an executive decision since 'a secular court deciding on religious disputes' would be 'explosive'.[218]

Christian groups expressed concern that the MRHA could be utilised to quench political dissent stemming from faith convictions.[219] Beyond assurances of ministerial prudence, a check through an EP veto over orders under article 22I was provided, although this operates only where the Presidential Council for Religious Harmony's (composed in part of religious representatives) recommendations contradict the cabinet's advice. While this tempers subjective ministerial discretion, the ultimate check resides in the blunt mechanism of the people's judgement in electing men of integrity.[220]

ISA and preventive detention orders

Legislation permitting the detention without trial of persons suspected of acts prejudicing Singapore's security[221] constitutes a 'blatant negation of the Rule of Law'[222] by mandating punishment contrary to personal liberty guarantees, sans judicial determination. Detention orders are renewable every two years, with Chia Thye Poh's 23-year detention for alleged communist activities being the most draconian example.[223]

These laws were primarily unleashed against communist insurgents and drug traffickers, and, more recently, alleged Marxist conspirators in the late 1980s and fundamentalist Islamic terrorists in 2001–2.

The ISA's precursor was the colonial Emergency Preservation of Public Ordinance. Exercising ISA powers against non-violent political dissenters attracted internal and external criticisms. Most notably, the 1987 detention of 22 so-called Marxist conspirators (including church workers and social activists) for allegedly plotting to establish a communist state elicited widespread scepticism. Accounts of coerced confessions and torture were made.[224]

Grappling with new security imperatives in their own countries after 9/11, the usual Western critics applauded the preventive detention of 15 people in December 2001 who were members of *Jemaah Islamiah* (JI) a terrorist group with Al Qaeda links.[225] Evidence of plots to bomb Yishun MRT (underground) station and US and Israeli properties was made public.[226] Though not constitutionally obliged to do so,[227] the government, cognisant of delicate race relations with the Muslim minority, supplied information on the arrests, held public dialogue meetings[228] to engage concerned parties and appeared supportive of the detainees' families.[229] JI members' filmed reconnaissance video clips were released,[230] schools were briefed[231] and a Home Affairs Ministry press release summarised the case against the detainees.[232] This strategy, based on government sensibility, provided some accountability, allaying public fears, diffusing emotive reactions.[233] This sensibility was starkly absent in the callous handling of 'Marxist' conspirators 15 years earlier.[234]

The ISA requires the constitution of an Advisory Board to hear detainee representations and to recommend to the president whether detention should continue beyond three months.[235] The three-member Board appointed by the president after consulting the chief justice must include one person with Supreme Court judge qualifications. This judicial element aside, the Board hearing falls short of an open court trial where natural justice rules and evidentiary and criminal procedure standards apply. But then preventive detention laws authorise expedient detentions, where proof is insufficient for criminal charges.[236] In May 2002, detention of the thirteen until at least January 2004 was recommended since they constituted an active threat to Singapore and their detention would facilitate continuing investigations to expose their network.[237]

Despite Communism's demise as a viable social threat, the ISA retains utility against terrorist threats, especially of the radical Islamic variety,[238] rehabilitated from its perception as an oppressive tool intimidating opposition politicians and the public into docility.[239] Its nation-building properties are celebrated by establishing an ISA heritage centre and informative book.[240] Nevertheless, preventive detention laws, while upholding one aspect of rule of law, that of public order, thwart effective checks on broad discretion. The attenuated conception of 'public order' as not necessarily involving violence renders differentiation between using the ISA to protect genuine security interests and for self-interested political purposes difficult.

Chng Suan Tze, *the truncation of judicial review, and 'freezing' the common law*

In response to the seminal December 1988[241] decision of *Chng Suan Tze v. Minister of Home Affairs*, which quashed an ISA order on technical grounds, Parliament moved swiftly to severely truncate judicial review over the ISA in January 1990.

After reviewing Commonwealth precedents, the court decided on principle that section 8's subjective wording ('if the President is satisfied') authorising the detention orders did not preclude an objective review test,[242] overruling the subjective test in *Lee Mau Seng v. Home Affairs Minister*.[243] Nevertheless, the court recognised that judicial self-restraint should be exercised over politically sensitive issues.[244]

The ISA amendments stipulated that the applicable judicial review test (broadly defined in section 8A to include prerogative writs and *habeas corpus* petitions) for reviewing ISA decisions was the law applicable in Singapore as of 13 July 1971, when *Lee Mau Seng* was decided. This attempts to 'freeze' the common law, which by nature evolves incrementally. The 'subjective' test was approved in the British wartime case of *Liversidge v. Anderson*,[245] where Lord Atkin's renowned dissent rebuking his brother judges for being 'more executive-minded than the executive' was later vindicated in Commonwealth jurisprudence.

Thus, a common law test formulated under wartime conditions was thought appropriate for peacetime Singapore. Furthermore, section 8B(2) limited review to ensuring compliance with procedural requirements. As ISA-related appeals to the Privy Council were excluded, this draconian executive power faced no substantial checks, besides the Advisory Board's non-binding recommendations. Further, article 149 of the Constitution was amended to include a 'notwithstanding clause', exempting laws enacted under Part XII (Special Powers against Subversion and Emergency Powers) from the operation of constitutional liberties, including articles 9 (life and liberty), 11 (retrospective laws), 12 (equality), 13 (banishment and free movement) and 14 (free speech, association, assembly). Furthermore, such laws are deemed not to be outside legislative power. The Constitution is not supreme in relation to 'Special Powers' laws; Parliament is. While these laws are exceptional, the danger lies in the extremely broadly drafted grounds authorising their enactment.[246]

Minister Jayakumar's justifications for these amendments illuminate the (marginalised) role of law in security matters, exhorting trust in executive judgement. The 'subjective' test was restored since the court had been unduly influenced by foreign, interventionist cases.[247] Since the colonial era, executive responsibility for national security decisions had been the norm, since objective judicial evaluation of security issues was impossible.[248]

Rather than trusting judicial self-restraint, Parliament preferred the externally sanctioned restraint of ouster clauses. Certainly, the reasoning of foreign cases manifested a more protective pro-individual bias, considered unsuitable for Singapore, in preferring authoritarian and unaccountable executive control reminiscent of colonial laws.[249] Thus Singapore security matters should not 'be governed by cases decided abroad',[250] rejecting the more liberal, robust human rights approach of UK courts, influenced by the European Court of Human Rights. The minister's view was that Singapore was developing its own unique common law.

The unfamiliarity of UK judges with Singapore's peculiar socio-political and economic conditions was cited to justify abolishing Privy Council appeals over 'matters of public law, especially defence and security'[251] Thus, the minister considered that laws – that is, *public* laws (since Singapore commercial law is essentially based on the British model) – had to be interpreted contextually by judges acquainted with local conditions,[252] which translates into a local prioritisation of community concerns. The minister also argued that judicial review was a 'highly illusory'[253] check against broad ISA powers since 'a bad government could abuse *all* discretionary powers' and indeed 'pack the courts'. He identified the best safeguard as the election of an honest government.

The constitutionality of these amendments was challenged in *Teo Soh Lung v. Minister of Home Affairs*[254] for transgressing judicial and legislative power and violating the rule of law. Judge Chua, in affirming the subjective ISA test, anaemically and formalistically stated that rule of law is that rule which Parliament stipulates![255] This stance eroded the currency of rights while maximising government discretion to ensure stability.

207

Logically, anointing legislation as a Special Powers law relating to national security lifts all limits on legislative power to enact the most repressive laws, consistent with a 'thin' emaciated positivist conception of 'law' as handmaiden to an authoritarian elite.

The court has also rejected arguments that detention orders breaching GCHQ grounds of review or made *mala fides* were reviewable as 'purported' rather than 'real' decisions in *Teo* and *Vincent Cheng v. Minister for Home Affairs*.[256] This stands at odds with the robust principles of administrative review lately developed by Malaysian courts. In principle, they recognise that, unlike the supreme UK Parliament, the Malaysian Parliament cannot by express words preclude any person from going to court, as an aspect of the constitutional right to personal liberty.[257] This is because 'Malaysia has a written constitution' fashioned in language 'that upholds the Rule of Law', with the personal liberty and equality clause demonstrating a 'government of laws' and not man. This is instructive, as the Singapore Constitution traces its genesis to the Malaysian Constitution. Thus, while the Malaysian courts recognise that they *can* review national security cases, they affirm that they *will not*, except perhaps on procedural grounds, in national security cases. [258]

The Singapore courts consider that the 1989 amendments effectively preclude substantive review of ISA cases, juridically normalising the 'regime of exception', occluding the line between exceptional regimes and normal legal processes.[259] In defence, it is argued that other safeguards exist.[260] Aside from the Advisory Board, which conducts private proceedings, the EP may withhold concurrence to a detention order or renewal.[261] However, the EP is not an across-the-board independent check, as his veto only operates where the cabinet disagrees with the Advisory Board's recommendation of release.[262] This cannot replace judicial review; thus the real issue is not over competing conceptions of the rule of law, but whether institutions and processes in fact meaningfully restrain power. The weakness of the non-legal institutional checks sustains de facto executive supremacy consonant with an illiberal order.

Conclusion

In Singapore, the assiduous adherence to the letter of the law is evident; law is viewed as an instrument of social engineering, a servant to stability and enterprise. The rule of law is dictated by efficiency and stability imperatives rather than social justice concerns, which a 'thicker' liberal conception might encompass. Instead, the background political theory supports a competing 'thick' version fashioned after an illiberal model which prioritises statist goals like economic growth and social control by a relatively incorrupt government. This is fuelled by 'neo-Confucian'-styled cultural arguments justifying soft authoritarian control. While the government follows the law, it is also able to change it easily and expeditiously within Singapore's managed democracy, with an undeveloped rights culture.

Within the commercial law realm, the efficiency, certainty and procedural fairness provided by the judicial framework buttress aspirations towards being an international trade and financial centre. Where public law issues are concerned, the judicial 'communitarian' approach consolidates state stability and social order in utilitarian terms, with less attention given to civil liberties. Rather than a robust principle of civilised governance, the rule of law strengthens state institutions, marginalising rights protection.

Dialogue over the quality of Singapore's legal system is often at cross-purposes. In replying to criticisms articulated by a UN Special Rapporteur (extra-judicial, summary or arbitrary executions) concerning alleged human rights violations in Singapore involving 'insinuations' of possible judicial wrongdoing, the Singapore Permanent Representative cited the 2001 *World Competitiveness Yearbook*'s ranking of Singapore among the top 15 countries in terms of fair administration of justice.[263] This reply fails to address the expressed concern, as the *Yearbook*'s methodology focuses on how conducive national environments are to 'the domestic and global competitiveness of enterprises'. None of the principles relates directly to human rights issues.[264] Thus, a strong rights component is discounted within illiberal notions of the rule of law.

Cabinet members,[265] the attorney-general[266] and the chief justice[267] have rejected Western liberal values, affirming the primacy of the public interest, citing the Latin maxim *Salus Populi Suprema Lex* – the people's safety is the supreme law. However, this is insufficient if a just, humane order is sought. While the constitution and rights were marginalised in the drive for economic takeoff, in contemporary Singapore society, increasingly, demands for intangible goods like a limited government, greater consultation and better protection of a citizen's liberty and security are evident. With political maturation, a wider vocabulary of justice may be related to, and temper, prevailing neo-authoritarian ideas of the rule of law.

Notes

1   See Thio Li-ann, 'The Right to Political Participation in Singapore: Tailor-Making a Westminster-Modelled Constitution to Fit the Imperatives of "Asian" Democracy', *Singapore Journal of International & Comparative Law*, vol. 6, no. 1 (July 2002 p. 181-243).
2   *Shared Values White Paper* (Cmd.1 of 1991) (hereafter *SVWP*).
3   The PAP captured 82 of 84 parliamentary seats in the 2001 general elections.
4   The National Trade Unions Congress. See Lee Kuan Yew, *From Third World to First: The Singapore Story: 1965–2000* (Singapore: Times Editions, 2000), pp. 103–15.
5   Thio Li-ann, 'Law and the Administrative State', in Kevin Y. L. Tan, ed., *Singapore Legal System*, 2nd edn (Singapore University Press, 1998 p. 160-239).
6   See Chapter 1.

7 PM Lee Kuan Yew, Speech, Singapore Law Academy, 31 August 1990, *Singapore Academy of Law Journal*, vol. 2 (1990), p. 155, at p. 156.

8 PK Ho, 71 *Singapore Parliament Reports*, 24 November 1999, col. 592 (hereafter *SPR*).

9 The Decline of the Rule of Law in Malaysia and Singapore Part II – Singapore, A Report of the Committee on International Human Rights of the Association of the Bar of the City of New York, *Record*, vol. 46 (1991), p. 5, at p. 17. (hereafter Record).

10 J. B. Jeyaretnam, 71 *SPR*, 24 November 1999, cols 569ff, 573–634. See also 'The Rule of Law in Singapore', in *The Rule of Law and Human Rights in Malaysia and Singapore, Conference Report*, European Parliament, March 1989 (Malaysia: Kehmas-s, 1989), pp. 30–8.

11 Lee Kuan Yew, Millennium Law Conference, 11 April 2000. The local press regularly report these accolades: see, e.g., 'Singapore's Legal System Rated Best in the World', *Straits Times (Singapore)*, 26 September 1993, 3 (hereafter *Straits Times*).

12 *Record*, *supra*, note 9. The decline was precipitated by the unleashing of preventive detention powers against the 1987 'Marxist Conspiracy', curbing the press and free speech, and measures intimidating bar and bench.

13 Asia Watch Report, *Silencing All Critics: Human Rights Violations in Singapore* (New York, 1989), p. 1.

14 Christopher Lingle, 'The Smoke Over Parts of Asia Obscures Some Profound Concerns', *International Herald Tribune*, 7 October 1994. This sparked a contempt of court suit: *AG v. Lingle* 1 *Singapore Law Report*, 696–712 (High Court, 1995).

15 William Safire, 'The MisRule of Law: Singapore's Legal Racket', *New York Times*, 1 June 1997, p. 17.

16 Attributed to exiled opposition politician Tang Liang Hoong, in 'A Historic Legal Battle: The Times', *Straits Times*, 16 August 1997, p. 37.

17 Attributed to the former solicitor-general Francis Seow, at a 1995 Williams College meeting: 'Parliament to Debate Chee Soon Juan Issue', *Straits Times*, 30 October 1995, p. 1. Two PAP MPs moved a motion regretting Chee's agreement with Seow's comments: 65 *SPR Reports*, 2 November 1995, cols 223–44.

18 On the dichotomous approach towards law in commercial (harmonisation and espousing legal rationality) and non-commercial fields (particularism and the cultural conditioning of the law), see Eugene K. B. Tan, 'Law and Values in Governance: The Singapore Way', *Hong Kong Law Journal* 30 (2000), pp. 91–119.

19 See Andrew B. L. Phang, *The Development of Singapore Law: Historical and Socio-Legal Perspectives* (Singapore: Butterworths, 1990), p. 84; P. N. Pillai, 'The Process of Legal Importation', in *State Enterprise in Singapore: Legal Importation and Development* (Singapore University Press, 1986), pp. 23–52.

20 Michael Hor has criticised the 'stark utilitarian calculus' underlying Singapore's criminal legal system: 'Singapore's Innovations to Due Process', *Criminal Law Forum*, 12 (2001), pp. 25–40. See also A. G. Chan Sek Keong, 'Cultural Issues and Crime', *Singapore Academy of Law Journal*, vol. 12 (2000), p. 1; 'The Criminal Process – The Singapore Model', *Singapore Law Review* 17 (1996), pp. 433–503.

21 Tommy T. B. Koh, 'Revisiting the "Asian Values" Debate', in *The Quest for World Order: Perspectives of a Pragmatic Idealist* (Singapore: Institute of Policy Studies, 1998), p. 358.

22 Neo-Confucianism is particularly thought to appeal to the majority Chinese group, constituting 77 per cent of Singapore's multi-racial population. It has discomfited other communities, particularly Malays.

23 L. C. Green, 'Native Law and the Common Law: Conflict or Harmony', *Malaya Law Review*, vol. 12 (1970), p. 59.

24 See Thio Li-ann, 'An I for an I: Singapore's Communitarian Model of Constitutional Adjudication', *Hong Kong Law Journal*, vol. 27, no. 2 (1997), pp. 152–86.

25 Michael F. Rutter, 'The Future of the Common Law', in The Applicable Law in Singapore and Malaysia: A Guide to the Reception, Precedent and the Sources of Law in the Republic of Singapore and the Federation of Malaysia (Singapore/Malaysia: Malayan Law Journal, 1989), p. 575.

26 Interview, E. W. Barker; Kevin Tan, 'The Legalists: Kenny Byrne & Eddie Barker', in Lam Peng Er and Kevin Y. L. Tan, eds, *Lee's Lieutenants: Singapore's Old Guard* (Allen & Unwin, 1999), p. 70, at 90.

27 Reproduced in Appendix D, Kevin Y. L. Tan and Thio Li-ann, *Constitutional Law in Malaysia and Singapore*, 2nd edn (Singapore/Malaysia/Hong Kong: Butterworths Asia, 1997) (hereafter Wee Report).

28 The Constitution continued to authorise the enactment and application of extraordinary legislation under Part XII (Special Powers against Subversion and Emergency Powers), including the Internal Security Act. This reflects a high premium on security and order issues.

29 Land Acquisition Act (Cap 152).

30 Federation of Malaya Constitution, art. 3. The Singapore Constitution does not define ' Malay', unlike art. 160, Malaysian Constitution; it excised the Malaysian constitutional prohibition against propagating other faiths among Muslims. Para. 38, Wee Report, *supra*, note 27, affirmed Singapore was a 'democratic, secular state'.

31 *Ibid.*, para. 12.

32 Administration of Muslim Law Act (Cap 3).

33 See Thio Li-ann, 'The Impact of Internationalisation on Domestic Governance: Gender Egalitarianism & the Transformative Potential of CEDAW', *Singapore Journal of International & Comparative Law*, vol. 1, no. 1 (1997), pp. 299–305.

34 See Thio Li-ann, 'The Constitutional Framework of Powers'; Kevin Tan, 'Parliament and the Making of Law in Singapore', both in *Singapore Legal System, supra*, note 5 at 67-159.

35 See William Dale, 'The Making and Re-Making of Commonwealth Constitutions', *International & Comparative Law Quarterly*, vol. 42 (1993), pp. 67–83.

36 See *R v. Home Secretary ex p Khawaja* AC (Appeals Court), vol. 1, 74 (England Court of Appeal, 1984), at 105, followed in *Re Fong Thin Choo*, Singapore Law Report, vol. 1, 120 (High Court, 1992). This approach was evident in pre-Human Rights Act (2000) cases.

37 *Cheong Seok Leng v. PP, Malayan Law Journal*, vol. 2., p. 481, at 487f (High Court, 1988).

38 The constitutions of new, multi-racial states struck compromises, particularly in protecting minority concerns from majoritarian politics.

39 Singapore Constitution, Part VII.

40 Singapore Constitution, art. 68.

41 Thio Su Mien, 'The Presidential Council', *Singapore Law Review*, vol. 1 (1969), p. 2.

42 Singapore Constitution, art.46.

43 See, generally, Thio Li-ann, 'The Post-Colonial Evolution of the Singapore Legislature: A Case Study', *Singapore Journal of Legal Studies* (July 1993), p. 80, at 97–102; Thio Li-ann, 'Choosing Representatives: Singapore Does It Her Way', in Graham Hassall and Cheryl Saunders, eds, *The People's Representatives: Electoral Systems in the Asia–Pacific Region* (Allen & Unwin, 1997), p. 57.

44 See, generally, Kevin Y. L. Tan and Lam Peng Er, eds, *Managing Political Change in Singapore: The Elected Presidency* (London and New York: Routledge, 1997), chs 3–5.

45 Singapore Constitution, art. 98.

46 Judges Remuneration Act (Cap 147). On other judicial perks, see Ross Worthington, 'Between Hermes and Themis: An Empirical Study of the Contemporary Judiciary in Singapore', *Journal of Law and Society*, vol. 28 (2001), p. 490, at 512.

47 Section 18, Supreme Court of Judicature Act (Cap 322).

48 Jury trial, a colonial import, was abolished in Singapore by 1970: Andrew B. L. Phang, 'Jury Trial in Singapore and Malaysia: The Unmaking of a Legal Institution', *Malayan Law Review*, vol. 25 (1983), 50.

49 Primarily, it was thought that after 30 years of statehood the Singapore legal system had achieved sufficient investor confidence, no longer needing the Privy Council 'safety net'. The law minister stated that continued reliance would stultify local legal development: Jayakumar, 62 *SPR*, 23 February 1994, cols 388–9.

50 *Singapore Parliamentary Debates*, 15 March 1967, cols 1,294–5. The Court of Appeal became Singapore's highest appeal court.

51 Lord Diplock, 'Judicial Control of Government', *Malayan Law Journal*, vol. 2 (1979), cxl.

52 1803 (1 Cranch 137). Article 4 proclaims constitutional supremacy.

53 To my knowledge, the High Court has only voided as unconstitutional one legislative provision (Prevention of Corruption Act), though this was overturned on appeal: see Karthigesu J, in *Taw Cheng Kong v. PP, Singapore Law Report*, vol. 1, 493 (High Court, 1998); 2 *Singapore Law Report*, vol. 2, 410 (Court of Appeal, 1998).

54 Or whether the EP was bound by Westminster convention, embodied in article 21, to act in accordance with the cabinet's advice. See *In the Matter of Articles 5(2), 5(2A) and 22H(1) of the Constitution of the Republic of Singapore*, Constitutional Reference no. 1 of 1995, *Singapore Law Report*, vol. 2 (1995), 201.

55 'Constitutional Tribunal Plea Rejected', *Straits Times*, 30 January 1999, 54. Jeyaretnam argued, in relation to charging Chee Soon Juan for speaking in public without a licence at Raffles Place on 29 December 1998, that the Act violated article 14 (free speech) and was an 'eminently suitable question' for a constitutional reference. The president, on cabinet's advice, refused this request as improperly interfering with the on-going judicial process by a letter, made public.

56 This question turned on the wording of article 144(1), Constitution: 'Send US$5b Loan Case to Constitutional Court, Says Jeya', *Straits Times*, 24 November 1997, 28.

57 Para. 218, UN Doc. E/CN.4/1996/37.

58 *Goh Chok Tong v. Jeyaretnam Joshua Benjamin, Singapore Law Report*, vol. 1., p. 547, at 562H (High Court, 1998). Here, Judge Rajendran stated that Singapore had 'an open system of justice', there being 'no private directives to a judge from the executive or from anyone one else on how a case is to be conducted': paras 31–2.

59 'Judges: Enough Evidence for Case against Lingle, Four Others', *Straits Times*,10 January 1995, 2.

60 65 *SPR*, 2 November 1995, cols 223 ff.

61 S. M. Lee Kuan Yew, JFK School of Government (Harvard University), 17 October 2000, 'For Third World Leaders: Hope or Despair?' Available at http://www.gov.sg/sprinter/search.htm (accessed 27 May 2002).

62 Attorney-General Speech, Opening of Legal Year 2002, available at http://www.sal.org.sg/media—speeches—oly2002AG.htm (accessed 25 May 2002).

63 See 'Spore Courts Have World Class Stature', *Straits Times*, 11 April 1999, 1, with the chief justice pointing out that the World Bank has recommended the subordinate courts as a model.

64 P. K. Ho, Speech, Launch of Singapore Statutes Online, 15 November 2001.

65 *Chan Hiang Leng, Colin v. Minister for Information and the Arts*, Singapore Law *Report*, vol. 1, p. 609, at 614C–F (Court of Appeal, 1996).

66 'Appeal Limit Not Meant to Deny Access, Says CJ', *Straits Times*, 10 January 1999. An amendment to the Supreme Court of Judicature Act restricted the automatic right of appeal to the High Court for civil cases involving less than $50,000, and $250,000 for appeals: 'Has the Price of Justice Gone Up?', *Straits Times*, 27 November 1998, 52. See Francis T. Seow, 'The Judiciary: Courts for the Rich', in Michael Haas, ed., *The Singapore Puzzle* (Westport, Connecticut: Praeger Publishers, 1999), p. 106, at 119–20.

67 Karen Blochlinger, 'Primus Inter Pares: Is the Singapore Judiciary First Among Equals?', *Pacific Rim Law & Policy Journal*, vol. 9 (2000), pp. 591–618.

68 'CJ Yong appointed for 3 Years', *Straits Times*,16 March 2001, 1.

69 For example, G. P. Selvam left the bench at 65: 'Retired Judge Back to Practicing Law', *Straits Times*,13 July 2001, H7.

70 This is particularly the case since contract judges, whose contracts are renewable at the government's discretion, are paid their full salary rather than their pension, which gives them a financial incentive to toe the political line. *Record*, *supra*, note 9, at pp. 64–5.

71 Singapore Constitution, art. 94(5).

72 This relates to a close consultative relationship between the executive and judiciary: Kanishka Jayasuriya, 'Corporatism and Judicial Independence within Statist Legal Institutions in East Asia', in *Law, Capitalism and Power in Asia: The Rule of Law and Legal Institutions* (London and New York: Routledge, 1999).

73 Ross Worthington, *supra*, note 46, pp. 495–7.

74 Article 45(e) disqualifies a parliamentarian convicted and fined more than $2,000 for an offence, unless he receives a free pardon. For details surrounding Jeyaretnam's disqualification and his being struck off the rolls (and later reinstated), see *Record*, *supra* note 9, pp. 56–8, 65.

75 'The AG's Four Examples', *Straits Times*, 18 November 1995, 27.

76 'Law Society Failed to Defend Legal System: AG', *Straits Times*, 18 November 1995, 1. See also 'Law Society Explains Its Reasons for Silence', *Straits Times*, 27 November 1995, 3; 'Law Society Council to Discuss AG's Comments', *Straits Times*, 19 November 1995, 33.

77 The rule of law within the British context has developed a more substantive content: Jeffrey Jowell, 'The Rule of Law Today', in Jeffrey Jowell and Dawn Oliver, eds, *The Changing Constitution* (Oxford: Clarendon Press, 1994), p. 57.

78 Chandra Mohan asserted that two of the three aspects of the rule of law to Englishmen were constitutionally embodied: that law predominates over power; and equality under the general law. A *Straits Times* journalist speculated that this flowed from discomfiture with the AG's assertion that the rule of law as stipulated by Parliament would serve political expediency. Leslie Fong, 'Law Society

Chief Could Do Better than Talk in Riddles', *Straits Times*, 13 January 1996, 35; 'CJ "Mystified" by Law Society Chief's Response to AG's Criticism', *Straits Times*, 7 January 1996, 21.

79 See, generally, R. Sen and S. S. Pattanayak, 'The Challenges Before the Singapore Economy', *Fletcher Forum for World Affairs*, vol. 24 (2000), 15.

80 See the distinction between ordinary and management shares: sec. 9, Newspaper & Printing Press Act (Cap 206).

81 Kanishka Jayasuriya, 'Understanding "Asian Values" as a Form of Reactionary Modernisation', *Contemporary Politics*, vol. 4 (1998), 77–91.

82 The PAP prefers to enhance assets rather than redistribute wealth through subsidies. It sought to avoid welfare benefits-related dependency and 'to reinforce the Confucian tradition that a man is responsible for his family': Lee Kuan Yew, *supra*, note 4, p. 126.

83 The Housing and Development Board (HDB) was charged with building low-cost housing. Today, about 90 per cent of Singaporeans live in HDB apartments. See Kevin Tan, 'Economic Development, Legal Reform and Rights in Singapore and Taiwan', in Joanne R. Bauer and Daniel. A. Bell, eds, *The East Asian Challenge for Human Rights* (Cambridge: Cambridge University Press, 1999), p. 264, at 268–70.

84 Lee Kuan Yew, *supra*, note 4, pp. 126–8.

85 *Ibid.*, pp. 127–8.

86 'Confucian Values Helped S'pore Prosper: SM Lee', *Straits Times*, 6 November 1994, 1.

87 Foreign Minister K. S. Wong, *The Real World of Human Rights*, Vienna, 16 June 1993, *Singapore Journal of Legal Studies* (July 1993), 605–610 (lauding Singapore's superior standard of living).

88 Michael C. Davis writes of the trend towards the 'Singaporeanisation' of Hong Kong in these terms: 'Constitutionalism under Chinese Rule: Hong Kong after the Handover', *Denver Journal of International law & Policy*, vol. 27 (1999), p. 275, at 297.

89 See, generally, Kevin Y. L. Tan, 'Economic Development and Prospects for Constitutionalism', in Anthony Chin and Alfred Choi, eds, *Law, Social Sciences and Public Policy: Towards a Unified Framework* (Singapore University Press, 1998), pp. 186–206. See also Christopher Lingle, *Singapore's Authoritarian Capitalism: Asian Values, Free Market Illusions & Political Dependency* (Barcelona: Edicions Sirocco, 1996) (characterising the Singapore system as one of rule by and for rulers).

90 See Antony Langlois, *The Politics of Justice and Human Rights: Southeast Asia and Universalist Theory* (Cambridge University Press, 2001).

91 This view is opposed as being both empirically unsustainable and ethically untenable by Amartya Sen, who argues for a holistic vision of human welfare and that democracy is both instrumental in and constitutive of the development process: *Development as Freedom* (New York: Knopf, 1999).

92 Chief Justice, P. H. Yong, Speech. Legal Service Dinner, 6 April 2001 (available at the Singapore Supreme Court website: http://www.supcourt.gov.sg/speeches/speechesindex.htm).

93 'Confucian Values Helped S'pore Prosper: SM Lee', *Straits Times*, 6 October 1994, 1.

94 Numbering some 136 in 1954, the labour unions were reined in: Raj Vasil, *Governing Singapore* (Singapore: Mandarin, 1992), pp. 146–63. Elizabeth Surin, 'Government Influence on Labor Unions in a Newly Industrialized Economy: A Look at the Singapore Labor System', *Comparative Labor Law*, vol. 18 (1996), 102.

95 The Bloomberg financial news services published a web article alleging 'nepotism' in the appointment of Deputy Prime Minister Lee's wife, Ho Ching, to Temasek Holdings. It subsequently apologised for making false allegations, concluding a \$338,067 financial settlement with Singapore's PM and two other ministers: see William Safire, 'Bloomberg News Humbled', *New York Times*, Editorial/Op-Ed, 29 August 2002; 'Nepotism Not the Real Issue, It's Performance', *Straits Times*, 12 June 2002.

96 66 *SPR*, 21–22 May 1996, cols 184–240, 323–52, 257–323.

97 Subsequently, the PM issued new rules on purchasing properties by government leaders to safeguard government integrity. 'SM Lee Defends Clean Image of S'pore', *Straits Times*, 30 May 1996, 52; 'Debate Showed that No One Is Above the Law', *Straits Times*, 24 May 1996, 52.

98 Lee Kuan Yew, *supra*, note 4, 197–8.

99 P. K. Ho, 71 *SPR*, 24 November 1999, col. 592.

100 'Let the People Decide through a Referendum', *Straits Times*, 1 November 1994, 18; 'Referendum Used "Only by Weak Leaders" – SM Lee', *Straits Times*, 12 November 1994, 32; 62 *SPR*, 1 November 1994, cols 752–88.

101 'I Would Have Failed S'pore If...', *Straits Times*, 21 August 2000, 35.

102 The PAP monopolised Parliament between 1968 and 1980, until J. B. Jeyaretnam won the 1981 Anson by-elections. Since then, opposition politicians have only won between one and four parliamentary seats.

103 '75.3% – Resounding Win for PAP', *Straits Times*, 4 November 2001, 1. Voting percentages only relate to those voters living in contested electoral wards.

104 Only 29 of the 84 parliamentary seats were contested in 2001. On Singapore elections information, see http://www.ecitizen.gov.sg/.

105 Co-option is by way of entry into the PAP or the Nominated MP scheme, which composes critical but friendly opponents of the government: see 'After November 3, What Next for Singapore Politics?', *Straits Times*, 10 November 2001, H12–H13.

106 The 'responsible journalism' model exhorts against a media acting as watchdog. Statutory provisions to restrict foreign media circulation where domestic politics is deemed to have been interfered with keep the foreign press reined in: see Li-ann Thio, 'Human Rights and the Media in Singapore', in Robert Haas, ed., *Human Rights and the Media* (Malaysia, AIDCOM: 1996), 69, at 72–5; 'Be Fair, Be Truthful, Be Part of a Virtuous Cycle', Straits *Times*, 16 July 1995, Sunday Review 1, SR4.

107 Chan Heng Chee, *The Politics of One Party Dominance: PAP at Grassroots* (Singapore University Press, 1976).

108 PM Goh made this promise to Potong Pasir residents during the 2001 elections. 'SDA Distances Itself from Chee's Behaviour', *Straits Times*, 1 November 2001, H4. See James Chin, 'Anti-Christian Chinese Chauvinists and HDB Upgrades: The 1997 Singapore General Election', *South East Asia Research*, vol. 5, no. 3 (1997) 217–241.

109 Low Thia Khiang (Workers' Party), 71 *SPR*, 24 November 1999, col. 622; K. S. Wong's reply at col. 622.

110 *Record*, *supra*, note 9, at 27.

111 P. K. Ho, 71 *SPR*, 24 November 1999, at col. 592: He said NCMP Jeyaretnam was insulting Singaporeans 'by alleging that the Rule of Law does not prevail in Singapore because this Government which stands on the Rule of Law has been repeatedly re-elected in 10 general elections since 1959'. This is a *non sequitur*.

112 Para. 41, *SVWP*, *supra*, note 2.

113 '[I]f our integrity is attacked, we defend it', noted by PM Goh before the court when suing Jeyaretnam for libel: 'Many People Around the World "Embrace *Junzi* Principle"', *Straits Times*,22 August 1997, pp. 36–7.

114 PM Goh called Chee Soon Juan a 'cheat and a liar, a slippery character': 'Found: Team of Good People to Join Politics', *Straits Times*, 14 November 1995, 1. He stated that if Francis Seow was elected into Parliament 'other scallywags and charlatans [would] follow him', entailing a loss of 'moral respect' for the governors: 51 *SPR*,31 May 1998, col. 287. Lee labelled Tang Liang Hong an 'anti-English and anti-Christian' Chinese chauvinist at a December 1996 rally: see *Goh Chok Tong v. J. B. Jeyaretnam, Singapore Law Report*, vol. 1, p. 547, at 557, para. 7 (High Court, 1998). He dubbed Jeyaretnam a 'mangy dog' and 'political riff raff': *Singapore Parliamentary Debates*, 19 March 1986, cols 688–9, 720.

115 SM Lee has praised Low Thia Khiang as a 'good MP' who 'looks after his constituency': 'To Get a Good Government, You Need Good Men in Charge', *Straits Times*, 2 November 1994, 17.

116 *SVWP, supra*, note 2, p. 10.

117 President's Speech to Parliament, January 1989, quoted in *SVWP, supra*, note 2, p. 1. A 2001 study on national identity concluded that Singaporeans numbered among the most materialistic, money-obsessed people in the world: 'S'poreans First but Ethnic Ties Still Strong', *Straits Times*, 12 June 2002, H3. Arguably, industrialisation rather than human rights and democracy precipitated excessive individualism.

118 Art Lee, 'Singapore's Maintenance of Parents Act: A Lesson to be Learned from the United States', *Loyola Los Angeles International & Comparative Law Journal*, vol. 17 (1995), p. 671; 'Parent's Tribunal an Important but Sad Milestone', *Straits Times*, 30 May 1996, 54.

119 Eddie Kuo, 'Confucianism as Political Discourse in Singapore: The Case of an Incomplete Revitalization Movement',in Tu Wei-ming, ed., *Confucian Traditions in East Asian Modernity: Moral Education and Economic Culture in Japan and the Four Mini-Dragons* (Harvard University Press, 1996), pp. 294–319, at 304, 307.

120 For example, the gender inequality advocated by traditional Confucian family relationships was recognised as needing 'updating', *SVWP, supra*, note 2, paras 42, 44.

121 Stephanie Lawson, 'Confucius in Singapore: Culture, Politics and the PAP State', in Peter Dauvergne, ed., *Weak and Strong States in Asia–Pacific Societies* (Canberra, ACT: Allen & Unwin, 1998), p. 123.

122 J. B. Jeyaretnam, 'Human Rights in Singapore: The Social, Ideological and Judicial Mechanisms of Control', in *The Rule of Law and Human Rights in Malaysia and Singapore* (Malaysia: Kehma-s, 1989), 30, at 38.

123 *SVWP, supra*, note 2, para. 29.

124 Kenneth Christie and Denny Roy, *The Politics of Human Rights in East Asia* (London and Sterling, VA: Pluto Press, 2001), at 57.

125 Max Weber's influence is obvious in prescribing that a poor country adopt a narrow form of Protestantism, supportive of minimal spending and honest public administration, as an economic salve: Kwok Kian-Woon, 'The Social Architect: Goh Keng Swee', in *Lee's Lieutenants, supra*, note 26, p. 63.

126 'Spore "Strict, Not Authoritarian"', *Straits Times*, 9 October 1996, 32. Goh made his 'Big Brother' analogy in a *Le Mondev* interview: 'PM to Forge Europe–E. Asia Link Deeper Insight into What Makes Switzerland Tick', *Straits Times*, 20 October 1994, 1.

127 'Debate Yes, But Do Not Take on Those in Authority as "Equals"', *Straits Times*, 20 February 1995, 19.

128 'Govt to Open Up Political Space Gradually', *Straits Times*, 9 February 2002, 4.

129 The Law Society, under the presidency of the currently fugitive Francis Seow, had commented on proposed legislation (Newspaper and Printing Presses Bill) and was thereafter criticised as becoming politicised: Lee Kuan Yew, *supra*, note 4, p. 149.

130 ' "Join a Party" If You Want to Contribute', *Straits Times*, 9 September 1993, 33.

131 PM Goh Chok Tong, 'PAP Loss Would Be "Hard to Contemplate Given the Grave Consequences"', *Straits Times*, 10 December 1992, 22.

132 SM Lee has noted that 'We had open debates, it ended up in riots', 'No Single Asian Value System: SM', *Straits Times*, 8 September 1998, 2.

133 Lord Diplock, 'Judicial Control of Government', *Malayan Law Journal*, vol. 2 (1979), cxl. T. R. S. Allan noted that the rule of law as a juristic principle 'embodies the liberal and individualistic bias of the common law in favour of the citizen': 'Legislative Supremacy and the Rule of Law: Democracy and Constitutionalism', *Cambridge Law Journal*, vol. 44 (1985), pp. 111–43, at 119.

134 *Malayan Law Journal*, vol. 1, p. 64 (Privy Council, 1984).

135 *Ibid.*, 70C–E.

136 1994 Practice Statement (Judicial Precedent), *Singapore Law Report*, vol. 2 (1994), p. 689.

137 *Singapore Law Report*, vol. 3, p. 662, at 688E–G (High Court, 1994). For a critical analysis, see Thio Li-ann, 'The Secular Trumps the Sacred: Constitutional Issues Arising Out of Colin Chan v. PP', *Singapore Law Review*, vol. 16 (1995), pp. 26–103, reproduced in Garry Rodan, ed., *International Library of Social Change in Asia Pacific: Singapore* (Ashgate, 2001), p. 135.

138 *Singapore Law Report*, vol. 3, p. 682, at 683C–D (High Court, 1994).

139 *Ibid.*, p. 684F–G.

140 *Ibid.,*, p. 678B.

141 Chief Justice Yong noted a government official's argument that recognising JW beliefs meant that persons enjoying the benefits did not bear the responsibilities of Singapore citizenship, *ibid.*, p. 684I.

142 Singapore Constitution, art. 9: 'No one shall be deprived of life or liberty save accordance with the law'.

143 *Supra*, note 135, p. 71B–D. Whether these fundamental principles are substantive or procedural has been debated;see A. J. Harding, 'Natural Justice and the Constitution', and T. K. K. Iyer, 'Article 9(1) and "Fundamental Principles of Natural Justice" in the Constitution of Singapore', *Malaya Law Review*, vol. 23 (1981), pp. 266 and 213, respectively.

144 *Singapore Law Report*, vol. 1, p. 617 (High Court, 1995).

145 *Ibid.*, p. 631B.

146 *Singapore Law Report*, vol. 1, p. 943 (High Court, 1998); subsequently overturned by the Court of Appeal: *Singapore Law Report*, vol. 2, p. 410.

147 *Singapore Law Report*, vol. 1, p. 943, at 955, para. 24H–I (High Court, 1998).

148 *Ibid.*, p. 965G–H.

149 *Ibid.*, pp. 964D–I to 965 A–I.

150 *Ibid.*, p. 965D–E.

151 CJ Yong, approving Government of the *State of Kelantan v. Government of the Federation of Malaya, Malayan Law Journal*, 355 (1963), in *Colin Chan v. PP, Singapore Law Report*, vol. 3, 662, at 681D (High Court, 1994). This disregards

the guidelines in Haw Tua Taw v. PP, Malayan Law Journal, vol. 1, p. 49 (Privy Council, 1981).

152 'I think the issues here are best resolved by a consideration of the provisions of the Constitution, the Societies Act and the UPA alone'. Yong CJ, *Colin Chan v. PP*, *Singapore Law Report*, vol. 3., 662, at 682A (High Court, 1994).

153 *Ibid.*, p. 681E-H. This cursory invocation of local conditions was also apparent in the contempt of court case of *AG v. Wain*, *Malayan Law Journal*, vol. 2., p. 525, at 531H (High Court, 1991).

154 For example, the Court of Appeal in *J. B. Jeyaretnam v. Lee Kuan Yew Yew* cited two Canadian cases that stressed the importance of the public character of institutions: *Campbell v. Spottiswoode, Queen's Bench (Law Reports)* 185 (1863) and *Tucker v. Douglas, Dominion Law Report*, vol. 2 (1950), 827.

155 In *Colin Chan v. PP*, Yong CJ approvingly cited the Australian case of *Adelaide Company of Jehovah's Witnesses Inc. v. Commonwealth, Commonwealth Law Reports*, vol. 67 (1943), 116, where the Governor under emergency wartime regulations had seized the premises of a JW group, declaring their pacifism prejudicial to the defence of the Commonwealth. *Singapore Law Report*, vol. 3, 662, at 683E–I (High Court, 1994).

156 Contempt of court and defamation are two express limits to the article 14 free speech guarantee.

157 PM Goh Chok Tong was awarded $700,000 for libel in *Tang Liang Hong Lee Kuan Yew*, *Singapore Law Report*, vol. 1, p. 97 (High Court, 1998). Opposition politicians have sued each other and compensatory damages of $120,000 have been awarded; see *Chiam*. See *Tong v. Ling How Doong*, *Singapore Law Report*, vol. 1, p. 97 (High Court, 1997).

158 *New York Times v. Sullivan*, 376 U.S. 254 (1964). The Court of Appeal rejected the 'actual malice' test.

159 *Lingens v. Austria*, 8 EHRR (1986) 407. The Court of Appeal rejected the idea that the acceptable limits of criticism were wider for politicians than for private citizens.

160 *Singapore Law Report*, vol. 2, p. 310 (Court of Appeal, 1992).

161 Approvingly quoting *Gatley on Libel and Slander, Singapore Law Report*, vol. 2, p. 310, at 333H–I (Court of Appeal, 1992).

162 *Singapore Law Report*, vol. 1, p. 547, at 561F–H (High Court, 1998).

163 *Ibid.*, p. 561G–H.

164 *Ibid.*, p. 592D–H.

165 See *AG v. Wain*, *Malayan Law Journal*, vol. 2, p. 525 (High Court, 1991).

166 *Ibid.*, p. 533I.

167 39 CCC (3d) 2 (1987).

168 R. H. Hickling, The Influence of the Chinese upon Legislative History in Malaysia and Singapore, Malaya Law Review, vol. 20 (1978), 265.

169 Joel T. B. Lee, 'The ADR Movement in Singapore',in *Singapore Legal System*, *supra*, note 5.

170 71 *SPR*,24 November 1999, cols 611 and 618. See article 93(A), Singapore Constitution and Part IV (Elections Petitions), Parliamentary Elections Act (Cap 218).

171 Singapore Constitution, art. 4.

172 Singapore Constitution, art. 5(2).

173 Calls for a referendum on the proposed EP scheme were ignored; the PAP located in their 61 per cent electoral win a mandate to introduce the EP: See Kevin Y. L. Tan, 'The Elected Presidency in Singapore: Legislation Comment and List', *Singapore Journal of Legal Studies* (1991), p. 179, at 191–3. Though no referendum was called prior to this scheme's introduction, a two-thirds vote

at a national referendum is needed to amend or abrogate it: see article 5(2A), which is still not in force a decade after its introduction. The government still wishes to further fine-tune an institution which it claims was 'carefully drafted' and debated before its introduction in 1991: 'SM Lee: Elected President Not the Second Centre of Power', *Straits Times*,12 August 1999, 32–3.

174 Goh Chok Tong, 70 *SPR*,17 August 1999, col. 2,034.
175 *Malayan Law Journal*, vol. 1, p. 418. (High Court, 1985).
176 Singapore Constitution, art. 12(1): 'All persons are equal before the law and entitled to the equal protection of the law'.
177 Convention for the Elimination of All Forms of Discrimination against Women: G.A. Res. 34/180, UN Doc A/34/46 (1981). See, generally, Thio Li-ann, 'Recent Constitutional Developments: Of Shadow and Whips, Race, Rifts and Rights, Terror and Tudungs, Women and Wrongs', *Singapore Journal of Legal Studies* (July 2002), p. 328, at 348–52.
178 See also the failure by the Manpower Ministry to treat discriminatory complaints as rights violations, preferring the road of educating employers: 'Education Can Curb biases', *Straits Times*, 28 January 1999, 40.
179 'Malay Rights Group "Could Damage Racial Harmony"', *Straits Times*, 27 June 1997, 50.
180 'Third Tudung Girl Suspended', *Straits Times* 12 February 2002, H3. A Malaysian lawyer offered his services gratis to the parents of the suspended girls: 'Karpal to File Papers for S'pore Tudung Case', *Straits Times*, 20 April 2002, H4.
181 It remains unclear whether litigation will proceed: 'Tudung Girl's School Return Welcome', *Straits Times*, 16 June 2002, 23; 'Muslims Urged to Discuss Tudung Issue: Legal Action Is Not the Way to Resolve Matters', *Straits Times*, 28 January 2002.
182 *Bridges Christopher v. PP*, *Singapore Law Report*, vol. 1, 406 (High Court, 1997).
183 *Stansfield Business International Pte Ltd v. Minister for Manpower, Singapore Law Report,* vol. 3, 742 (High Court, 1999).
184 See C. M. Chinkin, 'Abuse of Discretion in Malaysia and Singapore', in Andrew Harding, ed., The Common Law in Singapore and Malaysia: A Volume of Essays Marking the 25th Anniversary of the Malaya Law Review 1959–1984 (1985), 261. Contrast this with more vigorous Malaysian law developments: S. Pillay, 'The Emerging Doctrine of Substantive Fairness – A Permissible Challenge to the Exercise of Administrative Discretion?', *Malayan Law Journal,* vol. 3 (2001), p. 1.
185 *Singapore Law Report*, vol. 3, 662 (High Court, 1994).
186 See Kevin Tan, *The Legalists: Kenny Byrne & Eddie Barker*, *supra*, note 27, p. 89.On how constitutions should be tailored to fit the wearer, see Lee Kuan Yew, *Singapore Parliamentary Debates*, 24 July 1984, col. 1735.
187 Singapore Constitution, art. 39(b), provides for a maximum of six NCMP seats while §52 of the Parliamentary Elections Act (Cap 218) currently allows for three seats.
188 Singapore Constitution, art. 39(1)(c). The Fourth Schedule stipulates that NMPs be chosen from 'as wide a range of independent and non-partisan views as possible'.
189 'Join a Party, If You Want to Contribute', *Straits Times*, 9 September 1993, 33; 'Only Those Elected Can Set OB Markers', *Straits Times*, 3 February 1995, 22. Lately, registered civil society groups like the Roundtable and Think Centre have been allowed some space to comment on public policy.

190 Singapore Constitution, art. 39(2), provides that NCMPs (and NMPs) cannot vote on constitution amendment bills, supply and money bills, and 'no-confidence' votes.

191 Steve Chia, who polled 34.7 per cent of his ward's votes, accepted an NCMP seat in the Tenth Parliament: 'Chia's Call – BG [Brigadier-General] Lee Hopes He'll Accept NCMP Seat', *Straits Times*, 3 November 2001, 3.

192 Section 8A of the Parliamentary Elections Act (Cap 218) provides for a minimum of eight SMCs. In 1988, when the scheme was introduced, there were 13 three-member GRC teams (yielding 39 MPs), with the rest of the wards remaining SMCs under the simple plurality system. By 2001, there were only nine SMCs (all contested); of the 14 GRCs, only four were contested (20 seats), with the PAP enjoying walkovers in 10 GRCs (yielding 55 seats).

193 Singapore Constitution, art. 39A (Malay, Indian or 'Other').

194 A voter in a GRC ward casts one vote that will take four to six candidates into Parliament, while a voter in an SMC casts his one vote for one candidate – votes thus differ in terms of power, a potential breach of article 12 'cured' only by a 'notwithstanding' clause in article 39(A)(3).

195 This has allowed the government to be returned to power on Nomination Day. For example, in the 2001 general elections, 55 of the 75 GRC seats went uncontested. Singapore elections history information is available at http://www.ecitizens.gov.sg.

196 Section 8(1A), Parliamentary Elections Act (Cap 218) provides for at least eight non-GRC electoral divisions. §8(2) provides that a floor of at least 25 per cent of the total MP numbers shall be returned by GRCs. In 1988, 50 per cent of elected MPs were to come from GRC wards (13 three-member teams), to ensure that opposition parties unable to contest GRCs would not be precluded from electoral contest since they could stand in the 40 SMC wards. With the increase in size of GRC teams, SMC wards number only nine today.

197 See Kevin Y. L. Tan, 'Constitutional Implications of the 1991 General Elections', 26 *Singapore Law Review*, vol. 23 (1992), p. 46, on how the GRC affects election strategies and operates in practice.

198 The GRC scheme has been buttressed through its association with other programmes like Town Council management and Community Development Councils, which serve residents' welfare through disbursing government funds like educational subsidies, not all of which are naturally aligned.

199 '"Why No By-Election? PM Must Explain", Says WP Chief', *Straits Times*, 19 June 1999, 48; 'By-Election Secondary to Crisis Recovery', *Straits Times*, 5 June 1999, 2.

200 For example, Christopher Neo (of the Singapore Democratic Alliance [SDA]) found that Bukit Gombak ward was merged into a GRC two weeks before polling day: 'More Level Playing Field Needed, to Be Fair', *Straits Times*, 11 November 2001, 42.

201 'Should S'pore Have an Independent Elections Agency', *Straits Times*, 22 December 2001, H10–11.

202 This misappropriates the nomenclature, as the 'shadow cabinet' in a Westminster system is understood as the leading parliamentary opposition group, whose leaders have shadow portfolios, in preparing for future government roles.

203 Other self-regulatory restraints being the NMP scheme, the Government Parliamentary Committee scheme, or the past function of PAP backbenchers as internal critics. See Kevin Tan, 'Parliament and the Making of Law in Singapore', in *Singapore Legal System, supra*, note 5, pp. 123–59.

204 'Can a Shadow Play Have Real Impact', *Straits Times*, 15 December 2001, H16–17.

205 SM Lee, 'Elected President Not the Second Centre of Power', *Straits Times*, 12 August 1999, 32–3.

206 PM Goh Chok Tong, *Singapore Parliamentary Debates*, 4 October 1990, cols 462–3 and 469.

207 Section 8A, Presidential Elections Act (Cap 240A). In 1999, of three candidates, the PEC granted only S. R. Nathan an eligibility certificate. The PEC is not obliged to give reasons in its decisions: 'Only Nathan Gets Eligibility Cert', *Straits Times*, 18 August 1999, 2.

208 Singapore Constitution, art. 19(2)(g).

209 It was only after judicial review had been ousted under these Acts that discussions for a substitute check were entertained: Jayakumar, 56 *SPR*, 9 November 1990, cols 596–7. Financial but not human rights expertise is required for the office.

210 Singapore Constitution, art. 22G.

211 See Thio Li-ann, 'Working Out the Presidency: The Rites of Passage', *Singapore Journal of Legal Studies* (1995), p. 509–57; for a reply, see AG Chan Sek Keong, 'Working Out the Presidency: No Passage of Rights', *Singapore Journal of Legal Studies* (1996), pp. 1–39.

212 E.g., art. 151A, amended in 1994, removed presidential review over 'defence and spending' measures.

213 Low Thia Khiang, quoted in 'Govt Not Sincere, Says Opposition', *Straits Times*, 19 August 1999, 29.

214 Interview with Lee Kuan Yew, agreeing with the *Straits Times* assessment: 'Knowing President's Limits', *Straits Times*, 12 August 1999, p. 32.

215 EP Ong Teng Cheong, a former cabinet minister, demonstrated that his office could be independent, albeit weak. At a press interview, he detailed the difficulties faced in getting government cooperation in discharging his office. For example, the accountant-general evidenced reluctance towards his request for a statement of all government assets he was elected to protect. The PM felt compelled to address the EP's criticisms before Parliament and consequently a binding *White Paper on Safeguarding Accumulated Reserves* was adopted: 70 *SPR*, 18 August 1999, cols 2207ff.

216 *Singapore Law Report*, p. 132, at 156B–C (Court of Appeal, 1989). This decision was legislatively overruled a few weeks later by amending the ISA (Cap. 143) in January 1989, reinstating the 'subjective' test of review with respect to ISA decisions applied in *Lee Mau Seng v. Minister of Home Affairs*, *Singapore Law Report*, 508–26 (High Court, 1969–71). On these developments, see Thio Li-ann, 'Trends in Constitutional Interpretation: Oppugning Ong, Awakening Arumugam', *Singapore Journal of Legal Studies* (1997), p. 240, at 241–6.

217 Prof. Jayakumar, 56 *SPR*, 9 November 1990, col. 599.

218 Dr John Chen, 54 *SPR*, 22 February 1990, col. 1,128.

219 Dr Aline Wong, 54 *SPR*, 22 February 1990, cols 1,075–76.

220 Prof. Jayakumar, 54 *SPR*, 22 February 1990, col. 1,205.

221 For example, the Internal Security Act (Cap 143), Criminal Law Temporary Provisions Act (Cap 67) and Misuse of Drugs Act (Cap 185). Part XII, Singapore Constitution.

222 J. B. Jeyaretnam, 71 *SPR*, 24 November 1999, col. 576, stating that the ISA shows that 'even an Act of Parliament can violate the Rule of Law'.

223 Chia, a former Barisian Socialis MP, was detained in October 1966 at a demonstration protesting US involvement in Vietnam. He never admitted to being a

member of a communist party: 'Letters: Bogus Reasons for 22 Year Detention', *Far Eastern Economic Review*, 16 November 1989.

224 See Francis.T. Seow, *To Catch a Tartar: A Dissident in Lee Kuan Yew's Prison* (New Haven, Connecticut: Yale University Southeast Asia Studies, 1994).

225 'Pentagon "Pleased" with S'pore's Response', *Straits Times* 13 January 2002, 6. A further 21 Singaporeans were later detained for terrorist-related activities in September 2002: 'Don't Put Us on the Defensive Again: Muslims', *Straits Times*, 19 September 2002, H4.

226 See Thio Li-ann, 'Recent Constitutional Developments', *supra*, note 177, pp. 352–5.

227 Singapore Constitution, art. 151(3), allows authorities not to disclose facts contrary to the national interest.

228 'Ministers Hold Sessions on ISA Arrests', *Straits Times*, 25 January 2002, H5.This contrasts with not holding public meetings over the 1987 detentions since the detainees, in issuing press releases about coerced confessions, had engaged in political propaganda.

229 'ISA Detainees Co-operative, Coping Well', *Straits Times*, 24 January 2002, H4: The newspapers reported that detainees were allowed weekly familial visits and could perform religious obligations. Minister K. S. Wong spoke of Internal Security Department officers forming family support groups to get in touch with the families/wives of detainees and allay fears of government persecution: 'Don't View Muslims with Suspicion...Carry on Life as Before', *Straits Times*, 1 February 2002, H10–11.

230 'More Videotape Evidence of Terror Plot Here', *Straits Times*, 2 March 2002, 3.

231 'Schools Get Guide to ISD Arrests', *Straits Times*, 13 January 2002, H1.

232 'The Case Against the Jemaah Islamiah', *Straits Times*, 31 May 2002, H2.

233 Minister K. S. Wong said that information about the arrests was made public to 'ensure that both Muslims and non-Muslims did not react in emotional and distorted ways which could undermine ethnic trust and social peace'. 'Museum to Give a Glimpse of ISD Work; It's not open to the public, but select groups will be allowed to view political banners, bombs and classified exhibits', *Straits Times*, 21 March 2001.

234 Only Opposition MP Chiam See Tong questioned the 1987 detentions before Parliament, with all PAP MPs toeing the party line. 51 *SPR*, 31 May 1988, cols 238–9. Chiam asked officials to meet with the detainees' families to answer their queries and called for a public inquiry, which was dismissed as the detentions were apparently mandated by the PAP's 1988 electoral success, it having campaigned on retaining the ISA: Y. Yusof, col. 249.

235 Article 151(1) and (2). Under the 1955 Preservation of Public Security Ordinance, detention orders had to be renewed every three years. There was an Appeal Tribunal, which is more powerful than the current Advisory Board, composed of two High Court judges and one district judge, which could order release. The PAP in 1959 changed the Tribunal to the Advisory Committee, with recommendatory powers only.

236 In 1989 Lee Kuan Yew stated that the ISA serves Singapore's political stability and that subversives could not be allowed to escape simply because the government could not prove a case in accordance with 'strict rules of evidence in a court of law' against them. *Straits Times*, 5 June 1987.

237 'Review Board Upholds ISA Detentions', *Straits Times*, 31 May 2002, 6. It was reported that the president received a 90-page report containing information about the detainees' admission of involvement in terrorist activities, their

perception that America and Israel and their allies were 'enemies of Islam', and four witness testimonies.

238 See para. 10, President's Opening Address to Tenth Parliament, warning of spreading narrow, radical interpretations of Islam in South East Asian countries: http://www.gov.sg/istana/sp-020325.html.

239 See 69 *SPR*, 31 July 1998, cols 675–84; Asia Watch Report, *supra*, note 13, pp. 1–32.

240 'Museum to Give a Glimpse of ISD Work', *Straits Times*, 21 March 2001; 'Book on ISA to Be Released Later This Year', *Straits Times*, 14 April 2002.

241 *Singapore Law Report*, 132 (1988); 1 *Malayan Law Journal*, 69 (1989).

242 Review is available on the basis of precedent fact review and the *GCHQ* (UK Government Communications Headquarters) grounds, AC 374 (English Court of Appeal, 1985), of illegality, irrationality and procedural impropriety.

243 *Malayan Law Journal*, vol. 2, p. 137 (1971).

244 Where national security issues were concerned, the court, while not evaluating the evidence, would ensure the relevant decision was in fact based on national security considerations, not bad faith or caprice: *Malayan Law Journal*, vol. 1, p. 69, at 83F–H (High Court, 1989).

245 AC 206 (English Court of Appeal 1941).

246 Singapore Constitution, art. 149(1)(a)–(e). Notably, the court has since favoured an open-ended approach, maximising executive discretion in this regard in determining whether an activity prejudices national security: Judge Chua, *Teo Soh Lung v. Minister for Home Affairs*, *Singapore Law Report*, p. 499, at 508B (High Court, 1989).

247 S. Jayakumar, *Singapore Parliamentary Debates*,25 January 1989, cols 532, 467.

248 *Ibid.*, 527.

249 Jayakumar affirmed that the government's position on the limited judicial role in security matters was consistent that extant in October 1959, when Singapore was still a self-governing colony: *ibid.*, col. 470.

250 *Ibid.*, at col. 468.

251 *Ibid.*, at cols 471–3.

252 *Ibid.*, at col 526.

253 *Ibid.*, at col. 524.

254 *Supra*, note 247.

255 'It is erroneous to contend that the Rule of Law has been abolished by legislation and that Parliament has stated its absolute and conclusive judgement in applications for judicial review.... Parliament has done no more than *to enact the Rule of Law relating to the law applicable to judicial review* [emphasis mine].' *Supra*, note 247, pp. 15A–C.

256 *Malayan Law Journal*, vol. 1, 449 (High Court, 1990).

257 Malaysian Constitution, art. 5(1), upon which art. 9(1) of the Singapore Constitution is modelled.

258 Gopal Sri Ram JCA (judge of the Court of Appeal), *Sugumar Balakrishnan v. Pengarah Imigresen Negeri Saah*, *Malayan Law Journal*, vol. 3, p. 289, at 305A–D, 309B–D (Kuala Lumpur Court of Appeal, 1998).

259 Kanishka Jayasuriya, 'The Exception becomes the Norm: Law and Regimes of Exception in East Asia', *Asia–Pacific Law & Policy Journal*, vol. 1, p. 108, at 110, 114 (2001).

260 P. K. Ho, 71 *SPR*, 24 November 1999, col. 594.

261 Singapore Constitution, art. 21(2)(g).

262 Singapore Constitution, art. 151(4).

263 E/CN.4/2002/74; Singapore Permanent Representative Letter to UN Commission on Human Rights Chairperson, UN Doc E/CN.4/2002/170 (3 April 2002): see para. c.
264 *World Competitiveness Report* (1993), at 30–1.Principles include whether trade is internationalised, the degree of state intervention in business, labour-force skills and infrastructure quality.
265 Lee Kuan Yew claimed that Singapore 'shook ourselves free' from discordant English values where individual rights enjoyed 'paramount consideration' as 'our traditional Asian value system' prioritised community interests. *Supra*, note 7, at 156.
266 The AG castigated the Law Society for not rebutting foreign media allegations that harsh Singapore criminal law precluded fair trials, reinforcing 'the absurd thinking of libertarian academics and the Western liberal press': 'Law Society Failed to Defend Legal System: AG', *Straits Times*,18 November 1995, 1.
267 The chief justice stated that 'our heritage' emphasised individual duty and the primacy of community interests, while, conversely, 'less conservative beliefs have promoted the rights of individuals as being of greater importance'. 'CJ Defends Tough Laws, Punishment in Legal System', *Straits Times*, 5 November 1995, 1.

7

COMPETING CONCEPTIONS OF RULE OF LAW IN MALAYSIA

H. P. Lee

Introduction

In Malaysia, the idea of the 'rule of law' has never been subjected to extensive public debates or rigorous analysis. Yet it is an idea which does occupy a place in the Malaysian legal and political system. The adoption of a 'Westminster' form of government and the legacy of British colonial rule have fostered this idea.[1]

The idea of the rule of law permeates the constitutional framework which provided the foundations of the new Federation, first of Malaya, then of Malaysia. This idea, for instance, is manifested in the form of Article 4(1), which provides for the supremacy of the Constitution. However, the phrase 'rule of law' was stamped onto the public consciousness when it was embodied as one of five key principles constituting the *Rukunegara*, or the pillars of the nation. Following the racial disturbances of 13 May 1969, the government enumerated the *Rukunegara* as 'a five point national philosophy' to promote national unity.[2] These principles comprised the following:

* belief in God
* loyalty to king and country
* upholding the Constitution
* rule of law
* good behaviour and morality

One conception of the rule of law was explained by Dr Rais Yatim:

> The *Rule of Law* in the *Rukunegara* did not necessarily mean the same as the rule of law conceived by Dicey or the various ICJ [International Commission of Jurists] congresses. It was not particularly concerned with the checks and balances necessary in the popular notion under a modern democratic system. It was proclaimed to mean no more than that the rules and regulations made by the government must be followed.[3]

The explanation provided by Dr Rais Yatim reflects, to a large extent, the view of the rule of law from the standpoint of the government. The *Rukunegara* was formulated in the wake of a communal crisis which threatened national security. The overriding emphasis given to the promotion of national unity was regarded by the government as justification for invoking repressive laws to curb the inflammation of racial hatred and bigotry. However, opposition parties and dissidents saw the resort to such laws as an excuse to restrict the activities of critics of the government. Before embarking on an analysis of these competing conceptions in Malaysia, a conspectus of constitutional developments and the key institutions of government is set out. This is followed by a reference to some areas which illustrate the tensions in viewpoints about the rule of law.

From Malaya to Malaysia

Before the Second World War, the political structure which had existed in peninsular Malaya comprised a varied grouping of states: the 'Federated Malaya States' of Perak, Selangor, Negri Sembilan and Pahang; the 'Unfederated Malay States' of Johor, Kedah, Kelantan, Perlis and Tyrengganu; the 'Straits Settlements' of Penang, Malacca and Singapore. In Borneo, North Borneo (now 'Sabah') and Sarawak existed as protected states, whilst Brunei remained a sultanate receiving British protection.

After the Second World War, the nine Malay states and Penang and Malacca were grouped together in 1946 to constitute the new controversial Malayan Union. Concerns over the position of the Malay rulers and liberal notions of a proposed common citizenship led to the demise of the Malayan Union before 'the ink of the signatures [of the Malay rulers] endorsing the MacMichael Treaties was hardly dry'.[4] The Malayan Union was replaced by the Federation of Malaya, with a Federal Government being set up in Kuala Lumpur under a British high commissioner. The Federation of Malaya Agreement of 1948, which created the new Federation, also established a Federal Legislative Council in which the Malays were to be strongly represented. The Council also included representatives from other races.

In July 1955 the first federal elections were held for seats on the new Federal Legislative Council; 51 of the 52 unofficial seats were captured by the Alliance, which consisted of UMNO (United Malays National Organisation), the MCA (Malayan, later Malaysian, Chinese Association) and the MIC (Malayan, later Malaysian, Indian Congress). Tunku Abdul Rahman as president of UMNO and head of the Alliance, became chief minister.

A mission was led by Tunku Abdul Rahman to London to negotiate for independence. The talks from 18 January to 6 February 1956 culminated in the appointment of an Independent Constitutional Commission, which was entrusted with the task of drawing up a Constitution to provide for full self-government and independence for the Federation of Malaya.

The Independent Constitutional Commission, chaired by Lord Reid (United Kingdom) and also comprising Sir Ivor Jennings (United

Kingdom), Sir William McKell (Australia), B. Malik (India) and Justice Abdul Hamid (Pakistan), was instructed to examine the existing constitutional arrangements throughout the Federation of Malaya, and 'to make recommendations for a federal form of constitution for the whole country as a single self-governing unit within the Commonwealth based on Parliamentary democracy with a bicameral legislature'. The new constitution was to include provisions for the following:

*   the establishment of a new strong central government with the states and the settlements enjoying a measure of autonomy;
*   the safeguarding of the position and prestige of the Malay rulers;
*   a constitutional head of state for the Federation to be chosen from among the Malay rulers;
*   a common nationality for the whole of the Federation;
*   the safeguarding of the special position of the Malays and the legitimate interest of other communities.

In drawing up the constitutional framework the Independent Constitutional Commission (hereinafter referred to as the 'Reid Commission') had two broad objectives in mind:

1   There must be 'the fullest opportunity for the growth of a united, free and democratic, nation'.
2   There must be 'every facility for the development of the resources of the country and the maintenance and improvement of the standards of living of the people'.

The Commission also acknowledged that its recommendations had to be both 'practical in existing circumstances' and 'fair to all sections of the community'. The Federation of Malaya was enlarged into the Federation of Malaysia in 1963. The Malaysia Act (Act no. 26 of 1963) passed by the Malayan Parliament effected extensive changes to the Malayan Constitution to accommodate Singapore, Sabah and Sarawak within the restructured constitutional framework. Singapore was ejected from the Federation on 9 August 1965. This event was the culmination of escalating tensions between the Federal Government and the State Government of Singapore.

Key features of the political and legal system

The Federal Parliament

The 'legislative authority of the Federation' is vested in a bicameral Parliament consisting of the *Yang di-Pertuan Agong* (the king), the *Dewan Negara* (the Senate) and the *Dewan Rakyat* (the House of Representatives).[5]

Money bills can only originate in the *Dewan Rakyat* and the Senate has only delaying power of one month.[6] In the case of a Bill which seeks to amend the Constitution, such a Bill must obtain the approval of a two-thirds vote in the *Dewan Negara*, in addition to a two-thirds vote in the *Dewan Rakyat*.[7] The Reid Commission explained:

> Amendments should be made by Act of Parliament provided that an Act to amend the Constitution must be passed in each House by a majority of at least two-thirds of the members voting. In this matter the House of Representatives should not have power to over-rule the Senate. We think that this is a sufficient safeguard for the States because the majority of members of the Senate will represent the States.[8]

The intended role of the Senate to act as a protector of state interests is no longer an effective one, as a result of a number of changes. Under the 1957 Constitution, each state was to elect two senators, whilst the *Yang di-Pertuan Agong* was empowered to appoint 16 other senators. This meant that there were then 22 state-elected senators to 16 appointed senators. In 1963, the number of appointed senators was increased to 22. With the formation of Malaysia, the proportion of state-elected senators to appointed senators stood at 28 to 22. In 1964, the number of appointed senators was further increased to 32. With the separation of Singapore from the federation in 1965, the number of state-elected senators was reduced to 26. 'In these circumstances, it is extremely difficult for the State Senators to "block" any amendment.'[9]

Prime Minister and Cabinet

The 'executive authority of the Federation' is vested in the *Yang di-Pertuan Agong* and is exercisable, subject to the provisions of any federal law and of the Second Schedule of the Constitution, by him or by the Cabinet, or any minister authorised by the Cabinet.[10] The Constitution provides for the appointment from among the members of the *Dewan Rakyat*, by the *Yang di-Pertuan Agong*, of a prime minister. The *Yang di-Pertuan Agong*, on the advice of the prime minister, appoints other ministers from among the members of either House. In accordance with the 'Westminster' model, if the prime minister ceases to command the confidence of a majority of members of the *Dewan Rakyat*, then, unless at his request the *Yang di-Pertuan Agong* dissolves Parliament, the prime minister shall tender the resignation of the Cabinet.[11] It has been observed that in Malaysia, as in a parliamentary democracy, 'there is no real separation of powers between the legislature and the executive, as there is between these two branches on the one hand, and the judiciary on the other'.[12]

The Yang di-Pertuan Agong *and the rulers*

The Constitution provides for a constitutional monarchy. The king of the Federation, entitled the '*Yang di-Pertuan Agong*', was first created under the 1957 Constitution. It is an office which is 'both hereditary and elective'.[13] The king is elected by the Conference of Rulers, which, for this specific purpose, comprises only the nine hereditary rulers. In exercising the function of electing the king, the Conference of Rulers relies on an 'election list'. The election list for the first election in 1957 comprised the Malay states ranked in the order in which the state rulers recognised precedence among themselves based on the dates of accession to the thrones of the several states. The office of king is offered to the ruler qualified for election whose state is first on the election list, and, if he does not accept the office, to the ruler whose state is next on the list, and so on until a ruler accepts the office.

The Constitution envisages a constitutional monarchy, and clearly states that the *Yang di-Pertuan Agong* 'shall act in accordance with the advice of the Cabinet or of a Minister acting under the general authority of the Cabinet'.[14] In 1979, the constitutional role of the *Yang di-Pertuan Agong* was clearly explained by the Privy Council:

> [The *Yang di-Pertuan Agong*'s] functions are those of a constitutional monarch and except on certain matters that do not concern the instant appeal, he does not exercise any of his functions under the Constitution on his own initiative but is required by Article 40(1) to act in accordance with the advice of the Cabinet. So when one finds in the Constitution itself or in a Federal law powers conferred upon the Yang di-Pertuan Agong that are expressed to be exercisable if he is of opinion or is satisfied that a particular state of affairs exists or that particular action is necessary, the reference to his opinion or satisfaction is in reality a reference to the collective opinion or satisfaction of the members of the Cabinet, or the opinion or satisfaction of a particular Minister to whom the Cabinet have delegated their authority to give advice upon the matter in question.[15]

The certain matters in respect of which the *Yang di-Pertuan Agong* is empowered to act in its discretion relate to:

- the appointment of a prime minister;
- the withholding of consent to a request for the dissolution of Parliament;
- the requisition of a meeting of the Conference of Rulers concerned solely with the privileges, position, honours and dignities of their Royal Highnesses, and any action at such a meeting;
- and in any other case mentioned in the Constitution.

In addition, the ruler of a state has discretionary powers pertaining to his function as the head of the Muslim religion or relating to the customs of the Malays, the appointment of heirs, consorts, regent, or Council of Regency, the award of honours, and the regulation of royal courts and palaces.

The judiciary

Closely allied with the notion of a written constitution is the concept of the 'supremacy' of the constitution. As Chief Justice Marshall in *Marbury v. Madison*[16] said:

> All those who have framed written constitutions contemplate them as forming the fundamental and paramount law of the nation, and consequently, the theory of every government must be, that an act of the legislature repugnant to the constitution, is void. This theory is essentially attached to a written constitution, and is consequently to be considered by this court as one of the fundamental principles of society.[17]

These words of Chief Justice Marshall are all the more applicable to Malaysia in view of the fact that the Malaysian Constitution is expressly declared to be the 'supreme law of the Federation'.[18]

An open declaration of supremacy has no meaningful content unless the supremacy can be effectively secured. Indubitably, that role must be performed by the courts. Hence, it is vital that the Constitution provides for an independent judiciary.

The chief justice of the Federal Court, the president of the Court of Appeal, and the chief judges of the High Courts and the other judges of the Federal Court, or the Court of Appeal and of the High Courts, shall be appointed by the *Yang di-Pertuan Agong*, acting on the advice of the prime minister, after consulting the Conference of Rulers. Until the 1988 convulsion in the judiciary, judicial appointments were often regarded as non-controversial affairs. The impact of that convulsion led to a degree of politicisation of the appointment process, especially in relation to the higher courts.

In the case of the appointment of the chief justice of the Federal Court, the prime minister is required to consult the Conference of Rulers only. However, in the case of other judicial appointments to the various courts, the prime minister is required to consult the heads of the relevant courts concerned.

To ensure independence of the judiciary, the Constitution ensures tenure in office until the attainment of the age of retirement of 65, unless that judge has been removed through the removal mechanism of Article 125. Furthermore, the remuneration and other terms of office (including pension rights) may not be altered to the disadvantage of a judge after his or her appointment.[19]

It is also provided in the Constitution that the conduct of a judge of the Federal Court, Court of Appeal or High Court shall not be discussed in either House of Parliament except on a substantive motion of which notice has been given by not less than one-quarter of the total number of members of that House, and shall not be discussed in the Legislative Assembly of any state.[20] It is also expressly provided that the Federal Court, Court of Appeal or the High Court shall have power to punish any contempt of itself.[21]

An elaborate removal mechanism is set out in the Constitution. In order to maintain the independence of the judiciary, the Reid Commission recommended that:

> a judge cannot be removed except by order of the Yang di-Pertuan Agong in pursuance of an address passed by a majority of two-thirds of each House of Parliament; and before any such motion is moved there must be proved misconduct or infirmity of mind or body.[22]

The provisions of Article 125(3), following an amendment in 1994, now provides as follows:

> If the Prime Minister, or the Chief Justice after consulting the Prime Minister, represents to the Yang di-Pertuan Agong that a judge of the Federal Court ought to be removed on the ground of any breach of any provision of the code of ethics prescribed under Clause (3A) or on the ground of inability, from infirmity of body or mind or any other cause, properly to discharge the functions of his office, the Yang di-Pertuan Agong shall appoint a tribunal in accordance with Clause (4) and refer the representation to it, and may on the recommendation of the tribunal remove the judge from office.

The provisions of Article 125 apply also to judges of the Court of Appeal and of a High Court.

The tribunal must consist of not less than five persons who hold or have held office as a judge of the Federal Court, Court of Appeal or a High Court, or who hold or have held equivalent office in any other part of the Commonwealth. The tribunal is to be presided over by the member first in the following order, namely:

> the Chief Justice of the Federal Court, the Chief Judges according to their precedence among themselves, and other members according to the order of their appointment to an office qualifying them for membership (the older coming before the younger of two members with appointment of the same date).

It is also provided that, pending any reference and report under Article 125(3), the *Yang di-Pertuan Agong* may, on the recommendation of the prime minister and, in the case of any other Federal judge, after consulting the chief justice, suspend a judge from the exercise of his functions. In the case of a judge of the Court of Appeal and of a High Court, the consultation is with the president of the Court of Appeal and with the chief judge of a High Court, respectively.

Election system

A system of free elections is a fundamental feature of a true democracy. To provide for an election process whereby the Malaysian Parliament would comprise genuine representatives of the people, the Reid Commission had recommended various safeguards. One such safeguard was the creation of an independent Election Commission entrusted with the functions of delimiting constituencies, conducting elections to the House of Representatives, and preparing and revising the electoral rolls for such elections. In 1962 the power of delimiting electoral constituencies was removed from the Election Commission and transferred to the House of Representatives. Professor R. H. Hickling warned against such reduction of the powers of the Election Commission:

> The abolition of the powers of an independent Commission smacks a little of expediency: and expediency can be a dangerous policy.... The original architects of the Constitution may have been wiser than we know, in creating a complex division of powers designed to frustrate the politicians and alarm the law-students. To transfer all powers to the myth of a legislature and the reality of an executive is to make the way straight for authoritarian rule. This may not be a fear for today, but what of tomorrow, when these powers may be in other hands?[23]

The extent to which gerrymandering is perpetuated is a good indication of the strength of a democracy. When the Reid Commission had taken into account factors such as the sparseness or density of population, the means of communication, and the distribution of different communities, it recommended 'that the number of voters in any constituency should not be more than 15 per cent above or below the average for the State'. In 1962, as a result of a constitutional amendment, the 15 per cent disparity was enlarged to 'as little as one-half of the electors of any urban constituency'.[24] In 1973 this constitutionally prescribed disparity of 50 per cent was deleted altogether. The bland explanation given was that such an amendment was 'merely intended to give the Election Commission more room to exercise their discretion in deciding the measure of weightage in respect of rural areas which, because of prevailing circumstances, suffer disadvantage as compared with urban areas'.[25]

Quite clearly, the changes had the effect of diminishing the prospects of the opposition parties winning power. The identification of the Malays with rural areas and non-Malays with the urban areas was particularly accentuated in the early years after Independence. The weighting of rural constituencies to favour the Malays ensured UMNO dominance in the Parliament. This was fine as long as the Malays remained a united community. However, the split within UMNO at one stage and the Anwar imbroglio[26] threatened UMNO's grip on the reins of government, although post-September 11 developments indicate a resurgence of support for the Barisan Nasional. Many non-Malays and moderate Malays were clearly scared off by the fundamentalist policies of PAS (an opposition Islamic party which currently controls two of the states of the Federation).

A spectrum of factors

The state of constitutionalism in Malaysia is influenced by a number of factors. The rejection by the largest racial group, the Malays, of the Malayan Union was the result of a feeling of insecurity arising from the proposed creation of a common citizenship. It was proposed, for instance, that any person could qualify as a citizen of the Malayan Union by virtue of being born in Malaya or in Singapore and, in other cases, by fulfilling a requirement of a 10-year period of residence in Malaya or in Singapore in the 15 years preceding 1942. The fear was that Malay power would be diluted by a swelling in the number of citizens of other races, particularly the Chinese and Indians. That the racial factor is significant in understanding the notion of rule of law in Malaysia is reinforced by the omission of Singapore from the 1948 Federation of Malaya. Again, there was the fear that the Malays would be dominated by the Malayan Chinese if Singapore's 1 million Chinese acceded to Malaya. The inclusion of Singapore in the enlarged Federation of Malaysia in 1963 was counterbalanced by the proposed inclusion of Sabah, Sarawak and Brunei (a predominantly Muslim state), where the Chinese were not in the majority. This counterbalancing was skewed by the fact that Brunei backed out in the closing stages of the negotiations

The race factor is also very pertinent in the context of the Malaysian economy. The Malays dominate the bureaucracy and various institutions such as the police, the military and the judiciary. At Independence, the Chinese had dominated the economic sphere. A combination of these communal, social and economic factors has a major impact on the development of democratic rule in Malaysia. A dimming of constitutionalism occurred with the outbreak of racial riots in Kuala Lumpur in May 1969.

The racial clash of 1969 took place against the background of 'Malay "backwardness" and festering resentment against Chinese "wealth"'.[27] In the wake of the riots the government formulated the NEP (or 'New Economic Policy') with the aim of restructuring Malaysian society so as to erode the identification of race with economic function. As Dr Harold Crouch observed:

> The NEP was designed to create the foundations for intercommunal harmony in the long term, but it inevitably aggravated tensions in the short term. It discriminated in favour of Malays and against non-Malays, with the result that non-Malays believed they were treated as second-class citizens...
>
> The NEP was accompanied by cultural policies that symbolised the ascendancy of the Malays. Malay replaced English as the language of administration and education (except at the primary level where Chinese and Tamil continued to be used). Malay culture was given increased prominence in official ceremonies and television programs, and Islam became more fully identified with the state. In practice, non-Malays continued to speak Chinese and Tamil, there was still plenty of scope for non-Malay cultural expression, and religious freedom continued to be respected.[28]

Rapid changes have taken place in Malaysia. The impressive economic growth at an annual average rate of more than 6 per cent from 1957 until 1990 has effected a transformation in Malaysian society: improved living standards, an expansion of a Malay middle class and also growth of the non-Malay middle class. In analysing all these changes to Malaysian society, Dr Crouch concluded:

> In the long run, however, observers commonly assume that economic development in Third Word countries will lead to fuller democratization. Economic development produces a modern social structure in which new social classes emerge and demand political influence. Thus, the power of authoritarian and semi-authoritarian governments is undermined by countervailing forces created by the process of economic development. In the Malaysian case, the development of the middle class, especially the Malay middle class, is particularly important and might be expected to stimulate political competition and make the government more responsive to pressures from society. Nevertheless, the communal division of Malaysian society represents an enduring obstacle to full democratization, making it likely that Malay-dominated governments will retain authoritarian powers to ensure the continuation of Malay preeminence and prevent political stability's [sic.]being undermined by intercommunal violence. Whatever the eventual outcome, the Malaysian case shows that economic and social change can proceed

for many decades without leading to fundamental change in the political system. In practice, authoritarian and democratic characteristics have coexisted within a coherent political order in which the government has been both repressive and responsive to pressures from society.[29]

Rule of law

As the rule of law entails the idea of limited government it is necessary to explore a few contentious areas to highlight the varying notions of the rule of law in Malaysia. The key areas include the following: that there should be a tolerance of those who dissent from the government's viewpoints; that the fundamental rights of the citizens are not easily trampled upon; that the judiciary plays an independent role as arbiter in disputes between the various entities in the Malaysian Federation. Furthermore, there must be respect for the constitutional document to ensure that it is regarded as the basic norm of the Federation.

Emergency powers

The constitutions of many emergent nations have a conspicuous common feature. Most of them have an elaborate set of provisions empowering a government to invoke extraordinary powers to cope with a crisis. Such provisions are found in Article 150 of the Malaysian Constitution.[30]

It is thus provided that if the *Yang di-Pertuan Agong* 'is satisfied that a grave emergency exists whereby the security, or the economic life, or public order in the Federation or any part thereof is threatened, he may issue a Proclamation of Emergency, making therein a declaration to that effect'. A Proclamation of Emergency may be issued

> before the actual occurrence of the event which threatens the security, or the economic life, or public order in the Federation or any part thereof if the Yang di-Pertuan Agong is satisfied that there is imminent danger of the occurrence of such event.

The *Yang di-Pertuan Agong*'s power extends to issuing different Proclamations on different grounds or in different circumstances, regardless of the existence of other Proclamations.

When a Proclamation of Emergency is in operation, the *Yang di-Pertuan Agong* is empowered to promulgate ordinances, except when both Houses of Parliament are sitting concurrently. The ordinances have full force and effect as if they were Acts of Parliament. A Proclamation of Emergency and any promulgated ordinance are required to be laid before both Houses of Parliament. The Constitution, as it originally stood, provided that a

235

Proclamation of Emergency should cease to have force at the expiration of two months from the date on which it was issued, and, similarly, any ordinance promulgated by the *Yang di-Pertuan Agong* automatically lapsed, and ceased to have effect, at the expiration of 15 days from the date on which both Houses of Parliament were first sitting. As a result of a 1960 constitutional amendment, the Proclamation of Emergency and the ordinance, if not sooner revoked, only cease to have effect if resolutions are passed by both Houses annulling them.[31] An ordinance or any law made while a Proclamation was in force ceases to have effect at the expiration of six months from the date that a Proclamation of Emergency ceases to be in force.

The scope of the law-making powers of the Federal Parliament is considerably enlarged while a Proclamation of Emergency is in force: 'the Parliament may, notwithstanding anything in this Constitution, make laws with respect to any matter, if it appears to Parliament that the law is required by reason of the emergency.'[32] Such laws cannot be invalidated on the grounds of inconsistency with any provision of the Constitution. However, the enlarged law-making power of the Federal Parliament cannot extend to any matter of Islamic law or the custom of the Malays, or with respect to any matter of native law or customs in the states of Sabah or Sarawak. Furthermore, emergency legislation inconsistent with constitutional provisions relating to religion, citizenship or language will not be valid.[33] Apart from these specified exceptions, all the fundamental rights set out in the Constitution can be derogated in times of an emergency.

Any role for the judiciary in overseeing the exercise of emergency powers is precluded by the following provisions of Article 150(8):

Notwithstanding anything in this Constitution –

(a) the satisfaction of the Yang di-Pertuan Agong mentioned in Clause (1) and Clause (2B) shall be final and conclusive and shall not be challenged or called in question in any court on any ground; and
(b) no court shall have jurisdiction to entertain or determine any application, question or proceeding, in whatever form, on any ground, regarding the validity of –
(i) a Proclamation under Clause (1) or of a declaration made in such Proclamation to the effect stated in Clause (1);
(ii) the continued operation of such Proclamation;
(iii) any ordinance promulgated under Clause (2B); or
(iv) the continuation in force of any such ordinance.

The emergency powers were invoked in 1964, 1966, 1969 and 1977. They were used in 1966 and 1977 to overcome political crises in the states of Sarawak and Kelantan, respectively. Professor Andrew Harding rightly pointed out that in both cases 'there was no real security problem to justify federal intervention' and that 'the federal authorities acted to their own political advantage, securing control of the State Government'.[34] The 1964 state of emergency was proclaimed to respond to the launching of a 'confrontation' by Indonesia during the Sukarno era. The outbreak of communal riots in the midst of a general election led to a nationwide state of emergency on 15 May 1969. To deal with the racial disturbances of 1969, the Emergency (Public Order and Prevention of Crime) Ordinance 1969 was promulgated. This ordinance confers on the police wide powers to arrest and detain persons for 60 days and, in the case of the minister, two years. The following observation was made by a mission of external observers:

> The Emergency (Public Order and Prevention of Crime) Ordinance was proclaimed in 1969 when there were serious racial disturbances in the country. This Ordinance remains in place. After a brief ten day visit, spent entirely in Kuala Lumpur, the mission was not best placed to make judgmental remarks about the need for a State of Emergency. But everything the mission saw, heard and read suggested that Malaysia is a stable and prosperous country. The continuation of the Emergency Ordinance after the need for it has passed can have an insidiously brutalising effect upon the administration of justice in any country. We suspect that the Malaysian malaise may be due in no small measure to the gradual acceptance of a state of emergency as the norm of government. It is time for this ordinance to be repealed.[35]

A more positive aspect is that since 1977 no new Proclamation of Emergency has been made. Nevertheless, the fact that the 1969 Proclamation of Emergency, which was effected in a different time period for a different occasion, has not been revoked or annulled to date means that extraordinary laws are still operative despite the clear view that the factual basis for that Proclamation is no longer in existence. Professor Harding made the following wry observation:

> It appears therefore as though emergency laws have become a permanent, if strange, feature of the legal landscape. Undoubtedly this situation casts doubt on the continuing relevance of the rule of law in Malaysia.[36]

He reiterated this point:

> [W]hat has become normal is the existence of emergency laws in parallel with the operation of the ordinary constitutional and legal

systems. This means that the rule of law has become simply one option rather than the entire basis of the constitutional order.[37]

More fundamental to the rule of law is the ability of the courts to intervene when there has been a clear case of abuse of the emergency powers provisions. A significant issue is the justiciability of a Proclamation of Emergency. The Proclamation provides the legal foundations for the invocation of extraordinary powers, powers which cut across the fundamental liberties guaranteed by the Constitution. On one occasion when the validity of a Proclamation of Emergency was challenged on the basis that it was not made *bona fide* but 'in *fraudem legis*' the Privy Council simply dealt with the issue on the *assumption* that it was a justiciable issue.[38] The Privy Council found on that occasion the appellant had not discharged the onus on him to show that the Proclamation of Emergency was in *fraudem legis*. Lord MacDermott, in delivering the reasons for the Privy Council's decision, said:

> Whether a Proclamation under statutory powers by the Supreme Head of the Federation can be challenged before the courts on some or any grounds is a constitutional question of far-reaching importance which, on the present state of the authorities, remains unsettled and debateable.[39]

However, the Federal Court judge (as he then was), Ong Hock Thye, in the Federal Court phase of the *Ningkan* litigation, said:

> The inbuilt safeguards against indiscriminate or frivolous recourse to emergency legislation contained in article 150 specifically prove that the emergency must be one 'whereby the security or economic life of the Federation or of any part thereof is threatened'. If those words of limitation are not meaningless verbiage, they must be taken to mean exactly what they say, no more and no less, for article 150 does not confer on the Cabinet an untrammelled discretion to cause an emergency to be declared at their mere whim and fancy. According to the view of my learned brother, however, it would seem that the Cabinet have *carte blanche* to do as they please – a strange role for the judiciary who are commonly supposed to be bulwarks of individual liberty and the Rule of Law and guardians of the Constitution.[40]

Constitutionalism in Malaysia is weakened by the enactment of article 150(8), for the excision of the courts' jurisdiction in relation to the validity of a Proclamation of Emergency or an emergency ordinance creates a situation whereby 'the Cabinet have *carte blanche* to do as they please'.

In 1983 Article 150 was amended by the Constitution (Amendment) Act 1983 to provide for the issuance of a Proclamation of Emergency by the *Yang di-Pertuan Agong* if the *prime minister* is satisfied that a grave emergency exists whereby the security, or the economic life, or public order in the Federation, or any part thereof is threatened. The amendment replaced the 'satisfaction' of the *Yang di-Pertuan Agong* with the satisfaction of the prime minister. This amendment was subsequently repealed by the Constitution (Amendment) Act 1984 as part of the agreement reached between the Mahathir government and the hereditary rulers to bring to an end the constitutional crisis of 1983–4.[41]

Constitutional amendments

Although the Constitution is declared to be the supreme law of the Federation, the extensive changes which have been effected to it and the frequency of amendments have diminished its standing as a sacrosanct document. In 1970 Dr Mahathir was quoted as saying: 'The manner, the frequency and the trivial reasons for altering the Constitution reduced this supreme law of the nation to a useless scrap of paper.'[42]

Whilst a number of amendments can be justified on the basis of changing circumstances (such as the constitutional amendment to provide for the establishment of the Federation of Malaysia or the amendment to provide for the exclusion of Singapore from the Federation), many other amendments which occurred in the history of the Federation were simply motivated by political considerations. Indeed, one of the main complaints of parliamentarians and members of the public relates to the hastiness with which fundamental amendments were effected.

The constitution provides for a two-thirds majority vote in each House of Parliament to effect a valid constitutional change. Since Independence in 1957, the government in power has maintained and continues to maintain more than two-thirds of the seats in Parliament. In the period since Independence, the lack of restraint in resorting to the amendment process in Article 159 in order to increase executive power highlights the development of a 'limited democracy'.[43]

Fundamental liberties

The degree of respect accorded to the protection of fundamental liberties signifies the degree of deference which is given to the rule of law. The use of preventive detention laws (under the Internal Security Act 1960), sedition and official secrets laws and the imposition of controls on the media foster an image of a political system which is becoming increasingly authoritarian. The panoply of restrictive legislation led to the following conclusion in the *Justice in Jeopardy* report:

Although the Malaysian Constitution guarantees important rights, these rights are often deprived of their meaning and force by constitutional restrictions, many of which also deny judicial review of the executive action. A body of restrictive legislation exists in Malaysia that requires major change if Malaysia is to be ruled in accordance with a just rule of law.[44]

Article 149 of the Malaysian Constitution empowers the Parliament to pass laws which can override certain fundamental guarantees provided the law contains one of the following recitals:

that action has been taken or threatened by any substantial body of persons, whether inside or outside the Federation –
(a) to cause, or to cause a substantial number of citizens to fear, organised violence against persons or property; or
(b) to excite disaffection against the Yang di-Pertuan Agong or any Government in the Federation; or
(c) to promote feelings of ill-will and hostility between different races or other classes of the population likely to cause violence; or
(d) to procure the alteration, otherwise than by lawful means, of anything by law established; or
(e) which is prejudicial to the maintenance or the functioning of any supply or service to the public or any class of the public in the Federation or any part thereof; or
(f) which is prejudicial to public order in, or the security of, the Federation or any part thereof.[45]

The provisions of a law enacted under Article 149 which were designed to stop or prevent that action would be valid even if they were inconsistent with the constitutional provisions guaranteeing liberty of the person (Article 5), prohibition of banishment and freedom of movement of citizens (Article 9), freedom of speech, assembly, or association (Article 10), a right to 'adequate compensation' for compulsory acquisition or use of private property (Article 13).

The Internal Security Act 1960 (ISA) and the Dangerous Drugs (Special Preventive Measures) Act 1985 are two significant pieces of restrictive legislation enacted under Article 149. Both provide the minister of home affairs with the power of executive detention for a period not exceeding two years, a period which can be renewed indefinitely. Furthermore, the police are empowered under the ISA to arrest and detain any person for up to 60 days 'pending inquiry into the belief that he has acted in a manner prejudicial to security'. The ISA has been described as 'the most feared piece of legislation in Malaysia'.[46] It is beyond the scope of this chapter to canvass the full scope of the spectrum of discretionary powers conferred under the ISA.[47]

Apart from the legislation enacted pursuant to Article 149, other pieces of legislation operate to restrict the exercise of the fundamental guarantees embodied in the Malaysian Constitution. Thus, under the Printing Presses and Publications Act 1984, the minister has 'absolute discretion' to grant, refuse or revoke a licence for a printing press or to permit to print and publish a newspaper or other publication. Printing or producing any publication which 'contains an incitement to violence against persons or property, counsels disobedience to the law or to any lawful order or which is or is likely to lead to a breach of the peace or to promote feelings of ill-will, hostility, enmity, hatred, disharmony or disunity' is rendered a criminal offence. It is also an offence under the Act to publish 'false news' maliciously. A presumption of malice requires the accused to establish that, prior to publication, he or she took reasonable measures to verify the truth of the news. In respect of the minister's decision regarding an application for a licence or permit, or its suspension or revocation, judicial review is precluded by a finality clause, and the rules of natural justice pertaining to the right to be heard would not be applicable.

Another piece of legislation which severely restricts the right to freedom of speech is the Sedition Act 1948, which makes it an offence to utter words or to print or publish any material having a 'seditious tendency'. The broad scope of the Act can be seen from §3(1), which defines 'seditious tendency'. The definition includes in its ambit a tendency 'to bring into hatred or contempt or to excite disaffection against any ruler or against any Government' and a tendency 'to bring into hatred or contempt or to excite disaffection against the administration of justice in Malaysia or in any State'. In the wake of the 1969 racial violence, §3(1) was amended in 1970 to include a tendency to question four 'sensitive' issues: citizenship; the national language and the languages of other communities; the special position and privileges of the Malays, the natives of Sabah and Sarawak, and the legitimate interests of other communities in Malaysia; and the sovereignty of the rulers.

In the early years after the 1970 amendment to the Sedition Act 1948, the government sought to show that it was even-handed in its operation of the new law. Since then, the prosecution of some prominent Malaysian citizens under the Act has generated considerable concern that the law has been used to stifle criticism, whether of the government or of the judiciary. *Public Prosecutor v. Param Cumaraswamy*[48] involved a 1986 prosecution of Dato' Param Cumaraswamy, the then vice-president of the Malaysian Bar Council, for allegedly raising disaffection against the *Yang di-Pertuan Agong* through a purported suggestion of discrimination on the part of the Pardons Board, which was chaired by the *Yang di-Pertuan Agong*. In this case, the accused was eventually acquitted. In *Lim Guan Eng v. Public Prosecutor*,[49] the accused, who was an opposition Member of Parliament, was prosecuted under the 'false news' provision of the Printing Presses and

Publications Act 1984 and also under the Sedition Act 1984. The charges arose centrally from 'an allegation of selective prosecution' by the accused. The trial judge, in convicting the accused, sentenced him to a fine of RM 10,000, in default six months' imprisonment, in respect of the first charge; and a fine of RM 5,000, in default three months' imprisonment, in respect of the second charge, under the Sedition Act. On appeal, the Court of Appeal raised the sentence to eighteen months' imprisonment on each charge.[50] The *Justice in Jeopardy* report commented that the Lim Guan Eng episode 'shows in fact that anyone who dares to criticise the legal or judicial process may have to pay a very high price'.[51] In 2000, prosecution under the Sedition Act 1948 was launched against Karpal Singh, a lead defence counsel for the former Malaysian deputy prime minister, Anwar Ibrahim, 'with respect to statements made in court on 10 September 1999 in the defence of Anwar Ibrahim'.[52] The charge against Karpal Singh was eventually withdrawn.[53]

Other episodes involving the use of contempt powers and claims for huge amounts in damages in defamation suits were commented upon in the *Justice in Jeopardy* report.[54] In relation to defamation actions, the report recommended that 'Courts should not allow claims for or awards of damages in defamation cases to be of such magnitude as to be a means of stifling free speech and expression'.[55] Professor Andrew Harding commented:

> Fundamental Liberties have declined, especially the liberty of the person and political liberties. There has been some justification for exceptional restrictions being placed on these rights during the period of the emergency and other times of danger, but the strictures of circumstances have become the common place of the law.[56]

Judicial independence

Among the principles, articulated by Joseph Raz, which are required for the identification of the existence of the rule of law in a state are the following:

1   The independence of the judiciary must be guaranteed, otherwise the judiciary could not be relied upon to apply the law and the citizen should therefore not be guided by it.
2   The principles of natural justice such as the requirements of open court, absence of bias, the right to be heard etc. must be observed if the law is to be able to guide action.
3   The courts should have the power to examine the actions of the other branches of government in order to determine if they conform with the law.[57]

Using these guiding principles, it could be said that the rule of law has been considerably weakened by a number of episodes involving the judiciary. The major of these episodes is the well-known judiciary crisis of 1988, when in a confrontation with the Mahathir government the top judge of the land and two senior Supreme Court (now Federal Court) judges were removed from office. On paper the independence of the judiciary is formally guaranteed. However, the manner in which the mechanism for removal was manipulated led to an erosion of judicial independence. The sorry saga has been commented upon extensively elsewhere.[58] The point to note is that after 1988 confidence in the judiciary was also undermined by divisions within the higher courts. As Poh-Ling Tan observed: 'Events post-1988 also show a growing public unease concerning the true independence of certain judges.'[59] She cited the *Ayer Molek* case[60] as an example.

This was a case in which the Court of Appeal had found that the manner in which the case was handled in the High Court gave the impression to right-thinking people that litigants could choose the judge before whom they appeared. The Federal Court overruled the Court of Appeal and, in an unprecedented move, ordered that certain portions of the remarks contained in the judgement of the Courts of Appeal be expunged: an order unprecedented in Malaysian legal history.

Prior to 1988, Article 121 of the Malaysian Constitution declared that 'the judicial power of the Federation shall be vested in two High Courts of co-ordinate jurisdiction and status...and in such inferior courts as may be provided by federal law etc.' As a result of the Constitution (Amendment) Act 1988, Article 121 simply states that '[t]here shall be two High Courts of co-ordinate jurisdiction and status...and such inferior courts as may be provided by federal law etc.' The deletion of the phrases 'judicial power of the Federation' and 'vested' was construed by Professor Wu as amounting to a *'coup de grâce'*.[61] He said: 'The amendment purportedly restricts the constitutional role of the judiciary.' Professor Wu added:

> The co-equal status of the judiciary with the other branches as enshrined in the original Constitution has been de-emphasised or perhaps 'downgraded', a direction not contemplated by framers of the Constitution.[62]

However, Professor A. J. Harding remarked that the 'precise effect' of the amendment was 'a matter of some doubt'.[63]

The concern about the amendment to Article 121 should not be about the formal 'downgrading' of the judiciary. The expression 'judicial power of the Federation' is one which carries a lot of potential for the judiciary to develop a strict separation of judicial power doctrine. Australian constitutional developments are pointers in that direction.[64] The amendment has pre-empted any possible future move by the Malaysian judiciary in that direction.

The strength of the rule of law in the context of the administration of justice in Malaysia varies depending on the degree of government interest in the cases before the courts. In the vast majority of cases which come before the courts daily, there has been no display of public concern over the manner in which the cases are handled, the integrity of the presiding judges and magistrates and the eventual outcomes. This is so regardless of whether the cases involve commercial or family law litigation or criminal prosecution. The *Justice in Jeopardy* report stated that there were well-founded grounds for concern as to the proper administration of justice in Malaysia in cases which were of particular interest, for whatever reason, to the government. The report added:

> Plainly, this is only a small proportion of the total number of cases which arise, but they are of vital importance to the well-being of the entire system of justice in Malaysia. The central problem appears to be in the actions of the various branches of an extremely powerful executive, which has not acted with due regard for the other essential elements of a free and democratic society based on the just rule of law.[65]

The rule of law in Malaysia – a summation

Malaysia in one sense can count itself as one of the few 'fortunate' countries which emerged as independent entities after the Second World War. It is lucky in the sense that it has weathered a number of crises and controversies without setting the Constitution aside permanently. This, however, does not mean that in Malaysia the rule of law prevails to the same extent as in Western democracies. The reality is that the rule of law is constantly jostling with authoritarianism, which is attractive to a government which places greater emphasis on governmental stability. As Dr Harold Crouch put it, Malaysia is a country 'whose significant democratic and authoritarian characteristics are inextricably mixed'.[66] The prevalent notion floated by the government is that governmental stability and continuity is essential to economic and social achievements. Hence, the argument goes that the price to be paid for that stability is some diminution in the strength of the rule of law – that fundamental liberties may have to be constrained to some extent and that the executive must be strong and powerful for the good of the people. The notion that there must be some sacrifice in the enjoyment of the rule of law in order to achieve economic and social advancement appears to have considerable support in Malaysia, as reflected in successive electoral triumphs of the government since Independence in 1957. An opposition Member of Parliament sought to explain the paradox of governmental electoral triumphs despite the erosion of fundamental liberties:

It may be asked why people continue to vote for the government if the situation is so bad. The answer lies, in my opinion, in the way politics works in Malaysia. Malaysia is a mixed society, made up of different ethnic groups. Being an Asian society, appeal is made on the basis of identification to group or community rather than on an individual by individual basis. Indeed, whenever the government is attacked for being 'undemocratic', the standard reply is that democracy is a western concept which has restricted relevance to an Asian context. More relevant is the concept (it is claimed) that people elect their government who then carry out whatever actions they see fit for the good of the people.[67]

Professor Bradley and Professor Ewing described one sense of the rule of law in the following terms: 'First, the rule of law expresses a preference for law and order within a community other than anarchy, warfare and strife. In this sense, the rule of law is a philosophical view of society that is linked with basic democratic notions.'[68] Whilst the 'law and order' aspect of the rule of law would be subscribed to generally in Malaysia, there is, however, a conflict of views over the purported linkage to 'basic democratic notions'. The debate has been skewed by equating 'basic democratic notions' with the imposition of 'Western' values. It has been argued that these 'Western' values may not necessarily accord with the cultural norms and traditional values of 'Eastern' societies. A great champion of this line of argument is Dr Mahathir. In an address to a human rights conference in 1994, Dr Mahathir lamented the attempts by a post-Cold War international order to impose on every country values of a 'multi-party system of government' and 'the liberal views on human rights as conceived by the Europeans and the North Americans'.[69] He added:

Developed countries can do with weak governments or no government. But developing countries cannot function without strong authority on the part of government. Unstable and weak governments will result in chaos, and chaos cannot contribute to the development and well-being of developing countries. Divisive politics will occupy the time and minds of everyone, as we can witness in many a developing country today.[70]

Dr Rais Yatim, who had been in the faction which lost out in the tussle against Dr Mahathir, described the 'seemingly calm and patronising attitude' of the Malaysian people in accepting the erosion of fundamental rights as 'perplexing'.[71] He added:

It is as if Malaysians have lost touch with their basic rights in a country that prides itself in being democratic and leading the voice of liberation within the third world countries. Even with the increasing number of the young and well-educated in the country there appears to be little interest in the importance of civil liberties. We have noted how excessive executive powers, omnipresent and far-reaching as they have been, have rendered constitutional freedoms meaningless. And yet there appears to be little or no resistance from the man on the street to counter these inroads. There can be only one explanation to this: the culture of fear has set in. The underlying fear of executive reprisals has slowly but surely reduced Malaysians into being reluctantly submissive in many respects of their daily life.[72]

The rule of law has gone through different phases in Malaysia since the attainment of Independence. Measured by the degree of independence of the judiciary, a 'thick' rule of law operated during the term of office of the first three prime ministers of Malaysia. The tussle between the judiciary and the Mahathir administration, culminating in the 1988 judiciary crisis, led to a diminution in public confidence in the judicial institution and, consequently, a weakening of the rule of law. Measured by the constraints placed on the exercise of fundamental freedoms in the context of the political dynamics of the Malaysian polity, it is unlikely that a thick rule of law as obtained in a liberal democracy will operate in the foreseeable future. The imperatives of national unity and economic development are still viewed and propagated by the government as antithetical to the full enjoyment of fundamental liberties. To redress the economic imbalance in Malaysia and to achieve national unity, the government – which remains unchanged since Independence – claims that strong government is essential. Unfortunately, the perceptible trend in Malaysia is to equate the notion of strong government with 'arbitrary power'.[73] As Dr Rais Yatim remarked: 'A government can certainly be strong even when basic rights are comprehensively guarded by the courts.'[74]

Notes

1 A significant factor in this equation can be attributed to the prime ministerial personality in power at a particular point in time. For instance, the predecessors of the current prime minister, Mahathir, were educated in the law in England. Having studied abroad and observed the workings of the British legal and political system, they were, most likely, inculcated with a greater sense of the importance of observing, at the least, some limits to government consistent with the idea of the rule of law. Tun Mohamed Suffian, the highly respected Lord President of Malaysia from 1974 to 1982, in a public lecture in 1987 made the following observation: "So far the independence of the judiciary has never been in jeopardy, thanks mainly to the fact that our first three Prime Ministers were lawyers who understood the importance of having a judiciary that enjoys public confidence".
(Tun Mohamed Suffian, 'The Role of the Judiciary', *Malayan Law Journal*, no. 2 (1987), pp. xxiii–iv)

2 Rais Yatim, *Freedom Under Executive Power in Malaysia: A Study of Executive Supremacy* (Kuala Lumpur: Endowment Publications, 1995), p. 27, fn 7, fn 8.
3 *Ibid.*, at p. 28.
4 B. Simandjuntak, *Malayan Federalism 1945–63* (Kuala Lumpur: Oxford University Press, 1969), p. 41.
5 Malaysian Constitution, article 44.
6 Malaysian Constitution, article 68(1).
7 Malaysian Constitution, article 159.
8 Report of the Federation of Malaya Constitutional Commission, p. 31, para. 80.
9 S. Jayakumar, 'Constitutional Limitation on Legislative Powers in Malaysia', *Malaya Law Review*, vol. 9 (1967), p. 109.
10 Malaysian Constitution, article 39.
11 Malaysian Constitution, article 43(4).
12 Tun Mohamed Suffian, *An Introduction to the Legal System of Malaysia* (Petaling Jaya: Penefit Fajar Bakti Sdn Bhd, 1988), p. 43.
13 Wu Min Aun, *The Malaysian Legal System,* 2nd edn (Petaling Jaya: Longman, 1999), p. 49.
14 Malaysian Constitution, article 40(1).
15 *Teh Cheng Poh v. Public Prosecutor* (1979), 1 *Malayan Law Journal* 50, (1979) p. 52.
16 I *Cranch* 137: (1803).
17 *Ibid.*, at p. 177.
18 Malaysian Constitution, article 4(1).
19 Malaysian Constitution, article 125(7).
20 Malaysian Constitution, article 127.
21 Malaysian Constitution, article 126.
22 Report of the Federation of Malaya Constitutional Commission, p. 53, para. 125.
23 R. H. Hickling, 'The First Five Years of the Federation of Malaya Constitution', *Malaya Law Review*, vol. 4 (1962), pp. 183, 191–2.
24 Report of the Federation of Malaysia Constitutional Commission, p. 29, para. 74.
25 Jabatan Penerangan Malaysia, *Siaran Akhbar* (PEN 7/73/78 (PARL)), p. 2.
26 Anwar Ibrahim, the deputy prime minister of Malaysia, was sacked by Dr Mahathir in 1998. He was 'subsequently arrested, tried on charges of corruption and sodomy, and jailed'. See Ian Stewart, *The Mahathir Legacy* (Sydney: Allen & Unwin, 2003), p. 10; Wu Min Aun, 'Anwar Ibrahim: Epilogue', *Lawasia Journal* (2002), p. 45.
27 Harold Crouch, *Government and Society in Malaysia* (St Leonards: Allen & Unwin, 1996), p. 238.
28 *Ibid.*, at p. 239.
29 *Ibid.*, at p. 247.
30 See, generally, S. Jayakumar, 'Emergency Powers in Malaysia', in Tun Mohamed Suffian, H. P. Lee and F. A. Trindade, eds, *The Constitution of Malaysia – Its Development: 1957–1977* (Kuala Lumpur: Oxford University Press, 1978), pp. 328–68; H. P. Lee, 'Emergency Powers in Malaysia', in F. A. Trindade and H. P. Lee, eds, *The Constitution in Malaysia: Further Perspectives and Developments* (Singapore: Oxford University Press, 1986), pp. 135–56; Andrew Harding, *Law, Government and the Constitution on Malaysia* (Kuala Lumpur: Malayan Law Journal Sdn Bd, 1996), pp. 153–66; Rais Yatim, *Freedom Under Executive Power in Malaysia: A Study of Executive Supremacy*, pp. 183–238; Cyrus Das, *Governments and Crisis Powers* (Kuala Lumpur: Malaysian Current Law Journal Sdn Bhd, 1996).

31 Constitution (Amendment) Act 1960 (Act no. 10 of 1960).
32 Malaysian Constitution, article 150(5).
33 Malaysian Constitution, article 150(6A).
34 Andrew Harding, *Law, Government and the Constitution in Malaysia*, p. 163.
35 *Justice in Jeopardy: Malaysia 2000* (Report of a Mission on Behalf of the International Bar Association, the ICJ Centre for the Independence of Judges and Lawyers, the Commonwealth Lawyers' Association, and l'Union Internationale des Avocats). This report will hereinafter be referred to as the *Justice in Jeopardy* report.
36 Andrew Harding, *Law, Government and the Constitution in Malaysia*, p. 154.
37 *Ibid.*, at p. 159.
38 Stephen Kalong Ningkan v. The Government of Malaysia, 2 Malayan Law Journal 238 (1968).
39 *Ibid.*, at p. 242.
40 1 *Malayan Law Journal* 119 (1968), p. 128.
41 H. P. Lee, *Constitutional Conflicts in Contemporary Malaysia* (Kuala Lumpur: Oxford University Press, 1995), pp. 35–6.
42 Mahathir bin Mohamed, *The Malay Dilemma* (Petaling Jaya: Federal Publications, 1981), p. 11.
43 Andrew Harding, *Law, Government and the Constitution in Malaysia*, p. 271.
44 *Justice in Jeopardy* report, p. 74.
45 Malaysian Constitution, article 149(1).
46 Rais Yatim, *Freedom Under Executive Power in Malaysia: A Study of Executive Supremacy*, p. 239.
47 *Ibid.*, at pp. 239–99.
48 1 *Malayan Law Journal* 512 (1986); 1 *Malaya Law Journal* 518 (1986).
49 3 *Malayan Law Journal* 14 (1998) (Court of Appeal).
50 An appeal from the decision of the Court of Appeal was dismissed by the Federal Court – 2 *Malayan Law Journal* 577 (2000).
51 *Justice in Jeopardy* report, pp. 21–30, 36–9.
52 See Wu Min Aun, 'Anwar Ibrahim: The Fall and Fall of a Favoured Son', *Lawasia Journal* 46 (2000/1), p. 68, note 44.
53 Ian Stewart, *op. cit.,* at p. 172.
54 *Justice in Jeopardy* report, pp. 21–30, 36–39.
55 *Ibid.*, at p. 54.
56 Andrew Harding, *Law, Government and the Constitution in Malaysia*, p. 272.
57 J. Raz, 'The Rule of Law and its Virtue', 93 *Law Quarterly Review* 195 (1977), p. 198.
58 For an analysis of the 1988 judiciary crisis, see H. P. Lee, *Constitutional Conflicts in Contemporary Malaysia* (Kuala Lumpur: Oxford University Press, 1995), pp. 43–85, and for other writings on the crisis, see references in fn 1, p. 77 of the same text.
59 Poh-Ling Tan, 'Malaysia', in Poh-Ling Tan e.d., *Asian Legal Systems* (Sydney: Butterworths, 1997), p. 299.
60 *Ayer Molek Rubber Co. Bhd v. Insas Bhd*, 2 *Malayan Law Journal* 734 (1995). See Wu Min Aun, 'Judiciary at the Crossroads', in Wu Min Aun, ed., *Public Law in Contemporary Malaysia* (Petaling Jaya: Longman, 1999), pp. 96–9.
61 Wu Min Aun, *The Malaysian Legal System*, 2nd edn (Petaling Jaya: Longman, 1999), p. 58.
62 *Ibid.*, at p. 59.
63 Andrew Harding, *Law, Government and the Constitution on Malaysia*, p. 134.
64 See H. P. Lee, 'Judges and Constitutional Government', *Lawasia Journal* 30 (2000/1), pp. 41–4.

65 *Justice in Jeopardy* report, p. 77.
66 Harold Crouch, *Government and Society in Malaysia*, p. 5.
67 Sim Kwang Yang, 'Democracy in Malaysia?', in *The Rule of Law and Human Rights in Malaysia and Singapore*, a Report of the Conference held at the European Parliament, 9 and 10 March 1989, p. 41.
68 A. W. Bradley and K. D. Ewing, *Constitutional and Administrative Law*, 12th edn (London and New York: Longman, 1997), p. 105.
69 Speech by Dr Mahathir Mohamed at the Just International Conference on Rethinking Human Rights (Legend Hotel, Kuala Lumpur, 6 December 1994), p. 4. See H. P. Lee, 'Constitutional Values in Turbulent Asia', 23 *Monash University Law Review* 375 (1997).
70 *Ibid.*, at pp. 4–5.
71 Rais Yatim, *Freedom Under Executive Power in Malaysia: A Study of Executive Supremacy*, p. 387.
72 *Ibid.*, at p. 387–8.
73 *Ibid.*, at p. 388–9.
74 *Ibid.*, at p. 389.

8

DEBATING RULE OF LAW IN THE HONG KONG SPECIAL ADMINISTRATIVE REGION, 1997–2002

Albert H. Y. Chen and Anne S. Y. Cheung

Introduction

Hong Kong was in the international limelight on July 1, 1997, the day that it shed its colonial identity as a British dependent territory and assumed its new identity as a Special Administrative Region (SAR) of the People's Republic of China (PRC). In this SAR, capitalism was going to flourish, existing side by side with the Communist regime across the border, in accordance with Jiang Zemin's saying that "the river water will not interfere with the well water." Protected by the late Deng Xiaoping's mandate of "one country, two systems," Hong Kong was to enjoy a high degree of autonomy. The fundamental freedoms and rights enjoyed by its residents were enshrined in the 1984 Sino-British Joint Declaration, a treaty creating binding obligations in international law, and the Basic Law, the "mini-constitution" of the Hong Kong SAR (HKSAR).

Yet despite the promise of "one country, two systems," the shift from British liberal-colonial rule to a Chinese "neo-authoritarian"[1] regime has caused waves of anxiety among the locals and stirred curiosity in the international scene. People, inside and outside Hong Kong, are eager to learn whether the British-style rule of law that was transplanted to Hong Kong during its colonial age can survive the handover. Regardless of whether the rule of law is indeed a truly positive colonial legacy or pure rhetoric,[2] it has become for post-1997 Hong Kong both a litmus test for the success of "one country, two systems" and an ideal that the people cherish and aspire to.

Some years have passed since the handover, and Hong Kong has witnessed several major debates in which critics alleged that the Special Administrative Region government has failed to uphold the rule of law. Famous controversies include the right of abode saga, the executive's decision not to prosecute certain members of the elite class, the condemnation of Falun Gong activities by the chief executive and the prosecution of Falun Gong demonstrators, the attempt to enact an anti-subversion law under the Basic Law, the arrest and prosecution of activists under the Public Order Ordinance, and the Cyberport contract dispute. All are crucial stories in telling of the assumptions and expectations of members of the public in Hong Kong regarding the rule of law. They also shed light on the dynamic relationship between the three branches of the Hong Kong government, and the relations between the authorities and the citizens of Hong Kong, in this period of political transition and integration.

Before this chapter analyzes the relevant incidents, it will first describe, by way of introduction, the historical, political and economic context of the legal system of Hong Kong (pp. 000–00). It will then discuss the right of abode saga (pp. 000–00), the debate on freedoms of religion and the press (pp. 000–00), the incidents of non-prosecution (pp. 000–00), the controversy surrounding the Public Order Ordinance (pp. 000–00), and the dispute regarding the Cyberport Project (pp. 000–00). Finally, we reflect on the meaning and significance of these controversies and debates, and on how they reveal competing conceptions of the rule of law in Hong Kong (pp. 000–00).

Historical, political and economic contexts

The modern legal history of Hong Kong is usually traced back to 1842, when the British colony of Hong Kong was founded under the Treaty of Nanjing, which was concluded between Imperial China (under the Qing dynasty) and Britain after China's defeat in the "Opium War." As in the case of other British colonies, English common law and the British conception and tradition of the rule of law were imported to Hong Kong.[3] The geographical territory and hence British jurisdiction of the colony were subsequently extended to the Kowloon Peninsula (in 1860) and the New Territories (in 1898).[4]

In 1984 the PRC and Britain signed the Joint Declaration on the Question of Hong Kong, which provided for Hong Kong's return to China on July 1, 1997. In April 1990 the Basic Law of the Special Administrative Region of Hong Kong – a "mini-constitution"[5] for post-1997 Hong Kong – was enacted by China's legislature, the National People's Congress (NPC). This Basic Law has come into effect since July 1, 1997.[6] The Basic Law provides for the continuity of the legal and judicial systems in Hong Kong after the handover. For example, Article 8 stipulates that the laws previously in force in Hong Kong shall continue to survive. Article 18 provides that only those mainland Chinese laws listed in Annex III to the Basic Law are applicable to Hong Kong, and they must be confined to those relating to defense and foreign affairs.[7] The Basic Law also confers a high degree of autonomy on the HKSAR and outlines the division of power between the central government in Beijing and the HKSAR government.

As in other constitutional instruments, the Basic Law stipulates the constitution of the executive, legislative, and judicial branches of the HKSAR government, and guarantees the protection of human rights. It contains provisions that guarantee the continuation of the existing social and economic systems and policies of Hong Kong after the handover. Hong Kong has had one of the most free-market economies in the world, and the Basic Law has been described as a charter for capitalism.[8]

The political system established by the Basic Law is commonly described as an "executive-led" system, with the chief executive exercising powers akin to those of a president under a presidential system of government, and with restrictions on the power of members of the legislature to introduce private members' bills. Unlike the case in liberal democratic states, the chief executive of the HKSAR is not elected by universal suffrage. The first chief executive was chosen by a selection committee of 400 Hong Kong residents, all of whom were chosen by the Preparatory Committee for the HKSAR appointed by the Beijing government. Tung Chee-hwa, HKSAR's first chief executive,[9] was successfully re-elected without any competitors in 2002 by an 800-member election committee elected in Hong Kong on the basis of occupational and functional constituencies. However, it is stated under Article 45 of the Basic Law that the ultimate aim in the gradual development of the political system of the HKSAR is to select the chief executive by universal suffrage. The chief executive is advised by the Executive Council, members of which are appointed by him.

Under the colonial system,[10] the top level of the executive branch of government consisted of the governor, appointed by London, and senior civil servants appointed by the governor. After the handover, the senior civil servants (like other ranks of the civil service) of the colonial regime remained in office. In 2002 the SAR government put forward a reform proposal regarding greater "accountability" of the policy-makers in the government.[11] According to the proposal, the chief executive would appoint "ministers" to head the various policy bureaus of the government. The ministers, unlike the senior civil servants who previously headed the policy bureaus, will hold a political appointment for a fixed term of office. They may be recruited either from existing senior civil servants or from outside the civil service. This proposal received the support of the Legislative Council and has been implemented as of July 1, 2002 – the beginning of Mr Tung Chee-hwa's second term of office as chief executive of the Hong Kong SAR.

The current Legislative Council is composed of 60 members: 24 are elected by universal suffrage in geographical constituencies – with free and fair elections by international standards and intense competition among several political parties, the most important of which are the Democratic Party (generally perceived as an anti-Beijing party) and the Democratic Alliance for the Betterment of Hong Kong (generally perceived as a pro-Beijing party); 30 by functional constituencies; and six by the 800-member election committee. In the next election, in 2004, half of the members will be directly elected.[12] The Basic Law envisages that a review of the political system will be conducted before 2007 to determine whether there should be any change in the composition of the Legislative Council (in terms of the numbers of legislators elected by different means) and in the mode of election of the chief executive in 2007. These are controversial issues, on which heated debates are expected in the next few years.

As in the case of the English common law that is applicable in Hong Kong, the legal profession in Hong Kong has also survived the handover, although it is currently suffering from the economic downturn that has overtaken Hong Kong since the Asian financial crisis of 1997. As in the case of England, and unlike the case in many other common law jurisdictions, the legal profession in Hong Kong is still divided into barristers (forming the Hong Kong Bar Association) and solicitors (forming the Law Society of Hong Kong). Lawyers qualified in mainland China have no right to practice in Hong Kong. English is still the predominant language in the operation of the legal system in Hong Kong, particularly in the drafting of legal documentation, in advocacy before the higher courts and in legal education.

After the handover, the highest court of Hong Kong's legal system is no longer the Privy Council in London but the Court of Final Appeal of the HKSAR, which enjoys final adjudication power. Under section 5 of the Court of Final Appeal Ordinance,[13] the Court of Final Appeal may invite other judges from common law jurisdictions overseas to sit on the bench as non-permanent members. In practice, one non-permanent judge sits together with four permanent Hong Kong judges in each case. All the judges of the pre-1997 legal order have been allowed to continue in office after the handover. In the upper courts judges are still predominantly expatriate, and most judgments are still written exclusively in English.[14]

Human rights are entrenched under Chapter III of the Basic Law. Article 39 specifically states that the provisions of the International Covenant on Civil and Political Rights and the International Covenant on Economic, Social and Cultural Rights "as applied to Hong Kong shall remain in force." This provision provides the basis for judicial review of the constitutionality of Hong Kong legislation in the post-1997 era.[15]

While the above blueprint is aimed at maintaining the autonomy of Hong Kong, and may have presented an impressive profile in terms of the rule of law and the protection of human rights, the real test has to be provided by reality.

A government of laws? The right of abode saga

Few will dispute that the "right of abode" cases are the best cases to illustrate the ambiguous nature of the rule of law at the interface of the "two systems" under the framework of "one country, two systems," the delicate relations between the central government and the HKSAR, the precarious balance among the three branches of the HKSAR government, and the suspicious nature of government–citizen relations in post-colonial Hong

Kong. The fanfare of the controversy can be traced back to the late-colonial period, and the related litigation extends across the whole of post-1997 history to this very date. The battle for the right of abode has also caused tragedies in Hong Kong society.[16] And this fight has lingered on, and has been carried out both in the courtroom and on the streets of Hong Kong. This chapter attempts to capture this struggle through three landmark cases.

The right of abode saga is the product of family and social problems. Many Hong Kong men form their families in mainland China. Their wives and children, however, cannot immediately join them in Hong Kong. Before July 1, 1997, these children had no right of residence in Hong Kong, although they and their mothers could apply for a one-way exit permit from the mainland authorities to settle in Hong Kong. The queue was long and it took many years for the dream of family reunion to be realized. The coming of July 1997, however, apparently presented a glimpse of hope to this group of people, for Article 24 of the Basic Law prescribes six categories of persons who may be considered permanent residents of Hong Kong and entitled to the right of abode. In particular, Article 24(2)(3) provides that children of Chinese nationality born outside Hong Kong to a parent who is a Hong Kong permanent resident are qualified to be Hong Kong permanent residents. Hence, in the months before July 1, 1997, and in the days thereafter, many of these children either entered Hong Kong clandestinely or overstayed the limit of stay under their two-way permits for short visits to Hong Kong. After July 1, 1997, they approached the Immigration Department seeking recognition of their status as permanent residents.

It was when their applications were turned down that a whole series of litigation was triggered.

Cheung Lai Wah and others v. Director of Immigration

Fearing a large influx of migrants, the Immigration Ordinance[17] was amended on July 9, 1997, requiring children in the mainland of Hong Kong permanent residents to follow, before they could come to Hong Kong, the procedure of proving their identity and applying to the mainland authorities for the usual one-way exit permit plus a certificate of entitlement to reside in Hong Kong issued by the Hong Kong authorities. The children's exercise of their right of residence in Hong Kong was in effect postponed until they have applied for and obtained the necessary documentation. As regards children who had already been smuggled into Hong Kong without such documentation before the enactment of the new legislation, the legislation requires them to be sent back to the mainland, where they are supposed to apply to come again in accordance with the proper procedure. In essence, the Ordinance operated retrospectively.

The first constitutional crisis took place when the Immigration Ordinance was challenged by lawyers acting for the parents of some of the children who had already entered Hong Kong before the enactment of the legislation on July 9, 1997, in the famous case of *Cheung Lai Wah and others v. Director of Immigration*.[18]

Of particular relevance to the rule of law is the retrospective nature of the amendment. As pointed out by Johannes Chan, the requirement of having been in possession of a certificate of entitlement before one can enjoy the right of abode is a "fiction," an "impossible requirement which [one] could in no way comply with before July 10, 1997."[19] The Court of First Instance and the Court of Appeal, however, rejected this reasoning. Rather, it was held that the legislation was justified under Article 22(4) of the Basic Law, which provides that people from other parts of China must apply for approval before they can enter the Hong Kong SAR. It was pointed out that Articles 22(4) and 24 should be read together, and that such provisions in the Basic Law should be interpreted broadly and purposively. The majority judgment of the Court of Appeal nevertheless conceded that the new certificate system should not affect any person who had arrived in Hong Kong before July 1, 1997, since Article 22(4) only came into effect on that date. In addition, the court pointed out that the Basic Law is a constitutional document setting out basic principles, and detailed implementation is a matter left to the SAR legislature. In this case, the objective of the legislation is to provide for the orderly settlement in Hong Kong of the children concerned in a staggered manner. The legislation therefore implements the Basic Law and is not inconsistent with it.

The case then went before the Court of Final Appeal (CFA) under the name of *Ng Ka Ling and others v. Director of Immigration*.[20] Simultaneously, the case of *Chan Kam Nga* was also before the CFA.[21] The judgments rendered in these cases by the CFA on January 29, 1999, became the most important and famous judicial decisions in Hong Kong since the 1997 transition, and have far-reaching implications for both the constitutional-political and the socio-economic domains.

In *Ng Ka Ling*, the CFA rejected the interpretation of Article 22(4) adopted by the two courts below and consequently held that the immigration amendment legislation of July 9, 1997, was unconstitutional for its retrospective effect; it was also unconstitutional and invalid insofar as it mandated the possession of the one-way exit permit issued by the mainland authorities (in addition to the certificate of entitlement issued by the SAR government) as a condition precedent for entry to Hong Kong on the part of those mainland residents who, on the commencement of the Basic Law on July 1, 1997, became entitled to the right of abode in Hong Kong.

Under Article 158 of the Basic Law, the CFA is bound, before deciding a case, to refer basic law provisions touching on the relationship between the central authorities and the HKSAR, or on "affairs which are the responsibility of the Central People's Government," to the NPC Standing

Committee for interpretation if the court needs to interpret such a provision and its interpretation would affect the judgment. The CFA in *Ng Ka Ling*, recognized that Article 22(4) of the Basic Law may be a provision of the above nature since it requires people from other parts of China to apply for approval before they can enter the HKSAR. However, in the present case, the CFA decided that it was *not* necessary to refer Article 22 to the Standing Committee because the "substance" of the case was such that Article 24 rather than Article 22 was the "predominant provision" being interpreted by the court.[22]

Chan Kam Nga

On the other hand, in *Chan Kam Nga* the court was asked to rule on the issue of whether Chinese nationals who were born on the mainland before at least one of their parents became a permanent resident of Hong Kong should be granted the right of abode. Here it was argued by the applicants that under Article 24 of the Basic Law Hong Kong permanent residents' children who had the right of abode in Hong Kong included not only persons who were born at a time when at least one of their parents was already a Hong Kong permanent resident, but also any person whose parent subsequently became a Hong Kong permanent resident. Overruling the Court of Appeal judgment in this case, the CFA held that the right of abode of the applicants should be duly recognized, irrespective of the timing of their parents' acquisition of permanent resident status in Hong Kong.

National People's Congress v. Hong Kong Court of Final Appeal

What was most controversial and most provocative in these cases, at least from Beijing's perspective, was that the CFA declared in *Ng Ka Ling* that the Hong Kong courts have full authority (subject to the provisions of the Basic Law) to review the legislative acts of the NPC and its Standing Committee for the purpose of determining whether they are inconsistent with the Basic Law, and to declare such acts invalid if they are determined to be so inconsistent.[23] This particular statement ("Statement") of the constitutional jurisdiction of the Hong Kong courts to review the validity of acts of the NPC and its Standing Committee opened a Pandora's box of constitutional controversy and political struggle, thus precipitating the first constitutional crisis in Hong Kong since the 1997 transition. In a highly publicized seminar reported in Hong Kong and mainland media on February 7, 1999, four leading Chinese law professors, who were also former members of the Drafting Committee for the Basic Law and the Preparatory Committee for the establishment of the SAR, vehemently attacked the Statement, even to the point of saying that it had the effect of placing the Hong Kong courts above the NPC (which is the supreme organ of state power under the

Chinese Constitution) and of turning Hong Kong into an "independent political entity." It was reported that Chinese officials also criticized the Statement as "unconstitutional" and called for its "rectification."

The mainland reaction to the CFA Statement aroused international as well as local concern regarding the rule of law and judicial independence in Hong Kong. The British Consulate in Hong Kong, the U.S. Consulate in Hong Kong and the American Chamber of Commerce in Hong Kong all issued statements expressing concern about the matter and support for the CFA and for judicial autonomy in Hong Kong. These were implicit warnings to the Chinese government against intervention.

Initially, when the judgments were first handed down on January 29, 1999, the SAR government published statements that it would accept the decisions, abide by the principle of the rule of law and implement them. However, in the coming five months, the government retracted its position step by step. On February 24, 1999, the SAR government made the controversial move of applying to the CFA for the relevant part of the judgment of January 29, 1999 (containing the Statement), to be "clarified" on the grounds that the matter was of "great constitutional, public and general importance." The application was heard on the morning of February 26, and in a judgment issued on the afternoon of the same day the CFA exercised its "inherent jurisdictio" to state that:

1   The Hong Kong courts' power to interpret the Basic Law is derived from the NPC Standing Committee under Article 158 of the Basic Law.
2   Any interpretation made by the Standing Committee under Article 158 would be binding on the Hong Kong courts.
3   The judgment of January 29 did not question the authority of the NPC and its Standing Committee "to do any act which is in accordance with the provisions of the Basic Law and the procedure therein."[24]

It was generally accepted by the legal community and public opinion in Hong Kong that the CFA's statement of these additional points did not imply any retreat from its original position as defined in the judgment of January 29, 1999, but it only made explicit what was implicit in the original judgment.[25]

On February 27, 1999, the Legislative Affairs Commission of the NPC Standing Committee issued a statement referring to the CFA's "clarification" and pointing out that it had been essential. A comment made to the press the following day by Vice-Premier Qian Quichen indicated that the constitutional dispute had been brought to an end.

Yet, although Beijing was apparently satisfied, the HKSAR government was not. Making a U-turn from its own statement that it would honor the CFA's judgment, and claiming on the basis of a survey done after the judgment was handed down that 1.67 million mainland Chinese residents would be eligible to enter Hong Kong under the CFA's ruling and could only be accommodated by public spending of HK$700 billion in the next 10 years, the HKSAR government decided to appeal to the Beijing authority nearly four months after the CFA's judgment. It requested that the NPC Standing Committee interpret the relevant provisions of the Basic Law on May 21, 1999. On June 26, 1999, the NPCSC interpreted the Basic Law's Article 24 and Article 22, de facto overturning the CFA's interpretation of the articles. The Interpretation reiterated that the right of abode under Article 24 was subject to Article 22, so that persons falling under Article 24(2)(3) must apply for approval from the mainland authorities to enter the HKSAR. The Interpretation also stated that for a person to qualify under Article 24(2)(3) at least one of his or her parents must already be a Hong Kong permanent resident at the time of the child's birth. The Interpretation stated how the relevant provisions of the Basic Law should be interpreted, but expressly mentioned that the parties to the earlier litigation before the CFA would not be affected by the Interpretation but would be allowed to benefit from the CFA's decisions.[26]

Effectively, the NPCSC's ruling overturned the CFA judgment, and it was perceived by critics as a severe blow to judicial independence in Hong Kong, although it is also possible to see it as a necessary compromise or a situation of no alternative. In any event, the CFA acknowledged the overriding and binding authority of the NPC Standing Committee in subsequent cases.[27]

Executive v. judicial power: Ng Siu Tung & others v. Director of Immigration[28]

The matter did not rest easily with the final verdict of the NPC Standing Committee. On the same day that the NPC Standing Committee's Interpretation was issued in June 1999, the HKSAR government publicly announced that it "will allow persons who arrived in Hong Kong between July 1, 1997 and January 29, 1999, and had claimed the right of abode, to have their status as permanent resident verified in accordance with the [two CFA judgments]."[29] This policy sparked off another round of litigation represented by the case of *Ng Siu Tung*. What was significant about it was that the CFA was ultimately invited to face squarely its own decisions in *Ng Ka Ling* and *Chan Kam Nga* in the context of the NPC Standing Committee's Interpretation.

About 5,000 applicants claimed that they should benefit from the two previous CFA decisions and should not be affected by the NPCSC Interpretation. They argued that, since the two cases were litigated as test cases and the government had on various occasions assured them that their rights would be determined by the court rulings in 1999, they had a "legitimate expectation" to be treated in the same way as the parties in these previous cases. Indeed, the government, including the chief executive, had on at least six different occasions publicly stated that it would respect the court rulings.[30]

Facing the above arguments, the CFA trod a very fine line between NPC directions, the SAR government's policy and the common law doctrine of precedent. Four out of the five judges of the court delivered a cautious judgment in recognizing the rights of about 1,000 claimants. The winners were those who had actually received letters from the Legal Aid Department or the Secretary for Security informing them that it was unnecessary to commence further proceedings or join the actions initiated by Ng or Chan since the government would accept and implement the HKSAR courts' decisions in these cases.

The distinction between written letters and verbal promises from senior officials in the HKSAR was at best technical. Subconsciously, the CFA may have realized this but felt compelled by policy considerations to arrive at this final decision. The Court urged the Director of Immigration to exercise his discretion to mitigate "the unfairness of resiling from representations which have given rise to the legitimate expectation in question"[31] and "the unfairness of disappointing the legitimate expectation to the extent permissible by the law, without undermining the basic statutory scheme."[32] In addition to those who had legitimate expectations, the Court also ruled in favor of those claimants who arrived before the handover but were born before at least one of their parents had become a Hong Kong permanent resident. Other claimants who only relied on the oral statements made by government officials lost their case.

The final chapter of the right of abode saga was, however, not immediately in sight. The struggle still persisted: for instance, 88 abode-seekers filed another action against the government, claiming loss and damages due to maladministration, misrepresentations and mis-statements on the part of the government.[33] Ronny Tong, the former chairman of the Bar Association, accused the government of failing to exercise the discretion imposed by the CFA.[34] Despite the various personal plights of many individual claimants, the government has insisted on a firm stance of repatriation.[35]

Regardless of the outcome of the based on individuals' litigation circumstances, many could not hold back their grievances against the government. Understandably, the abode-seekers "harbour a profound sense of injustice."[36] From their perspective, the final outcome of the *Ng Siu Tung* case rewards those who sneaked into Hong Kong or overstayed there before July 1, 1997, and penalizes those who followed government advice not to initiate legal proceedings. From the perspective of others, the executive's immigration policy and the legislature's decree have trumped the rights upheld by the courts. Though the government has argued that the right of abode case was a very exceptional one, in which it was compelled to seek the intervention of central authority, and that the rule of law has not been compromised because the Basic Law itself authorizes the NPC Standing Committee to interpret it, critics have concluded that judicial autonomy and the rule of law in the HKSAR are, in the final analysis, dependent on executive restraint and Beijing's hopefully developing constitutional convention of non-intervention. In other words, contrary to the practice of common law systems, the Hong Kong judiciary may not always have the final word on what the law means. The critics have highlighted the risk that the rule of law in Hong Kong may be easily reduced to an instrument of the SAR executive and of Beijing and become "rule by law," in the sense that whenever policy or efficiency so demands the rule of law has to yield.

The rule of law and human rights: freedom of religion and freedom of the press

Closely related to the right of abode dispute, the anti-subversion clause under Article 23 of the Basic Law also enables one to appreciate the sensitive nature of the rule of law and human rights in Hong Kong, particularly on issues touching upon the mainland China–HKSAR relationship. The HKSAR government is required by this article to enact laws prohibiting treason, sedition,[37] subversion, secession and theft of state secrets.[38] For five years, the HKSAR has delayed the matter and has successfully warded off any suggestion to enact a law in the above regard.[39] Relying on the rule of law principles of certainty and predictability, critics have pointed out that the most problematic aspect of Article 23 is its vagueness, breadth and unknown parameters. Subversion and secession are alien concepts to the common law system. Under Chinese law, they used to be classified broadly under the vague but omnipotent umbrella of "counter-revolutionary offences."[40] At present, they are grouped under the offenses of "acts endangering state security."

Before 1997, the British Hong Kong government made an attempt to adapt the Crimes Ordinance to the requirements of Article 23.[41] The attempt failed became of Beijing's opposition and the lack of local consensus. Thus, there is a vacuum in the existing legislation.

Despite the uncertainty, most Hong Kong people are familiar with the famous Chinese dissidents Wang Dan and Wei Jingshen, who were sentenced to imprisonment for "subverting" the Chinese government.[42] China has warned Hong Kong repeatedly not to be a subversive base for Chinese dissidents, and Hong Kong citizens understand that part of Article 23 was inserted into the Basic Law after the 1989 Tiananmen students' movement.

The absence of a definitive interpretation coupled with an authoritarian attitude on the part of the mainland government has rendered the rights of certain groups uncertain. The potential victims at this time are Falun Gong and the press.

Freedom of religion: Falun Gong

Falun Gong is mainly a breath-taking exercise group, which claims to inherit the wisdom of Buddhism, Taoism, and Chinese *qigong*.[43] Despite its seemingly benign nature, the Chinese government has condemned the group as an "evil cult" and is determined to wipe out its existence. As a result of the large-scale gathering of more than 10,000 followers of Falun Gong surrounding Zhongnanhai, the Chinese leadership's compound in Beijing, on April 25, 1999, the mainland government was alarmed and since has viewed the group as a serious threat to the stability of the country.[44] Through various statements issued by the ministries of the State Council, the Supreme People's Court,[45] and the Standing Committee of the National People's Congress,[46] Falun Gong has been banned on the mainland since July 1999.

While Falun Gong is theoretically a lawful group in Hong Kong, its activities have come under increasing scrutiny by the HKSAR government, and pressure is mounting to enact laws under Article 23 of the Basic Law. On the mainland, the movement against Falun Gong intensified after an incident in early 2001, where on the eve of the Chinese New Year five people who were believed to be Falun Gong members set themselves on fire in the middle of Tiananmen Square, Beijing. While the group denied any connection with the act, the Chinese government hardened its stance against Falun Gong.

The tense atmosphere in the north gradually had its impact felt in the HKSAR. In February 2001, Tung Chee-hwa, the chief executive, finally broke his silence on Falun Gong and branded the group as "more or less bearing some characteristics of an evil cult."[47] In March 2001 President Jiang Zemin reminded Tung and Hong Kong that Falun Gong was an "evil cult" and of the importance of "stability" for the territory.[48] In June 2001 the chief executive echoed President Jiang's condemnation and relabeled the group as "undoubtedly an evil cult."[49]

Tung's escalation of comments was matched by parallel government actions. It was revealed that, between June 2001 and February 2002, Falun Gong had applied to rent venues under the Leisure and Cultural Services Department and two universities 36 times, but had been rejected 27 times without substantive reason.[50] It was also alleged that police officers had taken an unusually active role in soliciting citizens' opinions on the protest activity of Falun Gong so that they could consider possible reasons for arrest.[51] These types of political censorship may prove harder for the group to tackle than legal crackdown. Their freedom is shrinking but there is no legal mechanism that they can use to challenge the authorities. Freedom of religion may easily turn out to be an empty guarantee.

In April 2002, speculation had it that Beijing had given its signal that a law should be passed to ban any subversive activities, and the law was likely to affect the status of Falun Gong in Hong Kong.[52] In an interview with

Hong Kong journalists in late June 2002, the Chinese vice-premier, Qian Qichen, discussed the Falun Gong issue in the context of Article 23 of the Basic Law, and pointed out that if the Hong Kong Falun Gong association "creates many problems through its continuous links with overseas Falun Gong," then it will fall foul of the legislation under Article 23.[53]

The Falun Gong issue in Hong Kong attracted international attention in August 2002. On August 15, a 26-day trial of 16 Falun Gong activists (including four Swiss nationals and one New Zealander) was concluded, and the magistrate convicted all the activists for causing obstruction to a public place.[54] Some of them were also convicted for obstructing the police or assaulting police officers. Fines ranging from HK$1,300 to HK$3,800 (U.S.$165–485) were imposed on the offenders. The prosecution related to a peaceful and small-scale demonstration staged by the activists outside the building of the Liaison Office of the central government in Hong Kong on March 14. After persisting for four hours, during which the police issued repeated warnings that they should leave, the demonstrators (some of whom were performing Falun Gong meditation and some of whom were standing behind them and holding a banner) were forcibly removed by the police. Falun Gong spokesmen and human rights activists in Hong Kong condemned the prosecution as politically motivated and as a form of persecution of the Falun Gong in Hong Kong. Lawyers pointed out that the charge of public obstruction (mainly used against illegal hawkers in practice) has seldom been used against protestors in the past, and the decision bodes ill for freedom of public demonstration in Hong Kong. Falun Gong activists have vowed to appeal the decision to the higher courts in Hong Kong.

Freedom of the press

If Article 23 is a time bomb for Falun Gong, it is a sword of Damocles for the Hong Kong press. Journalists were concerned about the subversion and secession clauses, fearing that reporting on "sensitive" issues in Tibet, Taiwan, and Xinjiang would amount to "advocating" the "splitting up" of China. Stein describes Article 23 as an "unnervingly ambiguous section"[55] that contributes to self-censorship in the coverage of political news in the above dangerous zones.

As early as 1995, mainland leaders had already warned the Hong Kong media not to "advocate" "two Chinas" and not to "put forward political attacks on Chinese leaders."[56] After the handover, the first test came when the former president, Lee Teng-hui, of the Republic of China (Taiwan) announced his "state to state" theory in July 1999, implying that Taiwan was an independent state.[57] The media was very careful to position its stance. When Hong Kong's official radio station (RTHK) gave airtime to Cheng An-guo, Taiwan's representative in Hong Kong, during which he reiterated the view of President Lee, the radio was condemned by pro-Beijing forces in Hong Kong. China's premier, Qian Qichen, warned Hong Kong's media not to "advocate" any speech against the one-China policy.[58] On March 29, 2000, Cable TV of Hong Kong interviewed the vice-president of Taiwan, Annette Lu, who referred to mainland China as a "remote relative and a close neighbor." Though Cable TV is a private organization, this did not exempt it from the attack of Beijing officials. Wang Fengchao, the deputy director of the central government's Hong Kong SAR Liaison Office, warned Hong Kong's media not to "advocate" or disseminate" pro-Taiwan independence views. He also called for speedier legislation on anti-subversion activities for the purpose of the implementation of Article 23 of the Basic Law.[59]

A note on Article 23 and the rule of law

In the light of the above discussion, the publication on September 24, 2002, of the government's Consultation Document on *Proposals to Implement Article 23 of the Basic Law* was one of the most important constitutional and legal developments in the Hong Kong SAR since it was established. The three-month consultation exercise on this Document ended in December after a demonstration on December 15, 2002, of nearly 60,000 people against the legislative proposal. In response the government amended the proposal by giving several major "concessions" on its substance, but rejected the call for a White Bill – a bill published for public consultation but not yet introduced into the Legislative Council. The National Security (Legislative Provisions) Bill, designed to implement Article 23, was introduced into the legislature in February 2003. During the Bills Committee's deliberations the government agreed to some amendments. However, critics said that the amendments were insufficient, and in any event the government's timetable of passing the Bill in the Legislative Council's week-long meeting beginning on July 9 did not allow sufficient time for deliberation. Meanwhile, the onslaught of SARS (severe acute respiratory syndrome, or atypical pneumonia) in March 2003 distracted public attention from the Bill. As Hong Kong began to recover from the SARS crisis in June, opponents of the Bill woke members of the public up to the fact that the Bill was to be pushed through the legislature in early July. On July 1, 2003, a hot summer day which was also a public holiday marking the sixth anniversary of Hong Kong's return to China and the last day of the new Premier Wen Jiabao's visit to Hong Kong, half a million Hong Kong residents took to the streets to demonstrate against the Article 23 legislative exercise and to express other grievances against the Tung Chee-hwa administration. Surprised themselves by the large turnout, opponents of the Bill demanded that the Bill be shelved, and planned to organize a rally of tens of thousands surrounding the Legislative Council on July 9 if proceedings on the Bill were to go ahead on that day. The SAR government finally decided to postpone the Bill – the decision came three hours after the Liberal Party withdrew from the "governing coalition" of political parties in protest against the Tung administration's original decision on July 5 to give three major "concessions" on the content of the Bill and at the same time to adhere to the July 9 deadline for the passage of the Bill.[60]

The legislative exercise on Article 23 has become a major test of whether the concept of "one country, two systems" as enshrined in the Basic Law can be implemented in such a way that a proper balance is struck between the "one country" principle and the "two systems" principle, between which a tension has always existed. The issues at stake are large, fundamental and controversial ones. They have also attracted widespread international attention, particularly after the march of half a million Hong Kong residents on July 1, 2003.[61] Will civil liberties and the rule of law continue to thrive in the HKSAR? Or will the mainland control over words, activities, and organizations that are perceived to challenge the regime or otherwise threaten the "sovereignty, territorial integrity, unity, and national security" of China[62] be extended to the SAR? History will soon witness how these questions are to be resolved.

Equality before the law: the discretion not to prosecute

Another core ideal of the rule of law as understood by the Hong Kong community is equality before the law. Those who have committed the same offense under like circumstances should be given the same treatment. This simple principle faced its challenge shortly after 1997. On several occasions, the government has decided not to prosecute individuals belonging to the elite in society. Such decisions are perceived by many to have cast serious doubt on the impartiality of the government and the neutrality of the legal system.

The political elite: the Sally Aw case

The most notorious among these decisions is probably the Sally Aw Sian case in 1998. At the time of the controversy, Aw was the chairperson of the newspaper group that published the *Hong Kong Standard* and the *Sing Tao Daily News*.[63]On March 17, 1998, the Department of Justice initiated the prosecution of one former and two current members of the senior management of the *Hong Kong Standard* newspaper. One of the charges was that they conspired with Sally Aw to artificially inflate the circulation record of the newspaper in order to defraud purchasers of advertising space in the newspaper. Although Aw was named in the charge, she herself was not prosecuted. A huge uproar was immediately caused among members of the public. The matter was especially alarming in view of the fact that Aw used to have close business ties with Tung Chee-hwa, the chief executive; she is a member of the National Committee of the Chinese People's Political Consultative Conference, and is highly respected by the mainland authorities.

When the three defendants were later convicted of the offenses of conspiracy to defraud and false accounting and were sentenced to imprisonment, there was mounting pressure from the public on the Secretary for Justice, Elsie Leung, to offer an explanation for her decision not to prosecute Aw. Eventually, on February 4, 1999, Leung appeared before the Legislative Council's Panel on the Administration of Justice and Legal Services to present a statement on her decision. Leung cited various evidential considerations and public-interest considerations in defending her decision. While one might not be convinced by her analysis on the evidential point, what was most outrageous was her interpretation of what constituted public interest. Leung explained that the prosecution of Aw would aggravate the Sing Tao group's financial difficulties, thus causing serious obstacles to its negotiation with the banks on the prospect of restructuring. This would in turn lead to the laying-off of staff and more unemployment in Hong Kong. Leung also pointed out that the collapse of a famous media group in Hong Kong shortly after the handover would send a bad message to the international community.[64]

Leung's explanation proved only to be counterproductive and worsened her position. The logic of her reasons would imply that the government should not prosecute any big companies as this would affect their business planning and their employees. If one stretches this logic, one may conclude that the rich and powerful should enjoy special privileges in society. The reasoning of not prosecuting a media group for fear of sending the wrong signals to the international community was equally not persuasive. The international community would probably be more alarmed and disturbed by the fact that Hong Kong's government was willing to shelter the corrupt and unscrupulous practices of a media giant.

A motion of no confidence in Leung was introduced in the Legislative Council and was debated on March 11, 1999. Leung survived by a narrow margin of 30 to 21 votes, with eight abstentions. This incident, however, was only the first of a series of controversial incidents involving the exercise of prosecutorial discretion in post-1997 Hong Kong.

Family ties

Later incidents have added to the public perception that the prosecuting authorities in Hong Kong do not always exercise their power in a fair manner. In July 2000 they decided not to prosecute Godfrey Nguyen, the son of Mr. Justice Nguyen, a judge of the Court of First Instance of the High Court. Godfrey Nguyen was found to be in possession of two tablets of Ecstasy, a well-known party drug. He was 21 years old at that time, with a clean record. What concerned the public was that the prosecution had decided not to offer evidence against him upon his agreeing to be bound over for good behavior for the sum of HK$2,000 for two years. The explanation by the government was that the "consequences of prosecution would be out of proportion to the seriousness of the offence" and "it was not necessary in the public interest to pursue [the] prosecution."[65] Yet this was apparently inconsistent with the previous approach, whereby the government had stressed that punishment must be levied so that the correct message could be sent to deter youngsters from abusing drugs.[66]

Senior government officials

During the same year of 2000, Poon Kai-tak, the then assistant director of housing, was found to have stolen a computer magazine from a bookstore and assaulted a shop assistant when confronted. Once again, the prosecution decided not to offer evidence against him upon his agreeing to be bound over for one year for $2,000. The explanation offered by Poon was that he was under immense work pressure and was on medication due to psychiatric problems at the time of the alleged shoplifting. Magistrate Peter White remarked that the decision not to prosecute Poon was consistent with government policy, which had taken into account the suspect's good character and the small likelihood of re-offending.[67]

A similar incident happened in 2001 concerning a senior government counsel, Au Yuen-hwa, who was caught stealing a handbag in a department store in August 2001. It was later revealed that Ms. Au had a previous record of committing the same type of offense. In April 2002 the prosecution decided to drop the case against Ms. Au as she had a history of psychiatric disorders and was under treatment at the time of the alleged incident.[68] Ms. Au had also agreed to be bound over for one year for HK$2,000. The director of public prosecutions, Grenville Cross, explained that the Department of Justice had sought independent legal advice from private barristers before coming to the decision. Furthermore, Cross also pointed out that there were 4,734 cases of shoplifting, and the Department of Justice had exercised the discretion not to prosecute in 81 cases.[69] The government argued that this discretion was not a privilege reserved for the rich, the powerful, or those who are perceived to be "friends" of the ruling hierarchy.

Confusing signals

While all these explanations may be valid, critics argue that it is essential to have a consistent prosecution policy, and like cases should be treated alike so that the principle of rule of law is upheld and seen to be upheld. After the Nguyen incident, 36 people who were arrested for possessing small quantities of soft drugs or shoplifting asked the Department of Justice to drop the charges against them, but only three have succeeded.[70] Magistrate White himself, who was on the bench for the Poon case, confessed openly that he was confused by the prosecution policy. Relying on the principle of consistency and rule of law, he felt that he was compelled to let 40 suspected shoplifters go free. Nevertheless, he was reprimanded by the Court of Appeal for setting his own standard in sentencing.[71] Though the government has repeatedly stressed that its role is "prosecutor not persecutor," unless everyone can escape the fate of prosecution upon the production of medical evidence in a shoplifting offense, it is difficult to see how the above cases do not constitute a departure from the norm for like cases. Such leniency in selected cases has apparently shaken public confidence in the legal system in Hong Kong. For example, immediately after the Nguyen incident, an opinion poll showed that over 67 per cent of the respondents admitted that they now had less confidence in the legal system.[72]

The controversy surrounding the Public Order Ordinance

Another burning issue in the post-handover era concerns the rights of assembly, procession, and demonstration. These rights are popularly asserted as civil rights of citizens, and, as they may be used to challenge those in power, the legal limit of such rights reflects the regime's level of tolerance of dissenting voices. Under Article 27 of the Basic Law, Hong Kong residents are entitled to the above rights. After the handover in 1997, the locals are eager to exercise and assert these rights, which has resulted in frequent confrontations between police and protestors, and a test for the rule of law in Hong Kong.

Famous stories that have hit the headlines include the police attempt to drown out protestors' voices when they were shouting slogans against leaders in the mainland right at the moment of political transition on July 1, 1997;[73] the discovery that the police were filming prominent activists during demonstrations with video cameras in 1999;[74] the arrest of student leaders for illegal assembly in 2000;[75] and the forced partition of demonstrators into small groups of 20 and the zoning of demonstrations into districts far from the conference site during the Fortune Global Forum in May 2001.[76] The year 2002 was a volatile one marked by high tensions. The police banned the proposed demonstration outside the Central Government Office to commemorate the 13th anniversary of the June 4 Tiananmen event, although the demonstration was allowed at a nearby spot.[77] They handcuffed news reporters in their coverage of a protest staged by abode-seekers when the reporters refused to stay within the designated area.[78] They arrested and prosecuted a high-profile social campaigner and two student leaders for organizing a demonstration without complying with the legal requirement of prior notification of the police.[79] Some suspected the government's tightening attitude might have been related to the preparation for the fifth anniversary celebrations of the handover on July 1, 2002, when President Jiang Zemin visited Hong Kong.

Regardless of the heat and noise in different encounters between policemen and protestors, the core of the debate is the Public Order Ordinance.[80] Before its amendment in 1995, the Ordinance had been perceived as an instrument of suppression ever since its enactment at the time of the pro-communist riots against colonial rule in 1967. The 1967 version of the law[81] was itself a consolidation of various pieces of pre-existing legislation. Under the Public Order Ordinance as revised in 1980, there existed a licensing system for gatherings in public places in Hong Kong.[82] But in 1995 the Ordinance was amended as part of an exercise to bring Hong Kong law in line with the International Covenant on Civil and Political Rights, and a simple notification system was introduced to replace the license system.[83] However, the sudden liberalization in late-colonial days only convinced the Chinese government that the reform was maliciously motivated and aimed at reducing the legitimate public order regulatory powers of the SAR government. The NPC Standing Committee, when exercising its power under the Basic Law to determine which Hong Kong laws were inconsistent with the Basic Law and could not survive the handover, nullified the amendments in February 1997.[84] The Provisional Legislative Council of Hong Kong enacted a new version of the Public Order Ordinance in mid-1997,[85] which was believed to be a halfway house between the licensing and notification systems.

Under the present system, organizers of public assemblies of more than 50 people and marches of more than 30 must obtain a letter of no objection from the police seven days in advance.[86] Under Section 17A of the Ordinance, any failure to do so is a criminal offense and one may face up to five years' imprisonment. The government argued that the existing Ordinance was not a license system as there was a deeming clause in Section 14(4), which provides that if the commissioner of police does not notify the applicant of his objection within the time limit specified, then notice of no objection is deemed to be given.[87] However, the requirements of notification and approval have been criticized as a license system in disguise.[88] Moreover, under the 1997 version of the law the government also has the power to prohibit a public meeting or procession on the grounds of "national security" and "the protection of the rights and freedoms of others," in addition to the pre-existing grounds of "public safety" and "public order."[89]

While the ground of "national security" remains untested after the handover, the requirement of obtaining notice of no objection has proved to be controversial. Of particular difficulty and relevance to the debate in Hong Kong about the rule of law is that the Public Order Ordinance has vested much power in the authorities, which has apparently been applied by the HKSAR government in a selective manner. The heart of the problem

may lie in the inherent nature of the Ordinance itself. The stringent requirements of the Ordinance are such that if the government were to practice the
rule of law strictly and to enforce the legal requirement of notification vigi-
lantly, then large numbers of people would have to be prosecuted, with the
likely consequence that the law would be condemned by local and international public opinion as an "evil" or "unjust" law. According to official
figures in the period between July 1997 and March 2002, about one in seven
public rallies were in fact held without notifying the police in advance.[90] On
the other hand, if the law is not enforced it will become a dead letter in the
statute book, and this would be contrary to the rule of law principle that the
government should faithfully put the law into practice and implement it
without discrimination. As the government tried hard to resolve this legal
quagmire, it apparently chose to tread a midway path[91] by selectively
enforcing the Ordinance. This inconsistency in the government's approach
towards unauthorized demonstrations makes a mockery of the Ordinance
and adds fury to the public debate, as can be seen in the following cases.

Arrest of student leaders in 2000

The first case when the HKSAR government flexed its muscles in reliance
on the notification clause under the Public Order Ordinance took place in
2000, when seven student leaders were arrested. This caused a huge uproar,
and the arrest eventually ended in a decision not to prosecute.

The incident started on April 20, 2000, when 60 students demonstrated
against a proposal to alter university tuition fees. This was closely followed
by another demonstration where students showed their support for abode-
seekers on the anniversary of the reinterpretation of the Basic Law by the
NPC Standing Committee on June 26, 2000.[92] This latter event turned into
a bitter and violent confrontation when pepper spray was used by the
police against protestors.[93] On both occasions, prior notice of the demonstration was not given to the police. It was not until August 2000 that the
police arrested some suspects involved in these two incidents for organizing and joining illegal assemblies and obstructing the police. These
suspects included seven student leaders, eight abode-seekers, and one
supporter.

The arrest of the students immediately provoked a heated debate and
aroused general sympathy for the students. More than 500 academics and
researchers signed a petition to support them,[94] about 1,000 people marched
on the street without notifying the police in open defiance of the Public
Order Ordinance,[95] and the Hong Kong Bar Association condemned the
police for singling out students for arrest.[96]

Under mounting pressure, by the end of October 2000 the Secretary for
Justice decided not to prosecute the student leaders and other protestors,[97]
though the student leaders vowed once again to exercise their right of civil

disobedience against the Ordinance.[98] As an attempt to cure the "headaches" caused by the Public Order Ordinance,[99] the government initiated a motion debate in the Legislative Council on the retention of the Ordinance in its existing form on December 20, 2000. After a vigorous debate, the majority voted in favor of the status quo.[100]

The arrest and prosecution of the trio in 2002

While the student protestors narrowly escaped prosecution in 2000, the government had apparently hardened its stance and lost its patience by 2002. The first case that the HKSAR government decided to prosecute protestors for violation of the non-notification clause under the Public Order Ordinance was launched on May 9, 2002. On that day, veteran protestor Leung Kwok-hung (who belonged to the April 5 Action Group, a Trotskyite group) and two student activists were charged with organizing an unauthorized public assembly or assisting in organizing one on May 9, 2002.[101] Rather than issuing a court summons against the suspects, two of them were arrested at their homes in the early morning, while the third gave himself up to the police. The cause of the arrest and subsequent prosecution was that in February 2002 the three defendants had staged a protest against the imprisonment of Sunny Leung Chun-wai, who was jailed for obstructing the police and assaulting a police officer by shouting into his ear through a loudhailer at an earlier protest.[102] On November 25, 2002, the three activists were convicted for organizing an unauthorized public procession and for failing to notify the police under section 17A(3)(b)(i) of the Public Order Ordinance.[103] Each of them was fined HK$500 and was required to be bound over for three months. Magistrate Mr. Patrick Li held that the "notification system" for processions was a reasonable requirement for maintaining the *ordre public* of Hong Kong society. However, he did not address the question of whether "selective prosecution" under the Public Order Ordinance was a violation of the cardinal spirit of the rule of law. The three activists decided to appeal. Due to the significant constitutional implications of the case, the appeal will be heard before the Court of Appeal rather than the High Court.[104] Thus the final outcome of this case on the right to peaceful assembly in Hong Kong remains to be seen.

Although the government has denied vehemently that the decision to prosecute in this case was politically motivated,[105] it is hard to convince the public that this unprecedented move against a few high-profile protestors is the result of a consistent and fair policy in the implementation of the Public Order Ordinance. On the contrary, critics view it as the government's attempt to silence opposing voices, since Leung is often seen as a professional protestor and a leader of a radical political group, and the student activists are prominent members of the Hong Kong Federation of Students, a vocal critic of government policy.

The significance of the Public Order Ordinance

In targeting specific persons or groups for arrest and prosecution, the government seems to have moved beyond the maintenance of public order and the prevention of breaches of the peace. What is now at stake is the citizens' right to peaceful demonstrations as a way of expressing opinions. The authorities' obsession with the technical rule of notification and its enforcement makes people wonder whether Hong Kong is now no better off than it was in colonial days, when under the licensing system the police had extensive control over public demonstrations. In these circumstances, the act of protesting easily escalates into a gesture of civil disobedience, by which protestors deliberately and blatantly violate unreasonable legal rules in order to arouse social awareness and sympathy so as to put pressure on the government to change an unjust law.[106] The story of the Public Order Ordinance is thus a vivid illustration of the ambiguous relationship between the rule of law and human rights: Where the law does not uphold a human right but is perceived to have infringed it, does the rule of law require that the law be enforced uniformly and consistently? Is selective enforcement or complete non-enforcement consistent with the rule of law? Is the law itself consistent with the rule of law?

Despite the fact that decades have passed, it seems that little has changed in terms of the right to demonstrate in Hong Kong. Describing the ordinance in the 1970s, Mushkat remarked that freedom of assembly was marked by the "arbitrary exercise of police power and selective enforcement of the law."[107] Thirty years later, Loh echoed this view by describing the post-handover right to demonstrate as characterized by "planned intimidation...prominent deployment of force and selective targeting."[108] The only consolation in the pending case of the trio is that there is chance that the case will be appealed all the way up to the Court of Final Appeal, so that the constitutionality of the Public Order Ordinance can be fully argued and reviewed.

The Cyberport dispute

Hong Kong prides itself in being a capitalistic, free, and open economy. Nevertheless, the events since 1997 discussed earlier in this chapter have to some extent tarnished the image of Hong Kong. According to the Economist Intelligence Unit's (EIU) forecast, Hong Kong's position in the global ranking of best business environment has fallen from fifth place in 1997 to 11th in 2002.[109] It was estimated before 1997 that Hong Kong would have had the best business environment in Asia from 1997 to 2001. But in the 2002 study Hong Kong's place in Asia had been taken by Singapore. The EIU attributed the downgrading of Hong Kong's position to the erosion of Hong Kong's political autonomy from the mainland, the continuously deteriorating economic condition, the lack of relevant skills among workers, and the concerns regarding favoritism by the government towards certain firms.

The lack of government transparency in granting projects may best be illustrated in the Cyberport Project. The project aimed to develop in Hong Kong an equivalent of the Silicon Valley in the U.S. It was planned in 1999 that an ultra-modern high-tech complex equipped with the latest telecommunication, information, and computer facilities would be built so as to attract the world's leading information technology (IT) firms to the HKSAR. The project was to take up two-thirds of a 26-hectare complex, while the rest would be residential developments to be sold. The cost of the project was estimated to be $13 billion. The project was awarded to the Pacific Century Group, owned by Richard Li Tzar-kai, son of the property tycoon Li Ka Shing, without public tender.[110]

The deal was under attack for alleged cronyism, but the government defended it as a "practical approach" to save time.[111] Some legislators and local firms questioned the decision, but the government remained resolute. As critics point out, if the essence of the rule of law is transparency and fairness, the style in which the HKSAR government has run its political, legal, and economic affairs leaves much to be desired.

Reflections on competing conceptions of the rule of law

In the light of the twists and turns, ups and downs since the handover, the story of the rule of law in the HKSAR may be interpreted as a continuing and evolving debate about the meaning and significance of the rule of law in Hong Kong. When Hong Kong was a colony, it was for the British "borrowed time, borrowed place." For the Hong Kong Chinese, the English-style legal institutions imported into Hong Kong constituted no more than a borrowed legal system. Operated in a foreign language by predominantly expatriate judges, lawyers, and law draftsmen, the legal system was perceived as an alien imposition. It was also an instrument of colonial rule rather than a protector of rights and liberties, for until the 1980s the standards of legal protection of human rights in Hong Kong were lower than those in Britain itself.

The irony of history is such that since the 1980s the people of Hong Kong have embraced the transplanted legal system as their own. They have become more and more vigilant regarding their human and legal rights; they increasingly cherish and are more eager than ever before to defend what they believe to be the ideals of the rule of law. The battle for the defense of the rule of law in Hong Kong has been fought against the background understanding or assumption that there is no rule of law across the border in mainland China. Ever since the conclusion of the Sino-British Joint Declaration in 1984, which provided for Hong Kong's eventual return to Chinese rule in 1997, the people of Hong Kong have identified themselves as a people under the rule of law, which constitutes their distinctive identity vis-à-vis the people living in mainland China.

Hong Kong is a small jurisdiction with only a small legal profession, and an even smaller community of legal academics. Very few among them have written about the theory or philosophy of the rule of law. Those who do write usually confine themselves to popularizing notions of the rule of law in Western jurisprudence and have not ventured to develop original ideas relating to the rule of law in the Hong Kong context. The "Hong Kong conception of the rule of law," if there is one, is thus not to be found in the legal literature of Hong Kong.

This does not mean, however, that it is entirely meaningless or futile to talk about the Hong Kong conception of the rule of law. The Hong Kong community, or at least its more reflective and vocal members, does have its own ideas of the rule of law. Those in Hong Kong have not explicitly formulated them in academic articles or books, but the public discourse and debate there about issues relating to the rule of law do reveal their assumptions, presuppositions, and beliefs regarding what the rule of law is and what it means for Hong Kong.

What Hong Kong can feel proud of is that there has been, ever since the 1980s, a lively and vigorous public discussion about issues relating to the rule of law, and this discussion not only has not declined, but has actually intensified since the handover in 1997. The incidents mentioned in this chapter are but some examples of such discussion, and this chapter has by no means provided an exhaustive account. However, even on the basis of the limited evidence provided in this chapter, one can glimpse the vitality of the public debate on the rule of law in Hong Kong.

For the sake of analysis and further research, we venture to suggest that the public debate regarding the rule of law in Hong Kong, particularly as it has developed in the post-1997 era, can be analyzed in terms of two dimensions:

- the distinction between what Peerenboom, in Chapter 1, calls the "thin" conception and the "thick" conception of the rule of law;
- the distinction between what we call the "fundamentalist" conception and the "pragmatic" conception of the rule of law.

As defined by Peerenboom, the "thin" conception of the rule of law understands the rule of law in formal and procedural terms. "Lon Fuller's influential account that laws be general, public, prospective, clear, consistent, capable of being followed, stable and enforced"[112] is a classic statement of this conception of the rule of law.

Peerenboom also points out that the "thin" conception of the rule of law is often embedded in a particular version of the "thick" conception of the rule of law, which prescribes substantive ideals regarding political, economic, and social arrangements with which law and legal institutions are inextricably intertwined. Referring to the case of contemporary China, Peerenboom distinguishes between four versions of the "thick" conception: Statist Socialism, Neo-authoritarian, Communitarian, and Liberal Democratic.[113] He also points out that the liberal democratic version of the rule of law predominates in the Western world: "Indeed, for many, 'the rule of law' *means* a liberal democratic version of rule of law."[114] Central to this version of the rule of law are "free market capitalism," "multiparty democracy" and "a liberal interpretation of human rights that gives priority to civil and political rights over economic, social, cultural and collective or group rights."[115]

We now turn to the second dimension – the distinction between "fundamentalist" and "pragmatic" conceptions of the rule of law. According to what we call the fundamentalist conception of the rule of law, certain principles that form integral components of the rule of law (in either its thin version or its thick version) are sacred and inviolable, and cannot be sacrificed even if there are weighty policy considerations that suggest otherwise. The "fundamentalists" (defined here as adherents to the fundamentalist conception of the rule of law) will criticize any departure from these principles as a serious violation of the rule of law. They are also extremely vigilant regarding any speech or action that may ultimately lead to a violation of the rule of law, even if the speech or action does not in itself amount to such a violation.

The "pragmatists" (defined here as adherents to the pragmatic conception of the rule of law) recognize the importance of these principles as forming parts of the concept of the rule of law (in either its thin version or its thick version) but are open to other considerations that also deserve to be taken seriously. According to this pragmatic approach, whether an action should be criticized as a violation of the rule of law should not be determined exclusively by reference to these principles, but should be determined after the other considerations have been fully taken into account. The pragmatists are also willing to be more flexible in their interpretation of the principles of the rule of law. The concept of the rule of law is not a closed system, but is open to interaction with other considerations.

Using the two dimensions mentioned above, we may classify the following schools of thought which are of particular relevance to Hong Kong:

- fundamentalist adherents to the thin conception of the rule of law ("fundamentalist thin theorists");
- pragmatic adherents to the thin conception of the rule of law ("pragmatic thin theorists");
- fundamentalist adherents to the liberal democratic version of the thick conception of the rule of law ("fundamentalist liberals");

- pragmatic adherents to the liberal democratic version of the thick conception of the rule of law ("pragmatic liberals");
- adherents to a non-liberal version of the thick conception of the rule of law ("non-liberals"), who can also at the same time be thin theorists (of either the fundamentalist or pragmatic blend).

The experience of Hong Kong in recent years seems to suggest that the most vocal critics of the government on rule of law issues (such as the Democratic Party, the Hong Kong Bar Association, and a number of legislators, including Margaret Ng, Audrey Eu, and Emily Lau) are what we call "fundamentalist liberals" or "fundamentalist thin theorists," whereas most defenders of the government (such as the Democratic Alliance for the Betterment of Hong Kong and legislators who are regarded as "pro-China" or "pro-establishment") are "pragmatic thin theorists" or "non-liberals." One of the co-authors of this chapter would consider himself a "pragmatic liberal" – someone who believes in the liberal democratic version of the rule of law (and not just the thin conception), but who also believes that this should not be turned into a dogma in a fundamentalist manner.

Take the example of the "right of abode" cases. The fundamentalist thin theorists and fundamentalist liberals have been extremely critical of the SAR government's application to the Court of Final Appeal for "clarification" of its judgment *Ng Ka Ling* (after Beijing expressed its displeasure), and of the government's reference of Articles 22 and 24 of the Basic Law to the NPC Standing Committee for interpretation. They believe that both moves constitute serious violations of the rule of law in both its thin and its liberal democratic version. In their view, the "clarification" application was unprecedented and was not clearly provided for in the law of procedure, and could only be regarded as politically motivated. They also believe that the invitation to the NPC Standing Committee to interpret the Basic Law is a flagrant violation of the rule of law principle that the independent judiciary should be the ultimate interpreter of the law and guardian of constitutional rights (which principle can be regarded as forming either part of the thin conception of the rule of law or part of the liberal democratic conception).

On the other hand, the pragmatic thin theorists, pragmatic liberals and non-liberals believe that the "right of abode" episode should not be interpreted as a grave departure from the rule of law in Hong Kong. It is true that Beijing expressed displeasure regarding the Court of Final Appeal's assertion in *Ng Ka Ling* that it had the power to review the validity of the acts of the NPC and its Standing Committee, but the question raised by Beijing was a legitimate one regarding the scope of the jurisdiction of the Hong Kong courts relative to the national legislature. There was, at least potentially, a genuine constitutional dispute between Beijing and Hong Kong, and a means had to be found of resolving this constitutional crisis. In these circumstances, the application for a "clarification" from the court itself was an innovative but lawful and acceptable solution. As for the reference to the NPC Standing Committee for interpretation of the Basic Law, the pragmatists believe that this is also an acceptable means of dealing with the social crisis of massive immigration, particularly in view of the fact that the Basic Law and the Chinese Constitution do authorize the NPC Standing Committee to interpret the Basic Law.

With regard to the other incidents described in this chapter, there is also divergence of perception among the different schools of thought identified above. The fundamentalist liberals believe that Article 23 of the Basic Law itself, the SAR government's rhetoric regarding Falun Gong, its prosecution of Falun Gong demonstrators, as well as officials' comments regarding media reporting of Taiwanese independence views constitute grave threats to the rule of law and human rights. Thin theorists take a more relaxed view of the matter, pointing out that Article 23 is not directly enforceable in the Hong Kong courts and its implementing legislation has not yet been enacted, and that officials' rhetoric – at least in Hong Kong – does not have legal force and cannot result in legal sanctions. In their view, nor do the prosecution, conviction, and fine of a few Falun Gong demonstrators for several minor offenses constitute a departure from the rule of law. Pragmatic liberals tend to agree with the thin theorists regarding the issues of Article 23 and the officials' rhetoric, but would have reservations about the wisdom of prosecuting the Falun Gong demonstrators for obstruction in a public place, given that the actual extent of obstruction was minimal and the "obstruction" caused was in the context of a peaceful and small-scale demonstration. On the other hand, non-liberals do not see a problem at all with Article 23, the officials' rhetoric, or the prosecution.

As regards the decisions not to prosecute discussed in this chapter, fundamentalist thin theorists have been quick to criticize them and to conclude that the rule of law has been violated. Pragmatic thin theorists are more willing to listen to the official explanation, and to accept that the general principle of equality cannot always be absolutely applied and can be made subject to discretion exercised on the basis of individualized circumstances. Similar considerations are applicable to the Cyberport dispute.

The debate surrounding the Public Order Ordinance and its implementation provides an interesting illustration of the intersection and interaction between the fundamentalist–pragmatic dichotomy and the liberal–non-liberal dichotomy. The liberals (including the authors of this chapter, and therefore including a pragmatic liberal) believe that the Public Order Ordinance fails to give sufficient recognition to freedom of demonstration and is thus inconsistent with human rights. Consequently, prosecutions for unauthorized assembly under this Ordinance would be unjust, even if they are made selectively – in which case the equality principle of the rule of law would also be violated and the fundamentalist thin theorists also would find this to be objectionable. The pragmatic thin theorists, however, are willing to accept a more flexible approach to the implementation of the Public Order Ordinance, taking into account the different circumstances in which demonstrations occur. They may therefore be willing to accept some kind of selective prosecution. On the other hand, non-liberals do not find the Public Order Ordinance problematic at all – they are willing to attach greater weight to public order considerations in the balancing of freedom of demonstration and public order. Non-liberals who are pragmatic thin theorists find the government's approach of selective prosecution acceptable, whereas non-liberals who are fundamentalist thin theorists would prefer a strict enforcement of the Ordinance by prosecution in all cases of suspected violation.

It would be easy to criticize the pragmatists (pragmatic thin theorists and pragmatic liberals) for compromising too much and betraying the principles and ideals of the rule of law (in either its thin or its thick sense, as the case may be). In the climate of "one country, two systems," the fundamentalists (particularly the fundamentalist liberals) have gained the upper hand in the public discourse in Hong Kong. They are able to express the genuine concern and fear of the people of Hong Kong about deterioration in or erosion of the rule of law in Hong Kong as a result of mainland influence. They have so far played a healthy and positive role in the public domain, alerting both the local and international communities to critical issues affecting the rule of law in Hong Kong. But this does not mean that the fundamentalists are always right and the pragmatists always wrong. Indeed, sometimes the truth will only emerge after both sides have been heard. Each side has its role to play in the dialectics of legal history. The fundamentalists constantly remind us that the rule of law is a rare achievement of human civilization that can easily wither away if we do not treasure it and are not vigilant. The pragmatists impart to us a broader perspective on things: the abstract and general principles of the rule of law are not all that matters in this world; we should also care about the actual context, the real circumstances, the diverse interests and values in this world, and the concrete well-being of the human beings who live in it.

Notes

1 See Peerenboom's discussion of the "soft-authoritarian form of rule of law," which rejects a liberal interpretation of rights but allows limited democracy at lower levels of government: Randall Peerenboom, "Let One Hundred Flowers Bloom, One Hundred Schools Contend: Debating Rule of Law in China," *Michigan Journal of International Law*, vol. 23, no. 2 (2002), pp. 471–544.

2 One example of this view is Richard Klein, "The Empire Strikes Back: Britain's Use of the Law to Suppress Political Dissent in Hong Kong," *Boston University International Law Journal,* vol. 15 (1997), pp. 1–70, which is highly critical of British colonial governance in Hong Kong.

3 See, generally, Peter Wesley-Smith, *The Sources of Hong Kong Law* (Hong Kong: Hong Kong University Press, 1994).

4 See, generally, Peter Wesley-Smith, *Unequal Treaty 1898–1997: China, Great Britain and Hong Kong's New Territories* (Hong Kong: Oxford University Press, 1983).

5 Under colonial rule, the constitutional instruments of Hong Kong were the Letters Patent and Royal Instructions, as supplemented by certain Acts of Parliament that applied to Hong Kong by their express terms or by necessary implication. See, generally, Norman Miners, *The Government and Politics of Hong Kong*, 5th edn (Hong Kong: Oxford University Press, 1995); Peter Wesley-Smith, *Constitutional and Administrative Law in Hong Kong* (Hong Kong: Longman Asia, 1995).

6 On the drafting of the Basic Law, see Peter Wesley-Smith and Albert Chen, eds., *The Basic Law and Hong Kong's Future* (Singapore: Butterworths, 1988). On the constitutional, political and legal systems established by the Basic Law, see Yash Ghai, *Hong Kong's New Constitutional Order: The Resumption of Chinese Sovereignty and the Basic Law*, 2nd edn (Hong Kong: Hong Kong University Press, 1999).

7 Currently, there are 11 national laws that apply in the HKSAR.

8 See Yash Ghai, "The Rule of Law and Capitalism: Reflections on the Basic Law," in Raymond Wacks, ed., *Hong Kong, China and 1997: Essays in Legal Theory* (Hong Kong: Hong Kong University Press, 1993), pp. 343–65.

9 For an assessment of Hong Kong under the first five years of the Tung administration, see Lau Siu-kai, ed., *The First Tung Chee-hwa Administration: The First Five Years of the Hong Kong Special Administration* (Hong Kong: Chinese University Press, 2002).

10 See the works cited in note 5 above.

11 For a condensed version of the text of the chief executive's speech to the Legislative Council introducing this proposal, see "Lending an Ear to Public Accountability," *South China Morning Post*, 18 April 2002, p. 14.

12 During the first year of the life of the HKSAR, the legislature was the Provisional Legislative Council (PLC), which was not composed of all the members of the last colonial legislature. This was because of the breakdown in 1994 of the Sino-British negotiation on the pace of political reform and the development of representative government in Hong Kong. The Beijing authorities abandoned the "through-train model" (which was originally contemplated) and "derailed" the last legislature. For one year from July 1, 1997, Hong Kong was governed by the PLC, whose members were "elected" by members of the Preparatory Committee for the SAR, who were themselves appointed by the Beijing authorities. For discussion on the historical background, see Lo Chi-kin, "From 'Through Train' to 'Second Stove,'" in Joseph Y. S. Cheng and Sonny S. H. Lo, eds., *From Colony to SAR: Hong Kong's Challenges Ahead* (Hong Kong: Chinese University Press, 1995), pp. 25–38. For discussion of the laws passed by the PLC, seeAlbert H. Y. Chen, "Hong Kong's Legal System in Transition 1997–99," in Wang Gungwu and John Wong, eds., *Hong Kong in China: The Challenges of Transition* (Singapore: Times Academic Press, 1999), pp. 287–320, at pp. 290–2.

13 Cap. 484, Laws of Hong Kong.

14 On Hong Kong's legal system, see, generally, Peter Wesley-Smith, *An Introduction to the Hong Kong Legal System,* 3rd edn (Hong Kong: Oxford University Press, 1998).

15 See, generally, Albert H. Y. Chen, "The Interpretation of the Basic Law: Common Law and Mainland Chinese Perspectives," *Hong Kong Law Journal*, vol. 30 (2000), pp. 380–431, at pp. 417–23.

16 The most common type of tragedy is the separation of families. In extreme cases, death occurs when abode-seekers resort to violence. In August 2000 a group of abode-seekers attempted to force the government to grant their wish by setting fire to paint thinner in the immigration office. In the end, one officer and one abode-seeker were killed in the fire, and others injured. See Angel Lau, "Life for Arson Attack Ringleader as Six Others Given 12–13 Years," *South China Morning Post*, February 5 2002 (available in *Wisenews* database).

17 Immigration (Amendment) (No. 3) Ordinance 1997 (Ordinance no. 124 of 1997, Cap. 115, Laws of Hong Kong).

18 [1997] 3 HKC 64, [1997] HKLRD 1081 (Court of First Instance); [1998] 1 HKC 617, [1998] 2 HKC 382 (Court of Appeal) (reversed in part in the case cited in note 20 below). *Cheung* is a consolidation of four test cases litigated at roughly the same time.

19 Johannes Chan, "A Search for Identity: Legal Development since 1 July 1997," in Wang Gungwu and John Wong, eds., *Hong Kong in China: The Challenges of Transition*, pp. 245–86, at p. 274.

20 [1999]1 HKC 291 (Court of Final Appeal). As Cheung arrived in Hong Kong before July 1, 1997, she could benefit from the Court of Appeal's ruling. As far as she was concerned, the only issue in dispute in the CFA was whether her status of illegitimacy would affect her right of abode. Cheung's mother died before she could marry his father. See [1999] 1 HKC 319.

21 *Chan Kam Nga and 80 others v. Director of Immigration* [1998] HKLRD 142 (Court of First Instance), [1998] 2 HKC 405 (Court of Appeal), (1999) 2 HKCFAR 82 (Court of Final Appeal).

22 For a critical analysis, see Albert H. Y. Chen, "The Court of Final Appeal's Ruling in the 'Illegal Migrant' Children Case: A Critical Commentary on the Application of Article 158 of the Basic Law," in Johannes M. M. Chan, H. L. Fu, and Yash Ghai, eds., *Hong Kong's Constitutional Debate: Conflict Over Interpretation* (Hong Kong: Hong Kong University Press, 2000), pp. 113–41. A revised version of this article appears in "Ng Ka-ling and Article 158(3) of the Basic Law," *Journal of Chinese and Comparative Law*, vol. 5, no. 2 (2001–2), pp. 221–47.

23 [1999] 1 HKC 324.

24 [1999] 1 HKLRD 577 (Court of Final Appeal).

25 For a critical analysis, see Albert H. Y. Chen, "The Court of Final Appeal's Ruling in the 'Illegal Migrant' Children Case: Congressional Supremacy and Judicial Review," in Chan, Fu and Ghai, eds., note 22, pp. 73–96.

26 See "Interpretation of Articles 22(4) and 24(2)(3) of the Basic Law of the Hong Kong Special Administrative Region by the Standing Committee of the National People's Congress," *Gazette of the Standing Committee of the National People's Congress*, 15 July 1999 (in Chinese, also available at http://www.chinainfobank. com).

27 *Lau Kong Yung v. Director of Immigration* [1999] 3 HKLRD 778 (CFA); *Director of Immigration v. Chong Fung Yuen* [2001] 2 HKLRD 533 (CFA); and *Tam Nga Yin and others v. Director of Immigration* [2001] HKLRD 644 (CFA).

28 [2002] 1 HKLRD 561 (Court of Final Appeal).

29 Quoted in the judgment of *Ng Siu Tung*, id., pp. 579–80, para. 11.

30 Id., pp. 592–3, para. 65(1).

31 Id., p. 615, para. 142.

32 Id., p. 616, para. 143.

33 See Magdalen Chow, "Writ Challenges Repatriation Orders," *South China Morning Post*, April 5, 2002 (from *Wisenews* database); Magdalen Chow, "Abode

Seekers in Last-Ditch High Court Fight," *South China Morning Post*, April 3, 2002 (*Wisenews* database).

34 Ronny Tong Ka-wah, "Director of Immigration Must Clarify Why He Refused to Exercise His Discretionary Power," *Ming Pao*, April 11, 2002, p. D11 (in Chinese).

35 See, for example, the stories of a 70-year-old man who hoped to stay to take care of his 90-year-old ill father, a 34-year-old daughter who wished to take care of her half-paralyzed 68-year-old father, and 19-year-old twin sisters who had to face separation from their family members. See Tong, id.

36 Phrase used by Mr. Justice Stock of the High Court, quoted in Cliff Buddle, "Abode Saga Turns to Final Chapter," *South China Morning Post*, May 25, 2002, p. 16.

37 Treason and sedition are already provided for in the Crimes Ordinance (Cap. 200, Laws of Hong Kong).

38 Article 23 provides as follows:The Hong Kong Special Administrative Region shall enact laws on its own to prohibit any act of treason, secession, sedition, subversion against the Central People's Government, or theft of state secrets, to prohibit foreign political organizations or bodies from conducting political activities in the Region, and to prohibit political organizations or bodies of the Region from establishing ties with foreign political organizations or bodies.

39 Finally, on September 24, 2002, the Security Bureau of the HKSAR government published a Consultation Document on *Proposals to Implement Article 23 of the Basic Law*. For discussion of the issues by one of the co-authors of this chapter, see Albert H. Y. Chen, "Existing Law May Be Good Enough," *South China Morning Post*, September 23 2002, p. 18; "Giving a Score to Hong Kong's Human Rights Record," *Yazhou Zhoukan (Asia Weekly)*, 7–13 October 2002, p. 22 (in Chinese); "Proposals a Credit to '1 Country, 2 Systems,'" *China Daily (Hong Kong edition)*, October 7 2002, pp. 3–4; "Will Our Civil Liberties Survive the Implementation of Article 23?," *Hong Kong Lawyer*, November 2002, pp. 80–8. For developments after the end of the three-month consultation period in December 2002, see the section below in this chapter on "A note on Article 23 and the rule of law"

40 In March 1997 the Criminal Code of the People's Republic of China (originally adopted at the Second Session of the Fifth National People's Congress on July 1, 1979) was extensively revised at the Fifth Session of the Eighth National People's Congress. The phrase "Counter-revolutionary crimes" in the original version was replaced by "crimes endangering state security" (see chapter I, part 2 of the new Code). The change, however, does not mean that the content of crimes such as subversion, sedition or secession is now different. For example, it is still a crime to collude with a foreign state and conspire to jeopardize the sovereignty of the state (article 102); one who "organizes, plots, or acts to split the country or undermine national unification" commits a crime (article 103). In addition, it is a crime to subvert the government or to overthrow the socialist system (article 105), or to collaborate with overseas groups in a manner likely to endanger the state (article 106). See, generally, Wei Luo, *The 1997 Criminal Code of the People's Republic of China: With English Translation and Introduction* (New York: W. S. Hein,1998).

41 See the Crimes (Amendment) (No. 2) Bill 1996 and the Crimes (Amendment) (No. 2) Ordinance 1997. The latter ordinance has never been brought into force.

42 For further discussion of the crimes of subversion, sedition and counter-revolution in the Chinese context and the case of Wei, see Fu Hualing, "Sedition and Political Dissidence: Towards Legitimate Dissent in China?," *Hong Kong Law Journal*, vol. 26 (1996), pp. 210–33.

43 See, for example, the webpage of Falun Gong at http://minghui.org. The accuracy of such claims is hotly contested.

44 Benoit Vermander, "Looking at China Through the Mirror of Falun Gong," *China Perspectives* vol. 35 (May–June 2001), pp. 4–13, at p. 4.

45 Explanations of the Supreme People's Court and Supreme People's Procuratorate Concerning Laws Applicable to Handling Cases of Organizing and Employing Heretical Cult Organizations to Commit Crimes (adopted at the 1,079th Meeting of the Judicial Committee of the Supreme People's Court, October 9, 1999, and at the 47th Meeting of the 9th Procuratorial Committee of the Supreme People's Procuratorate, October 8, 1999).

46 Decision of the Standing Committee of the National People's Congress on Banning Heretical Cult Organizations, and Preventing and Punishing Cult Activities (adopted at the 12th Session of the Standing Committee of the 9th National People's Congress, October 30, 1999).

47 Angela Li, "Tung Pledges to Monitor Sect," *South China Morning Post*, February 9, 2001 (*Wisenews* database).

48 Carmen Cheung, "You Deal with 'Evil Cult,' Jiang Tells Tung," *Hong Kong IMail*, March 6, 2001 (*Wisenews* database).

49 "Who is to Define Evil?," English Editorial, *Ming Pao*, June 16, 2001.

50 The Department explained that priority had to be given to the performing arts. See May Sin-mi Hon, "Sect Seeks Probe of Censorship Fears," *South China Morning Post*, February 28, 2002, p. 6.

51 Stella Lee, "Police Accused Over Sect's Sit-in," *South China Morning Post*, November 17, 2001, p. 1.

52 Cliff Buddle, "Rights Time Bomb Ticking," *South China Morning Post*, April 12, 2002 (*Wisenews* database).

53 "Qian Qichen Points Out that Article 23 Can Deal with the Falun Gong," *Hong Kong Economic Journal (Xin bao)*, June 26, 2002 (in Chinese); "There Must Be Legislation on Article 23," *Ta Kung Po*, June 29, 2002 (in Chinese); Political Desk, "Falun Gong 'Should Be Banned If Foreign Links Kept," *South China Morning Post*, June 26, 2002, p. 1 (*Wisenews* database).

54 The case was headline news in Hong Kong on August 16, 2002, and was widely reported by international news agencies. See, generally, Thomas Crampton, "Hong Kong Convicts 16 Falun Gong Protesters," *International Herald Tribune*, August 16, 2002, pp. 1–4; Patrick Poon and Stella Lee, "Falun Gong Activists Convicted," *South China Morning Post*, August 16, 2002, p. 1; Cliff Buddle, "No Keeping Politics Out of Court," *South China Morning Post*, August 16, 2002, p. 14; "Falun Gong Guilty for Obstruction," *Ming Pao*, August 16, 2002 (in Chinese); editorial, "The Mistake Lies in the Prosecution and Not in the Verdict," *Ming Pao*, August 16, 2002 (in Chinese).

55 Peter Stein, "Hong Kong's Press: While Debate Rages About Media Ethics, Self-Censorship Quietly Thrives," *Nieman Reports*, vol. 53, no. 1(1999), pp. 49–50, at p. 49. Stein is the managing editor of the Hong Kong-based *Asian Wall Street Journal*.

56 The warning was expressed by Lu Ping, then director of the State Council's Hong Kong and Macau Affairs Office, in May 1996; and Qian Qichen, then foreign minister of China, in August 1995. See Hong Kong Journalists' Association, *1996 Annual Report: China's Challenge – Freedom of Expression in Hong Kong* (1996), p. 19.

57 Seith Faison, "Taiwan President Implies His Island Is Sovereign State," *New York Times*, July 13, 1999, p. A1.

58 Angela Li, Jimmy Cheung, and Ng Kang-chung, "Qian Instructs Media Not to Back Calls for Taiwan Split," *South China Morning Post*, August 20, 1999, p. 1.

281

59 Josephine Ma and Political Desk, "Media Warned on Taiwan Reports," *South China Morning Post*, April 13, 2000 (*Wisenews* database).

60 For comments on the aftermath of the 1 July march and on the Liberal Party's move by one of the co-authors of this chapter, see Albert Chen, "A Defining Moment in Hong Kong's History", *South China Morning Post*, "July 4 2003; Albert Chen, "How the Liberals Stopped a Constitutional Crisis", *South China Morning Post*, July 8 2003.

61 Even though the Bill was dropped from the agenda of the Legislative Council for 9 July, an estimated 50,000 people still responded to a call for and attended a demonstration outside the Legislative Council building on the evening of 9 July 2003 to protest against the article 23 law and to call for further democratization in Hong Kong. On Sunday 13 July, another mass rally of approximately 20,000 outside the Legislative Council building added its voice to the call for democratization – election of the Chief Executive by universal suffrage in 2007, and election of all members of the Legislative Council by universal suffrage in 2008 (according to Hong Kong's Basic Law, in the 2004 election, half of the legislators will be elected by universal suffrage, and the other half by "functional constituencies" consisting of professional and occupational groupings).

62 Quoted from para. 1.7 of the Consultation Document.

63 The *Hong Kong Standard* was closed down in late 1999 (but subsequently re-published). Aw sold her shares in the Sing Tao Group to an American Company, the Lazard Group. In 2001, the shares were sold to Global China Ltd.

64 For a quotation from Leung's statement and further details of the event, see Albert H. Y. Chen, "Hong Kong's Legal System in Transition, 1997–99" (note 12 above), pp. 313–14.

65 The explanation was offered by Esther Mak, prosecutor of the case. See Shirley Lau, "Drug Charge Against High Court Judge's Son Dropped," *South China Morning Post*, December 19, 2000 (*Wisenews* database).

66 See Angela Li, "Prosecutor's Office 'Won't Go Soft on Drug Offenders,'" *South China Morning Post*, January 17, 2001 (*Wisenews* database).

67 See Shirley Lau, "'Drugged' Official Wins Leniency on Theft," *South China Morning Post*, December 12, 2000 (*Wisenews* database).

68 See "Credibility of Professional Advice," English Editorial, *Ming Pao*, April 17, 2002, p. D10. In 2002, however, Ms. Au was prosecuted and convicted in 2003 for failing to disclose her previous conviction when she first applied for her position in government.

69 See Magdalen Chow, "Shoplifting Charge Against Government Lawyer Dropped," *South China Morning Post*, April 16, 2002, p. 4.

70 Most of the offenders were Secondary Four and Five students, all first-time offenders aged between 16 and 30. See Edward Chan, "Just 3 Win Court Reprieves Since Case of Judge's Son," *Hong Kong IMail*, April 3, 2001 (*Wisenews* database).

71 See Ali Lawlor, "Don't Rewrite the Law, Magistrate Who Freed Shoplifters Told," *Hong Kong IMail*, July 31, 2001 (*Wisenews* database).

72 The survey was conducted by the Hong Kong Policy Research Institute; 891 respondents were interviewed. See Wan Wai-kwan, "Poll Shows Less Faith in Legal System," *South China Morning Post*, January 6, 2001 (*Wisenews* database).

73 See Christine Loh, "Human Rights in the First Year – Genuine Restraint, or Buying Time?," in Larry Chuen-ho Chow and Yiu-kwan Fan, eds., *The Other Hong Kong Report 1998* (Hong Kong: Chinese University Press, 1999), pp. 48, 51–2.

74 Police officers were believed to have targeted certain radical pro-democracy leaders, like Leung Kwok-heung, during rallies, where video teams were

dispatched and slogans and messages were recorded. One such event occurred during President Jiang Zemin's visit to Hong Kong in July 1998. See Hong Kong Journalists' Association, *The Ground Rules Change: Freedom of Expression in Hong Kong, Two Years After the Handover to China*, 1999 Annual Report (June 1999), p. 12.

75 See"Authorities Ought to Rein In," English Editorial, *Ming Pao*, August 18, 2000, p. E7 (*Wisenews* database).

76 See"Police Used Excessive Force," English Editorial, *Ming Pao*, May 11, 2001, p. E8 (*Wisenews* database).

77 The protest was organized by the Hong Kong Alliance in Support of the Patriotic Democracy Movement in China as a prelude to the large-scale annual gathering at Victoria Park to commemorate the June 4 massacre. The group applied to protest in front of the Central Government Office but the police only allowed it to hold rallies outside the West Gate of the government building, which was far from the main entrance and would be out of the sight of arriving and departing officials. The group appealed against the police decision and eventually succeeded in the appeal. See Ambrose Leung, "Police Ban on CGO Rally Overruled," *South China Morning Post*, May 22, 2002, p. 6 (*Wisenews* database).

78 The incident happened after a group of abode-seekers who lost their case in court and more than 100 people surrounded the car of Regina Ip, the Secretary for Security, outside the Legislative Council in Central District on April 24, 2002. On the following day, the police proceeded to clear all abode-seekers who had been staging their long-term silent protest in the nearby Chater Garden. Reporters who were already in the park were forced into a small designated zone. Two reporters were handcuffed and a third was detained without being handcuffed. See the press statement of the Hong Kong Journalists' Association, "The Handcuffing and Beyond," at http://www.freeway.org.hk/hkja/press—statement/Position.htm (accessed June 10, 2002).

79 Alex Lo, Patrick Poon, and Klaudia Lee, "Landmark Case Launched over 'Illegal Protest,'" *South China Morning Post*, May 10, 2002, p. 3.

80 Cap. 245, Laws of Hong Kong.

81 Public Order Ordinance, Ordinance no. 64 of 1967. The Ordinance consisted of a combination of the Peace Preservation Ordinance, the Summary Offenses Ordinance and the common law. For a historical survey, see Roda Mushkat, "Peaceful Assembly," in Raymond Wacks, ed., *Human Rights in Hong Kong* (Hong Kong: Oxford University Press, 1992), pp. 410–38. For a brief account of how stringent the standard was, see Johannes Chan, "Human Rights in the Hong Kong Special Administrative Region: the First Four Years," *Kobe University Law Review*, no. 35 (2001), p. 75, at pp. 85–6.

82 Sections 7, 8, and 13 of the Public Order Ordinance, Cap. 245 (1987 edn).

83 Sections 8 and 13A, Public Order (Amendment) Ordinance 1995 (Ordinance no. 77 of 1995).

84 For a brief account of the political and legal debate, see Albert H. Y. Chen, "Hong Kong's Legal System After the 1997 Handover," *Kobe University Law Review*, no. 35(2001), p. 49, at pp. 52–3.

85 Ordinance no. 119 of 1997. The current version of the Public Order Ordinance is in Cap. 245, Laws of Hong Kong.

86 Sections 7 and 8 govern notification of public meetings, while sections 13 and 13A are on public processions.

87 For further details, see the press release on the speech by the Secretary for Security, Mrs. Regina Ip, in moving a government motion on the Public Order Ordinance in the Legislative Council on December 20, 2000, at http://www.info.gov.hk/gia/general/20012/20/poo20.htm.

88 See comments by Johannes Chan, note 81 above, p. 86.

89 Section 6 of the Public Order Ordinance.

90 In this period, official figures show that out of 4,408 public rallies, the organizers of 677 of them did not notify the police. Out of 6,388 public assemblies, 944 were held without prior notification. See Chris Yeung and May Sin-Mi Hon, "No Police Notice for Hundreds of Public Rallies," *South China Morning Post*, May 13, 2002, p. 4 (*Wisenews* database).

91 In response to criticisms of the Public Order Ordinance, the Security Bureau issued a statement in which it described the existing notification system as a "middle-of-the-road approach." See HKSAR Press Release, "Response to Frequently Asked Questions on Public Order Ordinance," December 14, 2000, at http://www.info.gov.hk/gia/general/200012/14/poo.htm (accessed June 10, 2002).

92 See Quinton Chan, "We Protest," *South China Morning Post*, October 4, 2000 (*Wisenews* database).

93 An inquiry was conducted after the event, as a result of which the officers were given a verbal warning for the use of excessive force by the Independent Police Complaints Council. See Joan Yip, "Riot-spray Officers to Be Warned: Protestors Faced 'Excessive Force,'" *Hong Kong iMail*, December 12, 2000, p. 10 (*Wisenews* database).

94 Stella Lee, "Academics Lend Weight to Student Protesters," *South China Morning Post*, October 24, 2000 (*Wisenews* database).

95 Chow Chung-yan and Ng Kang Chung, "Marchers Defy Protest Law," *South China Morning Post*, October 26, 2000, p. 1 (*Wisenews* database).

96 See Angela Li and Stella Lee, "Students Targeted for Arrest, Says Bar," *South China Morning Post*, October 10, 2000, p. 1 (*Wisenews* database). For the position of the Hong Kong Bar Association on the Public Order Ordinance, see Hong Kong Bar Association, "The Bar's Submissions on the Right of Peaceful Assembly or Procession," November 25, 2000, at http://www.hkba.org/whatsnew/press-release/20001125.html.

97 See Stella Lee, Niall Fraser, and Kong Lai-fan, "Protest 16 Won't be Charged," *South China Morning Post*, October 25, 2000, p. 1 (*Wisenews* database).

98 See Stella Lee, Wan Wai-Kwan, and May Sin-Mi Hon, "Defiant Activists Vow New Protests," October 26, 2000, p. 1 (*Wisenews* database).

99 Government officials sometimes refer to the student protestors as "headaches" to the authorities. One example was a comment uttered by Regina Ip, the Secretary for Security: see Stella Lee, "Stern Words Scare Off Students," *South China Morning Post*, November 6, 2000, p. 1 (*Wisenews* database).

100 The motion was passed by 36 to 21 votes. See Motions IV. 4, Government Motion by Secretary for Security, Legislative Council (Agenda), December 20, 2000, at http://www.legco.gov.hk/yr00–01/english/counmtg/agenda/cmtg2012.htm.

101 Leung and Christopher Fung Ka Keung, a student activist, were both arrested. Another student leader, Chris Lo Wai-ming, gave himself up after alleged threats by the police. See "Police Powers Threaten Human Rights," editorial, *Ming Pao*, May 11, 2002, p. 9 (*Wisenews* database).

102 For an account of the incident, see Alex Lo, Patrick Poon, and Klaudia Lee, "Landmark Case Launched Over 'Illegal Protest,'" May 10, 2002, p. 3 (*Wisenews* database).

103 [2003] 1 HKLRD 468.

104 See Sara Bradford, "Activists' Appeal Goes to Higher Court," *South China Morning Post*, June 24, 2003, p. 2.

105 See Patrick Poon and Stella Lee, "Prosecutions 'Not Politically Motivated,'" *South China Morning Post*, May 11, 2002, p. 3 (*Wisenews* database).
106 If the government were to decide to adopt a stringent approach towards the enforcement of the Ordinance, not only would organizers be prosecuted, but participants in unauthorized assemblies would have to face the same fate. Section 17A(3) of the Public Order Ordinance stipulates that those who knowingly take part in an unauthorized demonstration commit an offense. The police recently decided to warn protestors through banners in addition to loud-hailers so that protestors are more likely to be aware of the unlawful nature of the demonstration. See Stella Lee, "Police Banners Heighten Fears of Crackdown," *South China Morning Post*, May 18, 2002, p. 3 (*Wisenews* database).
107 Roda Mushkat, "Peaceful Assembly," p. 414.
108 Christine Loh, "Human Rights in the First Year," p. 57.
109 Stephen Seawright and May Sin-mi Hong, "Singapore 'Overtakes HK as Asia's Top Spot for Business,'" *South China Morning Post*, April 25, 2002, p. 1.
110 "Cyberport Scheme Linked to First Pacific Group," *Hong Kong Standard*, March 3, 1999, p. A2.
111 Tessi Cruz, "Open Tender Process 'Too Slow', Cyberport Rush 'to Chase Rivals,'" *Hong Kong Standard*, March 6, 1999, p. A4.
112 Randall Peerenboom, "Let One Hundred Flowers Bloom, One Hundred Schools Contend: Debating Rule of Law in China," *Michigan Journal of International Law*, vol. 23, no. 2 (2002), pp. 471–544, at p. 472.
113 Id., p. 473.
114 Id., p. 472.
115 Id., p. 472.

9

INDONESIA

Devaluing Asian values, rewriting rule of law

Tim Lindsey[1]

Introduction

The Bangkok Declaration was the high tide of the 'Asian values' argument, at least at the formal policy level. Whatever the niceties of its phrasing,[2] the instrument was widely understood as based on the argument that Asians shared distinct values that were incompatible with values shared by Westerners and that therefore the West[3] should not rely on its construction of human rights to intervene in affairs of Asian[4] states. The argument has been summarised by Inoue:

> Asia has its own cultural essence, fundamentally different from that of the West; and...this essence penetrates all Asian societies and their history so that they constitute a uniform and perennial cultural whole despite their phenomenal differences and constant changes. This dualism enables Asian advocates to charge Western concerns about human rights with cultural imperialism and to make the cultural relativist response: 'Asia will go its own way.'[5]

The Declaration was signed in 1993 by leaders including Lee Kuan Yew of Singapore, Dr Mahathir Mohammad of Malaysia and Soeharto of Indonesia. Under Soeharto's rule, the Indonesian state thus formed part of an ASEAN[6] ideological project that, implicitly – sometimes explicitly – rejected the universalism of human rights as an innately Western concept that was alien to East Asia. As part of the same project, Indonesia also developed a sophisticated narrative of *Rechtsstaat* (law state) that asserted the irrelevance of separation of powers and elevated the state to a position of almost unchecked authority.

Yet, within five years of the signing of the Bangkok Declaration, Soeharto's Asian values discourse was gone from Indonesian public life, as suddenly and as completely as the 'old man' himself. And within nine years, Indonesia had reconstructed its *Rechtsstaat* on liberal democratic principles. It had radically revised its longstanding and authoritarian Constitution to include, almost intact, that anathema of the Bangkok Declaration, the

Universal Declaration of Human Rights.[7] It had also stripped back the power of all state institutions, locating them (in theory at least) in a web of institutionalised checks and balances.

How did this happen? Will the liberal democratic version of the *Rechtsstaat* work? Is it, in fact, really the end of the Asian values discourse in Indonesia? And, if so, why were 'Asian values', which had seemed so central to the anti-democratic Indonesia polity, in fact so vulnerable?

Crime as policy

To answer these questions, it is useful to begin with an examination of why Soeharto's regime was concerned to prevent Western criticism of the treatment of human rights in Indonesia. Why 'Asian values' at all? The simple answer is that it was because the state system depended on institutionalised and state-sponsored abuse of human rights.[8]

Soeharto's regime called itself the 'New Order' (1966–98), a name that had become ironic by the 1980s, when the regime seemed rusted in place. The retrospectively renamed 'Old Order' (1945–66) of Indonesia's first President, Soekarno, that the New Order displaced had been a leftist state, albeit never formally Marxist. The New Order was thus a product of the Cold War, initially a US-sponsored bulwark against the Communist 'dominoes' of Indo-China. It was a right-wing, military-bureaucratic regime that consciously based its legitimacy on a deeply engrained rhetoric of militant anti-communism,[9] expressed through state-endorsed violence (examples of which are considered below). The state, to justify the fundamentally extralegal violence of its rule, had to construct a greater evil. This is because the New Order's basic brutality, though rarely acknowledged by the state, was pervasive and widely evident to its citizens – so much so that only a widespread sense of imminent crisis could make it acceptable.

This is part of the explanation for the potent political construction of Indonesian history since 1945 – but more so since the New Order began in 1966 – to justify the trope of the embattled republic, powerful but perpetually vulnerable from within: from NICA[10] traitors during the revolution (1945–9), to the communist 'stab in the back' at Madiun during the revolution (1948), to Darul Islam (1948–62) and PRRI/Permesta (1958) as the dark threats that forced 'Guided Democracy' on the *rakyat*,[11] through to the paradigmatic constructed betrayal from within, the 'GESTAPU[12] coup attempt' of 1965, which became the justification for the army takeover of 1966. All of these were used under Soeharto to persuade Indonesians that nameless subversives were on the verge of toppling the republic and that they could act in a way that was virtually incapable of detection and produced no evidence. The quintessence of this genre was the notion of *organisasi tanpa bentuk*, 'organisations without form', which must be destroyed by aggressive state force in order to maintain the union of state and people.

287

Siegel's description of the New Order fetishising of invisible enemies[13] includes his account of Attorney-General Ali Said banning a book by Pramoedya Ananta Toer on the grounds that it was an example of the 'infiltration of society that went unfelt by it'. He went on to say that communists had now decided that 'organisations without form are best'. Siegel describes Admiral Sudomo, Soeharto's one-time security chief, as arguing, in effect, that if the book was not banned, then, because it hid within a secret code form of instructions on Marxism–Leninism, 'it is obvious that public order will be at an end'.[14]

It is easy to find examples of these sorts of statements from senior New Order politicians and security and enforcement officials because they were so central a part of the state's public dialogue. They were common – however absurd they seemed at times – because they justified state violence. War against some Indonesians was presented as required to prevent the far worse descent into chaos and national slaughter that those particular Indonesians threatened. In this sense it was not just likely that from time to time 'enemies of state' would have to be attacked. It was actually *necessary* that this happen, to give some weight to the state's constant polemic of brinkmanship. The New Order was thus based on a security model, but perhaps the more appropriate description was the 'insecurity state', because it relied on a constant and official state of precariousness to justify acting in an essentially extra-legal – or, to put it more simply, 'lawless' – way.

Siegel has described the consequence of this as the violent state effectively becoming criminal, describing the Indonesian state, and Soeharto in particular, as 'the new criminal type of Jakarta'.[15] Examining the state-managed *Petrus* murders of thousands of 'gangsters' between 1983 and 1985, Siegel focuses on Soeharto's justifications for ordering these extra-legal executions. The tattooed *gali*[16] victims were, the President claimed, 'inhuman'.

> Criminals went beyond human limits. They not only broke the law, but they stepped beyond the limits of human endurance. For instance, old people were first robbed...and then killed. Isn't that inhumane? If you are going to take something, sure take it, but then don't murder. Then there were women whose wealth was stolen and other people's wives even raped by these criminals in front of their husbands yet. Isn't that going too far?...Doesn't that demand action? Automatically we had to give *shock treatment* [in English].

This inhumanity, or *sadis* (sadism), that Soeharto attributed to the *gali* was then matched by the state's brutality. The threat established that the law was irrelevant to the state's right to act. Disguised members of the military were sent to abduct and murder selected *gali*, usually with multiple bullet shots or stab wounds,[17] leaving the corpses in streets and rivers, as Soeharto

REWRITING RULE OF LAW IN INDONESIA

said, 'just like that. This was for *shock therapy* [in English]. So the masses would understand that faced with criminals there were still some who would act and who would control them.'[18]

Here the state has not only matched criminality, Siegel argues; it has appropriated it to secure its unity with its citizens. Siegel describes Soeharto and the state as having 'implicitly identified themselves with their victims even as they asserted their difference from them. It is the imitation of the criminal that is predominant, while the assertion of difference at this point was mere camouflage'.[19]

The state emerged from these events as the unchallenged possessor of lawless power, the mediator of violence – as Soeharto had clearly intended and believed was its right.

General Prabowo's remarks on his role in the abduction and torture of at least nine perceived dissidents in the months leading up to the fall of his father-in-law, Soeharto, in 1998[20] demonstrate precisely the same ideas. Prabowo has described himself as a 'good soldier' 'inculcated with the values of *ksatria* – the warrior – and patriotism',[21] who 'love[s] the army'. It was thus his duty, when instructed by the state (that is, the President, who, according to the pre-amendment formulation of the 1945 Constitution was the mandatory of the *Majelis Permusyawaratan Rakyat* (MPR) or People's Consultative Assembly, then the supreme sovereign body), to use violence to protect the authority of the New Order, like the 'samurai' he likens himself to, who will not 'leave your lord'.[22] This entitled Prabowo to remove and neutralise the threat presented by dissidents he saw as attempting to desta- bilise and destroy the state through a 'campaign of terror'.[23] For these high purposes, he saw no restraints applying – the interests of the government transcended the law – and so he was entitled to use criminal tactics against criminals 'already on the police wanted list' if necessary. In doing so, his actions, however illegal, should not, he says, be seen as 'betraying Pak Harto [Soeharto]...I never betrayed my country'.[24] The two, in his mind, were conflated.

An ambidextrous lawlessness

The violent nature of the New Order was well known in the West. Most governments – like those of the United States and, more particularly, Australia, Indonesia's near neighbour – turned a blind eye, however, for most of the Cold War. They did so for strategic reasons and because the Indonesian economy offered rich opportunities for their investors. Criticism was nonetheless constant from Western non-governmental organisations (NGOs) and some scholars. Occasionally this would be enough to lead Western governments (and, in particular, the Dutch) to pressure Indonesia for human rights reforms. The Asian values discourse then became a useful tool for the New Order, both as grounds to reject 'foreign' demands for reform, human rights protection and 'rule of law' as irrelevant and as grounds to attempt to prevent these values from 'taking root' in Indonesia.

Paradoxically, the New Order's rejection of Western ideas of human rights and rule of law, as Western only, had much in common with the approach of the pseudo-Marxist Old Order that it crushed so violently in 1966 and then reconstructed rhetorically as its bogeyman. It was Soekarno, of course, who famously said, 'Go to hell with your aid', formed the so-called 'Pyonyang-Beijing-Hanoi-Phnom Penh-Jakarta Axis' that lay at the heart of his alternative to the United Nations, the Conference of New Emerging Forces, and 'confronted' the imperialist West for creating a 'puppet state' in Malaysia.[25] It was Soekarno who had declared a 'State of War and Siege' in 1997 and then, two years later, unilaterally revoked the provisional parliamentary Constitution of 1950 in favour of a return to the authoritarian 1945 Constitution, suspended the legislature, ruled by decree, and systematically degraded and disempowered the judiciary.[26] By doing so, he thus established the basic pillars of the authoritarian and repressive state adopted by the New Order after it toppled him in 1966.[27]

Formal ideological hostility to rule of law and Western ideas of human rights had thus enjoyed a long and bloody pedigree in Indonesia – and indeed had sat at the very centre of two regimes – when Soeharto was finally forced by riots, military pressure and, more directly, the resignation of his ministers and his inability to find replacements, to step down after three decades of rule. It had been the basis of the two systems, left and right, Old and New Order, that had dominated Indonesian politics since independence was declared in 1945, for all but the brief interregnum from 1950 to 1957. Four decades of government propaganda taught in schools, mandatory workplace and public service training, 'P4' propaganda sessions and the public discourse of military-backed historians like Nugroho Notosusanto,[28] government lawyers and 'tame' politicians had resulted in the integration into the New Order's virtual state religion of security and order[29] of a sophisticated legal and political narrative that justified rejection of Western notions of democracy and rule of law: the *Integralisticstaatsidee*.[30]

Nowhere was this more clearly manifested than in the skeletal revolutionary Constitution of 1945. Originally created as an 'express' and explicitly temporary constitution drafted hastily to deal with the exigencies of the war of independence against the returning Dutch colonial forces at the end of the Second World War, it became the instrument by which this huge and complex archipelagic state[31] was governed for all but 10 of the next 53 years.[32]

Integrating the 1945 Constitution

The chief author of the 1945 Constitution was Professor Raden Soepomo, one of 62 experts forming the committee charged with the production of the basic statute in the months leading up to the Japanese surrender and the declaration of Indonesian independence in August that year.[33] He was an impassioned opponent of Western socialist and liberal ideas, and it was he who was given the task of actually drafting the statute as Indonesia's leaders awaited the surrender of the occupying Japanese and the arrival of the recolonising Allies.

Soepomo consciously set out to create a constitution which 'can give the greatest accent to the government', while being itself 'also accountable to the government and primarily the head of state'.[34] Take, for example, Soepomo on the state and individual rights:

> There will be no need for any guarantee of *Grund- unde Freiheitsrechte* of individuals against the state, for the individuals are nothing else than organic parts of the state, having specific positions and duties to realise the grandeur of the state.[35]

This was based on the fantastical notion that the integralist state – because it was 'integrated' – could never be at odds with individuals comprising it 'because the state is not a powerful body or political giant standing outside the sphere of individual freedom'.[36] As Soepomo said:

> [A]ccording to the meaning of the Integralist State, as a regulated nation, as the organised unity of the people, then fundamentally there is no dualism between state and society, there is no conflict between the structure of the state and the legal structure pertaining to individuals. There is no dualism of *Staat und statsfreier Gesellschaft* (state and society free from state intervention).[37]

On this view, there is no need for a civil (private) legal sphere independent of the state and thus able to check the state, because the state *is* all citizens and their interests are therefore identical. As Nasution says:

> Evidently, there was no fear of abuse of power by the state nor any doubt that the state would always use its power appropriately. The state functionaries were assumed to be good and wise persons taking seriously the interests of the people as a whole, never thinking of their interests. It was not astonishing that given these assumptions, Soepomo thought there was no need to put limits on state power or to guarantee individual rights.[38]

The democratic metaphor of the state as the people because it is chosen by the majority through a constitutional process of government is not the reference here. Rather, as Bourchier[39] and Burns[40] before him have shown, the Germanic Romantic notion of the state as the spiritual manifestation of the people, as a quasi-religious emanation of their racial and ethnic essence, is what is meant: the *Volksgeist*. Von Savigny and Puchta's ideas of the nation 'as an entity possessing an organic unity above and beyond the concerns of individuals'[41] were filtered through the Leiden School of Law into Indonesia via van Vollenhoven.

Soepomo, a graduate of Leiden, was a strong supporter of this school's notion of *Volksrecht*, the people's law, as opposed to *Juristenrecht*, lawyers' law. From his thinking sprang the so-called *adat* school of law, which saw Indonesian traditions as the only appropriate source of law because, he argued, it was the essence of Indonesianness, of the 'national identity'. This *Rechtsgeschichte* (legal genealogy) he interpreted as based around notions of an imagined traditional village 'family' as the model of the state, with decisions made by consensus and the villagers' communal life rendering them identical with the village, represented by its leaders. He 'maintained that there was no place for divisive concepts of political rights in the constitution'. He proposed instead a totalistic state philosophy he called 'integralism'.[42]

On Soepomo's reading, the state, being the people, cannot be wrong. It therefore is the source of law because, in the Romantic tradition, the only valid law is that which expresses the *Volksgeist*, the spirit of the people. It follows that, if the state does embody the *Volksgeist*, then all state acts are *inherently* legitimate and legally correct. If the state's actions conflict with legislation, then the legislation is in conflict with the *Volksgeist* and is to that extent without authority. This is a common approach in Indonesian statutes, which typically reserve discretion in the hands of the executive to overrule regulating provisions 'in the national interest'.[43] Equally, individuals acting against the state, manifest as the government, are therefore acting against society – the *rakyat*.

One consequence of this is the legal system's relative lack of interest in civil dispute resolution (that is, addressing grievances between citizens) and a continuing preoccupation with the authority of the state, manifest in a dominating concern for security and criminal regulation and administrative issues. So, violence is formally dealt with almost exclusively as a criminal problem or an issue of regulating the state structure and officers within it. Even this is done, however, with an overarching interest in protecting state institutions from damage caused by state officials, rather than dealing with acts of violence themselves. Again, Prabowo is an example *par excellence*. A symptom of this is that officials in agencies charged with preventing violence – the prosecutors (*jaksa*), intelligence agencies, the police and the courts – often actively work to sabotage the prosecution of 'political' acts of violence (that is, in Indonesian terms, ethnic or religious violence or the violence of state officials) when they feel that it could somehow, even indirectly or trivially, weaken the state. In other words, acts or events of violence are legally re-imagined not as wrongs involving perpetrators and victims but, rather, as issues of faulty administration and threats to state stability.

At its extreme, to the extent that the legal process itself is seen as having the potential to damage confidence in the state by dealing with 'political' violence, the legal process itself is, ironically, perceived as a threat. On this view, 'political' trials (for example, of soldiers for murders or human rights violations in Aceh and East Timor), if not controlled, may be more dangerous and serious than the crimes themselves. They are therefore manipulated. On the other hand, acts of violence without political content are opportunities for the state to assert its authority. Relatively few civil actions proceed, but routine – and politically relatively uncontroversial – criminal trials (non-'political' thefts, assaults, kidnapping, murders, drug cases) nearly always result in a guilty verdict and are publicised as evidence of the state performing its function. They become legitimisers.

A second important political result of Soepomo's state model follows from the state's monopoly on legitimacy and authority: citizens are component parts of the state entity and have no voice except through the state, as their duty is to obey it. Individuals who act contrary to the state government are simply, by doing so, outside the law, whether they are dissenters or criminals. This is not a legal status but it is implicit in Article 27 of the Constitution (see Appendix, pp. 000–00), which still provides simply that 'all citizens...shall uphold the law and the state without exception'.[44] The state is therefore not constrained by law or any other state system in acting against its perceived 'enemies'. They have placed themselves outside the *Volk* by opposing the state and thus no longer have rights. In this sense, then, there is no real role for law in dealing with opponents of the government. The government has an absolute right to punish its opponents and, of course, through armed forces, a virtual monopoly on the power to use violence to do so, so there is no need for law as a tool to deal with the disputes between the state and its dissenters.

This means that state violence, or violence which suits those who control the state, usually did not reach the courts (witness the failure to bring persons involved in the Tanjung Priok shootings or the May 1998 Jakarta rapes to trial). When state violence did reach the courts, the state could determine the outcome as it wished, regardless of the law, as in the Kedung Ombo case.[45] Examples of the use of state violence to resolve disputes in its own favour are manifold, but more notorious examples include the murder of trade union activist Marsinah by military figures,[46] the sacking of PDI[47] headquarters in 1996 under the auspices of the military, and General Prabowo's abductions and tortures.

Rechtsstaat in a lawless state

A third significant feature of integralism was its reading of *negara hukum* (literally, 'law state'). This is the Indonesian version of the German *Rechtsstaat* ('law state'), but since the fall of Soeharto the term is often used loosely as a synonym for the Anglo-American idea 'rule of law', both by Indonesian reformers and by foreign donors and lenders. In Anglo-American common law jurisdictions 'rule of law' is, of course, a term of art, laden with jurisprudence, and is, Clark[48] argues, to be distinguished from 'rule by law'. The latter merely implies standards prescribed by legislation or judicial decision-making that are applied in a universal and consistent fashion[49] and, in Indonesia, is a model derived historically from the civil law systems originated under Napoleon. This notion applies to the system of law-making and the process of implementation of those laws, rather than the larger political system in which the law operates. It is what contemporary theory might describe as the 'thin' (procedural, formal) account of rule of law.[50]

By contrast, 'rule of law' in the 'thick' (substantive) Anglo-American sense embraces 'rule by law' but is usually understood to extend beyond it to embrace representative democracy,[51] although there has never been any international consensus on what electoral system most perfectly implements government by the people. 'Rule of law' also usually assumes some degree of separation of powers or, put more specifically, divided responsibilities and bounded discretion.[52] The Indonesian term is *trias politika* (political triad).

Of course, Montesquieu's model of mutually independent executive, legislature and judiciary has rarely been fully realised anywhere. As in England, Australia and most Westminster systems, the most common departure is that the executive sits in the legislature rather than being independent of it. The United States is perhaps the most influential example of a true separation of powers, in theory at least. It could, however, be argued that, regardless of the formal structure in these jurisdictions, the divided responsibilities and bounded discretion of Gray's analysis are in reality, achieved by broad political consesus that support sophisticated constitutional and legislative schema of checks and balances on power whereby 'no individual has a total monopoly over a decision, without possibility of review by another, and final review rests with the top level of the formal legal system'.[53]

In Indonesia, however, the governments of Soekarno and Soeharto claimed to have implemented *negara hukum* in circumstances where there was no real representative democracy, certainly no separation of powers, and where final review sat formally in the hands of the *Mahkamah Agung*, or Supreme Court, but was consistently exercised in accordance with the dictates of the executive.[54]

International and Indonesian opponents therefore frequently criticised Indonesian governments for failing to implement the 'rule of law', but the use of common law traditions of 'rule of law' to understand *negara hukum* is problematic[55] because there has never been any theoretical consensus as to precisely what *negara hukum* means. Reform activists have long asserted, without recourse to much jurisprudence, that *trias politika* is self-evidently implicit in the notion of *negara hukum*, equating it with the 'thick' reading of rule of law. Leading orthodox Indonesian law professors and government lawyers, however, for decades countered with sophisticated arguments drawing on civil law tradition to support the 'thin' interpretation; that is, that *Rechtsstaat* and *negara hukum* do not necessarily imply either representative democracy or separation of powers.[56]

They had some authority for this in the very silence of the 1945 Constitution. It simply states that Indonesia shall be a *Rechtsstaat* (General Elucidation[57] to the Constitution) but gives no real definition of that term. In its body it established a judiciary, executive and legislature but essentially left their operation to future regulation. In other words, the statement of principle in the Elucidation, like so many Indonesian laws, is not given clear content or binding authority. In this sense, *negara hukum* was interpreted in the narrower and more formalistic sense that is closer to 'rule by law',[58] or, to use the hoary Indonesian joke, 'law of the rulers, rather than rule of law'. In practice this system implies a hierarchy, rather than a separation, of powers.

Gray[59] describes government on this model as operated by multiple levels of principals and agents, fixed by law. Authority is concentrated in the superior administrators, be they bureaucrats or the judiciary, who hold broad discretion fettered only by the superior discretion of their superiors. This system, although formal in structure, is necessarily informal in practice, and its combination of hierarchical structures and discretionary powers obviously lends itself to both patrimonialism and bureaucratisation. That this model prevailed in New Order Indonesia was obvious from even a superficial examination of government, and was acknowledged in official constitutional discourse by the controversial notion of 'distribution' or 'division' of powers. On this analysis, all power originated from the MPR[60] as supreme sovereign body[61] and is exercised by its 'mandatory', the President, in conjunction with the DPR[62] or parliament and the judiciary, whose powers are circumscribed by law and subject to the intervention of the MPR (and thus, implicitly – and explicitly under Soekarno – by the President).

Unravelling integralism

This was a system that both Soekarno and Soeharto had valorised as innately Indonesian,[63] claiming it reflected deep-seated, paternalistic and communitarian indigenous traditions of government, that it was the essence of an Indonesian *Volksgeist*. Under Soeharto it acquired added legitimacy as the supposed protective shell for *pembangunan*, national economic development. It is therefore remarkable how quickly and how far this decades-old and sophisticated panoply of theory, propaganda and practice disintegrated once Soeharto was gone.

And disintegrate it certainly has. On 10 August 2002, Indonesia's supreme sovereign body, against the expectations of most observers,

Indonesian and foreign, amended the country's 1945 Constitution for the fourth time since 1999.[64] With this amendment the members of the MPR produced a new statute that was more than three times longer than Soepomo's; that resolved a series of debates that have divided Indonesia since independence in 1945; and that vastly diminished both their own authority and that of the now slimmed-down presidency.[65] They also completed a formal constitutional transition from authoritarianism to liberal representative democratic system, with a new institutional framework that would allow separation of powers, thus settling the *negara hukum/trias politika* debate for the time being in favour of the historically weak, but now politically irresistible, Anglo-American 'thick' interpretation of rule of law. This new model, as mentioned, also implicitly, but unequivocally, rejected the 'Asian values' ideas enshrined in the Bangkok Declaration.

This result is all the more remarkable for Indonesia because it was the result of a genuinely democratic process. The MPR that made these amendments was the first ever truly democratic assembly in Indonesian history. No specialised or independent Constitutional Commission was established. Instead, members made the amendments through lengthy and difficult debates between parties and factions on the floor of the House – and through inevitable backroom horse-trading. Few countries have achieved so elaborate a transformation of their systems of government and politics and law so quickly, solely through parliamentary process.

Of course, constitutional reform does not necessarily mean that systems of administration and governance are immediately transformed. The reality is that Indonesia's far-reaching formal changes are only slowly being implemented. Despite this, the reforms are, nonetheless, important in their own right for the examination of the 'Asian values' debate that this volume presents. This is because they demonstrate that the implicit claim of the Bangkok Declaration that 'Asian values' in relation to human rights are inherent in Asian societies is, at least in Indonesia, no longer sustainable.

The persistence of memory

The spectacular results of the amendment process, and the speed with which they were attained, can be explained, in part, by how law reacted to its marginalisation and replacement by ideology and violence as prime means of ordering society under Soeharto and Soekarno. Law operated in the public life of New Order Indonesia as not much more than a series of hortatory statements that were treated as guidelines by the government. But it did not disappear. Marginalised, it became the property of those who inhabited the margins of the New Order, opposition figures, independent scholars and Indonesia's tenacious NGO sector.[66] It operated as a form of memory, a reminder of alternatives, a statement of what might be.

Indonesia's abandoned democratic course of the 1950s, and in particular the deliberations of the *Konstituante*, Indonesia's Constituant Assembly,[67] dissolved by Soekarno in 1959, saw the development of the typically wide range of alternative and sometimes divisive visions of political, constitutional and social arrangements that appeared whenever Indonesia's diverse groups had the opportunity to express themselves freely. The New Order was able, to some extent, to marginalise the democratic tradition of the pre-Guided Democracy 1950s through its ideological programme and, more particularly, by reinventing accounts of that period[68] as a political failure that jeopardised the state, but it could never silence the discourse.

Subversion trials were the most dramatic legal forum for the expression of alternative imaginings of the Indonesian community under Soeharto The trials of dissidents such as Muchtar Pakpahan,[69] Ratna Sarumpaet[70] and Sri Bintang Pamungkas[71] became set pieces where arguments on democracy and the rule of law were regularly and aggressively aired,[72] in a tradition established, ironically enough, by Soekarno's own trial by the Dutch under similar provisions in the 1930s. The inevitable convictions in all these cases were, in fact, political victories for the convicts because they focused attention on the illegitimacy of the final result, rather than the subject of the dispute.

This sort of persistent assertion of rule of law and universal values on the margins of public life is why Indonesians, once given a voice in policy and law-making by the reforms introduced by the New Order politicians clinging to power in Soehartos' wake, could rapidly dismantle the integralist state and repudiated the attached 'Asian values' dogma imposed on them for almost half a century. Even Soeharto's own chosen successor, protégé and de facto foster son, Dr B. J. Habibie, was at pains to demonstrate that he, unlike his patron, was, in his own words, 'a democrat, a Western educated man'[73] and a supporter of international notions of human rights. He ushered in a massive legislative reform programme and took unilateral decisions, sometimes without cabinet or government consultation, to move Indonesia toward compliance with the standards of multilateral global organisations like the United Nations (ordering the referendum in Timor against the army's wishes) or the International Labour Organisation (ILO) (making Indonesia the first Asian nation to sign all core ILO Conventions).

The result has been that integralism and its implicit claim to particularism, once so central to the Indonesian polity, have vanished from public discourse. And this has happened with virtually no contest. Accordingly, 'Asian values' seem to have been simply part of the baggage taken by the departing Soeharto. There are now no voices raised in the legislature or the media to defend the Bangkok Declaration and 'Asian values' or the New Order model. Indeed, 'human rights' has become part of the language of public life. So, for example, when corruptors are named in public or members of the armed forces charged with violent crime, they accuse their accusers of violating their human rights by defaming them. Likewise, the government defends it repression of regional separatists in Aceh and West Papua, for example, on the grounds that its enemies are committing human rights violations.

As these examples themselves demonstrate, the Indonesian state is, of course, still marked by problems of human rights abuses, crime and violence – as are most states, developing and developed and confusion about the substance of human rights. The point is, however, that the formal, institutionalised and intellectualised resistance to the universality of human rights that characterised the New Order is no longer part of formal state policy. This has led to a significant rethinking of the nature of the state and the beginning of a shift away from the impunity of the elite and armed forces of the state that marked the New Order. Indonesia may now appear to be a weak state, threatened, according to some, by Islamic extremism and the countervailing possibility of a military resurgence, and it certainly has a damaged and fragile economy, but is no longer an overtly and deliberately criminal system dependent on officially sanctioned and institutionalised human rights abuse for its survival.

It should not, however, be assumed that the transition from integralism to Indonesia's present ramshackle but functional democracy was simple or that it is complete. The balance of this chapter surveys the four troubled and difficult amendments to the 1945 Constitution that took place from 1999 through to 2002. In doing so, it traces the process by which the Soepomo's integralistic state was dismantled and a new universalist approach to rights constructed. An attempt to identify unresolved issues will be made before concluding with an assessment of whether *reformasi* will 'stick'.

The First Amendment

The First Amendment to the 1945 Constitution was passed on 19 October 1999 following the first true free and democratic election in Indonesia, held in June that year.[74] The MPR[75] that sat four months after the election was therefore the first truly independent, elected parliament in Indonesian history. It had a strong mandate to introduce reforms that would prevent the emergence of another dictatorial presidency. This mandate the MPR carried out by introducing constitutional amendments that strengthened the authority of the elected legislators as against the executive – that is, the President and cabinet – by handing the elected legislators greater control of the legislative process.

Defining the separation of legislative power between the executive and Indonesia's twin legislative bodies was a preoccupying concern for the MPR because of the absence of separation of powers between the three branches of government in the 1945 Constitution and because that Constitution did not clearly establish either a parliamentary or a presidential political system but instead created a blended and vague hybrid. On the one hand, the MPR was, nominally, the supreme sovereign body. In the words of the original Article 1 of the Constitution, 'sovereignty is in its hands and is exercised in full by it'. Chapter III of the Elucidation to the Constitution[76] even stated that, 'since the MPR is vested with the sovereignty of the state, its power is unlimited'. Section 6 (III)3 of the Elucidation deals with the implications of this for the presidency:

> It is the MPR that holds the highest power of the state, whereas the President shall pursue the state policy as outlined by the MPR. The President who is appointed by the MPR shall be subordinate and accountable to the MPR. He is the mandatory of the MPR; it is his duty to carry out its decisions. The President is not in an equal position to, but subordinate to the MPR.

The MPR thus had in theory unfettered[77] discretion to select the President and Vice-President.[78] It could also dismiss the President on the basis of an 'interpolation'[79] reference from the DPR.[80] Read on their own, these provisions made the Indonesian system appear parliamentary. On the other hand, the 1945 Constitution also unambiguously stated that the 'President shall hold the power of government' (Article 4). The Indonesian executive was thus at once both head of state and head of government. This suggested a strongly presidential system when read with the fixed five-year term of the presidency (which knew no limit on additional terms) (Article 7); the power of the President to make laws (Article 5(1)) and the regulations to implement them (Article 5(2)); the President's exclusive powers in respect of ambassadors, amnesty and pardon; the President's exclusive authority over ministers and the formation of cabinet (Articles 13, 14 and 17); and the President's broad emergency powers (which could allow suspension of the legislature and rule by decree) (Article 12). The presidential bias of these provisions was also supported by a clear statement in the Constitution that the President and ministers were not accountable to the legislature (the DPR) but only to the MPR (Chapter 6, Parts V and VII of the Elucidation).[81] And in reality, of course, the MPR had historically rarely been able to assert its authority against the two Presidents who had ruled prior to 1998.

The First Amendment did not completely resolve the tensions between presidential and parliamentary government, but it did significantly refine the formula, to the benefit of the legislature. The notion that the system was, in principle, presidential was affirmed, but the President's power to make laws was removed. This shift was expressed in changes to Articles 5 and 20, which in their original wording read: 'the President holds the power to make statutes [*undang-undang*] in conjunction with the DPR.' The new article 20 now states that the DPR 'holds the power to make statutes' (Article 20(1)), while the President merely has the right 'to present Bills to the DPR' (Article

5), a power he shares with all members of the DPR (Article 21(1)). Likewise, Article 20(2) requires that Bills be 'debated by the DPR and the President to reach joint agreement'.

The First Amendment also gave the DPR more influence in the appointment of ambassadors (Article 13) and the grant of amnesties (Article 14), while giving the Supreme Court (*Mahkamah Agung*) a role in the grant of pardons.

Finally – and of great political resonance – the new Article 7 also limits future Presidents to two five-year terms, a measure clearly responding to the 23-year reign of Soekarno and the 30 years enjoyed by Soeharto. Perhaps more than any other, this amendment was a clear statement of the political transition from authoritarianism.

The strengthening of the legislature's power at the expense of the presidency did not, however, completely resolve the problem of preventing another dictator. Rather, it created a strong parliament in a system still top-heavy because of a structural focus on a weakened executive. The result was still a strange hybrid, replete with tensions (albeit new ones) between these two branches of government – a hybrid shifting from favouring the President toward favouring the legislature.

The Second Amendment

On 18 August 2000, the Second Amendment was passed, together with a complementary set of MPR TAP (*Ketetapan*: Decision or Decree). Only one significant amendment focused on the tussle between presidency and legislature that marked the First Amendment: the President's ratification required for Bills to become law now became a mere courtesy. If approval of a Bill duly passed by the DPR is withheld by a President's refusal to sign it into law, then after 30 days it automatically becomes law in any case (Article 20(5)). This radical change left the DPR as the principal legislature, with the MPR, which retained its own law-making powers through the TAP mechanism,[82] as a sort of supervisory assembly with special responsibility for the Constitution.

The balance of the Second Amendment was concerned with issues not addressed by the First Amendment, all of which were critical to dismantling integralist state of Soepomo.

Bill of Rights

For Indonesia's newly legitimate MPR in 2000 – was the product of a democratic process triggered when the Indonesian people and a government parted ways so dramatically in 1998. For this new MPR, the addition to the Constitution of a new chapter on human rights to protect the people from the government was obviously an essential step toward reinventing the polity.

As mentioned, the new Articles 28A–28J of the Constitution (which form Chapter XA, a copy of which appears in the Appendix, pp. 000–00) therefore delivered perhaps the most radical change to the original philosophy of the Constitution. Soepomo's paternalist and authoritarian presidential model was tempered with clauses lifted directly from the Universal Declaration of Human Rights (UDHR). Chapter XA is lengthy and impressive, granting a full range of protections extending well beyond those guaranteed in most developed states. These range from the right to have a family; the right to self-development; the right to collective action; the right to education; a right against violence and discrimination; a right to equal opportunity; a right to access to information; and so forth. This is a radical reinvention of the basic assumptions on which the Indonesian state was founded.

In the first month after the Second Amendment, however, one of the new articles in Chapter XA became the subject of controversy. Paragraph 28I(1) of the amended Constitution was seen as presenting a political dilemma for human rights activists that related back to the question of unravelling *dwifungsi* and bringing the military more fully under civilian control. Although it is now widely accepted by Indonesian human rights reformers that the UDHR sets the international standard for the protection of human rights, the adoption of Article 11(2) of the Declaration (which prohibits prosecution under retrospective legislation) in Paragraph 28I(1) was seen as placing an obstacle in the path of efforts to make the armed forces account-able for human rights abuses.

The argument is that existing criminal statutes inherited from the New Order do not recognise crimes against humanity or human rights abuses in the sense of Articles 28A–28J. The new rule against retrospectivity would therefore prevent new, tougher laws from being applied, to New Order abuses thus maintaining the impunity the military had enjoyed under Soeharto.

Paragraph 28I(1) had been inserted without attracting much debate during the MPR session. The military, it has been widely said, had thereby 'stolen' protection from prosecution for abuses committed under Soeharto, in particular over the quarter-century of the East Timor occupation. Whether or not this does, in fact, prove to be the case, there can be little doubt that the military did see this amendment as a way of ensuring that the questions of responsibility for many of the human rights abuses that form 'dark sides of Indonesia's recent history'[83] are never decided.

The role of the military

Although Soeharto eventually emerged as absolute ruler independent of the military, his government had always relied heavily upon it for political support, social control and business partnerships.[84] For these reasons, the New Order had elevated the *dwifungsi* concept – the military's doctrine that its revolutionary struggle from 1945 to 1949 justified it exercising ongoing socio-political functions in addition to its defence function – to the level of a state religion.[85] For three decades the army was able to sit at the centre of national life, controlling public life with virtual impunity, despite its reputation for both profound corruption and routine human rights abuse.[86]

The fall of Soeharto was, however, accompanied by revelations as to the full extent of the military complicity in state terrorism and private gangsterism, including terrorist bombings, inciting ethnic violence and the murder and torture of civilians. It became clear that these events occurred not just in rebellious provinces like East Timor, Aceh and Irian Jaya (now Papua) but also in urban centres in Java, including the capital itself, and that even the children of the elite – university students at Trisakti University shot in pro-reform demonstrations in early 1998 – were potential targets. The military thus emerged from the chaos that surrounded the end of the New Order as a deeply shamed institution, understanding that it had little choice but to accept a significant lessening of its formal role in government and thus of its real political power. These issues came to a head at the MPR Annual Session in 2000, where, for the first time in decades, the role of the military was openly questioned by legislators.

Some of the most important reforms introduced by the Second Amendment are now set out in Article 30, 'National Defence and Security'. Paragraphs 30(2)–(4), for example, create a distinction between external defence, on the one hand – this remains the responsibility of the TNI – and, on the other, internal security, law enforcement and maintenance of public order – now handed to the Indonesian Police Force or Polri (*Polisi Republic Indonesia*), newly separated from the military to form a civilian organisation. Significantly, Paragraph 30(5) also handed the power to regulate the respective authority and jurisdictions of each of TNI and Polri to the legislature.

Other fundamental changes aimed at dismantling *dwifungsi* were introduced as TAP MPR rather than as constitutional amendments. These included the introduction of a new mechanism for appointing and dismissing the TNI commander and Polri chief, which now require DPR approval rather than being the gift of the President; and the subjection of the armed forces (police fully, military in part) to the civil and criminal jurisdiction of the General Courts.[87] The Military Courts (*Pengadilan Militer*), which had previously routinely whitewashed military abuses, are now left with a much-truncated jurisdiction which gives them authority only over breaches of the Military Code rather than any offence involving members of the military, as in the past.

The removal of the armed forces' privileges and their subjection to civilian authority was not, however, complete. As seen above, the Second Amendment did not fully remove the effective legal impunity the military

302

had long enjoyed in relation to human rights abuses. Likewise, although the MPR had decided in 1999 that the military's longstanding privilege of a guaranteed number of the appointed seats in the MPR would cease in 2004, the 'sunset' period was extended by TAP MPR until 2009, a backdown that drew widespread protest.[88]

Decentralisation

As mentioned, the New Order was characterised by a highly centralised political and economic system. McLeod,[89] Goodpaster[90] and Dick[91] have vividly demonstrated that it was, in fact, effectively a political and commercial corruption 'franchise' in which Soeharto, as 'head franchiser', distributed largesse and appointments in return for political support and access to national accounts. This system required that the benefit of Indonesia's huge natural resources, largely located in the outer regions, be directed almost entirely to the centre, in particular, to the ruling elite in Jakarta and, above all, to Jalan Cendana, where the Soeharto family compound is located. Consequently, it was essential for the centre to exercise sweeping political and economic control over the regions to secure the transfer of wealth that underpinned the elaborate structure of New Order state cronyism.

A result of this was, first, a loss of access to the benefits of local trade and industry by regional communities and, second, the creation of a highly intrusive regional bureaucracy controlled by Jakarta.[92] The sophisticated, centralist and rapacious *beamtenstaat*[93] inherited from the Dutch was thus placed at the disposal of a small group of politically, commercially and militarily well-positioned families: the New Order elite, clustered around Soeharto.

It is therefore not surprising that decentralisation of power was one of the central demands of the reform movement. President Habibie, who stood at the head of government with little popular legitimacy, responded with a policy of 'wide-ranging regional autonomy'. This resulted in Law 22/1999 on regional government and Law 25/1999 on financial balance between the central and regional governments.[94] Both statutes are vague in definition and are seriously inadequate in many critical respects, such as defining precisely the new financial and administrative relations between the central government and the newly empowered *kabupaten* or district governments and, in particular, as regards regulation of resources industries. The laws were also criticised by the regions they empowered on the grounds of insecurity: they were seen as gifts from the centre that could be revoked at any time. Constitutional form was therefore demanded to provide a hedge against policy reversal by a future government, and this was granted in Chapter VI (Articles 18, 18A and 18B), which mirrors the spirit of the laws.[95]

The Third Amendment

The Third Amendment was passed in the aftermath of a national constitutional crisis in which the newly strengthened constitutional authority of legislators was tested in direct confrontation with the President who replaced Habibie, Abdurrahman 'Gus Dur' Wahid, the charismatic, eccentric and blind leader of the world's largest Islamic organisation, *Nahdlatul Ulama*. The winner of the 1999 elections was, however, not Wahid's political vehicle, PKB, [96] but Megawati Soekarnoputri's PDI–P.[97] PDI–P's plurality of 33.7 per cent (33.1 per cent of seats) put it well ahead of its nearest rival, GOLKAR[98] (the former party of Soeharto), with only 22.4 per cent (26 per cent of seats). Wahid's PKB scored a distant 12.6 per cent (11 per cent of seats). Yet Wahid became President, with Megawati as his Vice-President. This was possible because appointment of the President remained a matter left to the absolute discretion of the MPR, pursuant to Article 6 of the Constitution. It was obliged only to choose the President from any 'native Indonesian citizen'. GOLKAR members – perhaps fearing prosecution for the rampant abuses of the Soeharto years – teamed up with PKB and other small Muslim parties to secure the numbers necessary to defeat Megawati.

The instability and administrative paralysis that marked Wahid's rule were therefore not surprising, as he never controlled a significant minority, let alone a majority, in the newly strengthened legislature. Instead, he was forced to extraordinary lengths to piece together weak coalitions to implement even routine decisions or pass laws. By mid-2001, government had virtually ceased to function and, in the words of one observer, '[c]ronyism has...cut deeply into the entire cabinet...the presidential office is beginning to become rather like a KKN[99] stock exchange'.[100]

As a consequence, the DPR moved to exercise its right of *interpolasi* (interpolation, a form of impeachment) pursuant to Part VII of Chapter 6 of the Elucidation, TAP MPR III of 1978 and TAP II of 1999.[101] It followed the procedures and timetable set out in the TAP, issuing two memoranda seeking an account from the President of his actions in relation to the so-called Bulogate and Bruneigate corruption scandals, both involving large sums missing from state coffers. In the memoranda, the DPR stated that 'it is reasonable to suspect' that the President had played a role in these corruption affairs. Wahid both aggressively rejected the allegations and challenged the procedure for interpolation, which was, indeed, vague in parts, especially as regards criteria for dismissal.

Events degenerated rapidly into a political standoff between President Wahid and law-makers in which the government became paralysed. On 28 May 2001, in the lead-up to the MPR special session called to consider his dismissal, the President issued an 'executive order' in terms eerily reminiscent of Soeharto's authoritarian turn of phrase, requiring the TNI to 'take necessary special actions and steps, by coordinating with all elements of the security forces, to overcome the crisis and uphold order, security and the law as quickly as possible'.

The crisis he referred to was described as 'the emergency political situation that we are facing because of controversies over the possibility of the Special session of the MPR and the possibility of a Presidential Decree'. He then purported to order the dissolution of the DPR/MPR. In carrying out these acts, Wahid was acting unconstitutionally and illegally, and, as it happened, the armed forces ignored his orders.[102] The MPR convened more quickly than planned and, as was by then politically inevitable, dismissed the President, replacing him with his deputy, Megawati, pursuant to Article 8 of the Constitution.[103]

These events were a watershed in the development of democracy in post-Soeharto Indonesia. The legislature had survived the crisis, had asserted its constitutional authority over a President seeking military support to act in an authoritarian and undemocratic fashion and had retained the support of the armed forces. However, in the process weaknesses in the definition of relations between the executive and the law-makers surviving from the First Amendment had been clearly demonstrated, as regards both the interpolation process and the relations between branches of government, as well as the root cause of the problem: the MPR's selection of a President whose party had, in fact, lost the election and lacked a workable presence in the legislature. In addition, the chaotic process had, to some extent, discredited all actors – including the MPR – in public perceptions. Accordingly, the Third Amendment was to deliver revolutionary change in these areas, principally to democratise and clarify the processes of government still further, but also to prevent another such crisis.

Election of the President

Perhaps the most radical change to the original scheme of the Constitution was the removal of power to appoint the President and deputy from the MPR. Instead they would now be directly elected from pairs of candidates proposed by political parties, on the basis of a minimum requirement that the winners score more than 50 per cent of the vote, plus at least 20 per cent of the votes in at least half of the provinces of Indonesia (Article 6A). This amendment was, however, incomplete. No consensus was reached on what would happen if, as is likely, no pair of candidates achieved so high an initial score. The question of whether there would be a second-round direct election between the two highest-scoring pairs or whether the MPR could then step in and decide between them was deferred to the next annual session of the MPR.

Dismissal of the President

A lengthy and detailed series of provisions (Articles 3, 7A, 7B and 8) were introduced to establish a clearer impeachment process for the President and Vice-President that excluded removal from office on policy grounds but specifically included corruption as a ground. The old procedure of a reference from the DPR to the MPR was retained, but the final decision was now made subject to review by a newly created Constitutional Court. Clarification was also introduced regarding succession by the Vice-President upon dismissal of the President (Paragraph 8(1)). Finally, the new Article 7C expressly restated the basic principle – moved now from the Elucidation to the text – that the President could not suspend or dismiss the DPR.

Formation of the cabinet

Reforms that minimised opportunities for any branch of government to act alone characterised the Third Amendment. As part of this, important changes to Article 20 were introduced. Paragraph 20(5) now provided that although the President may appoint and dismiss ministers, the formation of the cabinet and the change and dismissal of ministers is 'to be determined through law'; in other words, it can be controlled by the legislature (Article 17). This effectively gave the legislature the ability to control who will become members of the executive arm of government, and it marks a significant reduction in the power of the presidency, one that may prove important in the future, given that direct election will greatly increase the legitimacy of future presidents.

The Constitutional Court

Articles 24(2) and 24C established the new Constitutional Court, with jurisdiction over judicial review of legislation; conflict of interest among state institutions relating to constitutional powers of state institutions; actions for the dissolution of political parties; and actions with respect to election results. These articles also granted the new Court the power to rule on the new impeachment process. It is obvious that the creation of this Court was a direct answer to the crisis provoked by Wahid's dismissal, but it was also a response to the long absence of judicial review in Indonesia.

Soeharto's Law No. 14 of 1970 confirmed that Indonesian courts could not exercise such power, and for the long judicial winter of the New Order legislation was routinely rubber-stamped by the DPR, without any prospect of judicial assessment or interpretation.[104] Likewise, the absence of a power of constitutional review vested in the courts meant that there has been no development of doctrines of constitutional interpretation by the judiciary.[105] The unfortunate result was that much of the Soeharto-era web of regulation was, in fact, unconstitutional but also unimpeachable. This was one of the critical factors that has contributed to the steadily worsening dysfunction, corruption and political exploitation of Indonesia's legal system since 1959.[106]

If effective, the new Constitutional Court has the potential radically to transform the Indonesian judicial and legislative relationship and create a new check on the conduct of law-makers and the presidency. Unfortunately, however, the amendments did not deal in detail with the standing of the new Court within the system. How would cases be referred to it. Would it be truly independent? How would judges be appointed and, more importantly, dismissed? These critical issues have been left, pursuant to paragraph 24C(6), to later regulation by statute, but they remain largely unresolved and the Court was only constituted on August 17, 2003, and has not yet sat .Although Article 1 of the Constitution's new 'interim regulations' now fixes a deadline of 17 August 2003 for this to happen. Until then, the Supreme Court can exercise the Constitutional Court's powers. To date it has not yet done so.

Redefining the Role of the MPR

Ironically, the MPR's victory in its struggle with President Wahid resulted in still further erosion of its constitutional standing.

First, its previous authority to set the Broad Guidelines of State Policy (GBHN, *Garis-garis Besar Haluan Negara*) – which the President, as its 'mandatory', was charged to implement and account to it for – was lost completely (Article 3). With the passing of the accountability speech system, setting policy is now – presumably – the sole province of the executive.[107] More significantly from a theoretical perspective, the MPR's previously unlimited power to exercise the sovereignty of the people 'in full', granted by Article 1, has now also been removed. Instead, sovereignty is now nominally 'in the hands of the people' and seems to float with no specific locus, presumably above all three branches of government. The new paragraph 1(1) now simply states that the sovereignty of the people is to be 'exercised in accordance with the Constitution' (although the President still 'holds the power of government' under Article 4).

The regional 'senate'

A further major reform that will inevitably reduce the power of both the presidency and the legislature was the establishment of a regional 'senate'. The MPR the electorate will choose at the next election in 2004 will now be very different from its predecessors.

Chapter VIIA establishes the Regional Representatives Council (the *Dewan Perwakilan Daerah*, or DPD) with the power to submit laws to the

DPR on issues relating to regional autonomy, centre–region relations, and financial balance and natural resource management (Paragraph 22D(1)). In addition, it possesses the right to submit considerations to the DPR on the state budget and draft laws relating to tax, education and religion (Paragraph 22D(2)). Under Article 22C its members are to be elected from each province at the general election and must sit once a year, the same criteria as apply to the DPR (Article 19). The members of the DPD may not exceed one-third of the numbers of the DPR (Article 22C).

Reflecting the newly expanded nature of the general election – which will now choose President, Vice-President and the regional 'upper house', the DPD, as well as the members of the DPR (and thus together the entire membership of the MPR) – the General Election Commission (KPU, *Komisi Pemilhan Umum*) was established as a body independent of government (Paragraph 22E(5)). It will now no longer be under the control of the Minister for Internal Affairs.

Judicial Commission

For similar reasons, the new Article 24B provided for a new system for appointment of justices to the Supreme Court. Paragraph 24A(2) and 24B(1) establish an independent Judicial Commission that would have the role of proposing candidates to the DPR. The DPR would then select its preferred candidates from the Commission's list and they would 'then be confirmed' (*selanjutnya ditetapkan*) by the President. This was a reaction to controversies under President Wahid regarding the appointment of new judges under the exhausting new 'fit and proper' scrutiny system applied by the DPR, post-Soeharto. Claiming he did not like any of the candidates proposed, Wahid had refused to fill the vacant chief justice's position for months on end. The use of the words 'then confirmed' in the new Article 24A now seems to have removed presidential discretion from the process, although at the time of writing the Commission was yet to be formed. The Judicial Commission is also empowered to 'guard' (*menjaga*) and 'enforce' (*menegakkan*) judicial ethics (Paragraph 24B(1)), but these provisions are general in the extreme. Does this power extend as far as the dismissal of judges? If not, what sanctions are available to the Commission? If there are none, as Chapter 24B seems to suggest by its silence, then the Commission will be toothless.

Indeed, all the new provisions on the judiciary are disappointing when viewed from the perspective of judicial independence. Paragraph 24(1) states that the judicial power is 'independent' and is to be used to administer the courts and to enforce law and justice. However, the balance of the article then qualifies this, providing that the power is to be exercised by the Supreme Court, the various existing courts and 'other bodies connected with the judicial power *as provided in statute*' (Paragraphs 24(2) and (3); emphasis added). The same is true of the position, structure, membership and procedure of the Supreme Court (Article 24A(5)) and, indeed, the Judicial Commission (Paragraph 24B(4)), all of which are, again, left to statute, that is, the DPR. The grant of independence is thus nominal at best, as the judicial power is not actually vested in the highest court, but, ultimately, reserved to the legislature for allocation by statute.[108]

Constitutional Commission

The Third Amendment was far broader and more ambitious than its predecessor, but it was still not enough to recast the integralist, centralised and authoritarian New Order as a modern, devolved and plural democracy. This is because the changes required were so numerous and the document used as the basis for reconstruction – the 1945 Constitution – was so inadequate.

This meant that, despite the swathe of changes introduced in 2001, the Third Amendment resulted in frustration for reformers. Each new amendment created a need for further legislation and debate and little seemed to be finally resolved in detail. A range of reformed agencies remained without real structure or detailed substance (KPU, *Badan Pengawasan Keuangan* [BPK, State Audit Agency], Constitutional Court, Judicial Commission, DPD), and other amendments created a list of complex new statutes that would be required before the reforms could even begin to operate (for example a new election law, a decision on how the second round of presidential elections would be conducted and so forth). In this sense, the Third Amendment was more a 'shopping list' of future amendments than the start of a new system. Many felt that the detailed work required by that list was beyond the reach of the MPR special session, and many thought it would be beyond the normal procedures of the DPR as well.

One option considered to resolve these problems was the creation of a Constitutional Commission, sitting independently of the legislatures to debate the changes and make detailed proposals to the MPR. However, while scholars, lawyers and NGOs demanded an independent commission, political parties were divided. But, in the face of the absolute majority that Golkar and PDI–P together commanded, the three factions in the MPR that had supported a Commission did not put up a fight[109] and the proposal was, for the time being, defeated. This meant that, once again, a large range of unresolved but critical, politically sensitive and complex issues were deferred to the following year's MPR annual session, without a special-purpose body sitting in the interim to take submissions and refine the debate.

The Fourth Amendment

By comparison to the Third Amendment, the Fourth Amendment was of a lesser scope. Once again, however, the problem of the relative positions of the presidency and the MPR overshadowed all else and the MPR failed to deal with the growing list of urgent constitutional problems before it. The critical relationship between the DPR, the DPD and the MPR, for example, was not clarified. The status of the still unformed Constitutional Court and the extent of its powers were not resolved. The question of who now holds the power to dismiss judges and whether it should be in the hands of the not yet established Judicial Commission was also left untouched. It nonetheless made changes that were critical to ending integralism.

Direct election of the President

By unanimous vote, the MPR voluntarily finally stripped itself of the last remnants of the power it had enjoyed since 1945 to appoint the President (Article 6A). It was agreed, after bitter debate, that if none of the candidates receive an absolute majority in the first round of a direct election, then a second, direct, election would be held between the two highest-scoring candidates (Paragraph 6A(4)).

This reform will finally prevent the drawn-out horse trading, riddled with allegations of corruption, that has characterised the selection of Presidents since Soeharto's resignation, and it was passed despite initial reluctance from PDI–P, the largest party, which could have expected to have had a large say in the selection of the President under the old system.

MPR: the end of appointed members and dwifungsi

In the past, 195 members were added (200 prior to the departure of East Timor) to the DPR to form the MPR. Under legislation passed pursuant to former Article 2 (which simply left details of membership 'to be provided for by statute'), these additional members were made up of 122 regional party representatives (associated with the party groupings in the DPR), 65 appointed members and eight non-party regional representatives. The newly confirmed Article 2 now provides that the non-elected members will be replaced entirely by the DPD. Although, again, 'further organisation' is left to later regulation, it is now at least clear that there will be no appointed members after 2004.

Before the Fourth Amendment, the non-elected MPR seats included 38 reserved for representatives of the armed forces. In return, members of the armed forces were unable to vote. Since guaranteed appointed representation in the MPR has now been lost for the armed forces, it was agreed that they will now be given the right to vote as individuals. This represents the formal end to *dwifungsi*, at least in terms of its public political role.[110]

The task ahead

By the end of the 2002 MPR session it was obvious that the job of recreating the state system produced by the vestigial 1945 Constitution still had far to go, despite four years of radical constitutional amendment. As one observer said, 'this is the end of one chapter, the constitutional review, but the beginning of a lot of detailed work to take us into the next stage'.[111]

Take, for example, the laws now required by the Constitution itself to fill the gaps created by the four amendments to date:[112]

Law on Political Parties (or amendments)	Article 6A
Law on General Elections (or amendments)	Articles 6A, 22E
Law on Composition of the MPR	Article 22E
Law on Composition of the DPD	Articles 22C, D, E
Law on the Advisory Council	Article 16
Law on the Judicial Commission	Article 24
Law on the Constitutional Court	Article 24C
Law on the Central Bank (or amendments)	Article 23D
Law on Currency	Article 23B
Law on National Education	Article 31
Law on the Economy	Article 33
Law on Social Welfare	Article 34

If it is not part of the Law on General Elections, the following will also be necessary:

Law on Presidential Election	Article 6A

More problematic still, this array of major organic laws must be passed to meet the very tight deadline created by the elections and legislatures of President scheduled for April 2004. The dilemma was simply stated by Chusnul Mar'iyah of the General Election Commission (KPU): 'Indonesia has one and a half years to prepare for its first ever twin elections for the legislature and the presidency in what should take at least two years of preparations'.[113]

MPR or Constitutional Commission?

The enormity of the legislative and institutional tasks created by the four amendments have finally led the MPR to accept that Indonesia must have a specific-purpose Constitutional Commission to coordinate the enormous

and complex process of amendment, legislation, debate and public education now triggered.

Although the MPR has been willing – despite predictions to the contrary
– to divest itself of much of the power it enjoyed under Soekarno and
Soeharto, it has not been prepared to release its exclusive authority over
constitutional amendment. The proposal that an independent commission
guaranteed by a constitutional provision – a recreation of the Constituent
Assembly or *Konstituante* of the 1950s – be established was therefore
defeated. Instead, a Commission will, at last, be established, but it will be set
up by TAP MPR and will report to the MPR. Two-thirds of its members
will be regional and academic delegates appointed by the MPR, but one-
third will be MPR members. It will be a mere meeting place for technical
experts rather than a fully fledged Commission like that of Thailand, for
example.[114] Its proposals will be subject to the political process of the MPR.
This is very far from the ideal outcome, but it does at least mean that there is
now more opportunity for a broader, more inclusive and more public
process than occurred with the first four amendments.

Conclusion: the return of 'Asian values'?

The radical reinvention of Indonesia's constitutional arrangement sparked
by Soeharto's resignation has resulted in an unequivocal rejection, in constitutional principle at least, of the *Integralisticstaatside* and the 'thin' reading
of *Rechtsstaat* as 'rule by law'.

The result is, admittedly, still a long way from being satisfactory. The
new amended Constitution is an incomplete document and few of the
changes it has already mandated have even begun to be implemented
legislatively or institutionally. There are major problems to be
surmounted. First, the democratic ideal is now clearly agreed by almost
all parties as being the necessary outcome, but there is little understanding and less consensus on the detail of what that democratic ideal
might look like in Indonesia. The debate is fragmented and often
confused.

Second, for deep-seated historical reasons that are unlikely to alter in the
short term, none of the political protagonists are likely to be able to muster
a decisive majority sufficient to prevail over the cacophony. Compromise,
deal-making and an uneven patchwork approach are thus inevitable, as
democracy is negotiated clause by clause.

Third, to move from Soepomo's integralist authoritarian state to a plural
democracy, the executive and legislature – the groups that ultimately control
the reform process – must continue to divest themselves of significant power,
in particular to the long-repressed and still corrupt and poorly skilled judicial branch. The amendment process so far has been marked by intense
competition between the executive and judiciary as, while recognising the

need to reduce power, each continues to jostle and haggle, seeking to keep a relative advantage over the other branches of government.

Fourth, the fledgling democratic system in Indonesia faces revived attack from small but violent radical Islamic groups, which seek to destabilise the current moderate secular government of President Megawati and replace it with a hardline Islamic administration. These groups are, in a sense, proponents of a form of 'Asian values', although of a very different sort to that in the Bangkok Declaration or of Soeharto's New Order. Certainly a radical Islamic government would reject universalism of Western derivation for its own perception of Islamic absolutist universalism. It would seek to qualify human rights – which are recognised in most Islamic traditions – with the religious filter drawn from the Manichean intolerance of Saudi Wahabbism that informs most Islamic extremism today. This is, of course, a prospect that terrifies most of Indonesia's moderate, secularist Muslims, and it is therefore unlikely to succeed in the long run. But what is more likely – and no less threatening for the rule of law in Indonesia – is the possibility that the threat of Islam will be exploited by the military to engineer its own return to control of the state, just as it exploited a perceived communist threat to create the New Order in the 1960s, after killing and jailing millions. Certainly radical Islamic groups like Jema'ah Islamiyah seem to fit the New Order trope of shadowy subversive groups dedicated to overthrowing the state through violence. It is not impossible to imagine the New Order redux, with radical Islam conjured up in place of Marxism as the new bogeyman justifying a return to old 'Asian values' authoritarianism and legally institutionalised abuse.

But there are grounds for guarded optimism. The first is simply that Indonesia has come so far in so few years, from such a low base. Likewise, in that time its people have developed considerable legislative experience. The blossoming of civil society and, in particular, NGOs, coupled with the unmuzzling of Indonesia's now-voracious media, means that there is more capacity now for awareness-raising and educational campaigns than ever before. Likewise, the flood of post-Soeharto reforms and the widespread examination and criticism they have received have created a much broader public understanding of the importance of legal change and institutional reform than at any time since the 1950s and the mid-1960s. Political debate is sustained, widely followed and often subtle. Likewise, Indonesia's legal profession, although extremely small and largely irrelevant to public life, has begun to move more towards centre-stage, both with the emergence of a larger private profession and, more significantly, through a flourishing of effective legal NGOs.[115] All of these issues represent significant departures from the context in which the *Konstituante* was formed and extinguished in the first decade after the Revolution of 1945–9. Perhaps this 'muddling through' to democracy is in itself a democratic solution, and all the more likely to survive for that reason.

The 1945 Constitution of the Republic of Indonesia,
before amendment (1945 to 18 October 1999)117

The 1945 Constitution of the Republic of
Indonesia, as amended at 17 August
2002118

Article 27

1   All citizens have equal status before the
law and in government and shall uphold the law and
the government without any exception.

2   Every citizen has the right to work and to   *Article 27*
live in human dignity.

1   All citizens have equal status before the
law and in government and shall uphold the law and
the government without any exception.

2   Every citizen has the right to work and to
live in human dignity.

3   Every citizen has the right and duty to
participate in the defence of the nation.

Chapter XA. Human Rights

Article 28A

Each person has the right to live and has the right to
defend their life and their living.

Article 28B

1   Each person has the right to form a
family and to continue their family line through
legitimate marriage.

2   Each child has the right to viable life,
growth and development, and to protection from
violence and discrimination.

Article 28C

1   Each person has the right to develop
themselves through the fulfilment of their basic
needs, the right to education and to obtain benefit
from science and technology, art and culture, in
order to improve the quality of their life and the
welfare of the human race.

2   Each person has the right to advance
themselves in struggling to obtain their collective
rights to develop their community, their people, and
their nation.

1   Each person has the right to the recognition, the security, the protection and the certainty of just laws and equal treatment before the law.

2   Each person has the right to work and to receive just and appropriate rewards and treatment in their working relationships.

3   Each citizen has the right to obtain the same opportunities in government.

4   Each person has the right to citizenship.

1   Each person is free to profess their religion and to worship in accordance with their religion, to choose their education and training, their occupation, their citizenship, their place of residence within the territory of the State and to leave it and to return to it.

2   Each person has the freedom to possess convictions and beliefs, and to express their thoughts and attitudes in accordance with their conscience.

3   Each person has the freedom to associate, gather, and express their opinions.

Each person has the right to communicate and to obtain information in order to develop themselves and their social environment, and the right to seek out, obtain, possess, store, process, and transmit information using any means available.

1   Each person has the right to the protection of themselves, their family, their honour, their dignity, the property that is in their control, and the right to feel safe and to be protected from the threats of fear from doing or not doing something that is a basic right.

2   Each person has the right to be free from torture or treatment that lowers human dignity and has the right to obtain political asylum from other countries.

1   Each person has the right to physical and spiritual welfare, to have a home, to have a good and healthy living environment and to obtain health services.

2   Each person has the right to assistance and special treatment in order to gain the same opportunities and benefits in the attainment of equality and justice.

3   Each person has the right to social security that allows their full personal development as a human being.

4   Each person has the right to private property and this right may not be arbitrarily interfered with by anyone at all.

Article 28I

1   The right to live, the right not to be tortured, the right to freedom of thought and conscience, the right not to be enslaved, the right to be individually recognised by the law, and the right not to be prosecuted under retrospective laws are basic human rights that may not be interfered with under any circumstances at all.

2   Each person has the fright to be free from discriminatory treatment on any grounds and has the right to obtain protection from such discriminatory treatment.

3   Cultural identity and the rights of traditional communities are respected in accordance with the continuing development of civilisation over time.

4   The protection, advancement, upholding and fulfilment of basic human rights are the responsibility of the State, especially the government.

5   In order to uphold and protect basic human rights in accordance with the principle of a democratic State ruled by laws, the implementation of human rights shall be guaranteed, regulated and provided for in regulations and legislation.

Article 28J

1   Each person is obliged to respect the basic human rights of others in orderly life as a community, as a people, and as a nation.

2   In the enjoyment of their rights and freedoms, each person is obliged to submit to the limits determined by law, with the sole purpose of guaranteeing recognition and respect for the rights of others and to fulfil the requirements of justice and taking into consideration morality, religious values, security, and public order in a democratic community.

Notes

1 Associate Professor of Law and Director, Asian Law Centre, the University of Melbourne.

2 See Randall Peerenboom, 'Beyond Universalism and Relativism: The Evolving Debates about "Values in Asia",' (forthcoming) *Indiana International and Comparative Law Review* (2003) for an account of the Bangkok Declaration.

3 By 'West' I mean the USA, Canada, Western Europe, the British Isles, Australia and New Zealand.

4 'Asian' is a term that is almost impossible to define in a completely satisfactory way. Here I use it to refer to states that self-identify as 'Asian', and that certainly includes the 30-odd signatories to the Bangkok Declaration.

5 Tatsuo Inoue, 'Liberal Democracy and "Asian Values",' in M. Yasutomo, ed., *Law in a Changing World: Asian Alternatives* (Stuttgart, Frans Steiner Verlag, 1998), p. 59. See also Tim Lindsey, 'History Always Repeats? Corruption, Culture and "Asian Values",' in Tim Lindsey and Howard Dick, eds, *Corruption in Asia: Rethinking the Governance Paradigm* (Sydney, Federation, 2002), pp. 1–23.

6 Association of South East Asian Nations.

7 It now forms the new chapter XA of the 1945 Constitution, as amended: see Appendix (pp. 000–00) for details.

8 This part draws on material in Tim Lindsey, 'From Soepomo to Prabowo', in Charles Coppel, ed., *Violence in Indonesia* (forthcoming).

9 Merle Ricklefs, *A History of Modern Indonesia since c.1200*, 3rd edn (Basingstoke: Palgrave, 2001), p. 10.

10 Netherlands Indies Civil Administration, the Dutch government of the East Indies during the revolution, 1945–9.

11 *Rakyat*: the people, masses.

12 *Gerakan September Tiga Puluh*: the 30th September Movement; see, generally, Ricklefs (2001), ch. 21.

13 James T. Siegel, 'A New Criminal Type in Jakarta: The Nationalisation of Death', in Vicente L. Rafael, ed., *Figures of Criminality in Indonesia, the Philippines, and Colonial Vietnam* (Southeast Asia Program Publications, Ithaca, Cornell University, 1999), p. 215.

14 Id.

15 Id., p. 218.

16 *Gabungan Anak Liar*, groups of wild youths, a New Order euphemism for criminal gangs.

17 For more on the killings, see John Pemberton, *On the subject of 'Java'* (Ithaca, Cornell University Press, 1994).

18 This and the previous quote are taken from Soeharto's autobiography, as cited in Siegel (1999) pp. 227–30. I have substituted 'masses' for Siegel's rendering of '*orang banyak*' as 'crowds'.

19 Siegel sees this as an attempt to appropriate the power of the gali by asserting that it is the only institution that can go beyond limits (1999, p. 228). In my view this appropriation was unnecessary, because the integralist state has rarely, as a matter of fact, experienced real limits on its authority. It does not need more power. But this is a quibble.

20 Jose Manuel Tesoro, 'The Scapegoat?', *Asiaweek*, 3 March 2000.

21 Id.

22 Id.

23 'The "Coup",' *Asiaweek*, 3 March 2000.

24 Tesoro, 'The Scapegoat?'

25 See, generally, Ricklefs (2001), ch. 20.

26 Daniel Lev, 'Between State & Society: Professional Lawyers and Reform in Indonesia', in Tim Lindsey, ed., *Indonesia: Law and Society* (Sydney, Federation, 1999), pp. 227–46.
27 By 1966 Soeharto had appropriated effective ruling authority through the controversial Supersemar (*Surat Sebelas Maret*: Letter of 11 March) decree, and in 1968 he had formally replaced Soekarno; see, generally, Ricklefs (2001), ch. 21.
28 Kate McGregor, 'A Soldier's Historian', *Inside Indonesia*, October 2001.
29 On this 'state religion', see Pemberton (1994) and Clifford Geertz, '"Popular Art" and the Javanese Tradition', *Indonesia* (1990), p. 77.
30 'The integralist state idea' (Dutch).
31 Indonesia has over 17,000 islands, a population of over 217 million and between 200 and 300 separate ethnic groups and languages.
32 1945–1949; 1959–continuing (amended 1999, 2000, 2001, 2002; see Appendix, pp. 000–00). On the 1945 Constitution generally, see Adnan Buyung Nasution, *The Aspiration for Constitutional Government in Indonesia: A Socio-legal Study of the Indonesian Konstituante 1956–1959* (CIP–Gegevens Koninklijke Bibliotheek, Den Haag, 1992).
33 This part draws on material in Tim Lindsey, 'From Soepomo to Prabowo', in Charles Coppel, ed., *Violence in Indonesia*, forthcoming; and in Tim Lindsey, 'Indonesia's Negara Hukum: Walking the Tightrope to the Rule of Law', in Arief Budiman, Barbara Hately and Damien Kingsbury, eds, *Reformasi: Crisis and Change in Indonesia* (Monash Asia Institute/Centre for Southeast Asian Studies, Clayton, 1999), pp. 363–81.
34 Dr Muhammad Ridhwan Indra, *The 1945 Constitution: A Human Creation* (details not known – copy in possession of author), 1990.
35 H. Muhammad Yamin, *Naskah Persiapan Undang–Undang Dasar 1945*, vol. I (Jakarta, Yayasan Prapanca, 1959), p. 114.
36 Id.
37 Id.
38 Nasution (1992), p. 93.
39 David Bourchier, 'Positivism and Romanticism in Indonesian Legal Thought', in Tim Lindsey, ed., *Indonesia: Law and Society* (Sydney, Federation, 1999), pp. 186–96.
40 Peter Burns, 'The Myth of Adat', *Journal of Legal Pluralism and Unofficial Law*, no. 28 (1989), p.1. See also Peter Burns, *The Leiden Legacy: Concepts of Law in Indonesia* (Jakarta, PT Pradnya Paramita, 1999).
41 This paragraph draws on Bourchier (1999) and Burns (1989, 1999).
42 Bourchier (1999), p. 191.
43 Lindsey (1999), ch. 1.
44 Note, however, as discussed below, that the post-Soeharto amendments have now introduced a comprehensive Bill of Rights in Chapter XA of the 1945 Constitution, which largely replicates the Universal Declaration of Human Rights (see Appendix, pp. 000–00).
45 Daniel Fitzpatrick, 'Beyond Dualism: Land Acquisition and Law in Indonesia', in Tim Lindsey, ed., *Indonesia: Law and Society* (Sydney, Federation, 1999), pp. 74–93.
46 Ian Fehring, 'Unionism and Workers' Rights in Indonesia – the Future', in Tim Lindsey, ed., *Indonesia: Law and Society* (Sydney, Federation, 1999), pp. 367–80.
47 Partai Demokratis Indonesia (Indonesian Democratic Party).
48 David Clark, 'The Many Meanings of Rule of Law', in Kanishka Jayasuriya, ed., *Law, Capitalism and Power in Asia: the Rule of Law and legal Institutions* (Routledge, London and New York, 1999).
49 C. Gray, 'Legal Process and Economic Development: A Case Study of Indonesia', *World Development*, vol. 19, no. 7 (1991), p. 765; see also Clark (1999).

50 For an excellent description of 'thick' and 'thin' accounts of the rule of law, see Chapter 1.
51 Clark (1999).
52 Gray (1991), p. 765; Clark (1999).
53 Gray (1991), p. 766.
54 For a discussion of the political subordination of the *Mahkamah Agung* see Tim Lindsey, 'Paradigms, Paradoxes and Possibilities: Towards Understandings of Indonesia's Legal System', in Veronica Taylor, *Asian Laws Through Australian Eyes: Australian Perspectives on Asian Legal Systems* (Sydney, Law Book Company, 1997), pp. 90–110; and Lev (1999); Daniel Lev, 'Judicial Institutions and Legal Culture in Indonesia', in Claire Holt, ed., *Culture and Politics in Indonesia* (Ithaca and London, Cornell University Press, 1972).
55 See, generally, Gunter Frankenburg, 'Critical Comparisons: Re-thinking Comparative Law', *Havard International Law Journal*, vol. 26 (1985), pp. 411–55.
56 Bourchier (1999).
57 The Elucidation is the explanatory memorandum that accompanies most Indonesian legislative and regulatory instruments and, although not a formal source of law on its own, is usually read as part of the text of the instrument. It is routinely used by the courts in interpreting the meaning of any statute and it plays an essential role in interpreting the Constitution.
58 Some caution is required here. Indonesian laws have rarely been applied universally or consistently, as Gray (1991) would require for true 'rule by law'.
59 Id.
60 *Majelis Permusyawaratan Rakyat*, People's Consultative Assembly.
61 The MPR voluntarily surrendered sovereignty in the Third Amendment (see below).
62 *Dewan Perwakilan Rakyat*, People's Representative Council.
63 See Burns (1989, 1999).
64 The following discussion of the amendments to the 1945 Constitution draws on Tim Lindsey, 'Indonesian Constitutional Reform: Muddling Towards Democracy', *Singapore Journal of International & Comparative Law* 6 (2002), pp. 244–301.
65 See, for example, Kurniawan Hari and Tertiani Z. B. Simanjuntak, 'Time Running Out for Constitutional Reforms', *Jakarta Post*, 6 August 2002; Berni K. Moestafa 'MPR Annual Session, 2004 Election Not Important: Winters', *Jakarta Post*, 15 July 2002.
66 The following passages draw, in part, on Tim Lindsey, 'From Rule of Law to Law of the Rulers – to Reformation?', in Tim.Lindsey, ed., *Indonesia: Law and Society* (Sydney, Federation Press, 1999), pp. 11–21; on NGOs, see Tim Lindsey, 'Anti-Corruption and NGOs in Indonesia', in Richard Holloway, ed., *Stealing from the People:16 Studies on Corruption in Indonesia: Book 4 – the Clampdown: In Search of New Paradigms* (Partnership for Governance Reform, Jakarta, 2002), pp. 29–71.
67 On the *Konstituante*, see, generally, Nasution (1992).
68 David Bourchier, 'The 1950s in New Order Ideology & Politics', in David Bourchier and John Legge, *Democracy in Indonesia: 1950s and 1990s* (Centre of Southeast Asian Studies, Monash University, Clayton, 1994), pp. 50–60.
69 The leader of the formerly banned trade union, SBSI (*Serikat Buruh Sejahtera Indonesia*).
70 A well-known Indonesian dramatist.
71 A former legislator and staunch critic of Soeharto who established his own, unsuccessful opposition party.
72 For an engaging narrative of political trials of the late New Order, see Spencer Zifcak, 'But a Shadow of Justice: Political Trials in Indonesia', in Tim Lindsey, *Indonesia: Law and Society* (Sydney, Federation, 1999), pp. 355–66.

73 Personal communication to the author, Jakarta, April 1999.
74 The only real election held prior to the Soeharto era (which began in 1966) was in 1955. This election, with 91.5 per cent of registered voters participating, was more fair and open than the sham elections held every five years under Soeharto, but it has also been criticised for not being truly democratic, due to religious and military pressures. Under Soeharto all elections were heavily manipulated; see Ricklefs (2001), pp. 303–4.
75 At that time, the legislators comprised the elected members of the legislature, the DPR (and those same members, sitting with additional appointed members as a parliament, formed the MPR, then the only entity with the authority to amend the Constitution [Article 37 of the Constitution]).
76 On the Elucidation, see note 57, above.
77 The only control mechanism to restrain the MPR was the requirement that it meet once every five years (Article 2(2)), presumably a minimum. For most of Soeharto's rule, however, it was read as maximum and his rubber-stamp MPR therefore met only once every five years.
78 Indonesia's Road to Constitutional Reform – The 2000 MPR Annual Session, Assessment Report by the National Democratic Institute for International Affairs (2000), p. 7; copy on file with author.
79 *Interpolasi*: this is essentially a form of impeachment; see Tim Lindsey, 'The Criminal State: Premanisme and the New Indonesia', in Grayson Lloyd and Shannon Smiths, eds, *Indonesia Today* (Singapore, ISEAS, 2001), pp. 283–294 and note 17.
80 Part VII of Chapter 6 of the Elucidation provided for a process equivalent to impeachment. Specifically, it stated that if the DPR considered that the President has truly (*sungguh*) violated the *haluan Negara*, or national will (sometimes translated as national policy), as fixed either by the Constitution or by the MPR, then the DPR could call the MPR into session in a special sitting to ask the President to account for his actions. More specific regulation of the impeachment process is contained in MPR *Ketetapan* (TAP) or Decision III of 1978 and in TAP II of 1999. These instruments were intended to enlarge on the rights provided for in the Constitution. Most significantly, MPR TAP II of 1999 added 'the violation of the Constitution' as an additional ground for convening the special session of the MPR. The two MPR TAPs together required that two successive memoranda of censure be issued by the DPR before the MPR could be called into session. The TAP also established a two-month timetable for the memorandum and special sitting – the timetable was not fixed by the Constitution, contrary to most press reports. This was the mechanism used by the DPR and MPR to dismiss President Wahid in 2001.
81 Constitutionally, the President was on the same level as the legislature, the DPR, and as Chapter 6, Part V of the Elucidation to the Constitution states, 'the President is not responsible to it'. It also provides, however, that 'he/she must pay full attention to the voice of the DPR'.
82 *Indonesia's Road to Constitutional Reform* (2000), p. 7.
83 Id. See also Ross Clarke, 'Will the Guilty be Punished? Retrospectivity and the Constitutional Validity of the Bali Bomb and East Timor Trials', *Australia Journal of Asian Law*, vol. 5, no. 2 (forthcoming).
84 Ross McLeod, 'Soeharto's Indonesia: A Better Class of Corruption', *Agenda*, vol. 7, no. 2 (2000), pp. 99–112.
85 Pemberton (1994).
86 McLeod (2000); Richard Tanter, 'The Totalitarian Ambition: Intelligence and Security Agencies in Indonesia', in Arief Budiman, ed., *State and Civil Society in Indonesia*, Monash Papers on Southeast Asia, no. 22 (Clayton, Centre of

Southeast Asian Studies, Monash University, 1990), pp. 215–88; Pemberton (1994).

87 See *Indonesia's Road to Constitutional Reform*, 2000.

88 Similarly, paragraphs 30(1) and (2) explicitly recognised the army's prized 'total people's defence system' (*sishankamrata*) doctrine. Derived from the revolutionary experience of guerrilla war in the early 1940s, this notion places an obligation (*wajib*) on citizens to support the army in its carrying out its national defence and – more ominously – security roles. It may therefore one day provide a constitutional platform for a return of a de facto *dwifungsi* system.

89 Ross McLeod (2000), pp. 99–112.

90 Gary Goodpaster, 'Reflections on Corruption in Indonesia', in Tim Lindsey and Howard Dick, ed., *Corruption in Asia: Rethinking the Good Governance Paradigm* (Sydney, Federation Press, 2002), pp. 87–108.

91 Howard Dick, 'Corruption and Good Governance: The New Frontier of Social Engineering', in Tim Lindsey and Howard Dick, ed., *Corruption in Asia: Rethinking the Good Governance Paradigm* (Sydney, Federation Press, 2002), pp. 71–86.

92 Tanter (1990), pp. 215–88.

93 'Bureacratic state' (Dutch).

94 Blair A King, 'Constitutional Tinkering – The Search for Consensus is Taking Time', *Inside Indonesia*, January–March 2001, p. iii.

95 Id.

96 *Partai Kebangkitan Bangsa*, National Awakening Party.

97 *Partai Demokrasi Indonesia – Perjuangan*, Indonesian Democratic Party – Struggle.

98 *Golongan Karya* – Functional Group.

99 'Corruption, collusion, nepotism': *korupsi, kolusi, nepotisme* (Indonesian).

100 Hukumonline, 'ICW: Politik Uang di DPR Makin Marak', 23 January 2001, cited in Gary Goodpaster (2002), p. 96.

101 Together, these provisions required that two successive memoranda of censure be issued by the DPR before the MPR could be called into a special session by the DPR to consider the memoranda and any reply from the President and decide whether or not he should be dismissed.

102 Wahid appeared to rely on Article 12 of the Constitution, which provides that '[t]he President may declare a state of emergency. The conditions for such a declaration and the measures to deal with the emergency shall be governed by law'. The Law then governing states of emergency was Government Regulation in lieu of a Law (Perpu) 23 of 1959 (confirmed as a statute by the DPR in 1961). An attempt to introduce new emergency legislation in 1999 was passed by the DPR amid widespread protest and it has never been signed into law. Article 1 of Perpu 23 of 1959 requires that there be a declaration by the President of a state of civil emergency, a state of military emergency or a state of war before the President can exercise emergency powers in Article 10. However, it appears that such a formal declaration never occurred – not even according to Wahid – so the constitutional and statutory authority he needed was never invoked. Likewise, the order expressed itself as a *maklumat*, an order or decree. The *maklumat* was a commonly used form of law under President Soekarno's 'Guided Democracy' dictatorship, effective from 1957 to 1966. After his fall, in 1966 the MPR fixed a new hierarchy of laws in a TAP later confirmed in MPR TAP No. 3 of 2000. Presidential Decisions (*Keputusan Presiden* or *Keppres*) – which have a particular form – have a place in the hierarchy as the lowest level of legislation above other 'implementing regulations'. Presidential Decrees or *maklumat*, however, were specifically removed from the hierarchy by the MPR, with the result that the 'executive order' in fact

probably had no binding legal standing or could easily be overruled by DPR statute or MPR TAP. In any case, it was clear from chapter 6, Part VII of the Elucidation to the Constitution that the 'position of the DPR is strong. The DPR cannot be dissolved by the President'. As regards the MPR, the position was not expressly stated, but was arguably the same. As argued above in the discussion of the First Amendment, the Constitution was clear on the MPR's absolute superiority to the President.

103 There was some debate as to the meaning of this provision, as, while it covered generally what happened when a President could not perform his duties, it did not explicitly mention succession in the case of dismissal.

104 Lev (1999).

105 This poverty of constitutional jurisprudence is itself one of the difficulties the MPR has faced in trying to amend the Constitution.

106 Simon Butt, 'The Eksekusi of the Negara Hukum: Implementing Judicial Decisions in Indonesia', in Tim Lindsey, ed., *Indonesia: Law and Society* (Sydney, Federation Press, 1999), pp. 247–57; Lev (1999).

107 This power was more significant than it might seem at first blush, because it was the source of the MPR's right to demand that the President account for his or her implementation of the GBHN. This right in turn gave rise to the power to dismiss a President whose 'accountability speech' was deemed lacking. In 1966, in the aftermath of the army's annihilation of his leftist supporters, President Soekarno gave an accountability speech that the then (interim) MPR found 'fell short of fulfilling the expectations of the people'. It revoked the Presidency for Life it had previously conferred on him, and in 1967 it stripped him of the capacity to exercise his powers and appointed Soeharto acting President, confirming the latter as full President in 1968. This episode made it clear that the presidency was effectively in the gift of the MPR and that it could shorten the term of its gift in response to an inadequate accountability speech. The significance of the MPR refusing to accept an accountability speech was underlined more recently when the incumbent B. J. Habibie responded to rejection by withdrawing his candidature for a further term.

108 This reluctance to grant the Supreme Court real independence or to release the legislature's and executive's control over its activities – and, in particular, the dismissal of judges (which seems to remain vested in the Minister of Justice for the time being) – is a response to deep public mistrust in the institutional integrity of the Supreme Court. This Court is widely regarded as being one of the most corrupt institutions in Indonesia and its competence is also subject to much criticism. Although the stewardship of Professor Bagir Manan, the chief justice ultimately accepted by Wahid, has recently produced signs of improvement in Supreme Court decisions, it remains a profoundly troubled jurisdiction. The result is that many in the legislature and the government think it would be dangerous to fully release it too quickly from the oversight by the Ministry of Justice. The dilemma is a real one: the democratic *trias politika* obviously demands an independent third branch, but is it prudent to place the final level of appeal in the hands of an unchecked rogue court?

109 Kurniawan Hari, 'MPR Unlikely to set up Constitutional Commission', *Jakarta Post*, 24 October 2001.

110 It may, however, not be the end of the long tussle between civilians and the military for political power. Because, as mentioned, one outcome of the MPR session that produced the Third Amendment was an extension of the military's tenure in the MPR until 2009, some officers consider the now-reinstated deadline of 2004 to be a betrayal that may still be reversible.

111 Andrew Ellis, in Radio Netherlands, *Constitutional Changes in Indonesia*, 13 August 2002; copy on file with author.

112 List developed from Berni K. Moestafa and Hari Kurniawan, 'Time, the Next Hurdle for the 2004 General Election', *Jakarta Post*, 13 August 2002.

113 Id.

114 Andrew Harding, 'May There be Virtue: "New Asian Constitutionalism" in Thailand', 3 *Australian Journal of Asian Law* 236 (2001).

115 See, generally, Tim Lindsey, 'Anti-Corruption and NGOs in Indonesia' (2002), pp. 29–71.

116 This version was translated and developed by Helen Pausacker, Rohan Gould and Tim Lindsey, Asian Law Centre, University of Melbourne.

117 Developed from the translation of the first edition, published by the then Yogyakarta-based Information Ministry of the Republic of Indonesia in 1950: http://asnic.utexas.edu/asnic/countries/indonesia/ConstIndonesia.html,courtesy, Embassy of the Republic of Indonesia, Washington, DC.

118 Developed from the version published in Kompas newspaper, 12 August 2002.

10

RULE OF LAW IN INDIA
Theory and practice

Upendra Baxi

Anxieties

A new explosion of the rule of law discourse understandably marks the advent of the twenty-first century CE. Heady currents of contemporary post-Cold War globalization in part induce it. This new discourse is also heavily and poignantly now imbricated in a post-9/11 reconfigured world 'order'.[1] The tumultuous rise of global civil society and new social movements contributes a great deal to people-oriented multitudinous scrutiny; this new discursivity assuredly reveals that the rule of law, assumed to be a 'good thing' all round, means different things to different peoples, in ways that render any general theory about it inchoate/impossible. Its histories differ not just across legal and social cultures but also within same-law regions. Its prescriptive bases also remain contested sites. The diversity may seem desirable even for its own sake in a postmodern world. Even so, all this poses some formidable tasks for understanding and judgement. One thing is indeed clear: unexamined notions of rule of law may not be *not* a 'good thing' at all, if only because, understood in minimalist procedural terms, the rule of law may also authorize Holocaustian practices of politics.[2] Avoidance of this dreadful conflation names the task of defining rule of law as the 'rule of *good law*'. But elucidating 'good' law entails 'a complete social philosophy' which deprives the rule of law notion of 'any useful function'. As Joseph Raz acutely reminds us, '[w]e have no need to be converted to rule of law in order to discover that to believe in it is also to believe that good should triumph'.[3] But the 'good' that triumphs, as a 'complete social philosophy', may be, and indeed has often been, defined in ways that perpetuate states of Radical Evil. Complete social philosophies have justified, and remain capable of justifying, varieties of violent social exclusion.

Is this the reason why contemporary postmetaphysical approaches invite us to tasks of envisioning justice – qualities of the basic structure of society, economy and polity – in ways that render otiose the rule of law languages? Neither John Rawls' assemblage of 'constitutional essentials', 'reasonable pluralism' and 'overlapping consensus'[4] nor Jurgen Habermas' concern with modes of discursive (dialogical) production of 'legitimate law',[5] in which 'human rights' embody the newfound powers of 'communicative reason' and fashion the foundational ways instituting 'deliberative democracy', remain overly concerned with the rule of law. The ways in which recent political philosophy and social theory have refused to converse with the inaugural contribution of Michael Oakeshott, who strove all his life to provide us with a 'non-instrumental' understanding of the rule of law, testify to the 'poverty of theory'.[6]

'The germ of doubt', to evoke J. M. Cootze, 'gnaws at the heart of conviction'.[7] At best, our notions of rule of law remain 'empty signifiers'.[8]

While the variegated rule of law notions convey a sense of constraints upon lawmaking (legislative) power,[9] they rarely speak to any ethical *obligation* to make law, a public 'right' to have a law made for disadvantaged, dispossessed and deprived peoples. These remorseless non-decisions impact upon many a human future. It is only when we pour the content of contemporary human rights norms, standards and values into our notions about the rule of law that such an obligation begins to take shape.

Similarly, the rule of law notions do not entail pertinent constraints concerning sovereign, life and death, decisions. Indeed, the separation of powers component only invests the executive with sovereign discretion in the realms of macro- and micro-development planning, arms production (inclusive of weapons of mass destruction), decisions to wage many types of (covert as well as overt) war, or management of insurgent violence. Our rule of law talk, unsurprisingly, but still unhappily, ends more or less where the militarized state (the 'secret' State, to evoke E. P. Thompson)[10] begins. In terms of a substantive theory of the 'good', our rule of law talk fails, on the whole, the task of elucidating notions of *just* governance.

Further, differentiation of governance functions fosters the belief that relatively autonomous spheres constituting legislative, executive and adjudicatory powers actually *deliver* limited governance. On this view, dispersal of governance powers constitutes a sure antidote to tyranny signified by concentration of powers. And histories of domination ineluctably guide us to privilege dispersal. But what follows from logics of such dispersal is far from clear. The following summarily put interrogations, I hope, are not impertinent.

Does the rule of law in this mode privilege 'good' and ethically viable ways of structuring representation? Does it speak to us of the inherent 'good' of proportional and preferential voting as against first-past-the-post electoral arrangements? How may it address tasks of delimitation of constituencies in ways that avoid gerrymandering?[11] Does it authorize recall of errant or corrupt legislators? Does it favour *federalism* over *unitary*, *republican* over *monarchical*, *secular* over *theological*, *flexible* over *rigid* constitutional formats? Does it privilege plenary judicial review over forms of legislative, executive and administrative action? In what ways do the rule of law languages speak prescriptively to the constitution of adjudicative power? How may hierarchies of administration of justice devised, justices appointed and their autonomy and accountability be concretely defined? In what ways may the rule of law prescribe the structuration of legislative power: should this be accompanied by an integral ethical minimum, such that there may be said to exist critical ethical thresholds to 'parliamentary sovereignty'? Ought the sphere of legislation to be constitutively defined in terms of 'constitutional engineering' that casts specific human rights obligations on the activity of governance through legislation and administration? Ought popular participation in the administration of criminal justice, for example, emerge as an enshrined value of the rule of law, such that it entails consultation with affected interests in the making of criminal law and its dispensation in real life (for example trial by jury)?

Indeed, the notion of limited government becomes insensible when we recall, with Louis Althusser, that the languages of the separation of powers mark not so much the vaunted dispersal of power but rather the 'centralized unity' of state?[12] And, as Julius Stone, in another vein, reminded us, 'separation of powers', at the end of the day, consists in no more than a 'division of functions' in modes of governance,[13] a task that does not go beyond the recurrent repair of governance deficit and all too often involves 'short-changing' citizens through practices of judicial restraint and the consequent systemic under-enforcement of human rights. Further still, how may we understand in our rule of law languages 'legal' conceptions of sovereignty that, in Carl Schmitt's phrase regime, consist *not* so much in the power to name the 'normal', but the 'exceptional', as its very definitive moment;[14] that is, the power of regimes to incarnate the Reason of the State against all protestations under the banner of human rights?

The other of governance stands insufficiently addressed by the rule of law talk. It is a social fact that the ruled have very different notions of what this means.

A multitude of mass illegalities historically enact forms of citizen understandings and interpretations of the rule of law notion. These divergent insurgencies define forms of popular sovereignty; the rule of law, on this register, is a terrain of struggle of the multitudes against the rule of the minuscule.[15] What space may we provide, and how may 'we' (the 'symbol traders' of the rule of law languages and rhetoric) provide it, for the militant particularisms in our narratives?

Finally (and without being exhaustive) the rule of law narratives mark and map diverse human histories. No 'universal' history of the rule of law exists. Yet we are constantly asked to believe that it does, and to subscribe to the myth of origins in the Euro-American tradition of modern law.[16] The standard narratology of rule of law remains insufficiently situated in the combined and uneven development of modern capitalism; it has very little space for Marxian critique[17] or subsequent socialist and postsocialist reconstruction.

The progress narratives that celebrate core normative constraints on power and domination remain regressively Eurocentric. As such, they do not locate the historic renovation of that notion made possible by the world historic peoples' struggles. If today self-determination, dignity and equality of peoples and states possess historic significance, this owes little to the classical liberal theory of human rights and the rule of law. People's movements from Mahatma Gandhi to Nelson Mandela and beyond have contributed enormously to ethical refinement of our rule of law notions. The originary foundational moments of the rule of law capaciously accommodated forms of colonial predatory legality and violent social exclusion.[18] Only popular, mass 'illegalities' endowed the rule of law with future historic, even messianic, social power.

Many jurisprudential movements (critical legal studies, feminist jurisprudence, critical race theory, lesbian, gay, transgender and human rights movements) demonstrate even today that the promise of the rule of law stands constituted (like all promises) only by the possibility of its betrayal.[19] How may we incorporate this form of critique in our reconstruction of the rule of law discourse?

And the rule of law notion becomes somewhat inchoate in a rapidly globalizing world where nation-states remain compelled by many doctrines of 'good governance' to pay more attention to the needs of the communities of foreign investors over those of their own citizens, and where transactional corporations and international financial institutions owe very little democratic accountability and human rights responsibilities. There is no parallel development of a global rule of law in the making. Insofar as September 11 and its aftermath may be said to have yielded such a notion, it remains frankly a cause of concern rather than celebration.[20]

This summary checklist of anxieties is *not* intended to suggest that we dispense altogether with the languages and logics of the rule of law. Rather, it invites sustained labours that handle the normative and ideological histories and frontiers of rule of law with very great care and strict scrutiny.[21]

The rule of law notion remains a veritable conceptual minefield. This volume testifies richly, in the present view, to diverse histories of rule of law, as sites both of state formative practices and of resistance.[22] All I can do here is to combine both the courage of conviction and courage of confusion in tracing the itinerary of the rule of law 'theory' and practice in Indian constitutionalism.

Both forms of courage derive from an aphoristic utterance: the *rule of law is always and everywhere a terrain of peoples' struggle to make power accountable, governance just, and state ethical.* Undoubtedly, each romantic/radical term used here (accountability, justice and ethics) needs deciphering.[23]

Beyond mimesis? Postcolonial Indian construction of the rule of law

Despite many a colonially induced historic continuity,[24] the Indian Constitution inaugurates marked discontinuity in theory and practice of contemporary rule of law. Its revisionist liberal conceptions assume distinctive forms of constitutional life of the South.[25]

Contemporary niche epistemic markets regard rule of law doctrine as a prize commodity for cultural export. Thus, peoples of postsocialist societies, for example, have to begin to read A. V. Dicey's notions and to learn how flawed they turned out to be in the country of origin! Indeed, the dominant North epistemic entrepreneurs successfully prevent meaningful transfer of social, comparative constitutional learning from South experience in the making of constitutions of the so-called 'transitional societies', even when postcolonial and postsocialist histories of theory and practice of rule of law demonstrate some considerable 'elective affinities' (in Goethe's phrase). I suggest, for example, that contemporary Russia and the former 'East European' constitutionalism have more to learn from the experience of judicial activism (say in India and South Africa) than from the rather sanitized discourse concerning the legitimacy of judicial review in the United States. I hope that contributions to this volume bring home this important truth.

I may here address only the uniqueness of the Indian constitutional conception of the rule of law. It inaugurally enunciates linkages between four core notions of rule of law. These are 'rights', 'development', 'governance' and 'justice.' Its rule of law conception addresses all these notions in their dynamic and dialectical relationships. Of necessity, the practice of theory (to borrow a fecund phrase from Pierre Bourdieu) remains both complex and contradictory. I present it in different strokes and rather summarily (given reasons of space).

Rights

Even when the Indian rule of law notion casts rights as a corpus of limitation on state and public power, it also innovates the received Euro-American theory of human rights. It contemplates a progressive state and polity that name not just politically organized power but also the civil society as a potent source of promotion and protection of human rights, and enable a rather encyclopaedic variety for naming (and shaming) rule of law violation.

It thus outlaws practices of 'untouchability', and social conduct that results in imposition of disability and discrimination on the grounds of 'untouchability' (Article 17) as an integral aspect of the fundamental right to equality before the law and 'equal protection of law'. In enunciating a human right against 'exploitation' (Articles 23, 24), the Constitution outlaws bonded or slave labour, agrestic serfdom, traffic in human beings, and certain forms of child labour.

Rule of law stands here normatively conceived not just as a sword against state domination and violation, but also as a continual constitutional combat against historic civil society norms and practices. In so doing, it engages in simultaneous disempowerment and re-empowerment of the Indian state in ways that complicate governance, politics and constitutional development. In terms of the social psychology of yesteryear, the Constitution thus inaugurates 'cognitive dissonance' in ways that necessarily mark its rather schizoid course of development.

This schizophrenia, rather 'creatively', anticipates future international law human rights dichotomies and hierarchies. The Directive Principles of State Policy (Part IV, codifying relatively non-justiciable livelihood rights, but still casting constitutional duties of governance and lawmaking that affirm, respect, protect and promote these) are set against here-and-now, as it were, judicially enforceable civil and political Fundamental Rights (Part III.) Of course, the Indian Constitution here derives inspiration from its Irish counterpart. But its normative audacity distinctive, even unique. It also by now generally informs, for weal or woe, theory and practice of South constitutionalism.

Conceptions of equality before the law and equal protection of law, this dominant software of constitutionalism, begin their long and tumultuous journey soon upon the adoption of the Indian Constitution. The First Amendment, hardly before the ink on the Constitution dries, reprogrammes constitutional conceptions of the right to equality by enshrining basic rights to affirmative action programmes for the millennially deprived peoples, the 'untouchables' and the First Nations peoples (described, respectively, as 'Scheduled Castes' and Scheduled Tribes, a governance and rights device to name the deprived peoples.) Unlike the United States' constitutionalism, affirmative action in India is not a pre-eminent gift of judicial review, subject to its manifold vagaries. Indian justices no doubt invent ways of adjudication that draw bright lines between and among various notions of equality (equality of opportunity/equality of results/horizontal equality versus 'vertical' forms, for example), but affirmative action ('compensatory', 'preferential' and 'reverse' discrimination; and these descriptions do make and mark an important difference) remains the leitmotiv of the Indian rule of law, defining its core of 'good governance'.

Indian constitutional theory and practice innovate writing of rights. All fundamental rights in Part III stand explicitly subjected to parliamentary powers of 'reasonable regulation' on specified grounds. This marks a deeply troubled and conflicted site, because the conferral of rights serves also and at the same time to register grants of plenary legislative powers. In rich pre-Foucault modes, the 'authors' of the Indian rule of law authorize a citadel of 'reasonable restrictions' that confer meaning for fundamental freedoms and human rights.[26]

There exist no near-absolute rights like those typified by the First

Amendment of the United States Constitution in the Indian Constitution. Extraordinarily, Article 21, granting equivalent due process rights of life and liberty, is followed by a code of explicit powers to legislate for preventive detention! Understandable in the moment of constitutional origin marked by the Holocaustian violence of the Indian Partition, Article 22 powers have been used to make preventive detention a paradigmatic mode within which rights to life and liberty stand imbricated. The Indian Supreme Court has thus constructed a magnificent edifice of preventive detention jurisprudence, subjecting acts of detention to strict scrutiny while sustaining legislative constitutionality of such measures.

The evolution of Indian rule of law has thus to be understood in terms of (what Julius stone named as) administrative law explosion; that is, steady and substantial growth of the micro powers of judicial review. Michel Foucault would have warmed to this narration, which provides a perfect example of 'disciplinary' judicial powers gnawing at the very heart of 'sovereign' power!

Even when Indian justices proclaim the public virtue of drawing bright lines between permissible 'regulation' and offensive 'abrogation', they may only do so amidst case-by-case contestation. The spectacle of midwifery of judicial review process and power that delivers human rights and limited governance indeed fascinates, until we recall, as we all must, that judges and courts, always and everywhere, resymbolize the sovereign power of the state. The spectacle and the truth are not uniquely Indian; what is distinctive to the Indian story is that justices increasingly believe, and act on the belief, that basic human rights are safer in their interpretive custody than with representative institutions. This belief and practice combine to produce a distinctive type of 'constitutional faith' (to borrow a fecund expression from Sanford Levinson), which renders legitimate expansive judicial review.

It is, however, not always even tolerably clear when and whether judicial interpretation of regulated fundamental rights to freedoms helps sustain, rather than abrogate, these. For close to three decades large landholders (the *zamindars*) complained that the Indian Supreme Court abrogated their fundamental right to property by acquiescing with predatory land and agrarian redistribution laws. Ever since the judicial affirmation of a fundamental right to affirmative/compensatory discrimination for socially and educationally backward classes, people belonging to dominant ethnic majority have contested as a violation of their basic right to equality the Court's meandering affirmation of quotas in education and state employment. Muslim religious minority groups have contested and condemned judicial decisions that are based on the arrogation of the right of secular justices to interpret the Holy Koran. Missionary religions, especially Christianity in India, have never fully accepted the Supreme Court sustenance of state legislation that prohibits religious conversion on the grounds of force and fraud. Expansively interpreted, such prohibition eats away the vitals of the right to practice and propagate religion, because it would constitute either 'force' of 'fraud', or both, to invoke visions of heaven or hell in the performance of proselytization. This last offers a rather poignant example of the current forms of Hindutva – oriented ways of Indian governance.

These large examples point to the inherent tension in any constitutional theory of 'regulated' rights. For those affected, judicial determination that legislative 'regulation' of fundamental rights is permissible 'reasonable regulation' appears as 'abrogation' of their constitutional estate. In the process, 'rights' often lose their vaunted trumping feature because rights themselves get represented/reconstituted as so may rolled-up considerations of public policy, which other kindred considerations may with remarkable felicity outweigh.

On the whole, it remains doubtful that judicial interpretive communities and styles, have educated Parliament and, more importantly, executive power in the wisdom of deference to judicial interpretation. If by rule of law we signify constant conversation between adjudicatory powers of the state towards the creation of constitutionally/human-rights-oriented governance cultures, the movement, at best, has been one step forward, two steps back.

Development

The Indian constitutional rule of law defines human and social development variously and in complex and contradictory modes. A standard narrative frame is provided by the tension and contradiction, already noted, between Parts III (Fundamental Rights) and Part IV (Directive Principles of State Policy). The justiciability/non-justiciability distinction sustaining these dichotomous recognition of 'rights in actual experience stands judicially mutated.

Although explicitly declared non-justiciable, the Directives cast a 'paramount' duty of observance in the making of law and policy. Because of this, Indian courts have deployed the Directives as a technology of constitutional interpretation: they have favoured interpretation that *fosters*, rather than *frustrates*, the Directives. This 'indirect' justiciability has contributed a good deal towards fructification of the substantive/'thick' versions of the Indian rule of law.

In the process, much constitutional heat and dust has also been generated, in the main over a 'conservative' judiciary that seemed to frustrate a 'progressive' Parliament committed to agrarian reforms and redistribution leading to judicial 'packing', Indian style.[27] This constitutional gigantomachy has resulted in the transformation of 'development' discourse in terms of redefinition of governance powers. This signifies, overall, contestation of 'leadership' over the 'last'/ final rule of law 'saying power'.

Thus, adjudicatory power (fostered by social and human rights activism constituencies) contests, principally, some of the following 'development' issues. In large metanarrative terms, the Indian Supreme Court had had to negotiate 'rights' and 'development' binaries (to take a few examples) as follows:

1   In what ways may the judiciary say that mega irrigation projects are constitutionally rights offensive?
2   How may courts and justices square (as it were) the human rights to livelihood, and lifestyle diversity, in terms provided by the logic and rhetoric of 'sustainable development'?
3   When may courts and justices agree with citizen contestation that policies of privatization/deregulation remain anti-developmental and are offensive to/violate human rights?
4   How may they locate/relocate the logics/rhetorics of the current motto 'Women's rights are human rights'?
5   How may the adjudicatory voice promote 'the composite culture' (Article 51–A) of rights and governance?

Participation in governance is the leitmotiv of the constitutional conception of the Indian rule of law. What are distinctive to its theory and practice are the histories concretizing equality of opportunity and access for the millennially deprived peoples. Educational quotas in state-administered/aided educational institutions and state and federal employment provide a wealth of Indian narrative constructions the rule of law.[28] On this register, the Indian case provides a more fecund register of judicial activism than the United States' 'affirmative action' jurisprudence.

More crucial is the unique device of legislative reservations. Initially conceived as only a decade-long provision, decennial constitutional amendments now render irreversible electoral reservations for members of the communities of the Scheduled Castes and Tribes. These alone may contest elections from 'reserved' constituencies where all may vote. The Supreme Court of India has sustained this derogation from the principle of adult suffrage under the title of 'equality before the law'. As a result, these communities enter the stage of politics, not as 'extras', but as integral populous actors on the stage of constitutional development. They acquire a voice in Parliament and state legislatures; the same principle continues to operate in grassroots governance (at village and city municipal levels), with the addition of reservations for women as well. The issue of representation for women in national and state legislatures currently dominates the agenda of national constitutional reform and renovation.[29]

The Indian rule of law conception authorizes exacting solicitude for group/collective rights to language, culture and religion. This is indeed striking because the Indian Constitution and constitutional development occur in an era where newfangled notions of 'multiculturalism' were nowhere in sight! It grants a whole array of rights for linguistic, educational and cultural minorities, and provides distinct regimes of identity rights. Understandably, the modes of constitution of 'minorities', and the range of rights they may thus enjoy and exercise, have consumed the energy of India's most articulate and concerned justices. But, overall, they have not just arrested the tyranny of electorally constituted legislative majorities but also protected the individual rights of the minority within the dominantly configured minorities claiming invincible autonomy rights.

All this occurs within the fractured idiom of forms of social toleration in the 'rolled-up' languages of constitutional secularism.[30] Indian constitutional development transcends in many crucial ways the rule of law genre of the American First Amendment's 'Wall of Separation' between state and religion. Instead, it obligates the Indian state specifically to reform the 'dominant'/'majoritarian' 'Hindu' religious traditions in a fast-forward mode, while leaving the reform of 'minority' communitarian/religious traditions to slow-motion, minuscule change Thus the bulk and generality of tradition-constituted women of these communities still remain hostages to governance 'fortunes'. The Indian rule of law model, in this respect, remains stymied. On the one hand, the logics of group/collective rights invite tolerance of violations of women's rights as human rights; on the other, these entail constitutionally ambivalent endeavours to promote and protect these rights.[31] We should not fail to mention the paradigmatic constitutional provisions (through the constitutional Fifth and Sixth Schedules) that authorize the prevalence of regimes of indigenous customary law over local, regional and national enactments.[32]

Governance: emplotting federalism

The dominant rule of law talk, as already noted, does not quite regard federalism as a necessary condition for the accomplishment of its lofty objectives. This raises a rather large question concerning the value of public participation in governance, a question that decisively emerges in the career of Indian constitutional development as a defining mark of the rule of law.

Understanding Indian federalism requires recourse to a distinction between the federal *principle* and *detail*. No matter how governance ridden, the federal principle is (in the sense that Robert Cover gave it) jurisgenerative: it privileges the *local* within the *national* timeplace. In this, it respects the geography of difference in ways that authorize local knowledge, cultures, powers and voices to inform and shape governance. Unlike unitary constitutional forms, the Indian federal principle respects self-determinative autonomy within the national timeplace. It also authorizes forms of public participation/insurrection usually not available in unitary constitutionalisms that place the local at the largesse of the national.

The federal principle stands besieged on all sides by what I here call the federal *detail*. The federal detail seeks to consummate a Nietzschean Will to Power. It seeks to devour the federal principle itself. Indian constitutionalism is replete with stories about ways in which adjudication dissipates this Will to Power and fashions the federal principle as so many subaltern narratives.

The federal detail concerns, in the main, distribution of legislative, administrative and adjudicatory powers. If the detail too often privileges the national over the local/regional timeplace, it remains reversible, too, in the pursuit of values of autonomy and participation. In terms of values of participation, it is this zone of contestation that matters.

If the Indian federal principle promotes internal/sub-national populist (in a non-pejorative sense) practices of self-determination, its detail also confers overweening power on the federal government. History here, however, avenges mere theory. In theory, Parliament has the power of redrawing the federal map, creating/diminishing the boundaries, even the names, of states without the need for any democratic deliberation. In reality, it is the people's movements that exercise this constituent power. New states are almost constantly born within the Indian federation, along linguistic/cultural/identity axes. No doubt, both insurgent and state violence mark the birthing of new state 'communities'. This violence is constantly at stake in Indian constitutional development in ways that nourish cultures of human rights and service the emergence of subaltern conceptions of rule of law. 'Normal'/'dominant' rule of law talk does not usually foreground such histories; the Indian case does.

The usual cocktail of the federal detail, drawing heavily on the experience of comparative federalism, displays a rather minute regard for distribution of legislative and executive powers through a division among the Union, State and Concurrent powers, which may only be changed by constitutional amendments. Powers not thus listed invest the federal centre with a generous residue of undefined authority. Judicial interpretation of the division of powers tends to be informed by comparative interpretive histories of federalism. And within these margins, the Indian Supreme Court constantly innovates interpretation.

Three features of the Indian federal detail, however, are distinctive. First, Parliament retains the power to override the detail in pursuit of nationwide power to enforce outlawry of millennially imposed disabilities and discriminations and innovative ways of structuring both representation and administration.

Second, cooperative federalism seems to be the norm. The constitutionally ordained National Finance Commission constructs human rights normativity in the allocation of federal resources to states. Union–state relations tend to be cast in the wholesome dominant image of 'cooperative federalism', ways through which responsive policies meeting the basic needs

of the impoverished masses furnish a resource for the legitimation of governance. The constitution and the law create India-wide national agencies[33]
entrusted with the tasks of protection and promotion of the human rights of
'discrete and insular' minorities. The comptroller and auditor-general of
India, assisted by the Central Vigilance Commission, at least help fashion
the discourse concerning corruption in high places. And, overall, the Indian
Election Commission has incrementally pursued the heroic tasks of attaining
a modicum of integrity in the electoral process. The ways these and related
agencies actually perform their tasks is the subject of lively political discourse,
both within legislatures and through the practices of investigative journalism, made constitutionally secure by the exertions of State High Courts
and the Supreme Court of India. All this enables continual rearticulation of
the people's power confronted by a heavily militarized polity and state
formation. Never regarded as adequate or just by the affected peoples, these
processes, institutions and networks of governmentality (in the heavy Foucauldian
sense) remain marked by genuine democratic deficit.

This deficit, third, stands structured by the federal power to suspend the
federal principle in at least two situations. In situations of armed rebellion
and of external aggression, proclamations of emergency may lead to suspension of the fundamental rights enshrined in Part III. Over time, the scope
and severity of this suspension have been curtailed by judicial review power
as well as by explicit constitutional amendments. The same may be said
concerning the unique federal power (through the device of the President's
Rule) that enables the national government to suspend or dissolve state legislatures on the grounds of manifest inability of state governance in accordance
with the constitutional provisions. This power, once liberally exercised, has now
been attenuated to vanishing point by various decisions of the Supreme Court.

Overall, it seems to be the case that the federal principle holds the federal
detail within normative restraints. Put another way, Indian federalism
contributes to the rule of law discourse not just as facilitating governance
but also as empowering participatory forms of citizen resilience and self-
reliance. This experience needs to be accorded a measure of dignity of
discourse in our 'comparative' conversations.

Justice: the 'jurispathic' dimensions

All this being said, comparative studies of histories of constitutional
conceptions of rule of law remain cruelly abstract without the manifold
narratives of pathologies of power that these also shelter. Concerns with
issues of 'justice' do not integrally inform of dominant rule of law narratives. At best, these are informed by wholly proceduralist, though not for
that reason unimportant, notions about justice.

Although conceptually pre-dating the enunciation of the now famous
Rawlsian 'difference principle', the Indian constitutional rendering of the

rule of law actually enshrines it. My privileged reading of Indian constitutionalism suggests a distinctive conception wherein development is
defined as that set and series of public policy measures under which the
most impoverished Indian peoples benefit *disproportionately* from development. On this score, the evolution of the practices of Indian rule of
law must be said to have enhanced the *injustice* of development.

It is beyond the bounds of this chapter to provide even a meagre sense
of the violence and violation embedded in the histories of rule of law in
India. Not merely have the impoverished been forced to cheat their way
to meagre survival, 'jurispathic' (to evoke Robert Cover's phrase) dimensions of the Indian rule of law at work have continually evolved new
means to disenfranchise them. These stories of violent social exclusion
may be told in various ways. I have recently narrated the institutionaliza-
tion of 'rape culture' in the context of violence and violation in Gujarat
in 2002.[34]

But it is to literature rather than law that we must turn to realize the full
horror of the betrayal of the Indian rule of law. Mahasweta Devi's *Bashai
Tudu*[35] speaks to us about the constitutive ambiguities of the practices of
militarized 'rule of law' governance and resistance in contemporary India.
Rohinton Mistry's *A Fine Balance*[36] educates us in the constitutional misery
of untouchables caught in the ever-escalating web of 'constitutional' governance. These two paradigmatic literary classics invite us to pursue a
distinctively Indian law and literature genre of study, outside which it
remains almost impossible to grasp the lived atrocities of Indian rule of law
in practice.

They also make the vital point (with the remarkable Indian *Subaltern
Studies* series, Delhi: Oxford University Press/Permanent Black) that the
pathologies of rule of law governance are located outside the dominant
narrative frame of the constitution and the law, which by definition mystify
the experience of disenfranchisement of citizens. In various modes, these
critical narratives educate us in the ways in which the very banner of the rule
of law mirrors (to evoke Hannah Arendt's favourite phrase) 'rightless'
peoples. The jurispathic attributes of the Indian rule of law at work can best
be explained in terms of social reproduction of rightlessness. It is on this
register that Indian judicial activism begins to make and mark a modest
reversal. It is to this that we now turn.

Adjudication as a kiss of life for Indian constitutionalism and the rule of law

The historic practices of Indian adjudication reincarnate different visions of
limited government. I name this 'historic' for two reasons. First, the stunning verbosity of the text of the Indian Constitution (the Indian
Constitution is arguably the largest constitutional text in the history of

humankind) was designed to limit the scope for interpretation. The confounding Fathers of the text (because there were *no* founding Mothers) intended, for good and bad reasons, a marginal voice for adjudicatory power in national governance. Innocent of hermeneutics, they altogether over-looked the simple truth: the more text there is, more the leeway of interpretation. Second, they overlooked the potential for judicial courage, craft and contention. The 'original intention' served, in wholly unanticipated ways, the fateful mission of judicial recrafting and retooling of the Indian rule of law.

I state here summarily (for reasons of space) the adjudicatory 'goings-on' (to evoke Michael Oaekshott's imagery[37]). First, and simultaneously with the adoption of the Constitution, Indian justices strove to erect boundaries to the power of delegated legislation (processes by which the executive power seeks to legislate.) They conceded this power, but with a significant accompanying caveat: the rule-making power of the administration ought not to usurp the legislative function of enunciation of policy accompanied by prescriptive sanctions. Thus came into being the 'administrative law explosion', where justices did not so much invalidate delegated legislation as vigorously police its performance. The executive may make rules that bind; but courts made it their business to interrogate, and even invalidate, specific exercises of administrative rule-making. That explosion also put in view a stunning array of judicial techniques for the review of administrative action.[38]

Second, and coeval with the promulgation of the constitution, the Supreme Court enunciated the germinal principle of the rule of law: the exercise of legislative/executive power is valid (and legitimate) only when its exercise is consistent with the purposes for which power is conferred. The doctrine of *ultra vires* was thus at its very birth constitutionalized. Justices ruled that conferral of such power by definition may not be construed as intending violation of fundamental rights, and thereby began exercising vast judicial power over the grants of power. Rule of law considerations thus furnished a warrant for expansive, and later on activist, judicial review powers.

In, and through, these performative acts of adjudicatory power, the Indian Supreme Court installs a unique form of 'originalism'. That term, as understood in the staple American constitutional theory talk, marks, in sum, the borders of legitimate judicial review. What the Indian discourse achieves in the main, however, is the reconstruction of originalism to signify the judicial re-authorship of the originally written constitution. Put another way, 'originalism' in the Indian constitutional discourse refers not so much to the 'original' intendment of the historically first collective authors, but rather to the ensemble of high adjudicative 'original intent'.

Third, justices asserted judicial review power over the constitutionality of legislative performances. Laws that transgressed fundamental rights or the principle and detail of Indian federalism activated the 'essence' of judicial review powers. When tormenting judicial endeavours failed to reconcile the forms of transgression (by the standard repertoire of 'reading down' the statutory scope and intendments so as to avoid conflict and by recourse to the peculiar judicial doctrine of 'harmonious construction'), enacted laws were declared constitutionally null and void. And even when resuscitated by legislative reaffirmation, these were subjected again to the judicial gauntlet of strict scrutiny. The instances of judicial invalidation of statutes far exceed in number and range the experience of judicial review in the North.

Fourth, going beyond this, Indian justices assumed awesome power to subject constitutional amendments to strict judicial scrutiny and review. They performed an audacious innovation through the judicially crafted doctrine of the Basic Structure of the Constitution, which stood, in judicial and juridical discourse, as definitive of the 'personality' – defined, from time to time, as the 'essential features' – of the Constitution. They proclaimed the 'rule of law', 'equality', 'fundamental rights', 'secularism', 'federalism', 'democracy' and 'judicial review' as essential features of the Basic Structure, which amendatory power may not ever lawfully transgress.

Initially articulated as a judicial doctrine crafting the limits of amendatory power, the regime of the Basic Structure limitation has spread to other forms of exercise of constitutional, and even legislative, powers. The ineffable adjudicatory modes also mark a new and a bold conception: 'constituent power' (the power to remake and unmake the Constitution through the exercise of majoritarian performances of political will) is conjointly shared with the Indian Supreme Court to the point of declaring certain amendments constitutionally *invalid*.

This judicial, and juridical, production then momentously (because justices undertook the task of protecting the constitution against itself!) traversed the constitutional jurisprudence of Pakistan, Bangladesh and Nepal. The 'comparative' rule of law theory discourse wholly passes by this germinal renovation, because it regards all this as exotic variation worthy of epistemological violence through acts of organized oblivion.

Fifth, exponential forms of Indian judicial activism remain biophilic. They enhance the life of the subaltern (in a global economy of knowledge production) rule of law conceptions. Since the early 1980s, through the device of Social Action litigation (where disempowered citizens seek to co-opt state adjudicatory power to make governance just, power accountable, and state ethical) Indian courts and justices have renovated inherited notions of standing and justiciability. Impoverished and disenfranchised citizens stand now possessed (through what I have named 'epistolary jurisdiction') of the power to marshal judicial voice through the simple device of writing letters to courts complaining of violations of their *right to be, and to remain, human*.[39] Everyone possesses the power to activate forms of Indian judicial review power and process that invigilate practices and habits of governance.

In the process, the 'bright lines' demarcating standing and justiciability become blurred, often in creative ways.

Lay citizens are thus enabled/empowered to activate judicial process and power to combat inimical forms of governance. Through the processes of epistolary jurisdiction and jurisprudence, they not merely ventilate grievances against governmental lawlessness and official deviance but also enable reconceptualization of adjudicative state power as a *form of fiduciary power*, where justices are summoned to use their constitutional authority to serve the civil liberties and democratic rights of the disenfranchised and impoverished Indian citizen masses. In the process, judicial power and process reconstitute themselves as a forum for redemocratization of Indian governance and polity.

Courts and justices have responded to people-oriented struggles to rearticulate the rule of law is several different ways. In sum, they have:

- reinterpreted, in expansive ways, rights enshrined in the Constitution beyond the 'original intent';[40]
- reinserted rights excluded, after 'due' deliberation, from the formative prose of the originary constitutional provisions;[41]
- scripted judicial enunciation of rights unanticipated by the Constitution;[42]
- devised forms of invigilation and monitoring of governance respect/deference of rights thus enunciated;[43]
- assumed, almost daily, superintendence of institutional governance performance, in ways often supplanting it;[44]
- privileged the values of popular participation over governmental monopolistic definitions of public interest defining ways of Indian development;[45]
- fashioned novel narratives of adjudicative lawmaking.[46]

I state all this rather summarily and certainly in no *celebrationist narrative* mode; Indian social and human rights activist communities recoursing judicial power and process remain familiar with the meandering nature of judicial activism. Even as they engage the activist judiciary in the tasks of Indian democratic renewal, their politics of hope remains moderated by an acknowledgement of the brute institutional fact that courts and justices remain, at the end of the day, state-bound and -permeated beings. People's re-enchantment with judicial process and power in the refashioning of state power and ideology remains marked by the experience of the dynamic of disenchantment. All the same, judicial activism, for them, is not a rope of sand. It has contingent, and often strategic, uses that symbolize the last best hope there is for participative rearticulation of the rule of law in India, and the redemocratization of Indian governance.[47]

In lieu of a conclusion

The Indian story at least situates the significance for contemporary rule of law theory and practice of the forms of creationist South narratives. The time is surely at hand for constructions of multicultural (despite the justified reservation that this term evokes[48]) narratives of the rule of law.

Precisely because it is being loudly stated that 'history' has now ended, and there remain on the horizon *no* meaningful 'alternatives' to global capitalism, we need to undertake to decipher the popular and multitudinous understandings that recontextualize the rule of law in the current conjuncture and circumstance of globality, now manifest in the anti-globalization protest movement.[49]

We need to participate in new marathon tasks that facilitate the emergence of a 'global' conception of rule of law, which extend human rights responsibilities to new networks of domination and governance (the transnational corporations, international financial institutions, the WTO, and regional and bilateral trade and investment treaty regimes[50]). Through wholly insincere languages, these proselytize good governance and the rule of law not so much with a view to promoting the paradigm of universal human rights of all human beings everywhere, but to promote the paradigm of trade-related market-friendly human rights.[51]

The authentic quest for the renaissance of rule of law has just begun its world historic career. Rule of law epistemic communities have choices to make. Our ways of talking about the rule of law may either wholly abort or aid to a full birth conceptions of rule of law now struggling to find a voice through multitudinous people's struggles against global capitalism that presage alternatives to it.

We need after all, I believe, to place ourselves once again under the tutelage of Michael Oakeshott. He reminds us, preciously, that far from being a 'finished product' of humankind's history, the rule of law discourse 'remains an individual composition, a unity of particularity and generosity, in which each component is what it is in virtue of what it contributes to the delineation of the whole'.[52] That virtue of the 'whole' may not any longer legitimate Euro-American narratology that de-privileges other ways of telling stories abut the rule of law, as a form of participative enterprise by myriad 'subaltern' voices.

Notes

1   See Upendra Baxi, 'Operation Enduring Freedom: Towards a New International Law and Order?,' in A. Anghie, B.S. Chimni, K. Mickelson, and O.C. Okafor (eds) *The Third World and International Law* (2003 in press; Kluwer Law International)
2   Giorgio Agamben, *Homo Sacer: Sovereign Power and Bare Life* (Stanford: Stanford University Press, 1998).

340

3   Joseph Raz, 'The Rule of Law and its Virtue', 93 *Law Quarterly Review* 208 (1977):

> It has now become attractive to seek to derive 'good' from the languages, logics and paralogics of human rights oriented governance and public culture. At a most general level, 'good governance' is then presented as a set of normative and institutional processes that best enable sustained forms of recognition, respect, and reaffirmation of human rights.

But this merely names the problem. Internationally enunciated, as well constitutionally crafted human rights norms and standards (and these vary a great deal) remain contingent products of intergovernmental and intra-NGO politics of desire. Not all human rights stand endowed with equal worth, some being presented as here-and-now judicially enforceable entitlements, others as 'programme' or 'manifesto' human rights subject only to regimes of 'progressive realization'. Human rights languages and logics, by enacting hierarchies of rights, situate socially vulnerable human beings in actually existing forms of production/reproduction of rightlessness. They do not always provide institutional designs for addressing 'just' ways of handling the problem of conflict of rights. And many arenas remain as yet untouched by human rights normativity (to take just one example, the human right to immunity from governance corruption). Rights talk, contrary to naïve widespread activist founding faith, fails to enunciate visions of the good and the just society, economy and polity. 'Positivist' human rights notions remain the playthings of domination and power; 'transcendent' theories evoke postmodernist *angst* concerning metaphysical metanarratives of universality. The endeavour to define rule of law in terms of privileging the 'good' via languages of actually existing human rights normativity remains fraught with difficulties.

4   John Rawls, *Political Liberalism* (New York: Columbia University Press, 1993).

5   Jürgen Habermas, *Between Facts and Norms: Contributions to a Discourse Theory of Law and Democracy*, trans. William Rehg (Cambridge, Massachusetts: MIT Press, 1995).)

6   See Guri Aderni, ' Legal Intimations: Michael Oakeshott and the Rule of Law', 1993 *Wisconsin Law Review* 838:The message that those in power should somehow construct and respect constraints on their own power is surely an important one. But the import of this sensible requirement is not clear enough. To be sure, rulers as well as ruled ought to remain bound by the law (conceived here as a going legal order, order of legality) regardless of the privilege of power. But ought they to so do because legality (rule following conduct) is posited as an ethical value and virtue? Is merely instrumental (purpose rational, even expedient) rule following an equally worthy rule of law performance? The 'rulers' often comply with Rule of Law constraints on their power instrumentally, as a means of 'legitimating' power relations and structures. In that sense, government *of* laws presents itself merely as an *instrumentality for government of men*. If that is all that we choose to signify by this slogan, the rule of law talk marks pathways of perfection of many a hegemonic credential. But most of us, the epistemic wonder-working communities, do not wish to represent our Rule of Law discourse this way.

7   The germ that gnaws at the heart of the dominant rule of law narratologies is the flippant, when not dangerous, aphorism, reiterated ad nauseam,that rule of law means *'government of laws, not of men'*. Useful as a deconstructive device where authority is based on, or claimed from, divine power, it makes very little sense outside these contexts. Indeed, it mystifies. Common sense and collective human

experience compel acknowledgement that government of laws does not exist anywhere and that we do not quite know whether it can ever exist. All that exists is government of *men* (and feminist theory and movement educate us about what *this* means!). Prescriptively, I am not sure whether many of us would commend any transhuman, robotic forms of governance, governmentality and law.

We may then need to translate this aphorism into another one: rule of law is *both, and at once, government of law and of men*. The rule of law notion heavily suggests that all power is legally determined and sovereign power dissipates within the contending spheres of executive versus adjudicative 'supremacy'. Men who govern, then, may only do so within the law. (Note that we do not quite manage to agree on whether, and which combination of, law signifies an assemblage, in a Deleuzean sense, of 'rules', distinguished from 'standards', 'principles', 'doctrines', 'values' and 'ideals'. But I must here resist the temptation of yet again enacting this parade of horribles!) Even so, *men* (because in the main the discourse carries its patriarchal birthmarks everywhere!) decide what *law* should be. See, for the interesting discourse in contemporary China, Peerenboom, note 8, *infra*.

8 Ernesto Laclau, *Emancipation(s)* (London: Verso, 1996). In contemporary terms this marks a distinction between 'thin' versus 'thick' theories about the rule of law: see Randall Peerenboom, 'Let One Hundred Flowers Bloom, One Hundred Schools Contend: Debating Rule of Law in China', 23 *Michigan Journal of International Law* 471 (2002).

9 Such as those elaborated in Lon Fuller's *Morality of Law* (New Haven, Connecticut: Yale University Press, 1964), developed variously further by Neil McCormick, 'Natural Law and the Separation of Law and Morals', in Robert P. George, ed., *Natural Law Theory: Contemporary Essays* (Oxford: Clarendon Press, 1992), pp. 105–33, and John Finnis, *Natural Law and Natural Rights* (Oxford: Clarendon Press, 1980); Geoffrey de Q. Walker, *The Rule of Law: Foundation of Constitutional Democracy* (Melbourne: Melbourne University Press, 1988).

10 E. P. Thompson, *Writing by the Candlelight* (London: Merlin Press, 1989).

11 See the incredibly rich narration in J. Morgan Kousser, *Colorblind Injustice: Minority Voting Rights and the Undoing of the Second Reconstruction* (Chapel Hill: University of North Carolina Press, 1999).

12 Louis Althusser, *Montesquieu, Rousseau, Marx: Politics and History*, trans. Ben Brewster (London: Verso, 1982).

13 Julius Stone, *The Social Dimensions of Law and Justice* (Sydney: Maitland, 1966), pp. 797–9.

14 Carl Schmitt, *Political Theology: Four Chapters on the Concept of Sovereignty*, trans. George Schwab (Cambridge: MIT Press, 1985).

15 I invite your attention to such diverse phenomena as, in May 1968, the campus protest in the United States against the Vietnam War, peoples demonstrations against the Uruguay round and the World Trade Organization (WTO), the Tiananmen Square massacre, the struggles against apartheid regimes in the United States and South Africa, and against perversions of the East and Central European socialist legality.

For befittingly amorphous notions of 'multitudes', see Antonio Negri, *Insurgencies: Constituent Power and the Modern State*, trans. Muarizia Boscagli (Minnesota: University of Minnesota Press, 1999); Antonio Negri and Michael Hardt, *Empire* (Cambridge, Massachusetts: Harvard University Press, 2000).

16 Peter Fitzpatrick, *The Mythology of Modern Law* (London: Routledge, 1992); *Modernism and Grounds of Law* (Cambridge: Cambridge University Press, 2000).

17 Bob Fine, *Democracy and the Rule of Law: Liberal Ideals and Marxist Critiques* (London: Pluto Press, 1984).
18 Upendra Baxi, *The Future of Human Rights* (Delhi: Oxford University Press, 2002), pp. 24–41.
19 Hans George Miller, '(In)Felicitous Speech Acts in Kafka's *The Trial*' (2001); copy on file with the author.
20 See Upendra Baxi, note 1, *supra*. See also notes 49, 50, *infra*.
21 Further, as Amartya Sen, in his *Development as Freedom* (Oxford: Oxford University Press, 1999), and Martha Nussbaum, in her *Women and Human Development* (Cambridge: Cambridge University Press, 2000), implicitly remind us, we may need to recast the old languages into those of promotion of human 'capabilities' and 'flourishings'. Discernment in deployment of this notion summons us to many sensitive distinctions thus framed variously.
22 Upendra Baxi, 'Constitutionalism as a Site for State Formative Practices', 21 *Cardozo Law Review* 1,183–210 (2000).
23 This theme stands addressed in my forthcoming work *Prefigurative Constitutionalism*, which seeks to trace the modes in which the five decades of people's struggles have sought to mutate the postcolonial heritage.
24 Granville Austin, *The Indian Constitution: The Cornerstone of Nation* (Delhi: Oxford University Press, 1964), *Working a Democratic Constitution – The Indian Experience* (Delhi: Oxford University Press, 1999) and the extensive literature therein cited, especially the corpus of H. M Seervai, Durga Das Basu and of P. K. Tripathi, M. P. Jain, S. P. Sathe and Rajeev Dhavan; Upendra Baxi, 'Postcolonial Legality', in Henry Schwartz and Sangeeta Roy, eds, *A Companion to Postcolonial Studies* (Oxford: Blackwell, 2000), pp. 540–55.
25 The Indian constitutionalism makes normative impact on postcolonial constitutionalism, illustrated most remarkably and recently by the post-apartheid South African Constitution. So inveterate, however, are Euro-American habits of heart that the dominant, even comparative, discourse represents the Indian and related South forms of constitutionalism as merely *mimetic*.
26 In his *History of Sexuality, Volume 1*, Foucault memorably begins by stating that freedom of speech makes sense only within regimes of interdiction that we name as 'censorship'. The 'outside' (reasonable restriction) is thus the very core of the inside (freedom of speech and expression).
27 See, S. P. Sathe, *Judicial Activism in India* (Delhi: Oxford University Press, 2002), and the literature there cited; Upendra Baxi, *The Indian Supreme Court and Politics* (Lucknow: Eastern Book Company, 1990); *Courage, Craft, and Contention: The Indian Supreme Court in Mid-Eighties* (Bombay: N. M. Tripathi, 1985).
28 See Marc Galanter, *Competing Equalities* (Delhi: Oxford, 1984). I refrain from adding citations of voluminous Indian writing on the subject, of which the corpus of Professors S. P. Sathe, P. N. Singh and M. P. Singh remain exemplary.
29 The various constitutional amendment bills providing reservation for women in national and state legislatures have yet to materialize. Their chequered contemporary legislative histories remain mired, in socially significant ways, over the issue of 'reservations within reservations'. That is, the issue of whether this device should be stratified so as to enable/empower women doubly/multiply oppressed by state and civil society, through provisions for a representational quota for women belonging to 'underclasses'.

How far these devices, in general, may result in redistribution of power and self-esteem remains contested: the question invites reading of fifty-plus years of histories of legislative reservations for the Scheduled Castes and Tribes. See Marc Galanter, *Competing Equalities* (Delhi: Oxford University Press); Upendra Baxi,

'Legislative Reservations for Social Justice', in R. B. Goldman and J. Williams, eds, *From Independence to Statehood: Managing Ethnic Conflicts in Five African and Asian States* (London: Pinter, 1984), pp. 210–24.

30 See Anthony Blackshield, 'Secularism and Social Control in the West' in G. S. Sharma ed., *Secularism: Its Implications for India* (Bombay: N. M. Tripathi, 1966), p. 9.

31 See, e.g., Rajeswari Sunder Rajan, 'Some Implications of the Uniform Civil Code Debates in India', 18 *Social Text* ? (2000); Kumkum Sangri, 'Politics of Diversity', XXX *Economic & Political Weekly* (1995), pp. 3,287–389; Sudipta Kaviraj, ed., *Politics in India* (Oxford: Oxford University Press, 1999), pp. 329–64; Nivedita Menon, 'State/Gender/Community', *Economic & Political Weekly*, PE3–9 (1998); Upendra Baxi, 'The Constitutional Discourse on Secularism', in Upendra Baxi, Alice Jacob, and Tarlok Singh, eds, *Reconstructing the Republic* (Delhi: Har Anand, 1999), pp. 211–32.

32 Mohammad Hidyatullah, *The Fifth and Sixth Schedules of the Constitution of India* (Gauhati: Ashok Publishing House, 1979).

33 Such as, for example, the Inter-State Development Council, the Planning Commission, Human Rights Commission, the Minorities and Women Commissions, the Scheduled Castes and Tribes Commission, the Central Vigilance Commission and the Indian Law Commission. See Austin, note 24, *supra*.

34 See Upendra Baxi, 'The Second Gujarat Catastrophe', XXXV11 *Economic and Political Weekly* (2002), p. 3,519; 'The (Im)Possibility of Constitutional Justice: Seismographic Notes on Indian Constitutionalism', in *India's Living Constitution* (New Delhi: Permanent Black, 2002), pp. 43–6, 51–4.

35 Calcutta: Thema Publishers, 1990.

36 London: Faber (1995).

37 Michael Oakeshott, *On Human Conduct* (Oxford: Oxford University Press, 1975), pp. 1–31.

38 The literature here is vast and manifold. See my Introduction to Professor M. P. Massey's *Administrative Law*, 5th edn (Lucknow, Eastern Book Company, 1999) and the literature there cited; and S. P. Sathe's book (in the current edition) of the same title (Delhi: Butterworth).

39 Upendra Baxi, 'Taking Suffering Seriously: Social Action before the Supreme Court of India', in Rajeev Dhavan Salman Kurshid and R. Sudershan, eds, *Judges and Judicial Power* (Bombay: N. M. Tripathi, 1985), pp. 289–315; 'From Human Rights to the Right to Be Human', in *Inhuman Wrongs and Human Rights: Unconventional Essays* (Delhi: Har Anand), pp. 1–17.

40 See S. P. Sathe, *Judicial Activism in India* (Delhi: Oxford University Press, 2002), and the literature there cited; Upendra Baxi, *The Indian Supreme Court and Politics* (Lucknow: Eastern Book Company, 1990).

41 In this and subsequent notes I do not cite in detail the relevant case law and literature, now well archived in Sathe, note 40, *supra*. Rather, I mention here the principal examples of judicial activism.

   The Supreme Court thus read in the textual (Article 21) prescription 'procedure established by law' whole notions of 'due process' specifically excluded by constitution-makers; it affirmed a right to speedy trial excluded from the constitutional text after much deliberation.

42 These include a right to bail; rights to livelihood, housing, shelter, health, literacy and education; environmental integrity rights; rights to restitution and rehabilitation for acts of governmental lawlessness.

43 Through innovative fact-finding procedures such as socio-legal commissions of enquiry into rights violations, acts of continuing jurisdiction, enactments of

frequent reportage obligations by the administration, compliance-inducing renovation of contempt jurisprudence.

44 Activist justices now not merely routinely manage/administer the implementation
of human rights in custodial institutions (prisons, juvenile homes, psychiatric
care institutions, women's remand homes), but also monitor the performance,
often on a day-to-day basis, of personnel invested with the duty of combating
corruption.

45 Through reading down the executive (Crown) privilege on confidentiality of
proceedings and government documents; affirming, incrementally, people's right
to know; mandating government to hear affected parties (especially in large irrigation and development projects) in making/remaking developmental decisions.

46 The Supreme Court now overtly legislates, especially in the field of environmental protection and the protection of women's rights as human rights. For
example, in the latter sphere it judicially enacted a law against sexual harassment
in the workplace; in the former sphere it ensured air-pollution control in Delhi by
insisting that public transport use CNG (non-polluting car fuel) rather than
polluting petroleum fuels.

47 Upendra Baxi, 'The *Avatars* of Judicial Activism: Explorations in the
Geographies of (In)Justice', in S. K. Verma and K. Kusum, eds, *Fifty Years of
the Supreme Court of India: Its Grasp and Reach* (Delhi: Oxford University
Press), pp. 156–209.

48 See Upendra Baxi, note 18, *supra*, pp. 91–118.

49 Leslie Sklar, *Globalization: Global Capitalism and its Alternatives* (Oxford:
Oxford University Press); *On Fire: The Battle of Genoa and the Anti-capitalist
Movement* (London: One-Off Press, 2001); Michael Edwards and John Gaventa,
eds., *Global Citizen Action* (London: Earthscan Press, 2001); John Braithwaite
and Peter Drahos, *Global Business Regulation* (Cambridge: Cambridge
University Press, 2000); Arturo Escobar, *Encountering Development: the Making
and the Unmaking of the Third World* (Princeton: Princeton University Press,
1995).

50 See Maxwell O. Chibundu, 'Globalizing Rule of Law: Some Thoughts at and on
the Periphery', 7 *Indiana Journal of Global Studies* 79–115 (1999).

51 See notes, 18, 49, 50, *supra*.

52 See note 37, *supra*, pp. 132–66.

11

RULE OF LAW AND ASPECTS OF HUMAN RIGHTS IN THAILAND[1]

From conceptualization to implementation?

Vitit Muntarbhorn

As in other parts of the world, the concept known as the rule of law is held in high esteem in academic literature on law and jurisprudence in Thailand.[2] At the very least, it is understood to imply basic guarantees for individuals and communities in the face of the nation-state. It is complemented by the axiom of the independence of the judiciary, particularly as a protector of rights and a bulwark against injustices from the executive branch of government. These elements are closely linked with human rights in that the inspiration for the rule of law cannot simply be based upon national law or "positive law"; rather, the rule of law is influenced by – indeed, contingent upon – various norms transcending the nation-state, particularly international human rights standards, often ascribed to "natural law."

The evolution of the rule of law in Thailand should be seen against the backdrop of monumental political changes in the 19th and 20th centuries. It may first be noted that the 19th century was a time when various European colonial powers were vying for influence in Southeast Asia. While Thailand's neighbors were all subjected to colonization, Thailand managed to retain her independence, although not without a price. As a buffer state, the country was pressured heavily to undertake key reforms as part of a survival strategy in the face of the colonization process. One of the results was legislative and judicial reforms – courts and written laws in the form of Codes were introduced in the 19th and early 20th centuries, derived from the European model, particularly the civil law system.[3] Components of the rule of law started to permeate the Thai legal system, for example in relation to the rights of persons arrested under the criminal law.

The political scenario from the 1930s onwards was a tug-of-war between authoritarianism and democratization. In 1932 the country's absolute monarchy was overturned and this was converted to a constitutional monarchy with the introduction of the first Constitution. Yet, subsequent developments – a multiplicity of *coups d'état* from the 1930s until the 1990s – led to military rule for many decades, although these left untouched the position of the monarch as the symbolic, unifying force at the apex of the system, a key institution to this very day.

One of the greatest preoccupations, and pretexts for the consolidation of military rule, after the Second World War was to counter Communism – amidst the fiery war in Indochina, particularly in the 1960s and 1970s, and the victory of Communist forces in Laos, Vietnam and Cambodia in 1975. Obviously this had an impact on the exercise of various rights related to the rule of law, such as freedom of expression and association in Thailand – a country at the geographical heart of an ideologically sensitive crucible. The 1970s witnessed a slight flowering of democracy when a student-led movement mobilized the public to eject a powerful military triumvirate from office on October 14, 1973. However, the transition to democracy was overturned by a conservative military backlash on October 6, 1976, which led to the reinstatement of military rule and its subsequent prolongation. In the early 1990s there was again a brief experimentation with the election of a civilian government, but the latter was overturned by a *coup d'état* staged by the military in 1991 on the grounds that the government was corrupt. Although the coup-makers then installed an unelected civilian government, the military took charge again in 1992. The gathering political storm meant that in May 1992 the public staged huge demonstrations calling for democracy. The ensuing bloody conflict, with the military using force to suppress demonstrators, led to a national and international outcry and enormous pressure for liberalization. This led to the demise of military rule, the return of civilians on the political stage, and the advent of new elections, ultimately leading to Thailand's first people-based Constitution of 1997 – its 16th Constitution – which has helped to entrench the rule of law in Thailand.

In such a volatile setting, the rule of law has been able to exist to some extent throughout the years in the form of an administration of justice under the judiciary established by law. As protected by national law, human rights have been enjoyed to varying degrees, for example freedom of expression through the written press, although television and radio channels were/are still largely in the hands of the state and the military. However, the judicial process has tended to leave untouched the power of the military, thus being able to render justice in a rather constrained manner – a dormant rather than active watchdog for the rule of law on several occasions.

With the benefit of hindsight, it is thus possible to generalize that, like many other countries, the country was very much under rule *by* law, especially military diktat or fiat, rather than the rule of law with democratic constituents, until the seminal year of 1992.

Second, although the rule of law finds a prominent place in academic thinking, the term has taken on a somewhat presumptuous air, in that when it is used people are presumed to know what it means – when in fact people often do not know what it means; nor has it been explained adequately to people. The Thai term for the rule of law is "*Luck*

Nititham" implying a precept of law based upon a sense of justice and virtue – not an easy notion to grasp in a concrete sense. There is thus a kind of mythification of the term as a linchpin of our society, when in reality it is steeped in popular incomprehension rather than comprehension. This mythification dilutes the impact of the notion of the rule of law, precisely because the distance between people and the notion itself is often extreme – and that gap results in what can be described as the *rule of lore*. It is compounded by this paradox: while, in principle, ignorance of the law is no excuse, why should we be presumed to know the law when no one disseminates it to us?

This chapter endeavors to examine the rule of law and its relationship with aspects of human rights in Thailand from two main angles, conceptualization and implementation, and it is to the first element that this article now turns.

Conceptualization

The notion of the rule of law is inevitably linked with the dichotomies outlined below.

Rights and duties

Historically, there has been a tendency to emphasize duties rather than rights in Thailand. Interestingly, Buddhism itself, the main religion of the country, calls for actions from individuals on the basis of their duties towards others rather than on the basis of an individual's rights.[4] However, it can be argued that one man/one woman's duties are merely the converse of another person's rights. From this religious angle, there is a transcendent element which cannot be computed in material terms. The notion of "karma" – the life-propelling force through one's good and bad deeds – shapes one's well-being through a process whereby the correlation between duties and rights is manifested ultimately in the cycle of reincarnation to which humans are subjected.

In secular terms, there has also been a tendency to emphasize duties rather than rights. In all the Thai constitutions to date, there has been such emphasis. At best, it may lead to an enhancement of the relationship between citizens and the state. For instance, under the current Constitution, there is a new duty – the duty of citizens to vote; if they fail to vote, certain rights will be forfeited temporarily. However, there has been a negative side, in that the notion of duties, particularly in the constitutions prior to the current one, was often used to undermine human rights. There was (and still is) a duty to pay tax, to take part in military conscription, to abide by the law, to report one's birth and death, to respect state symbols, etc. The notion of duties, towards state sovereignty in particular, was used by military governments to circumscribe and constrain the understanding of and enjoyment of human rights.

More directly on the notion of rights and human rights, it may be noted that in the past, the term "human rights" was seen as somewhat subversive by authoritarian governments. However, it now appears explicitly in the new Constitution, thus enjoying a degree of legitimacy. The pseudonym used in this Constitution for the term "human rights" is "human dignity," as per Section 4:

> The human dignity, rights and liberties of the people shall be protected.[5]

Moreover, the National Human Rights Commission was established by the new Constitution, thus linking human rights directly with a new constitutional mechanism. Interestingly, in semantic and jurisprudential terms, the term "human dignity" also provides a kind of preferred, local *raison d'être* for human rights, particularly because the "natural law" *raison d'être* for human rights may be seen as Western or Eurocentric.

Yet even the conceptualization of rights under the current people-based Constitution is more limited than the international perception of human rights. Intriguingly, Chapter III of the Constitution starts with the title "Rights and Liberties of the Thai People," rather than rights and liberties of all people. Such a rubric indicates a more nationalistic or parochial approach to rights which differs from the non-discrimination component of international human rights standards. However, several other parts of the Constitution pertain to all persons and not simply to Thai citizens. Importantly, Chapter VIII of the Constitution, which deals with the judiciary, guarantees many rights, particularly in the civil and political field, which accrue to the benefit of all persons in Thailand irrespective of citizenship. This converges well with international human rights standards.

Individuals and communities

There has been, for a long time, a debate on the relationship between human rights and communities, as contradistinguished from individuals. In its inception, the historical emphasis of human rights was very much predicated upon the rights of individuals. However, in recent years the debate has been broadened to advocate the rights of various groups, collectivities, or communities, for example indigenous peoples and minorities. In the international arena the debate is still unsettled, compounded by the fear that too much emphasis on the rights of groups may undermine the rights of individuals, especially from the angle of groups oppressing individuals. The ambiguities take on a more edgy tone

349

in the aftermath of the terrorist attack on New York in September 2001, especially in view of the fact that, clearly, human rights violations are committed not only by states but also by non-state actors, such as non-government armed groups.

The latest approach on the issue in Thailand is found in the current Constitution, which guarantees the rights of individuals and of communities. However, these rights are advocated very much *vis-à-vis* the state or vested interests rather than against each other (i.e. the individual *vis-à-vis* the community). In the Constitution there are a number of individual rights akin to international standards, for example, the presumption of innocence and the right of those arrested to have access to courts expeditiously – within 48 hours, according to the Constitution. On the other hand, the right of communities is guaranteed very much in the environmental field, such as in regard to access to information, environmental impact assessment and public hearings before decisions are taken by the authorities affecting people's lives. The complementarity between the rights of individuals and communities *vis-à-vis* the state is found particularly in Section 46 and Section 56 of the Constitution, as follows:

> Persons so assembling as to be a traditional community shall have the right to conserve or restore their customs, local knowledge, arts or good culture of their community and of the nation and partici-pate in the management, maintenance, preservation and exploitation of natural resources and the environment in a balanced fashion and persistently as provided by law.[6]

> The right of a person...and communities' participation in the preservation and exploitation of natural resources and biological diversity and in the protection, promotion and preservation of the quality of the environment for usual and consistent survival in the environment which is not hazardous to his or her health and sani-tary condition, welfare or quality of life, shall be protected, as provided by law.

> Any project or activity which may seriously affect the quality of the environment shall not be permitted, unless its impacts on the environment have been studied and evaluated and opinions of an independent organization, consisting of representatives from private environmental organizations and from higher education institutions providing studies in the environmental field, have been obtained prior to the operation of such project or activity, as provided by law.

> The right of a person to sue a State agency, State enterprise, local government organization or other State authority to perform the duties as provided by law under paragraph one and paragraph two shall be protected.[7]

Thus many environmental projects, for instance "damned dams," have been shelved as a result of protests and objections from communities affected by them. On another front, interestingly, there is currently a bill before parliament to allow community forestry whereby communities will be permitted to live in various national forest areas, rather than being evicted therefrom, while recognizing that these communities can contribute to the protection of forests. However, it may be noted that the rights of indigenous peoples and minorities are not expressly mentioned by the Thai Constitution.

Civil/political and economic/social/cultural rights

In a sense, the notion of the rule of law has always been closely related to civil and political rights, such as guarantees before a court of law in criminal proceedings, rather than by equal emphasis on economic, social, and cultural rights, especially anti-poverty measures. By contrast, a basic premise of human rights is the indivisibility of civil, political, economic, social, and cultural rights – all human rights have to be promoted in an interconnected sense. This nexus is taken further by one of the newer human rights recognized internationally – the right to development, which emphasizes social justice, particularly through equitable policies, national and international, leading to income distribution and resource allocations to help marginalized groups.

Transposed to the national setting, the bifurcation between civil/political rights and economic/social/cultural rights is even more marked: some governments prefer to promote economic, social, and cultural rights rather than civil and political rights. This is much linked with the Asian values debate dealt with below.

The response in the Thai setting is to promote a mixture of such rights as evidenced by the Constitution, depending upon the nature and policies of governments. Conceptually, the Constitution's emphasis on a variety of rights embodies the indivisibility of human rights, but there are major problems in relation to practical implementation. There are also various new angles which are not covered by international human rights standards. For instance, consumer rights are treated as part of the human rights framework at the national level, while consumer rights tend not to be treated as part of the human rights framework internationally. Likewise, the recognition of community rights in the Thai Constitution is perhaps more evolved than international human rights standards. There is also a linkage between the rule of law, human rights, and non-violence/peace in the Thai Constitution which is very much derived from the national experience and a bottom-up approach, deserving note, as per Section 65:

A person shall have the right to resist peacefully any act committed for the acquisition of the power to rule the country by a means which is not in accordance with the modes provided in this Constitution.[8]

Human rights/security and national security

One of the perennial difficulties faced by the rule of law and human rights is how to balance these rights with national security. The quest for this balance has become even more rickety with the current preoccupation with anti-terrorist measures globally. Many governments – both democratic and undemocratic (more often undemocratic?) – have at times had a field-day in constraining human rights by advocating wide discretion for the executive branch of government and broad interpretation of national security. Thailand is no exception to this. For instance, until the end of the previous millennium Communism was illegal in Thailand and the Anti-Communist Law enabled the authorities to detain people without trial for long periods. Martial law is still used in parts of Thailand. However, on a positive front, the Anti-Communist Law has now been reformed, with more of a green light for human rights and human security.

Another example of how the national security claim was abused in the past was that military coups and the bloody incident of May 1992 (when scores of civilians were injured, killed, or disappeared in street demonstrations against military rule) were all justified by the military, to a greater or lesser extent, under the pretext of national security. *En passant*, it is worth noting that if national security is to be seen as a response to threats, those threats may be actual, potential, or fictitious.

Likewise, all national Constitutions prior to the current one had broad provisions on national security which could be and were used to constrain human rights and the rule of law. The current Constitution fortunately plays down the national security argument and advocates that constraints on human rights cannot be used to destroy the substance of such rights. This is evidenced by Section 29, which stipulates that

> The restriction of such rights and liberties as recognized by the Constitution shall not be imposed on a person except by virtue of provisions of the law specifically enacted for the purpose determined by this Constitution and only to the extent of necessity and provided that it shall not affect the essential substance of such rights and liberties.[9]

However, globally and nationally there is a need for vigilance, in view of the tide of terrorism and counter-terrorism, both of which have enormous implications for human rights and the rule of law.

Universality and particularities

The term "universality" is used in the human rights context to advocate that there are basic minimum standards of human rights guaranteed internationally, especially through various international human rights instruments and international monitoring for accountability. In recent years, this notion has been queried by various ethnocentric trends, particularly to suggest that such universal standards should bear in mind various national and regional specificities or particularities, and even yield to them. The debate was volatile in the lead-up to the 1993 World Conference on Human Rights, held in Vienna. Thailand's own position on the issue was – like that of many other countries – ambivalent. While the Thai government was ready to bend to support the subjection of universality to particularities as part of the trend among Asia–Pacific governments, the non-governmental sector was much more protective of the notion of universality and wary of particularities.

This bifurcation was evident in 1993 and is still pervasive today. In the lead-up to the Vienna Conference, Asia–Pacific governments (including Thailand) adopted the Asia–Pacific Governmental Declaration on Human Rights ("The Bangkok Governmental Declaration"), which tried to dilute the universality of human rights by subsuming them under national and regional influences with the following provision:

> While human rights are universal in nature, they must be considered in the context of a dynamic process of international norm-setting, bearing in mind the significance of national and regional particularities and various historical, cultural and religious backgrounds.[10]

Asia–Pacific non-governmental organizations (NGOs), including the Thai organizations present in 1993 at the parallel NGO conference in Bangkok, rejected the governmental stance by adopting their own "Bangkok Non-governmental Declaration of Human Rights," reiterating the universality of human rights as follows:

> We affirm the basis of universality of human rights which accord protection to all of humanity.... While advocating cultural pluralism, those cultural practices which derogate from universally accepted human rights, including women's rights, must not be tolerated. As human rights are of universal concern and are universal in value, the advocacy of human rights cannot be considered to be an encroachment upon national sovereignty.[11]

A tenuous compromise was reached at the World Conference on Human Rights and the final text in the form of the Vienna Declaration and Program of Action adopted this formula:

All human rights are universal, indivisible and interdependent and interrelated. The international community must treat human rights globally in a fair and equal manner, on the same footing, and with the same emphasis. While the significance of national and regional particularities and various historical, cultural and religious back-grounds must be borne in mind, it is the duty of States, regardless of their political, economic and cultural systems, to promote and protect all human rights and fundamental freedoms.[12]

The structure of this formula would suggest that, although we should take into account national and regional particularities, the universality of human rights should prevail if there is a conflict with such particularities. Yet many less than democratic governments are still unconvinced of the primacy of human rights and the rule of law; they prefer to advocate national sovereignty and non-interference in the international affairs of a state. This ambivalence is appropriately linked with the claim of Asian values below, which is very much based upon various particularities in this region.

Asian values and values-in-Asia

The advocacy of Asian values is no longer new internationally. It flourished before the gargantuan economic crash in the region in 1997, but diminished in force subsequently as many of the protagonists became less confident and more preoccupied with economic restructuring at home in the wake of the debacle. However, although the fangs of the "Asian tigers" have become somewhat blunted in the process, the claim of Asian values is still influential in various circles and has various implications for the rule of law and human rights. Thailand has not been in the forefront of advocating Asian values, but the governmental sector is particularly malleable to such values, espe-cially when it acts in concert with Asia–Pacific governments, as is evident in regard to the particularities noted above.

Asian values in their various incarnations epitomize a whole variety of claims, including the following:[13]

- strong government and political stability;
- deference to authority;
- guided democracy or a soft brand of authoritarianism;
- economic development rather than broad-based political participation and democracy;
- economic rights rather than political rights;
- civic responsibilities at least on a par with human rights;
- advocacy against the Eurocentric perception of human rights, with its overwhelming emphasis on political rights;
- emphasis on the community and family rather than the individual;

- presence of extended family rather than the nuclear family;
- diligence and self-discipline;
- non-confrontational approach;
- informal interaction rather than rule-based and institution-based structure and decision-making;
- consensus-building;
- pragmatism;
- effective, clean government rather than democratic but unclean government.

When tested against the backdrop of the rule of law and human rights, obviously those who favor such Asian values are ready to sacrifice parts, if not all, of the rule of law and human rights in order to uphold such values. There is thus potentially or actually a conflict between the rule of law or human rights and Asian values. For example, a strong government and political stability are not a prerequisite for the rule of law or human rights – at times the former are antithetical to the latter.

The claim of Asian values is presumptuous and misleading in a variety of ways. First, it is not so much the conundrum concerning "what are Asian values?" but "who is making the argument?" which is really the key to unraveling the subject. A number of governments have, for their own political ends, capitalized upon the Asian values argument to legitimize their action against the population and as a testament to opportunism. In a sense, the Asian values argument is very much a state instrument – an *instrument d'état* – which some less than democratic governments use to gloss over their excesses and lend themselves credibility while dampening popular participation and democratic constituents. This is a process of politicization and instrumentalization, claiming to provide a homogenized approach for Asia, when in fact it does not represent the expectations of civil society and democracy in the heterogeneous setting which personifies Asia.

Upon scrutiny, such elements as strong government and political stability, respect for authority, economic development rather than political participation, and economic rights rather than political rights are all pretexts for undemocratic governments to prolong their rule and impose their fiat on the people. The interests of the community and family and civic responsibilities are also overplayed so as to impose constraints upon the rights and freedoms of individuals.

Second, some of the better elements of the list of Asian values are universal rather than particularistic. For example, the trait of diligence is a universal aspiration rather than a purely Asian characteristic. The concerns of the family are universal, especially as in all societies many families are now under pressure and disintegrating in the face of the less positive side of globalization, economic needs, dislocation, and migration. While it is true that extended families tend to be the norm in Asia, extended families are now breaking up in various parts of Asia, and there arises a question, similar to that appearing elsewhere, concerning who will provide safety nets for family members when the family is no longer able to sustain itself; hence the universal call in all regions for social development, social security, social insurance and social protection for families and their members.

A more constructive approach is to identify values-in-Asia which can help to enrich universal norms and practices rather than to undermine such norms by means of culturally relativistic opportunism embodied in Asian values. One value found in Asia – but which has not found a prominent place in the listing of Asian values – is equity, particularly to share resources between the haves and the have-nots. Yet, the value is well rooted in Asia. For instance, an important principle inherent in Islam, a key religion in Asia, is the need to contribute part of one's wealth to help the poor, known as *Zakat*. This reinforces the universal concern of social justice to share wealth more fairly across different strata of society. Likewise, the advocacy of kindness and consideration for one's neighbors in Buddhism converges with the belief of the world's religions to support a humane response to those in need. These values-in-Asia add much value to the rule of law and human rights, not only in material terms but also in spiritual terms.

The conceptualization of the rule of law and its linkage with human rights is thus inspired by the best traditions from Asia, which converge constructively with international standards. However, there is another key step in these building blocks: this perspective needs to be tested even more meticulously from the angle of implementation. Even if the norms exist, how they are enforced – or not enforced – is critical, and it is to this that we now turn.

Implementation

The picture is one of contrasts. While there are many positive examples of implementation, there is also lax enforcement of the rule of law and human rights in several settings, pointing to a chasm between principles and practice. The situation can be tested from the angles outlined below.

Processes/procedures

One of the intriguing developments of Thai law and policy is that they have become much more open to participatory processes as part of democratization. A key example is that when the military regime collapsed in 1992 huge public mobilization called for a new constitution to be drafted, not by parliamentarians – because the public was distrustful of many parliamentarians, who had colluded with the military or other vested interests – but by an independent drafting committee composed of non-parliamentarians drawn from respected members of civil society. The Constitution which was drafted by this committee was aired throughout the whole country by means of public hearings involving different parts of the community before it was finally put to parliament for adoption. As destiny would have it, although there were dissenting voices in parliament who wished to reject the draft Constitution, they were overcome by the impact of an unforeseen cataclysmic event – the economic crash in 1997. Since the dissident parliamentarians did not want to be seen as politically irresponsible in the wake of the crash by rejecting the popular support for the draft Constitution, they relented and passed the new Constitution.

The content of the Constitution is replete with many participatory processes and procedures which embody democratic aspirations while enhancing the rule of law and human rights. For instance, in addition to having the right to vote, the public is now able to enjoy procedures embodying direct democracy in at least three ways:[14]

- at least 50,000 people may submit a draft law to parliament for consideration;
- a similar number of people can petition parliament to investigate politicians for misconduct;
- the public has a right to participate in referendums.

At the local level also, a number of citizens can petition to investigate local politicians for misconduct. This goes hand in hand with greater decentralization. A number of laws have been passed to enable local authorities to decide upon projects of concern to the localities, as well as to oversee local resources and income from taxation, without having to pass through decision-making in Bangkok.

Another angle of participatory processes can be seen in the much-improved access of civil society to the selection panels for choosing candidates for national mechanisms under the Constitution. For instance, in the selection panel for candidates under the National Election Commission and the National Human Rights Commission, a number of the panel members must come from civil society. The same is true in relation to other independent bodies, including the judiciary.

There are other participatory processes. The Thai Parliament now consists of the lower House of Representatives, based upon those directly elected and those selected through proportional representation by means of a party list, and an upper house in the form of the Senate. For the first time ever, the Senate is now a directly elected body and acts as a balancing force for the lower house. As noted earlier, there are also provisions which open the door to public hearings, especially in the environmental field. The role of civil society as an advocate for the rule of law and human rights has become more legitimate, especially as it was instrumental in toppling the military in 1992 and propelling the process towards the new Constitution.

However, there are residues from the past which are still less than participatory. The extensive system of patronage, perverse influence, and corruption
is longstanding and undermines the rule of law and the aspiration to be
democratic. Despite the various modalities listed above as part of participatory processes, the reality is often different. For example, when people try to
propose laws under the 50,000-people procedure, technicalities are at times
used to block this, for example "not enough proof of the identity of the
proposers." The laws on decentralization have been hampered by slow implementation, especially as there are local vested interests which do not wish to
relinquish power. The Senate itself has been criticized for being politicized,
while the selection processes of some of the mechanisms under the
Constitution have been less than transparent.

Substantive law/policies

Given the fact that prior to 1992 Thailand was for many decades under
authoritarian rule, many laws and policies were and are inconsistent with the
rule of law and human rights. Military regimes in the past liked to bypass
parliament by issuing various decrees. Perhaps the most famous of these were
self-amnesty decrees passed by a number of military governments, exempting
themselves from responsibility and prosecutions upon leaving office.

On a positive note, the new Constitution embodies much-improved
substantive law on many fronts.[15] Chapter III of the Constitution, on rights
and liberties, has led to the review of many laws and policies, and its many
guarantees include the following:

- non-discrimination;
- right to life and freedom from torture;
- non-retroactive criminal law;
- presumption of innocence;
- right to privacy;
- liberty of movement;
- liberty of communications by lawful means;
- liberty to profess a religion;
- liberty of expression;
- radio and television frequencies as the common resources of the people;
- freedom from state interference in the presentation of news;
- academic freedom;
- right to receive 12 years of basic education;
- liberty of assembly;
- right of the community to protect the environment;
- right to form a political party;
- right to property;
- right to engage in an occupation;

- freedom from forced labor;
- right to standard public health service;
- right of children and family members to be protected from violence and unfair treatment;
- right of the elderly to receive state aid;
- right of those with disability to receive state aid;
- right to access public information.

Chapter V of the Constitution stipulates a variety of policies with particular impact on a range of rights, especially economic, social, and cultural rights, including the following:

- promotion of non-discrimination
- promotion of public participation in policy-making
- decentralization
- provision of a public health service
- fair distribution of income
- appropriate system of land holdings
- protection of labor
- a free-market system

Chapter VIII of the Constitution, on the courts, takes the position further by reinforcing a number of rights, especially in the civil and political field, concerning primarily criminal cases, including that:

- a court hearing requires a full quorum of judges, and any judge not sitting at the hearing of a case cannot give judgment;
- no arrest or detention of a person may be made except by a court warrant or, without a warrant, in the case of *flagrante delicto* or as provided by law;
- an arrested person must be sent to a court within 48 hours of the arrest;
- an application for bail of the suspect must be considered without delay;
- a complaint against unlawful detention can be lodged with the court by a person acting on behalf of the detainee;
- the suspect or the accused has a right to a speedy and fair trial;
- the suspect has the right to see a lawyer and to receive legal aid;
- there is a right against self-incrimination;
- witnesses and the injured person have a right to protection and appropriate remuneration from the state;
- a wrongfully accused person has a right to appropriate compensation from the state.

Many of the provisions above, of course, interlink with other laws, including the Criminal Code and Criminal Procedure Code. Since the passage of the Constitution, a number of law reforms have been adopted to implement the Constitution, including in relation to the criminal law. For instance, unlike in the past, when the police often took the law into their own hands, today writs to arrest persons and to search premises must be issued by the judiciary, almost without exception. The Criminal Procedure Code has now been reformed to provide more victim-friendly procedures, such as videotaping of the testimonies of children/youth as well as access to social workers, psychologists, and friends when being questioned by the police. Another reform dictates that in post mortem cases only a medically qualified person may carry out the post mortem. This helps to overcome the previous practice in some localities whereby for lack of medical personnel the post mortem was conducted by village leaders. A recent law has been enacted in line with the Constitution to offer compensation to those wrongfully convicted by the criminal justice system. New regulations are being considered by the courts concerning the granting of bail.

However, these welcome developments should not obscure the fact that law enforcement is weak or contradictory on many fronts. As in several other countries, Thailand is confronted with five Cs in the administration of justice: corruption, collusion, cronyism, clientelism, and crime. The good intentions of the Constitution demand effective law reform and jurisprudence to overcome old laws inconsistent with the Constitution and/or to enact new laws to help implement the rights guaranteed. Yet, at times, law reform and the drafting of new laws to help enforce the Constitution have been tardy, and conservative elements are trying to undermine the whole process of change.

Mechanisms/institutions

The rule of law and human rights in Thailand have to be tested from the angle of how national mechanisms, institutions, and related personnel respond to them. The record on this front has been mixed.

First, it should be noted that the new Constitution opens the door to the reappraisal of traditional institutions such as Parliament, the executive and the judiciary. There are new elements concerning these institutions in the Constitution, and some of them have already been referred to above, for instance an elected Senate and improved processes and substantive law relating to the courts. Second, new mechanisms have been introduced by the Constitution as a system of checks and balances.[16] The newly independent mechanisms or institutions (independent at least from the executive) include the Constitutional Court, the Election Commission, the Ombudsman, Administrative Courts, the National Human Rights Commission, and the National Counter Corruption Commission. The first is vested with the power to decide upon the constitutionality of laws and actions. The second supervises elections, while the third addresses maladministration of justice, particularly on the part of the executive, reports its recommendations to parliament and can cross-refer cases to the courts. The fourth deliberates on administrative cases between people and the public sector, such as when contracts between the government and individuals are questioned. The fifth has the task of promoting and protecting human rights, including monitoring of the situation. The sixth investigates allegations of corruption in the public sector and can cross-refer cases to the Constitutional Court.

How effective have the reforms been? A key example of how the new Constitution has impacted on the traditional institutions and personnel is that politicians, their spouses and children under the age of majority are now obliged to disclose their assets both before and after such politicians take up political office. This helps to provide transparency.

The courts system has been subjected to various reforms. For instance, prior to the new Constitution the administration of the courts was under the Ministry of Justice. This Ministry has now been separated from the courts, and the courts will be able to concentrate on judicial deliberation rather than enforcement of judgments. The Ministry of Justice is now in charge of the latter, and it is also charged with supervising prisons and juvenile detention facilities, as well as overseeing implementation of laws in general.

What of the principle of independence of the judiciary and the courts, and related reforms? In fact, there are four types of courts at stake, two old and two new:[17]

- the (old) courts of law, such as the criminal and civil courts and provincial courts, with the Court of Appeal and the Supreme Court as the second and third tiers, and a sprinkle of special courts such as Family Courts, Labor Courts, the Intellectual Property Court, the Bankruptcy Court, and the Taxation Court;
- the (old) Military Courts;
- the (new) Constitutional Court;
- the (new) Administrative Courts.

The (old) courts of law deal traditionally with civil and criminal cases among civilians. The Military Courts, by contrast, are courts which deal with criminal offences involving the military, even where one of the parties in the case is a civilian. The roles of the Constitutional Court and Administrative Courts have already been noted.

As seen above, an innovative step is the recent introduction of reforms to separate the executive branch from the judicial branch to enhance judicial independence. Yet the aim of judicial independence in itself is inadequate. There is a need to test the judiciary from the angle of effectiveness and transparency in rendering justice.

Some of the positive developments on this front can be noted. While prior to the Constitution several courts were willing to consider cases and render judgment without a quorum of the bench, today the need for a quorum is imperative and is being followed in practice. Various reforms at the instigation of the courts are being undertaken to ensure that police powers do not dilute the powers of the courts to issue writs, while the grant of bail should be eased with the introduction of new court regulations.

On the other hand, there is a huge backlog of cases and access to the courts is still difficult and expensive for many people. Court cases often take years to complete, and there is no fixed day in court when court proceedings will be dealt with expeditiously once and for all. In this era of democracy, the presence of Military Courts is also unnecessary, at least when one of the parties in the case is a civilian.

On another front, while lay judges have some access to sit in the special courts mentioned above, for instance in Family Courts, Labor Courts, etc., public participation in the administration of justice is too limited. Moreover, in litigation access to the courts depends upon *locus standi* – proof of grievances through being affected by the alleged misdeeds. The Thai legal system does not generally recognize class actions which would not require *locus standi* but general public interest, except in two cases which are rarely invoked – namely, consumer protection law and environmental protection law.

There has also been much talk of alternative dispute settlement to circumvent delays and expenses in court, and this has been implemented to some extent through a system of arbitration and mediation, but it still needs to be made more extensive. Moreover, from the angle of transparency, many court decisions are not reported at all to the public. For instance, not all Supreme Court decisions are published, and the decisions of the Court of Appeal and lower courts are generally not published. However, for the first time, a synopsis of Court of Appeal decisions will be appearing soon.

More concretely, in terms of case examples on the part of the traditional courts there are both constructive and less constructive lessons. For example, in a seminal case decades back, the Supreme Court upheld the right of Thais to marry displaced persons (refugees) from other countries, even though the Ministry of Interior tried to block this right.[18] Courts are also no longer willing to validate, *ex post facto*, the actions of the police to arrest persons without a proper writ from the courts. These examples are contrasted with the scenario whereby through a series of cases in recent years the courts rejected the claims of the families of the victims harmed by the military during the bloody May incidents of 1992.[19] Even more recently, the Judicial Commission, which oversees court appointments, had difficulties with the question of those with disabilities applying to become judges.[20] Its rejection of candidates on this front has been the subject of public criticism.

With regard to one of the newest courts – the Constitutional Court, which has the power to decide on the constitutionality of laws and actions when tested against the Constitution – the record has also been mixed. On a positive front, in one case it delivered a judgment indicating that it would be unconstitutional for the Election Commission to issue its own regulations depriving Thai citizens of various rights if they fail to vote at elections.[21] Subsequently, this led to a national law passed by Parliament, rather than a regulation from the Election Commission.

However, other cases are open to debate. In one case, the Constitutional Court decided that a minister who had been given a suspended sentence by a criminal court was not disbarred from political office.[22] The most controversial contrast among cases in this court has been among those cases concerning the false or incomplete declaration of assets by politicians. In several cases, the court found that various persons holding political appointments had failed to declare their assets in conformity with the law, thus leading to their disqualification from public office.[23] Yet in similar circumstances, in a case involving Thailand's billionaire prime minister, the court – by a very slim majority – did not find him guilty of misconduct.[24]

Another controversial issue was raised recently before the Constitutional Court on the question of those with disabilities seeking judicial positions. With an attitude similar to some other parts of the judiciary, this court turned down the appeal of two persons with disabilities who had questioned a ruling of the Judicial Commission to the effect that they were unsuited to become judges because of a limp due to childhood polio.[25] This was in spite of Section 30 of the Constitution, the spirit of which is against discrimination, as follows:

> All persons are equal before the law and shall enjoy equal protection under the law. Men and women shall enjoy equal rights. Unjust discrimination against a person on the grounds of the difference in origin, race, language, sex, age, physical or health condition, personal status, economic or social standing, religious belief, education or constitutionally political view, shall not be permitted.[26]

Another test case now before the courts concerns the question of gender discrimination. Currently, under an old law, women are obliged to change their maiden name upon marriage to that of the husband. A while ago, efforts to reform this law failed in Parliament, blocked by conservative groups. The question was then referred to the ombudsman, who then referred the case to the Constitutional Court to see whether this law is unconstitutional and discriminatory. This now awaits the deliberations of the Constitutional Court.[27]

Upon scrutiny, questions remain concerning whether this court and other courts are proactive enough in upholding the principle of non-discrimination which is entrenched in the Constitution.

From another angle, law enforcement touches upon a series of institutions and personnel beyond the courts system, and it is well known that many of them are less than transparent. Corruption is longstanding and rife in several quarters, and is well known and openly admitted among law enforcers.[28] From the angle of the rule of law, therefore, it may be asked how law enforcers are selected, trained, paid, and monitored. If the system allows the least qualified to enter the law enforcement system, offers them hardly any training on human rights and ethics, provides very low salaries, and fails to monitor them, the dim prospects for good governance are more than self-evident.

Checks and balances

One of the challenges facing the rule of law and human rights is to ensure that there are check and balances against the abuse of power. On the one hand, this implies the need for a variety of formal institutions, such as a number of courts to test the actions of the executive. It is linked with the need for separation of powers and functions between the different branches of government. Yet the formal institutions themselves may be deficient, and there should be room for non-formal or extra-systemic checks and balances such as a strong civil society, active NGOs, and a range of media.

On a positive front, Thailand has some of these checks and balances. For instance, in the case above, concerning discrimination against those with disabilities, the complainants first went to the Judicial Commission and, failing a response there, the ombudsman was later used to seek redress. The latter then transferred the case to the Constitutional Court. Although the decision of that court was not favorable to the complainants, since then the media has been actively criticizing the judicial position, and there is a possibility that the judiciary may reconsider its stance and rationalize itself more. Intriguingly, the Foreign Ministry recently came out with a more liberal position, opening the door to those with disabilities, thus enabling the public to make comparisons between the different approaches of state institutions.[29]

Another example of the importance of checks and balances is this: The relationship between the current executive branch of government and the media has not been a smooth one, with threats from the former against the latter in relation to freedom of expression. There have been problems between that branch and a number of those in the Thai and foreign press. In one case, the country's anti-money laundering body, established under an anti-money laundering law, started to pry into the bank accounts of various members of the mass media and their families. This snowballed into a huge furor related to the question of freedom of the press and fear of intimidation directed against the critics of the government, including the media personnel under investigation. Those members of the media took their complaint to the Administrative Court and an injunction was obtained against the action of the anti-money laundering body. The court has now rule against the anti-money laundering body on the issue.[30]

With regard to the National Human Rights Commission, this institution has only recently been functioning and is still under-resourced. It has great potential for acting as a monitor on all actors who have an impact on human rights and as a check and balance between different institutions. It is now working on its strategic plan for action in the next few years. It has already started to act as a mediator on various issues, for example in conflicts between the authorities and the public. In one instance it used a traditional means of reconciliation – Buddhist rites of forgiveness – to reach a compromise between the two protagonists.[31] However, the Commission is not a court of law and its findings are only in the form of recommendations, ultimately dependent on the prime minister and Parliament for pressure for accountability.

Upon analysis, despite all the mechanisms mentioned above, often the formal systems, mechanisms, and institutions are not easily activated to respond to grievances unless there is visible pressure from the public. One key example of the latter is the work of the Assembly of the Poor, a non-governmental movement linking different groups with grievances ranging from displacements to slow compensation from government agencies where government-backed programs have damaged such groups. A major strategy has been street demonstrations and long-term camping outside Government House to protest against government delays.[32] These have resulted in a number of compromises between the authorities and the aggrieved. Despite promises of redress from the former, annual demonstrations from the Assembly have taken place to maintain pressure for implementation of these promises.

Intriguingly, there is a sense of unease even in the face of a democratically elected government where the government is based upon a blend of populism and monied interests. Critically, there is fear of intimidation *vis-à-vis* the media and those who are critical of the regime. This implies that the mere fact of a democratically elected government does not necessarily ensure that it will respect the rule of law or human rights; hence the need for society to be vigilant towards all power groups so as to prevent them from committing abuses of power, as well to pressure for remedies.

Resources

This term is often understood to imply material resources, but it should not neglect the non-material resources available and needed in society to support the rule of law and human rights.

From another angle, the fact that even government-backed national economic and social development plans admit that nearly 60 per cent of the nation's material resources are in the hands of some 20 per cent of the population is not reassuring. This lack of equity has dire consequences for the rule of law and human rights, precisely because the inequity may breed violence, if not disrespect for the law. How can the rule of law help to foster equity and social justice?

To date, that question has not been at the heart of the notion of the rule of law, but it needs to be asked more prominently in that context; it is linked with the challenge of sustainable development, including rural development and access to marginalized groups. The current government in Thailand has tried to answer this question to some extent by adopting a series of populist policies, including a 30 baht (less than a dollar) medical scheme making health services available to all, a 1 million baht fund for each village, and debt moratorium for farmers. Despite the potentially positive impact of such intentions, there remain queries about the efficacy of implementation and financial/fiscal discipline, especially as the country is running a disconcertingly high public deficit and has already borrowed billions of dollars from the International Monetary Fund to offset the negative impact of the 1997 economic crash.[33]

Yet little is heard of how to address the issue of distortions of land holdings and how to redistribute wealth and resources on other fronts. By contrast, it is worth noting that some of the country's richest men and women (including the country's richest person) sit in Parliament, especially in the Cabinet.

International standards and cooperation

It was noted at the outset that the rule of law and human rights are linked with international standards. There is a variety of international instruments which help to provide the content behind these titles. How has Thailand participated in this standard-setting, related implementation, and cooperation on the issue?[34]

Like many other countries, Thailand voted for the 1948 Universal Declaration of Human Rights. Since then, its participation in key human rights treaties has grown. Currently it is a state party to the following:

- the 1979 Convention on the Elimination of All Forms of Discrimination against Women;
- the 1989 Convention on the Rights of the Child;
- the 1966 International Covenant on Civil and Political Rights;
- the 1966 International Covenant on Economic, Social and Cultural Rights.

It has ratified a number of treaties of the International Labor Organization and has signed, although not yet ratified, the 1998 Rome Statute of the International Criminal Court. Attempts to promote its accession to the 1965 International Convention on the Elimination of All Forms of Racial Discrimination were, however, foiled recently by conservative elements antithetical to international human rights treaties.[35]

The positive impact of this participation by the country is manifold. First, the standards expounded by these treaties help to promote law, policy, and practical reforms by offering an international barometer to test national standards. Second, the country is obliged to prepare and send periodic national reports on how it is implementing the treaties to the various international treaty bodies charged with monitoring the implementation of these treaties at the national level. This helps to provide transparency and channels for eliciting international recommendations to help the local reform process.

Third, the information and data gathered to prepare such national reports help to build a database system useful for planning and implementation. Fourth, the process of national report preparation may bring together both governmental and non-governmental actors to enhance cross-sectoral cooperation, which can assist in the implementation of the rule of law and human rights. Fifth, the opportunity of liaising between different sectors of the community to implement international standards at the national and local levels is an empowering process which may lead to the enhancement of cooperation through joint actions. In this context, there are avenues to share local experiences and wisdom which can provide added value to the international perspective.

Yet the negative side is that the process of implementing international standards is often slow and less than participatory. In acceding to some of the treaties, the country has entered a range of reservations and declarations which indicate a lack of readiness to accept, or a sense of unease in accepting, international standards on a number of issues, such as family rights, refugee rights, and the administration of justice, particularly in the criminal field. There has also been inadequate access by the public to the national monitoring process in regard to some of the treaties, especially on the implementation of civil and political rights, while the recent rejection of the convention concerning racial discrimination points to conservative elements which are possibly hostile towards pluralism in the country. On another front, precisely because in this era of globalization so many problems have a cross-border dimension (for example human trafficking), there is much more room for transnational cooperation.

Education / mindset

Behind the facade of the rule of law and human rights, there is a need to ask how a society nurtures a mindset favorable towards such concepts. This is linked with a socialization process and an educational system conducive to a sense of care and consideration towards others. Does this take place?

On the positive front, it should be recognized that human rights education has become a more legitimate notion. It is now found in national plans and is spreading on several fronts. For example, the *Rajabhat* institutes, which train teachers all over the country, have been experimenting with human rights education with the support of a United Nations agency. Several courses on human rights and humanitarian law are available in universities, while informal courses can be found addressed to a variety of disparate groups, including the military, NGOs, parliamentarians, and civil servants.

However, while the above are welcome, they tend to be ad hoc or unsystematic. What is needed is to integrate the rule of law and human rights systematically into all levels of the educational system for all groups and to train, prepare, and reward teachers accordingly. The bookish methodology, compounded by learning by rote, should also be avoided, while more daily life experiences should incorporated into the teaching process to foster the mindset and behavior responsive to the rule of law and human rights. This is currently seen in some of the human rights courses which emphasize field visits to broaden the experience of the students. They can be enhanced by community-oriented programs which take the young (and older) of different economic and social groups to visit and work with other groups to promote an ethical process of cross-cultural fertilization. Yet these developments are nascent rather than mainstreamed into the national psyche.

Orientations

In retrospect, the concepts of the rule of law and human rights are now at least verbally accepted in Thailand, and this is very welcome. Yet, while many positive developments can be identified in response to such concepts at the national and local levels, there remain major gaps in terms of principles and practices, particularly lax implementation on several fronts, as discussed above.

Some of the preferred orientations for the future include the following:

- more participatory processes and procedures for the population to take part in understanding and safeguarding the rule of law and human rights;
- more reforms of laws, policies, and practices which conflict with the rule of law and human rights;
- more expeditious enactment of laws and policies, and effective implementation measures, to enforce the rule of law and human rights;
- more mainstreaming of the rule of law and human rights into the work of national mechanisms, institutions, and related personnel;
- more integration of the rights of women, children, and marginalized groups who are actually or potentially victims of discrimination in the national and local settings;
- more promotion of not only the independence of the judiciary but also its efficacy and transparency;
- improved processes to select quality law enforcers, to train them on the rule of law and human rights, to monitor their performance, and to reward them adequately;
- greater participation of the public in the administration of justice;

- more checks and balances against abuses of power, not only between formal institutions but through non-formal interaction with civil society, the media, and other stakeholders, especially in this era, where both terrorism and counter-terrorism have an enormous impact on the rule of law and human rights;
- more attention to the promotion of equity and social justice in the advocacy of the rule of law and human rights, especially in relation to anti-poverty measures and redistribution of resources;
- more participation in international standard-setting and related implementation, while identifying and strengthening local wisdom and channels for cooperation not only between governments but also in civil society;
- more capacity-building through socialization, education, information, and life experiences to promote an ethical mindset and behavior responsive to the rule of law and human rights.

Notes

1 This chapter was prepared for the Conference on the Rule of Law in Asia: Comparative Conceptions, Hong Kong University, Hong Kong, June 20–21, 2002. Warmest thanks to Judge J. Pakditanakul, Khun Jiravudh, and Khun Damorn for providing some of the information used in this study. All views expressed are the personal views of the author.
2 For background reading, see R. Lingat, *Prawatisart Kotmai Thai* [History of Thai Law], vols. 1 and 2 (Bangkok: Thammasat University, 1983) (in Thai); M. B. Hooker, *A Concise Legal History of Southeast Asia*(Oxford: Oxford University Press, 1978); V. Muntarbhorn, "Human Rights in Thailand," in L. Palmier, ed., *State and Law in Eastern Asia*(Aldershot: Dartmouth Press, 1993), pp. 103–40; D. K. Wyatt, *Studies in Thai History*(Bangkok: Silkworm Books, 1994); V. Muntarbhorn and C. Taylor, *Roads to Democracy: Human Rights and Democratic Development in Thailand* (Montreal: Centre International des Droits et du Développement Démocratique,1994); K. Kittayarak, ed., *Tittang Krabuankarn Yutitham Thai Nai Satawat Mai* [Directions of the Thai Administration of Justice in the New Century] (Bangkok: Fund for Research, 2000) (in Thai); K. Kittayarak, ed., *Yuttasat Karn Patirup Krabuankarn Yutitham Tang Aya Thai* [Strategies for Reforming the Administration of the Thai Criminal Justice System] (Bangkok: Fund for Research, 2001) (in Thai).
3 Lingat, *ibid.*
4 Phra Dhammapitaka, *Human Rights: Social Harmony or Social Disintegration* (Bangkok: Sahamit Press, 1998).
5 Constitution of the Kingdom of Thailand, B.E.2540 (1997) (Bangkok: The Senate, 1997), §4, p. 3.
6 *Ibid.*, §46, at p. 15.
7 *Ibid.*, §56, at p. 18.
8 *Ibid.*, §65, at p. 20.
9 *Ibid.*, §29, at p. 9.
10 *Our Voice: Bangkok NGO Declaration on Human Rights*(Bangkok: Asian Cultural Forum on Human Rights, 1993), pp. 242–4.
11 *Ibid.*, at pp. 198–232, 199.

12 United Nations (U.N.), World Conference on Human Rights: The Vienna Declaration and Programme of Action, June 1993 (New York: U.N., 1993), p. 30.

13 V. Muntarbhorn, *ASEAN Summitry: The Asia–Europe Meeting (ASEM) 1996 and Beyond*(Bangkok: Child Rights Asianet and the Faculty of Law, Chulalongkorn University, Bangkok, 1998), p. 6.

14 See, further, V. Muntarbhorn, *Human Rights and Human Development: Thailand Country Study*, Occasional Papers (36) (New York: United Nations Development Programme (UNDP, 2000), p. 10.

15 M. Jumpa, *Kwam Ru Buangton Keo Kup Ratatamanoon Por Sor 2540* [Introduction to the Constitution B.E.2540] (Bangkok: Nititham Press, 1998) (in Thai).

16 *Ibid.*

17 W. Tuntikulanand, *Kam Atibai Kotmai Phrathammanoon Sanyutidham* [Textbook on the Law Concerning the Courts] (Bangkok: Pimaksorn Press, 2000) (in Thai).

18 Jaran Pakditanakul, "Sithi Kor Tung Kropkrua Kong Kon Tangdao" [The Right of Aliens to Found a Family], *Botbandit Journal*, vol. 37 (1982) 3, pp. 281–6 (in Thai).

19 Dika (Supreme Court) Decision No. 2015/2019(22 April 1999)(in Thai).

20 *Bangkok Post*, May 2, 2002, p. 11.

21 W. Wirachnipawan, Chintakorn Boonmark, and Boontiwa Porchcharoenroj, *Research on Analysis of the Decisions of the Court and Justices of the Constitutional Court*(Bangkok: Sititham Press, 2002), pp. 282–93 (in Thai).

22 *Ibid.*, pp. 477–515.

23 *Ibid.*, pp. 1,095–132.

24 *Kam Winichai Kong San Ratatamanoon Khadi Nayok Thaksin Shinawatra* [Judgment of the Constitutional Court in the Case Concerning Prime Minister Thaksin Shinawatra] (Bangkok: Sukarpjai Press, 2001) (in Thai).

25 *Bangkok Post*, May 2, 2002.

26 Constitution of the Kingdom of Thailand B.E.2540 (1997), p. 10.

27 Subsequent to the preparation of this study, in the middle of 2003 the Constitutional Court held that restrictions on Women's use/retention of their maiden name upon marriage are unconstitutional, thus strengthening women's rights in Thailand

28 For an external assessment, see *Country Reports on Human Rights Practices for 2001*, vol. 1 (Washington: United States Department of State, 2002), p. 1,183.

29 *Bangkok Post*, June 16, 2002, p. 1.

30 *Bangkok Post*, June 25, 2002, p. 4, reported as follows:

> The Administrative Court yesterday ruled as unlawful the order by the Anti-Money Laundering Office (AMLO) for 17 financial institutions to scrutinize transactions of 19 media figures. AMLO, however, escaped the wrath of the law by presenting a letter dated June 21, which revoked its Feb 25 order for the financial scrutiny, just before Judge Visanu Varanyu read his verdict.

31 The Human Rights Commission started operating fully in 2002. By mid-year, it had investigated, or was investigating, some 200 cases.

32 See, further, V. Muntarbhorn, Human Rights and Human Development: Thailand Country Study; UNDP, Human Development Report 2000: Human Rights and Human Development (Oxford: Oxford University Press, 2000).

33 For recent monitoring, see World Bank, *Thailand Social Monitor: Poverty and Public Policy*(Bangkok and Washington: World Bank, 2001).

34 Human Rights and Human Development: Thailand Country Study, pp. 15–16.

35 Subsequent to the preparation of this study, Thailand decided to accede to the International Convention on the Elimination of All Forms of Racial Discrimination.

12

THE PHILIPPINE "PEOPLE POWER" CONSTITUTION, RULE OF LAW, AND THE LIMITS OF LIBERAL CONSTITUTIONALISM

Raul C. Pangalangan[1]

Summary

Philippine constitutional discourse today is characterized by two competing tendencies. On one hand, a highly formalistic account of the rule of law, "a government of laws and not of men," had animated the anti-Marcos democratic movement and left its mark in the Filipino legal imagination. Because of such overweening trust in formal institutions, there is the urge to "juridify" policy debates – that is, to turn to the courts to advance social causes and to resolve political disputes. On the other hand, this constitutionally induced judicial activism has resulted in the relaxation of doctrine, for example, in liberalized rules of standing and justiciability. It has also produced an outcome-oriented jurisprudence, as if the courts were in a perpetual popularity contest refereed by polling groups and single-interest lobbies, all of them oblivious to the professional demands of the legal craftsman and attuned solely to the questions "who won?" and "are we on the same side?" Unwittingly, this has abetted an unabashed derision for law as "legal gobbledygook" (a term popularized during the impeachment trial of President Estrada), a readiness to bypass formal processes in favor of substantive results, and to see in law not fixed standards but movable goalposts as political seasons change.

Brief constitutional history

The Malolos Constitution

The "thin" version of the rule of law was idealized in the liberal aspirations of the Philippine revolution for independence against Spain, and in law was most authoritatively embodied in the Malolos Constitution,[2] the charter adopted in January 1899 by a fledgling Filipino republic following the

Declaration of Philippine Independence[3] on June 12, 1898, and before the American takeover of the Philippines.

The Spanish colonial government in the Philippines had only rudimentary legal and judicial institutions, and outside the city of Manila exercised power largely through the Catholic Church and its monastic orders. The Philippine revolution, which began in 1896, aimed to secure independence from the colonial power as much as it sought to protect individuals from the excesses of state, church and feudal power. The Malolos Constitution thus established a tripartite separation of powers[4] through a parliamentary government[5] and a Bill of Rights,[6] which included familiar, if not sophisticated, provisions on the right against unlawful arrest and detention,[7] the security of one's home,[8] and privacy.[9] It expressly provided for the separation of church and state,[10] and banned titles of nobility.[11] Most important of all, it established judicial power[12] – "the exclusive...power to apply the laws, in the name of the Nation, in all civil and criminal trials"[13] – and by which alone persons may be detained and punished.[14]

By these provisions, the Filipino revolutionists rejected the personalistic exercise of state power identified with Spanish rule in the Philippines, and in its stead created modern legal institutions that secured rights and not just privilege.

The American "organic acts" and the 1935 Constitution

The "thin" version, already expressed in Malolos, was strengthened by the new colonial power, which made the rule of law a secular religion embraced by many Filipinos.

America came to the Philippines as a consequence of the Spanish–American War. Spain ceded the Philippines, together with Cuba and Puerto Rico, to the United States in the Treaty of Peace, signed in Paris on December 10 1898,[15] and the U.S. President William McKinley proclaimed on December 21, 1898, his policy of "Benevolent Assimilation."[16] The triumphant U.S. forces governed the "new territories" through "issuances," starting with President McKinley's famous "Instructions" (as commander-in-chief), the subsequent executive and legislative "organic acts" for the Philippine Islands, and the 1916 Jones Law, which allowed the colony to write its own constitution in preparation for independence – that is, the 1935 Constitution. These organic acts were all characterized by a tripartite separation of powers as well, but modeled on the presidential system of government, and by an express Bill of Rights.[17]

These culminated with the 1935 Constitution, drafted by Filipinos and, as required by the United States, approved by the U.S. Congress, which was thus – not surprisingly – a faithful copy of the U.S. Constitution. It was a textbook example of liberal democracy: periodic elections; independent

courts; a bicameral congress; a vigorous free press; a free market; and hortatory clauses on social justice for the poor and disadvantaged.

Its biggest challenge came from the social ferment of the mid-1960s,
articulated by the intellectual Left and the student movement, which
presented a straightforward critique of the legal fictions of the liberal state
and the fraud of these fictions in a poor country beset by social inequality.
Note, therefore, that the main challenge to the "thin" rule of law idealized in
the 1935 Constitution took the form of a Leftist critique of liberalism – an
attack emanating from outside the rule of law framework, and indeed
rejecting law *in toto* as an instrument of the ruling classes – rather than an
immanent critique from a "thick" rule of law which accepted the values of
rule-based governance and asked merely that law fulfill its promise.

The Marcos Constitution

That challenge peaked in the early 1970s, with the rise of the local Maoist
rebellion, prompting then President Ferdinand Marcos first to suspend
the writ of *habeas corpus*,[18] and then to declare martial law.[19] (To this day,
the 1935 Constitution is the charter that was in force the longest in
Philippine history, from 1935 until 1973, when Marcos proclaimed his
new constitution).

By January 1973, a tired but pliant nation adopted a new Constitution,[20]
changing the presidency to a parliamentary government and providing a
transition period that effectively allowed Marcos to concentrate powers in
himself. In the historic case *Javellana v. Executive Secretary*,[21] the Court
recognized that the Constitution had not been ratified according to the
rules, which required approval by the people in a proper plebiscite. Yet the
Court declined to set aside the bogus ratification, deferring to the sovereign
people as the source of all authority and declining to second-guess that
sovereign's acquiescence as a valid, even if merely passive, choice: "There is
therefore no further judicial obstacle to the new Constitution being considered in full force and effect." Key passages are excerpted below, because the
reasoning of the Court in *Javellana* will return to haunt Philippine constitutional law for decades to come:

> Regardless of the modality of [ratification] – even if it deviates
> from...the old Constitution, once the new Constitution is
> ratified...by the people, this Court is precluded from inquiring into
> the validity of those acts.[22]

> If they had risen up in arms and by force deposed the then existing
> government...there could not be the least doubt that their act would
> be political and not subject to judicial review. We do not see any
> difference if no force had been resorted to and the people, in defi-

ance of the existing Constitution but peacefully...ordained a new Constitution.[23]

In 1976 Marcos had this 1973 Constitution amended, making him a one-man legislature, and in 1981 he fully "constitutionalized" his government by further amending the Constitution and declaring a "new" republic altogether.[24]

Marcos proceeded to establish what he himself referred to as a "constitutional authoritarianism," and promised to deliver, in fact and not merely in law, the equality promised by earlier liberal regimes.[25] The Marcos years exemplify either the demise of the "thin" rule of law ideal in Philippine constitutionalism or its extreme, positivist triumph. Demise, because on the classic promise of a trade-off – of formal liberties in exchange for economic growth and substantive equality – Marcos proceeded to dismantle the constitutional safeguards of liberty (including the right against unlawful searches and seizures, the right against warrantless arrests, the right of civilians to be tried only by non-military courts, etc.) and of democratic governance (including the tripartite separation of powers and especially the principle of judicial independence, the right to vote and to have one's ballots counted, to speak without fear of censorship or reprisal); positivist triumph, because Marcos made sure that his authoritarianism was constitutional, a dictatorship that was expressly provided for in the Constitution and, by all appearances, established in full compliance with proper procedure.

Cory Aquino's Freedom Constitution

The Marcos regime was brought to an end in 1986 by the People Power Revolution (hereinafter EDSA 1, EDSA representing the initials of the main highway where the protests converged, and the number 1 to distinguish it from subsequent People Power exercises). In August 1983 Ninoy Aquino was executed upon landing at the Manila International Airport and his death triggered off nationwide indignation. In October 1985, yielding to international pressure, Marcos called for special elections in February 1986 to secure a fresh mandate. Ninoy's widow Cory ran against Marcos but, despite overwhelming support, was cheated of victory. What ensued was EDSA 1, the peaceful uprising by citizens armed only with moral indignation and their readiness to sacrifice themselves for their cause.

Marcos fled to exile in Honolulu, Cory took her oath, and immediately promulgated her "Freedom Constitution"[26] – by "direct mandate of the sovereign Filipino people" – the interim charter by which the Philippines were governed between February 1986 (when Marcos was overthrown at EDSA 1) and January 1987 (when the present Constitution was adopted).

In the *Freedom Constitution* cases[27] the Supreme Court recognized that Cory Aquino became president "in violation of [the] Constitution" as

374

expressly declared by the Marcos-dominated parliament of that time (i.e. the *Batasang Pambansa*) and that her government was "revolutionary in the sense that it came into existence in defiance of existing legal processes":

> Mrs. Aquino's rise to the presidency was not due to constitutional processes; in fact it was achieved in violation of the provisions of the 1973 Constitution as a *Batasang Pambansa* resolution had earlier declared Mr. Marcos to be the winner in the 1986 presidential election.[28]

Thus the Court stated that, the people having accepted the Cory government, and Cory being in effective control of the entire country, its legitimacy was "not a justiciable matter [but] belongs to the realm of politics where only the people...are the judge."[29] She thus drew her legitimacy from outside the constitution, and all challenges raised political and non-justiciable questions.

Note that, once again, the Court exposed the limits of formal legality – this time, the extreme legalism that validated Marcos's spurious electoral victory – and the primacy of substantive norms.

Philippine constitutional traditions and crises

The Philippines' post-Marcos constitutional order aimed at two, often competing, goals: one, to end "personalistic rule"[30] identified with Marcos and restore the rule of law; and, two, advancing the EDSA Revolution by institutionalizing "People Power" – the direct but peaceful exercise of democracy that ousted the Marcos regime – by embodying in law a social reform agenda.

The current Philippine Constitution (hereinafter the 1987 Constitution) achieved the first goal by restoring constitutional checks and balances through a tripartite separation of powers,[31] detailing guarantees against a Marcos-style power grab, including congressional review of emergency measures,[32] and enhancing judicial power to enable the courts to review just about any abuse by government[33] (a direct response to the "judicial statesmanship" of an emasculated judiciary during the Marcos regime). These provisions reflect the restoration of the "thin" rule of law mechanisms in the pre-Marcos 1935 Constitution, and which people identified with the liberal democracy that Marcos extinguished.

The second goal, the codification of a social reform agenda, took the form of "directive principles" contained in an entire section of the Constitution called the "Declaration of Principles and State Policies" and scattered in many other places in the Constitution,[34] a virtual checklist of welfare claims against the state, including "social justice,"[35] the right to health[36] and to "a balanced and healthful ecology in accord with the rhythm and harmony of nature,"[37] and the duty of the state to foster "a self-reliant and independent national economy."[38] A Supreme Court Justice has referred to these norms as a "constitutional inventory of fundamental community values and interests," the equivalent in human rights discourse of non-traditional, aspirational and programmatic claims.

Juridifying social causes

The Constitution has enlarged the power of the courts to review decisions by the political branches of government, while at the same time codifying the norms that citizens may invoke before these courts. In the absence of norms of a "lower order of generality," we have thus pushed the courts "into the uncharted ocean of economy policy-making," thus prodding them to interfere too much by second-guessing government policy-makers and issuing injunctions against business decisions.

For instance, in *Garcia v. Board of Investments* the Court reversed a petro-chemical plant investor's decision to relocate a proposed plant, citing the duty of the state to "develop a self-reliant and independent national economy effectively controlled by Filipinos," and using policy arguments to explain why the investor's decision was bad for the nation. Strong dissenting opinions argued for judicial restraint:

> [C]hoosing an appropriate site for the investor's project is a political and economic decision which, under our system of separation of powers, only the executive branch, as implementer of policy formu-lated by the legislature ..., is empowered to make.[39]

> [The majority has] decided upon the wisdom of the transfer of the site... the reasonableness of the feedstock to be used...the undesir-ability of the capitalization aspect... and injected its own concept of the national interest.[40]

> By no means [does the Constitution] vest in the Courts the power to enter the realm of policy considerations under the guise of the commission of grave abuse of discretion.[41]

In the *Manila Prince Hotel* case[42], another highly controversial decision about the sale of the historic Manila Hotel, the Court held that the losing bidder, a Filipino company, had the right to match *post hoc* the winning bid of a Malaysian company. The Court held, first, that the hotel was part of the nation's cultural patrimony, this absent a prior administrative finding as required by law, and, second, that the state's constitutional duty to "give preference to qualified Filipinos" was "self-executory" and *"per se* judicially enforceable," even without implementing legislation enacted by the Congress:

A provision which lays down a general principle...is usually not self-executing. But a provision which is complete in itself and becomes operative without the aid of supplementary or enabling legislation, or which supplies sufficient rule by means of which the right it grants may be enjoyed or protected, is self-executing.[43]

[This provision] is a mandatory, positive command which is complete in itself and which needs no further guidelines or implementing laws or rules for its enforcement....It is *per se* judicially enforceable.[44]

These requirements notwithstanding, however, the Court has held in another case that the "right to a balanced and healthful ecology in accord with the rhythm and harmony of nature" is "self-executing and judicially enforceable even in [its] present form."[45] In *Minors Oposa v. Factoran*, a group of minors, represented by their parents, asked the trial court to cancel all existing, and stop issuing new, timber license agreements. The trial court had dismissed the case for failure to allege a cause of action, agreeing with the government's defense that the petitioners had failed to allege "a specific legal right" and had stated "nothing...but vague and nebulous allegations." The Supreme Court set aside the trial court's ruling, holding that the "right to a balanced and healthful ecology" sufficiently gave rise to an actionable claim. A separate opinion lamented the absence of "specific, operable norms and standards," of "a right cast in language of a significantly lower order of generality":

Where substantive standards as general as a "right to a balanced and healthful ecology" and the "right to health" are combined with remedial standards as broad ranging as "grave abuse of discretion", the result will be...*to propel the courts into the uncharted ocean of social and economic policy making.* [46]

Finally, in the *Oil Industry Deregulation Law* decision, the Court struck down the law deregulating the oil industry for not faithfully carrying out the anti-monopoly clause of the Constitution. The Court found that the tariff-differential inventory reserves requirement and predatory pricing schemes imposed substantial barriers to the entry of new players in the oil industry and inhibited the working of a truly competitive market.[47]

The Court has continued to agonize over the dilemma of promoting social causes while remaining faithful to its institutional mandate. It has insisted on implementing legislation for the protectionist clauses of the Constitution in the *WTO Ratification* case, saying:

These [economic principles]...are not intended to be self-executing... They are used by the judiciary as aids or as guides in the exercise of its power of judicial review, and by the legislature in the enactment of laws.[48]

In another case, upholding a government-sponsored lottery, the Court held that the "good morals" clauses were not self-executing:

the disregard of which can give rise to a cause of action in the courts [because t]hey do not embody judicially enforceable constitutional rights but guidelines for legislation.[49]

Creating new institutional checks

In the "thin" rule of law model, the people's rights are secured through the separation of powers – as it were, "*A Machine That Would Go of Itself*"[50] – a self-contained system of checks and balances that "would enable government to control the governed, and in the next place oblige it to control itself." The 1987 Philippine Constitution has taken two divergent paths. The first is to create more institutional checks, as if to perfect the "thin" model; the second is to discard institutions altogether and to allow the people to exercise their power directly.

The 1987 Constitution has superimposed a Commission on Human Rights (CHR) atop the tripartite separation of powers, forming yet another layer of oversight to secure people's liberties. Yet the Supreme Court has consistently barred the CHR from issuing binding orders, saying that it "simply has no place in this scheme of things,"[51] and demonstrating how oddly the CHR fits into the constitutional order precisely because it aims to vindicate the very same rights already protected by the courts.

In *Cariño v. CHR*, the Supreme Court declared that the Commission does not possess judicial power and could therefore shield public school teachers, who were protesting unpaid wages, from being fired. The most that can be conceded to the CHR is the power to investigate – that is, mere fact-finding – but not the power to apply the law upon those facts-that is, the judicial power, which belongs to the courts alone.

This was affirmed by the Court in another case, where the Commission attempted to bar a government agency from evicting "squatters," or illegal dwellers, in a special economic zone.[52] The Court explained why the CHR cannot issue even temporary and protective measures, because these aim to preserve the rights of the parties while proceedings are pending, which constitutes a judicial act.

Finally, the Court rejected an order by the CHR stopping a city mayor from carrying out a demolition order against squatter vendors occupying public land.[53] The vendors had invoked the constitutional right to decent housing, but only indirectly, by saying that their stalls were their way of earning a living and that they were thus deprived of a right to livelihood.

The Court found that the drafters of the Constitution had deliberately excluded economic and social claims from the scope of the CHR. They had established the CHR as a response to the civil and political rights violations under Marcos, and indeed were concerned that Marcos had justified those violations with the classic "trade-off argument" that economic and social rights were more important in a poor country like the Philippines.

The current Constitution has created a further institutional device to perfect the "thin" model of the rule of law, but the result has been to short-circuit the time-tested separation of powers.

De-institutionalizing democracy

The 1987 Constitution has expressly recognized the right of the people to exercise by "direct initiative" many powers hitherto reserved to the great departments of government. These powers are:

- to propose or repeal national and local laws;[54]
- to recall local government officials and propose or repeal local laws;[55]
- to propose amendments to the Constitution.[56]

Direct democracy has – depending on how you see it – either "institutionalized people power"[57] or, conversely, de-institutionalized democracy, resorting to the raw political power of the people and discarding institutional checks altogether.

The Supreme Court has since "rhapsodized people power"[58] in several cases where the "direct initiative" clauses of the Constitution had been invoked.

The Congress has passed implementing laws, which have been applied, tested, and affirmed before the Supreme Court. The Local Government Code[59] provided for the recall of local officials either by the direct call of the voters or through "preparatory recall assembly" consisting of local government officials, which was hailed by the Supreme Court as an "innovative attempt...to remove impediments to the effective exercise by the people of their sovereign power."[60]

The Congress has also enacted the Initiative and Referendum Act (hereinafter the Initiative Law),[61] which provided for three systems of initiative, namely: to amend the Constitution; to propose, revise, or reject statutes; and to propose, revise, or reject local legislation. In a case involving the creation and scope of a special economic zone created out of Subic Bay, a former U.S. military base,[62] the Supreme Court hailed the Initiative Law as "actualizing...direct sovereignty" and "expressly recogniz[ed the people's] residual and sovereign authority to ordain legislation directly through the concepts and processes of initiative and of referendum."

But the power of direct initiative has been tested in two cases which are historic for the Philippines' newly restored democracy. The first was in the PIRMA cases, the attempt by then President Fidel Ramos (Cory Aquino's successor), through willing cohorts, to amend the Constitution to lift term limits which banned him from remaining in office after his term ended in 1998. In what has been called the "acid test of democratic consolidation,"[63] he was rebuffed by the Supreme Court, following protests by people who saw a dark reminder of a similar maneuver by Marcos which led to the death of Philippine democracy in 1972. Since the proposal was politically unpopular, a shadowy private group called the People's Initiative for Reforms, Modernization and Action (PIRMA or, literally translated to Filipino, "signature") instead launched a signature campaign asking for that constitutional amendment, invoking the direct initiative law. That attempt was rejected twice by the Supreme Court,[64] which went to great lengths to say that the direct initiative clauses of the Constitution were not self-executory; that they thus required congressional implementation; and that Congress's response, the Initiative Law, was "inadequate" – notwithstanding the fact that it expressly referred to constitutional amendments – and thus cannot be relied upon by PIRMA.

The second test was with the case of the People Power protests (hereinafter EDSA 2), which ousted President Joseph ("Erap") Estrada in January 2001, where the Court truly cast off its "reticence" about what the sociologist Randolph David refers to as "the dark side of people power,"[65] while intellectually maintaining the test of strict legality.

Estrada, a former movie actor, became president by direct vote of the people, winning by an overwhelming margin in May 1998. By August 2000 he was linked to illegal payoffs from gambling lords. A high-profile impeachment trial ensued, in what was to be the shining moment of constitutional supremacy. Yet the senators (empanelled as the impeachment by jury, as required by the Constitution) and the public were often impatient with technical debates on the admissibility of evidence ("legal gobbledygook," a Senator said). When certain bank records to prove illicit payoffs were suppressed, the next EDSA uprising emerged, and a few days later President Estrada abandoned the Presidential Palace. Vice-president Gloria Arroyo was sworn in as president, and was immediately challenged before the Supreme Court.

In the case of *Joseph Estrada v. Gloria Macapagal-Arroyo*,[66] the Court could have taken the path of least resistance and declared the matter a political question and outside the scope of judicial review, exactly as it had done with earlier challenges to the legitimacy of Cory Aquino's government and, before that, to Marcos's martial law government. Or the Court could have institutionalized People Power unabashedly as a means of changing presidents, and rather elastically interpreted the Constitution to mean that Estrada was "incapacitated," not by sickness but by induced political paralysis through "withdrawal of support" by various centers of power in government, including the military, and by civil society. Instead the Court took the most careful legal path, declared the matter justiciable, found that Estrada had indeed resigned, and ruled that Arroyo's oath-taking was squarely covered by the Constitution. The Court found that the "totality of prior, contemporaneous and posterior facts and...evidence" showed an intent to resign coupled with the actual act of relinquishing office.

The Court thus refused to throw the gates wide open to extra-constitutional transitions, but insisted on the disciplined analysis of hard doctrine, as if EDSA 2 was not unusual at all and had fit so snugly into the existing constitutional framework. The irony of EDSA 2 is that it barely satisfied constitutional process yet it upheld the most deeply held norm that public office is a public trust. The deeper irony is that a "thin" rule of law – but for the deft and creative legal reasoning of the Court – could barely account in strict legalistic terms for the direct exercise of democracy at EDSA.

Emerging challenges in Philippine constitutional discourse

I have looked at the tension between rule-based governance, through periodic elections, representative institutions and independent courts ("thin" rule of law), and substantive claims to social reform and mass-based politics (toward a "thick" account of the rule of law). The rule of law tradition in the Philippines has been anchored in the primacy of the Constitution. Constitutionalism privileges certain norms and brings them above ordinary politics, beyond the reach of the ordinary give and take of periodic elections, and reserves them to a "higher politics," one that is debated only in the arcane language of the wise, becoming accessible to the lay public only in the rare, historic moments of constitutional revision.[67] Philippine constitutionalism, in codifying a social reform agenda, has not only taken "high politics" away from the people but also de-politicized the people's causes. It has shifted these causes away from the raw power of the masses and channeled it toward institutions – elected representatives and appointed judges – farther and farther away from the people.

But perhaps that is precisely why the Philippines has embraced constitutionalism with a passion. Given the volatility of Philippine politics, and the lack of a national consensus on values and policy preferences, the key function of constitutionalism is to mark, even if synthetically by law, the road that public power must take. If, at the time of the Malolos Constitution and the American "organic acts", constitutionalism was welcomed as a modern, meritocratic substitute for feudal despotism under Spanish rule; if after the first EDSA uprising constitutionalism was restored as the antidote to personalistic rule and human rights abuses; today constitutionalism and the rule of law tradition that it has fostered remain relevant as the non-negotiable, neutral framework for competing claims and powers. The fixity of the non-negotiable may be myth, for law's meanings are elastic and malleable, and neutrality may be an illusion, as law is partisan to the accidental bearers of constitutionalized values. But it is the possibility, the mere promise, of decision-making that is untainted by power and interests that explains the continuing Filipino idealization of "decision according to law."

Notes

1 Professor and Dean of Law, University of the Philippines.
2 S. Guevarra, ed., The Laws of the First Philippine Republic (The Laws of Malolos) (Manila, National Historical Commission: Manila, 1994), p. 104. See also C. Majul, The Political and Constitutional Ideas of the Philippine Revolution (University of the Philippines Press, 1967).
3 Id., p. 203.
4 Malolos Constitution, Title II (The Government), id.
5 Malolos Constitution, Title V (The Legislative Power), id.
6 Malolos Constitution, Title IV (The Filipino and their National and Individual Rights), id.
7 Malolos Constitution, Title IV, arts. 7, 8 and 9, id.
8 Malolos Constitution, Title IV, arts. 10 and 11, id.
9 Malolos Constitution, Title IV, arts. 12 and 13, id.
10 Malolos Constitution, Title III (Religion), id.
11 Malolos Constitution, Title IV, art. 32, id.
12 Malolos Constitution, Title X (The Judicial Power), id.
13 Malolos Constitution, Title X, art. 77, id.
14 Malolos Constitution, Title IV, arts. 14, 15 and 31, id.
15 O.D. Corpuz, The Roots of the Filipino Nation, vol. II (Manila: Aklahi Foundation, 1989), pp. 348, 358–60.
16 Id. p. 373.
17 See V. Mendoza, From McKinley's Instructions to the New Constitution (Manila: Central Law Books, 1974).
18 Lansang v. Garcia, G.R. No. 33964, December 11, 1971, 42 Supreme Court Reports Annotated (hereinafter, SCRA) 448.
19 Proclamation No. 1081, Proclaiming a State of Martial Law in the Philippines (September 21, 1972).
20 Proclamation 1102, Announcing the Ratification by the Filipino People of the Constitution (January 17, 1973).
21 Javellana v. Executive Secretary, G.R. No. L–36142, March 31, 1973, 50 SCRA 30.
22 Id., p. 205.
23 Id., p.164.
24 Proclamation No. 2045, Proclaiming the Termination of the State of Martial Law (January 17, 1981).
25 See F. Marcos, Today's Revolution: Democracy (Manila, 1971); F. Marcos, Revolution from the Center: Notes on the New Society of the Philippines (Manila, 1973); F. Marcos, The Democratic Revolution in the Philippines (Englewood Cliffs, N.J.: Prentice-Hall, 1974).
26 Proclamation No. 3, Promulgating a Freedom Constitution (March 25, 1986).
27 Lawyer's League for a Better Philippines v. President Aquino, G.R. No. 73748, May 22, 1986; In re Saturnino Bermudez, G.R. No. 76180, October 24, 1986, 145 SCRA 160; De Leon v. Esguerra, G.R. No. L–78059, August 31, 1987, 153

SCRA 602; and *Letter of Associate Justice Reynato S. Puno*, A.M. No. 90–11–2697–CA, June 29, 1992, 210 SCRA 589.

28 *Letter of Associate Justice Reynato S. Puno*, A.M. No. 90–11–2697–CA, June 29, 1992, 210 SCRA 589.
29 *Lawyer's League for a Better Philippines v. President Aquino*, G.R. No. 73748, May 22, 1986.
30 M. Thompson, The Anti-Marcos Struggle: Personalistic Rule and Democratic Transition in the Philippines (Englewood Cliffs, N.J., Yale, 1995).
31 Const. arts. VI (The Legislative Department), VII (Executive Department), and VIII (Judicial Department).
32 Const. art. VII §18.
33 Const. art. VIII §1.
34 Const, art. XII (National Economy and Patrimony), art. XIII (Social Justice and Human Rights) and art. XIV (Education, Science and Technology, Arts, Culture and Sports).
35 Const. art. II §10.
36 Const. art. II §15.
37 Const. art. II §16, as interpreted by the Court in *Oposa v. Factoran*, G.R. No. 101083, July 30, 1993, 224 SCRA 792.
38 Const. art. II §119, as interpreted by the Court in *Garcia v. Board of Investments*, G.R. No. 92024, November 9, 1990, 191 SCRA 288.
39 Id., p. 299.
40 Id., p. 301.
41 Id., p. 302.
42 Manila Prince Hotel v. Government Service Insurance System, Manila Hotel Corporation, Committee on Privatization and Office of the Government Corporate Counsel, G.R. No. 122156, February 3, 1997, 267 SCRA 408.
43 Id., p. 8.
44 Id., pp. 13–14.
45 *Minors Oposa v. Factoran*, G.R. No. 101083, July 30, 1993, 224 SCRA 792.
46 *Ibid.*, emphasis supplied.
47 *Tatad v. Secretary of Energy*, G.R. No. 124360, November 5, 1997, 281 SCRA 330.
48 *Tañada v. Angara*. G.R. No. 118295, May 2, 1997, 272 SCRA 18. See also *Tolentino v. Secretary of Finance*, G.R. No. 115455, August 25, 1994, 235 SCRA 630 and October 30, 1995, 249 SCRA 628
49 *Kilosbayan, Inc. v. Morato*, G.R. and *Basco v. PAGCOR*, G.R. No 91649, May 14, 1991, 197 SCRA 52
50 Michael Kammen, *A Machine That Would Go of Itself* (New York, St. Martin's Press, 1993).
51 *Cariño v. Commission on Human Rights*, G.R No. 96681, December 2, 1991, 204 SCRA 483.
52 *Export Processing Zone Authority v. Commission on Human Rights*,G.R. No. 101476, April 14, 1992, 208 SCRA 125.
53 *Mayor Simon v. Commission on Human Rights*, G.R. No. 100150, January 5, 1994, 229 SCRA 117.
54 Const., art. VI, § 32.
55 Const., art. X, § 3.
56 Const., art. XVII, § 2.
57 *Subic Bay Metropolitan Authority v. Commission on Elections*, G.R. No. 125416, September 26, 1996, 262 SCRA 492.
58 *Defensor-Santiago v. Commission on Elections*, G.R. No. 127325, March 19, 1997, 270 SCRA 106.

59 Republic Act No. 7160 (January 1, 1992).
60 *Garcia v. Commission on Elections*, G.R. 111511, October 5, 1993, 227 SCRA 100.
61 Republic Act No. 6753 (August 11, 1984).
62 *Subic Bay Metropolitan Authority v. Commission on Elections*, G.R. No. 125416, September 26, 1996, 262 SCRA 492.
63 Jose V. Abueva, "Philippine Democratization and the Consolidation of Democracy since the 1986 Revolution: An Overview of the Main Issues, Trends and Prospects," in Felipe B. Miranda, ed., *Democratization: Philippine Perspectives* (Quezon City, University of the Philippines Press, 1997), p. 22.
64 *Defensor-Santiago v. Commission on Elections*, G.R. No. 127325, March 19, 1997, 270 SCRA 106; *People's Initiative for Reform, Modernization and Action v. Commission on Elections*, G.R. No. 129754, September 23, 1997) (both cases hereinafter cited as the PIRMA cases).
65 Randolf S. David, "People Power and the Legal System: A Sociological Note," in *Supreme Court Centenary Lecture Series*, vol. I, pp. 405–11 (Manila, Supreme Court of the Philippines, 2002); see also Randolf S. David, "The Third Time as Farce," in *Philippine Daily Inquirer*, April 29, 2001.
66 G.R. No. 146738, March 2, 2001, 353 SCRA 452.
67 Richard Parker, *Here the People Rule: A Populist Manifesto* (Cambridge, Massachusetts, Harvard, 1996).

13

RULE OF LAW IN SOUTH KOREA

Rhetoric and implementation

Hahm Chaihark

Introduction

According to a noted legal historian of Korea, Park Byung-ho, one of the salient features of the legal system of Chosŏn dynasty (1392–1910) was its commitment to "rule of law."[1] As evidence for this proposition, he cites the Chosŏn government's continued efforts throughout its history to regularize and systematize its law codes. Indeed, the number of codes compiled by the government during the Chosŏn period is quite impressive. At the least, there seems to have been a commitment to clarify the legal basis and authorization for the activities of the bureaucracy. The Korean word used here for the idea of "rule of law" is *pŏp ch'ijuŭi*. This, in fact, is the standard term used in Korean legal discourse to translate the English term "rule of law" as well as the German *Rechtsstaat*.[2] The thrust of Park's argument is that, contrary to conventional wisdom, the pre-modern Korean polity, heavily informed as it was by Confucian norms and ideals, was not ruled by personalized autocratic power, but rather was marked by regularized governance achieved through some degree of legality. Although the bulk of the codes dealt with "administrative" matters, rather than what we would call "constitutional" issues, and were primarily directed at the officials who staffed the central bureaucracy, the successive codifications and revisions do reflect a commitment on the part of the ruling elite to give a legal grounding for their governance.

In a way, this argument is but one expression of a common theme among many scholars in East Asian legal studies, who have been waging as it were a sustained campaign against the strong presumption that, due to various reasons (most notably Confucianism), law did not figure prominently in the overall scheme of governance in East Asian countries of the pre-modern era. This theme is also evident in the argument that it is mistaken to try to find a supposed aversion to law and litigation in modern East Asia, and then attribute it to some allegedly prevalent cultural traditions. One of the implied ideological motivations in much of this line of arguments, at least for the native Korean scholars, is a nationalistic desire to "rescue" their past from a narrative that paints their political history as one of arbitrary rule or

385

"lawlessness."[3] Owing to the fact that rule of law has become what one observer calls an "honorific term"[4] in the recent rhetorical configuration of political disputations, many feel the need to represent their country as one that has known and practiced rule of law for a long time.

This is not to say that their "revisionist" history is therefore factually inaccurate or contrived in any way. The conventional view of the irrelevance of law in pre-modern or modern Korea certainly needs to be revised radically. On the other hand, portraying the Chosŏn polity as one marked by "rule of law," though understandable given the rhetorical import of "absence of rule of law" (lawlessness or arbitrary rule), should at least be done with caution. For the idea of rule of law has its own political history in the West, its own images, backgrounds, and cultural meanings, which cannot readily be transposed onto the Korean context. Perhaps most important among these is the idea of an independent court and a specialized profession of jurists who exert restraint on the holder of political power. While it is true that we need to develop a theoretical vocabulary for expressing the pre-modern, Confucian political ideal and practice of restraining the political ruler, it is doubtful how much conceptual clarity can be derived from using the language of rule of law to describe it. It is certainly conceivable that Chosŏn had developed its own institutional and political resources to contain the arbitrary exercise of royal power.[5] Yet it is difficult to frame them in terms of the power of autonomous courts and lawyers.

To be sure, the idea of rule of law as developed in the Western political tradition is a complex one.[6] Rule of law is merely shorthand for a whole constellation of related ideas and practices, and the element of independent courts and autonomous legal profession is perhaps not the most prominent one. Particularly in the recent global upsurge of interest in rule of law reforms, the usual emphasis seems to be on its potential to promote economic development and enhance liberal democracy.[7] Although independent and impartial courts and an autonomous legal profession are never neglected, they appear to be required for their incidental value of securing the benefits of economic prosperity and political liberalization. Yet in this chapter I will emphasize these elements for the purpose of highlighting the novelty of this ideal in the Korean context. That is, I take rule of law to refer to a particular form of political practice intended to restrain and discipline government powers, whose distinctiveness lies in the role played by the courts and lawyers.[8] As alluded to above, the Confucian polity of Chosŏn had its own method of restraining and disciplining the ruler, but it wasn't through the courts and the legal profession.

Also, while we could talk of rule of law in terms of its relation or contribution to economic development,[9] I shall for the most part focus on the political aspect of preventing abuse of government power. Obviously, rule of law could be defined in many ways. Under certain conceptions, a polity could be seen as practicing rule of law as long as the people's properties are protected and contractual rights are properly enforced and crime rates kept to a minimum. I happen to believe that without meaningful restraint on its political leaders a country cannot be said to be practicing rule of law. Particularly in the Korean context, I believe discussions on rule of law need to be separated from the country's capacity to achieve economic development, for it is generally agreed that economic development in Korea came during oppressive military regimes that showed little respect for rule of law.[10]

Thus, conceptualized as the practice of restraining and disciplining government power through the law, with the courts and the legal profession playing the leading role, rule of law must be acknowledged as a relatively new concept and ideal in Korean political history. It was probably first introduced from the West when the Chosŏn government started opening up the country in the late 19th century. Yet for most of the 20th century, rule of law remained an elusive ideal. The century opened with the loss of national sovereignty to Japanese imperialism, but even after regaining independence after the Second World War, Korea went through U.S. military government, a civil war, an increasingly authoritarian and corrupt civilian regime, and a succession of military dictatorships, until it embarked upon a momentous process of democratization that is still underway.[11] The rule of law ideal is therefore only recently beginning to be felt and discussed as a relevant ideal for Koreans.

In the following, I will start with a brief description of the legal system of Korea, and then proceed to analyze the current political context in which rule of law is being debated in Korea. As will be seen, rule of law has recently become a highly political and politicized issue, and therefore in order to get a taste of the "local" disputations regarding rule of law, it is necessary to understand the rhetorical and substantive political configurations surrounding the debate. The next section will be an analysis of a few select decisions of the Constitutional Court of Korea. Rule of law in the sense of judicial check on government actors became possible only with the recent political democratization, which also coincided with the establishment of the Constitutional Court. Therefore analyzing the major decisions of that Court will be a useful way of gaining a perspective on Korea's newly embarked upon journey toward the implementation of rule of law.

The legal system of Korea

The Korean legal system is generally categorized as a civil law system. Although, at the end of the 19th century there were some efforts on the part of the Chosŏn government to "modernize" its government and legal system, they were cut short by the Japanese annexation in 1910. The Japanese colonial administration transplanted its own legal system, which was itself based on the laws of Prussia, Austria, and France. The Japanese also investigated and enforced certain "native" Korean legal customs in such areas as marriage and inheritance laws. Nevertheless, the courts and the legal profession were entirely staffed by Japanese or Japanese-trained Korean lawyers. To this day, the influence of Japanese and German law is quite palpable in the way that law is taught and practiced. Of course, after Independence in 1945, the American influence in various areas of the law has been growing steadily.[12] Yet it is probably safe to say that this remains generally restricted to the contents of the law (e.g. individual doctrines), with little impact on the overall institutional structure of the court and the profession, and their culture.

The current government system, of which the courts are a part, is a unitary (i.e. non-federal) system with a unicameral legislature (National Assembly) and a popularly elected president. The members of the National Assembly consist of those elected at regional electoral districts as well as some elected through "national" constituency. The president is elected through a direct popular vote and is prohibited by the Constitution from seeking re-election. The courts are staffed by professional judges who have passed the national judicial examination and have completed the two-year course of the Judicial Research and Training Institute (JRTI), established under the Supreme Court. The judges are civil servants and are promoted through the bureaucratic, hierarchical structure that is the national court system. They typically serve three to five years at any given post and then move on to the next assignment. Practicing attorneys, in order to be licensed, must also pass the national judicial examination.[13] The same is true for the prosecutors who comprise the National Prosecutors' Office, another very hierarchical agency under the Ministry of Justice.

The judges, prosecutors, and practicing attorneys are commonly said to comprise the "three wheels of the legal profession" (*ppcho samnyun*). In terms of social prestige, the judges are still considered the cream of the crop, with the prosecutors enjoying some advantage over the practitioners, although in recent years the prosecutors appear to be losing their edge. This social gradation used to be readily discernible in the grades of the three groups of graduates of the JRTI who joined the three "wheels". Since there are far more graduates each year than the number of judges to be hired by the courts, the judiciary got – and still gets – to select those with the highest graduating scores. The next tier of graduates were recruited into the Prosecutors' Office, with the lowest tier becoming practitioners. This, however, may no longer be true given the changing perception of the prosecutors' as no longer such a glamorous profession. By contrast, the job of practicing attorney is becoming increasingly popular due to a number of factors. With the increasing "trendiness" of international practice, a handful of prestigious large-scale law firms are sometimes able to lure the top graduates away from judgeships to join their practice.[14] With the gradual "legalization" of Korean society in general, newer fields of law, such as consumer protection or environmental law, are also attracting graduates of the JRTI. This is also slowly transforming the composition of practicing attorneys. It used to be that most practitioners were litigators and that most successful litigators were retired judges and prosecutors. With the growing number of attorneys hired just out of the JRTI by the law firms, it is no longer the case that to be successful as a practicing lawyer one must have been a former government official.

One noteworthy feature of the Korean judicial system is the existence of a separate Constitutional Court outside the ordinary court hierarchy headed by the Supreme Court. Roughly modeled on the German Federal Constitutional Court (*Bundesverfassungsgericht*), the Court according to the Constitution has jurisdiction over five areas:

- review of the constitutionality of statutes;
- dissolution of political parties;
- impeachment of high-level officials;
- competence dispute among different state agencies;
- adjudication of constitutional petitions.[15]

As the bulk of the Court's cases fall under the first and the last categories, judicial review and constitutional petitions comprise the most important business of the Court.

The Constitutional Court gets to review the constitutionality of statutes via a number of routes. First, ordinary trial courts can refer the matter to the Constitutional Court if the outcome of the case depends on the constitutionality of a statute. The referral may be made at the request of the parties, or the court may do it *sua sponte*.[16] Second, according to Article 68(2) of the Constitutional Court Act (CCA), in cases where the court of original jurisdiction denies a party's motion to refer the matter to the Constitutional Court, the party may then lodge a constitutional petition with the Court to review the constitutionality of the statute at issue.[17]

Unlike the German Federal Constitutional Court, which has exclusive jurisdiction over the constitutionality of all forms of law, the Korean Constitutional Court shares its power of constitutional review with the Supreme Court. The Constitution itself envisions a "division of labor" in which the Constitutional Court reviews the constitutionality of statutes only, whereas the Supreme Court reviews the constitutionality of administrative regulations, presidential decrees, and other "lesser" forms of law. Also unlike its German counterpart, the Korean Constitutional Court's powers do not include "abstract review" (*Abstrackte Normenkontrolle*) of statutes; it cannot review statutes on their face value without a specific case or controversy being put before it.[18]

The CCA provides for another type of constitutional petition, whereby an individual whose constitutional rights have been violated by the exercise or non-exercise of government power may request of the Court a suitable remedy for the violation.[19] In order to bring this second type of constitu-

389

tional petition (which is actually the primary type in the scheme of the CCA), the petitioner must first exhaust all existing procedures of relief.[20] The Court has tended to interpret the term "exercise or non-exercise of government power" very broadly to include actions and inactions by the legislature, the executive, and the judiciary branches of the government.[21]

The Constitutional Court is comprised of nine justices who must be qualified to serve as judges in ordinary courts, and the three branches of the government are all involved in their selection. The president, the National Assembly, and the chief justice of the Supreme Court all nominate three justices each.[22] The justices of the Court serve for a term of six years, which may be renewed, and they are subject to a mandatory retirement age of 65, with the exception of the Court's head, called the "president," whose retirement age is 70.[23] The president of the Court is appointed by the president (of the country), and must be confirmed by the National Assembly.[24] At least six justices must concur before the Court can find a statute unconstitutional or accept a constitutional petition.[25]

One of the current issues facing the Korean judiciary and the legal profession as a whole is the overhaul of the system of licensing as well as the legal education system. Currently legal education is part of the undergraduate program in universities, and there are about 80 universities nationwide with law colleges.[26] Since the early 1990s, however, serious proposals to make legal education part of the graduate program, along the lines of American law schools, have been advanced by both the government and a number of academics.[27] Rationales for the idea include the need to improve the quality of legal services rendered by law graduates, to prepare for the increasingly transnational nature of legal practice in the interdependent, globalized world, and to enhance the level of legal scholarship, which is widely perceived to be mired in 19th century-style conceptual jurisprudence. While discussion on the matter has actually stalled for the time being for political reasons,[28] there is a gradually growing consensus that some change will ultimately be inevitable.

Overhaul of legal education, however, will not be complete without a parallel change in the licensing system for lawyers. Under the current system, no formal legal education is required in order to take the national judicial examination. Indeed, there is no requirement for any type of formal education, which means that, technically, one need not even have attended primary school to take the exam. Legal education is in some sense superfluous to the system of producing lawyers. Therefore many think that legal education will never be truly reformed until it is institutionally incorporated into the licensing system. Further, given the hyper-competitive nature of the judicial examination, its social meaning is akin to that of the civil service examination of the Chosŏn dynasty – that is, the "ladder of success" in Korean society. Many believe that the state must relax its tight control over entry into the legal profession, by dramatically increasing the number of those passing bar exams, and let the legal market take care of itself. Yet altering the way lawyers are licensed also implies changing the way judges and prosecutors are recruited. This obviously entails a major transformation of the entire government system.[29] This has naturally occasioned much resistance from the judiciary as well as the established members of the bar. As is the case in many countries, the judiciary and the bar tend to represent the more conservative segment of Korean society,[30] who do not wish to change the system that has hitherto served their interests. The only compromise reached so far has been to allow more people to pass the judicial examination, beginning in 1996 with 500, with 100 more added each year until the number reaches 1,000 per year. Thus, beginning in 2001, the state will admit 1,000 new lawyer candidates every year.[31]

Efforts to reform legal education and the licensing system can be understood as a part of Korea's transition to democracy. In fact, when Kim Young-sam, the first civilian to be elected president in 30 years, came to power in 1993, reform of legal education and the legal profession was included in his overall package of democratic reforms and "globalization" policy.[32] Then, in the early years of Kim Dae-jung's administration, a series of corruption scandals involving judges and prosecutors made the need for reform even more urgent. *Sabp kaehyk* (reform of the judiciary) and *ppcho kaehyk* (reform of the legal profession) have become familiar phrases commonly seen in newspaper headlines and heard in policy discussions. In a sense, Korean society for the first time is going through an open debate about law, role of the courts, and the legal profession – about "rule of law." It is still an ongoing debate, as the reform efforts have yet to bear tangible fruits.[33]

The politics of rule of law in Korea

As mentioned above, Korea's first experiment with a legal system in which independent courts and lawyers were needed took place during the final days of Chosŏn dynasty. This was unfortunate for the subsequent history of rule of law in Korea because the first Western-style court system and state-run law school were established as parts of "modernization" measures that were practically imposed on the Chosŏn court by the Japanese. Although this was before the actual annexation of Korea by the Japanese empire, the Japanese had already begun the steady process of seizing control of Korea. Thus, for many Koreans the modern legal system was from the beginning tainted with Japanese imperialism and therefore ideologically suspect.[34]

Thus began a long history of the politics of rule of law, in which the courts and the legal profession did not enjoy such high esteem. During the Japanese occupation (1910–45) the legal system was identified with the colonial power, and people naturally did not regard the legal system as a means by which they could restrain those in power.[35] Following Independence, the legal system and the law enforcement apparatus were staffed by those people who had experience in and knowledge of running the system, many of whom were regarded as having "collaborated" with the Japanese imperialists. This is not so say that the legal profession as a whole was considered unpatriotic. There were a number of well-respected jurists at that time, men of integrity and compassion who looked out for the interests of their less fortunate countrymen. Nevertheless, it is true that during the early years of the Republic the legal system did not exactly operate in a way that curbed the power of the increasingly autocratic presidency. In fact, little changed until the last decade of the 20th century. Law, including the Constitution, was generally regarded as a tool for carrying out the will of whoever was in power. As for the courts, they rarely showed any interest in restraining the power of the government or making sure that the government abided by the law. While the law colleges continued to attract, and feed the bench and the bar with, the brightest students of the nation, the ideal of restraining the political ruler through law failed to become a reality.

It is fair to say, then, that until very recently the term "rule of law" remained largely irrelevant to most Koreans. It was either a cover for legitimizing oppressive authoritarian regimes or the subject of naïve and sentimental musing on the part of law professors. The utterance of the term generally evoked fear or suspicion.[36] With the transition to democracy beginning in 1987, however, rule of law is being invoked with increasing frequency as Koreans seek to move away from their authoritarian past. Not surprisingly, this was made possible by the emergence of constitutional politics in Korea. Through the activities of the Constitutional Court, the Constitution has become a normative document regulating the lives of the people and the operation of the government. The term *hnjong jil s*, meaning "constitutional order," has become a familiar one in contemporary Korean political discourse. For example, the prosecution and conviction in 1995 of the two former presidents Chun Doo-hwan and Roh Tae-woo, who had come to power through a military *coup d'état* and a brutal massacre of civilians, were carried out in the name of restoring "constitutional order."[37] People of various political persuasions are learning to invoke the Constitution in support of their different positions. Especially when they are criticizing the government, people have started doing so in the name of the Constitution. A gradual change is taking place in the way that political discourse is conducted. A culture of political dispute is taking shape in which appeals to the law and the Constitution for the purpose of restraining the government are a regular part of normal discourse. Koreans are finally becoming familiar and comfortable with the rhetoric of "rule of law."

Interestingly, since President Kim Dae-jung took office in 1998 his critics, who tend to be politically conservative and economically pro-business, have frequently used rule of law rhetoric to attack the policies of his administration. Previously it was Kim and his friends, supposedly the more "liberal" or "democratic" group, who used to criticize their oppressors for disregarding the rule of law or destroying the constitutional order. Now that they are in power, their political opponents began applying the same rhetoric to them. A recent example is the statement by the Korean Bar Association in 2001 criticizing Kim Dae-jung's administration for disregarding "rule of law." In it, the lawyers charged that rule of law has taken a backseat to the "rule of force" since Kim came to power.[38] They were then joined by a number of prominent law professors and other "conservative" intellectuals. As evidence of Kim's disdain for rule of law, they pointed to the general tax audit of all the major news media companies undertaken by his government, which according to them was merely a cover for persecution of his political opponents. Under the guise of "reform," and of enforcing generally applicable rules, they said, Kim Dae-jung was actually singling out and punishing those newspapers that had been vocal in criticizing his policies. For them, this was a classic case of "rule of man" – the polar opposite of rule of law – in which the law was being used for political ends.

This was probably the first time that the Korean Bar Association had taken such an explicitly political stance criticizing the government. A cynic might criticize the association for being hypocritical, because during the period of authoritarian rule it had studiously avoided becoming involved in political matters. Both the government and the ruling party expressed their displeasure at the lawyers' group's overtly political action and their seeming opposition to the social and economic reforms.[39] The subtext of their response was that lawyers should not get involved in politics. Ironically, both the Korean Bar Association and the Kim Dae-jung government seem to share the assumption that law and lawyers should properly be segregated from politics. Apparently, rule of law required that law be above political contests and that lawyers refrain from expressing political views. Apparently, what has been criticized by the Critical Legal Studies in the U.S. as the myth of legal liberalism, or the illusion of law's autonomy from politics,[40] is becoming a common feature of the Korean political discourse on rule of law.

Even before the tax audit of newspapers, Kim Dae-jung drew fire for ignoring the Constitution and rule of law when he expressed favorable views toward the activities of certain civic groups during the 2000 general election. Many "progressive" civic groups joined in January of that year to form the Citizens' Alliance for the 2000 General Election (*2000 nyn Ch'ongsn Shimin Yndae*), with the intention of actively discouraging political parties from nominating as their candidates certain individuals whom they regarded as having authoritarian backgrounds or being otherwise unfit to hold public office, and then of aggressively dissuading the electorate from voting for those individuals in case they won a party's nomination.[41] According to the Law on Elections for Public Offices and Prevention of Election Frauds, however, no group or association was allowed openly to support or oppose (or encourage others to support or oppose) a particular candidate or polit-

393

ical party.[42] The activities of the Citizens' Alliance were therefore considered illegal, and the law enforcement agencies made it clear that anyone engaging in such activities would be treated as criminals. The citizens' group declared that their monitoring activities were justified to reform the undemocratic practices that plagued the electoral process, and that they would persist in the name of civil disobedience. It was at this juncture that President Kim Dae-jung expressed his support for the group's activities and urged the lawmakers to revise the laws to make them legal. Kim described their activities as an expression of the people's sovereign power and stated that the purpose of the legal system is to safeguard, rather than to outlaw, the exercise of that power.[43]

Kim's opponents invoked the rule of law rhetoric to criticize his statements. Although many agreed with the objectives of the Citizens' Alliance, the group's resolve to openly flout the law's prohibition was met with general disapproval. The president's encouragement of such disrespect for the authority of the law indicated for his opponents that he himself had no respect for the rule of law. Some even condemned the citizens' group as sycophantic running dogs of political power and likened them to the infamous Red Guards of China during the Cultural Revolution. For Kim's critics, even the expression of the people's sovereign will must be made within the parameters of the law. Even if it was true that the political parties were so corrupt and undemocratic, that was no justification for actively breaking the law. Democratic legitimacy by itself was not enough to override the value of the rule of law. Kim's supporters, on the other hand, argued that insisting on the rule of law when the underlying politics lack democratic legitimacy only promotes blind submission to authority. Rule of law cannot be valued for its own sake in isolation from the constitutional principle of democracy, and it cannot be the only criterion for evaluating the citizens' group's activities.[44]

The Law was actually revised in February 2000, a month after Kim spoke in support of the Citizens' Alliance, to permit a limited range of campaign activities by civic groups. Yet, from the perspective of the Citizens' Alliance, the "time, place, and manner" of the campaign activities they were allowed to engage in were still severely restricted. Its members thus continued their illegal activities until the elections were held the following April, and a number of their leaders were subsequently tried and convicted for violating the election law. The Supreme Court upheld the conviction.[45] On the other hand, the Citizens' Alliance brought a constitutional petition in the Constitutional Court alleging that the Law as revised infringed their constitutional right to express their political views regarding certain candidates. They also claimed that their activities must be differentiated from the campaigning by the candidates or their parties, and thus must be exempted from the complex regulations governing regular "campaign activities."[46] In August 2001 the Constitutional Court rejected their petition.[47]

The "growth" of rule of law rhetoric in Korea is thus intricately related to the emergence of democratic politics and constitutionalism. Ever since it was created in 1988, the Constitutional Court has been quite busy, with an ever-increasing number of cases filling its docket. Perhaps not all the cases decided by the Court dealt with cores issues of rule of law (understood here as disciplining government power through the law and the courts). Yet there is a substantial number of decisions since 1988 that merit examination. One way of discussing the establishment of rule of law might be to take each substantive areas of law – administrative law, criminal law, commercial law, etc. – and to see whether and how individuals' rights have been properly protected in each area. In the following, I shall take a different approach. I will introduce and discuss a number of cases which may not fall neatly into a readily defined area of law, but which can nevertheless be viewed as having significantly cut back the scope of government power and brought a measure of regularity to the exercise of that power.

The Constitutional Court and the rule of law

Prior to the creation of the Constitutional Court in September 1988, constitutional litigation was something Koreans had rarely seen or heard of.[48] Even after it began operation, the Court did not have much "business" for a while.[49] This was due in part to the people's skepticism about the Court's ability or willingness to do anything meaningful, but also in part to simple ignorance on the part of the people about how to utilize the Court's services. It thus had to gradually cultivate its business and reputation by showing the people that their complaints and grievances will be given careful consideration.[50]

In time, the Court became an extremely busy establishment. As of May 31, 2002, the total number of cases brought to the Constitutional Court since its establishment was 7,848, and it had given a disposition in one form or another for 7,338 of those cases. Of the 7,338 cases disposed, 3,516 were dismissed for failure to meet certain formal or procedural requirements.[51] In other words, only 3,822 cases were actually decided on their merit. Of these, the Court held in 507 cases that a statute or some (non-)exercise of government power was either unconstitutional or otherwise constitutionally deficient.[52] This means that in more than 13 percent of all cases received, the Court has found some constitutional infirmity with the actions of the state.

This has caused many commentators to describe it as an "activist" court championing the rule of law and the civil and political rights of the individual.[53] While this is not wholly inaccurate, I believe we need to be more cautious in using the term "judicial activism." Most commentators seem to laud the Court for being activist because they implicitly equate activism with liberal and democratic political positions. In point of fact, the ideological import of judicial activism depends entirely on the political orientation of pre-existing practices and doctrines. Depending on the baseline, an activist court could with equal logical consistency side with either progressivism or conservatism. Therefore, apart from its rhetorical effects, calling a court activist is unhelpful in understanding its political tendency or ideological inclination. In the Korean context, the baseline happened to be the legacy of authoritarian rule, which the Constitutional Court to a certain extent has been dismantling. Thus it is understandable why people would liken it to the Warren Court by using the label "judicial activism," as if that by itself indicated its political orientation. Even assuming, *arguendo*, that an activist court is by nature more progressive or liberal, a close analysis of the Court's decisions is required before we can conclude that it is in fact activist in that sense. Moreover, I believe that in Korea the meaning of words like "conservative," "liberal," and "progressive" is quite ambiguous and unstable.[54] In such a context, then, we would at least have first to clarify the definition of those terms before applying them to any person or entity.

Rather than attempt to label the Court's political position or identify its ideological shade, I shall in the following discuss a few select cases that are significant for establishing rule of law in Korea. I have chosen them because they deal most directly with the issue of restraining government power, which I take to be the core value of rule of law. They are particularly significant in that they were directed at practices which were once quite common, if not normal, features of Korean political life, but which are very problematic from the perspective of the ideal of rule of law.

The exercise of extra-legal government power

One of the very first cases filed with the Court when it first began operation was a constitutional petition brought by the former owner of a conglomerate (*chaebl*) called Kukje Group, which he claimed had been forced into bankruptcy and subsequently completely dissolved in early 1985 by the Chun Doo-hwan regime. At the end of 1984, Kukje Group was one of Korea's ten largest *chaebl*s, consisting of some 20 affiliated companies. Although the immediate cause of the bankruptcy was the decision by Jeil Bank, its primary lender, to withhold credit, its actions were, according to the petition, directed by the president through the minister of finance, who at the time exercised effective control over all commercial banks and other financial institutions. The petitioner therefore sought the nullification of a series of actions taken by the minister of finance, under the close supervision of the president, which directly led to the dissolution of Kukje.[55]

To put the case in context, it must be understood that during the 1970s and 1980s state control over economic affairs was pervasive in Korea. The state, through such agencies as the Ministry of Finance and the Economic Planning Board, intervened deeply in the economic activities of citizens. It decided which industry should be promoted, which company should be selected as the leader of that industry, and how much credit and foreign exchange should be allotted to whom. This, of course, is the classic developmental-state model of economic development. From the legal standpoint, however, much of the state's planning and intervention was often carried out through informal means the legal bases of which were at best ambiguous. Indeed, law was just another means of achieving the state's developmental objectives. Economic entities were constantly coerced, ordered, and threatened through legal and extra-legal means to conform to the priorities set by the state. In that regard the kind of treatment Kukje received from the state was not atypical.[56] To be sure, a total liquidation of a company as large as Kukje was rare. Yet the president allegedly "allowed" this conglomerate to go bankrupt precisely because it was deemed necessary to show the business community that even big corporations can be dissolved upon mismanagement.[57]

The Constitutional Court held that, although the dissolution of Kukje Group was ostensibly the result of a private entity's (Jeil Bank's) actions, there was no doubt that the Bank in this case was acting as a mere conduit for the actions of the government, which gave the Bank detailed instructions about how to liquidate Kukje's assets, who should be the new owners, and even what to say in a press release regarding Kukje's dissolution. That is, even though the violation of the petitioner's rights was not caused by an "exercise of government power" as anticipated by Article 68(1) of the Constitutional Court Act, the Court characterized the actions of the government as a naked (non-legal) act of power (*kwllykchk sashilhaengwi*)[58] that resulted in the loss of ownership and managing rights of the petitioner. The Court stated that government interventions into the economic activities of an enterprise must be based on predictable statutes, and that intervention without a statutory basis violates the procedural requirements of the rule of law. The state should in principle not interfere with such activities, and even when there is a pressing need to intervene it must do so through legal means. At the least, intervention must be based on an emergency decree that can be justified in terms of a need to avert a grave financial or economic crisis.[59] As the actions of the government in this case had no legal grounds whatsoever, the Court concluded that all the actions leading up to the dissolution of Kukje were unconstitutional.

Before reaching that conclusion, however, the Court had to decide, as a preliminary matter, whether the petition was filed in a timely manner. The Constitutional Court Act prescribes that a constitutional petition must be filed within 60 days of the day that the petitioner learned of the infringement of his/her rights and within 180 days of the day when the infringement took place.[60] The plan to dissolve Kukje Group was executed in February of 1985, and the petition was filed on February 27, 1989. Since the Court did not commence adjudicating cases until September 19, 1988, it held that for violations of constitutional rights that took place before the Court was created the period for filing a petition should run from that date. This satisfied the 180-day requirement, but the 60-day requirement could not be satisfied even after some virtual legal acrobatics to set the time when the petitioner "learned" of the violation at a later date.[61] In the end, the Court invoked a provision in the Administrative Litigation Act which allowed an exception to the timeliness requirement for administrative litigations in such cases as there was a legitimate reason. It did so on the basis of Article 40(1) of the Constitutional Court Act, which provided that provisions of the Administrative Litigation Act shall be applied *mutatis mutandis* in constitutional petition proceedings. In light of the circumstances under which Kukje was dissolved, the Court concluded that there was a sufficient legitimate reason to allow an exception in this case.

Thus, the Court in a way had to strain the interpretation of legal requirements for filing a constitutional petition, in order to deliver its pronouncement on the importance of rule of law. The Court also found a way to make an exception to the requirement that all other avenues of appeal must be exhausted before filing a complaint.[62] Of course, stretching the technical requirements somewhat absolutely pales when compared to the political and historical significance of proclaiming the unconstitutionality of those actions, and of upholding the sanctity of rule of law. Indeed, given the importance of the case for the cause of safeguarding and maintaining the constitutional order, the Court pointed out that there was a need to confirm the unconstitutionality of government actions even though those actions themselves have already ended. The justices evidently wished to take this opportunity to make clear the limits of the government's power to regulate and interfere with the activities of a business entity as a way of giving substance to the constitutional doctrine of private property and a free-market economy.[63]

The case was widely noted in the media for its importance in establishing the rule of law in Korea, especially in clarifying the principle that presidential authority must be exercised in accordance with the law. Yet, unfortunately, even after the case was decided, the petitioner was not able immediately to recover all of his previous assets. In a civil lawsuit in which he demanded the return of the stocks of a company that originally had belonged to him, the Seoul High Court held that a stock sales contract between private parties was neither void nor voidable just because the government's action towards one of the parties was unconstitutional. This decision obviously met with severe criticism from the public as well as the Constitutional Court itself. In a different suit to recover the stocks of another unit of the Kukje Group, the petitioner was successful when the court agreed that the original transfer of stocks had occurred under duress. In sum, while the Kukje Group case obviously represents a major step in Korea's progress toward rule of law, it is marked with some blemishes in that in the decision itself some casuistry had to be engaged in for it to reach its conclusion, and in that the case did not have the expected effect of restoring the petitioner's original property rights.

The coup d'état *and constitutional order*

In the mid-1990s Koreans witnessed a series of events which would have been utterly unimaginable in earlier decades. The leaders of the previous military regime, former presidents Chun Doo-hwan and Roh Tae-woo, were prosecuted and convicted of treason and corruption. That fact by itself might be proof enough for the proposition that rule of law is firmly established in Korea. Politically, it certainly indicates a major advancement of Korean democracy. Legally too it represents an enormous change, and perhaps development, on the part of the judiciary, which previously would in all likelihood never have touched such a politically sensitive case. Under previous regimes, the judiciary was noted for its studied avoidance of cases involving any actions of the president.[64] The mere fact that the judiciary, including the Constitutional Court, considered this issue a proper matter for adjudication in a court of law is a vast improvement. Of course, the change in their attitude was not entirely voluntary. Moreover, the entire process of prosecution was not without problems. The Constitutional Court was involved in three different phases of that process, and its behavior in each case needs to be scrutinized.[65]

On October 26, 1979, President Park Chung-hee was assassinated by the chief of the Korean Central Intelligence Agency, Kim Jae-kyu. The government immediately proclaimed martial law throughout the country, with the exception of the island province of Cheju. In the ensuing power vacuum, on December 12, 1979, Generals Chun Doo-hwan and Roh Tae-woo and their comrades arrested the Martial Law commander-in-chief, and took control of the military, thereby securing their first step toward controlling the entire country. (This is commonly called the 12/12 Incident.) Subsequently, Chun Doo-hwan served as the president from September 1, 1980, to February 26, 1988. Roh Tae-woo then succeeded him in the presidency and was in office from Febrary 26, 1988, to February 24, 1993, when Kim Young-sam, a civilian, took office.

The first case to come before the Constitutional Court was a constitutional petition filed by the former Martial Law commander-in-chief and other victims of the 12/12 Incident. In July 1993, after both Chun and Roh had left office, they had filed a criminal complaint with the Seoul District Prosecutors' Office accusing them of treason, mutiny, and other crimes. When the prosecutors' office disposed of their complaint by deciding not to indict, they filed a constitutional petition on November 24, 1994, seeking the cancellation of the decision not to indict the former presidents and their cohorts. The Kim Young-sam administration at that point had adopted a policy of not initiating any legal proceedings against Chun, Roh, and company, even though their actions were now characterized as a military *coup d'état*, which implied that they were unlawful. Kim Young-sam preferred to let history pass judgment on them rather than risk the appearance of political retribution.

Under such circumstances, the Court found that the prosecutors had not abused their discretion in reaching their decision, and rejected the petition.[66] Regarding the charges of mutiny and other crimes punishable by the Military Criminal Code, the prosecutors had found enough evidence to indict Chun and company, and even recognized that prosecuting them would be valuable in terms of rectifying past wrongs. Yet, against these findings, the prosecutors also recognized fact that an indictment would inevitably polarize the whole of Korean society and prolong political and social strife within the nation. In its decision the Constitutional Court said that the prosecutors had acted properly when they weighed these two conflicting considerations, and that they had acted within the limits of their discretion when they concluded that the latter consideration should take precedence. It is evident that the Court did not wish to go against the stated policy of President Kim Young-sam, who preferred not to charge his predecessors in a court of law.

On the other hand, the Court did contribute to the eventual trial of the ex-generals by clarifying a technical point about the statute of limitations in the context of prosecuting former presidents.[67] Article 84 of the Constitution provides that "[e]xcept for treason, or for waging a foreign war, the President shall not be criminally prosecuted while in office." This meant that a president could be indicted for treason and foreign war even during his term. What was unclear was whether this provision meant that for other crimes the statute of limitation was tolled against the president while in office. The Constitutional Court held that this provision should be interpreted to mean that statutes of limitation are tolled for crimes other than treason and waging of war. This in turn meant that, while Chun could no longer be tried for treason, he could still be tried for mutiny and other crimes specified in the petitioners' original complaint because the statute of limitation had not run during the period of seven years and five months when he was in office. In other words, while the Court was not willing to force the prosecutors to indict the former presidents, it made it clear that, for crimes other than treason, the prosecutors' office was free to withdraw its own decision and proceed with the indictment, if it so chose. In the end, the prosecutors' office was forced by public opinion to take that route.

The second case the Court was asked to decide on in relation to the prosecution of the former presidents was another constitutional petition seeking the cancellation of another decision not to indict by the prosecutors' office. The case dealt with the other tragic episode that took place in the process of Chun Doo-hwan's seizure of power. On May 18, 1980, hundreds of civilian demonstrators were brutally murdered by the military in the southwestern city of Kwangju when paratroopers were sent in to suppress protests against Chun's decision to impose a virtual ban on all political activities and to bring the entire country, including Cheju Island, under martial law. (This is commonly referred to as the 5/18 Incident.) Several victims of the 5/18

Incident filed criminal complaints at various times in 1994 with the Seoul District Prosecutors' Office charging Chun and others of treason, mutiny, and other crimes.

The prosecutors responded by deciding not to indict the accused. Their reasoning was that the accused had succeeded in a *coup d'état* and had already formed a new constitutional order. They further reasoned that a successful *coup d'état* could not be the object of indictment because the current prosecutorial power itself was derived from the new order created by the coup. Their conclusion, announced on July 18, 1995, was that in such a case they did not have the power to prosecute. In response, the victims filed a constitutional petition with the Constitutional Court in October 1995 seeking cancellation of the prosecutors' decision.

Before the Court delivered its decision, the political environment had changed dramatically. Faced with increasing demands to pass a special law to enable punishment for treason,[68] Kim Young-sam's government was in the process of changing its former stance that it would not seek legal actions on the issue of the 12/12 and 5/18 Incidents. Meanwhile, Roh Tae-woo was arrested on the charge of accumulating an astronomical "slush fund" in hidden bank accounts under a false name. This added to the demands to enact the special law. Also, it was rumored that the Constitutional Court would hold that a successful *coup d'état* could be subject to criminal prosecution, but that the statute of limitations had already run for the crime of treason. Kim Young-sam then announced his plans to enact the special law. And then, just days before the Court was scheduled to announce its decision, the petitioners withdrew their petition. They feared that if the Court delivered such a judgment the proposed special law to enable punishment of treason could be seen as retroactive legislation, which is specifically prohibited by the Constitution.[69]

Faced with the odd situation in which there was no longer a petition to adjudicate, the Court was forced to "announce the termination of adjudication" without discussing the merits. Yet, in a devious way, the Court did manage to announce the opinion it had prepared with regard to the punishability of a successful *coup d'état*. Although this was originally the majority view, after the withdrawal of the petition a new majority was formed in favor of merely announcing the termination of adjudication, and, as a result, what had been the original majority view was published as the opinion of the minority who still insisted on discussing the merits of the petition.

The minority opinion stated that the constitutional order of the state is not founded on the physical force of whoever is in power, but rather on the people's sovereign power. The Constitution actually requires, according to the minority, the punishment of even the president if he has committed the crime of treason, regardless of its success or failure. Granted that it might be practically impossible to punish the perpetrators of a successful coup,

401

they can and should be punished as soon as the practical impediments are gone and the prosecutorial power of the proper constitutional agencies is restored. The minority justices therefore berated the prosecutors for concluding that they lacked the power to prosecute, as that was clearly based on a gross misunderstanding of not only the criminal jurisprudence regarding treason, but also the ideals and principles of the Constitution.

On the issue of whether or not the statute of limitation for treason had already expired, the Court chose not to disclose its opinion. In light of the fact that there were numerous views expressed by politicians and law professors regarding the issue of when exactly the statute of limitations had started to run, and the fact that both the executive and legislative branches of the government were about to pass the special law permitting punishment of the ex-generals, the Court obviously did not wish to risk becoming unpopular by announcing its view on the matter. Even the so-called minority opinion of the Court affirming the punishability of a successful coup can be viewed as an expression of the Court's deference to growing public opinion, or outrage, regarding the prosecutors' line of reasoning. Such behavior of the Court could hardly be considered independent and autonomous, or conducive to the ideal of rule of law. Yet perhaps it did contribute to the larger ideal of bringing justice to the former leaders of the military regime and thereby establishing rule of law at a deeper level.

The third occasion on which the Constitutional Court got involved in this protracted story was after the National Assembly had passed, at the urging of President Kim Young-sam, the special legislation to prosecute Chun and Roh. With the passage of the Special Act Concerning the 5/18 Democratization Movement, which suspended the statute of limitations for "crimes destructive of the constitutional order" committed during the 12/12 and 5/18 Incidents, the prosecutors' office reopened its investigation. When the prosecutors requested arrest warrants from the Seoul District Court for the leaders of the *coup d'état*, Chun, Roh, and company argued that the special law constituted an *ex post facto* law specifically prohibited by the Constitution. The District Court agreed and referred the issue of the special law's constitutionality to the Constitutional Court for an authoritative determination.

In its decision, the Court stated that the special law would not be unconstitutional if at the time of its enactment the statute of limitations had not already run. In the case where the period had already expired, five of the justices stated that the law should be held unconstitutional, while the other four were willing to uphold it. Since a vote of six justices is required by the Constitution for a decision of unconstitutionality, the Special Act could not be held unconstitutional.[70] The upshot of the Court's decision was that, while the constitutionality of the law initially depends on how the ordinary courts interpret the statutes of limitation, ultimately it did not matter because the law was constitutional even as retroactive legislation. The minority justices (whose views prevailed) also emphasized that the overwhelming public interest in punishing criminals who destroyed the constitutional order and in restoring justice justified making an exception to the rule against retroactive legislation.

Essentially the same argument was made in response to the charge that the special law was a case-specific legislation – that is, a "private bill" directed at specific individuals. The Court stated that, while the principle of equality generally forbids case-specific legislation, it is not inherently unconstitutional. The discriminatory effect of case-specific legislation can be justified if there are legitimate overriding considerations. In this case, the Court held that the public interest in, and the historic demand for, cleansing the recent history of constitutional irregularities was enough to justify making an exception to the rule against private bills.

Again, it is possible to criticize the Court's decision for capitulating to public opinion in order to protect its own reputation. Any "activism" on the part of the Court can actually be seen as the result of consciously following the policies of the Kim Young-sam government. Also, the Court could afford to be "activist" in these cases because the people affected by the decisions were no longer in power. Some criticized the Court for trying to please everyone by indicating the unconstitutionality of the special law while upholding it in the end under the pretext of the procedural "technical" requirement for a six-vote majority.

On the other hand, regardless of its motivations the Constitutional Court is to be commended for reaffirming that prosecutorial discretion may be subject to constitutional review, and for proclaiming that a successful *coup d'état* does not establish a new constitutional order. For all its shortcomings, the Court did contribute to, and in a sense presided over, the long process of legal and political maneuverings which ultimately ended with the Supreme Court's confirmation in April 1997 of the convictions of the two former presidents and their accessories. There is no doubt that this string of events advanced democracy in Korea. Given that democracy is commonly seen as inextricably related to rule of law, the experience may be seen as having deepened the rule of law in Korea as well.

Emergency powers

One of the thorniest problems in any system of government is the issue of reconciling the need for effective "emergency powers" on the part of the executive with the requirement that the exercise of those powers be disciplined and justified according to the relevant norms. Particularly from the perspective of rule of law, such "extraordinary powers" cannot but be a threat to the postulate that government power be exercised according to clear, predictable, and predetermined rules. Frequent use of such emergency powers by the president was an all too common feature of Korea's recent political history. President Park Chung-hee issued a series of emergency decrees which virtually had the effect of overriding the Constitution. In fact, the Constitution at that time (the infamous *Yushin* Constitution) contained an express provision stipulating that the president's emergency decrees were exempt from judicial review.

With the progress of democratization, however, Korean presidents by and large had little occasion to utilize those powers. The new Constitution strengthened the conditions under which they could be exercised, and required the president to seek the National Assembly's subsequent authorization.[71] Yet, in August 1993, President Kim Young-sam issued the Emergency Financial and Economic Decree on Real Name Financial Transaction and Protection of Confidentiality.[72] The goal of the Decree was to abolish the pre-existing financial transaction system which allowed people to open bank accounts under false or borrowed names, and establish a new system that required people to use their real names. Under the old system, transparency of the entire financial system was difficult to attain, and since it was all too easy to conceal funds under another person's name, the system was deemed to facilitate corruption and money laundering.

Before Kim issued this Decree, his predecessor, Roh Tae-woo, had also tried to push through basically the same reform measures but had been thwarted due to opposition from both the political and business communities. While virtually everyone agreed on the necessity of the reform, particularly in light of the increasing globalization of Korea's economy, most people said that it was premature because the transition to the new system was expected to be too costly. Given the experience of his predecessor, Kim decided to proceed in utmost secrecy and let no one know of his plan to institute the real-name transaction system. Other than the minister of finance and a small group of officials selected to draft the reform measures, not even his cabinet members were informed of the plan. Kim was convinced that if he were to follow the normal procedure of presenting a bill to the National Assembly and have it subjected to the usual deliberations, as Roh had done, the measure would again be defeated.

Thus, on August 12, 1993, the president issued the Decree without any prior notice and sought the subsequent approval of the National Assembly, which was given on August 19. According to the Constitution, such a decree has the effect of a statute, but if the National Assembly refuses to give its approval, the decree immediately and automatically lapses. Yet on August 16 a constitutional petition was filed at the Constitutional Court alleging that the president acted unconstitutionally because he failed to satisfy the conditions for exercising his emergency powers, and that as a result the petitioner's constitutional rights had been violated.[73] In response, the minister of justice, representing the government, argued that the exercise of the president's emergency powers is an instance of *t'ongch'i haengwi* (act of reigning, or *Regierungsakt* in German) which cannot be the subject of judicial review; that the president had met all the requirements for issuing the Decree; that no constitutional rights of the petitioner were infringed; and that even if some infringements had occurred they were all within the permissible range as specified under Article 37(2) of the Constitution.[74]

The Constitutional Court rejected all of the petitioner's claims. Yet it did not completely agree with the minister of justice either. This case is important for it gave the Court an opportunity to expound upon an important issue of rule of law, the so-called "act of reigning." The Court acknowledged as a valid concept the idea of "act of reigning," which is generally defined as an act of a highly political nature by the ruler, whose political judgment must be respected by the judiciary. It also acknowledged that the president's issuance of an emergency decree could be counted as an instance of "act of reigning" which should be respected as much as possible. Yet the Court went on to state that all acts of state, including such "acts of reigning," must be executed within the limits set by the constitutional rights of the people, and that to the extent that it violates an individual's rights even an act of a highly political nature has to become the subject of review by the Court. Moreover, in the case of an emergency decree, because it has the same effect as a statute there can be no question but that it must conform to the Constitution.

Thus, the Court appears to have rejected any doctrine such as the American notion of "political question," which used on principle to preclude judicial review.[75] This decision is generally viewed as having established the principle that there can be no area of government power which is *a priori* non-justiciable. On the other hand, it is obvious that the Court was able to reject any notion of act of reigning, or executive prerogative, precisely because in this case it did not have to invalidate the president's actions. In other words, it was an easy case that did not require much courage to decide; nor did the high-sounding pronouncements cause any anguish in the actual deliberation of the merits. This is not to disparage the decision as insignificant for the ideal and practice of rule of law in Korea. The decision might have been even more valuable (in terms of gauging the practical limits the Court's power) if it had been a case where the Court had had to engage in genuine toil and was compelled to hold the executive's action unconstitutional.

The propriety of the legislative process

In the American context, another set of issues which courts would normally consider non-justiciable is how other branches of the government regulate themselves. For example, the separation of powers principle as well as the political question doctrine would probably preclude judicial review of the legislative process itself.[76] Yet, in Korea, the Constitutional Court recently had occasion to decide whether or not the circumstances under which a bill was passed in the National Assembly were constitutional.

On December 23, 1996, a special session of the National Assembly was convened to vote on several labor laws and certain revisions to the National Security Planning Agency Act. Members of the opposition parties were opposed to the bills. In order to prevent the vote from taking place, they forcefully occupied the office of the Speaker of the National Assembly and continued to make it physically impossible to commence the session. The Vice-Speaker, a member of the ruling party and acting on behalf the Speaker, convened the session at 6:00 a.m. on December 26, after having notified only those assemblymen who were members of his party. The 155 ruling-party assemblymen then proceeded to vote on the bills and passed them all within six minutes, whereupon the Vice-Speaker declared the laws passed. On December 30, members of the opposition parties filed a "competence dispute" with the Constitutional Court claiming that their rights as members of the National Assembly to review and vote on proposed bills were violated and that the Vice-Speaker's declaration of passage should be annulled.[77] They argued that that irregularity in the legislative process should render the law itself unconstitutional.

During the previous authoritarian and military regimes in Korea, such legislative irregularities could be seen quite frequently. It was a common tactic for the ruling party, which almost always commanded a majority, to "railroad" a bill through the legislature by convening a plenary session among its members and voting on it, usually without any discussion or deliberation. In certain situations, ruling-party legislators would hold a session outside the National Assembly building. Once, the Constitution was even revised under such procedurally irregular circumstances. Needless to say, the members of the ruling party were acting under the direction of the president, who usually had the power to pick and choose who would be elected to the National Assembly.[78]

In its decision, the Constitutional Court held that failure to notify the opposition members of the time and place of the session in accordance with the provisions of the National Assembly Act, which in turn deprived them of a chance to participate in the deliberation and voting process on a proposed piece of legislation, constituted a violation of their constitutional rights to deliberate and vote. The Court reasoned that those rights, though not explicitly mentioned in the Constitution, were nevertheless inferable from those articles which granted exclusive legislative power to the National Assembly and stipulated that the National Assembly shall be constituted by representatives elected by the people.[79]

After finding that the representatives' rights had been violated, however, the Court chose not to declare unconstitutional the bills passed under such circumstances. It stated that making such a declaration would mean retroactively voiding a law that had been in effect, and thereby causing a major threat to the legal order of the country. Further, it argued that in order to void a law on grounds of procedural defect, the defect must be so grave as to be a direct violation of the express provisions of the Constitution. The only constitutional provisions on legislative procedure being Article 49, prescribing the principle of majority vote, and Article 50, prescribing the principle of open session, the Court found no direct violation of those provisions. The fact that the opposition National Assembly members were unable to exercise their right to deliberate and vote was a defect of lesser magnitude, according to the Court.

This was the result of an internal disagreement among the justices. Three justices thought that the case should be dismissed for lack of standing. They argued that individual National Assembly members could not file a "competence dispute" because this was a form of dispute among different state agencies.[80] Of the six justices who thought the standing requirement was satisfied, and who all agreed that the representatives' rights had been violated, only three were of the opinion that the bills should therefore be annulled. Lacking the necessary votes, the Court could only declare the violation of National Assembly members' rights and reject the claim that the bills be held unconstitutional.

After taking the historic step of declaring that opposition members' right to participate in the deliberation and voting process must be protected, the Court then undercut the significance of that declaration by saying that the law passed in violation of those rights was nonetheless valid. Perhaps the justices did not wish to annoy the ruling party and the president by siding with the opposition. That would be understandable in view of the need to maintain the Court's institutional autonomy given that it is still a very weak agency without any power to enforce its decisions. Even if it had declared the law void, there was no guarantee that its decision would have been honored by the executive branch.[81] At any rate, it remains to be seen what the practical effect of this decision will be.

Conclusion

The Constitutional Court decisions discussed above are significant because they all proclaimed in one way or another that in a democratic society the government must operate according to and on the basis of well-defined law. Rule of law required that both executive and legislative branches of the government observe the law in exercising their powers, and that everybody respect the constitutional order. On the other hand, it was seen that in some cases the pronouncement of the Constitutional Court rang a bit hollow because it failed to produce the substantive effects sought by the parties. In other cases, the Court itself stretched the law somewhat in order to establish a "higher" legal principle. We may also say that, from a political standpoint, the Court was able to affirm those principles only because society had become more democratic. In a way, the growth of rule of law is a product, rather than the cause, of political democratization.[82]

Nevertheless, the Court's behavior in proclaiming these higher principles of rule of law may be viewed as a kind of preparatory work, laying the groundwork for future developments. These cases can be invoked by later courts for the general propositions established in them. In that sense, I agree with the following assessment:

> From a purely legal perspective, however, the Court's decision to rule on these "political matters" seems phenomenal. Laying a precedent itself is a ground-breaking event for the Korean judiciary, and in the long run, it will benefit both the judiciary and the people.[83]

As mentioned at the beginning, rule of law has many dimensions, and to focus too much on the institution of constitutional review is perhaps overly restrictive. For one thing, courts and the lawyers are but a small part of the larger society. As some Western scholars critical of rule of law are wont to remind us, rule of law has the danger of turning into a rule by judiciary and a rule by conservative elites, thereby impeding the process of further democratization.[84] This, of course, is related to the issue known in American scholarship as the "counter-majoritarian difficulty" – that is, the judiciary's relative deficiency in democratic legitimacy.[85] The Korean Constitutional Court also suffers from the same problem. Many scholars point to the fact that even as compared to the Supreme Court, whose justices must all be confirmed by the National Assembly, the Constitutional Court lacks democratic legitimacy because only its president is subject to the same requirement under the Constitution.[86] Also, the requirement that all justices should be licensed as ordinary court judges, with at least 15 years' practical experience, may make it more likely for people with a conservative and elitist outlook to sit on the Constitutional Court.[87] Yet, given the Court's attitude toward public opinion and its apparent desire to protect its reputation as a somewhat populist institution, it is conceivable that the problem might be to some extent mitigated by those tendencies.

In order to be fully rooted in society, any legal system or ideal must be supported and cherished by its people as their own. It was noted above that Koreans are beginning to regard the rule of law rhetoric as a natural part of their political and legal language. On the other hand, scholarly efforts to formulate a theory of rule of law "with Korean characteristics" have yet to appear. Most legal textbooks generally do not go much beyond introducing the German discussions on the concept of *Rechtsstaat*. Thus, the distinction between the "formal" and the "substantive" conceptions of the idea developed in German constitutional history are very familiar to most Korean law students. Efforts to draw on "indigenous" resources or formulate "indigenous" conceptions, by contrast, rarely occupy the mainstream scholarship.[88] Perhaps this is due to the relative novelty of the rule of law ideal in Korean society. It may be that it is still too early to expect sophisticated "native" debates and theories on rule of law to blossom. Or perhaps this is due to an implicit settled agreement on the desirability and superiority of the (imported) theories and conceptions of rule of law. This would not be surprising given the near-universal agreement that a modern democratic state must practice rule of law. Indeed, it may well be that most Koreans no longer regard rule of law as a "foreign" ideal. As we have seen, at least at the level of rhetoric, Koreans have become quite proficient in the language of rule of law. In addition, the growing jurisprudence of the Constitutional Court is slowly but surely contributing to the actual implementation of that ideal.

Notes

1 Park Byung-ho [Pak Pyŏngho], *Kŭnse ŭi Pŏp kwa Pŏp sasang* [Law and Legal Thoughts of the Modern Era] (Seoul: Chinwn, 1996).

2 Another term commonly used is *pŏp ŭi chibae*, which is perhaps a more literal translation of "rule of law." The term *pŏp ch'igukka* is also used for the German idea of *Rechtsstaat*. Almost all Korean constitutional law textbooks list the principle of rule of law as one of the fundamental principles underlying the Korean Constitution, and often include brief descriptions of the Anglo-American and German "versions" of the principle.

3 Note that in English the term "lawlessness" is a synonym for chaos and madness. This seems to reinforce the impression among English speakers that any society that does not practice the "rule of law" can only be a society in total disarray or one plagued by a war of all against all. Cf., René David, "On the Concept of 'Western' Law," *University of Cincinnati Law Review*, vol. 52 (1983), pp. 126–35 (stating that in the Western tradition order and justice are unthinkable apart from law).

4 Randall Peerenboom, *China's Long March Toward Rule of Law* (Cambridge: University of Cambridge Press, 2002), p. 140.

5 For an attempt to describe this as a form of constitutionalism without using the rhetoric of rule of law, see Chaihark Hahm, "Conceptualizing Korean Constitutionalism: Foreign Transplant or Indigenous Tradition?," *Journal of Korean Law*, vol. 1, no. 2 (2001), pp. 151–96.

6 Many writers use the term "essentially contested concept" to describe rule of law and other similarly complex legal ideals, with the customary invocation of works by W. B. Gallie and William Connolly. For example, Richard H. Fallon, Jr., "'The Rule of Law' as a Concept in Constitutional Discourse," *Columbia Law Review*, vol. 97 (1997), p. 7. Cf. Sanford Levinson, *Constitutional Faith* (Princeton: Princeton University Press, 1988), pp. 124–5 (referring to constitutionalism as an essentially contested concept).

7 Cf. Thomas Carothers, "The Rule of Law Revival," *Foreign Affairs*, vol. 77, no. 2 (March/April 1998), pp. 95–106.

8 This is nothing original, as the existence of an autonomous legal profession was a crucial element of Max Weber's definition of a legal order. Max Weber, *Economy and Society*, vol. 2 (Berkeley: University of California Press, 1978). In A. V. Dicey's portrayal of rule of law in England, too, independent common law courts that applied the same rules to everyone were vital to the concept of rule of law as he understood it. *Introduction to the Study of the Law of the Constitution*, 8th edn. (Indianapolis: Liberty Fund, 1982) (1915), pp. 114–15. Following Weber, Roberto Unger also counts institutional and occupational autonomy as elements

of the Western concept of rule of law, which requires that laws be public, positive, autonomous, and general. *Law in Modern Society* (New York: Free Press, 1976), pp. 52–4. By citing Unger's conception of rule of law I am not thereby endorsing his simplistic categorization of modern societies into "liberal/post-liberal modern" (Western countries), "traditionalistic modern" (Japan), and "revolutionary socialist modern" (PRC) countries. Id., at pp. 223–37. Apparently, the allure of such crude and simplistic, as well as orientalist, categorization scheme is difficult to resist, as can be seen more recently in Ugo Mattei, "Three Patterns of Law: Taxonomy and Change in the World's Legal Systems," 45 *American Journal of Comparative Law*, vol. 45 (1997), pp. 5–43. For a critique of such orientalist tendencies with regard to Asian law, see Veronica Taylor, "Beyond Legal Orientalism," in Veronica Taylor, ed., *Asian Law Through Australian Eyes* (Sydney: Law Book Company, 1997), pp. 47–62.

9 While the earlier law and development movement of the 1970s has largely been discredited, the recent efforts at economic liberalization and development through legal reforms appears to have rekindled scholarly interest in many issues that occupied writers in the law and development camp. With regard to East Asia on the connection between law and economic development, see Kanishka Jayasuriya, ed., *Law, Capitalism, and Power in Asia* (London: Routledge, 1999); Katharina Pistor and Philip A. Wellons, *The Role of Law and Legal Institutions in Asian Economic Development, 1960–1995* (New York: Oxford University Press, 1999).

10 It may be argued that even if rule of law was not established in the political sphere, it was nevertheless operating to a degree in the economic sphere. The very fact that Korea was successful in developing its economy may be argued as evidence of that. To be sure, it could be argued that rule of law existed in the sense that one could go to court to resolve a contract dispute and have the judgment enforced against the losing party. On the other hand, if we focus on issues like the accessibility of the courts to the average citizen and the degree of their independence and/or corruption, it becomes more difficult to make that argument. Another factor that must be considered is the heavy involvement of the state in Korea's process of economic development. As will be seen below the government was generally not too concerned about whether or not it had legal authorization to engage in such proactive planning and allocation of economic resources, as well as "guiding" economic actors to conform to its plans. This would tend to make it even harder to argue that rule of law, even in a very formalistic sense, existed in the economic sphere. For a critique of the rule of law rhetoric inspired by new institutionalist literature and promoted by many international development agencies, see John K. M. Ohnesorge, "The Rule of Law, Economic Development, and the Developmental States of Northeast Asia," in Christoph Antons, ed., *Law and Development in East and Southeast Asia* (New York: RoutledgeCurzon, 2003).

11 This paper deals with South Korea only. As is well known, the story of rule of law in North Korea is even worse than that in the South. Also, from the perspective of South Korea the North Korean regime is technically an "anti-state organization" which is unlawfully controlling the northern part of the peninsula. The South Korean Constitution proclaims that the entire Korean peninsula and its islands are the territory of the Republic of Korea.

12 See for example, Kyong Whan Ahn, "The Influence of American Constitutionalism in South Korea," *Southern Illinois University Law Journal*, vol. 22 (Fall 1997), pp. 71–115.

13 As of May 18, 2002, the *Taehan Byŏnhosa Hyŏphoe* (Korean Bar Association) had a membership of 5,055 attorneys licensed to practice law.

14 Jae-Won Kim, "Transnational Practice," in Dae-Kyu Yoon, ed., *Recent Transformations in Korean Law and Society* (Seoul: Seoul National University Press, 2000).
15 Hŏnpŏp [Constitution], art. 111(1) (Korea).
16 Hŏnpŏp Chaep'anso Pp [Constitutional Court Act] [CCA], art. 41(1).
17 CCA, art. 68(2).
18 On the powers of the German Constitutional Court, see Donald P. Kommers, *The Constitutional Jurisprudence of the Federal Republic of Germany* (Durham, N.C.: Duke University Press, 1997), pp. 10–15.
19 CCA, art. 68(1).
20 Id. In certain situations, when going through the existing appeals process would be futile or impracticable, the Court has considerably relaxed the requirement of exhausting all other remedies.
21 Acts of the judiciary are subject to constitutional petitions in exceptional cases only because the law itself excludes ordinary courts' decisions from the subject matter of constitutional petitions. CCA, art. 68(1). When a statute passed by the National Assembly directly (i.e. simultaneously with its promulgation, without any implementing regulation) violates a person's constitutional right, the Court is allowed to declare it unconstitutional, and this would be the third way in which the Court gets to rule on the constitutionality of a statute. A form of action by the executive branch that has become the subject of countless petitions is the prosecutors' decision not to indict a criminal suspect. Although few such petitions have actually resulted in the nullification of the prosecutors' decision, the Court has indicated that, at least in theory, where a victim's constitutional rights have been infringed by the prosecutors' decision and the Court finds that the prosecutor has abused his or her discretion in reaching the decision, that decision may be cancelled by the Court.
22 Constitution, art. 111(2) and (3).
23 CCA, art. 7.
24 Constitution, art. 111(4).
25 Constitution, art. 113(1).
26 For an insightful and critical account of the existing legal education system, see James M. West, *Education of the Legal Profession in Korea* (Seoul: Korea University, 1991). See also Dai-kwon Choi, "Legal Education in Korea: Problems and Reform Efforts," *Seoul Law Journal*, vol. 29, no. 2 (1988), pp. 104–22.
27 See Jae Won Kim, "The Ideal and Reality of the Korean Legal Profession," *Asian–Pacific Law & Policy Journal*, vol. 2, no. 1 (2001), pp. 45–68.
28 Id. Meanwhile, Japan has also started debating the idea of adopting graduate level law schools, and appears to have set the year 2004 has the date for the switch.
29 Some proposals included the abolition of the JRTI, which will have the political effect of diminishing the Supreme Court's influence over the licensing of attorneys.
30 An important qualification to this statement in the Korean context is the activities of a group of lawyers known as the *Minbyŏn*, whose full name in English would be "Lawyers' Group for a Democratic Society." Even before the formation of the group in 1988, its members had been active in defending political dissidents and were widely known as *inkwŏn byŏnhosa* (human rights lawyers). Members of the *Minbyŏn* are of course licensed members of the Korean Bar Association, have represented parties in many cases before the Constitutional Court.

31 Those passing the bar exam are lawyer "candidates" because they still have to finish the two-year JRTI course in order to be fully licensed. This sudden increase in the number of lawyers is expected to cause a major shift within the profession. Many predict (and even hope) that some lawyers will not be able to find employment and will be forced to leave the practice, which will in turn destroy the "myth" that passing the judicial exam will allow one to move up the social ladder and lead a comfortable life. "Pyŏnhosa Manmyŏng Shidae" [The Era of Ten Thousand Lawyers], *Chugan Han'guk* [Hanguk Weekly], April 18, 2002, pp. 24–7.

32 In some ways Kim Young-sam's judicial reform policies were spurred by the activities of certain civic groups. Specifically, a group formed in 1994 and known as *Ch'amyŏ Minjujuŭi rŭl Wihan Shimin Yndae* (People's Solidarity for Participatory Democracy) set up a watchdog agency, *Sabŏp Kamshi Sentŏ* (Justice Watch Center), which in addition to monitoring any irregularities at the courts and the prosecutors' offices also made concrete proposals for reform of the entire judiciary.

33 With Kim Dae-jung's term in the presidency nearing its end, the current administration appears no longer to be willing or interested in pursuing these reforms. The task of carrying them to some sort of fruition will likely be up to the next president and his administration.

34 For more on the early history of the importation of the modern legal system during Chosŏn Korea, see Hahm Pyong-choon, "Korea's Initial Encounter with the Western Law: 1866–1910 A.D.," in *Korean Jurisprudence, Politics, and Culture* (Seoul: Yonsei University Press, 1986), pp. 122–36.

35 This is not to say that Korean people during that time did not make use of the colonial legal system. See Chulwoo Lee, "Modernity, Legality, and Power in Korea Under Japanese Rule," in Gi-Wook Shin and Michael Robinson, eds., *Colonial Modernity in Korea* (Cambridge: Harvard Asia Center, 1999), pp. 21–51.

36 For a poignant account from an earlier generation of the predicament in which Korea found itself with regard to the problem of establishing the rule of law, see Hahm Pyong-choon, "The Rule of What Law? A Korean Conundrum," in *The Korean Political Tradition and Law* (Seoul: Royal Asiatic Society Korea Branch, 1967), pp. 205–17.

37 The name of a special law enacted to allow for the prosecution of the ex-generals included the phrase "[the] crime of destroying the constitutional order." Chun and Roh were convicted on treason and corruption charges, and served their sentences until early 1998, just before the inauguration of the newly elected president Kim Dae-jung, to which they were all invited as former presidents.

38 *Hanguk Ilbo* [Hanguk Daily], July 25, 2001.

39 Some members of the *Minbyŏn*, who were also officers of the Korean Bar Association, resigned from their positions in protest at the association's criticism of Kim's reform projects.

40 E.g. Duncan Kennedy, *A Critique of Adjudication* (Cambridge: Harvard University Press, 1999).

41 The group published a "blacklist" of such individuals, cataloguing the reasons why they should not be elected to the National Assembly. This group was not the only one to do so. Another civic group representing the ultra-conservatives also published a similar blacklist of politicians they regarded as being pro-North Korea. Such activities led many to comment that Korea's civil society had finally come of age.

42 Kongjik Sŏn'gŏ mit Sŏn'gŏ Bujŏng Bangji Pŏp [Law on Elections for Public Offices and Prevention of Election Frauds], art. 87. The Law made an exception for labor unions. While this may sound like a very "undemocratic" law in that it

restricts people's ability to express their views on candidates for elected offices, it actually has a quite democratic, or egalitarian, rationale. Koreans, or at least their representatives in the National Assembly, felt that with no such limitations the wealthier candidates, who can mobilize larger amounts of resources, both human and financial, would inevitably have an unwarranted advantage over the relatively indigent candidates. The legislative intent was to level the playing field, so to speak, for all who campaigned for public office. Apparently, money in Korea is not regarded as a form of political speech.

43 Yonhap News Agency, January 19, 2000.

44 E.g. Chǒng T'ae-uk, *Chǒngch'i-wa Pǒpch'i* [Politics and Rule of Law] (Seoul: Chaeksesang, 2002).

45 2000 Do 4576 (decided 16 January 2001).

46 Their major concern was that they be allowed to publish their lists and inform the public prior to the beginning of the prescribed "campaign period," which they regarded as too short.

47 2000 HǒnMa 121 and 202 (consolidated) (decided August 30, 2001).

48 For a detailed account of the constitutional revision process that resulted in the creation of the Constitutional Court, see James M. West and Edward J. Baker, "The 1987 Constitutional Reforms in South Korea: Electoral Process and Judicial Independence," in William Shaw, ed., *Human Rights in Korea: Historical and Policy Perspectives* (Cambridge, Massachusetts: Council on East Asian Studies, Harvard University, 1991).

49 Yi Shiyun, "Hǒnpǒp Chaep'an 10 nyǒn-i Hoego-wa Chǒnmang" [A Retrospective and Prospective on the Ten Years of Constitutional Adjudication], *Kongpǒp Yǒn'gu*, vol. 27, no. 3 (1999), pp. 107–15.

50 The Court even went out of its way to write long and detailed opinions for what would now be seen as easy and insignificant cases. *Ibid.*, p. 109.

51 These are mostly constitutional petition cases that are dismissed for failure to file the petition within the prescribed time period; for failure to have attorney representation as required by the CCA, art. 25; for failure to exhaust other avenues of appeal, etc. The Court utilizes a small bench of three justices to do these preliminary screenings. CCA, art. 72. Yet this is different from a system of writ of *certiorari* utilized by the U.S. Supreme Court, for the Korean justices do not have discretion to pick and choose their cases.

52 Detailed statistics may be found at the Court's website: http://www.ccourt.go.kr/intro/i3.html/. In addition to the straightforward judgments of "constitutional" or "unconstitutional," the Korean Constitutional Court has developed a number of "modified judgments" (*pyǒnhyǒng kyǒlchǒng*). These include judgments of "incompatibility with the Constitution", "limited unconstitutionality", and "limited constitutionality". Although an instance of the German influence on Korean legal system, this practice of rendering modified judgments is, unlike in Germany, not authorized by any legislation, and its propriety is therefore the subject of continuing debate among scholars and commentators. At least one justice of the Constitutional Court, Justice Byun Jeong-soo, has consistently criticized this practice as a pretext for not discharging the Court's solemn duty of rendering final, authoritative judicial determinations. (In actuality, in Germany too the Federal Constitutional Court began rendering modified judgments without legal authorization, but the Federal Constitutional Court Act was later revised to give a legal basis for the practice.)

53 E.g. Kyong Whan Ahn, "The Influence of American Constitutionalism"; Gavin Healy (Student Note), "Judicial Activism in the New Constitutional Court of Korea," *Columbia Journal of Asian Law*, vol. 14 (2000), pp. 213–34.

54 In the political ideological terrain of Korea, "conservative" generally refers to a position characterized by strong anti-communism, nostalgia for the state-led, export-driven, economic policy of the 1970s and 1980s, a pro-business stance, and support for a strong state *vis-à-vis* society. "Progressive," on the other hand, connotes a more open attitude toward North Korea, a pro-labor stance, support for a stronger civil society, and perhaps ironically, a neo-liberal economic policy marked by deregulation and marketization. For an elucidation of the spectrum of political viewpoints currently found in Korea, see Mo Jongryn, "Segyehwa wa Han'guk i Yinyŏm Chŏngch'i" [Globalization and Korea's Ideological Politics], *Kyegan Sasang* [Thought Quarterly], winter 2001.

55 89 *HnMa* 31, 5–2 Hŏnpŏp Chaep'anso Pallyejip [Korean Constitutional Court Report; (KCCR)] 87 (decided July 29, 1993). For an in-depth analysis of this decision, see James M. West, "*Kukje* and Beyond: Constitutionalism and the Market," *Segye Hŏnpp Yŏn'gu* , pp. 321–51.

56 West, "*Kukje* and Beyond," pp. 325–8.

57 89 *HnMa*31, 5–2 KCCR, at 102. The petitioner also alleged that the whole affair was planned and carried out in retaliation against his refusal to comply with Chun Doo-hwan's demands for political contributions and other quasi-taxes. 5–2 KCCR, at 93. The Korean public found this all too plausible.

58 Some translate it as a "de facto exercise of power." At any rate, the Court noted that, as such, it went beyond even the problematic "administrative guidance" commonly issued by the government. 5–2 KCCR, at 105–6.

59 The president is given such powers under Article 76 of the Constitution.

60 CCA, art. 68(1).

61 There was room for maneuvering because the petitioner had received no formal notice from the government about the liquidation of his conglomerate at the time, and particularly because the government had tried persistently to conceal its involvement in the whole affair. The latest that the Court could set the date when the petitioner "knew" of the exercise of government power was December 21, 1988, which was the day when the petitioner had provided a document reporting his grievances to the National Assembly during a hearing convened to investigate wrongdoings of the Chun Doo-hwan regime. That still meant that the petition was filed eight days too late.

62 The Court argued that it need not wait for the outcome of certain other legal proceedings, because those cases were challenging the after-effects, as it were, of the exercise of state power, which was the subject matter of this case.

63 Article 119 of the Constitution proclaims the principle of a free-market economy as well as the conditions that must be met before the state can intervene in it. Also, Article 126 prohibits nationalizing private enterprises or controlling their management, except in cases of emergency involving national security or the national economy. For a commentary which suggests that the Court's decision may have overstated the case for the free market, especially in light of the subsequent need during the Asian financial crisis for the state's active role in meeting the exigencies of the moment (e.g. through restructuring and coordination), see James M. West, "*Kukje* and Beyond," pp. 329–35.

64 In the words of one Korean constitutional law scholar:

> The dubious concept of *Regierungsakt* [act of reigning] had provided theoretical justification for both the court's "hands-off" policy and the president's "above-the-law" attitude. Heavily influenced by pre-World War II German theories of state, justifying strong administrative powers, Korean courts had been content with self-imposed detachment from "political questions."

(Kyong Whan Ahn, "The Influence of American Constitutionalism," p. 94)

65 For an in-depth analysis of the legal proceedings against the former presidents, see James M. West, "Martial Lawlessness: The Legal Aftermath of Kwangju," *Pacific Rim Law and Policy Journal*, vol. 6 (1997), pp. 85–168.

66 94 HŏnMa 246, 7–1 KCCR 15 (decided January 20, 1995).

67 According to Article 249 of the Code of Criminal Procedures, the statute of limitation is 15 years for capital crimes and 10 years or less for less serious crimes.

68 Recall that in the Constitutional Court's first case in this saga, the statute of limitations for the crime of treason committed during the 12/12 Incident was held to have already run. In response people started demanding that the government should enact a special law to prevent the courts from reaching the same conclusion in relation to the crimes committed during the 5/18 Incident.

69 Constitution, art. 13(1).

70 96 HŏnKa 2 *et al.* (consolidated), 8–1 KCCR 51 (decided February 16, 1996). For an analysis of this case, see David M. Waters (Student Note), "Korean Constitutionalism and the 'Special Act' to Prosecute Former Presidents Chun Doo-hwan and Roh Tae-woo," *Columbia Journal of Asian Law*, vol. 10 (1996), pp. 461–85.

71 Constitution, art. 76.

72 Presidential Emergency Financial and Economic Decree no. 16 (August 13, 1993).

73 93 HŏnMa 186, 8–1 KCCR 111 (decided February 29, 1996). The petitioner also claimed that the National Assembly had acted unconstitutionally by not impeaching the president for violating the Constitution. This part of the petition was dismissed on that grounds that impeachment proceedings are a matter of discretion on the part of National Assembly and that the petitioner has no legal right to request impeachment.

74 Article 37(2) provides that:

> The freedoms and rights of citizens may be restricted by law only when necessary for national security, the maintenance of law and order, or for public welfare. Even when such restriction is imposed, no essential aspect of the freedom or right shall be violated

75 As mentioned, the Korean term *t'ongch'i haengwi* is a translation of the German notion of *Regierungsakt*. But the idea that there is an area of government action that is by nature not amenable to judicial evaluation is common to many different traditions. According to Charles McIlwain, English constitutionalism was a product of the continuous renegotiation of the boundary line between the realms of *jurisdictio* (jurisdiction of common law courts) and *gubernaculum* (royal prerogative). Charles McIlwain, *Constitutionalism: Ancient and Modern* (Ithaca, N.Y.: Cornell University Press, 1947). As is well known, the exact contours of the political question doctrine in the U.S. are the subject of ongoing controversy, and many scholars question its usefulness and even its existence. Louis Henkin, "Is There a 'Political Question' Doctrine?," *Yale Law Journal*, vol. 85 (1976).

76 Similarly, until the middle of the 20th century, the reapportionment cases were considered non-justiciable because they were too political.

77 96 HŏnRa 2, 9–2 KCCR 154 (decided July 16, 1997).

78 This case, however, occurred after the former military rulers had left office. The ruling party in this case was the party of President Kim Young-sam, who was particularly proud of the fact that he was the first civilian president in over 30 years. Old habits apparently die hard.

79 Constitution, arts. 40 and 41(1).
80 This had in fact been the established precedent of the Court. By holding that individual representatives had standing, the majority in this case were actually reversing their previous decisions.
81 A similar, and quite real, problem facing the Court is that ordinary courts, especially the Supreme Court, are sometimes unwilling to honor the Constitutional Court's decisions. In a couple of cases, the Supreme Court has applied a statute which had previously been found unconstitutional by the Constitutional Court. The Constitutional Court has responded by holding that in such situations the Supreme Court's decision itself may be the subject of a constitutional petition, thereby creating an exception to the explicit provision in the Constitutional Court Act exempting court judgments from the subject matter of constitutional petitions. Jongcheol Kim, "Some Problems with the Korean Constitutional Adjudication System," *Journal of Korean Law*, vol. 1, no. 2 (2001), pp. 17–36.
82 Dae-kyu Yoon, "New Developments in Korean Constitutionalism: Changes and Prospects," *Pacific Rim Law & Policy Journal*, vol. 4 (1995), p. 417 (political change precedes legal change, which in turn accelerates political change). Yoon also states that political democratization of the larger society is the primary explanation behind the phenomenal number of cases brought before the Court. He also refers to institutional changes that made it easier to adjudicate constitutional issues as major factors in accounting for the statistics.
83 Kyong Whan Ahn, "The Influence of American Constitutionalism," p. 95 (discussing the significance of the Court's decisions on the 12/12 and 5/18 Incidents).
84 E.g. Allan C. Hutchinson and Patrick Monahan, "Democracy and the Rule of Law," in *The Rule of Law: Ideal or Ideology* (Toronto: Carswell, 1987), pp. 97–123; Morton J. Horwitz, "Book Review: The Rule of Law: An Unqualified Human Good?," *Yale Law Journal*, vol. 86 (1977), pp. 561–6.
85 Alexander Bickel, *The Least Dangerous Branch* (New Haven, Connecticut: Yale University Press, 1962).
86 E.g. Jongcheol Kim, "Some Problems with the Korean Constitutional Adjudication System," pp. 24–5.
87 CCA, art. 5(1).
88 To a certain extent, Choi Dai-Kwon's writings constitute an exception to this state of affairs. E.g. Choi Dai-Kwon, "Sŏnhan Sahoe-ŭi Chokŏn: Pŏpch'ijuŭi-rŭl Wihan Shiron" [Conditions of a Good Society: Preliminary Discussions for the Rule of Law], *Pŏphak*, vol. 40, no. 3 (1999), pp. 62–87 (arguing that any attempt to revive and promote Confucian or other native values in Korea must be harmonized with the demand for rule of law).

14

THE EFFECTS OF RULE OF LAW PRINCIPLES IN TAIWAN[1]

Sean Cooney

Introduction

Taiwan seems to offer encouragement for those eager to see successful East Asian transitions to the 'rule of law'.[2] Until the late 1980s the state was subject to little legal constraint. However, since then a newly assertive judiciary has insisted that the executive – and even elected legislative bodies – must observe fundamental principles of legality. Further, recent administrative law amendments aim to render the state bureaucracy increasingly transparent, consultative and accountable.

Even more pleasing to many Western observers, the consolidation of 'thin' rule of law principles in the legal system has been accompanied by a strong judicial and political commitment to a liberal democratic 'thick' version of the rule of law. Judges have asserted the right to protect multi-party democracy and individual civil and political rights, and the executive and legislative arms of government have generally consented to them doing so.

However, while Taiwan is now operating essentially as a liberal democracy, its authoritarian history has continuing effects. One such effect is the different level of commitment to liberal democratic principles manifested by, on the one hand, legal and political elites, and, on the other, the bureaucracy and the general populace. This difference is reflected in considerable non-adherence to legal norms in certain areas of regulation.

This chapter explores the state of rule of law discourse in Taiwan. It first outlines the structure of Taiwan's legal and political institutions. It then examines the changing significance of the rule of law (in both thin and thick senses) in the legal and political discourse which has emanated from those institutions. The last part of the chapter explores the contrast between the currently dominant position which liberal democratic rule of law principles occupy at abstract and general levels of legal discourse and the difficulties those principles encounter in law's practical and specific interactions with other parts of society.

An overview of Taiwan's institutions of government

The basic legal framework of the (quasi-)state of Taiwan is found in the Constitution of the Republic of China (ROC), a document drafted by the Nationalists (or Kuomintang – KMT) in the last few years of their rule on the Chinese mainland.[3] In many ways, it resembles the constitutions of liberal democratic states; it provides for a separation of powers, the protection of basic human rights and for democratically elected political institutions. But the Constitution has spent most of its life in exile and in suspended animation.

The outcome of the Chinese Civil War saw the Nationalists and their Constitution transported to Taiwan, which had just experienced fifty years of Japanese colonial rule.[4] By this time, most of the Constitution had been rendered inoperative through the Nationalists' enactment of 'Temporary Provisions'[5] which granted extraordinary powers to the president, including powers to suspend basic freedoms. Taiwan was placed under martial law from 1949 until 1987. The Temporary Provisions continued in force until 1991.[6] During the martial law period, regime leaders such as Chiang Kai-shek insisted that the Republic of China upheld the 'rule of law' and 'democratic constitutionalism', in contrast to the 'Communist bandits'.[7] In fact, the civilian court system was often sidelined by military tribunals,[8] which exercised wide jurisdiction over the entire population and tried cases involving offences, including political offences, specified by the executive, not the legislature.[9]

One of the more bizarre measures that flowed from the Temporary Provisions was the postponement of national elections for more than forty years, on the grounds that sitting politicians (who overwhelming represented mainland areas) could not be subject to election until those areas were recovered from the Communists. This postponement, quite contrary to the text of the Constitution, which specifies fixed terms for elected officials, was approved by the Council of Grand Justices, Taiwan's constitutional court.[10] By the late 1980s the elected organs of the state[11] were still in the hands of elderly mainland gentlemen who had never been required to face the Taiwanese electorate.[12]

This farcical situation was ended by the Grand Justices in 1990 in a strongly worded ruling (or, as they are known, 'interpretation'). The justices emphasised the importance of regular elections in a constitutional democracy. Finding that circumstances no longer justified the suspension of general elections, they ordered that the terms of the representatives on the mainland be terminated and that new elections be held by the end of 1991 (by implication confined to Taiwan alone). Since that decision, Taiwan has held regular multi-party elections. These elections have seen a gradual shift in power away from the Nationalists to the Democratic Progressive Party (DPP), a party led by former dissidents which has now become the most significant political force on the island.

While the Taiwanese constitutional order can now be fairly described as liberal democratic, there are many quirks in its present arrangements, as might be expected given the Constitution's extraordinary history. One such quirk is that most of the provisions in the main body of the Constitution setting out the basic structure of government have no application to contemporary Taiwan. The provisions currently in force are to be found in 'Additional Articles' (AA) to the Constitution, first adopted in 1991 and amended five times since.[13] The AA effectively confine the operation of the Constitution to Taiwan as the 'free area' of the Republic of China. Unlike most constitutional amendments, the AA do not alter the original text of the Constitution. The original text has been preserved in order to maintain the pretence that the government of Taiwan is a[14] legitimate government of 'China'[15] and to avoid making it constitutionally obvious that Taiwan is an independent state.

A second quirk is that state power is divided into six rather than three organs. This reflects Sun Yat-sen's (awkward) attempt to merge Chinese and Western institutional forms. In the original constitution, a National Assembly was supposed to exercise 'political powers on behalf of the whole body of citizens'.[16] The Assembly never functioned as it was intended, and after the most recent revision of the AA it has ceased to be a standing body. It is elected on an ad hoc basis and sits only to vote on the legislature's proposals to amend the constitution, alter national boundaries or impeach the president or vice-president.[17]

There are five other government organs or 'Yuan':[18] the Executive Yuan, the Legislative Yuan, the Judicial Yuan (the Council of Grand Justices), the Examination Yuan, which as its name suggests oversees state examinations, and the Control Yuan, which monitors and sanctions the behaviour of public officials. The last two Yuan are based on institutions in Imperial China. The Constitution also provides for a president and vice-president; these were originally appointed by the National Assembly but are now directly elected.[19]

The legal relationship between the president, the head of the Executive Yuan (the premier, appointed by the president) and the legislature has been the subject of ongoing controversy. Since the early 1990s, attempts to resolve disputes about the nature of the relationship have led to three revisions to the AA and to several interpretations by the Council of Grand Justices. The tension between the bodies reached its height during the period between the presidential elections of May 2000 and the legislative elections of December 2001 (presidential and legislative elections are not synchronised). During this period, the presidency and the Executive Yuan were in the hands of the DPP but the legislature was controlled by the Nationalists. Deadlock ensued, especially after the premier, in accordance with DPP policy, cancelled the country's fourth nuclear power station, even though the legislature had passed a budget bill dedicating funds to the project. This action led to an unsuccessful attempt by some Nationalist members of the legislature to impeach the president. The issue was referred to the Council of Grand Justices, which issued an ambiguous interpretation enabling each of the disputants to save face.[20] The defeat of the Nationalists in the December 2001 legislative elections, which saw the DPP become the largest party in the legislature, somewhat improved relations between the two Yuan. However, the DPP still cannot control a majority of votes.[21]

With this institutional background in mind, I turn to examine the rule of law in Taiwan.

The thin conception of rule of law in Taiwan

The martial law period

When Western-style legal institutions were introduced into Taiwan under Japanese rule, their operation was generally limited to private law matters and to criminal law.[22] In these areas, Taiwanese came to invoke, or were subject to, Western notions of legality.[23] However, Japanese colonial law did very little to compel state organs in Taiwan to adhere to even a 'thin version' of the rule of law.[24]

This bifurcation between the implementation of legal norms in civil and (to a lesser extent) criminal[25] areas and their non-implementation in areas pertaining to state power persisted during the Nationalist martial law period. The similarity between Japanese and Nationalist civil, commercial and criminal law, and the retention of much of the Japanese court infrastructure, meant that there was little substantive change in the functioning of legal institutions. In particular, a formal legal framework complying with rule of law principles continued to operate in relation to purely private matters.[26] Thus, Taiwan had a Civil Code,[27] derived from the German model, which was clearly identifiable as a law and publicly set out extensive principles of general application pertaining to a range of social arrangements and transactions.

However, at least in the earlier period of Nationalist rule, Taiwanese legal institutions under the Nationalists constrained the regime no more than they had under the Japanese. The Nationalist regime was unwilling to operate according to rule of law principles and the courts could not compel it to do so. We have already seen that during the martial law period there was a glaring contradiction between the many liberal democratic features of the Constitution and actual practice. It is a straightforward conclusion that the liberal democratic 'thick' version of the rule of law did not operate in Taiwan at this time. At best, a neo-authoritarian (or perhaps state corporatist)[28] variant prevailed. In many respects, however, even adherence to rule of law in the thin sense was very weak. The militarised developmentalist state pursued its social and economic objectives with little regard for the law.[29] In turn, legal institutions adopted such a loose interpretation of legality that they enabled executive action to operate largely unchecked.[30]

Taiwan's legal system ostensibly provides forums both for constitutional review – the Council of Grand Justices – and administrative review – the Administrative Court. As illustrated most clearly by the 1954 decision already referred to which legitimated the suspension of democratic government,[31] the Council did little to ensure that the state complied with constitutional norms, even those that were not suspended by the Temporary Provisions.[32] Restrictions on standing in place during the martial law period meant that only one application lodged by an individual (as distinct from a governmental organ) was made before 1976.[33] Cases mainly dealt with legal interpretations for government organs, or disputes between those organs.[34]

In relation to the legality of administrative action, the Administrative Court placed few obstacles in the way of executive action.[35] This is illustrated in a recent article by Professor Wu Geng[36] tracing the history of the principle of 'administration according to law' (*yifa xingzheng*) over the period of Nationalist rule.[37] Wu Geng notes that this principle is an aspect of thin or 'narrow' rule of law.[38] He identifies two key doctrines associated with the principle: the 'negative' doctrine of 'precedence of statutes' (*falü youyue yuanze*), which prohibits administrative authorities from acting contrary to statute; and the 'positive' doctrine of 'reservation of statutory powers' (*falü baoliu yuanze*), which requires that the exercise of any administrative power to be supported by an authorising statute.[39] These doctrines are derived from the German administrative law concepts of *Gesetzesvorrang* and *Gesetzesvorbehalt*. They are recognised in the ROC Constitution.[40]

During the martial law period, the reservation of statutory powers doctrine, in particular, was regularly violated.[41] Many decisions of the Administrative Court upheld the validity of administrative acts and orders, including those imposing fees and penalties, notwithstanding the fact that they lacked any specific statutory basis. It was often sufficient if they were issued by an organ validly constituted under an 'organisation law', or if the measure did not directly contradict the Constitution or a statute.[42] For example, the Court held that Rules on Registering the Establishment of Factories, issued by the Ministry of Economic Affairs, were valid simply because:

- they fell within the Ministry's responsibility for formulating and implementing industry policy under the relevant Organisation Law;
- they were not inconsistent with any statute.[43]

Other administrative measures lacking statutory authorisation were justified on the basis that they were a private rather than a public law measure (what was in fact a penalty could be described as a bond subject to confiscation), or that they were in the 'public interest', or that they affected a 'privilege' rather than an existing property right.[44] Further, in some cases the Administrative Court ruled that persons affected by administrative measures unsupported by a specific statute had no standing to contest their validity.[45]

At best, then, only the 'negative' principle of precedence of statutes had practical operation. However, there was little work for this principle to do, since few statutes were produced by the inert legislature during the martial law period and many of those enacted prior to the martial law period were suspended.[46] Much public and private activity was thus regulated by various forms of executive orders.

In sum, then, during the martial law period the (thin) rule of law could be said to exist in substance only in relation to private areas of social action. In the public sphere there were, in Peerenboom's terms, few 'meaningful restraints on state actors'. The executive had *de facto* law-making power; it enjoyed wide discretion in its choice of procedures and regulatory content.

The post-martial law period

Since the late 1980s there has been radical revision of public law in Taiwan. The tenets of liberal constitutional and administrative legal theory have gained widespread acceptance in legal and political circles. The courts have taken a much more robust approach to the 'thin version' of the rule of law. This is illustrated in particular by the much greater scope given to the reservation of statutory powers doctrine.[47] The Council of Grand Justices has now repeatedly held that, as a matter of constitutional law, administrative instruments affecting individual rights and freedoms must be supported by a statute stipulating 'specifically and clearly the purpose, scope and content'[48] of such instruments. Instruments imposing sanctions (such as fines and disciplinary measures) will be subject to this principle. Thus, the Council has invalidated[49] certain rules made by the Ministry for Transport and Communications imposing penalties on airlines because they lacked a specific basis in the Civil Aviation Law.[50] The reservation of statutory powers principle has been applied to administrative measures implemented by private law mechanisms.[51] The Council has also forced the Administrative Courts[52] to take a much more generous approach to standing in administrative cases.[53] These various interpretations have the effect of greatly extending the reach of administrative review. And indeed the number of cases before the Administrative Courts has increased more than fivefold since the early 1990s.[54] Nevertheless, the Courts have not always demonstrated sound reasoning in applying the new broader judicial review principles, as perhaps might be expected from an institution with limited experience of them.[55]

This more expansive judicial approach to the thin rule of law has been complemented by important legislative reforms. Chief among these is the Administrative Procedure Law of 1999.[56] This law came into effect on 1 January 2001. Its purpose is to ensure, *inter alia*, that public administration respects the principles of fairness, transparency, democratic procedure and administration according to law. The law applies to various forms of administrative decision-making, including discrete administrative acts,[57] administrative contracts,[58] administrative regulation-making[59] and Japanese-style 'administrative guidance'.[60] It sets out a range of procedural and substantive requirements for these based on German, American and Japanese models.[61] For example, where an administrative act will have an adverse effect on an individual (such as depriving the person of a right), that individual is generally entitled to notice of the intention to carry out the act and to an opportunity to present a written case.[62] The administrative act cannot take effect unless the person is notified of the resultant decision, of the reasons for the decision and of the relevant appeal rights.[63]

Again, where administrative agencies propose to issue administrative regulations[64] (other than those regulations pertaining to military, diplomatic or national security matters), they must notify the public of the proposal and provide an opportunity for comment, for example through a public hearing.[65] Administrative regulations must be published in the government gazette or in newspapers.[66] The Law specifically applies the doctrines of precedence of statute and reservation of statutory powers to administrative regulations,[67] giving legislative recognition to these doctrines as recently developed by the Council of Grand Justices.

Apart from these specific requirements, the Law sets out basic normative standards for administrative decision-making. Administrative decisions must be clear,[68] must not discriminate without a legitimate reason,[69] must be proportionate,[70] and must be taken in good faith.[71] The Law also establishes a freedom of information process.[72]

The Administrative Procedure Law enshrines most of the principles on Peerenboom's list of the key 'thin' rule of law elements. The law appears to be having a significant impact on the administration, with agencies as diverse as the Securities and Futures Commission, the Central Personnel Administration, the National Police Administration and the Environmental Protection Administration all engaged in reviewing their procedures in the light of the Law.[73] However, it is too early to assess how effective the Law will be in rendering government more transparent and accountable. This will of course depend on how courts choose to apply it and on the extent to which the bureaucracy internalises its norms.

The ascendancy of the liberal democratic thick version of the rule of law in contemporary Taiwan

The post-martial law endorsement of rule of law principles on the part of Taiwanese legal institutions has not been limited to 'thin' issues. It has extended, at least at the highest level of the judiciary, to an apparently strong commitment to a liberal democratic 'thick' version.

The Council of Grand Justice's assertion of liberal democratic principles

Since the early 1990s, the Council of Grand Justices has moved to protect the civil and political rights[74] set out in Chapter II of the Constitution.[75] It has struck down legislation and administrative actions that it considered violated provisions concerning, for example, the protection of personal liberty,[76] freedom of expression,[77] freedom of association[78] and the protection of property rights[79] (although its interpretation of these provisions is often rather restrictive compared to some other liberal democratic jurisdictions).

However, the commitment to liberal democracy is best illustrated by a striking recent decision of the Council which asserts that liberal democracy is so fundamental to Taiwan that its basic principles cannot be impaired, even through a constitutional amendment passed by democratic processes.[80]

On 3 September 1999 the National Assembly amended Article 1 of the AA to the Constitution, replacing elections for future National Assemblies with a proportional appointment system.[81] The amendment also had the effect of extending the term of the Third National Assembly by two years, in order to synchronise the appointment of National Assembly representatives with elections for the Legislative Yuan. There were certain irregularities in the voting procedures adopted by the National Assembly.[82] Nevertheless, the amendment was passed in accordance with the amendment procedure set out in Article 174 of the Constitution (which requires, *inter alia*, a three-quarters majority vote) and promulgated by the president on 15 September 1999.

More than 100 members of the legislature then petitioned the Council of Grand Justices to overturn the amendment. The National Assembly disputed the justiciability of the issue, but the Council accepted the petition and ruled (Interpretation 499 of 2000) that the amendment was ineffective.

The decision is remarkable for the extensive procedural and substantive limitations it imposes on constitutional change.[83] First, the Council held that no amendment could take effect if the amendment process was 'clearly and grossly flawed' (*you mingxian zhongda xiaci*). The legitimacy of the constitutional state depended on 'rational communication' (*lixing goutong*) realised through open and transparent procedures.

Although the justices in their typically terse decision did not elaborate on what they meant by 'rational communication', this analysis suggests a link with procedural theories of legal legitimacy, and in particular Habermas' arguments on constitutional requirements flowing from communicative rationality.[84] Proceeding from this analysis, the Council identified many examples of clear and gross flaws in the amendment voting process.

Second, the Council found that the amendments violated substantive limitations on the power of the National Assembly to change the Constitution. The Council held that no organ of government could alter those provisions of the Constitution that ensured the existence of a liberal democratic political order (*ziyou minzhu xianzheng zhixu*).[85] Such provisions included those articles constituting the 'Republic of China' as a democratic republic,[86] vesting sovereignty in the entire populace,[87] stipulating fundamental rights and duties[88] and establishing the separation of powers and the system of checks and balances.[89]

The amendments violated these foundational principles. The appointment rather than election of National Assembly members violated the liberal democratic political order since the National Assembly was one of the constitutional bodies exercising political power on behalf of the people.[90] Further, the extension of terms violated the principle of representative democracy. The powers of National Assembly representatives were conferred on them by the electors in an implicit agreement, a key element of which was that at the end of their terms they would, except in an emergency situation,[91] be subject to re-election.[92]

The acceptance of the liberal democratic version of the rule of law among legal and political elites

The liberal democratic version of the rule of law articulated by the grand justices in Interpretation 499 is, at least on the surface, widely shared among Taiwan's legal and political circles. Competing versions of the rule of law, such as those contending in mainland China, are largely absent from the island.

Consider, first, legal academics. During the martial law period law professors were generally reluctant to question the state on rule of law practices. Although legal scholarship flourished under the Nationalists' rule on Taiwan,[93] this scholarship was largely concerned with civil and commercial law.[94] Quiescent in the shadow of the authoritarian regime, public law scholarship did not begin to reach a similar standard until the late 1970s.[95] This scholarship is now firmly based on liberal democratic premises. Contemporary constitutional and administrative law scholars, heavily influenced by German, Japanese and American theory, take for granted the appropriateness of the separation of powers, a multi-party democracy, constitutionally entrenched rights (with particular emphasis on liberty of the person, freedom of speech and association, and the right to vote) and sophisticated systems of judicial review. These assumptions first clearly emerged in the work of scholars who came to prominence in the final years of the martial law period, such as Li Hong-hsi,[96] Wu Geng[97] and Lin Ziyi.[98] This work continues with a younger generation of scholars who have analysed democratisation and the new judicial review. This group includes Yeh Jiunn-rong,[99] Tang De-chung,[100] Huang Jauyuan[101] and Chen Tsung-fu,[102] all of whom assume a liberal democratic state to be the appropriate form of government for Taiwan.[103]

The wider legal profession has also played a prominent role in advocating liberal democratic rule of law principles.[104] This is demonstrated most forcefully by the fact that the most prominent government figures are no longer from the military but lawyers. Indeed, both the president and vice-president are both former human rights advocates.

Further, liberal democratic rule of law ideals are apparently shared by Taiwan's three major political parties, although somewhat more equivocally.[105] The DPP grew out of the *Meilidao* (Formosa) activists who attacked authoritarian rule during the 1970s and 1980s. It is therefore hardly surprising that the party platform makes extensive reference to individual rights, multi-party democracy and the separation of powers.

The Nationalists in practice also promote Western-style liberal democracy. It is true that the Nationalist party charter adheres to Sun Yat-sen's Three Principles of the People,[106] with its emphasis on combining Western and Chinese institutions and its advocacy of strong and guiding government. Sun Yat-sen's thought, while not elaborated in a rigorous form, might be characterised as communitarian.[107] However, his works appear to have had very little influence on the Nationalists in recent years. Their implementation of democratic reforms in the 1980s and 1990s in fact constitutes a significant departure from Sun's vision in that those reforms brought Taiwan's constitutional arrangements much more in line with Western models.

The recently established third power in Taiwanese politics, the People First Party (*Qinmindang*), is committed to 'constitutional government', 'human rights' and 'judicial reform' but also to national security and greater police protection. It is not clear how the party would reconcile these, but this platform seems, on the surface at least, typical of conservative parties in liberal democratic societies.

It is also noteworthy that both the current DPP president and his KMT predecessor have explicitly rejected the communitarian 'Asian values' rhetoric of Singapore and Malaysia. In an interview with *Die Zeit* in November 2001, president Chen Shui-bian declared that democracy, freedom and human rights were 'universal values'[108] and that rulers who question them in the name of 'Asian values' were 'employing a ruse to keep power'.[109] President Lee Teng-hui at the end of his term welcomed the election of his DPP opponent as reflecting a 'clean break with Asian values'.[110]

We can see here an important factor in explaining the high level of enthusiasm among Taiwan's legal and political elites for liberal democracy; it can distinguish Taiwan from its 'Other' – the PRC.[111] In contrast to Singaporean and Malaysian leaders, concerned to differentiate themselves from Western nations, most Taiwanese leaders, especially the 'indigenous' Taiwanese (or '*benshengren*')[112] are keen to associate themselves with their Western allies, particularly the United States, and to emphasise the contrast with the 'communist' and authoritarian PRC. This enables them to delay reunification, and garner Western support for so doing. Thus, the 1991 Guidelines for National Reunification[113] state that 'China's unification should aim at promoting Chinese culture, safeguarding human dignity, guaranteeing fundamental human rights, and practicing democracy and the rule of law'.[114] More recently Dr Tsai Ying-wen, chairwoman of the Mainland Affairs Council, has stated that:

> If the Mainland Chinese Government can introduce democracy into its regimes, [and] the government's decisions are to be constrained by their governmental systems, as well as laws, and monitored by the people and the press…it would then be more comfortable for Taiwan and for the world at large to engage with China.[115]

The effects of rule of law discourse outside legal and political circles

The discussion so far has suggested that the elements of both the thin version of rule of law and the liberal democratic thick version are now well embedded in Taiwan's legal and political institutions. However, if we move from the abstract and generalised declarations of rule of law principles emanating from those institutions to a consideration of the practical operation of those principles as seen by the wider population, or to specific regulatory contexts, a more complex picture emerges. At these more concrete levels, the liberal democratic version of the rule of law no longer enjoys its discursive dominance.

Adherence to rule of law principles among the general populace

There is some evidence to suggest that 'thin' rule of law concepts have been broadly accepted in the Taiwanese community *when these concepts are presented at an abstract level*.[116] Taiwanese appear to be fairly comfortable with concepts of the binding effect of law and legal equality. Attitudinal surveys have shown more than 80 per cent agreement with the proposition that 'all members of society are equal'[117] and at least 60 per cent support for the proposition that 'all laws should be obeyed without exception'.[118] Over 70 per cent agreed that 'the law is the best protection against corruption'.[119] These results suggest that an obligation to obey the law has been largely internalised.

On the other hand, this adherence to abstract rule of law principles is heavily qualified by attitudes to the legal system in practice.[120] First, morality and reputation appear, at least in some circumstances, to be more important considerations than law in determining whether obligations should be enforced.[121] Second, there is significant resistance to the intrusion of law into family activities.[122]

Third, there appears to be a widespread reluctance to invoke the legal system. Thus, Chen Tsung-fu's analysis of litigation rates over the fifty years from 1949 to 1998 indicates, that, contrary to expectations that rapid economic development might have greatly increased use of the court system,[123] the ratio of cases to population has, since the beginning of the 1960s, shown only a slight to moderate rise.[124] Moreover, there has been a steady *increase* in the proportion of disputes taken to mediation outside the court system in preference to litigation.[125] Chen attributes this reluctance to use the courts both to considerable institutional obstacles to potential litigants and to a pervasive distrust of judges.[126] The institutional obstacles include the low number of judges, delays in concluding cases, high courts fees, the low quality of many judgments issued under the pressure of high caseloads, falling rates of effective enforcement, the small number of available lawyers, and high lawyer fees.[127] In relation to attitudes to the judiciary, surveys of public opinion suggest that only half of all Taiwanese believe that judges determine cases fairly.[128]

Turning to adhesion to 'thick' rule of law ideas, the general populace appears more lukewarm in its support for liberal democracy than the legal and political elites.

Democracy enjoys considerable, although not unqualified, backing; 75 per cent of respondents in a 1999 study indicated that democracy was important to them 'in their personal lives'.[129] Many Taiwanese involve themselves actively – and often passionately – in the democratic process. Participation rates of Taiwanese in national elections are high, even in comparison with mature liberal democracies; 82 per cent of eligible voters took part in the 2000 presidential elections and around 67 per cent in the 2001 legislative elections.[130]

However, a survey in 1998 found that 55 per cent of respondents believed it more important to develop the economy than to establish democracy, with only just over 30 per cent prioritising democracy,[131] and while there appears to be overwhelming support for public participation in public policy-making, this is tempered by a view among most Taiwanese that the primary input in policy-making should be from experts and officials.[132]

In any case, the Taiwanese are much less liberal than they are democratic. They appear to hold quite harsh social attitudes on some aspects of civil rights. Chen Tsung-fu points to continuities between severe punishments meted out to criminals in traditional China and contemporary views on sentencing.[133] He cites data from the 1990s showing 69 per cent support for the death penalty (and 58 per cent approval of executions in public), a similar level of support for the enactment of special laws to punish specific crimes,[134] and (in a later survey) 52 per cent support for tougher sentencing.[135] The extent to which this indicates the persistence of distinctly Chinese ideas is, however, unclear. Some of these illiberal results are replicated in Western countries, as the current popularity of 'tough on crime' political campaigns indicates. For example, equal support for the death penalty can be found in the United States,[136] and although the death penalty was abolished in Australia in 1975, around half of Australians are in favour of it.[137]

In sum, then, these (not entirely consistent) data suggest that, while Taiwanese show in principle support for the liberal democratic rule of law – or at least democratic rule of law – many of them do not seem to believe that the legal system delivers it; nor do they accept many of its implications for individual rights.

Rule of law discourse in specific regulatory contexts

The circumscribed power of liberal democratic rule of law rhetoric outside legal and political elites is also evident in specific regulatory fields. Even in Western societies, legislators, judges and law enforcers are often likely to fail in their endeavours to regulate particular social systems[138] (the state bureaucracy, the market, the family and so on) as they intend.[139] These systems often fail to acknowledge law's claims of its binding force or internalise its values of formal equality and consistency.

In Taiwan, the discrepancies between law and other social systems are greater than in the West. First, unlike most Western states, Taiwan does not have a rich experience in devising processes and agencies to implement law effectively in a liberal democratic context.

Second, Taiwan's laws, while to some extent adapted by drafters to local conditions, are essentially transplants – based on foreign models. Where law is transplanted from one country to another, the interaction between different social systems is disturbed,[140] and predicted regulatory effects may not eventuate. This is particularly so where there are very significant political, economic and cultural differences, as there are between Western and East Asian societies. Taiwan's move toward a liberal democratic legal and political order, its mature market economy and the exposure of most of the population to Western ideas through the island's effective public education system and diverse media mean that the discrepancy between its major social systems and those in the 'donor' countries has been significantly reduced. Nevertheless, differences persist, particularly where remnants of authoritarian or traditional mindsets remain.

Identifying law's impact in a specific legal context requires an exploration of the frames of references (including goals and distinct modes of reasoning) of those actors (including governmental agencies, commercial entities and 'civil society' groups) involved in the implementation of the relevant laws.[141] These frames of reference do not necessarily accommodate a liberal democratic view of law's role. Thus a regulatory agency may continue to adopt an authoritarian approach to administering the law, at least until subject to judicial review. Even then, an adverse judicial ruling may fail substantially to alter such an approach.

Two examples

The failure of liberal democratic rule of law principles to embed themselves strongly across all aspects of Taiwanese law can be illustrated by considering the implementation of law relating to work and the environment.

The law of work

Although based on Western models (derived largely from German law and from international labour conventions), the Taiwanese law of work has operated quite unlike its counterparts in Western countries.[142] This was unsurprising under the martial law period, when the formal legal norms governing employment and industrial relations were ignored and/or displaced by coercive executive instruments.

More interesting is the fact that after the emergence of a strong liberal democratic rule discourse in Taiwan many relevant labour law norms continue to lack traction. This is despite the express declaration by the Council of Grand Justices that the constitution protects fundamental labour rights[143] and the transfer of political power to a party with a historically strong commitment to human rights, including labour rights. Provisions of the Labour Standards Law requiring employers to provide employees with written contracts and unpaid maternity leave are violated by the majority of employers.[144] Most new union federations have been formed in violation of the Trade Union Law.[145] The legal mechanism for conciliating and arbitrating *collective* interest disputes was used only once between 1990 and 2002.[146] On the other hand, other provisions of the Labour Standards Law concerning the payment of overtime and annual leave are generally observed.[147] And the parties to employment contracts seem increasingly willing to bring their *individual* disputes before legal and administrative authorities (and especially labour mediation committees). The number of officially notified disputes rose fivefold between 1992 and 2002, to more than 10,000.[148]

This survey suggests that it is not possible to generalise about the impact of law of work. In some areas, laws are complied with and legal institutions are active; in others the law is irrelevant to many or most actors. It is not possible to say for certain why this variation occurs without a detailed examination of how law is perceived from, say, the point of view of 'rational actors' that treat legal norms as costs, social movements that view the bureaucracy as hostile, employees who persistently devalue women's work and so on. A further illuminating part of the examination would consider the 'bureaucratic culture' within administrative systems. Administrative agencies charged with communicating and implementing the law often continue to evince an authoritarian corporatist culture which favours – frequently ineffective – hierarchical bureaucratic enforcement over, for example, persuasion or the encouragement of decentralised party self-regulation.[149]

Environmental law

The Taiwanese environment has suffered greatly over the past half-century.[150] For example, the initial Nationalist policy of using Taiwan as a military base to retake the mainland diverted resources from essential sewage and transportation works. Land in water conservation areas was given to veterans of the Civil War.[151] Rapid industrialisation resulted in the pollution of coasts and rivers through the inappropriate use of dyes for the textile industry and chemicals for reprocessing scrap metal.[152] Under martial law conditions, there was little the population could do to prevent this.[153] As far as the law was concerned, the legislative framework for environmental protection was vague and weak,[154] the courts did little to challenge state action initiating or tolerating damage to the environment and there was no provision for public consultation in state decision-making on environmental matters.[155]

This situation has changed. Political liberalisation has subjected the state to much greater public, media and (as we have seen) judicial scrutiny. The importance of environmental protection is now recognised in the Constitution.[156] The legislative and Executive Yuans have produced a range of new regulatory instruments, based largely on American and Japanese models.[157] Some of these significantly improve agency accountability. The Environmental Impact Assessment Act of 1994, for instance, introduces requirements of transparency and public participation into many aspects of environmental decision-making.[158] Other new instruments diversify the regulatory measures which can be employed.[159]

However, while these measures have greatly increased state protection of the environment and improved agency accountability, it is not clear whether they will be able to overcome pervasive problems in the administration of environmental law. The administration is used to enjoying broad discretionary powers to make rules and implement them with little objection from the Administrative Court.[160]

Whatever the future direction of the environment bureaucracy, a technocratic 'command and control' culture involving selective enforcement of regulations[161] has hitherto prevailed.[162]

Professor Yeh Jiunn-rong[163] provides an illustration of the dysfunctional results produced by this bureaucratic approach, with a case study of the 'Four North Taoyuan Townships' incident.[164] Residents in the coastal townships alleged that the discharge of sulphur dioxide from a government-operated power plant had contributed to the withering of their rice fields and the surrounding trees which acted as a windbreak against salt-laden sea breezes. Reflecting typical reluctance to litigate on environmental issues,[165] the residents turned to the government rather than the courts for a remedy. When no assistance was forthcoming, they organised street protests and blockaded the plant.

The government bureaucracy, including the Environmental Protection Administration (EPA), responded by conducting thirteen scientific investigations, the last of which found that the plant emissions could have contributed to the loss but that it was not possible to determine the extent of the contribution.[166] The EPA then commissioned a further study.

Meanwhile, other government ministries oscillated between threatening criminal sanctions against the protesters and offering compromise payments. The EPA head refused to agree to any payment until 'scientific proof' of damage was established. Eventually, however, the further study was abandoned and a 'pay-off' agreed by the Economics Ministry, on the basis that it was 'assistance' and would 'not constitute a precedent'.[167]

Professor Yeh notes that this case follows an oft-repeated script. In particular, the environmental bureaucracy is caught between conflicting standpoints: a technocratic insistence that it not act except on the basis of 'scientific proof' (which, as in this case, is often impossible to attain within reasonable cost and time constraints) and a political imperative to respond quickly to social unrest.[168]

From the perspective of 'administration according to law' and the thin version of the rule of law more generally, this case is deeply problematic. As far as response of the administration was concerned, there does not seem to be any *clear* violation of the 'precedence of statutes principle' or the 'reservation of statutory powers' principle (although the language in the authorising statute is extremely loose).[169] However, the handling of environmental issues in this way is inconsistent with the (thin) rule of law. The decision-making was, from a legal point of view, arbitrary; the resolution had little or no reference to the basic objectives of the relevant legislation. It was unreasonable: the EPA's insistence on firm scientific proof was unreal in the circumstances.[170] The decision-making failed to follow a clear and predictable process. The respective responsibilities of administrative agencies were blurred, and the case fails to set any precedent that can be consistently applied in the future.

Now it may be replied that this is the very kind of situation that the most recent reforms to Taiwan's administrative law framework will be able to remedy.[171] Perhaps if it is combined with a much more sophisticated legislative framework[172] environmental decision-making might come to conform with these rule of law norms. Nevertheless, unless such reforms induce a fundamental reorientation of the bureaucratic frame of reference – something which even highly complex Western regulatory reforms have often failed to achieve – administrative agencies will continue to interpret their legal mandates in accordance with their own technocratic traditions.

Conclusion

There appears to be significant agreement about the meaning and importance of the rule of law in Taiwanese legal and political circles. At a general level, rule of law discourse, and specifically liberal democratic rule of law discourse, is now readily invoked. This means that the state feels generally bound by legal norms. It also means that Taiwanese can challenge adverse administrative decisions in the courts, that they can change their government through orderly electoral processes and that they can protect their civil and political rights from state violation.

However, despite the fact that the institutions asserting liberal democratic rule of law principles seek to ensure their application across different regulatory fields, general rule of law discourse has limited capacity to influence social interactions at the specific levels of public administration and private transactions. In this sense, then, the rule of law is context-sensitive. In many areas, legal norms do not always 'rule' bureaucratic implementation; nor do legal processes enjoy the complete confidence of the population. Laws, while usually having some discernible impact, are misread and reworked as they encounter different frames of reference and modes of reasoning. Thus, an account of rule of law discourse in legal and political institutions provides only a starting point for more specific, complex and intriguing enquiries about the relationship between law and other social systems in Taiwan.

Notes

1 I would like to thank Professors Wang Tay-sheng and Chen Tsung-fu for their assistance with this chapter. All mistakes, however, are mine.
2 The meanings attributed to the expression 'rule of law' are of course numerous. For present purposes, I will simply adopt Peerenboom's analysis and in particular the distinction between 'thin' and 'thick' versions of the rule of law.
3 The ROC Constitution was adopted on 25 December 1946 by the Nationalist 'National Assembly', was promulgated on 1 January 1947 and entered into force on 25 December 1947.
4 For a discussion of this period, see Tay-sheng Wang, *Legal Reform in Taiwan under Japanese Colonial Rule, 1895–1945: The Reception of Western Law* (Seattle: Washington University Press, 2000) (hereafter Wang 2000).
5 The 'Temporary Provisions Effective During the Period of the Suppression of the Communist Rebellion' were passed by the National Assembly in April 1948.
6 See, e.g.,Jau-yuan Hwang, 'Constitutional Change and Political Transition in Taiwan since 1986 – The Role of Legal Institutions', unpublished doctoral thesis(Harvard University, 1995).
7 Tsung-fu Chen, 'The Rule of Law in Taiwan: Culture, Ideology and Social Change', unpublished conference paper (The Mansfield Dialogue in Taiwan: 'Rule of Law and Its Acceptance in Asia', National Taiwan University, Taipei, September 2000) (hereafter Chen 2000a) . A shorter version of this paper has been published as Tsung-fu Chen, 'The Rule of Law in Taiwan', in Mansfield Centre for Pacific Affairs, *The Rule of Law: Perspectives from the Pacific Rim* (Washington: Mansfield Centre for Pacific Affairs, 2000) (hereafter Chen 2000b). Chen maintains that '[Chiang's] Rule of Law was nothing more than a government run according to the law, rather than a government governed by law'.
8 Despite constitutional restrictions on the application of military tribunals to civilians: Constitution of the Republic of China, arts 8 and 9.
9 Hwang, pp. 19–21.
10 See Council of Grand Justices Interpretation 31 of 1954. Note that a selection of the Grand Justices' interpretations (including this one) have been translated into English and are available at http://www.judicial.gov.tw/j4e/.
11 At that time the National Assembly, the Legislative Yuan and the Control Yuan.

12 This situation prompted the moniker 'the 10,000-year parliament' (*wannian guohui*) for the National Assembly. Note, however, that elections had, in the later martial law period, been held for casual vacancies and for supplementary positions in the National Assembly and the other representative bodies.

13 Most recently in April 2000.

14 Until 1991 the Nationalists claimed that the Republic of China was *the* legitimate government of China.

15 See, e.g., Tay-sheng Wang, 'The Impact of Modern Western Law on the Chinese in Taiwan', 1 *Australian Journal of Asian Law*, vol. 1 (1999) (hereafter Wang 1999), pp. 194, 205–6.

16 ROC Constitution, art. 25. This is based on Sun's division between 'political' and 'administrative' power (according to Sun, administrative power oddly encompasses legislative power): see Yat-sen Sun, *The Three Principles of the People* (Taipei: Government Information Office, 1990), pp. 130–49. Sun's key writings take the form of largely unreferenced public lectures and his understanding of Western democracy is confused on several points, such as in relation to the concepts of 'political' and 'administrative' power. These confusions, manifested in the problematic relationship between the National Assembly and the legislature, derive in part from Sun's incorporation of Soviet governmental elements: see Jau-Yuan Hwang and Jiunn-rong Yeh, 'Taiwan', in Cheryl Saunders and Graham Hassall, eds, *Asia–Pacific Constitutional Yearbook* (Carlton, Australia: Centre for Comparative Constitutional Studies, University of Melbourne, 1997), pp. 292–4; and Winston Hsiao, 'The Development of Human Rights in the Republic of China on Taiwan: Ramifications of Recent Democratic Reforms and Problems of Enforcement', *Pacific Rim Law and Policy Journal* 5 (1995), pp. 166–203, at p. 167.

17 AA, art. 1.

18 AA, arts 3–7.

19 AA, art. 2.

20 Interpretation 520 of 2001. The Council found, by majority, that the Executive Yuan's decision was not unconstitutional or unlawful because the relevant law was a 'budgetary' rather than a 'statutory' law and therefore conferred upon the executive discretionary power to alter the project. However, this matter was of such national importance that it should not have been dealt with by the executive alone. The executive should have advised the legislature of its intention to cancel prior to taking its decision. Its decision was therefore flawed. The legislature was also partly to blame because it had refused to allow the premier to address it. The Council instructed the premier to seek the legislature's approval for the cancellation a second time. If this was not forthcoming, there were various possibilities, including a vote of non-confidence against the premier in the legislature followed by the dissolution of the legislature and new legislative elections. In the event, work on the project was resumed.

21 The DPP, together with its allies in the Taiwan Solidarity Union, fell just short of a majority. The two main opposition parties, the Nationalists and the People First Party, are able, in combination, to control the legislature, although the DPP has attempted to persuade some opposition members to defect, or at least to 'cross the floor' and vote with them on certain issues.

22 Wang 1999, pp. 207–10. For more extensive account of Taiwanese legal history by Tay-sheng Wang, the pre-eminent historian of Taiwanese law, see: Wang 2000; Tay-sheng Wang, *Taiwan Falushi de Jianli* [The Foundation of Taiwanese Legal History] (Taipei: National Taiwan University Law Series, 1997) (hereafter 1997); Tay-sheng Wang, 'The Legal Development of Taiwan in the 20th Century:

Toward a Liberal and Democratic Country', *Pacific Rim Law and Policy Journal*, vol. 11

23 2002) (hereafter Wang 2002). Wang 2002, pp. 548–50, 554–5. Wang comments that for the KMT authorities arriving in 1945 'the most valuable legacy of the Japanese was that the native Taiwanese were law-abiding', at p. 550.

24 Wang 1999, p. 203. There was, for example, no colonial legislature. Wang 2002, p. 543.

25 Excluding 'political' crimes.

26 Wang 2002, pp. 212–13. The Taiwanese legal system provides separate legal institutions for hearing civil and criminal matters on the one hand and constitutional and administrative matters on the other. The highest civil court is the *Zuigao Fayuan* or Supreme Court. A concise, although out-of-date, English-language overview of the Taiwanese legal system is provided by Hungdah Chiu and Jyh-pin Fa, 'Taiwan's Legal System and Legal Profession', in Mitchell Silk, *Taiwan Trade and Investment Law* (Hong Kong: Oxford University Press, 1994), pp. 28–31.

27 The Japanese Civil Code became applicable to Taiwan in 1923. Taiwan's current Civil Code was enacted on the Chinese mainland in 1929.

28 See, e.g., Yuan Chu 'The Realignment of Business–Government Relations and Regime Transition in Taiwan', in Andrew MacIntyre, ed., *Business and Government in Industrialising Asia* (Sydney: Allen & Unwin, 1994).

29 For an extensive analysis of the relationship between the legal system and the Nationalists' economic objectives, see Wei-ceng Chen, *Falü yu Jingji Qiji zhi Dizao* [Law and the Creation of the Economic Miracle]. Chen traces the aims and modes of the Nationalist government's intervention in Taiwan's economy from 1945 to 1997. Over this period, the commanding role the state played in Taiwan's economy gradually diminished, particularly after the late 1980s when democratisation, economic globalisation and the increasing power of capitalists in the legislature weakened the state's capacity to intervene. In a parallel development, the ability of law to constrain the state in economic matters increased. Whereas initially the Nationalists simply considered law as no more binding than any other policy tool, they came to see the constraining capacity of law as important for their own legitimacy and for encouraging economic development. However, again, it was not until the late 1980s that law constituted a major constraint on the state, and even in the 1990s the state sought to use the porous nature of much Taiwanese legislation to evade attempts to subject it to legal control.

30 Chen Tsung-fu writes of this time: 'There was no rule of law, but rather rule of the KMT party'. Chen 2000a, p. 10.

31 See Hwang, pp. 44–53.

32 See, e.g., Lawrence Liu, 'Judicial Review and the Emerging Constitutionalism: The Uneasy Case for the Republic of China on Taiwan', *American Journal of Comparative Law* 39 (1991), pp. 509–58; Jiunn-rong Yeh 'Cong Guojia Fazhan yu Xianfa Bianqian Tan Dafaguan de Shixian Jineng: 1949–1998' [A Discussion of the Interpretative Function of the Council of Grand Justices from the Point of View of National Development and Constitutional Change], *Taida Faxue Luncong* [Taiwan Law Journal] 28 (1998), pp. 21–37. A limited exception is Interpretation 166 of 1980, which found that administrative detention and compulsory labour without trial were unconstitutional. The Council indicated that the legislature should amend the relevant law so that such matters were brought before the courts. However, the Council did not expressly declare the existing law invalid or set a time limit for reform. In a case on similar provisions in 1990, the Council noted that Interpretation 166 had not been properly

complied with. It held that the relevant law would be invalid on 1 July 1991 unless it had been amended to comply with the Council's decisions. Interpretation 251 of 1990.

33 Jyh-pin Fa, 'Constitutional Developments in Taiwan: the Role of the Council of Grand Justices', *International and Comparative Law Quarterly* 40 (1991), pp. 198, 203.

34 Id., p. 203.

35 One reason for the weakness of Taiwan legal institutions under the authoritarian period was that judges enjoyed only limited independence from other state organs: see Wang (1997), pp. 356–9.

36 Grand Justice and former Professor of Administrative Law at National Taiwan University.

37 Geng Wu, 'The Principle of Administration According to Law in Practice: Past and Future [Yifa Xingzheng Yuanze de Shijian – Huigu yu Zhanwang] *Xin Shiji Zhiku Luntan* [New Century Knowledge Forum] 12 (2000), pp. 24–32 (hereafter Wu 2000).

38 Id., p. 25.

39 These doctrines are discussed more fully in Geng Wu, *Xingzhengfa zhi Lilun yu Shiyong* [The Theory and Practice of Administrative Law] (Taipei: Sanmin, 1993) (hereafter Wu 1993), at pp. 75–85.

40 Articles 116, 125, 170, 171 and 172 all give effect to the precedence of statute doctrine, by establishing a hierarchy of legal norms (constitution, statutes, then administrative ordinances and regional and local regulations); Article 23 gives partial effect to the reservation of statutory powers doctrine by specifying the conditions under which rights and freedoms can be restricted by statute.

41 See also Wu 1993, pp. 85–100.

42 Wu 2000, p. 26.

43 Administrative Court Judgment Number 56 of 1982, cited in Wu 2000, p. 26.

44 Id., at p. 27.

45 Id., at p. 28.

46 For example, many pertaining to labour law.

47 Wu 2000, pp. 29–31.

48 Interpretation 402 of 1996. See also Interpretations 390 of 1994 and 394 of 1995.

49 The Council usually defers its invalidation order for a specific time period (such as a year) to enable appropriate legal regulation to be drafted.

50 Interpretation 313 of 1993. See also, for example, Interpretations 402 of 1996 (administrative order empowering officers to suspend or revoke an insurance broker's licence invalid for lack of a clear statutory basis) and 454 of 1998 (regulations affecting the residency rights of certain citizens invalid). On the other hand, instruments which are simply technical in nature or detail matters set out in the empowering legislation will be valid: see, e.g., Interpretation 344 of 1994 (regulations specifying amount of crop not entitled to subsidy valid).

51 See, e.g., Interpretation 324 of 1993 (administrative measures requiring shipping container yard owners to deposit a bond with customs need statutory basis).

52 In 1999 the Administrative Court was reorganised into a first-instance and an appellate division.

53 See, for example, Interpretation 338 of 1994 (overturning Administrative Court judgments 414 of 1968 and 400 of 1970 denying administrative appeal rights to officials on classification matters); Interpretation 328 of 1995 (overturning Administrative Court judgment 6 of 1952 denying administrative appeal rights to student discharged from a public school).

54 Matters nearly doubled from 4,433 cases in 1992 to 8,599 in 1998. The number of cases before the first-instance tribunal in 2001 was 27,516 (although there

appeared to be a significant fall occurring in 2002). These statistics are available from the Judicial Yuan statistical website: http://www.judicial.gov.tw/hq/juds/.

55 See the case studies in Jiunn-rong Yeh, *Xingzhengfa Anli Fenxi yu Yanjiu Fangfa* [Case Study Analysis and Research Methodology in Administrative Law] (Taipei: San Min Publishing, 1999) (hereafter Yeh 1999).

56 For a discussion of the background to this law, see Jiunn-rong Yeh, 'Zhuanxing Shehui de Chengxu Lifa: Woguo Xingzheng Chengxu Fa Sheji yu Lifa Yingxiang Pinggu [Administrative Procedure Legislation in a Transforming Society: Legislative Drafting and Impact Analysis of the Administrative Procedure Law in Taiwan] in *Dangdai Gongfa Lilun* [Contemporary Public Law Theory], a collection edited by the Committee to Celebrate the Birthday of Professor Chiu-sheng Weng (Taipei: Yuedan Legal Series, 1993] (hereafter Yeh 1993). There have also been radical revisions of the Administrative Litigation Law (amended in 1998) and the Administrative Appeals Law (amended in 1998 and again in 2000).

57 Administrative Procedure Law, Chapter II.

58 Id., Chapter III.

59 Id., Chapter IV.

60 Id., Chapter VI.

61 The need for an Administrative Procedure Law has also flowed from several decisions of the Council of Grand Justices holding that administrative measures must respect due process requirements. See, e.g., Interpretation 384 of 1995 (administrative measures *inter alia* enabling persons to be defined as 'hoodlums' without reference to court procedures invalidated); Interpretation 488 of 1999 (administrative measure concerning scope of authority of government agent appointed to manage a private financial institution flawed because they failed to require agent to consider views of shareholders and members); and Interpretation 491 of 1999 (procedures adopted in relation to discharge of a government officer must specify clear grounds for discharge, must provide for determination by an unbiased internal committee, must enable the officer to present a case and to rebut, must require reasons to be given for any determination and must inform the officer of appeal rights).

62 Administrative Procedure Law, Chapter II, Part 2.

63 Id., Chapter II, Part 3.

64 The law distinguishes between 'administrative regulations' (*xingzheng mingling*) having general application as delegated legislation and 'administrative rules' (*xingzheng guize*), which have effect only upon the agency itself: Id., arts 150 and 159.

65 Id., arts 154–6.

66 Id., art. 157.

67 Id., art. 158.

68 Id., art. 5.

69 Id., art. 6.

70 Id., art. 7.

71 Id., art. 8. Article 32 requires administrators to avoid conflicts of interest.

72 Id., Chapter I, Part 7.

73 This impression is gained from a survey of the relevant agency websites.

74 Article 15 recognises the social and economic rights to work and to live (which is understood as, in part, the right to a minimum standard of living). These are probably not justiciable: see Ziyi Lin, *Quanli Fenli yu Xianzheng Fazhan* [The Separation of Powers and Constitutional Development of Constitutional Government] (Taipei: National Taiwan University Law Series, 1993), pp. 145–67. However, the right to work *is* justiciable insofar as it protects labour

rights such as the rights to organise, to bargain collectively and to engage in industrial action: see Interpretation 373 of 1995.

75 These decisions are discussed in more detail in Sean Cooney, 'A Community Changes: Taiwan's Council of Grand Justices and Liberal Democratic Reform', in Kanishka Jayasuriya, ed., *Law, Capitalism and Power in Asia* (London: Routledge, 1999); and Sean Cooney 'Taiwan's Emerging Liberal Democracy and the New Constitutional Review', in Veronica Taylor, ed., *Asian Laws Through Australian Eyes* (Sydney: Law Book Company, 1997).

76 See, e.g., Interpretation 384 of 1995 (police powers violated Article 8 provision requiring deprivation of liberty to be authorised by a judicial body); Interpretation 535 of 2001 (police regulations required amendment to ensure that searches are based on reasonable grounds, are proportional and respect privacy rights etc. and to provide remedies for abusive searches); contrast Interpretation 528 of 2001 (forced labour in certain circumstances not in violation of the Constitution).

77 Interpretation 380 of 1995 (freedom of teaching violated by government imposition of compulsory courses); Interpretation 450 of 1998 (government requirement that all universities establish an office of military training unconstitutional); contrast Interpretation 509 of 2001 (criminal sanctions for defamation do not violate freedom of speech).

78 Interpretation 373 of 1995 (freedom of association and right to work violated by restrictions on certain educational workers' right to organise); Interpretation 445 of 1998 (law prohibiting assemblies advocating communism or division of Chinese territory unconstitutional); Interpretation 479 of 1999 (government requirement that social organisations include their district in their name unconstitutional).

79 Interpretation 434 of 1997 (government ordered to repay premiums paid by government employees into public insurance funds).

80 I note in passing that if this is so it creates a significant legal impediment to reunification. On this issue generally, see Sean Cooney, 'Why Taiwan is not Hong Kong: A Review of the PRC's "One Country Two Systems" Model for Reunification with Taiwan', *Pacific Rim Law and Policy Journal* 6 (1997), pp. 497–548.

81 The National Assembly representatives were to be appointed in proportion to the percentage of the national vote obtained by political parties at the legislative elections immediately preceding their appointment.

82 For example, a secret ballot was taken rather than a public vote as required by the rules pertaining to National Assembly proceedings.

83 The Council drew, in particular, on German, Austrian, Italian, Turkish and, to a lesser extent, American constitutional jurisprudence.

84 On a proceduralist view, only the state, as a political system invested with decision-making power, can "act". But its action is legitimate only if the formal decision-making procedures within the constitutional state have a discursive character that preserves, under conditions of complexity, the democratic sources of legitimacy.

(Jürgen Habermas, Between Facts and Norms
(Cambridge: Polity Press, 1996), p. 135)

85 Interpretation 499 of 2000 (no page number available). An English translation of this Interpretation is available at http://www.judicial.gov.tw/j4e/doc/499.doc.

86 Art. 1.

87 Art. 2.

88 Part II.

89 This is set up by the Constitution as a whole.
90 See art. 25.
91 Such as the Civil War defeat at the heart of Interpretation 31.
92 On 25 April 2000, in response to the decision, the National Assembly voted to disband itself, after passing a new constitutional amendment which re-established the National Assembly as a directly elected but non-standing body.
93 Yong-qin Su, 'Taiwan de Shehui Bianqian yu Falüxue de Fazhan [Social Change in Taiwan and the Development of Legal Studies], *Dangdai Faxue Mingjia Lunwenji* [A Collection of Works by Leading Scholars in ContemporaryLegalStudies], pp. 562–8. An outstanding example is Professor Wang Tze-chien's series on the Civil Code.
94 Id.
95 Id, p. 571.
96 See, e.g., Hong-xi Li, *Xianfa Jianshi* [Constitutional Law Classroom] (Taipei, Yuedan Publishing, 1994), p. 37 (constitutional government requires the separation of powers and protection of individual rights.
97 See, e.g., Wu 1993 and Wu 2000.
98 See, e.g.., Lin.
99 See, e.g., Yeh 1993 and Yeh 1999.
100 See, e.g., Dennis Te-chung Tang, 'New Developments in Environmental Law and Policy in Taiwan, *Pacific Rim Law and Policy Journal* 6 (1997) (hereafter Tang 1997), pp. 245–304.
101 See, e.g., Hwang.
102 See, e.g., Chen 2000a and Chen 2000b.
103 The scholars referred to here have been or continue to be professors at National Taiwan University Law School, Taiwan's leading law school.
104 Jane Kaufman Winn, and T. C. Yeh, 'Advocating Democracy: The Role of Lawyers in Taiwan's Political Transformation', *Law and Social Inquiry* 20 (1995), pp. 561–99.
105 Party charters and platforms can be accessed through their websites: www.dpp.org.tw; www.kmt.org.tw; www.pfp.org.tw. For a more sceptical view than that expressed here, see Winn and Yeh..
106 See art. 1 of the Charter.
107 See note 16 above.
108 The extent to which Taiwan's embrace of liberal democratic human rights is truly universal is questionable. Shih Chih-yu suggests that human rights rhetoric during the 1990s was used by the KMT government (which came to be dominated by indigenous Taiwanese) to refashion the separate identity of Taiwan *vis-à-vis* the mainland. One aspect of this 'boundary creation' was that the human rights of Taiwanese citizens were to be asserted and protected, especially when allegedly violated by the PRC, whereas those of PRC citizens were neglected, especially when they were apparently violated by Taiwan: Chih-yu Shih, 'Human Rights as Identities: Difference and Discrimination in Taiwan's China Policy', in Peter Van Ness, ed., *Debating Human Rights: Critical Essays from the United States and Asia* (London: Routledge, 1999). The pivotal importance of Taiwanese identity politics to the DPP would suggest that they, too, may be tempted to be selective in their application of 'universal' rights.
109 'Taiwan a Beacon for Mainland Democracy', *Taiwan Headlines,* 9 November 2001.
110 'Lee's Legacy Will Live On', *Taipei Times,* 10 May 2000. These views might not be reflected throughout the contemporary KMT, particularly as Lee is seen by some as too close to the DPP, and has mentored a split within KMT ranks, leading to the formation of the Taiwan Solidarity Party.

111 Shih.
112 This term (literally 'people of this province', as opposed to the '*waishengren*', '
people from outside the province [i.e. mainlanders]') refers to Taiwanese whose
ancestors immigrated to the island well before the Nationalist 'mainlanders' in
1949.
113 Adopted by the Executive Yuan on 14 March 1991.
114 Id., Part III, principle 3.
115 Ying-wen Tsai, 'Taiwan's Democracy in Action', paper delivered at the
Conference on Democratic Consolidation, Peace and Security (Grand Hotel,
Taipei, 2 December 2001).
116 The discussion in this section draws extensively from the ideas of Pitman Potter,
'Doctrinal Norms and Popular Attitudes Concerning Civil Law Relationships
in Taiwan', *UCLA Pacific Basin Law Journal* 13 (1995), pp. 265–88; and from
Tsung-fu Chen, 'Fayuan Susong yu Shehui Fazhan' [Litigation and Social
Development], *Guojia Kexue Weiyuanhui Yanjiu Huikan* [NationalScience
Council Research Compilation], vol. 10, no. 4 (2000), pp. 435–502 (hereafter
Chen 2000c).
117 According to a survey conducted by Pitman Potter in cooperation with the
National Taiwan University Psychology Department. Potter, above.
118 Id. A survey conducted by Academica Sinica, Taiwan's leading research institute, in July 1998 as part of the *Taiwan Diqu Shehui Bianqian Jiben Diaocha
Jihua* [Basic Survey Plan of the Social Change in the Taiwan Area] found that
75 per cent of respondents agreed that the law should be obeyed even if it was
unreasonable; less than 20 per cent disagreed. In a survey in the following year,
85 per cent of respondents stated that they believed obeying law was important
or very important. Note that data cited here have been rounded to whole
numbers.
119 Potter, p. 282.
120 It is not, of course, suggested here that the qualifications to rule of law adherence discussed here are peculiar to Taiwan, or East Asia.
121 Potter reports that while 20 per cent of respondents indicated that they would
repay a debt because of a legal duty, many more indicated that they would
repay debts on moral (48 per cent) or reputational (26 per cent) grounds. On the
other hand, only 11 per cent of respondents indicated that they would never sue
to recover a debt. Potter, pp. 282, 285.
122 In Potter's survey, 79 per cent of respondents stated that dishonest acts occurring within the family were more serious than those occurring outside, and 36
per cent stated that the family should remain beyond the scope of law. Id, p.
282. See also Li-Ju Lee, 'Law and Social Norms in a Changing Society: A Case
Study of Taiwanese Family Law', *Southern California Review of Law and
Women's Studies*, vol. 8 (1999), pp. 413–44. Lee identifies areas in which traditional social norms about gender roles, still persisting to some extent in Taiwan,
are incompatible with contemporary Taiwanese family law, which has been
substantially revised in recent years to reflect the formal equality of family
members. In some areas, social norms seem to prevail over legal norms. For
example, although provisions in the Civil Code have for over half a century
stipulated that sons and daughters should inherit equally, many families still
find ways to ensure that sons will inherit the bulk of family property (Id., at pp.
429–31).
123 There is a lively debate about the relationship between Taiwan's obvious
economic success and its legal system. Compare Jane K. Winn, 'Relational
Practices and the Marginalisation of Law: Informal Financial Practices of
Small Businesses in Taiwan', *Law and Society Review* 28(2) (1994), pp. 193–232

(arguing that many transactions are conducted outside the formal legal system), and Potter, above (economic growth may induce, rather than depend on, adherence to formal legal norms), with Tom Ginsburg, 'Does Law Matter for Economic Development? Evidence from East Asia', *Law and Society Review* 34 (2000), pp. 829–56 (suggesting that many informal transactions are dependent on the availability of sanctions through the formal legal system). See also Katharina Pistor and Philip Wellons, *The Role of Law and Legal Institutions in Asian Economic Development* (New York: Oxford University Press, 1999).

124 Chen 2000c. Thus, for the period 1959–63 there were around 35 cases for every 10,000 Taiwanese, whereas the proportion for 1989–93 was 36. However, in periods of economic recession the proportion of cases increased. Thus, in the early 1980s it rose to 38 and in the period 1994–98 to 47. Id., pp. 442–4. Chen found little difference between litigation rates in more 'modern' urbanised areas and more 'traditional' rural areas. Id, pp. 447–9. Note, however, the dramatic increase in the number of cases before the Administrative Courts, referred to above, at note 54.

125 In 1975, 82 per cent of cases were taken to court and only 18 per cent to mediation (which refers to mediation conducted through town and village mediation committees, labour mediation committees and court mediation). In 1997, the proportion was 50–50, with the long-term trend favouring mediation. Chen 2000c, pp. 449–59.

126 For Chen, distrust of judges is an aspect of 'legal culture'. As debates in relation to 'reluctant litigants' in Japan and other countries have shown, it is of course difficult to disentangle legal culture from institutional incentive effects. Compare the discussion of litigation and mediation practices in a small community in Michael Moser, *Law and Social Change in a Chinese Community: A Case Study from Rural Taiwan* (Dobbs Ferry, N.Y.: Oceana, 1982).

127 Chen 2000c, pp. 459–62. For an English discussion of these factors, see Chen 2000b, pp. 119–21. These obstacles exist to some extent in all legal systems, but the low number of lawyers and judges is a factor which distinguishes Taiwan (and Korea and Japan) from many other industrialised countries. Chen cites 1998 statistics indicating that there were fewer than 6 judges per 100,000 persons in 1998 and 14.6 lawyers. Only 5.6 per cent of applicants passed the bar examination in 1998. Most litigants are unrepresented, even in the higher courts and even in criminal matters. Id, at p. 120. By way of contrast, around one in every 750 Americans was a member of the American Bar Association and one in every 550 Australians was a member of the Law Council of Australia.

128 Chen cites a 1995 survey which found that only 40 per cent of Taiwanese believe that judges determine cases fairly; a 1999 survey showed that the proportion had risen to 55 per cent: Chen 2000c, p. 464.

129 Academica Sinica, above, survey carried out in July 1999.

130 Republic of China Central Election Commission data.

131 Academica Sinica, above, survey conducted July 1998. 40 per cent of the sample initially indicated that the economy was more important than democracy and 40 per cent indicated that the two were equal. When the later group were forced to choose, 63 per cent opted for the economy.

132 In Potter's survey, referred to above, 94 per cent disagreed with the proposition that law does not require input from ordinary people, but a majority of respondents (57 per cent) considered that law-making should receive primary input from experts and wise officials, compared to 43 per cent who thought that elected representatives should have primary input. Potter, p. 283.

133 Chen 2000a, p. 38.

134 Id., at pp. 38–9, citing Jiunn-rong Yeh, 'Minzhong de Falü Taidu' [The Public's Attitude towards Law], in National Science Council Research Report, *Taiwan Diqu Shehui Yixiang Diaocha* [The Social Image Survey: General Survey of Social Attitudes In Taiwan] (1991), p. 183.

135 Id., citing Chung-Wei Lee, *Guoren Fazhi Guannian Renzhi Chengdu Zhi Diaocha Yanjiu* [Investigation and Research on Citizen's Understanding of the Rule of Law Concepts] (2000), p. 73, figures 4–2–31, 4–2–32, 4–2–33.

136 Around two-thirds to three-quarters of Americans favour the death penalty: see the various polls collected at http://www.pollingreport.com/crime.htm.

137 The most recent opinion poll in Australia on the issue appears to be a Morgan Gallup Poll in June 1990 which found that a bare majority of Australians (51.4 per cent) were in favour of the death penalty; cited by Justice Michael Kirby, 'The Death Penalty: A Special Sign of Barbarity', unpublished paper presented to the Criminal Bar Association, Melbourne, 17 May 2001. The death penalty was abolished in Australia in 1975. Chen also refers to data suggesting a lack of support for freedom of speech and assembly. A 1985 survey found that 'almost 59 percent of respondents supported [restrictions] on freedom of speech for the sake of social stability, and 91 percent of them disagreed [with the proposition] that the people were entitled to assembly or parade without permission', cited in Yung-chin Su, *Fazhi Renzhi yu Taiwan Diqu de Zhengzhi Minzhuhua: Cong Renmin de Zhifa Xingwei Tantao* [The Cognition of Rule of Law and Political Democratization on Taiwan: A Discussion of Law Enforcement], p. 27, figure Q. 34 (1997); Chen 2000a, above. However, this data should be treated with caution. First, the survey was conducted before the end of martial law. Second, responses to questions about rights are likely to be heavily conditioned by the fact scenario presented to those surveyed. See, for example, the results of the 'State of the First Amendment Survey', conducted by the Center for Survey Research and Analysis at the University of Connecticut for the Freedom Forum First Amendment Center at Vanderbilt University (26 February–24 March 1999), available at http://www.pollingreport.com/civil.htm: 67 per cent of respondents disagreed with the proposition that 'the First Amendment goes too far in the rights it guarantees', but 80 per cent of respondents stated that people should not be allowed to burn or deface the American flag as a political statement.

138 This section is informed by contemporary systems theory, particularly the work of Gunther Teubner. Very briefly, according to this theory society is fragmented into discrete discursive social systems (such as law, party politics, moral and religious frameworks and markets). Many of these social systems are self-reproducing or 'autopoietic'. Thus, a person in 'economic mode' views a legal norm as imposing a cost or benefit, in 'ethical mode' as moral or immoral, and in 'legal mode' as, say, constitutional or unconstitutional or binding or nonbinding. There is no *direct* causality between many of these social systems, only 'interference'. Effective legal regulation of other social systems thus depends not on mere legal command (which may be ignored), but rather on context-specific alignment of ('reflexive') law to the particular configuration of social systems facing a regulator. See, e.g., Gunther Teubner, *Law as an Autopoietic System* (Oxford: Blackwell, 1993); Gunther Teubner, 'Juridification: Concepts, Aspects, Limits, Solutions', in Gunther Teubner, ed., *Juridification of Social Spheres: A Comparative Analysis in the Areas of Labor, Corporate, Antitrust, and Social Welfare Law* (Berlin: de Gruyter, 1987); Gunther Teubner, 'Substantive and Reflexive Elements in Modern Law', *Law and Society Review* 17 (1983), pp. 239–86. Compare Ian Ayres and John Braithwaite, *Responsive Regulation: Transcending the Deregulation Debate* (New York, Oxford

University Press, 1992). For a very helpful commentary, see Hugh Baxter, 'Autopoiesis and the "Relative Autonomy" of Law', *Cardozo Law Review* 19 (1998), pp. 1,987–2,090.

139 Questions about the operation – and especially application – of law in discrete contexts are a major concern of legal regulation theorists (of which Teubner is one). These theorists have, from different theoretical perspectives, pointed out the very wide gaps between law and practice in countries where the rule of law is commonly understood to have prevailed for very many years; see, for example, the articles collected in Robert Baldwin, Colin Scott and Christopher Hood, *A Reader on Regulation* (Oxford: Oxford University Press, 1998).

140 Gunther Teubner, 'Legal Irritants: Good Faith in British Law or How Unifying Law Ends Up in New Divergences', *Modern Law Review* 61 (1998), pp. 11–32.

141 For an example of such an investigation conducted from a systems-theoretical perspective, see John Paterson and Gunther Teubner, 'Changing Maps: Empirical Legal Autopoiesis', *Social and Legal Studies* 7 (1998), pp. 451–86.

142 See, generally, Huei-ling Wang with Sean Cooney, 'Taiwan's Labour Law: The End of State Corporatism?', in Sean Cooney, Tim Lindsey, Richard Mitchell and Ying Zhu, eds., *Law and Labour Market Regulation in East Asia* (Routledge: London, 2002). See also Sean Cooney, 'The New Taiwan and its Old Labour Law: Authoritarian Legislation in a Democratised Society', *Comparative Labor Law Journal* 18 (1996), pp. 1–61.

143 Interpretation 373 of 1995.

144 Wang with Cooney, pp. 206–7.

145 Id., at pp. 194–6.

146 Id., at p. 195.

147 Id., at pp. 206–7.

148 Id., at p. 210, n. 31. See statistics at Council of Labour Affairs http://www.cla.gov.tw/acdept/month/tab0305.xls.

149 Wang with Cooney, pp. 199, 205–6. Of course, this culture has its roots not merely in authoritarian practices associated with Japanese colonial rule and Nationalist martial law, but also in traditional Chinese approaches to government. Note also that labour statutes are still 'structurally coupled' with this culture in that they confer extensive discretion on the bureaucrats but provide few legal supports for workplace-based negotiation. It is, however, unclear to what extent amendment of the law would substantially change bureaucratic culture.

150 Jiunn-rong Yeh, 'Institutional Capacity-Building Towards Sustainable Development: Taiwan's Environmental Protection in the Climate of Economic Development and Political Liberalization', *Duke Journal of Comparative and International Law* 6 (1996) (hereafter Yeh 1996), pp. 229–72. See also Lester Ross, Mitchell Silk and Jiunn-rong Yeh, 'The Environmental Dimension of Trade and Investment in Taiwan', in Mitchell Silk, ed., *Taiwan Trade and Investment Law* (Hong Kong: Oxford University Press, 1994), pp. 622–4.

151 Yeh 1996, pp. 249–52.

152 Id., at p. 253.

153 Id., at p. 254–5. Social movements and the media were of course suppressed and/or controlled during the martial law ara so that the government could minimise agitation on environmental issues. As the legislature was not subject to election, there was little possibility of achieving environmental protection through political means.

154 Laws were passed in the mid-1970s pertaining to air and water pollution and waste disposal. The Bureau of Environmental Protection was not established

until 1982. The present Environmental Protection Administration was established in 1987. See Ross *et al.*, pp. 624–6.
155 Tang 1997.
156 Article 10 of the Additional Articles provides that:Environmental and ecological protection shall be given equal consideration with economic and technological development.
This amendment was inserted into the Additional Articles by Second Revision in May 1992.
157 See Tang 1997; and Ross *et al.*, pp. 624–33.
158 Available in English at http://www.epa.gov.tw/english/LAWS/ eiaact2.htm. This law, similar to equivalents in other jurisdictions, requires environmental impact assessments to be conducted for most development projects and submitted for review to the Environmental Protection Administration. Where significant adverse effects on the environment are likely, the law requires, *inter alia*, that development proposals be publicised and that the views of local residents, non-governmental organisations, experts and scholars be taken into account in the Administration's review of the project. The Administration is empowered to prevent a project proceeding. For a critique of this law, see Tang 1997, pp. 257–63; See also Yeh 1996, pp. 260–1.
159 See, e.g., the Settlement Law for Public Nuisance Disputes and Jiunn-rong Yeh, 'Falu yu Shili zhijian: Huanjing Baohu Xieyishu zai Taiwan de Fazhan [In Between Law and Power: The Development of Environmental Protection Agreements in Taiwan], in Jiunn-Rong Yeh, *Huanjing Lixing yu Zhidu Jueze* [Environmental Rationality and Institutional Choice] (Taipei: Editorial Board of the National Taiwan University Law Series, 1997) (hereafter Yeh 1997a).
160 Tang 1997, p. 281.
161 For example, well-established and politically sensitive industries such as fishing have been lightly regulated, while 'greenfields' projects attract closer scrutiny.
162 Dennis Te-Chung Tang, 'The Environmental Laws and Policies of Taiwan: A Comparative Law Perspective', *Pacific Rim Law & Policy Journal* 3 (1993), pp. s-89–s-132, at pp. 113–18; and Tang 1997, pp. 247, 280.
163 Professor at the National Taiwan University. Professor Yeh is one of Taiwan's leading constitutional and administrative law scholars. His work gives particular emphasis to environmental regulation.
164 Jiunn-rong Yeh, 'Beitao Sixiang Gonghai Qiucheng Shijian zhi Yanjiu: Cong Kexue Misi yu Zhengzhi Yunzuo zhong Jianli Falu de Chengxu Lixing' [A Study of the Four North Taiyuan Townships Demand for Compensation for Public Nuisance: Constructing Procedural Rationality in Law Amid Scientific Myths and Politics], in Jiunn-Rong Yeh, *Huanjing Lixing yu Zhidu Jueze* [Environmental Rationality and Institutional Choice] (Taipei: Editorial Board of the National Taiwan University Law Series, 1997) (hereafter Yeh 1997b).
165 Id, at p. 217.
166 Under the Clean Air Act, the EPA has wide discretionary powers to investigate allegations of air pollution, and to seek remedies for persons affected. See, e.g., art. 52: Victims of air pollution may request the Responsible Agency at the local government level to verify the cause of the air pollution damage; the local Responsible Agency shall, in conjunction with other relevant agencies, conduct investigations, order those emitting pollutants to make immediate improvements and request that appropriate compensation be awarded to the air pollution victims. After conclusion of an agreement with respect to the compensation mentioned in the preceding Section, the victims may directly file a petition with a court for enforcement if the polluter refuses to honor the agreement.

The EPA can also order a factory to cease discharging dangerous pollutants; art. 8.
167 It is not clear whether the payment was actually made.
168 Yeh 1997b, pp. 221–6.
169 See note 151, above.
170 Article 1 of the Air Pollution Act provides: 'The purpose of this Act is to prevent and control air pollution, safeguard public health and the living environment and improve the quality of life.'
171 This incident took place in the early 1990s, well before the passage of the Administrative Procedure Law and before the change of administrative personnel following the DPP's electoral success.
172 Indeed Yeh makes specific suggestions for legal reform: he argues that a more sophisticated legal framework which facilitated compromises through transparent procedures might assist in resolving such disputes. Yeh 1997b, p. 230.

15

RULE OF LAW IN JAPAN

John O. Haley and Veronica Taylor

Abstract

Japan today is a postindustrial economy with a mature legal system. In this chapter we trace the evolution of rule of law in Japan by focusing on judges and the courts. We begin with Japan's borrowing of legal institutions from China in the mediaeval period and then discuss the 19th-century use of the German concept of the *Rechtsstaat* by Meiji state-builders and the "reception" of European law and development of indigenous modern legal institutions in the interwar years. Following the Second World War an Anglo-American version of rule of law was introduced through the 1947 constitutional framework, ushering in decades of constitutional rights discourse and a new means of negotiating the relationship between state, individual and community. During the postwar high-growth era, until the economic downturn beginning in 1989, the conventional wisdom was that Japan had to some degree molded its law and legal institutions to the demands of economic growth. In the late 1990s, however, a new "justice system reform" discourse emerged and began to crystallize a set of wide-reaching policy reforms, including dramatic overhauls of the court system, the legal profession, and legal education. It remains to be seen whether Japan's "justice system reform" process is simply a continuation of earlier systemic reforms, or whether it marks a transition to a new set of debates about the parameters of law in Japan.

At each point in this history Japanese legal debates and institutions reference Chinese, European, and American counterparts, but do not mimic them. Significantly, Japan becomes the first Asian post-developmental state to face economic stagnation and Japanese elites respond by revisiting key legal institutional arrangements. We argue in this chapter that "rule of law" is a construct defined by the political and economic character of a particular state. In Japan, "rule of law" has resurfaced in legal discourse precisely because the system may be at a major institutional turning point. Rule of law as conceived by Peerenboom (Chapter 1) – both the "thick" and "thin" versions – is visible and vibrant in Japan. Multiple definitions of rule of law are well understood and deeply internalized by elite political and legal actors and are not at issue in the new "justice system reform" process. Whether the institutional forms of rule of law will dramatically alter as a result of the reform process in Japan, however, is an open question.

Rule of law and Japanese adaptations

Introduction

While economists condemn the stalled Japanese economy and a lack of political will to tackle structural reforms, many lawyers – both Japanese and foreign – claim that Japan is experiencing historic, convulsive and comprehensive legal change. Is law in Japan in the midst of the greatest upheaval since the postwar occupation? So it seems. Legal reforms that only a few years ago were dismissed out of hand as politically impossible are, if not already enacted, now thought to be inevitable.[1]

The list of key legal changes is significant: the 1993 Administrative Procedure Law;[2] the 1994 election law reforms;[3] the 1994 Products Liability Law;[4] the complete rewrite of the 1996 Code of Civil Procedure;[5] a new Freedom of Information Law;[6] major amendments of Japan's antitrust law,[7] additional foreign investment and trade reforms,[8] as well as new crime laws targeting bid-rigging and racketeering.[9] In the commercial law sphere the 1997 and 1998 banking and capital market reforms designed to produce Japan's "big bang" were highly significant,[10] while the 2001 and 2002 reforms to the Commercial Code fundamentally alter the form of corporate governance for large corporations operating in Japan.[11] Significantly, too, we see a new regulatory impetus in the 1990s, with new statutes in both the environmental[12] and consumer protection fields.[13] Other equally profound changes, including overhaul of Japan's system of legal education and judicial selection are underway within a wide-ranging process of "justice system reform" (*shihōkaikaku*).[14]

The bureaucracy – linchpin of Japan's "developmental state" – has not escaped reform.[15] New legislation consolidates and changes the names of some of Japan's principal ministries and administrative organs.[16] The famous acronym MITI (Ministry of International Trade and Industry) is now METI – a new Ministry of Economy, Trade and Industry. Government officials have been made subject to anti-bribery regulations. The hitherto powerful Ministry of Finance (*Ōkurasho*) was stripped of its jurisdiction over the banking and insurance industry and has become the *Zaimusho*. The nature and effect of these legal changes are vigorously debated.[17] Even as co-authors of this chapter, we have slightly different views about what they might represent. The catalysts for much of this reform, however, are not in doubt.

Japan was the first of Asia's economies to face post-development stagnation and the need for structural reform. Economic and political changes since the "bubble" economy burst in 1989 have been incremental and widely criticized outside Japan.[18] At home, public dissatisfaction with the government and with the hitherto enduring institutional features of postwar Japan has deepened. The targets of public criticism include "self-regulating" corporations, the bureaucratic elite, and a legal system that seems to some to be tilted toward the interests of business, industry and government rather than toward the needs of Japan's citizens.[19] Legal institutions are presented in the new justice system reform agenda as being partially the cause of Japan's social and economic malaise (for example lack of attorneys, resulting in poor access to justice; a remote and potentially unjust criminal justice system; sluggish court procedures; and a legal profession unable to service the corporate sector effectively due to lack of competitive skill in emerging areas of global regulation such as intellectual property and competition law). Paradoxically, though, legal institutions are also imagined to be a policy: they become the "linchpin" of Japan's economic structural reform.[20]

This chapter argues that "rule of law" in Japan, whether conceived of as a singular construct or separated into the "thick" and "thin" versions favored by Peerenboom,[21] are visible and vibrant in contemporary Japan. They have been internalized by political and legal elites and absorbed into conventional political and legal theory.[22] However, as in most mature legal systems, rule of law in Japan is frequently honored in the breach and those shortcomings are vigorously critiqued and debated domestically and internationally. It seems to us unhelpful to attempt to label or to "measure" Japanese "rule of law" by reference to American or European discourses, given that these are themselves products of particular historical periods and political and economic agendas.

Our approach in this chapter is to sample some of the thinking about rule of law in Japan – and ways in which this changes – with reference to courts and the judiciary from the seventh century to the 21st.[23] Of course a "court-centric" account of Japanese legal history may immediately prompt the criticism that this is an artificial story that ignores fundamental law and society insights about the dangers of reifying courts and formal processes of adjudication.[24] In the world of Japanese law, too,[25] this approach risks revisiting a profound and prolonged debate about the independence of the Japanese judiciary.[26] We confess and try to avoid these difficulties. Our justification for narrowing the focus is that it makes meaningful comparison with other legal systems somewhat easier and that the Anglo-American use of rule of law accords great importance to the role of the courts and questions of judicial independence. Moreover, these are also irreducible elements in many of the cross-system indicators of "rule of law" used by international financial institutions such as the International Monetary Fund (IMF) and the World Bank for the purposes of assessing economic development.[27]

Rule of law and institutional design in Japan

Conventional (or, if you prefer, "thin") notions of the rule of law in Japan, as elsewhere, encompass two separate but closely related ideas. The first is the requirement that governmental authority and its exercise have a basis in law. This is what the Germans understood in the late 19th century as the *Rechtsstaat*, the requirement of legality for governmental action. The second is a notion of law as a set of justiciable principles and rules equally binding on those who make and enforce them. Essentially an Anglo-American idea, this version of rule of law presupposes an independent judiciary with sufficient authority and power to ensure its efficacy. Thus the civilian and common law variants of rule of law are different. But, under both notions, the rule by and of law enables more predictable and less arbitrary exercises of governmental power. Japan invokes elements of both the *Rechtsstaat* and Anglo-American rule of law in the design and culture of its legal institutions and procedures. While rule of law of course remains an imagined ideal, Japan has been distinguished by its fidelity to both the formal ideal and its implementation in practice.

Japan's adaptation of Chinese legal concepts

Japan implemented rule *by* law from as early as the seventh century. By the 16th century, it had become one of the most densely governed societies in the world. By the end of the 19th century it was able to defend itself against the territorial ambitions of more powerful mercantile nations by voluntarily adopting modern European laws, institutions and processes.[28]

Japan's institutional history begins with the reception of T'ang Chinese political and legal institutions that culminated in the Taika reforms in the mid seventh century. Law was only one of many features of Imperial China's more advanced civilization introduced into Japan during this formative period. From China Japan received Buddhism, a new religion that would have profound influence on values and modes of thought. The imperial legal code of the newly established T'ang dynasty (A.D. 619–906), which itself reflected in both form and substance nearly a millennium of legal history, was adapted as Japan's first written law code. Chinese law thus provided a mode of legal ordering by which the ensuing *ritsuryō* age became known – compound characters denoting law as a combination of criminal penalties (*ritsu*) and administrative proscriptions (*ryō*). Within a relatively short period of time Japan replicated most of the institutional and cultural features of the neighboring Chinese imperium. In 662 a set of administrative instructions (*ryō*) was promulgated, followed by the introduction of a series of penal statutes (*ritsu*). The first known integrated "code" came in 702 with the promulgation of the *Taihō ritsuryō*, revised by what is now known as the *Yōrō ritsuryō* in 718. The rulers of the new Japan did not, however, slavishly borrow or fully implement Chinese forms and practice. The constraints of Imperial China's conception of a mandate of heaven as the basis of legitimate imperial rule had no place in Japan. Instead, a creation narrative ascribing the ancestry of a hegemonic clan chieftain newly transformed as

449

"emperor" (*tennō*) provided enduring legitimacy for a hereditary ruler. Nor was a Chinese-style examination system implemented to replace kinship and inheritance as the basis for access to political office and influence. As a consequence, Japan never fully established a system of centralized, administrative rule. Those with kinship ties to the imperial family, as well as local magnates whose influence and hold on power could not be displaced, continued to hold or gained sufficient control over local resources at the expense of the center. The expansion of large tax-exempt rice-producing estates (*shōen*) denied revenues and resources to the center and thereby contributed to the waning of imperial rule and public order. In the resulting disorder, a warrior class had emerged by the end of the 11th century. Yet, albeit continuously narrowed in jurisdictional application, the *ritsuryō* survived in form and as a foundational feature of warrior rule.

Warrior governance in Japan was not fully developed until the establishment, under Minamoto Yoritomo, of the Kamakura shogunate or *bakufu* (lit. "tent government") in A.D. 1185. As shogun (supreme military commander) he was granted an imperial mandate with the authority to appoint warriors to newly created offices in each province to exercise police functions (*shugo*) and tax-collecting and judicial functions (*jitō*) at the expense of the imperially appointed governors. A system of dual jurisdiction emerged, with adjudication by the Kamakura authorities of disputes involving conflicting claims among warrior rulers and adjudication of other disputes conducted under the auspices of imperial *ritsuryō* rule.

Procedurally, adjudication in medieval Japan was more rational and advanced than in Western Europe at that time. Adjudication was essentially an administrative process. Although the procedures followed were quite sophisticated, ineffective enforcement and delay were chronic problems. In terms of substantive law, the lack in the Chinese tradition (in contrast to Roman law) of a general conception of private law – or of contracts, property, and torts as legal categories – constrained the development of formal private law. The most important legislation of the period was a list of precedents (*shikimoku*) promulgated for warrior officials to apply in adjudicatory proceedings. As a result of these developments the practice of rule by law had become firmly implanted as a basic feature in Japanese governance.

The new breed of warlords that emerged from the carnage of the Onin war (1467–77) justified their rule by might; unlike their *shugo* predecessors, they had no title or other formal claim to authority. With the dawn of the 16th century imperial rule had reached it nadir. Warrior rule from the center had become hardly more than a formality. Japan was divided into over a hundred territorial kingdom-like domains. Each was controlled by a virtually independent warlord who proceeded to consolidate control over followers and peasantry alike by requiring their warrior retainers to live within the shadow and supervision of a newly constructed castle that each had begun to build in one of the more strategic locations of the domain.

These new *daimyo* began to legislate as territorial sovereigns, using law-making as both a means of control and a source of legitimacy.

During the 16th century a process of reconsolidating at the center began under Oda Nobunaga, the first of three unifiers. Through alliances and successful military campaigns, Nobunaga was able to establish control over one-third of Japan by the time of his assassination in 1582. Military unification was completed under his deputy and successor in arms, Toyotomi Hideyoshi. Within a decade of Nobunaga's death, Hideyoshi had successfully brought all of the military houses ruling Japan under his control. He completed the process that had begun at the local level, establishing a rigid system of hereditary status, disarming the peasantry and removing all warriors to the castle towns of their respective *daimyo*. He instituted a cadastral survey and established the framework for local government. And he assumed direct administrative supervision over Japan's major cities, foreign trade and final judicial authority.

Hideyoshi died in 1598, and in the struggle over succession Tokugawa Ieyasu emerged victor. Perfecting the patterns of federated rule and administration of his predecessor, Ieyasu and his heirs maintained a system of governance that provided Japan with two and a half centuries of order and peace. Under Tokugawa rule, patterns of law and governance that had been evolving for most of the century became even more deeply embedded. Both rural and urban areas were subject to extensive administrative regulation. All persons were registered with Buddhist temples by village or city ward. Free movement of persons, as well as alienation of land, was restricted. Nevertheless, for the vast majority of Japanese, direct contact with their warrior rulers was quite limited. A warrior officialdom emerged, with adjudicative magistrates (*daikan*) as the principal administrative officials, but they remained in urban centers. Japan's villages were largely self-governing. For each village a headman was administratively appointed. So long as taxes were paid and peace maintained, however, the villages were generally left alone. As a strategy for autonomy, villagers complied ostensibly in form, but not necessarily in substance, with the demands of their rulers. The result was the paradigm of a largely self-governing community maintaining a significant degree of collective autonomy by fostering consensus and order within.

The mechanisms of administrative adjudication expanded. Although officials attempted to relegate private disputes to consensual solutions, people continued to assert claims – especially in transactions related to land and commercial dealings – that resulted in well-defined categories of lawsuits. In the process a corpus of embryonic private law emerged.

By the end of the Tokugawa period in the early 19th century we see in Japan a legal system that is comparable in many respects to those of European states of the period. In the criminal and administrative spheres, the law comprises well-defined rules that are recorded in writing, communicated to a highly literate population, applied in adjudicated cases and intended to be universal in application within defined social classes. Indigenous private and commercial law exists primarily in the "parallel universe" of the village or town, or within merchant institutions. Official ideology and system design discouraging private legal actions give way over time to demands for justiciability of private and commercial disputes. In Japan's political transition from the 19th to the 20th century, law becomes a central organizing concept, as the Meiji reformers legitimate their rule through legal processes and use the development of a modern, European-style legal system to reposition Japan as an economic and military peer with England, the United States, France, Prussia (later Germany), and Russia.

The modernizing legal impulse

Tokugawa rule ended with the Meiji Restoration in 1867. After flirting briefly with a return to Chinese legal models, Japan's new leaders opted in the early 1870s to begin a process of transforming reforms based on Western law. In 1889 the emperor, at the behest of political reformers, promulgated the Constitution of the Empire of Japan, as a gift by the sovereign to his subjects. The Meiji Constitution became the fundamental law of the modern Japanese state, expressing principles that were to guide the emperor's conduct and to which, he declared in the preamble, he, his descendants and his subjects were "forever to conform." In a concomitant imperial oath the emperor then swore to his ancestors "never at this time or in the future to fail to be an example to Our subjects in the observance of the Laws hereby established." Few monarchs have expressed so eloquently or so explicitly their allegiance to a rule of law.

The framers of the Meiji Constitution consciously adopted a modern, European version of rule of law for Japan, but grafted this to the pre-existing institutional and bureaucratic culture, one that was well versed in rule-oriented legitimacy and accountability. The Meiji Constitution explicitly created legislative and judicial oversight of the executive by introducing the basic principle of representative government that all statutes required consent of the legislature (art. 37). It further provided that no administrative regulation or imperial ordinance could alter any statutory rule (art.9), that all crimes and punishments had to be determined by statute (art. 23), and that the fundamental rights of subjects, although not absolute, could only be restricted by statute.

By the time the era of modern legal reform ended in 1907, the year of enactment of the last of the basic codes – the Criminal Code – strict adherence to legal rules had become an ingrained feature of Japanese governance.

The period of "reception" of these new constitutional principles and the procedural changes that followed resulted in the flowering of interwar democracy, marked by political pluralism and the rise of organized labor. This was cut short as Japan began to militarize in the 1930s. However, even during the peak of wartime repression in the late 1930s and early 1940s – a period synonymous with secret police, widespread censorship, limits on freedom of speech, and harassment of organized labor and left-wing political activists – Japanese officials, including judges and lawyers, operated under the law and displayed extraordinarily care in complying with the applicable legal rules.

After 1945 the influence of the United States as the dominant force during the Occupation (1945–52) produced a hybrid of European and American approaches. The legacy is especially notable in constitutional, regulatory, and commercial law. The legal reforms of this period were, for the most part, carried out by a combination of Occupation and Japanese reformers under the rubric of "democratizing" Japan, and were intended to reinforce adherence to the rule of law, now redefined to emphasize American notions of judicial protection and enforcement of more absolute constitutional protections.[29]

Japan's Constitution, which came into force in 1947, was adopted under the Allied Occupation as an amendment to the Meiji Constitution, although significantly changing the role of the emperor and the design of the parliament and introducing universal suffrage and a Bill of Rights. The 1947 Constitution describes the emperor of Japan as the "symbol" of the nation and expressly grants the emperor responsibility for the exercise of functions performed by most heads of state. It provides for a bicameral parliament, the Diet (*kokkai*), with a politically accountable cabinet of ministers headed by a prime minister. The composition of the two houses of the Diet, the ministries and the electoral system is determined by a separate statute.[30] Members of the House of Representatives and House of Councilors are elected through a mix of proportional representation, party vote, single-seat constituencies and multi-member districts. In practice the Diet has, for most of the postwar period, been controlled by the Liberal Democratic Party ruling alone or in coalition.

Legal institutional design: the courts

Unlike its Meiji predecessor, the 1947 Constitution of Japan clearly contemplates a court system charged with oversight of the executive branch of government. The Constitution provides for a Supreme Court (*saikōsaibansho*) and such inferior courts as may be established by statute (art. 76(1)). Pursuant to this provision the 1947 Court Organization Law establishes four categories of courts below the Supreme Court: eight high courts (*kōtōsaibansho*) as the primary courts of first appeal, 50 district courts (*chihō saibansho*), and 50 family courts (*katei saibansho*), each with 203 branches as the primary courts of first instance, and 438 summary courts (*kan'i saibansho*) for relatively small claims and minor offenses. Like many civil law systems, an automatic right of appeal to have the case heard

453

de novo applied, and until the changes to the Code of Civil Procedure in 1996 subsequent appeals to the Supreme Court on questions of law were routinely allowed, resulting in a case overload at that level. All courts have the right to pronounce on questions of legality and constitutionality. The 1996 procedural reforms also alter the unified court structure somewhat by creating small-claims procedure in courts of first instance and creating specialized divisions for, for example, intellectual property and insolvency matters in certain district courts to speed proceedings and encourage judicial specialization.

Japanese implementation of constitutional guarantees

In Japan, as elsewhere, a common critique of law is the gap between stated statutory rights or implicit procedural protections and their implementation. The Constitution contains a long list of political, economic, and social rights. The list begins with a broad explicit guarantee of all fundamental human rights as "eternal and inviolate rights" (art. 11), subject, however, to an equally broad caveat that the exercise of such rights shall not be abused and are subject to the public welfare (art. 12). The enumerated rights include a guarantee of equality under the law and the prohibition of political, social, and economic discrimination based on ancestry, family, gender, social status, or occupation (art. 14); fundamental political rights (art. 15 and 16); a right to compensation for tortious acts of government officials (art. 17); prohibition against involuntary servitude (art. 18); freedom of thought and conscience (art. 19); freedom of religion and prohibition of state involvement in religion (art. 20); freedom of assembly, association, speech, the press, and other forms of expression (art. 21); freedom of occupation (art. 22); guarantee of academic freedom (art. 23); guarantee of gender equality (art. 24); a right to a minimum standard of living (art. 25); a right to equal education (art. 26); a right and duty to work (art. 27); a right of workers to organize and to bargain collectively (art. 28); guarantee of property rights (art. 29); due process rights in criminal proceedings (art. 31); a right of access to the courts (art. 32); and elementary criminal process rights (arts. 33–40).

Constitutional guarantees are taken seriously in Japan; there is a vast body of writing – both scholarly and popular – on the Constitution, on emerging rights, and on the implementation or otherwise of human rights in Japan.[31] Constitutional litigation is not uncommon.[32] However, some scholars discern a pattern in which cases that invoke constitutional rights or freedoms generate a more clear-cut response from the lower courts and a greater balancing of interests or tempering of the result at the Supreme Court level.[33] The cases in which this has been most controversial (and most widely recognized outside Japan) are those concerning the renunciation of war and prohibition of military establishment clauses of Article 9 of the Constitution. Although a few lower-court decisions have held Japan's Self-

Defense Forces to be unconstitutional, the Supreme Court has consistently refused to uphold these decisions on the grounds that this is essentially a "political question" for the legislative branch of government.

By avoiding the question of constitutional support for self-defense and its more recent extension into peacekeeping, however, the court has not called into doubt its constitutionally explicit authority of judicial review. Indeed, the Article 9 cases stand out as exceptions to the general public and political acceptance of the role of the Supreme Court as the final arbiter of constitutional questions and the legality of actions by the state. Nor is the legal status of Article 9 static. There is continued debate abut whether the *Peacekeeping Operations Law*, for example, which authorizes the dispatch of troops and equipment overseas, can validly coexist with Article 9 in its current guise or whether an explicitly Constitutional amendment is required.[34] Fuelling both the pro- and anti-reform discourse is the fact that the postwar Constitution has never been amended, even though it contains an explicit mechanism for doing so.[35] In 2000 the Koizumi government appointed a Constitutional Study Group to explore the range of views on whether constitutional reform is desirable and/or viable.

Perhaps as a result of emphasis on the Supreme Court's treatment of the Article 9 cases, much conventional wisdom and academic commentary holds that the Japanese judiciary is relatively powerless, or that it has been bent to the political purposes of the government. This perception in turn has provoked studies that seek to show that judges and the courts play a relatively active role in the development of legal norms and the process of legal and social change in Japan. Such studies are important, because they remind us that many of the "rights" enjoyed by Japanese citizens and resident non-citizens are not fashioned from a constitutional discourse, but emerge incrementally from judicial expansion of categories in regulatory law and in private law.

The procuracy and problems of criminal law

As with many mature legal systems, we see also in Japan the subordination of constitutional guarantees in practice where full implementation might conflict with a prevailing systemic or cultural norm at the time. This is hardly a unique problem, but in Japan much of the public comment and critical scholarship focuses on criminal procedure. The constitutional right to due process (art. 31) has not fared well in a country that boasts a highly professionalized procuracy and police force, a 99 percent conviction rate, and a regularly administered death penalty. There is intense debate both within and outside Japan today about the future of Japan's criminal procedure – indeed, it occupies almost one-third of the "agenda" within justice system reform documents. The conventional "story" of Japanese criminal justice is that it is distinguished by its emphasis on meticulous prosecutorial investigation to determine guilt (an intersection of traditional practice and the French-derived prewar preliminary investigatory proceeding) and a restorative emphasis on the effective correction of offenders and their reintegration into society. The techniques vary from police and prosecutorial diversion of many cases away from formal adjudication to the judicial imposition of relatively light fines or suspension of sentences.[36] In this story, the full force of the law is reserved for serious crime and for recidivists. We see this played out in the very careful prosecution of members of the Aum Shin Rikyo cult for murders, assaults, and the sarin gas attack on the Tokyo subway system. We also see this in procedural accommodations such as high-quality court interpreting and explanatory videos created for the growing number of non-Japanese accused processed through Japanese courts.[37]

The apparent success of Japan's restorative approach comes with costs. The vicarious social stigma that attaches to an offender's family and community provides powerful incentives for extralegal social control as well as outward expressions of offender remorse. Moreover, as David Johnson's outstanding study shows, the reputations of police, procuracy, and judiciary are now at issue.[38] Longstanding critiques of Japanese-style criminal justice concern the 23-day holding rule that allows police to detain suspects without charge, without access to legal counsel, and without a videotaped record for up to 23 days, and a very heavy reliance by police and prosecutors on confessional evidence. As Johnson points out, the foundational assumptions of the system are challenged now by the changing demographic of crime in Japan (you cannot reintegrate foreigners whose are structurally marginalized), the public awareness of not infrequent errors in the system, and new episodes of corruption that threaten the prestige and trustworthiness of police and procuracy. A further factor identified by prosecutors themselves is that the notoriously difficult national bar examination, which credentials judges, attorneys, and prosecutors alike, has not served them well. The median age of Japanese prosecutors is now above 40 and the profession faces a manpower shortage. In Johnson's view, it is not at all clear that the "Japanese way of justice" will survive intact the criticisms of a populace disenchanted with the modus operandi of a highly professional but insular legal elite.[39]

Constraints on access to justice in Japan

Direct comparison of Japanese courts and judges with their American counterparts is understandable, given that judicial review was an important element introduced in the Occupation reforms to the Constitution and legal system. Yet Japan's courts and key legal professions – judges, prosecutors, and attorneys – are products of a pre-modern Japanese administrative state, an adopted German institutional culture and mindset, and an Anglo-

American overlay.[40] The latter seems destined to strengthen in the wake of the decision to transform legal education in Japan, starting in April 2004, from a European undergraduate model to a graduate model that primarily references the United States.

Nevertheless, German legal influence remains quite strong in several doctrinal areas in Japan. Prewar German theory on administrative acts, for example, underlies the requirements for direct judicial review of administrative dispositions. German legal theory is similarly robust in much of Japanese contract, criminal, and procedural jurisprudence. Even areas of law that have no ostensible German or European roots, such as Japanese competition law, are often interpreted or revised in light of European ideas and practice.[41] Even corporations law, which began by borrowing some key features of German law and then was regularly revised with an eye to U.S. developments, has not entirely converged to a U.S. model.[42] Consequently, despite the postwar influence of the United States in constitutional, regulatory and commercial law, the Japanese legal *mentalité* remains grounded in the civil law tradition but in practice is quite hybrid.

Part of Japan's civil law tradition is the centrality of codified law. In Japan, the Codes today are supplemented by a burgeoning body of special laws and case law. There is no dearth of litigation. The average Japanese judge is an unelected, career public servant, who each year disposes of more than double the number of cases of the average federal judge in the United States. Japanese judges do "make law" in a real sense – there is a long tradition of judicial law-making though gradual rereading of statutory provisions. Nevertheless, as a civil law jurisdiction Japan has no Scalia or Posner – the individual judicial iconoclast seeking to make law where none exists. Remedies, too, tend to be constrained – at present Japan has no jury and no punitive damages. On the other hand, the unitary nature of the court system results in fairly predictable outcomes in cases that go to a full reported decision.

Constraining the capacity of Japan's courts

Viewed from the outside, Japan's courts seem remarkably ordered. However, they also suffer from institutional factors (or designed constraints) that limit their accessibility.[43] Haley suggests that one of the defining features of the postwar legal system in Japan is the weakness of law enforcement and the concomitant tendency to rely on the didactic effect of legal rules and a variety of extralegal, informal, and community mechanisms for their enforcement.

A telling characteristic of the court system in Japan is its limited capacity. All branches of the legal profession remain very small from the perspective of comparable legal systems, such as Germany, for example. Japan has less than one-tenth as many judges and as many prosecutors,[44] despite recent decisions to significantly increase the number of legal trainees for the bench, the procuracy, and the bar. Until recently Japanese *bengoshi* had an exclusive right to appear in court, although this is gradually being eroded by professional competitors such as patent attorneys (*benrishi*).[45] One consequence is that the proportion of unrepresented cases in summary courts is relatively high.

Similarly, costs have been used to systemically discourage litigation. When fees have been reduced – as in the filing fees for shareholder derivative suits against corporations – there has been a notable increase in litigation in these areas of the law. As Eiji Takahashi and Joachim Rudo note in their comparative study of abuse of shareholder rights in Germany and Japan, only one derivative action was brought in the 40 years between 1950 and 1990. In contrast, at least 174 suits were filed in 1995 alone.[46] Such gains are quite small, however, in comparison to the broader landscape of private law enforcement. The absence of private litigation insurance, the scope of attorney fees (and attorney availability),[47] and the absence of contingency fees are also notable features of Japanese civil litigation design, although they are not unique to Japan.

In regulatory disputes, such as administrative cases challenging government actions or in environmental suits, standing required a "directly affected" interest, which limited participation by third parties. Class actions of the kind familiar in the U.S. do not exist.

Neither recent substantive nor procedural law reforms have done much to alter pre-existing constraints on civil remedies or the problems of proof. The enforcement of private law rules is still discouraged by low awards that result in part from the prevailing emphasis on compensation as the exclusive aim of damages, ignoring completely any consideration of deterrence as an additional function. Problems of proof, especially continuing restrictions on discovery, also continue to diminish the usefulness of private damage actions as a means of private law enforcement. The question of delay is a more difficult one because aggregated figures for the duration of civil litigation in Japan are not vastly different from those for other industrialized countries. What is different, of course, is the system of discontinuous hearings and, until the recent introduction of a small-claims procedure, the inability to receive a swift resolution following oral argument or documentary submissions. An automatic right of appeal also has the effect of prolonging litigation in many cases, particularly when exercised by an unsuccessful defendant.

Reforms to civil procedure do not address the problems of enforcement of public law rules. The focus of administrative law reforms since the early 1990s has been the introduction of greater procedural controls to enhance the transparency of the administrative process. From an American viewpoint, critics may well fault the timidity of the drafters of the 1993 Administrative Procedure Law and the more recent Freedom of Information Law.[48] Yet, from European perspectives, the Japanese have progressed quite far in the American direction. Japan does not enjoy either the extensive array of civil enforcement mechanisms taken for granted by American agencies or the special administrative sanctions enjoyed by most European agencies. Moreover, unlike most civil law jurisdictions Japan still has no adequate substitute for contempt.

Still, however, no one in Japan has seriously addressed the weakness of administrative law enforcement. As a result, public law rules remain formally enforced almost exclusively through the criminal process. Discretion over prosecution rests exclusively with the procuracy. No agency can ensure prosecution. This fact alone makes reliance on criminal sanctions for the enforcement of administrative rules especially burdensome. With fewer than 2,300 prosecutors, the vast majority of administrative offenses cannot possibly be prosecuted. Only those considered significant by the procuracy and its parent agency, the Ministry of Justice, are likely to be enforced with regularity and dispatch. For example, only a handful of prosecutions have ever been brought for corporate fraud, insider trading, or violations of foreign exchange or foreign trade controls. The result was widespread flouting of the law. Japan's antitrust experience prior to the mid-1990s was similar. No criminal antitrust actions were brought for over two decades from the mid-1950s through the mid-1970s. And even though in recent years a series of bid-rigging cases have been prosecuted,[49] the number of criminal antitrust actions remains very small.[50]

Courts as venues of protest

These institutional and cultural constraints have not deterred claimants from actively using the courts in Japan, both in regular cases and as a forum in which to stage political protests – often resulting in remedial action by government in the form of compensation schemes or new statutes.[51] Well-established patterns of "protest" litigation have progressively legitimated new types of claim and groups of claimants. Since the early 1990s alone we see the a wave of claims by forced laborers from the Second World War; claims from "comfort women" forced into military prostitution during the Second World War; claims against the Japanese government by people with HIV infected through contaminated blood products; mass torts claims against corporations and their government supervisors; administrative actions by local communities protesting national or regional development projects; and shareholder derivative suits against large public corporations.

Constitutional rights in Japan are ostensibly framed as individual rights. Group rights are not contemplated in the Constitution, although recent case law reopens the question of rights for ethnic minorities who were subsumed within the boundaries of the modern Japanese state during the Meiji period. Illustrative examples are the administrative challenge by an indigenous Ainu community in Hokkaido to the construction of a dam in a place of cultural and religious significance[52] and the (largely symbolic) threats by the

Governor of Okinawa Prefecture (until the 19th century the separate kingdom of the Ryukyus) to discontinue leasing public land in the prefectural capital, Naha, to the United States for use as military bases at the behest of the national government.

We also observe the courts used as a venue of last resort by those at the periphery of Japanese society. Upham's groundbreaking analysis of the *burakumin* protest movement and its legal accommodation is an early example of this.[53] Mainstream scholarly opinion accepts that constitutional guarantees apply equally to non-citizens. However, the neat bifurcation between ethnically Japanese "citizen" and non-Japanese "non-citizen" is now deeply complicated both by the permanent residence in Japan of Koreans and Chinese whose families, once colonial subjects, were stripped of Japanese nationality at the end of the Second World War, and by progressive waves of migrant laborers to Japan, primarily from Asia, who are destined to become long-term, if not permanent, residents. These tensions were highlighted in the baby Andrew case, where the Supreme Court found that the Ministry of Justice erred in its refusal to recognize the entitlement to Japanese nationality of a child born out of wedlock to a Filipina mother and a (presumed) Japanese father.[54]

A valid criticism of Japan's courts is that they have been relatively timid in the direct application of international law obligations contained in conventions ratified by Japan. Although the conventions of themselves could furnish a source of legal norms for Japanese judges,[55] the pattern seems to have been to wait until the principles are formally adopted into domestic legislation and then interpret and expand these gradually.[56]

Protest litigation and the use of courts by social "outsiders" implicates rule of law in at least two ways. First, it is clearly permitted in Japan and supported institutionally by attorneys (often in a *pro bono* role) and by the courts willing to hear the cases, albeit with a variety of results. Second, the claims themselves often emerge from a governmental failure to deliver on, or a corporate failure to honor, formal legal protections.

Many legal scholars in Japan tacitly accept that law reform in the postwar period was sequenced in a way that supported government economic priorities, large corporations and their bureaucratic advisors. Thus, for example, the statutory auditor (*kansayaku*) scheme of independent oversight of large corporations borrowed from German law was progressively "strengthened" from the 1950s onward, but with no real legislative belief that auditors would emerge as strong independent monitors. The Japan Fair Trade Commission did not (and was not resourced to) enforce the Antimonopoly Law vigorously until the mid-1990s.[57] Environmental regulation entered a hiatus after the antipollution suits and legislation of the 1970s but was revisited once multi-generational problems such as nuclear waste and dioxin emerged in the 1990s.[58] The Product Liability Law and Consumer Contracts Law followed the direction of EU

Directives, but lagged behind counterpart protections in other postindustrial systems. Similarly, the tolerance of administrative guidance and administrative decision-making without reasons is now constrained by the 1996 Administrative Procedure Law, but this too was the product of a brief window of opportunity provided by a (short-lived) non-Liberal Democratic Party (LDP) cabinet.[59]

The instrumental use of law and legal institutions and their selective non-use can be traced back to the pre-modern Japanese administrative state, and they echo the processes of Meiji reform and also government attempts to undercut civil litigation in the interwar period.[60] So, if indeed the postwar legal system in Japan privileged large corporations and favored informal rather than litigated outcomes for conflicts, this would be no anomaly.

Debate about the role of law in the course of Japan's economic development can be found in numerous places in Japanese legal scholarship. Tatsuo Inoue , for example, looks at the way in which the construction of Japanese "non-litigiousness" can be harnessed for the purposes of the "Asian values" debate – the consensus-oriented community versus the litigious individual. He draws attention to the way in which this juxtaposition obscures the functions and effects of formal public adjudication, including the protection it may provide against an opportunistic use of power in an informal setting. These themes, and the considerable ambivalence they arouse in Japanese academics, resurface in questions about the "Japanese model" for law and development purposes, as Japan enters the ranks of countries actively exporting technical legal assistance to transitional economies, primarily in Asia.[61]

A related and important discourse relates to how law has been used in Japan in pursuit of the "modern," in particular the privileging of formal, often bureaucratically mandated law over social norms that might (or should) inform law. Kyoto University legal scholar Takao Tanase, drawing in part on Teubner, has been particularly influential in articulating this tension from a sociology of law perspective.[62] Legal pluralism seems widely understood and accepted in Japan, both in the sense of there being identifiable remnants of customary law still existing and in the sense that this is a state in which parallel normative orders are both important and relied upon by the formal legal system. There is ongoing debate and considerable empirical research in Japan about the link between social and legal norms, and inquiry into how communities formulate informal and formal rules (some of which may be adopted or ratified within the formal legal system) and how people design private and commercial dealings to fall outside the reach of formal law.

Indeed, the Japanese experience also reminds us that law is never the sole basis for governance and legitimate rule. Nor are legal rules ever as fully binding in fact on those who make and enforce them as on those who have no control over either their creation or enforcement. In Japan, as elsewhere, this forces us to consider parallel legal regimes,[63] both formal and informal, and the differential impact of formal law on people and organizations with different statuses.[64]

Private claims, community concerns

The interplay between formal legal institutions and social norms can be seen in cases that reflecting a distinctively communitarian orientation. By "communitarian" we mean something other than the American political formulation of the term or the way in which it is used by neo-Confucian technocrats in, say, Singapore or Korea.[65] Terao points out, for example, that the ideographs for "public" and "private" in Japan are, respectively, the characters for "administrator/administration" and "private (individual)." She goes on to argue that there is no linguistic – or indeed legal – formulation of "public" in the sense of "public interest" or "public benefit" as it is used in English to denote the accrual of a benefit to "we, the non-state actors."[66] Her argument gains some strength if we consider that the use of "public comment" in regulatory agency documents and in legislation – particularly in the environmental field – is a late 1990s phenomenon and "public comment" is actually rendered in *katakana* (i.e. as a foreign loan word), denoting a newly coined word and legal concept.[67]

By "communitarian" we also mean something less than a universal norm. What we see in court decisions importing social norms is that these are applied in the particular case rather than articulated as an ideology. They may also change over time. So, for example, the no-fault divorce right created through changes to the Civil Code in 1947 was sternly rejected by the courts as being corrosive of public morality until formally accepted in 1987.[68] In the public law realm we see the celebrated constitutional case where, for example, the wishes of a widow concerning the religious form of memorialization of her husband were overridden by both the husband's family and a local military veteran's group.[69] Some recent surveys also show that since the early 1990s the Japanese have come to place even more emphasis on the nation and society rather than a fulfilling personal life.[70]

Scholars of private law have been attentive to the way in which judges discern and apply "community norms" in contract and tort. Tanase, for example, is highly critical of recent trends toward legal formalism in Japan, arguing that more weight needs to be given to norms arising from everyday interactions.[71] At the most abstract level, we see judges routinely making use of broad doctrines such as "good faith and public morals" and "abuse of rights" to balance claims according to perceived social standards.[72] At least until very recently, this balancing has not been articulated in terms of market transactions conducted by rational actors, or the need to promote market-based efficiencies.[73] Case decisions, however, show diverse outcomes.[74] Nottage argues that Japanese contract case law is less formalist than, say, its English or New Zealand counterparts, but more formalist than the substantive legal realism seen in many U.S. cases. In some cases we see a kind of European-style welfare liberalism pervading the decision. This is evident in Visser 'T Hooft's excellent study of how contract and antitrust law intersect in Japan in the realm of terminated distributorship contracts.[75] Japanese views on this, however, diverge. Kashiwagi suggests, for example, that Japanese judges are unacceptably interventionist in continuing transactions (e.g. franchises) and apply an equity-like concern for the "weaker party" which is at odds with commercial reality in many situations.[76] Uchida argues, by contrast, that the arm's length, atomistic contract that forms the conceptual starting point of new Japanese contract legislation (and perhaps the case law that it will give rise to) is at odds with what empirical studies show about the nature of relational business ties within the Japanese economy.[77]

Legal institutional design: judges

The question of whether judges in Japan are more or less interventionist in different kinds of cases and precisely what sets of norms they may reference in their decision-making begs the question "Who judges in Japan?"

The Supreme Court comprises 15 justices, 10 of whom by law must have served for not less than 10 years as a career judge or not less than 20 years as a judge, prosecutor, lawyer, or law professor, or combination thereof. In practice, the plurality of justices are career judges, nearly all of whom serve at the time of appointment as the president (*chōkan*) of a major high court (usually either Tokyo or Osaka, occasionally Fukuoka or Nagoya). Of the six career judges on the court in 2002, at the time of appointment two were serving as president of the Tokyo High Court; two, of the Osaka High Court; and two, of the Fukuoka High Court. Similarly, the two former prosecutors were chief high court prosecutors when appointed. Four lawyers are currently on the court, all of whom held prominent positions in their respective local bar associations as well as the Japan Federation of Bar Associations.[78] To date there have been only two female Supreme Court justices, Justice Takahashi and Justice Yokoo.[79]

The consistency in the pattern of appointment of Supreme Court judges belies any assertion that the justices are appointed on the basis of partisan political considerations. Party membership could hardly play a role in the appointment of career judges since by law they are not permitted to affiliate with any political party. Nor do Japanese judges or Supreme Court justices stand for election.[80] The process of judicial appointments to Japan's highest court instead reflects recommendations emanating from the Japanese legal establishment – senior judges, senior prosecutors, and the leaders of the organized bar. In this sense, it is meaningless to talk of "liberal" or "conservative" judges in the American sense of judges being identified with political parties, political platforms, or personal policy preferences. Rather, the justices reflect the intrinsic conservatism of Japan's bureaucratic elite – especially the senior judges who control the administration of the judiciary. For these judges, adherence to the rule of law – understood as the independence, professionalism, stability, and consistency of judicial decision-making – has long been a fundamental value.

The Supreme Court is subtly constrained by the career judiciary in other respects as well. First, the caseload is heavy. Assigned to the court is cadre of about 30 research judges (*chōsakan*) selected from the career judiciary to serve normally for three-year terms. Even working in three petty benches, each with five justices, the Court could hardly function without the assistance and consequent influence of the research judges. The Court's caseload is overwhelming, with over 4,000 new appeals filed each year. In 1996 reforms to the Code of Civil Procedure led to the abolition of the automatic appeal as of right to the Supreme Court in ordinary cases – the Court now exercises some choice over cases that will be accepted for decisions. Given this caseload, the influence of the research judges becomes especially great as the justices rely on them for advice and analysis of the issues and applicable precedents.

Compounding the caseload is the turnover. The mandatory retirement age for Supreme Court justices is 70, and nearly all justices have been at least 60 when appointed, with most the their mid-60s. Thus few justices ever spend more than eight or nine years on the Court. For example, all but two of the justices serving on the Court in 2003 had been appointed within the previous five years. The justice with the most seniority, Hiroshi Fukuda, had served for only eight years; the next longest-serving justice, Toshiro Kanatani, had served for only six. Five justices, one-third of the Court, were appointed in 2002. The reliance on career judges assigned to the Court as research judges contributes to the conservative cautious style in the Court's decisions. For all concerned to adhere to precedent and past practice, thereby reaching predictable outcomes, avoids the time, effort, and energy that a more active and less cautious approach would involve.

Finally, the size and structure of Japan's career judiciary further ensure a rarely matched degree of consistency with prior decisions and adherence to legal rules in adjudication. The number of judges is small – less than 3,000. They are reassigned and transferred to different courts nationwide at three-year intervals for most if not all of their careers. Young judges are literally apprenticed to older judges in the early phase of their careers, when they sit as part of a three-judge panel and craft joint judgments. A shared set of professional experiences inculcate what judges refer to as "the legal mind." In the words of one young judge, "[W]hen you find, through discussion, your opponent's legal theory superior and more persuasive than your own, you must accept it. This is true even though…it contradicts your own personal principle or political viewpoint." How better could the rule of law be expressed?

Japanese judges generally live together in apartment buildings that in effect form judicial compounds.[81] All hiring, assignments and promotions are determined by senior judges in the personnel office of the general secretariat in Tokyo, who carefully monitor the progress of individual judges. District, regional and national judicial conferences are held regularly, enabling judges to air solutions to common problems and set common standards that enable consistent outcomes among disparate courts.

The net effect of this institutional design is a public perception in Japan that judges are highly professional, but very distant. There is no sense in which a judge is expected to become part of a local community, or represent a distinct set of religious, political or social beliefs, or a particular constituency. This remoteness and some recent high-profile cases, such as the criminal prosecution of the Aum Shin Rikyo cult members, have piqued public interest in the identity of judges. We now see more "legal" and court-centered Japanese television dramas and more publishing about the courts and judges, for example.[82]

In the 21st century, then, Japan seems to embody a system design that imports all the attributes of rule of law – universal, widely promulgated laws, a legitimate government that submits to judicial review, a professionalized bureaucracy that can be checked through judicial oversight, and a judiciary that seems to be a paradigm of apolitical independence with strong internal controls on consistency of decision-making. At the substantive level, we see a fairly lengthy list of constitutional guarantees being gradually fleshed out in case law and a steadily growing body of specialized statutes that respond to social crises or emergent areas of entitlement. Although the shifting nature of "rule of law" makes accurate comparisons over time and space difficult, we suggest that Japan's trajectory of law and development in the 19th and 20th centuries includes a fairly full realization of the formal attributes of both the civil and common law versions of rule of law in the West.

The "justice system reform" process

If our account of how Japan embraces "rule of law" in its different guises is correct, what is it that causes a prominent legal commentator to declare that "Japan democratized after the war, but never really achieved rule of law....We have a chance to do so now"?[83] As the prime architect of the initial "justice system reform" agenda, Sato points up the need to improve and refine existing legal institutions, including the judiciary. The agenda itself is a varied one. It embraces increased numbers in the three major branches of the profession – attorneys, prosecutors, and judges – but is silent on the even larger number of legal paraprofessionals and in-house counsel. It enables radical reform to legal education by adding a graduate law school to exiting law faculties, but retains the national bar exam, albeit with an increased pass rate. It opens debate on the criminal justice system, canvassing lay assessors, reopening debate on juries, and recommending victim impact statements. Yet, however dramatic the "reform" process launched by the Obuchi Cabinet in 1998 appears, it is also the latest in a century of continuous reform projects.

Japan maintains a continuous debt to outside sources for internal innovation. Even during the Tokugawa Era, at the point of Japan's greatest isolation from external contacts, Japanese were learning everything they could from abroad, including foreign law, as exemplified by Ming law influence on the *Osadamegaki*.[84]

From the 19th century onward, the Japanese drafters examined every relevant legislative source in the United States and Europe. Advisory committees sent delegations to the United States and Europe to interview government officials, scholars, and others with expertise in the area of reform. Included on these committees or regularly consulted were Japanese scholars, generally expected as a matter of course to keep abreast of any significant legal developments abroad in their fields. Each of the 1990s legal reforms, from products liability to freedom of information, banking reform to legal education, reflects the influence of American and European experience.

The influence of foreign models does not mean that Japanese legislators function simply as data collectors and legislative conduits. Japan heeds but does not mimic foreign experience. Rather, the process is selective, adaptive, and, above all, political. Armed with examples from abroad, Japanese interests – bureaucratic, business, academic, and political – seek to craft reforms in ways that satisfy public welfare aims but are usually equally self-serving (or at least not self-defeating).

Tanase, however, reads this process very differently. In his English-language essay "The Emptiness of Japanese Modernization" and in his extensive scholarship on Japanese law and society, he highlights what he regards as a harmful conflation of legal institutional reform with "modernization,"[85] so that the formal, imposed structure becomes the "modern." Other commentators seem more optimistic, or at least see the reform process as a chance to carve out a space to agitate for the opening of the policy debate to the ordinary citizen.[86] This critique becomes more important when we consider the accelerated pace and scope of legal reform during the 1990s, particularly the institutions reforms contemplated by the "justice system reform" agenda.[87]

Japan today is a diverse, complex society with a sophisticated modern legal system. It resembles many other postindustrial nations in that its laws and legal institutions reveal the kind of internal contradictions and inconsistencies that typify politically plural, multicultural states.[88] What does seem somewhat different in the 21st century is that Japan is now a "transition economy," in the sense of being the first Asian post-developmental state facing economic stagnation and an uncertain future. Rule of law in the 19th or 20th century sense does not preoccupy Japanese elites today. Instead, "rule of law" is much more likely to be invoked as an umbrella term in broader debates about regulation or public policy that ameliorates social friction during economic downturn. So, as Linnan points out, the "justice system reform" agenda itself seems to borrow freely from concepts derived from the *Rechtsstaat* or civil law version or rule of law (such as concern with reframing the authority of bureaucrats) *and* to invoke Anglo-American rule of law debate staples (e.g. the debate about whether to (re)introduce the jury to Japan).[89] In response, some Japanese legal academics simply admit: "Yes, but we are not particularly interested in analyzing the contradictions. 'Rule of law' is just a loose term that allows everyone to take part in the debate."[90]

Some may argue that profound change is truly in the air and that we are witness, in fact, to a true transition of historical magnitude. They may be correct. The extent of recent reforms suggests that Japan is in the midst of an institutional transformation akin to the Meiji Restoration, the 1930s, or the immediate postwar period. Thus, the argument runs, the past decade of political and economic malaise, like the 1850s or the 1920s and the late 1940s, may indeed herald a new era on the horizon. Perhaps so, but in retrospect what again stand out are the elements of continuity rather than change and the seized-upon opportunity to make legislative or institutional reforms, often following a long gestation. As in past instances of major reform in the 1930s, 1940s, 1950s and 1970s, political upheaval and weakness provided the opportunity. From this perspective, very little may have changed. Or has it?

Notes

1 John O. Haley, "Japanese Law in Transition," paper presented at a conference, Change, Continuity and Context: Japanese Law in the Twenty-First Century, April 6–7 2001, University of Michigan, April 2001(unpublished), pp. 1.

2 *Gyōsei tetsuzuki hō* (Law No. 88, 1993), translated into English by Mark A. Levin in 25 *Law in Japan: An Annual* (1995). For an English-language analysis, see Lorenz Ködderitzsch, "Japan's New Administrative Procedure Act: Reasons for Its Enactment and Likely Implications," 24 *Law in Japan: An Annual* 105 (1994).

3 Surprisingly little has been written in English on the 1994 election law reform. In January 1994, after two decades of debate, in the first of a series of revisions the Diet amended the Public Office Election Law (*Kōshoku senkyo hō*, Law No. 100, 1950) (as amended by Law No. 2, 1994), replacing the former system of multi-member districts by one in which 300 winner-take-all single-member districts were combined with 200 (later reduced to 180) seats allocated by proportional representation from 11 regional blocks. The reform was challenged in a number of cases under various provisions of the Constitution but upheld in a trio of related *en banc* decisions handed down on November 10, 1999. See *Yamaguchi, et al., v. Tokyo Prefectural Election Commission*, 53 Minshū 1441 (Sup. Ct., G.B., November 10, 1999); *Okura, et. al, v. Central Election Administration*, 53 Minshū 1577 (Sup. Ct., G.B., November 10, 1999); *Koyama, et al., v. Tokyo Prefectural Election Commission*, 53 Minshū 1577 (Sup. Ct., G.B., November 10, 1999).

4 *Seizōbutsu sekinin hō* (Law No. 85, 1994). For translation and critical commentary, see Thomas Leo Madden, "An Explanation of Japan's Product Liability

Law," 5 *Pacific Rim Law & Policy Journal* 299 (1996), and Andrew Marcuse, "Why Japan's New Products Liability Law Isn't," 53 *Pacific Rim Law & Policy Journal* 365 (1994).

5 The new Code of Civil Procedure (*Minji soshō hō*, Law No. 109, 1996) is perhaps better described as a revision rather than a reform. The new Code was designed as a linguistic updating of the Code to make it more accessible to contemporary readers. The new version made few major substantive changes. Among these was to be a broadening of discovery. However, whatever the intended changes may have been, in light of the Supreme Court's decision in *K.K. Fuji Bank v. Maeda*, 53 Minshū 1787 (Sup. Ct., 2nd P.B., November 12, 1999), denying discovery of a bank memo evaluating a loan application as an "internal" memo under CCP article 220 (4)(c), suggests that the most significant pre-existing limits on discovery remain.

6 *Jōhō kōkai hō* [Public Disclosure of Information Act], Law No. 42 of 1999. For a detailed discussion of the statute and local government experience with similar disclosure requirements, see Lawrence Repeta, "Local Government Disclosure Systems in Japan," *NBR Executive Insight*, No. 16, October 1999.

7 See John O. Haley, *Antitrust in Germany and Japan: The First Fifty Years, 1947–1998* (Seattle: University of Washington Press, 2001), pp. 63, for a brief description of all amendments of the Antimonopoly Law (the Law concerning the Prohibition of Private Monopoly and Maintenance of Fair Trade) [*Shiteki dokusen no kinshi oyobi kōsei kakuho ni kansuru hōritsu*, Law No. 54, 1947] through 1999. The most significant of the recent amendments were the elimination of the international contract reporting and review requirement and the easing of the prohibition against holding companies.

8 For details on the results of U.S.–Japan bilateral trade negotiations, see United States Trade Representative, Reports on Japan <http://www.ustr.gov/pdf/2000—japan.pdf>.

9 E.g. *Bōryokudan taisaku hō* [Anti-Organized Crime Measures Act], Law No. 77 of 1991.

10 For a sample of comments and more provocative studies on various aspects of the financial reforms over the past decade, see Jessica C. Wiley, "Will the 'Bang' Mean 'Big' Changes to Japanese Financial Laws?" 22 *Hamline Journal of Public Law & Policy* 379 (1999); Hideki Kanda, "Securitization in Japan," 8 *Duke Journal of Comparative & International Law* 359 (1998); Ernest T. Patrikis, 24 *Brooklyn Journal of International Law* 577 (1998); Note (Brian Arthur Pomper), 28 *Cornell International Law Journal* 525 (1995); Colin P. A. Jones, "Japanese Banking Reform: A Legal Analysis of Recent Developments," 3 *Duke Journal of Comparative & International Law* 387 (1993); Curtis J. Milhaupt, "Financial Reform in Japan: Recent Legislation Leaves Some Issues Unresolved," 14 *East Asia Executive Reports* (No. 12) 9 (December 1992); Yoshirō Miwa, "*Kin'yū seido kaikaku no seijikeizaigaku*" [Political economy of financial system reform], in K. Takarazuka and K. Ikeo, eds., *Kin'yū riron to seido kaikaku* [Financial theory and institutional reform] (Tokyo: Yuhikaku, 1992), pp. 307–41.

11 For a useful tabular presentation of the changes, see Dan W Puchniack, "The 2002 Reform of the Management of Large Corporations in Japan: A Race to Somewhere?," *Australian Journal of Asian Law* (in press, 2003).

12 See *Kankyō kihon hō* [Basic Environmental Law], Law No. 91 of 1993; *Dojō osen taisaku hō* [Soil Contamination Control Law], Law No. 53 of 2002. For a full commentary on the changes, see Lara Fowler, "From Technical Fix to Regulatory Mix: Japan's New Environmental Law," 12 *Pacific Rim Law and Policy Journal* 441 (2003).

13 E.g. *Shōhisha keiyaku hō* [Consumer Contracts Law], Law No. 61 of 2000.

14 The Justice System Reform Council, *Recommendations of the Justice System Reform Council – For a Justice System to Support Japan in the 21st Century*, June 12, 2001. For an overview of the preliminary agenda, see Veronica Taylor, "Re-regulating Japanese Transactions: The Competition Law Dimension," in Peter Drysdale and Jennifer Amyx, eds., *Japanese Governance: Beyond Japan, Inc.* (New York: Routledge, 2003), pp. 134–55.

15 Compare earlier works by Chalmers Johnson, *Japan: Who Governs?: The Rise of the Developmental State* (New York: W. W. Norton, 1996), on Japan as developmental state, with the essays in Peter Drysdale and Jennifer Amyx, eds., *Japanese Governance: Beyond Japan, Inc.* (New York: Routledge, 2003).

16 The number of ministries has been reduced to 10 with consolidation of Home Affairs and Posts and Telecommunications into a new Ministry of Public Management, Home Affairs and Posts and Telecommunications, of Labor and Health and Welfare as the Ministry of Health, Labor and Welfare. A new Ministry of the Environment was created, and two ministries were reorganized and renamed – the Ministry of Education as the new Ministry of Education, Culture, Sports, Science and Technology and in the new Ministry of Economy, Trade and Industry.

17 E.g. Peter Drysdale and Jennifer Amyx, eds., *Japanese Governance: Beyond Japan, Inc.* (New York: Routledge, 2003)

18 E.g. Edward J. Lincoln, *Arthritic Japan: The Slow Pace of Economic Reform* (Washington, DC, Brookings Institution, 2001).

19 Media coverage of corporate, bureaucratic and legal institutional scandals and shortcomings has been influential in constructing this dissatisfaction. See examples cited in Veronica Taylor, "Re-regulating Japanese Transactions: The Competition Dimension," in Peter Drysdale and Jennifer Amyx, eds., *Japanese Governance: Beyond Japan, Inc.* (New York: Routledge, 2003), p. 137. For an example of the media itself coming under attack for poor corporate governance, see Michiyo Nakamoto, "Nikkei Tackles a Scandal of Its Own," *Financial Times*, April 10, 2003.

20 Veronica Taylor, "Re-regulating Japanese Transactions: the Competition Dimension," in Peter Drysdale and Jennifer Amyx, eds., *Japanese Governance: Beyond Japan, Inc.* (New York: Routledge, 2003), p. 139.

21 Peerenboom, this volume.

22 The Japan Federation of Bar Associations' journal, for example, is simply called *Hō no shihai* [Rule of Law] – an unselfconscious adoption of a fundamental jurisprudential concept.

23 Following Upham, we could equally well talk about the "invention" and "re-invention" of rule of law and its institutional form in Japan. Frank Upham, "Weak Legal Consciousness as Invented Tradition," in Stephen Vlastos, ed., *Mirror of Modernity: Invented Traditions of Modern Japan* (University of California Press, 1998).

24 Two fundamental essays on the role of formal legal adjudication and its alternatives in Japan are John O. Haley, "The Myth of the Reluctant Litigant," *Journal of Japanese Studies* 4, 1978, 359, and J. Mark Ramseyer and Minoru Nakazato, "The Rational Litigant: Settlement Amounts and Verdict Rates in Japan," *Journal of Legal Studies* 18, 1989, 263.

25 Tom Ginsburg, Luke Nottage, and Hiroo Sono, eds., *The Multiple Worlds of Japanese Law: Conjunctions and Disjunctions*, Proceedings of a CAPI Colloquium, University of Victoria (Victoria BC: Center for Asia Pacific Initiatives, University of Victoria, 2001).

26 For an extended debate about the independence of the Japanese judiciary, see J. Mark Ramseyer and Frances Rosenbluth, *Japan's Political Marketplace*

(Cambridge: Harvard University Press, 1993); John O. Haley, *The Spirit of Japanese Law* (Athens: University of Georgia Press, 1998); and J. Mark Ramseyer and Minoru Nakazato, *Japanese Law: An Economic Approach* (Chicago: University of Chicago Press, 1999).

27 See examples of this in Veronica Taylor, "Measuring Legal Reform in Transition Economies: the 'Legal Olympics,'" in Timothy Lindsey, ed., *Law Reform in Asia* (forthcoming).

28 The text of this section is adapted from John O. Haley, *Authority Without Power: Law and the Japanese Paradox* (Oxford: Oxford University Press, 1991), pp. 29–77.

29 Following from the language of the Potsdam Declaration; for a detailed discussion of the Occupation reforms, see Alfred C. Oppler, *Legal Reform in Occupied Japan: A Participant Looks Back* (Princeton, Princeton University Press, 1976)

30 At present (2003) the House of Representatives (*Shūgi-in*) has 500 seats, 200 of which are elected on a proportional representation basis from 11 regional blocks. The remaining 300 seats are elected from single-seat constituencies. The upper House of Councilors (*Sangi-in*) has 252 seats. One half are elected every three years to serve fixed six-year terms, with 76 members elected from the 47 prefectures as multi-member districts and 50 elected by party vote from a single nationwide list.

31 For an example of a range of views among Japanese constitutional scholars under 50 designed for a popular, literate audience, see Masako Kamiya, *Nihon koku kempō o yominaosu* [Re-reading the Japanese Constitution] (Tokyo, Nikkei Shimbun, 2000), and the essay in that volume by Junji Annen, "Constitutionalism as a Political Culture," (translated by Lee H. Rousso, 11 *Pacific Rim Law & Policy Journal* 561–76 (2002).

32 Major constitutional cases are digested annually in leading law journals such as *Jurisuto Jūyō Hanrei* [*Jurisuto*: leading cases].

33 Hiroshi Itoh and Lawrence Beer, *Constitutional Case Law of Japan, 1970 through 1990* (Seattle, University of Washington Press, 1996); and Percy Luney, *The Constitution of Japan: The Fifth Decade, Law and Contemporary Problems* (special edn.) (Durham, NC, Duke University Press, 1990).

34 See Glenn D. Hook and Gavan McCormack, *Japan's Contested Constitution* (New York: Routledge, 2001).

35 See Glenn D. Hook and Gavan McCormack, *Japan's Contested Constitution* (New York: Routledge, 2001).

36 John Braithwaite, *Crime, Shame and Reintegration* (Cambridge: Cambridge University Press, 1989), and John O. Haley, *Spirit of Japanese Law* (Athens, GA, University of Georgia Press, 1998), pp. 70–89.

37 Veronica Taylor, Personal observations of Tokyo District Court and High Court trials involving foreigners, 1996–2000.

38 David T. Johnson, *The Japanese Way of Justice* (Oxford University Press, 2002).

39 David T Johnson, "Criminal Justice in Japan," in Daniel Foote, ed., *Law in Japan: A Turning Point* (working title) (University of Washington Press, in preparation).

40 American law is now the dominant form of foreign law taught in Japanese law faculties, but Japanese lawyers have, up to this point, been educated as civilian lawyers. Moreover, their training is geared toward Japan's unitary state with its parliamentary political framework, rather than to an American-style federated, presidential system with a multiplicity of legal jurisdictions.

41 See the Antimonopoly Act of 1947.

42 See, for example, Richard O. Kummert and Misao Tatsuta, *U.S./Japan Corporations Law* (Seattle: University of Washington Press, in preparation).

43 On this point generally, see the foundational article by John O. Haley "The Myth of the Reluctant Litigant," 4 *Journal of Japanese Studies* 359 (No. 2, Summer 1978).

44 For the most recent statistics on the legal professions in Germany, see <http://www.statistik.bund.de.>

45 The new scope of the patent attorneys' work is described in Lee Rousso, "Japan's New Patent Attorney Law Breaches Barrier Between the 'Legal' and 'Quasi-Legal' Professions," in 10 *Pacific Rim Law and Policy Journal* 3 (2001).

46 Takahashi Eiji and Rudo, Joachim, "Mißbrauch von Aktionärsrechten in Japan und Deutschland," 12 *Recht in Japan* 71, 75 (2000). See also Shishido, Zenichi, "Japanese Corporate Governance: The Hidden Problems of Corporate Law and Their Solutions," 25 *Delaware Journal of Corporation Law* 189 (2000); Shiro Kawashima and Susumu Sakurai, "Shareholder Derivative Litigation in Japan: Law, Practice, and Suggested Reforms," 33 *Stanford Journal of International Law* 9 (1997); West, Mark D., "The Pricing of Shareholder Derivative Actions in Japan and the United States," 88 *Northwestern University Law Review* 51 (1994).

47 In summary courts up to 70 percent of cases are typically unrepresented litigants (personal communication, Osaka High Court judge, 2002).

48 *Gyōsei tetsuzuki hō* [Administrative Procedure Law], Law No. 88 of 1993; *Jōhō kōkai hō* [Public Disclosure of Information Act], Law No. 42 of 1999.

49 For a summary of these cases, see John O. Haley, *Antitrust in Germany and Japan: The First Fifty Years, 1947–1998* (Seattle: University of Washington Press, 2001), pp. 165–8.

50 E.g. Ulrike Schaede, *Cooperative Capitalism: Self-Regulation, Trade Associations, and the Antimonopoly Law in Japan* (Oxford: Oxford University Press, 2000).Taylor argues that we can discern a shift in enforcement in this field from about 1996 onwards: Veronica Taylor, "Re-regulating Japanese Transactions: The Competition Law Dimension," in Peter Drysdale and Jennifer Amyx, eds., *Japanese Governance: Beyond Japan, Inc.* (New York: Routledge, 2003).

51 The classic study of this process is Frank Upham, *Law and Social Change in Postwar Japan* (Cambridge: Harvard University press, 1989); see also more recent work on health rights by Eric Feldman, *The Ritual of Rights in Japan* (Cambridge: Cambridge University Press, 2000).

52 The challenge succeeded in the court of first instance, but too late to prevent construction. The significance of the case lies in its explicit recognition of the Ainu plaintiffs as having a distinct cultural identity that may vest in them specific rights: Mark Levin, "Essential Commodities and Racial Justice: Using Constitutional Protection of Japan's Indigenous Ainu People to Inform Understandings of the United States and Japan," in 33 *NYU Journal of International Law and Politics* 2 (2001): 419.

53 Frank Upham, *Law and Social Change in Postwar Japan* (Cambridge: Harvard University press, 1989).

54 Supreme Court, 49 Minshu (1) 56 (1995), also translated in 40 *Japanese Annual of International Law* 129.

55 Yuji Iwasawa, *International Law, Human Rights, and Japanese Law* (Oxford: Clarendon Press, 1998).

56 Examples include the Equal Employment Opportunity Law 1985 (as amended) and revisions to the Nationality Law, following Japan's ratification of the 1980 Convention on the Elimination of All Forms of Discrimination Against Women.

57 John O. Haley, Antitrust in Germany and Japan: The First Fifty Years, 1947–1998 (Seattle: University of Washington Press, 2001); Ulrike Schaede, Cooperative Capitalism: Self-Regulation, Trade Associations and the Antimonopoly Law in Japan (Oxford University Press: 2000).

58 Lara Fowler, "From Technical Fix to Regulatory Mix: Japan's New Environmental Law," 12 *Pacific Rim Law and Policy Journal* 441 (2003).

59 Tom Ginsburg, "System Change? A New Perspective on Japan's Administrative Procedure Law," in Tom Ginsburg, Luke Nottage, and Hiroo Sono, eds., *The Multiple Worlds of Japanese Law: Conjunctions and Disjunctions,* Proceedings of CAPI Colloquium, University of Victoria (Victoria, BC, Center for Asia Pacific Initiatives, University of Victoria, 2001).

60 John O. Haley, *Authority Without Power: Law and the Japanese Paradox* (New York: Oxford University Press, 1991).

61 E.g. Yasutomo Morigiwa, "*Ajia no hō to nihon no hōtetsugaku*" [Asian Laws and Japanese Legal Philosophy], in Hiromichi Imai, Yasutomo Morigiwa, and Tatsuo Inoue, *Henyō suru ajia no hō to tetsugaku* [Law in a Changing World: Asian Alternatives] (Tokyo, Yuhikaku: 1999).

62 Takao Tanase, *Hermeneutics of Japanese Law: Modernity and Community* (forthcoming).

63 The insights of legal pluralism suggest that we should distinguish between ideas of "rule of law" that construct and constrain state-controlled or state-sponsored legal institutions, and those institutions, binding rules or social or transactional norms beyond the immediate reach of the state. Contemporary theories of regulation suggest that this binary divide between state and non-state actors and institutions is somewhat illusory – both are interdependent and combine to build and enforce regulatory regimes – but for the purposes of this project we leave these debates to one side.

64 There is a growing and extensive body of work on the legal treatment of minorities and vulnerable groups in Japan. A good starting point is Yuji Iwasawa, *International Law, Human Rights, and Japanese Law* (Oxford: Clarendon Press, 1998).

65 See the essays in Hiromichi Imai, Yasutomo Morigiwa, and Tatsuo Inoue,*Henyō suru ajia no hō to tetsugaku* [Law in a Changing World: Asian Alternatives] (Tokyo, Yuhikaku: 1999).

66 A "public benefit" legal person (or *kōekihōjin*) exists, but these tend to be quasi-public welfare or educational institutions. Private Communication with Professor Terao, University of Tokyo.

67 See, e.g., *Dojō osen taisaku hō* [Soil Contamination Control Law], Law No. 53 of 2002.

68 Supreme Court, September 2, 1987, Minshu 411–6–1423, discussed in Hiroshi Oda *Japanese Law* (Oxford: Oxford University Press, 1999), p. 385.

69 Discussed in John O. Haley, *The Spirit of Japanese Law* (Athens: University of Georgia Press, 1998); and Norma Field, *In the Realm of a Dying Emperor* (New York: Pantheon, 1991).

70 See <http://jin.jcic.or.jp/stats/220PN11.html>.

71 Takao Tanase. "The Hermeneutics of Japanese Law: Modernity and Community' (in preparation).

72 E.g. Takashi Uchida, "*Gendai keiyakuhō to arata na tenkai to ippan jōkō*" [General clauses and new developments in contemporary contract law], *NBL*, vol. 514, pp. 6–11; vol. 515, pp. 13–21; vol. 516, pp. 22–32; vol. 517, pp. 32–40; vol. 518, pp. 26–32, describing the growth and importance of this jurisprudence.

73 Although this may change as judges and lawyers become more conversant with law and economics thinking, see, e.g., J. Mark Ramseyer, *Hō to keizaigaku: Nihon hō no keizai bunseki* (Tokyo, Japan, Kobundo, 1991).

74 E.g. Veronica Taylor, "Continuing Transactions and Persistent Myths: Contracts in Contemporary Japan," 19 *Melbourne University Law Review* (1993) 352; and Luke Nottage, *Form, Substance, and Neo-Proceduralism in Comparative Contract*

Law, thesis submitted in fulfillment of the requirements of the PhD in Law, Victoria University of Wellington, August 1999.

75 Willem M. Visser 'T Hooft, *Japanese Contract and Antitrust Law: A Sociological and Comparative Study* (London: RoutledgeCurzon, 2002).

76 Noboru Kashiwagi, "I Can't Turn You Loose: The Termination of Distributors and Agents in Japan," paper presented at a conference, *Change, Continuity and Context: Japanese Law in the Twenty-First Century*, April 6–7 2001, University of Michigan (unpublished)

77 Takashi Uchida and Veronica Taylor, "Re-regulating Japanese Contacts" (working title), in Daniel Foote, ed., *Law in Japan: A Turning Point* (working title) (University of Washington Press, forthcoming).

78 Two of the remaining three justices were career civil servants, one a diplomat (Ministry of Foreign Affairs), the other a former Ministry of Health and Welfare official, Kazuko Yokoo.

79 Neither were law graduates. The Supreme Court may be composed of up to one-third of justices selected for their "experience," and this permits the appointment of non-lawyers.

80 Newly appointed judges are ratified by voters at the time of the next general election, but this is a ritualized process. Voters seldom have sufficient information or cause not to approve an appointment.

81 The Chief Justice of the Supreme Court has an official residence, but this is also tucked away in an inconspicuous inner-city residential precinct.

82 Recent examples include the autobiography of a legal practitioner appointed to the Supreme Court that was somewhat controversial – perhaps because it reveals the consummate tedium of the job, see Masao Ōno, *Bengoshi kara saibankan e: Saikōsai hanji no seikatsu to iken* [From Attorney to Judge: The Life and Views of a Supreme Court Judge] (Tokyo: Iwanami Shoten, 2000).

83 Carol Lawson and Simon Thornley, " 'Perceptions of the Current State of the Japanese Legal System': Interview with Koji Sato, Chairman of Japan's Judicial Reform Council,' " in 4 *Australian Journal of Asian Law* 1 (2002), pp. 76–91.

84 See Dan Fenno Henderson, "Chinese Influences on Eighteenth-Century Tokugawa Codes," in J. A. Cohen, R. R. Edwards, and F. C. Chen, eds., *Essays on China's Legal Tradition* (Princeton: Princeton University Press, 1980), pp. 270–301.

85 Takao Tanase, *Hermeneutics of Japanese Law: Modernity and Community* (forthcoming).

86 Setsuo Miyazawa, "Legal Education and the Reproduction of the Elite in Japan," 1 *Asian Pacific Law and Policy Journal* 1 (2000), e-journal, article available online at <http://www.hawaii.edu/aplpj/pdfs/02-miyazawa.pdf>; and the new popular magazine, *Kausa* [Causa].

87 Until the 1990s, much of Japan's legal reform was routed through a Legal System Consultative Council (*hōsei shingikai*), a peak advisory body with representation from a range of stakeholder groups. Since the second half of the 1990s the composition of the *shingikai* has changed slightly in favor of those with an economics background, and the scope of the review has been narrowed to particular reform projects, such as the overhaul of Japan's insolvency law regime; see, e.g., Gregory Noble, "Reform and Continuity in Japan's *Shingikai* Deliberation Councils," in Peter Drysdale and Jennifer Amyx, eds., *Japanese Governance: Beyond Japan, Inc.* (New York: Routledge, 2003), p. 113.

88 On Japanese multiculturalism, see Donald Denoon, Gavan McCormack, Mark Hudson, Tessa Morris-Suzuki, eds., *Multicultural Japan: Palaeolithic to Postmodern* (Cambridge: Cambridge University Press, 2002).

89 David Linnan, comments from the floor, *Law in Japan: A Turning Point*, Conference at the University of Washington, Seattle, August 2002.

90 Comments from the floor, *Law in Japan: A Turning Point*, Conference at the University of Washington, Seattle, August 2002. This seems to echo the Peerenboom comments from Chinese scholars (this volume) about using rule of law as a cover for debate, but with a slightly different nuance, since the Japanese are engaged in a public, official debate with some tolerance for strong dissent.

INDEX

administrative law xxi, 19, 39, 40; in
China 8, 17, 115, 117-18, 120, 129,
133; in Japan 14, 457-458; in Vietnam
15, 149; in Singapore 19, 184, 186,
189, 201; in Germany 80, 89, 420; in
India 329, 336; South Korea 394; in
Tawain 416, 424, 431
affirmative action 31, 43, 73, 328, 331
Amnesty International 22
Amsterdam Treaty (1997) 98, 99, 100,
101, 102
Aquino, Cory 10, 11, 373-74, 379
Asian Development Bank 147
Asian developmental state 4, 121
Asian values x, xiii 4, 18-20, 27-28, 44,
114, 119; in China 124; in Indonesia
286-313; in Singapore 184, 186, 194;
in Thailand 353-55; in Taiwan 425; in
Japan 426 as construct xiv, 5; see also
Values in Asia
assembly, freedom of xix, xxi, 20, 42; in
Singapore 197, 207; in Malaysia 240;
in Hong Kong 267, 269, 271, 277;
Thailand 357; in Japan 453; in the
United States 57; in France 89; in
Malaysia 240; in Taiwan 423-4; in
Japan 453
association, freedom of xii, xix, xxi, 3, 7,
20, 42, 129; in the United States 57;
in France 92; in China 129
authoritarianism xx, 1, 18-19, 24, 27, 44,
244, 296, 300, 313, 345, 353, 373; in
China 119; in Vietnam 146; in
Singapore 202; in Malaysia 244; in
Indonesia 296, 313; in Thailand 345,
353; in Philippines 373 soft
authoritarianism xvii, 1, 9, 16, 18, 19,
20, 46-47, 183, 202; neo-
authoritarianism 113, 119, 146, 250

Bangkok declaration 286, 296-97, 313,
352
Bill of Rights: in general (not U.S.) 58,
96, 98; in United States 60; in
Indonesia 300-01; in Philippines 371;
in Japan 452; in Singapore 187
Bodin, Jean 83
Buddhism xvii, xxii, 9, 46; and Falun
Gong 261; in Thailand 347, 355; in
Japan 448
Bush v. Gore 14, 25

capital punishment xi, 134
capitalism xvii, xviii, 4, 17, 29, 61-62,
113, 121; in China 113, 121; in
Vietnam 154; in Singapore 186; in
Hong Kong 250, 252, 274; in India
325, 339
Chen Shui-bian 425
child custody xii
child labor xii, 31; in India 327
Chun Doo-hwan 21, 391, 395, 398-99
civil disobedience 10, 36-37; in Hong
Kong 269-271; in South Korea 393
civil law xvii; in South Korea 386, 397; in
Indonesia 294-95; in Thailand 345; in
Japan 452, 456, 458, 466
clientelism xviii, 26; in China 121-23; in
Thailand 359
commercial law xix, xx, 39, 42; in
Vietnam 161-62, 164-66, 168; in
Singapore 186, 207, 209, in South
Korea 394, 424; in Japan 446, 451-52,
456
common law xvii, 20, 27, 46, 120, 151,
294; in Singapore 186-7, 196, 199,
206-7; in Hong Kong 251, 253, 259,
260; in Japan 448, 464
Communaute de droit 99

INDEX

Indonesia 287; in Thailand xii, 29,
346, 351; Chinese Communist Party
(CCP) 115; Communist Party of
Vietnam (CPV) 146
communitarianism xii, xiii, 4, 5, 9, 17-20,
27-28, 31-32, 46, 47, 68, in China
113-14, 118-19, 121-5, 127, 130-34; in
Vietname 146, 161, 171-72, ; in
Singapore 183-209; in Hong Kong
274, 295; in India 332; in Taiwan 425;
in Japan 461; Asian communitarians
xii
Confucianism xvii, xxii, xv, xvii, xxii 19,
27, 29, 114, 127, 155, 159, 192-6, 200,
203, 384-85; Neo-Confucians 9, 149-
150, 155, 164, 171, 172, 183, 195, 208,
461; New Confucians 9, 113, 119, 183
conscience, freedom of see religion,
freedom of
Consent: as basis for legitimacy 43
constitutional law xxi, 14; in the United
States 40, 82, 328; in France 40, 82,
84-98; and European Union 98-103;
in China 133; in Singapore 186-87,
199; in Malaysia 225, 230, 235-40; in
Hong Kong 251, 263-64; in Indonesia
289, 290-93 298-300, 303-04, 310-11;
In India 328, 335-38, 357-59; in
Thailand 357-59; in Philippines 370-
75, 374-75, 377-81; in South Korea
388, 398-404; in Tawain 417-19; in
Japan 445, 451, 453-54; emergency
powers 235-39, 402-04; constitutional
amendments 239, 298, 418
Convention for the Elimination of All
Forms of Discrimination Against
Women (United Nations) 43, 187
corporate law xviii, xxi, 8; in Vietnam
164; in Japan 446
corporatism xviii, 123, 67; in China 121-
23; in Vietnam 159
criminal law 8, 21, 32-33, 39-42, 57, 72,
79, 451, 454; in France 93; in China
131, 134; in Singapore 186, 189, 190,
192, 206; in Malaysia 241, 244, 268,
in Indonesia 288-9, 292-3, 298, 301-2;
in India 325; in Thailand 345, 350,
357-60, 362, 366; in the Philippines
371; in South Korea 393-94, 398-402;
in Taiwan 419, 427, 431; in Japan
454, 447-48, 450-51, 453, 454-56, 458,

464; in Vietnam 147, 149, 154-6, 165,
168-70; criminal procedure 42, 134,
192, 206, 358, 359
critical left 4, 65, 67, 68
Critical Legal Theory 36, 69, 128, 326,
392
Critical Race Theory 36, 326
cruel and unusual punishment xi
Cultural Revolution (PRC) 120, 126,
128, 132, 393

Daoism xvii, 9, 43
David, Rene xiv
De l'Esprit des Lois (The Spirit of the
Laws, 1748) 84
de Malberg, Raymond Carre 80, 86-87
democracy: defined xix
Deng Xiaoping 132, 250
Dewey, John 119
distributive justice 4, 29, 47, 64, 72
doi moi reforms 15, 146, 148-9, 151, 158,
165, 167
domestic violence xii
Du Contrat social (The Social Contract,
1762) 85
due process 3, 153-54, 329, 453; in
Vietnam 148, 153-54; in India 329; in
Japan 453-54
dwifungsi 301-02, 310-11
Dworkin, Ronald 11, 57, 72-74

East Timor 22, 293, 301-02, 310, 319
education xviii, xxi, 30, 44, 366; in China
131, 134; in Vietnam 164; in
Singapore 183, 192, 200, 234; in
Hong Kong 253; in Indonesia 301,
308, 311-15; in India 329, 331-2; in
Thailand 349, 357, 362, 366-68; in
South Korea 389-90; in Taiwan 428;
in Japan 453, 456, 465; legal
education 14, 32, 253 389-90, 445-46,
453, 456, 464-65
Enlightenment (European) 17, 43, 84,
131
Enlightenment (European) see liberalism
environmental law xii, xx, 39, 387, 429,
430
equal protection of law see equality
before the law
equality before the law 35, 41, 64, 88, 93,
152, 194, 264, 327, 328, 331, 362
Estrada, Joseph 24-25, 370, 379-80
Etat de droit: origins in France 33

476

24689533R00278

Printed in Great Britain
by Amazon